COMPARATIVE ECONOMIC SYSTEMS

SECOND EDITION

COMPARATIVE ECONOMIC SYSTEMS

SECOND EDITION

H. Stephen Gardner
Baylor University

The Dryden Press
Harcourt Brace College Publishers

Fort Worth Philadelphia San Diego New York Orlando Austin San Antonio

Toronto Montreal London Sydney Tokyo

Publisher	George Provol
Acquisitions Editor	Gary Nelson
Product Manager	Kathleen Sharp
Developmental Editors	Cinda Cheney and Stacey Sims
Project Editor	Dee Salisbury
Production Manager	Lois West
Art Director	Jeanette Barber

Address for Orders
Harcourt Brace College Publishers
6277 Sea Harbor Drive
Orlando, FL 32887-6777
1-800-782-4479

Address for Editorial Correspondence
The Dryden Press
301 Commerce Street, Suite 3700
Fort Worth, TX 76102

ISBN: 0-03-032822-5

Library of Congress Catalog Card Number: 96-83886

Printed in the United States of America

8 9 066 9 8 7 6 5 4 3 2

The Dryden Press
Harcourt Brace College Publishers

*To my parents, Evelyn Gardner and the late C. E. Gardner,
and my "other" parents, Lynn and Joy Stokes
—my bridges to the past;
and to my son and daughter, Danny and Jessica
—with hope for the future.*

THE DRYDEN PRESS SERIES IN ECONOMICS

Baldani, Bradfield, and Turner
Mathematical Economics

Baumol and Blinder
Economics: Principles and Policy
Seventh Edition
(also available in Micro and Macro
paperbacks)

Baumol, Panzar, and Willig
*Contestable Markets and the Theory of
Industry Structure*
Revised Edition

Breit and Elzinga
*The Antitrust Casebook: Milestones in
Economic Regulation*
Third Edition

Brue
The Evolution of Economic Thought
Fifth Edition

Edgmand, Moomaw, and Olson
Economics and Contemporary Issues
Fourth Edition

Gardner
Comparative Economic Systems
Second Edition

Gwartney and Stroup
Economics: Private and Public Choice
Eighth Edition
(also available in micro and macro
paperbacks)

Gwartney and Stroup
*Introduction to Economics: The Wealth
and Poverty of Nations*

Heilbroner and Singer
*The Economic Transformation of America:
1600 to the Present*
Third Edition

Hess and Ross
*Economic Development: Theories,
Evidence, and Policies*

Hirschey and Pappas
*Fundamentals of Managerial Economics:
Theories, Evidence, and Policies*
Sixth Edition

Hirschey and Pappas
Managerial Economics
Eighth Edition

Hyman
*Public Finance: A Contemporary
Application of Theory to Policy*
Fifth Edition

Kahn
*The Economic Approach to Environmental
and Natural Resources*
Second Edition

Kaserman and Mayo
*Government and Business: The Economics
of Antitrust and Regulation*

Kaufman
The Economics of Labor Markets
Fourth Edition

Kennett and Lieberman
*The Road to Capitalism: The Economic
Transformation of Eastern Europe and the
Former Soviet Union*

Kreinin
*International Economics: A Policy
Approach*
Eighth Edition

Lott and Ray
Applied Econometrics with Data Sets

Mankiw, *Principles of Economics*
(also available in Micro and Macro
paperbacks)

Marlow
Public Finance: Theory and Practice

Nicholson
*Intermediate Microeconomics and Its
Application*
Seventh Edition

Nicholson
*Microeconomic Theory: Basic Principles
and Extensions*
Seventh Edition

Puth
American Economic History
Third Edition

Ragan and Thomas
Principles of Economics
Second Edition
(also available in Micro and Macro
paperbacks)

Ramanathan
*Introductory Econometrics with
Applications*
Fourth Edition

Rukstad
*Corporate Decision Making in the World
Economy: Company Case Studies*

Rukstad
*Macroeconomic Decision Making in the
World Economy: Text and Cases*
Third Edition

Samuelson and Marks
Managerial Economics
Second Edition

Scarth
*Macroeconomics: An Introduction to
Advanced Methods*
Third Edition

Stockman
Introduction to Economics
(also available in Micro and Macro
paperbacks)

Walton and Rockoff
History of the American Economy
Eighth Edition

Welch and Welch
Economics: Theory and Practice
Sixth Edition

Yarbrough and Yarbrough
The World Economy: Trade and Finance
Fourth Edition

PREFACE

These are the days of lasers in the jungle

Lasers in the jungle somewhere

Staccato signals of constant information

A loose affiliation of millionaires . . .

The way we look to a distant constellation

That's dying in a corner of the sky

These are the days of miracle and wonder

And don't cry baby, don't cry

—PAUL SIMON, "THE BOY IN THE BUBBLE,"
GRACELAND, 1986

Nothing endures but change.

—HERACLITUS, C. 500 B.C.

According to scholarly tradition, the modern historical era began around 1500 A.D. Within fifty years of that date, the last citadel of ancient Rome was overthrown in Constantinople, a despotic Mongol regime collapsed in Russia, Christopher Columbus and Vasco da Gama created new links between Europe and the outside world, Gutenberg launched an era of mass communication, Copernicus rearranged the known universe, Luther and Calvin transformed the institutions of Christendom, and Michelangelo, Raphael, and da Vinci led a High Renaissance of the arts.

Today, five centuries later, the world seems to be passing through another radical phase of reinvention. Left-wing and right-wing despotisms have fallen in Central Europe, Latin America, Africa, and Asia, clearing the way for unthinkable opportunities and unpredictable challenges. Communication technologies and trade agreements have unleashed the movement of information, ideas, people, and products. The world market is open for business.

What is the current economic condition of the world and its regions? What historical, cultural, and ideological forces are shaping the economy of the future? What institutional options do we have as individuals, countries, and regions in an intensely competitive world? In Comparative Economic Systems, I attempt to provide the conceptual tools, historical background, and current information needed to explore these questions.

This book is designed to serve as a basic text for undergraduates or as a supplementary survey text for graduate students. My approach is non-technical; most of the book can be understood by readers with limited backgrounds in economics. This is important because all of us—business people, journalists, public servants, educators, and students—need to understand the rich diversity and mutability of economic institutions in the world around us.

NEW AND DISTINCTIVE FEATURES

Although some important features of the first edition have been preserved, this edition of the book has been completely reorganized, expanded, updated, and rewritten to reflect the new and changing shape of the world economy. Several unique features should distinguish it from the first edition or from other books in the field.

REGIONAL ORIENTATION. In the past, comparative economics texts were organized along ideological lines, emphasizing the differences between capitalist and socialist societies. Some authors have continued to emphasize ideological divisions, and I have addressed them in this book. Today, though, the more important distinctions between countries seem to be related to geography. If two countries are located in the same region, they are more likely to share elements of culture, climate, history, and colonial heritage, and they are more likely to be united by a free trade agreement or another international arrangement. Hence, I have reorganized this book along regional lines, with new chapters added to introduce the Western Hemisphere, Western Europe, Central Eurasia, South and East Asia, and Africa. Each of these chapters includes a survey of economic and cultural factors that unite and/or divide the region, and a survey of institutions promoting regional economic integration.

BROAD COUNTRY COVERAGE. Many individual countries are given full-chapter coverage. These include the United States, Great Britain, Germany, Sweden, France, Japan, and China. Four chapters devoted to the transitional economies of the former Soviet Union and Central and Eastern Europe. Thus, instructors should be able to accommodate individual interests and time constraints.

PEDAGOGICAL APPROACH. Conceptual material is integrated into chapters that discuss actual economies. The theory of the labor-managed firm, for example, is incorporated in our discussion of former Yugoslavia; input-output economics is connected to the former Soviet economy; the theory of the share economy is connected to Japan. When necessary, technical issues are discussed in chapter appendices. Several chapters also include boxed items to provide living applications of broader concepts.

When possible, the country chapters follow a common outline to facilitate comparisons. Each chapter opens with a map, and includes a survey of economic institutions related to the socioeconomic environment, industrial organization, labor market and relations, financial sector, and the government. Key terms appear in bold type. Each chapter ends with a summary, a set of discussion questions, a list of suggested readings, and a list of Internet resources. An updated collection of resources will be maintained at my personal Web site: <http://hsb.baylor.edu/html/gardner/>.

STATISTICAL EMPHASIS. A unique chapter on comparative economic statistics is included early in the book to introduce students to the methods and definitions used by professionals. Numerous charts and tables are supplied throughout the book to provide breadth and depth of information.

HISTORICAL PERSPECTIVE. It is impossible to understand the roots of American individualism, Russian authoritarianism, British economic decline, or African and South Asian poverty without exploring the distant past. Thus, I have included more historical material than is common in common in books like this one. Full chapters are included on the institutional and theoretical histories of capitalism and socialism. The largest part of the book, however, is devoted to current conditions, trends, and issues.

ACKNOWLEDGMENTS

Many people contributed to this book and I cannot possibly thank them all. First, I am ever mindful of my debt to the late Ed Hewett (when he was at the University of Texas, Austin) and to Gregory Grossman and Benjamin Ward (at the University of California, Berkeley), who introduced me to the field of comparative economics in the early 1970s. In subsequent years, my students at Baylor University have influenced my opinions on the scope and teaching of this subject. During the preparation of this edition, Boris Jordanov, Elena Sklyadneva, and Zheng (Frank) Hongfeng provided invaluable assistance as research assistants and as manuscript reviewers on chapters relating to Central Eurasia and China. Several drafts of the manuscript were tested in my classes, and my students provided many helpful suggestions. Dan Alinange, Sergei Koltovich, David Paredes, Jens Rosmus, and Gwénaëlle Ruault provided particularly useful insights on conditions, respectively, in Uganda, Belarus, Chile, Germany, and France.

I am particularly grateful, of course, to faculty members at more than ninety colleges and universities who adopted the first edition of this text, and who, in some cases, continued to use it long after a new edition was needed. Many cheered me on during the preparation of a new edition. This rewrite progressed slowly because I refused to offer an edition that was not genuinely new, and because I could not resist the temptation to participate in several time-consuming educational and social projects in Russia and Central Europe.

I must also thank the 215 faculty members who responded to a survey The Dryden Press conducted for me in 1995, indicating their preferences concerning the content, structure, and organization of comparative economics and global economy courses. We were amazed and heartened by the high response rate, and by the number of respondents who included extensive written comments. This academic discipline is passing through a major transition, together with its object, and many of you have strong and penetrating views on its evolving architecture. I cannot respond adequately to all the advice offered by 215 people, but the survey had a major impact on the finished product.

Information and specific suggestions on portions of the manuscript were provided by many scholars, based, in a few cases, on pilot testing in their classrooms. These include: Senyo Adjibolosoo (Trinity Western University), Vasili Babunashvili (Georgian Ministry of Foreign Affairs), Michael Beaty (Baylor University), Steven Cobb (University of North Texas), Sergei Komlev (formerly at the USA-Canada Institute of the Russian Academy of Sciences, now at the United Financial Group, Moscow), Joseph McKinney (Baylor University), Robert W. Mead (University of Pittsburgh), Vladimir Popov (WIDER Institute, Helsinki, and Academy of National Economy, Moscow), Thomas Rawski (University of Pittsburgh), Vitaly Tcherenkov (St. Petersburg University of Economics and Finance), and Robert Welch (Midwestern State University).

In 1995, I was privileged to participate in an intensive week-long session of the Salzburg Seminar on "Transitioning Economies: Comparative Models." Olin Robison, President of the Salzburg Seminar, played a most important role in arranging my participation. The seminar was attended by 55 wonderful scholars and officials from 35 countries. In spirited discussion and human interaction, this was among the most exciting intellectual experiences of my life, and the Salzburg experience has an important influence on the formulation of this book. I offer particular thanks to our session leader, William Glade (University of Texas, Austin), and to our discussion leaders: Ivo Bicanic (University of Zagreb), Rolf Lüders (Pontificia Universidad Católica de Chile), Charles-Albert Michalet (World Bank), Bruno Rubess (Volkswagen, ret.), and Alexander Schaub (European Commission).

I owe special thanks to the administration of Baylor University, the Hankamer School of Business, and the Herman Brown Foundation for supporting this project. Once again, the staff at The Dryden Press provided unrelenting encouragement, creativity, and attention to detail. I was particularly aware of the efforts of Jeanette Barber, Cinda Cheney, Dee Salisbury, Stacey Sims, and Lois West.

A most special word of thanks is reserved for my colleague, Mahamudu Bawumia, who wrote the first draft of Chapter 21, "Africa: The Challenge of Development," and worked closely with me on Chapter 18, "Asia and the Pacific Area: An Overview." Dr. Bawumia, a native of Ghana, holds degrees in economics from the University of Buckingham, Lincoln College of Oxford University, and Simon-Fraser University.

Finally, I want to thank my family—Kathy, Danny, and Jessica—for their patience and support during this project. Hundreds of times during the past few years, they have allowed me to say, "We'll do that right after I finish the book." Soon, I will begin repayment of those debts.

H. Stephen Gardner

INTERNET RESOURCES

Dryden Economics
http://www.dryden.com/econ/index.html

Gardner's World Economics
http://hsb.baylor.edu/html/gardner/

Salzburg Seminar
http://www.salsem.ac.at/

CONTENTS

BASES OF COMPARISON

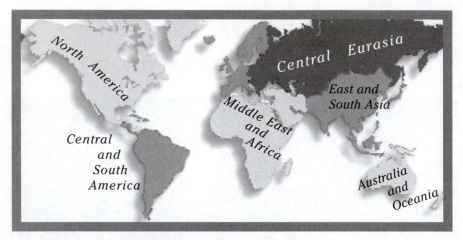

North America

Central Eurasia

East and
South Asia

Middle East
and
Africa

Central
and
South
America

Australia
and
Oceania

World Continents and Regions

ECONOMIC SYSTEMS: CLASSIFICATION AND PERFORMANCE

All that Adam had, all that Caesar could, you have and can do. . . . Build, therefore, your own world.

—RALPH WALDO EMERSON,
NATURE, 1836

conomics, we say, is all about making choices. The realities of life require each of us to make economic choices every day. Where will I live and work? What goods and services will I produce? How much of my income will I spend and save? What will I buy? Where will I buy it?

Some of the most important economic choices must be made by or imposed upon entire societies. What, for example, should individuals be allowed to own? Should we have the right to own simple consumer goods, factories, farms, slaves, rivers, foreign currency, debt claims, creative ideas, trademarks, and songs? How should we establish, protect, and regulate these ownership rights? What kind of monetary system, if any, should we use? What should be the economic roles of local and national governments, professional organizations, labor unions, educational institutions, churches, and the news media? What, in other words, should be the nature of our economic system?

In this introductory chapter we will first explore the concept of an "economic system" and consider its role in the broader social system. Next, we will survey the various criteria that are used to classify economic systems. Finally, we will discuss a few of the problems involved in comparisons of national economic performance.

THE ECONOMIC SYSTEM, THE ENVIRONMENT, AND POLICIES

According to the useful framework suggested by Tjalling Koopmans and John Michael Montias, the **economic performance** of a country is determined by its economic system and environment, and by the policies of its leaders.[1] Let us briefly consider what is meant by each of these terms.

---

[1]Tjalling Koopmans and John Michael Montias, "On the Description and Comparison of Economic Systems," in *Comparison of Economic Systems: Theoretical and Methodological Approaches,* ed. Alexander Eckstein (Berkeley: University of California Press, 1971), 27–38. Koopmans and Montias usually use the term *outcomes* where we use *performance.*

An **economic system** is an interactive set of institutions that constrain, facilitate, and coordinate the economic behaviors of a society.[2] An **institution** is an organization, practice, convention, or custom that is material and persistent in the life or culture of a society. The most familiar institutions are formal organizations, such as business corporations, labor unions, and government agencies. Equally important, however, are practices, conventions, and customs, such as the profit motive, property rights, racial discrimination, market exchange, queues, planning, and taxation.[3] We may think of the economic system in France, for example, as a unique collection of these institutions.

Within the institutional framework of an economic system, we attempt to influence economic performance by setting **policies**, which are implemented through the employment of policy **instruments**. Suppose, for example, that the current policy of the Bundesbank, the German central bank, is to slow the growth of the money supply. It may employ any of three instruments: an increase in open-market sales of securities, a reduction in Bundesbank lending to commercial banks, or an increase in the reserve requirements of commercial banks.

The **environment**, in the broad sense that we use the term, consists of all the factors that affect the economic performance of the society, but are beyond the control of participants in the economic system. For example, annual rainfall has a major impact on agricultural performance, but we have little control over the clouds. In a similar way, we cannot control the abundance or scarcity of our natural resources, the cultural heritage of our society, the economic policies and performances of our trading partners, or the existence of military rivals and allies.

The boundaries between system, policies, and environment are not always clear and they may depend on the time period of analysis.[4] A persistent practice, such as the collection of an income tax in the United States, eventually becomes a component of the economic system. A less persistent practice, such as a temporary reduction in tax rates, represents a mere change in policy. In a short-run analysis, the educational level of the population may be considered an environmental variable. In a long-run analysis, education becomes an important policy variable.

The distinctions between an economic system, environment, policies, and performance may be clarified with a simple analogy. An automobile is a sys-

---

[2]Our definition is closest to that of Gregory Grossman in *Economic Systems*, 2d ed. (Englewood Cliffs, N.J.: Prentice-Hall, 1974), 3. The notion that our behavior is *constrained* by systems and institutions is emphasized by Douglass North in "Institutions," *Journal of Economic Perspectives* 5 (Winter 1991): 97–112.

[3]Institutions are sometimes divided between conventions, which arise from the need to solve shared problems (i.e., avoiding collisions by driving on a particular side of the street), and entitlements, which arise from the need to settle disputes (i.e., laws of ownership and inheritance). For an extended discussion of institutional forms, see Daniel W. Bromley, *Economic Interests and Institutions* (Oxford: Basil Blackwell, 1989), 82–104.

[4]This problem is recognized and discussed by Koopmans and Montias, "Description and Comparison," 33.

tem composed of several persistent mechanisms (institutions), each of which is designed to perform a particular task. The driver uses her steering wheel and other controls (instruments) to guide (set policy for) her car through changing road, weather, and traffic conditions (environment).

If an automobile performs badly, this may be the result of a deficiency in the car itself, or it may be caused by the manner and environment in which the car is driven. Likewise, poor performance of an economy may or may not represent a failure of the economic system. Also, an individual's decision to purchase a particular car depends on the kind of performance desired (such as rapid speed, fuel economy, or safety) and on the environment in which the car will be driven (a large radiator may be preferable in a hot climate). Similarly, it is not likely that a single economic system could be optimal for all purposes, populations, times, and places.

MODES OF CLASSIFICATION

There are far too many countries in the world to analyze carefully in a single book. Instead, we will begin in this chapter by formulating a broad conceptual basis for classification and analysis of economic systems. In later chapters, we will use this scheme to analyze the evolution and operation of economic systems in major regions and representative countries of the world.

We can classify economic systems in many different ways. Just as we can classify people according to their height, weight, sex, age, nationality, political philosophy, and temperament, we can classify economic systems according to a wide range of overlapping criteria. Furthermore, the economic systems of actual countries are never purely capitalist or socialist, market or planned, free or controlled. Real countries have mixed institutional structures that change from year to year through evolution and revolution.

Nevertheless, for a period of time, the actual economic system in a particular country may roughly approximate one of the pure, idealized, theoretical economic systems, and may provide some indication of the relative merit of that theoretical system. Conversely, an economic theory based on an idealized economic system (such as the theory of perfect competition) may contribute to our understanding of the operation of actual economic systems. We should always remember, however, that theory is theory, and reality is reality.

CLASSIFICATION ACCORDING TO OWNERSHIP

The economic and political power structure of a society is largely a reflection of its systems of ownership and property rights. Thus, the most durable classification of economic systems, dating back at least to Karl Marx, distinguishes between economies according to the predominant form of ownership of the factories, farms, and other productive assets. Accordingly, **feudalism** is an economic and social system wherein all ownership rights are ultimately held by a queen, king, or other monarch, and are delegated down through a hierarchy of princes, dukes, barons, and serfs, subject to their loyalty, payment of tribute, and military and civil service. In a **capitalist** system, the greater part of the means of production are owned outright (not subject to feudal obligations) by private individuals, and in **socialism** most of the means of production are owned "socially."

In practice, it is sometimes difficult to distinguish among these different forms of ownership. What do we mean, after all, when we say that we "own" property? We may mean that we have any or all of the following rights: (1) the right to control how the property will be used; (2) the right to retain income generated by the property; and (3) the right to transfer ownership of the property to others. Even in countries with traditions of free-enterprise capitalism, individual property rights are limited by zoning and inheritance laws, environmental and safety regulations, and other legal and social restrictions. On the other hand, even the most repressive societies usually make some formal or informal allowance for individual ownership (see "When Is an Owner an Owner?" on page 7).

Individual and social ownership can take many different forms. A capitalist enterprise may be owned by a sole proprietor, by a group of partners, or by a group of corporate shareholders. A socialist enterprise may be owned by the national government, by a local commune, or by a cooperative of producers or consumers.[5] In practice, the distinctions between these different forms of ownership can be quite subtle; for example, a "capitalist" partnership may be functionally similar to a "socialist" producer cooperative.

We distinguish between economic systems in terms of the "predominant" form of ownership because very few countries have ever been purely capitalist or socialist. In the high-income capitalist world, publicly owned enterprises account for a share of gross investment that ranges from about 4 percent in the United States and the United Kingdom to nearly 30 percent in Norway.[6] In the mid–1980s, when they still referred to themselves as "socialist" countries, the private sector accounted for 14 percent of national income in Yugoslavia, 20 percent in Poland, and 48 percent in Vietnam (Table A.16).

Finally, we should note that private ownership alone does not guarantee the full development of capitalism. Many developing countries have a system of private property, but they often lack the entrepreneurial talent, capital resources, stable monetary system, and other institutions that are needed for successful capitalist development. On the other hand, social

---

[5]Under Soviet socialism, for example, the government maintained effective ownership rights over most of the means of production, whereas Yugoslav socialism delegated most of these rights to the workers' councils of individual factories. As we shall see in later chapters, this is a distinction of considerable operational importance.

[6]These are estimates for 1991 calculated from data in Organization for Economic Cooperation and Development, *National Accounts: Detailed Tables* (Paris, 1993).

WHEN IS AN OWNER AN OWNER?

Beginning in the 1930s, most agricultural land in the Soviet Union was owned and controlled by large collective and state farms. Each rural family was allowed to rent a small plot of land near their house, cultivate it in their spare time, and sell food and livestock from the plot with considerable freedom. Although they used only 3 percent of the sown land, the plots accounted for about 26 percent of the gross value of agricultural output. In the mid–1980s, the ambiguous legal and psychological nature of private plot ownership was described vividly by Viktor Kulinich, a collective farm worker in southern Russia: "The house is my personal property, and the land belongs to me. Well, it's not really mine; we rent the land—nominal rent, about $30 per year. The state owns all of the land, but if the land is attached to my house, it sort of belongs to me."

Subsequent changes have done little to simplify the system of land ownership in the Soviet Union or in Russia. In 1990, the Soviet legislature adopted a plan to make leaseholding the dominant form of ownership in the countryside. The state would maintain legal ownership of the land, but individual farmers would be able to lease it for up to fifty years, and would be able to bequeath their leasing rights to their children as an inheritance.

In 1993, after the disintegration of the Soviet Union, a presidential decree declared that farmers would now have a right to own private property, and within a year the country had more than 100,000 farmers. Most of the private farms, though, were small and financially weak, and the situation of the old socialist sector was now ambiguous. According to Oleg Polukeyev, though, many of the old socialist directors have been able to maintain power: "As far as the land of collective farms and state farms is concerned, the most important considerations affecting the ownership of land are the intrigues . . . of people who do not want to lose power over the land or, in effect, over those who work it."

Sources: "October Harvest," an installment of the "Comrades" series aired on the PBS television program, "Front Line," in 1986; "One Land for All," *Pravda*, February 21, 1991, 2; and Oleg Polukeyev, "Land Decree: How Much Reform Does It Entail?" *Nezavisimaya Gazeta*, October 29, 1993, 1.

ownership alone does not guarantee the fulfillment of socialist ideals. Seventy years of Soviet experience demonstrated that state ownership, wedded with a totalitarian government, does not deliver Marx's promise of a "society in which the full and free development of every individual forms the ruling principle."[7]

---

[7]Karl Marx, *Capital*, vol. 1 (Moscow: Progress Publishers, 1956), 555.

CLASSIFICATION ACCORDING TO COORDINATING MECHANISM

In any economic system, a large number of decisions must be made each year concerning the production and exchange of commodities and resources. Since millions of people may be involved in making and implementing these decisions, every economic system must employ one or more **coordinating mechanisms** to insure some degree of consistency. Ideally, intended purchases of each commodity should equal intended production, the number of people who enter a given occupation should roughly equal the number of jobs available in that occupation, and so on. Economic systems are often classified, therefore, according to their predominant coordinating mechanism.

A **traditional economy** is one in which coordination is maintained through simple perpetuation of the status quo.[8] What products will be produced? Those that were produced last year. How will they be produced? The way they were produced in the past. The sons follow their fathers in their choice of occupation, and the daughters follow their mothers.

Tradition can predominate as a coordinating mechanism only in rather small, simple, and stationary economies. In fact, it would be contradictory to speak of a dynamic and growing economy that is coordinated primarily by tradition. Nevertheless, elements of tradition can be found in any functioning economy. Racial and gender discrimination, for example, have traditionally influenced the patterns of employment in the United States and many other countries. In Japan, large corporations have traditionally maintained long, stable relationships with their suppliers and subcontractors. In the old Soviet Union, economic plans were not prepared in a vacuum; they always built on the results achieved in the previous year.

A **market economy** is one in which coordination is predominantly achieved through the free and spontaneous movement of market prices, responding to the forces of supply and demand. Thus, under competitive conditions, a shortage (or surplus) of any commodity will cause its relative price to rise (fall). The resulting increase (decrease) in the quantity supplied and decrease (increase) in the quantity demanded will reduce or eliminate the shortage (or surplus).

Ideally, a market economy also provides for **consumer sovereignty**. Consumer demand, the largest component of final demand during peacetime, ultimately determines what is produced in the economy. John Kenneth Galbraith and others have noted that the sovereignty of the consumer is manipulated by the marketing programs of producers. Nonetheless, if consumers cannot be convinced to buy a particular product, production will not continue. This is not always true in centrally planned economies, where

---

[8]Notice that tradition cannot, in itself, coordinate decisions, but can only perpetuate a set of decisions that has been coordinated in some other way.

shortages and surpluses of products may arise from a mismatch between planners' priorities and consumer demand.

A **planned economy** is, quite simply, one in which coordination of long-run and/or short-run decisions is attempted by means of a central plan, which is designed to guide the economy toward certain goals or objectives.[9] Given the generality of this definition, a planned economy can take any of several forms.

Directive planning (or **command planning**), which has been employed in the former Soviet Union, China, Eastern Europe, and the U.S. military, is a system whereby the most important long-run *and* short-run decisions are made by a central planning authority and are then passed down to subordinates in the form of instructions, directives, or commands. A directive plan typically includes an annual target for each factory and each important product, and compliance is compulsory. A **centrally planned economy (CPE)** is a country that employs directive planning as its predominant coordinating mechanism. Countries that are attempting to replace directive planning with market institutions are now commonly known as **transitional economies (TEs)**. When we speak collectively about CPEs and TEs, we call them **historically planned economies (HPEs)**.[10]

Indicative planning, employed in France, Japan, and a number of other countries, is a hybrid system that uses the market to coordinate short-run decisions (how many apples to pick this week) in combination with a plan to coordinate long-run decisions (how many apple trees to plant this year). Unlike a directive plan, which must provide detailed instructions to individual producers, an indicative plan typically includes broad goals for entire industries over a long (usually five-year) time horizon. Private companies are not legally required to comply with plan targets, but the government may use fiscal and monetary policy instruments to encourage compliance. Ideally, if it sets goals that are beneficial to all segments of society, an indicative plan should evoke voluntary compliance — it should be a self-fulfilling prophecy.

Quite often, countries that engage in indicative planning also conduct an active **industrial policy (IP)**. An IP may include several different kinds of programs. First, a list of "winning" and "losing" industries may be formulated, with measures designed to support the former and phase out the latter. For example, the Japanese government supported development of the

---

[9] We reject John Kenneth Galbraith's assertion that corporate planning *within* each major industry has transformed the United States into a planned economy. By our more restrictive definition, the plan must, in some sense, be formulated to achieve coordination *between* industries. See John Kenneth Galbraith, *The New Industrial State* (Boston: Houghton Mifflin, 1956).

[10] This terminology was introduced by Paul Marer. See his "Conceptual and Practical Problems of Comparative Measurement of Economic Performance," in *Economic Statistics for Economies in Transition: Eastern Europe in the 1990s,* proceedings of a conference sponsored by the U.S. Bureau of Labor Statistics and Eurostat, Washington, D.C., 1991, 5–23.

steel and auto industries in the 1950s, consumer electronics in the 1960s, computer chips in the 1970s, and "knowledge-intensive" industries in the 1980s. Second, an IP may include measures to strengthen industrial stability and/or competition. Where monopoly power is pervasive, existing companies may be regulated, nationalized, or split into smaller units. Conversely, small companies may be merged into larger units to enhance their financial strength, production efficiency, and competitive position on the world market.

CLASSIFICATION ACCORDING TO INCENTIVE SYSTEMS

Any coordinating mechanism must include a system of incentives to reward socially desirable behavior and to discourage inappropriate actions. These are usually divided into three broad classes: coercive, material, and moral incentives.

Coercive incentives, which attempt to modify behavior through actual or threatened force and punishment, played a historic role in ancient Egypt, the American South, Hitler's Germany, Stalin's Soviet Union, and Pinochet's Chile. Slavery was not legally abolished in Mauritania until 1980, and forced labor is still reported in Burma, Cambodia, Haiti, Namibia, Sudan, and several other countries. According to Antislavery International in London, as many as 200 million people in the world are working under conditions outlawed by international agreements.[11] Local officials in China employ coercive methods to hold down the growth rate of the population.[12] Even the most libertarian societies use force to raise tax revenues, enforce contracts, and prevent theft, fraud, violence, and other illegal actions.

Material incentives are those that reward desirable behavior with a claim over material goods, usually through some form of monetary payment. In a competitive market economy, material incentives arise more or less automatically from the operation of the system. If there is a shortage of any product, the resulting increase in its relative price will give producers a material incentive to increase the quantity they supply, and it will give consumers a material incentive to reduce the quantity they demand.

Systems of material incentives become more complicated in the presence of **principal-agent relationships**. Suppose that a "principal," perhaps the owner of a capitalist shoe factory, hires a group of "agents," or employees. What kind of material incentive system should the principal design to elicit the most desirable behavior from the agents at the lowest cost? A system of profit sharing, for example, may encourage the agents to respond more ap-

[11]"Millions Around the World Still Work in Bondage, Group Says," *The Dallas Morning News*, March 9, 1993, 5A. A similar estimate is given in Robert Senser, "Outlawing the Crime of Child Slavery," *Freedom Review* 24 (November–December 1993): 29–35.

[12]For information on these and other human rights abuses recorded by the U.S. State Department, see U.S. Senate, Committee on Foreign Relations, *Country Reports on Human Rights Practices* (Washington, D.C.: U.S. Government Printing Office, annual).

propriately to market signals, such as an increase in the price of shoes, but it may also be costly.[13]

In an economy coordinated by a directive plan, principal-agent relationships can be even more complex. A material incentive system must be consciously designed and administered to elicit compliance with the plan. Customarily, this has involved bonus pay arrangements tied to fulfillment of production targets. We shall find, however, that countries like the former Soviet Union found it very difficult to design an incentive system that would simultaneously encourage accurate reporting of economic information to central planners and compliance with both the letter and the intent of the plan.

Moral incentives are designed to elicit desired behaviors by appealing to an emotional cause, such as nationalism, company or personal pride, compassion for the sick and the poor, or the desire for acceptance by one's peers. Moral incentives have been employed in "socialist competitions" between factories in the former Soviet Union, in the singing of company songs in Japan, and in the use of slogans, such as "Buy American."

Again, economic systems can be classified according to their dominant incentive systems. Karl Marx predicted that goods would be distributed according to the principle, "to each according to his labor," during the early stages of socialism, whereas the ultimate communist system would be characterized by distribution "to each according to his needs." In other words, immature socialism would be based on material incentives, but full communism would be based on moral incentives. Similarly, distinctions may be drawn between **command socialism**, which makes extensive use of coercion; **utopian socialism**, which leans heavily on moral incentives; and **market socialism**, with its stronger reliance on material incentives.

CLASSIFICATION ACCORDING TO OBJECTIVES

Earlier we noted that automobiles are often classified according to the purposes they are meant to serve: race cars, economy cars, military vehicles, etc. Similarly, different economic systems are established to pursue different objectives, and they may be classified accordingly. Among the objectives that nations may choose to pursue are the following:

- Individual freedom
- High levels of personal consumption
- High rates of economic growth
- Economic and military power
- Equity in income distribution

[13]David E. M. Sappington, "Incentives in Principal-Agent Relationships," *Journal of Economic Perspectives* 5 (Spring 1991): 45–66.

■ Full employment
■ Protection of the natural environment
■ Price stability

As its name implies, a **free-enterprise economy** is one in which protection of individual freedom is a dominant objective. Proponents of free enterprise—from Adam Smith, Ludwig von Mises, and Friedrich von Hayek, to Milton and Rose Friedman—have always drawn a close connection between economic and political freedoms:

Economic freedom is an essential requisite for political freedom. By enabling people to cooperate with one another without coercion or central direction, it reduces the area over which political power is exercised. In addition, by dispersing power, the free market provides an offset to whatever concentration of political power may arise. The concentration of economic and political power in the same hands is a sure recipe for tyranny.[14]

Today, some of the strongest advocates of free enterprise are found in Russia and Eastern Europe, where the interplay between political and economic freedom is most evident. Janos Kornai, a well-known Hungarian economist, insists that a "free economy is, of course, a market economy," and it must be "embedded in a democratic political order, characterized by the free competition of political forces and ideas."[15]

Advocates of free enterprise usually place a top priority on individual freedom, but they argue that other objectives, such as economic growth and an equitable distribution of income, are also best achieved by the market system. "A society that puts freedom first," according to Milton and Rose Friedman, "will, as a happy byproduct, end up with both greater freedom and greater equality."[16]

In a **welfare state**, an equitable distribution of income and full employment are among the leading objectives, and positive governmental action is employed to pursue those objectives. Advocates of the welfare state find it hard to believe that free and unregulated capitalism will best promote the welfare of society. In the words of John Maynard Keynes, "The outstanding faults of the economic society in which we live are its failure to provide for full employment and its arbitrary and inequitable distribution of wealth and incomes."[17] Governmental programs, including countercyclical monetary and fiscal policy, redistribution of income, health and employment insurance, and many other services are supported in the welfare state.

---

[14]Milton Friedman and Rose Friedman, *Free to Choose: A Personal Statement* (New York: Harcourt Brace Jovanovich, 1979), 2–3.

[15]Janos Kornai, *The Road to a Free Economy* (New York: W. W. Norton, 1990), 22–23.

[16]Friedman and Friedman, *Free to Choose,* 148.

[17]John Maynard Keynes, *The General Theory of Employment, Interest, and Money* (New York: Harcourt, Brace, and World, 1964), 372.

Of course, equity, like beauty, is in the eye of the beholder. Is an equitable income distribution one that divides the national income equally across the population? Is it one that divides income according to work performed? If so, should inherited wealth be confiscated by the government? How can the work of carpenters, lawyers, artists, and legislators be reduced to a common denominator to divide the national income equitably? These are among the questions that must be considered in the welfare state.

A number of different labels have been attached to economic systems that set the attainment of economic and military power as a preeminent objective. **Mercantilism**, which held sway in England and much of Europe during the sixteenth, seventeenth, and eighteenth centuries, was a system of economic thought and policy that held that national economic power could be augmented by governmental support of domestic monopolies, subsidization of exports, and restriction of imports, all aimed toward the accumulation of wealth embodied in gold and silver. The preoccupation of the mercantilists with gold and silver was explained by Jacob Viner, an eminent economic historian:

With wealth one could finance and equip armies and navies, hire foreign mercenaries, bribe potential enemies, and subsidize allies. Power could be exercised to acquire colonies, to win access to new markets, and to monopolize trade routes, high-seas fisheries, and the slave trade with Africa.[18]

When capitalist ownership is combined with a totalitarian government bent on national economic and military power, the result is an exaggerated form of mercantilism, known as **fascism** or **nazism**. The relationship between individual rights and the national interest under such a system was described by the Fascist Labor Charter of 1927:

The Italian Nation is an organism having ends, a life and means superior in power and duration to the single individuals or groups of individuals composing it. . . . In view of the fact that private organization of production is a function of national concern, the organizer of the enterprise is responsible to the state for the direction given to production.[19]

AN OPERATIONAL CLASSIFICATION SYSTEM

Again, classification of economic systems is an imprecise enterprise that invites disagreement. We have considered four dimensions along which economic systems may be classified: ownership, coordinating mechanisms, incentive systems, and objectives. Many other dimensions can be considered,

---

[18] Jacob Viner, "Mercantilist Thought," *International Encyclopedia of the Social Sciences* (New York: Macmillan, 1968), 4:438.

[19] This translation is given in Earl Sikes, *Contemporary Economic Systems* (New York: Henry Holt, 1940), 670–675.

including centralization of decision making, modes of distributing information, the role of money in the economy, and the state of excess supply or excess demand in product markets.[20] Furthermore, when we attempt to classify economic systems, we should remember the following:

1. Economic systems may be either real or theoretical.
2. Theoretical systems may be "pure," but real systems generally include a mixture of different forms of ownership, coordination, incentives, and objectives.
3. Theoretical systems may stand still, but real systems change through time.
4. Reasonable persons will disagree on the assignment of actual countries to conceptual categories.
5. Ideally, assignment of actual countries to categories should be based on objective criteria, not on the rhetoric of politicians.

Pushing aside all the ambiguities, in Table 1.1 we identify eight very broad categories of economic systems that encompass most of the real and theoretical cases we will consider in this book. Countless numbers of other subcategories could be created by filling in more detail. For example, we could say that democratic socialism is a form of market socialism with a democratic set of objectives. Command socialism could be divided into its Stalinist, Maoist, and reformed variants, and so forth.

We shall examine countries that represent each of these systemic varieties in the following chapters. Our brief study of the developing world will explain the difficulties involved in breaking out of traditional and feudal modes of organization. A pure system of free-enterprise capitalism has never existed outside of textbooks and our closest approximation to that archetype is probably the U.S. economy. Among our examples of regulated capitalism, the United Kingdom, West Germany, and Sweden will represent the capitalist welfare states, and France and Japan will demonstrate the operation of indicative planning.

After the 1917 revolution, the Russians adopted a form of command socialism known as War Communism. They experimented with market socialism during the 1920s, under Lenin's New Economic Policy (NEP), but returned to command socialism in 1928, with the adoption of the first five-year plan. After World War II, the Soviet Union imposed command socialism on its Eastern European satellites. Today, of course, all these countries are in transition, but their destinations are unclear.

The Chinese leaders adopted the Stalinist version of command socialism after World War II, but developed their own Maoist variety during the Great Leap Forward (1958–1960) and the Cultural Revolution (1966–1976). Today,

---

[20]For a discussion of this last criterion, see Janos Kornai, "Resource-constrained versus Demand-constrained Systems," *Econometrica* 48 (1979): 801–819.

■ **TABLE 1.1**

AN OPERATIONAL CLASSIFICATION OF ECONOMIC SYSTEMS

	Dominant System of Ownership	Dominant System of Coordination	Dominant System of Incentives	Dominant System of Objectives
Traditional	Tribal	Tradition	Various	Various
Feudalism	Shared with superiors	Tradition, Market	Material, Coercion	Various
Free-Enterprise Capitalism	Private	Market	Material	Individual freedom
Regulated Capitalism	Private	Market, Indicative plan	Material	Various
Fascism, Nazism	Private	Market	Coercion, Material	National power
Command Socialism	Social	Market, Indicative plan	Material	Various
Market Socialism	Social	Market, Indicative plan	Material	Various

the Chinese economic system exhibits tremendous regional diversity; some regions have clung to command socialism and others have moved to a system approximating free-enterprise capitalism.

COMPARISONS OF SYSTEM PERFORMANCE

Given our competitive, nationalistic, and ideological leanings, we inevitably wish to know which economic system is best—capitalism or socialism, American or Japanese, German or Swedish? Let us briefly consider some of the problems involved in making such comparisons.

ISOLATION OF THE ECONOMIC SYSTEM

Earlier we noted that economic performance is influenced jointly by the economic system, the environment, and policies. If the economic performance of a country is relatively good or bad, we should not automatically conclude that the economic *system* is better or worse than that of other countries.

Before its disintegration in 1991, for example, Yugoslavia had a unique system of market socialism, based on worker participation in the ownership and management of enterprises. By all accounts, the performance of the Yugoslav economy was very poor during the 1980s, characterized by high unemployment and inflation rates, chronic balance of payments deficits, and deterioration in the standard of living.

Based on this information, can we quickly conclude that the system of worker-managed market socialism was a failure? This is the conclusion suggested by Ivan Ribnikar of the University of Ljubljana: "The lesson of Yugoslavia is that there is no compromise between a market economy and a centrally planned economy. One must have a true market economy."[21] On the other hand, we may ask whether *any* economic system would have performed successfully in the Yugoslav environment of regional conflict and political instability.

ACTUAL AND IDEAL ECONOMIC SYSTEMS

Polemical defenders of capitalism and socialism are often guilty of comparing a theoretical version of one system with a description of the actual problems of the other. During the Cold War, for example, American commentators often discussed the shortages of goods that existed under Soviet socialism, and then described how those problems could be solved in a perfectly competitive free-enterprise economy. Soviet writers emphasized the unemployment, inflation, and social injustice of capitalist economies, and argued that perfect coordination of economic activity could be achieved under a central plan. If we remember their limitations, abstract models of idealized economic systems can be quite useful in our understanding of actual economic systems. However, they should be handled with care when performance comparisons are made.

MEASUREMENT PROBLEMS

The statistical problems involved in making international comparisons of income, unemployment, income distribution, and the like are so important and complex that we will devote an entire chapter to their discussion. Differences in monetary systems, accounting standards, and data collection systems, as well as international secrecy, all contribute to the problems. Furthermore, many important performance criteria, such as individual freedom, are not readily quantifiable.

ASSIGNING PRIORITIES

Finally, even if we could isolate the influences of economic systems and quantify them fully, any broad performance comparison must be based on value judgments. Is the "better" economic system the one that provides more individual freedom, more economic growth, less inflation or unemployment,

---

[21]Craig Forman, "Yugoslavia's Problems Show Risks in Reforms of Socialist Systems," *The Wall Street Journal,* February 20, 1990, A1.

more technological progress, or more equitable distribution of income? If a single economic system does not excel according to all these and other criteria, then people or groups of people with different values may disagree on the question of performance. Indeed, even if one system outperforms the other according to all objective criteria, the "loser" may still maintain support on ideological grounds. In other words, as you read the remainder of this book, you are invited to draw your own conclusions.

SUMMARY

The economic performance of a country is determined by its economic system and environment, and by the policies of its leaders. An economic system is a set of institutions involved in making and implementing economic decisions.

Economic systems can be classified according to ownership of productive assets (feudalism, capitalism, or socialism), according to the mode of coordination (tradition, market, plan, or industrial policy), according to incentive systems (coercive, material, or moral), or according to objectives (free enterprise, welfare state, fascism, utopianism). Economic systems can be either real or theoretical, and real systems generally employ complex mixtures of ownership relations, coordination mechanisms, incentive systems, and objectives.

When we compare the performance of two economic systems, we should remember that: (1) poor economic performance of a country may be caused by environmental factors or poor policies, rather than a faulty economic system; (2) it is unfair to compare the real system in one country to a theoretical model of the system in the other country; (3) international statistical comparisons should be handled with care; and (4) performance comparisons ultimately are based on a system of values and priorities, about which opinions may differ.

DISCUSSION AND REVIEW QUESTIONS

1. In addition to those we have discussed in this chapter, what other criteria could be used to classify economic systems?

2. Who owns your college, university, or business? Does that system of ownership have a significant influence on the way the institution is governed?

3. Countries that rely on the market system during times of peace have been known to use rationing and central control during times of war. How might this be explained?

4. What is the difference between a directive plan and an indicative plan? What are the different purposes they serve?

5. According to *Nation's Business* magazine (April 1991), Modern of Marshfield, one of the best American furniture companies, relies heavily on

suggestions from its employees for improvements in manufacturing techniques. Twenty percent of the cost savings from these suggestions are distributed to the employees, and the employees who offer the best suggestions are named Colleague of the Month at a monthly luncheon, are given gifts, and are allowed to use a special parking space in the company lot. The annual winner, the Colleague of the Year, is awarded an expense-paid vacation. What categories of incentives are used by Modern of Marshfield, and which of these would be most effective with you?

6. According to your own system of values and priorities, what are the most important performance criteria for an economic system?

SUGGESTED READINGS

Comparative Economic Studies (CES) and *Journal of Comparative Economics* (JCE). *These are two professional journals that are devoted to the field of comparative economic systems. The articles in JCE tend to be more mathematically technical than those in CES.*

Bromley, Daniel W. *Economic Interests and Institutions.* Oxford: Basil Blackwell, 1989. *Aimed at readers with an intermediate knowledge of economic theory, this book provides an excellent discussion of institutional arrangements, institutional change, and economic policy analysis. The author's "primary purpose," he says, is to explore how our understanding of efficiency is molded by the existing institutional structure.*

Dahl, Robert A., and Charles E. Lindblom. *Politics, Economics, and Welfare.* New York: Harper & Row, 1953. *Written by a political scientist and an economist, this book examines economic and political systems under four broad categories: the price system, hierarchy, polyarchy, and bargaining.*

Kornai, Janos. *The Road to a Free Economy.* New York: W.W. Norton, 1990. *Written by a well-known Hungarian economist, the primary purpose of this book is to present the author's reform proposals, but it also includes an extended discussion of alternative forms of ownership.*

Wiles, Peter J. D. *Economic Institutions Compared.* New York: John Wiley, 1977. *Written with insight and biting wit by an iconoclastic professor (one of several in this field) at the London School of Economics. Long and sometimes difficult, but rewarding, this book is organized by institutions rather than by national case studies.*

INTERNET RESOURCES

AmosWorld
http://qmos.bus.okstate.edu

Economics Working Paper Archive
http://wuecon.wustl.edu/wpawelcome.html

International Affairs Resources
http://www.pitt.edu/~ian/ianres.html

International Political Economy
http://csf.colorado.edu:80/ipe/

Political Economy
http://sosig.esrc.bris.ac.uk/Subjects/polecon.html

Resources for Economists on the Internet
http://COBA.SHSU.edu/EconFAQ/EconFAQ.htm

The World: Income Groups Based on GDP per Capita

 Low-Income Countries

Lower-Middle-Income Countries

Upper-Middle-Income Countries

High-Income Countries

Source: World Bank, *World Development Report 1997*.

COMPARATIVE ECONOMIC STATISTICS

Thou shalt not have in thine house divers measures, a
great and a small. But thou shalt have a perfect and just
weight, a perfect and just measure shalt thou have.

—DEUTERONOMY 25:14–15

A s we compare the operation and performance of economic systems, we will base many of our judgments on statistical data. Comparisons of this kind are important for many reasons. First, statistical measurements lend greater objectivity to a field of study that provokes strong opinions. They help us to formulate and test complex hypotheses and to check our preconceived notions. In which country, for example, would you expect that exports represent a larger proportion of national income—Japan or France? You may be surprised to learn that the answer is France. In which of these countries is gross government debt larger in relation to national income? The answer this time is Japan.

International comparisons are particularly important when they are used to guide public policy. For many years, decisions concerning U.S. defense spending were influenced by comparisons with Soviet expenditures, prepared by the U.S. intelligence community. The International Financial Corporation, an arm of the World Bank, provides aid to low-income countries that can pass a needs test based on GDP per capita. Voting rights of member nations of the Commonwealth of Independent States are distributed according to national shares of regional GDP. Comparisons of national income, inflation, and other economic and social statistics are used to guide selection of partners for free trade agreements.[1]

Because of their importance and complexity, international statistical comparisons should be handled with caution. They are complicated, first of all, by differences in the definitions and accounting methods that are used by different countries. Second, there are major national differences in statistical reporting and collection systems. Third, there are difficult theoretical and methodological issues involved in the interpretation of international data.

---

[1]See, for example, Paul Kelash, "So Barbados Is Better? Economists Say Caribbean Should Be Next into NAFTA," *LDC Debt Report/Latin American Markets* 7 (July 11, 1994), passim.

Finally, because of state secrecy and a number of other considerations, many important statistics simply are not available.

In this chapter we will examine the methods and problems involved in making international comparisons for several broad classes of data, including national income, unemployment, inflation, and income distribution statistics. Our examination of the actual data will raise several questions to be discussed in later chapters.

NATIONAL INCOME COMPARISONS

Since 1665, when Sir William Petty compiled the first estimate of the "income of the people" of England, measures of national income have played a prominent role in international comparisons, and international comparisons have played an important role in national income measurement. John W. Kendrick notes that "the most frequent motivation of the individual scholars" who developed national income accounting before 1920 "was nationalism—the desire to compare the economic performance of rival nations."[2]

Today, national income comparisons are used for a number of purposes. Total national income or product is the most common measure of the economic size or power of a country. Ratios of imports or exports to national income are commonly used to measure the "openness" of countries to foreign trade, ratios of military spending to national income are used to measure the "burden" of defense, and so on. When we speak of the economic growth of a country, we usually mean growth of real national income and product. Finally, national income per capita is the yardstick most commonly used to compare levels of economic development or standards of living.

NATIONAL INCOME DEFINITIONS

When we attempt to compare the incomes of nations, we must be aware of the fact that countries and international agencies employ several different concepts and definitions of national income. For our purposes, the three most important measures are gross national product, gross domestic product, and net material product. It is not meaningful to compare, for example, the gross national product of one country with the net material product of another. Furthermore, if we compare the gross national products of two countries, we are likely to obtain different results from those that would arise from a comparison of net material products.

Gross national product (GNP) is the principal measure of aggregate production in the National Income and Product Account (NIPA) system that was developed by the U.S. Commerce Department. GNP is defined as the market value of all final goods and services produced by the nation in a year. In this case, the *nation* does not refer to the geographical confines of a country, or to its citizens, but rather to its residents—those who resided in the country for more than 6 months of the year. The income of a U.S. resident is included in

---

[2]John W. Kendrick, *Economic Accounts and Their Uses* (New York: McGraw-Hill, 1972), 10.

the U.S. GNP even if it is earned abroad. A U.S. resident may, for example, spend part of the year working abroad, or she may obtain income from investments abroad. In either case, her income would be included in the U.S. GNP. On the other hand, the income of a U.S. citizen, whether it is earned in the United States or abroad, is not included in U.S. GNP if that citizen is not also a resident.

Gross domestic product (GDP) is the central measure of national product in the System of National Accounts (SNA) developed by the United Nations. Members of the European Community, Japan, and many other nations have used the SNA since the 1970s. During the 1990s, the United States, China, and other countries of the former Soviet Union and Eastern Europe have gradually shifted to this system. Thus, the SNA is quickly becoming a world standard for national income accounting, which will facilitate international comparisons.

GDP is defined to be the annual market value of final goods and services produced within the geographic boundaries of a nation, whether it is produced by citizens, residents, or migrant workers.[3] The income generated by international investments is included in the GDP of the country where production of goods or services is conducted, which may not be the country where the recipient of that income resides.

Therefore, if we want to know where production is taking place, we should perform GDP comparisons. If, instead, we want to know where income is being received, GNP comparisons should provide more accurate results. In practice, though, the difference between GNP and GDP is relatively small for most countries — less than 3 percent of GDP (see Table 2.1). However, in countries that pay or receive large incomes from international investments or remittances, such as Bahrain, Fiji, Jamaica, and Kuwait, the difference between GNP and GDP can be quite substantial.

Net material product (NMP) is the central measure of national income in the Material Product System (MPS), until recently the official system of national accounts in the former Soviet Union, Eastern Europe, China, and other centrally planned economies. A few of these countries have shifted entirely to the SNA, but most are reporting a mixture of statistics from the SNA and the MPS.[4]

NMP is equal to the total value, measured in final selling prices, of final material production, net of depreciation of fixed assets.[5] Unlike GNP and

---

[3]Kendrick, *Economic Accounts*, 33–34. For a discussion of the shift from the NIPA to the SNA in the United States, see Carol S. Carson, "Replacing GNP: The Updated System of National Economic Accounts," *Business Economics* 27 (July 1992): 44–48. For a discussion of the transition in the former Soviet Union, see Youri Ivanov, Boris Rjabushkin, and Tatjana Homenko, "Introduction of the SNA into the Official Statistics of the Commonwealth of Independent States," *Review of Income and Wealth* 39 (September 1993): 279–294.

[4]For example, official reports of Russian economic performance are now primarily based on GDP and GNP, but official reports from the Commonwealth of Independent States, of which Russia is the largest member, are still based on NMP. Compare the reports in *Ekonomika i Zhizn*, No. 35, August 1994, supplement, and *Delovoi Mir*, No. 123, June 1994, 6.

[5]For a full discussion, see Abraham S. Becker, "National Income Accounting in the USSR," in *Soviet Economic Statistics*, ed. Vladimir Treml and John Hardt (Durham, N.C.: Duke University Press, 1972).

■ TABLE 2.1

GNP AS A PERCENTAGE OF GDP IN SELECTED COUNTRIES, 1995

Country	Percentage	Country	Percentage
Argentina	99.0	Japan	100.8
Bahrain	80.0	Kuwait	118.5
El Salvador	98.8	Philippines	102.8
Fiji	87.4	Singapore	100.7
France	99.7	Switzerland	104.3
Germany	99.6	United Kingdom	101.1
Jamaica	94.1	United States	99.9

Source: International Monetary Fund, *International Financial Statistics*, June 1997.

GDP, NMP does not include the value of nonmaterial services. Generally, services are included in NMP only if they contribute to the value of a material product, such as the services of repair technicians. Governmental, medical, educational, and recreational services are among those excluded from NMP. On a philosophical level, services are excluded in keeping with the classical notion, propounded by Adam Smith and amplified by Karl Marx, that service workers do not create anything of lasting substance—they are "unproductive."[6] On a practical level, the MPS was originally developed to meet the demands of central planners who were preoccupied with the structure of material production.

The differences between international comparisons based on GNP (or GDP) and NMP measurements can be quite substantial. In 1988, for example, when the Soviet NMP was reported at about 64 percent of the U.S. level, their GNP was only about 52 percent of the American total.[7] The main reason for the difference is quite clear. Because the U.S. economy has a highly developed service sector, NMP calculations excluded a much larger portion of economic activity for the United States than they did for the Soviet Union. (See "Economic Statistics for Economies in Transition," p. 25.)

---

[6]In their recent book, *Measuring the Wealth of Nations* (Cambridge: Cambridge University Press, 1994), Anwar M. Shaikh and E. Ahmet Tonak propose a system of national accounts, based on Marxian categories, that falls between the "polar extremes" of the SNA and MPS systems. They include many nonmaterial services in social consumption, but not in production.

[7]The NMP estimate is from Goskomstat SSSR, *Narodnoe khoziaistvo SSSR v 1988 g.* (Moscow: Finansi i Statistika, 1989), 681. The GNP estimate is the geometric mean of dollar and ruble comparisons in U.S. Central Intelligence Agency, *Handbook of Economic Statistics, 1990* (CPAS 90–10001, September 1990), 38. In reality, the relative size of the Soviet national income probably was much smaller than either of these figures suggests. According to unofficial estimates, if proper adjustments were made for low product quality and false reporting by managers, Soviet GNP would be only 15 to 35 percent of the U.S. level. See "Is the Economy as Bad as the Soviets Say?" *Orbis* 34 (Fall 1990), 509–525.

Among the many challenges that face the transitional economies (TEs) of Eastern Europe, one of the most urgent is to reform their systems of economic statistics. According to Vadim Kirichenko, chairman of the Russian State Committee for Statistics, "Our current policy in the field of statistics . . . is to overcome the vestiges and distortions imposed by the system of administrative command. In the past, statistical and theoretical work had to praise the system of administrative command, reporting its successes and hiding its weaknesses." Today, the statistical agencies are operating more independently, free to collect and publish statistics relating to crime, unemployment, infant mortality, drug addiction, strike activity, and many other social problems that were not reported a few years ago.

Under the central planning system, many products were produced by only a few large state enterprises, all of which were required to provide detailed reports to the authorities on their output, employment, sales, purchases, and financial condition. Thus, it was possible to base national statistics on *universal* coverage. Today, the TEs are experiencing rapid growth in the number of small, market-oriented enterprises that are not controlled by central planners. Under these circumstances, it is necessary to base national statistics on partial coverage, derived from random surveys. These sampling methods have been used for many years in the West, but they are relatively new in the TEs.

Undoubtedly, the economic reforms will cause business enterprises to change their reporting biases. In the past, enterprises concealed information about their production capacities, hoping to obtain easy assignments from the central planners. Today, with a stronger profit motive, enterprises are more likely to conceal information about new products and production methods, hoping to protect their competitive advantage, and about their profitability, hoping to avoid taxation.

The TEs are adopting statistical methods and definitions that were developed in the industrial West. For example, they are shifting toward the use of GDP rather than NMP as their basic measure of national income. These changes are sometimes required for membership in organizations, such as the International Monetary Fund, and they will make it easier to perform international comparisons. On the other hand, they will make it more difficult to compare the present performance of the TEs with their past, when a different statistical system was used.

In addition to these we have mentioned, economic reform presents many other problems to the statistical services. How much confidentiality should be granted to the private sector? How should we account for improvements in product quality and selection that result from the market reforms? Which statistics should be collected and reported by the state, and which should be handled by the private sector? The TEs can look to the West for suggestions, but they will have to find their own answers to questions such as these.

Source: Papers by Vadim Kirichenko, Paul Marer, Jozef Olenski, and Leszek Zienkowski in *Economic Statistics for Economies in Transition: Eastern Europe in the 1990s*. Washington, D.C.: U.S. Bureau of Labor Statistics and Eurostat, 1994.

UNCOUNTED PRODUCTION AND INCOME

Certain forms of production and income are not fully included even in the broader measures of national income, such as GNP and GDP. Generally speaking, GDP measurements include only the value of goods and services that are produced legally and sold on open markets. Let us briefly consider how this restriction affects international comparisons of income.

First, GNP measurements exclude most of the goods and services produced by families for their own consumption because these are never sold on an open market. Thus, when we perform our own housework, care for our children, or grow vegetables in our backyards, our efforts are seldom reflected in GNP calculations. If these goods and services were counted, they would enlarge American GNP by about 20 to 33 percent.[8] Nonmarket activities are even more significant in underdeveloped subsistence economies, accounting for about 40 to 45 percent of total labor time.[9] This helps explain how the World Bank can report, with a straight face, that GNP per person in Mozambique was $80 (25 cents per day!) in 1995.[10] Clearly, a great deal of production in Mozambique is never sold on a market and is not included in GNP.

In addition to the problem of unmarketed output, national income estimates also exclude the value of goods and services produced in the **underground** (or **informal** or **second** or **shadow**) **economy**—production that is hidden from governmental authorities to escape taxation, regulation, and prosecution for criminal activities. Inclusion of the underground economy would increase measured GDP by about 4 percent in Japan, 6 percent in the United States, 12 percent in the European Union, and 20 to 25 percent in the transitional economies of Eastern Europe. In many African and Latin American countries, between 40 and 50 percent of the nonagricultural labor force is employed in the informal sector.[11] In general, the underground economy seems to be largest in countries that have high tax rates and cumbersome systems of business registration, poor systems of statistical reporting and tax

---

[8]This is the range of contributions of "unpaid household labor" in the studies surveyed in Robert Eisner, *The Total Incomes System of Accounts* (Chicago: The University of Chicago Press, 1989), 55–85.

[9]Luisella Goldschmidt-Clermont, *Economic Evaluations of Unpaid Household Work: Africa, Asia, Latin America, and Oceania*, Women, Work, and Development Series, No. 14 (Geneva: International Labour Office, 1987), 58.

[10]World Bank, *World Development Report 1997* (New York: Oxford University Press, 1997), 214.

[11]These estimates were gathered from a number of sources, including the following: David Turnham, Bernard Salome, and Antoine Schwarz, *The Informal Sector Revisited* (Paris: OECD Development Center, 1990); Peter S. Spiro, "Invisible, Outlawed, and Untaxed: America's Underground Economy," *Business Economics* 29 (July 1994): 75; David Manisan, et. al., "Europe's Booming Black Economy," *International Management* 42 (July–August 1987): 24–30; Anna Marszalek, "Report on the Parallel Economy," *Polish News Bulletin* (April 22, 1994), 1; and Richard Bruner, "Unreported Business in Hungary Spreads Budget's Red Ink," *Christian Science Monitor*, November 15, 1993, 10.

enforcement, and high rates of inflation and unemployment. In countries that fit this description, national income may be seriously understated.[12]

CONVERSION OF NATIONAL INCOMES TO A SINGLE CURRENCY

Before national incomes of various countries can meaningfully be compared, they must be measured in a single currency, usually the U.S. dollar. A simple and obvious solution is to convert all the other currencies into dollars (or some other common currency) with market exchange rates. This simple method of currency conversion will yield fairly accurate income comparisons if: (1) the countries under comparison have free and open market economies, (2) the countries are at similar levels of economic development, (3) capital flows (international saving and investment) between the countries are small compared to volumes of international trade, (4) inflation rates in the countries are fairly low and stable, and (5) exchange rates are relatively stable during the comparison period.

Under these conditions, the market exchange rates should be roughly equal to **purchasing-power-parity (PPP) exchange rates.** That is, each exchange rate should roughly translate the prices of one market economy into the prices of another. Suppose, for example, that a particular bundle of goods can be purchased in the United States for $100. If the dollar/yen exchange rate is currently at PPP, we should be able to purchase a similar bundle of goods in Japan by exchanging $100 for yen at the market exchange rate and paying Japanese prices.

Why, under the conditions listed above, do market exchange rates gravitate toward PPP levels? Basically, because of the forces of international competition. Suppose, for example, that the price of a ton of steel is presently lower in Japan than in the United States. That is, the yen price, converted to dollars at the market exchange rate, is lower than the dollar price. What will happen? International competition will tend to cause a decrease in the dollar price, and/or an increase in the yen price, and/or an increase in the exchange rate of the yen. In any case, after these adjustments occur, the market exchange rate will reflect the relative purchasing powers of the two currencies.

Realistically, though, anyone who has traveled abroad knows that exchange rates tend to stray, more or less, from PPP levels. In countries where the currency is undervalued, travelers easily find bargains. In countries where the currency is overvalued, prices may seem exorbitant. If departures from PPP are large, the conditions listed in the first paragraph of this section have probably been broken.

---

[12]An important exception to the rule is Italy, which has a relatively large underground economy, but deliberately attempts to include it in measured GDP. Italy began this practice in the mid-1980s, attempting to demonstrate that it had overtaken the United Kingdom as the Western world's fifth largest economic power.

For example, exchange rates may depart significantly from PPP during periods of price instability and speculative activity in foreign exchange markets. To reduce the impact of temporary exchange rate fluctuations on its national income comparisons, the World Bank, for many years, has used a procedure called the **Atlas Method.** According to this method, the national income of a country in year t is converted into dollars with a calculated exchange rate, equal to an average of the exchange rates in years t, t − 1, and t − 2, adjusted for general price movements.[13] As the data in the first two columns of Table 2.2 indicate, the results derived from the Atlas Method are similar in most cases to those obtained from a simple application of the exchange rate in year t to the national income data in year t. Still, in comparisons of GNP per person for 1995, Mexico was ahead of Hungary according to the simplest exchange rate method, but Hungary was ahead of Mexico according to the Atlas Method.

The Atlas Method reduces the effect of temporary exchange rate movements, but it does not solve measurement problems caused by long-term departures from PPP caused by economic regulation, long-term capital flows, and structural differences between countries at different levels of economic development. To deal with these problems, the **U.N. International Comparison Project (ICP)** has devised a repricing procedure that is much more complex than the Atlas Method.[14] The output of each country is divided into 151 product groups and the value of each group is calculated according to a set of average **international prices** (expressed in terms of U.S. dollars). When the product groups are added together, the resulting comparisons of national income should be roughly equal to those obtained by application of PPP exchange rates.

The data in the third column of Table 2.2 demonstrate that international comparisons based on the ICP repricing method can differ substantially from those based on market exchange rates. Switzerland, which has a much larger income per capita than the United States according to the other two methods, falls slightly below the United States according to the ICP method. On the other hand, middle-income and low-income countries, such as Mexico, Hungary, Poland, India, and China, seem to have much larger dollar incomes according to the ICP method.

THE INDEX NUMBER PROBLEM

Although international comparisons of national income based on the ICP repricing methods are, in principle, superior to those based on market or official exchange rates, they still do not solve one nagging problem. As we

---

[13]For a fuller explanation of the Atlas Method, see World Bank, *World Development Report 1997*, 262.

[14]See Irving Kravis et al., *World Product and Income: International Comparisons of Real Gross Product* (Baltimore: Johns Hopkins University Press, 1982); and Robert Summers and Alan Heston, "A New Set of International Comparisons of Real Product and Price Levels Estimates for 130 Countries, 1950–1985," *Review of Income and Wealth* 34 (March 1988): 1–25.

■ TABLE 2.2

CONVERTING GNP PER CAPITA TO DOLLARS: THREE METHODS COMPARED (U.S. DOLLARS PER PERSON IN 1995)

	Simple Exchange Rate Method	World Bank Atlas Method	ICP Repricing Method
Switzerland	44,392	40,630	25,860
Germany	29,431	27,510	20,070
United States	26,980	26,980	26,970
United Kingdom	18,838	18,700	19,260
Mexico	5,999	3,320	6,400
Hungary	3,040	4,120	6,410
Poland	3,003	2,790	5,400
China	564	620	2,920
India	328	340	1,400
Nigeria	77	80	810

Sources: First column: Calculated by the author from GNP, exchange rate, and population data in International Monetary Fund, *International Financial Statistics* (June 1997), passim. Second and third columns: World Bank, *World Development Report 1997* (New York: Oxford University Press, 1997), Appendix table 1.

have seen, national products can be converted to a single currency by applying a single set of prices to the outputs of the various countries. The question remains: Whose prices do we use? The so-called **index number problem** refers to the fact that comparisons of macroeconomic aggregates can be greatly influenced by the prices used to add the values of products together.

Suppose, for example, that we wish to compare the national products of the United States and the former Soviet Union, and, for the sake of simplicity, suppose that both countries produced only two products—wheat and steel. According to the hypothetical data in Table 2.3, U.S. agriculture was highly productive; thus, U.S. wheat production was greater than Soviet wheat production and the price of wheat was relatively low in dollars. Suppose on the other hand, that the Soviet Union had a relatively efficient steel industry, with a high level of production at a relatively low price.

If we calculate the U.S. GNP using rubles, we apply the relatively high ruble price for wheat to the high level of U.S. wheat production and thus derive a U.S. GNP that is nearly twice the Soviet level. The Soviet Union, however, looks better if the comparison is done in dollars: the Soviet GNP includes a large volume of steel production valued at the high U.S. steel price.

Our hypothetical example illustrates the **Gershchenkron effect**—when the production levels of two countries are compared, the GNP of country X

■ **TABLE 2.3**

HYPOTHETICAL GNP CALCULATIONS

	Final Output (billion tons) USSR	U.S.	Prices per Ton Rubles	Dollars
Wheat	10	50	16	15
Steel	50	30	8	20

Gross National Product

	USSR	U.S.	USSR/U.S.
Rubles (billion)	(10)(16) + (50)(8) = 560	(50)(16) + (30)(8) = 1040	.54
Dollars (billion)	(10)(15) + (50)(20) = 1150	(50)(15) + (30)(20) = 1350	.85

will appear to be relatively larger if the prices of country Y are used to sum the products of each of the countries. This regularity is supported by the actual, rather than hypothetical, estimates of U.S. and Soviet GNP. According to the Central Intelligence Agency, Soviet GNP was 37 percent of the U.S. level in 1990 when measured in rubles and about 64 percent of the U.S. level when measured in dollars.[15] Which estimate is more meaningful or valid? The one in dollars? The one in rubles? Some average of the two? Unfortunately, this question has no straightforward answer.

As we noted before, the U.N. International Comparisons Project (ICP) handles the index number problem by employing a set of average international prices. In principle, this is better than using the prices of any single country. In practice, though, the prices used in the ICP studies are closer to those of the industrial countries than they are to those of the developing countries. The Gershchenkron effect would suggest that application of industrial world prices is likely to impart an upward bias to the estimates of national income for the developing countries. Indeed, the estimates of developing-country incomes that are obtained by the ICP studies are several times larger than those obtained by simple market exchange rate conversions (Table 2.2). Thus, the ICP estimates have been criticized by Third World economists, who fear that the larger income estimates may reduce their nations' access to foreign aid.[16]

---

[15]Central Intelligence Agency, *Handbook of Economic Statistics, 1991,* CPAS 91–10001, September 1991, 36. Beginning with the 1992 *Handbook,* the CIA has not provided this kind of information for the former Soviet Union or for any of its successor states.

[16]See, for example, Xin Dun, "China's Strength Is Overestimated," *Beijing Review* (June 14–20, 1993): 9–10.

MILITARY SPENDING: THE INDEX NUMBER GAME

In any comparison of broad aggregates, such as industrial production, agricultural production, or the general crime rate, we must deal with many of the same problems that occur in GNP comparisons. For many years, the CIA used a repricing procedure to compare U.S. and Soviet defense spending. Each year, they would use satellite reconnaissance and other intelligence sources to compile a list of military purchases in physical terms—numbers of personnel, aircraft, ships, missiles, and so on. Next, they would attach approximate dollar prices to each of those items (wage rates paid to U.S. military personnel and prices of American weapons that were more or less similar to Soviet weapons) and add them together. Thus, the CIA calculated the approximate number of dollars that the Soviet Union would have to spend in American prices to pay for its military. This dollar amount was compared to the actual level of U.S. military spending.

From time to time, CIA analysts would also prepare comparisons in rubles, but they had less confidence in these estimates because of uncertainty about ruble prices. Thus, the ruble estimates were given little publicity.

According to the Gershchenkron effect, the relative size of the Soviet military should have been somewhat larger in the dollar estimates than in the ruble estimates. Indeed, according to the CIA estimates for 1981, the Soviet military cost 45 percent more than the American military in dollar prices and 25 percent more in ruble prices. By 1985, after an American defense buildup, the CIA estimated that U.S. and Soviet spending were roughly equal in dollars. Ruble comparisons were not published after the early 1980s, but apparently they would have indicated that the United States was outspending the Soviet Union. According to some critics, the CIA overestimated the relative size of the Soviet military, and according to others, they seriously underestimated the Soviet threat.

Sources: The CIA estimates were reported in annual hearings of the Joint Economic Committee of the U.S. Congress, titled Allocation of Resources in the Soviet Union and China. For critical analyses of the CIA estimates, see Dmitri Steinberg, "Trends in Soviet Military Expenditure," *Soviet Studies* 42 (October 1990): 675–699; Franklyn D. Holzman, "How the CIA Distorted the Truth about Soviet Military Spending," *Challenge* 33 (March–April 1990): 27–36; and Daniel Berkowitz et. al., "An Evaluation of the CIA's Analysis of Soviet Economic Performance, 1970–90," *Comparative Economic Studies* 35 (Summer 1993): 41–56.

ALTERNATIVE MEASURES OF THE STANDARD OF LIVING

As was mentioned earlier, national income per capita is the measure most commonly used for international comparisons of economic development and living standards. However, because of the deficiencies discussed above—disagreements over how national income should be defined, exclusion of unmarketed and hidden output, and the problems involved in converting national incomes to a common currency—the search is under way for alternative measures of the standard of living.

For a number of years, many international aid agencies and scholars have used the **Physical Quality of Life Index (PQLI)** as an alternative to national income. Developed by the Overseas Development Council, the PQLI is meant to measure economic and social development in terms of human results (health and education) rather than in terms of inputs (consumption of food and other goods and services). The PQLI is a simple unweighted average of index numbers for three development indicators: infant mortality rate, life expectancy, and adult literacy.[17] It is attractive in its simplicity, in its apparent lack of bias toward any economic system, and in its emphasis on results. Furthermore, because public health and literacy are positively correlated with income equality, the PQLI tells us something about the distribution as well as the average level of real income in each country. Indeed, given the high priority that socialist countries supposedly placed on income equality and public health, a planned economy with a particular level of per capita income may be expected to have a higher PQLI than a market economy at that same level of income. Statistical tests have yielded mixed results, but they provide some support for this hypothesis.[18]

A relatively new and interesting measure of the standard of living is the **Human Development Index (HDI)**. Introduced in 1990, the HDI has gained recognition quickly because it is sponsored by the United Nations Development Program, and is the centerpiece of that agency's annual *Human Development Report*. HDI, like PQLI, is an unweighted average of three other indexes. First, a health index is based on life expectancy at birth. Second, an educational attainment index is formed by combining an index of adult literacy (two-thirds weight) and a composite index of primary, secondary, and college-level school enrollment (one-third weight). Third, an index of "access to resources" is based on GDP per capita at PPP (the ICP repricing method), adjusted to reflect diminishing marginal utility derived from higher levels of income. Thus, HDI differs from PQLI because it excludes the infant mortality rate, includes school enrollment, and includes GDP per capita.[19] Neither PQLI nor HDI includes indicators specifically related to leisure, crime,

[17]The PQLI is fully explained in Morris D. Morris, *Measuring the Condition of the World's Poor* (New York: Pergamon Press, 1979). Also, see the explanatory note under Table 2.4.

[18]Edward F. Stuart, "The PQLI as a Measure of Comparative Economic Performance," *The ACES Bulletin* 26 (Winter 1984): 43–53; and John P. Burkett, "PQLI as a Measure of Comparative Performance: Comment," *Comparative Economic Studies* 28 (Summer 1986): 59–68.

[19]For a full explanation of HDI, see the United Nations Development Program, *Human Development Report 1997* (New York: Oxford University Press, 1997), 122. For a critique, see Arnab Acharya and Howard J. Wall, "An Evaluation of the United Nations' Human Development Index," *Journal of Economic and Social Measurement* 20 (1994): 51–65.

ALTERNATIVE MEASURES OF THE STANDARD OF LIVING, 1995

	Real GDP per Capita (PPP$)	Physical Quality of Life Index	Human Development Index
United States	26,980	96	.942
Hong Kong	22,950	96	.914
Japan	22,110	100	.940
Canada	21,130	98	.960
France	21,030	98	.946
Germany	20,070	96	.924
United Kingdom	19,260	97	.931
Sweden	18,540	99	.936
Chile	9,520	90	.891
Mexico	6,400	84	.853
Russia	4,480	85	.792
China	2,920	79	.626
India	1,400	57	.446
Ethiopia	450	32	.244

Source: World Bank, *World Development Report 1997; and* United Nations Development Programme, *Human Development Report 1997* (New York: Oxford University Press, 1997). Figures in the second column were calculated by the author according to the formula: PQLI = (Adult Literacy Rate/3) + [(Life Expectancy at Birth − 40/1.2)] + [(179 − Infant Mortality Rate)/5.25].

mental health, unemployment, environmental disruption, or many other dimensions of the quality of life.

In Table 2.4, we see that the relative performances of countries are quite different according to GDP per capita (at PPP), PQLI, and HDI. For example, the United States leads the world in GDP per capita, but follows behind Canada and France in PQLI and HDI. Japan leads the world in PQLI, but follows the United States in GDP per capita and HDI. The developing countries compare more favorably with the industrial market economies in terms of the PQLI than they do in terms of per capita national income.

INCOME DISTRIBUTION COMPARISONS

We noted in the previous chapter that the performance of an economic system may be assessed not only by the size and growth of the national income it generates but also by the equity with which that income is distributed across the population. We also noted, however, that one person's equity is another person's injustice. An equitable income distribution may be one that divides income evenly, or according to work, inheritance, market forces, or any number of other standards. We should establish at the outset, therefore, that measures of income *equality* may not be the same as measures of income *equity*.

MEASURES OF INCOME INEQUALITY

Data relating to the distributions of income in the United States, Sweden, and Brazil are presented in Table 2.5. Based on these data, the Swedish distribution of income is more even than that of the United States, and the Brazilian distribution, like that of many Third World countries, is less even. These observations can be illustrated in several ways. First, and most simply, the poorest decile (tenth) of households received only 0.6 percent of total income in Brazil, compared to 1.6 percent in the United States and 2.6 percent in Sweden.

Another simple measure of income inequality is the **decile ratio**—the share of income received by the richest decile of the population divided by the share of the poorest decile. A larger decile ratio would, of course, denote a less equal distribution of income. According to the data in Table 2.5, the decile ratios are 18.1 for the United States, 8.2 for Sweden, and 84.3 for Brazil. Although the decile ratio is a simple and useful measure of inequality, it utilizes data concerning only the richest and poorest members of the population, ignoring those in the middle.

A second tool for analysis and comparison of income distributions is the **Lorenz curve,** which illustrates the percentage of total income received by each cumulative percentage of the population. Lorenz curves based on the data in Table 2.5 are presented in Figure 2.1. Clearly, all Lorenz curves must pass through points A and B on the graph, because zero percent of households must logically receive zero percent of total income, and 100 percent of households must logically receive 100 percent of income. It is the *shape* of the Lorenz curve between these points that reflects the degree of income inequality.

If there were a country in the world with a perfectly even distribution of income (there is not), its Lorenz curve would be the straight diagonal line, AB. Along that line, the poorest 20 percent of households receive 20 percent of total income, the poorest 40 percent of households receive 40 percent of total income, and so forth. The greater the income inequality in a country, the more the Lorenz curve will bend away from the line of equality. Thus, it is clear by inspection that Brazilian income is distributed less equally than American income, and Swedish income is distributed more equally. In the extreme and unsustainable case of perfect income inequality (one person receives all the income) the Lorenz curve would be the right-angled line, ACB.

A third tool for comparison of income distributions is the **Gini ratio,** named for the Italian statistician who introduced it in 1912. The Gini ratio is equal to the measured area between the diagonal line of equality, AB, and the Lorenz curve, divided by the total area of the triangle, ABC. In the case of

■ **TABLE 2.5**

DISTRIBUTION OF HOUSEHOLD INCOME IN THE UNITED STATES, SWEDEN, AND BRAZIL

Percentage of Total Household Income Received by Each Decile

	United States	Sweden	Brazil
Poorest Decile	1.6	2.6	0.6
Second Decile	3.4	4.6	1.4
Third Decile	4.7	6.1	2.1
Fourth Decile	6.1	6.7	2.9
Fifth Decile	7.5	7.5	4.0
Sixth Decile	8.9	9.9	5.4
Seventh Decile	10.6	11.8	7.1
Eighth Decile	12.6	13.6	9.9
Ninth Decile	15.6	16.0	16.0
Tenth Decile	29.0	21.2	50.6

Source: Wouter van Ginneken and Jung-goo Park, *Generating Internationally Comparable Income Distribution Estimates* (Geneva: International Labor Office, 1984), Tables 1 and A.1. Reference years are 1971 for the United States, 1972 for Brazil, and 1979 for Sweden.

perfect equality there would be no area between the Lorenz curve and the diagonal line (they would be the same line) and the Gini ratio would equal zero. In the case of perfect inequality, the Gini ratio would equal the area of triangle ABC divided by itself, or 1. For any real country, the Gini ratio falls somewhere between 0 and 1, with a larger coefficient denoting more income inequality.

Because the curved area between a Lorenz curve and the line of equality can be difficult to measure, exact calculation of the Gini ratio is somewhat complex, and several different estimation techniques are available. The simplest formula is:

$$\text{Gini ratio} = 1 - 2 \sum_{i=1}^{n} \left(\frac{1}{2n} + \frac{(n-i)}{n} \right) P_i$$

Where:

n = number of income groups (n = 10 in Table 2.5)

i = a particular income group (I= 1 for poorest group)

P_i = fractoin of total income received by income groupe I, expressed as a decimal fraction rather than a percentage (P_1 = .016 for the United States).

If the population is divided into ten income groups (as in Table 2.5), then:

■ FIGURE 2.1

LORENZ CURVES

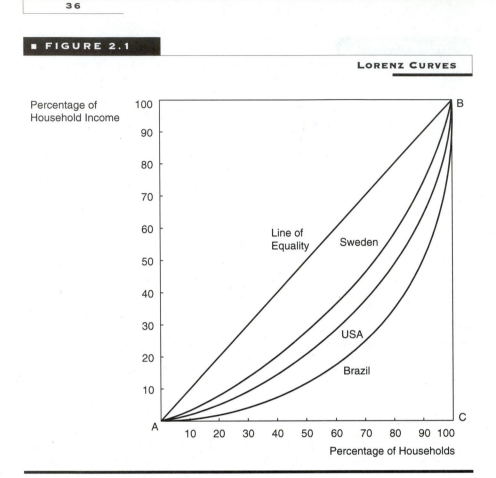

$$\text{Gini ratio} = 1 - (1.9P_1 + 1.7P_2 + 1.5P_3 + 1.3P_4 + 1.1P_5 +$$
$$.9P_6 + .7P_7 + .5P_8 + .3P_9 + .1P_{10})$$

Applying this formula, the Gini ratios calculated from the data in Table 2.5 are 0.30 for Sweden, 0.39 for the United States, and 0.61 for Brazil. Data for several other countries are presented in Table 2.6. These data have been selected and adjusted to ensure a reasonable level of comparability, but they should be treated with caution.

Closely related to the concept of income inequality is the **poverty rate**— the percentage of the population living below a level of income that provides for basic needs. International comparisons of poverty may be based on an "absolute" approach, with a single poverty line for all countries, or a "relative" approach, with higher poverty thresholds in countries that have higher average incomes. In Table 2.6, for example, the estimates in the Absolute column are based on a uniform threshold of $7,392 in 1985 U.S. dollars, converted to each currency on a PPP basis. In the Relative column, the poverty

■ TABLE 2.6

ABSOLUTE AND RELATIVE POVERTY RATES

	Year	Absolute Percentage Poor	Relative Percentage Poor
Australia	1987	29.9	15.2
Austria	1987	26.3	8.4
Canada	1987	11.3	11.5
France	1984	29.8	7.6
Germany	1984	30.6	6.6
Italy	1986	42.8	10.4
Luxembourg	1985	13.7	5.6
Netherlands	1987	42.4	5.0
Sweden	1987	34.9	9.1
United Kingdom	1986	35.9	9.2
United States	1986	17.7	17.7

Source: LIS data sets presented in McKinley L. Blackburn, "International Comparisons of Poverty," *American Economic Review* 84 (May 1994): 372.

line in each country is taken to be one-half of median income in that country. On an absolute scale, Italy has the highest poverty rate in the group and Canada has the lowest. On a relative scale, the United States has the highest incidence of poverty and the Netherlands has the lowest.

Estimated poverty rates for developing countries are presented in Table 2.7. These are estimated by the World Bank according to an absolute poverty line of $370 per person per year at 1985 PPP prices. In 1985, these figures suggest that the South Asian countries had the highest incidence of poverty in the world. By the end of the century, though, their rates are expected to be significantly lower than those in Sub-Saharan Africa.

PROBLEMS IN MAKING INCOME DISTRIBUTION COMPARISONS

If international comparisons of income inequality are to be made—whether we employ decile ratios, Lorenz curves, Gini ratios, or poverty rates—we must consider the comparability of the underlying income distribution data. First, the data should be comparable in their coverage and segmentation of the population. For example, data that cover only employed persons or workers will indicate a greater degree of income equality than data that include retired persons, the unemployed, and others with low incomes. With regard to segmentation, the distribution of income among households can be quite different from the distribution of income among families or individual

■ TABLE 2.7

POVERTY RATES IN DEVELOPING REGIONS

	1985	1990	2000 projected
All Developing Countries	30.5	29.7	24.1
Sub-Saharan Africa	47.6	47.8	49.7
East Asia	13.2	11.3	4.2
South Asia	51.8	49.0	36.9
Eastern Europe	7.1	7.1	5.8
Middle East , North Africa	30.6	33.1	30.6
Latin America, Caribbean	22.4	25.2	24.9

Note: The rates in this table should not be compared with those in Table 2.6, which are based on much higher income thresholds. See explanation in text.
Sources: First two columns are from World Bank, *World Development Report 1993* (New York: Oxford University Press, 1993), 42. Projections for 2000 are from *World Development Report 1993*, 30.

people.[20] Inequality is significantly greater between households in Bangladesh and Sweden, but it is greater between individuals in South Korea and Mexico.[21]

Second, the data should be comparable in terms of income coverage. That is, the data should have similar coverage of wages, profits, rents, capital gains, transfer payments, income in kind, and so forth. Inclusion of capital gains, for example, usually increases measured income inequality. Comparisons are preferably based on income after taxes and transfer payments, because many countries design these programs to redistribute income.

The significance of these considerations can be illustrated with data relating to the United States. In 1989, the Gini ratio for money income received by families was 0.40, and for households it was 0.43. If government transfer payments were removed from household income, inequality would be much greater, yielding a Gini ratio of approximately 0.48. If household incomes were adjusted to reflect the effects of taxes and noncash transfer payments, measured inequality would be considerably lower, reflected in a Gini ratio of 0.39.[22]

---

[20]According to definitions used by the U.S. Bureau of the Census, a "household" consists of all persons who occupy a housing unit. A "family" consists of two or more related people who reside together. A single person can constitute a household, but he/she cannot constitute a family.

[21]For a comparison of household and individual income distributions for twenty countries, see R. M. Sundrum, Income Distribution in Less Developed Countries (London: Routledge, 1990), 77.

[22]U. S. Department of Commerce, Bureau of the Census, *Money Income and Poverty in the United States, 1989*, Current Population Reports, P–60, no. 168 (September 1990), 30; and U. S. Department of Commerce, Bureau of the Census, *Measuring the Effect of Benefits and Taxes on Income and Poverty: 1989*, Current Population Reports, P–60, no. 169-RD (September 1990), 5.

For industrial capitalist countries, the most careful comparisons of income inequality and poverty have been prepared under the auspices of the **Luxembourg Income Study (LIS)**. The heart of the LIS project is a huge unified database of household income surveys from the participating countries. The national data sets have been adjusted to yield comparable values for 42 income variables and 28 demographic variables. After completion of a training program, researchers around the world are able to obtain and manipulate the data through the Internet.[23]

Estimates of income inequality in developing countries are made difficult by poor statistical reporting systems. For reasons that we shall consider in the following section, unemployment is often underestimated in low-income countries, possibly causing an underestimation of income inequality. On the other hand, nonmarket incomes are also underestimated in these countries, possibly causing an overestimation of inequality. According to estimates for Malaysia, the Gini ratio falls from 0.62 to 0.57 (denoting greater equality) when in-kind income, transfer payments, and the value of housing services are included in income.[24]

UNEMPLOYMENT COMPARISONS

International comparisons of unemployment are facilitated by the fact that international agreements were reached in 1954 and 1982 under the auspices of the International Labour Organization on a standard definition for unemployment.[25] Nevertheless, national practices vary with respect to age limits, reference periods, criteria used to determine whether a person is actively seeking work, treatment of persons who are temporarily laid off, handling of military personnel, and other details that are not included in a standard definition. Moreover, some nations have ignored the international agreements.

Aside from definitional problems, the international comparability of unemployment rates is also damaged by differences in the methods of data collection. The United States, Japan, and several other high-income countries base their unemployment estimates on periodic labor force surveys. These probably yield the best estimates of unemployment because they take account of demographic groups that are usually missed by other methods.

A much larger number of countries, including Germany, the United Kingdom, and most of the developing nations, base their monthly unemployment figures on registrations at governmental employment offices. These may, of

---

[23]For a full description of the LIS project, see Timothy M. Smeeding, Lee Rainwater, and Rick Simpson, "Comparative Cross-National Research on Income and Economic Well-Being: The Luxembourg Income Study," *Survey of Current Business* 69 (March 1989): 62–68. The data in Table 2.6 are based on an LIS study.

[24]Michael Kusnic and Julie Davanzo, "Accounting for Non-Market Activities in the Distribution of Income," *Journal of Development Economics* 21 (May 1986): 211–227.

[25]The standard definition and a description of the various systems of data collection are given in *Yearbook of Labour Statistics* (Geneva: International Labour Office, 1988), 617–618.

course, overlook unemployed persons who choose not to register. In low-income countries where the government employment service has few convenient offices, provides few job placement services, and offers little unemployment compensation, workers have little incentive to register their unemployment. Thus, the employment office in Singapore counted only 8,000 registrations in 1987, but the labor force survey estimated that 59,000 were unemployed.[26]

In Table 2.8, four sets of unemployment estimates are assembled. The first column lists the rates that are commonly reported by each of the countries, reflecting their various definitions and methods of data collection. A set of standardized estimates, adjusted for comparability by the Organization for Economic Cooperation and Development (OECD), is reported in the second column. For most countries, the differences between official and standardized rates are rather small. Standardized rates are significantly lower than official rates in Germany and Canada, but they are higher than the official rates in Sweden.

In the third column of Table 2.8, we have information about "discouraged workers." These people are excluded from the conventional measures of unemployment because they have abandoned their active search for jobs. According to these estimates, inclusion of discouraged workers raises the unemployment rate by more than two percentage points in Italy, Japan, and Sweden.[27]

Suppose that a large number of workers in Country One are unemployed for very short periods of time, and a small number of workers in Country Two are unemployed for very long periods of time. The two countries may have the same average rate of unemployment, but their conditions are very different. Perhaps the short spells of unemployment in Country One are explained by simple movement between jobs (frictional unemployment) in a dynamic economy. Long spells of unemployment are evidence of deeper structural flaws in the economic and social system, and they cause more disruption in people's lives. According to the data in Table 2.8, Italy had a relatively high rate of unemployment in 1992, and about two-thirds of the unemployed had been jobless for a year or more. At the other extreme, Sweden had a low rate of unemployment, and also a low incidence of long-term unemployment.

In a similar way, published unemployment rates do not reflect the underutilization of labor that occurs when workers are forced to accept part-time

---

[26]Employment offices in countries such as Sweden, which provide extensive job training and placement, report registrations that are much closer to the numbers derived from surveys.

[27]If discouraged workers had been included, the BLS estimates that the Japanese unemployment rate would have been about 7.2 percent in 1989, compared to a rate of 7.9 percent in the United States. See Constance Sorrentino, "International Comparisons of Unemployment Indicators," *Monthly Labor Review* (March 1993): 6.

■ TABLE 2.8

ALTERNATIVE MEASURES OF UNEMPLOYMENT, 1995

	Officially Reported Rates	OECD Standardized Rates	Discouraged Workers (1993)	Long-Term Share of Total Unemployment*
Canada	9.6	8.7	0.9	13.8
Finland	17.2	17.1	1.5	32.3
France	11.5	11.6	0.2	45.6
Germany	9.4	8.2	n.a.	48.3
Italy	12.0	12.2	2.6	62.9
Japan	3.1	3.1	2.2	18.1
Netherlands	7.1	6.5	0.6	43.2
Sweden	7.7	9.2	2.0	15.7
United Kingdom	8.1	8.7	0.6	43.5
United States	5.6	5.5	0.9	9.7

*The percentage of unemployed persons who have been jobless for twelve months or more.

Sources: Organization for Economic Cooperation and Development (OECD), *Employment Outlook*, 1995; *OECD in Figures 1997*, supplement to *OECD Observer*, July 1997; and *OECD Economic Outlook*, June 1997.

jobs or jobs below their skill levels, or when employers are forced to retain unproductive workers.[28] In Japan, the permanent commitment system of employment causes a substantial amount of "unemployment within the company." According to one estimate, the total unemployment and underutilization of Japanese labor during the late 1970s was about 10 percent of the labor force, while the official unemployment rate was only 2 percent.[29]

International comparisons of unemployment are also complicated by the existence of underground, unreported employment. Those who hide their incomes in order to obtain welfare benefits, to hide illegal activities, or to avoid taxation are often counted as unemployed. We might hypothesize, therefore, that reported unemployment rates are inflated in countries with high tax rates, large welfare systems, and high crime rates, because of the prevalence of underground employment.

---

[28]For more on the growing significance of part-time employment, see Joseph E. Thurman and Gabriele Trah, "Part-Time Work in International Perspective," *International Labour Review* 124 (January 1990): 23–40.

[29]For example, see Koji Taira, "Japan's Low Unemployment: Economic Miracle or Statistical Artifact?" *Monthly Labor Review* 106 (July 1983): 9.

COMPARISONS OF INFLATION

Few international comparisons are more dramatic than those for price inflation. In 1996, inflation rates ranged from 0.1 percent in Japan to about 4,000 percent in Angola. During the single month of November 1993, prices reportedly increased by more than 20,000 percent in Serbia.[30] Unlike unemployment, GDP in constant prices, and other "real" economic statistics, the only technical limit on the inflation rate seems to be our ability to create large volumes of money.

Several considerations should be kept in mind when international comparisons of inflation are made. First, there is significant variation across countries in the quantity and quality of price data collected. In Rwanda, for example, the consumer price index (CPI) is based on data for only 54 products collected from 50 markets and retail outlets in Kigali, the capital city. In the United States, CPI data are collected for 359 product categories in 85 cities from 57,000 housing units and 19,000 retail establishments.[31]

Even in countries where comprehensive data are collected, the "true" rate of inflation is uncertain. Different estimates will be obtained, for example, if price indexes are based on different systems of quantity weights.[32] In the United States, the annual rate of consumer price inflation between 1970 and 1993 was 5.5 percent according to the fixed-weight price index for consumer expenditures, or 5.7 percent according to the implicit deflator for consumer expenditures (which uses variable quantity weights), or 5.9 percent according to the consumer price index (which uses another system of fixed weights).[33] These may seem to be small differences, but they can have a major impact on the economy when price indexes are used to adjust wages, social security benefits, and other payments.

Another difficult issue involves the adjustment of price indexes for changes in product quality and introduction of new products. In most countries, the statistical agencies take little account of these changes. For many years, American price indexes indicated that the average prices of office computers were gradually *increasing*. When new methods were introduced in 1986 to take fuller account of technological improvements, the new index indicated that computer prices had *fallen* by about 55 percent between 1972 and 1983.[34] To this day, the U.S. consumer price index does not

---

[30]Estimate of the Serbian Federal Statistics Office, cited in *RFE/RL Daily Report*, December 2, 1993.

[31]For a detailed comparison of CPI statistics around the world, see *Statistical Sources and Methods, Vol. 1: Consumer Price Indices* (Geneva: International Labour Office, annual).

[32]This is another application of the "index number problem" we discussed earlier. For a comparison of inflation rates based on different systems of quantity weights, see Mary Kokoski, "Experimental Cost-of-Living Indexes: A Summary of Current Research," *Monthly Labor Review* 113 (July 1989): 34–39.

[33]Calculated from index numbers in the *Economic Report of the President* (Washington: USGPO, 1994), 272, 274, and 335.

[34]David Cartwright, "Improved Deflation of Purchases of Computers," *Survey of Current Business* 66 (March 1986): 7–10.

account for changes in the quality of most services, such as medical care. Thus, if the average quality and technological sophistication of goods and services are increasing, our price indexes tend to overestimate the rate of inflation.

Special care must be taken when international comparisons include countries that exercise price controls. Many countries, including the United States during the 1940s and 1970s, have imposed price controls at one time or another. Under the system of central planning, the vast majority of prices in the former Soviet Union and Eastern Europe were set and controlled by governmental agencies. During periods of price control, inflation takes three forms: (1) open, reported inflation, (2) hidden inflation, and (3) repressed inflation.

Price control is seldom universal, it usually allows for some **open, reported inflation**. In centrally planned economies, for example, part of agricultural output was usually sold on farmers' markets where it was legal to charge any price the market would bear and other prices were adjusted from time to time.

Hidden inflation occurs when there are violations or evasions of price regulations. These can take many forms. For example, producers may obtain approval for price increases by introducing "new" products, supposedly higher in quality, that are in fact very similar to the old ones. Or, producers may reduce the quality of a product, but continue to sell it at the old price. Or, producers may reduce the availability of their lower-priced models, forcing consumers to purchase higher-priced models.[35] Finally, suppliers may simply engage in "black market" sales of their goods at prices that exceed controlled levels. In any of these cases, the resulting inflation is not likely to be reflected in official price indexes.[36]

Repressed inflation is a condition in which price controls are effective, so inflationary pressures (such as rapid growth in the money supply) cannot be relieved by open or hidden price increases. Instead, the inflationary pressures manifest themselves in the form of shortages, requiring the distribution of products through queues or rationing.[37] Repressed inflation has a cumulative effect on the economy. If excessive monetary growth continues year after year, the financial imbalance of the economy will grow larger and larger, eventually requiring a large adjustment in the price level or the monetary system.

---

[35]This practice, known as forced substitution, was analyzed in a classic article by Nicholas Kaldor, "Rationing and the Cost of Living Index," *Review of Economic Studies* 8 (1940–41): 185–87.

[36]See H. Stephen Gardner, "Product Quality and Price Inflation in Transitional Economies," in *Economic Statistics for Economies in Transition: Eastern Europe in the 1990s*, proceedings of a conference sponsored by U.S. Bureau of Labor Statistics and Eurostat, Washington, D.C., 1991, 178–192.

[37]Shortages, we should note, do not necessarily indicate the presence of repressed inflation. They may be caused by a faulty set of *relative* prices rather than a low *general* price level.

In Russia, for example, monetary growth during 1981–1990 was consistent with an average annual inflation rate of nearly 8 percent. Every year, though, less than half of this inflationary pressure was allowed to express itself openly in higher prices; the remainder was hidden in quality deterioration or accumulated in repressed inflation (Table 2.9). These imbalances grew far worse in 1991, when the breakup of the Soviet Union led to a loss of monetary control and a collapse of production. Finally, most price controls were released by the Russian government in January 1992, and consumer prices more than tripled in a single month. Prices quickly adjusted to their market-clearing levels, and long lines for products largely disappeared: "Whereas last year there was a shortage of commodities on the market, in 1994 . . . the market is saturated with many goods in spite of a precipitous decline of production."[38]

SUMMARY

Statistical information is invaluable in assessing economic systems, but it should always be handled cautiously. First, there are problems of definition. National income can be defined as gross national product, gross domestic product, net material product, or in a number of other ways. Income distribution and poverty statistics may cover the incomes of households or individuals, before or after taxes. Unemployment statistics may or may not include those who have failed to look for a job in the past month. Inflation may be measured at the consumer, wholesale, or GDP level.

Second, there are inconsistencies between countries in the methods and quality of data collection. In the case of national income measurement, a significant amount of output may not be reported if it is produced for home consumption or the underground economy. Unemployment statistics may be collected through market surveys or from employment office statistics. Price indexes may be based on large or small numbers of geographic areas and commodity groups, and they may or may not account for changes in product quality. Price increases may be hidden or repressed in countries that exercise price controls.

Finally, there are problems of interpretation. The very meaning of national income comparisons is clouded by the index number problem. The significance of income distribution statistics depends on one's concept of social equity. The dividing lines between the unemployed, the underemployed, and the "discouraged workers" may be difficult to draw. The rate of repressed in-

---

[38]V. Prokhina, S. Rogova, and G. Filimonovskaya, "Household Appliances, Furniture, Housewares; Everything Is Available Now Except Customers," Torgovaya gazeta, no. 4 (August 1994), 3, translated in Foreign Broadcast Information Service, *Daily Report: Central Eurasia,* September 14, 1994, 23–27.

■ **TABLE 2.9**

**OPEN AND REPRESSED INFLATION IN RUSSIA
(ANNUAL PERCENTAGE GROWTH)**

	Total Inflationary Pressure	Open Inflation	Hidden/Repressed Inflation
1981–1985 average	6	2	4
1986	6	3	3
1987	7	3	4
1988	8	4	4
1989	11	5	6
1990	19	5	14
1991	367	95	272

Sources: Data for 1981–1988 are from A. Shmarov and N. Kirichenko, "Inflayatsionnyi vsplesk: masshtaby i prichiny," *Ekonomicheskaya gazeta*, no. 13 (1989), 12; data for 1989–1990 are from private communication of the author with Andrei Shmarov. Data for 1991 are rough approximations by the author, based on retail trade, consumer price, and disposable money income indexes in *Planecon Report* 10 (April 28, 1994): 10, 14, and 17.

flation may be impossible to measure. These are analytical problems that, even while unsolved, must not be ignored.

DISCUSSION AND REVIEW QUESTIONS

1. What is the difference between GNP and GDP? Between GNP and NMP?

2. How should the value of services performed by lawyers, accountants, and college professors be measured for inclusion in GDP? How should we measure changes in their productivity?

3. In national income comparisons, what is the advantage of using a common set of average international prices to evaluate each nation's output, rather than converting total national incomes with exchange rates? What problems are not solved by this procedure?

4. If you were asked to prepare a comparison of national standards of living, and you were given an unlimited budget, how would you proceed?

5. Suppose that you are appointed Minister of Propaganda for your country and you wish to say that your country has an even distribution of income. Without actually falsifying the data, how will you collect and arrange them to make your point? What forms of income and taxation will you include? What population unit will you use? With what country will you compare your country's income distribution?

6. What are the differences between open, hidden, and repressed inflation? For the general population (or for various segments of the population), what would be the advantages and disadvantages of living in a country with repressed inflation rather than open inflation?

7. If you have a background in statistics or econometrics, how would you test the hypothesis that a socialist country at a particular level of per capita income tends to have a higher PQLI than a capitalist country at the same level of income?

Suggested Readings

Dallago, Bruno. *The Irregular Economy.* Hanover: Dartmouth Press, 1990. *Probably the best book available on the definition and measurement of the underground economy, and on its operation in market and centrally planned economies.*

Economic Statistics for Economies in Transition: Eastern Europe in the 1990s. Proceedings of a conference sponsored by U.S. Bureau of Labor Statistics and Eurostat, Washington, D.C., 1991. *In eighteen chapters contributed by an international team of authors, this book surveys the existing statistical systems in transitional economies and analyzes their needs, but also provides a wealth of information about these systems in the United States and Western Europe. See, for example, the discussion of poverty rates in Chapter 13.*

Kravis, Irving, et al. *World Product and Income: International Comparisons of Real Gross Product.* Baltimore: Johns Hopkins University Press, 1982. *Gives a full description of the objectives, methods, and results of the U.N. International Comparisons Project.*

Pryor, Frederic L. *A Guidebook to the Comparative Study of Economic Systems.* Englewood Cliffs, N.J.: Prentice-Hall, 1985. *Pryor has collected an enormous amount of comparative data for capitalist and socialist countries and is a pioneer in the kind of hypothesis testing mentioned in discussion question 7.*

Shaikh, Anwar, and E. Ahmet Tonak. *Measuring the Wealth of Nations: The Political Economy of National Accounts.* Cambridge: Cambridge University Press, 1994. *A provocative and careful analysis of classical and Marxian approaches to national income theory and measurement.*

Sundrum, R. M. *Income Distribution in Less Developed Countries.* London: Routledge, 1990. *This book focuses on less developed countries, but it provides a clear and full analysis of income inequality that has general application.*

Following are a few of the many sources of current comparative statistical data. You can learn much about comparative statistics by reading their explanatory notes and appendices.

Historically Planned Economies: A Guide to the Data. Washington, D.C.: The World Bank, annual.

International Financial Statistics. Washington, D.C.: International Monetary Fund, monthly, with annual compilations and supplements.

Monthly Bulletin of Statistics. New York: United Nations Statistical Office, monthly.

OECD Economic Outlook. Paris: Organization for Economic Cooperation and Development, biannual.

United Nations Statistical Office. *Statistical Yearbook.* New York: United Nations, annual.

United Nations Development Program. *Human Development Report.* New York: Oxford University Press, annual.

World Bank. *World Development Report.* New York: Oxford University Press, annual.

World Bank. *World Tables.* Baltimore: Johns Hopkins University Press, annual.

World Economic Outlook. Washington, D.C.: International Monetary Fund, annual.

Yearbook of Labour Statistics. Geneva: International Labour Office, annual.

INTERNET RESOURCES

Consortium for International Earth Science Information Network (CIESIN)
http://www.ciesin.org/home-page/ciesin-home.html

International Monetary Fund
http://www.imf.org/

Luxembourg Income Study
http://www-cpr.maxwell.syr.edu/lis_part/lisintro.htm

Manchester Information Datasets and Associated Services (MIDAS)
http://midas.ac.uk/

Penn World Tables (national income data from the U.N. International Comparisons Project)
http://nber.harvard.edu/pwt56.html

United Nations Development Program
http://www.undp.org/undp_data.html

U.S. Central Intelligence Agency (including World Factbook)
http://www.ic.gov/

World Bank
http://www.worldbank.org/html

World Economic Window
http://nmg.clever.net/wew/

ECONOMIC SYSTEMS

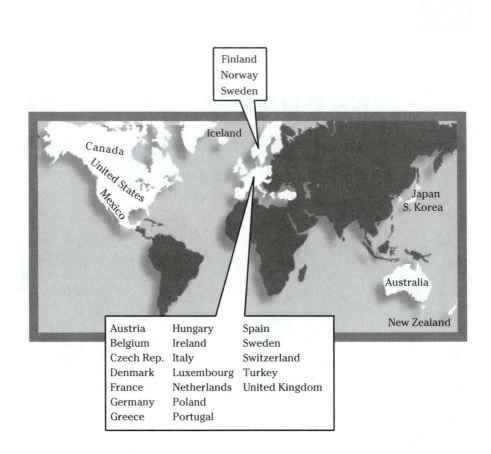

Finland
Norway
Sweden

Iceland

Canada
United States
Mexico

Japan
S. Korea

Australia

New Zealand

Austria	Hungary	Spain
Belgium	Ireland	Sweden
Czech Rep.	Italy	Switzerland
Denmark	Luxembourg	Turkey
France	Netherlands	United Kingdom
Germany	Poland	
Greece	Portugal	

3

HISTORY AND THEORIES OF CAPITALISM

Less than seventy-five years after it officially began, the contest between capitalism and socialism is over: capitalism has won. . . . Yet I doubt whether the historic drama will conclude, like a great morality play, in the unequivocal victory of one side and the ignominious defeat of the other. The economic enemy of capitalism has always been its own self-generated dynamics, not the presence of an alternative economic system.

—ROBERT HEILBRONER
THE NEW YORKER, JANUARY 23, 1989

apitalism is an economic and social system in which the nation's farms, factories, and mines are owned predominantly by private individuals, partners, and stockholders. Although social ownership may be present, and it may be substantial, it is a deviation from the rule. The market system is the basic coordinating mechanism under capitalism, but each country modifies the forces of supply and demand with its own assortment of traditional behaviors, industrial policies, social welfare programs, and other instruments of social and governmental control. Thus, there are clear distinctions among the economic systems in the United States, Germany, Japan, and the scores of other capitalist nations.

To those of us who live in high-income capitalist countries, many of the institutions of market exchange and private property are so familiar that we take them for granted. We must be reminded that checking accounts, credit cards, patent rights, and markets for stocks, bonds, and real estate are relatively recent innovations in the history of civilization; indeed, they barely exist in many parts of the world today.

As we open this chapter, we will discuss the nature of precapitalist systems, and note a few of the historical forces that gave rise to modern capitalism. Next, we will survey the development of economic analysis of capitalism from the eighteenth century to the present. Finally, we will discuss the nature and significance of the growing internationalization of capitalism.

PRECAPITALIST ECONOMIC SYSTEMS

At the dawn of civilization, beginning in the fifth millennium B.C., capitalism did not play a noticeable role in the societies that developed along the Tigris, Euphrates, and Nile river valleys. After centuries of tribalism and tradition, an early version of authoritarian central planning was adopted by the Babylonians, Egyptians, Assyrians, Hittites, and Persians. Institutional structures differed from one dynasty to another, but the land and other productive assets were generally owned by the state, individual freedoms were severely restricted, and huge public bureaucracies were maintained to build public works, distribute irrigation water, and manage flood control. The pyramids and the walls of Babylon demonstrated the ability of strong central authorities to mobilize society toward the fulfillment of high-priority projects.[1]

GREECE AND ROME

Beginning in the twelfth century B.C., the rise of the Greek and Roman city-states ushered in a new era of individual freedom, including economic freedom, for a significant segment of the population. Although perhaps 50 percent of the Greek and 80 percent of the Roman population lived in slavery, a significant number of people were free to choose their occupations; the crafts, merchant, and banking professions began to thrive in the cities. Indeed, their prosperity gained the attention of the classical philosophers. Aristotle, for one, was quite disturbed by the fortunes amassed by merchants and bankers:

> Gaining wealth through retail trade] is justly censured; for it is unnatural, and a mode by which men gain from one another. The most hated sort, and with the greatest reason, is usury, which makes a gain out of money itself, and not from the natural object of it. For money was meant to be used in exchange, but not to increase at interest. Wherefore of all modes of getting wealth this is the most unnatural.[2]

Interestingly, although Aristotle argued that the unlimited capitalist pursuit of wealth was "unnatural," he argued in favor of the right of individuals to own private property. Property should be held privately, he said, because "when every one has a distinct interest, men will not complain of one another, and they will make more progress, because every one will be attending to his own business."[3] In other words, Aristotle noted in the fourth century B.C. that an economic system based on private property rights would provide stronger incentives for production than a communal society. On the other hand, he believed that the inequities caused by private property should be balanced with charity: "It is clearly better that property should be private,

---

[1]Stephan Viljoen, *Economic Systems in World History* (London: Longman, 1974), 16; and Rondo Cameron, *A Concise Economic History of the World: From Paleolithic Times to the Present* (New York: Oxford University Press, 1989), 30.

[2]Aristotle, *Politics* 1.10.1258a38–1258b7.

[3]Aristotle, *Politics* 2.5.12663a25–29.

but the use of it common; and the special business of the legislator is to create in men this benevolent disposition."[4]

Although one author contends that "the Graeco-Roman economy was a free economy in the sense that a number of markets were more or less free to regulate themselves," the system was still quite unlike modern market capitalism.[5] Again, the use of slave labor was a dominant characteristic of the system and retail trade existed for little more than the provision of luxury goods to the upper class. Most of the important economic achievements of the Greek and Roman societies were prompted by governmental commands rather than by market forces, and surplus productive power was used to build impressive public buildings, city walls, and standing armies, rather than factories, machinery, and equipment.

THE MIDDLE AGES

Progress toward the establishment of a market capitalist system was interrupted when the western part of the Roman Empire fell in the fifth century A.D. The relative peace and unity that had been imposed by Rome disintegrated into chaos. Long-distance trade became extremely hazardous and it was further restricted by the lack of a common language, legal code, or currency. The countryside was carved into a large number of small, self-sufficient, feudal estates. Each estate was held in trust by a feudal lord, who was responsible for the physical and economic welfare of his vassals. In turn, the serfs were required to work in the lord's fields and shops and to provide him with a portion of their product. Little money changed hands and little trade was conducted with neighboring estates.

The system of mutual obligations between lords and servants in the countryside was paralleled by the craft guilds in the cities. Master craftsmen and their apprentices were bound by a system of indentures, which required faithful service by the apprentices in exchange for instruction by the masters, together with suitable provision of food, clothing, and shelter. The guild organizations enforced a rigid set of regulations concerning everything from hours of work, methods of production, tools, prices, and raw materials that could be used, to the number of apprentices and journeymen that could fall under a single master's control. Thus, labor mobility, entrepreneurship, market flexibility, and technological progress were seriously restricted.[6]

The medieval social structure was legitimized and maintained in the West by the dominant institution of the era, the Roman Catholic church. Thomas Aquinas and other church theologians maintained that the master-servant authority structure, including the institution of slavery, was ordained by God. Indeed, the theologians of the day believed that charitable contributions should be limited in order to allow the upper class to live "in keeping

---

[4]Ibid., 1263a38.

[5]Viljoen, *Economic Systems in World History*, 55.

[6]For an extended discussion of the Roman and medieval economic systems, see James Angresano, *Comparative Economics* (Englewood Cliffs, N.J.: Prentice Hall, 1992), Chapters 3 and 4.

with their social station," because "no man ought to live unbecomingly."[7] On the other hand, Aquinas declared that inordinate accumulation of wealth was sinful, particularly if it was accomplished by selling goods above their "just price" or by charging interest on loans.

A number of developments caused the slow demise of the feudal system. The gradual rebuilding of strong centralized governments in Europe and England restored the unity of languages, monetary systems, and laws, and reopened trade routes. In the countryside, the slow substitution of money rents for labor services transformed the relationship between lord and serf.

In the thirteenth century, the **enclosure movement** began, whereby the landed aristocracy "enclosed" lands for their exclusive use that had previously been accessible to peasant farmers. As a result, a new class of landless peasants was formed—a class dependent on the wages they could earn by working for others. Thus, the enclosure movement began the stage of development that Karl Marx called "primitive capitalist accumulation," which, in his opinion, "plays in Political Economy about the same part as original sin in theology."[8]

According to Werner Sombart, a German economic historian, the "spirit of capitalism" first manifested itself in the thirteenth century in Italy; by the fourteenth century the Florentines "were filled with a feverish (I had almost said an American) desire for gain, and a devotion to business that almost amounted to passionate love."[9] Italian commerce was facilitated by the substitution of Arabic for Roman numerals in the early thirteenth century, allowing quick and exact calculation, and by the development of a well-ordered system of bookkeeping by the end of the century.[10]

RENAISSANCE AND REFORMATION

The end of the Middle Ages and the beginning of the Renaissance are usually associated with the fall of Constantinople, the capital of the Byzantine Empire, in 1453. Refugees from Byzantium, where the study of Greek and Roman literature and art had continued, reintroduced those ideas in the West and a new era of creativity began. The inventiveness and vision of Leonardo da Vinci and his peers laid the necessary groundwork for the Industrial Revolution that would follow three centuries later.

As the Renaissance continued, Martin Luther unwittingly initiated the Protestant Reformation in 1517 when he attacked the papal practice of indulgences. The rise of Protestantism may have contributed to the rise of capitalism in a number of ways. First, it weakened the legitimizing force behind the

---

[7]Thomas Aquinas, *Summa Theologica*, quoted in Jacob Viner, *Religious Thought and Economic Society* (Durham, N.C.: Duke University Press, 1978), 74.

[8]Karl Marx, *Capital*, vol. 1 (New York: International Publishers, 1967), 713.

[9]Werner Sombart, *The Quintessence of Capitalism* (New York: Howard Fertig, 1967), 132. In this, Sombart agreed with Marx, who also believed that capitalism originated in Italy. See Marx, *Capital*, 716.

[10]Sombart, *Quintessence*, 126–127.

feudal order—the Roman Catholic church. Second, the new Protestant theology was more individualistic than Catholic doctrine—confession and interpretation of scripture did not require the intervention of the clergy. The new spirit of individualism may have encouraged the replacement of hierarchical social systems with decentralized markets. Third, according to the German sociologist Max Weber, the Calvinist belief that worldly success was a sign of divine favor inspired a work ethic and an attitude toward thrift that supported economic development more effectively than Catholic doctrine and practice.

THE DEVELOPMENT OF CAPITALISM

The forces of Renaissance, Reformation, enclosure, urban growth, international trade, mathematics, and monetary exchange converged in the late sixteenth and early seventeenth centuries as capitalism spread from the merchant sphere to the productive sphere of the Western economies. In its early stages, a large part of capitalist production was organized around the so-called **putting-out system**, whereby the capitalists bought raw materials, "put them out" to artisans working in their own homes for a piece-wage, and then sold the final product. The scale of such operations could be quite large, as was the case of a British clothier who employed 3,000 home laborers.[11]

In the late 1700s, Britain was shaken by the Industrial Revolution and the American Revolution. The former was initiated by an amazing succession of technical innovations. After 1760, for example, British iron production expanded rapidly as methods were developed that made it possible to use relatively abundant coke, rather than scarce charcoal, in the smelting process. In 1770, James Hargreaves patented the first machine capable of spinning more than one cotton thread at a time and in 1776 James Watt constructed his first successful steam engine. In all, 976 patents were granted in Great Britain for new inventions between 1760 and 1789, compared to only 230 patents between 1730 and 1759.[12]

The new technologies necessitated and supported a number of other developments. First, their effective use required that laborers move their places of work from their homes to mechanized factories. The capitalist or entrepreneur, who previously provided his workers only with raw materials under the putting-out system, became an owner of factories and machinery. Thus, the share of capital formation in British national income rose from approximately 3 percent during the first half of the eighteenth century to 5 percent in 1780, and to 10 percent in the mid-nineteenth century.[13] The result? Between 1770 and 1800, British iron production increased fivefold and cotton textile production increased twelvefold. Overall industrial production, which had

---

[11]E. A. J. Johnson and Herman E. Krooss, *The American Economy: Its Origins, Development, and Transformation* (Englewood Cliffs, N.J.: Prentice Hall, 1960), 58.

[12]Viljoen, *Economic Systems in World History*, 176n.

[13]Ibid., 178.

risen by only 1.0 percent per year between 1700 and 1783, grew by 3.4 percent per year between 1783 and 1802.[14]

The Industrial Revolution had begun in England. At Manchester, cartloads and boatloads of people of both sexes and all ages poured into the city to work in the new factories. Of the 12,000 houses in Birmingham in 1790, two-thirds were built after 1760.[15] The share of the British labor force working in agriculture dropped from 60 percent in 1700 to 40 percent in 1820 and to 16 percent in 1890.[16]

Similar movements toward industrialization, mechanization, and urbanization occurred in France, Germany, and the United States after 1830, and in Sweden, Japan, and Russia after 1860. As the volume of world trade grew approximately tenfold between 1830 and 1900, the resulting diffusion of new technology, creation of new markets, and growth of specialization and competition caused industrial development to spread from one country to another. Just as important, in stark contrast to the slow, unsteady pace of economic development before the 1780s, economic growth in the newly emerging capitalist countries was *self-sustaining*. The surplus capacity that had been used to build pyramids by the Egyptians, coliseums by the Romans, and castles by the feudal lords was used by the new capitalist class to build machines and factories, which could be used to build even more machines and factories. Real GDP per capita roughly tripled in England, France, Germany, and Sweden between 1820 and 1913 and it grew more than fourfold in the United States.

EARLY VIEWS OF CAPITALISM

MERCANTILISM

We noted previously that the late feudal era was marked by the consolidation of national governments and by the rise of a merchant class with considerable economic and political power. Beginning in the fifteenth century, legislation was passed throughout Europe and England that served the purposes of the ascending civil servants and merchants. The new governments raised needed revenues, for example, by selling "patents of monopoly," which granted the exclusive right to trade with certain foreign countries to a few favored merchants. As a result, by about 1600, the ordinary Englishman could trade only with France, Spain, and Portugal without the intervention of the East India Company or one of the other monopolistic trading companies.

An equally important source of governmental revenue was the collection of tariffs on imported goods. Once again, import tariffs served the purposes of domestic manufacturing and merchant interests by protecting

---

[14]Walter G. Hoffmann, *British Industry, 1700–1950* (Oxford: Basil Blackwell, 1955), 331.

[15]Witt Bowden et al., *An Economic History of Europe Since 1750* (New York: Howard Fertig, 1970), 190.

[16]Angus Maddison, *Phases of Capitalist Development* (Oxford: Oxford University Press, 1982), 35.

them from foreign competition. Their interests were served so well that the merchants put forth an influential—if self-serving—argument for further import protection.

The **mercantilist** foreign trade doctrine was based on the proposition, stated most clearly by the French finance minister Colbert, that "the quantity of gold in a state alone determines the degree of its greatness and power."[17] A large stock of monetary gold was believed to stimulate trade within the nation, and it could be used to hire mercenaries and purchase munitions in wartime. Because gold was earned through the sale of exports and was sacrificed through the purchase of imports, the mercantilists argued that active measures should be taken by the government to encourage the former and limit the latter. In short, the mercantilists maintained that the wealth of a nation was advanced most effectively by active governmental intervention in the economy, promotion of monopolies, and restriction of imports.

ADAM SMITH AND CLASSICAL THEORY

Just as many modern-day proponents of governmental regulation of the capitalist economy can trace their roots to the mercantilists, advocates of laissez-faire capitalism can draw inspiration from the Scottish philosopher and economist, Adam Smith (1723–1790). In *The Wealth of Nations* (1776), Smith declared that provision of consumer goods, not accumulation of gold, "is the sole end and purpose of production."[18] What kind of economic system would serve the needs of consumers most efficiently? Certainly not the mercantile system, which placed limits on imports and encouraged the formation of monopolies. Instead, Smith proposed a system of "natural liberty"—a system that would mobilize the self-interested acts of individuals to pursue social goals:

> It is not from the benevolence of the butcher, the brewer, or the baker, that we expect our dinner, but from their regard to their own self-interest.[19]
>
> Every individual necessarily labours to render the annual revenue of the society as great as he can. . . . He intends only his own gain, and he is in this, as in many other cases, led by an invisible hand to promote an end which was no part of his intention. . . . By pursuing his own interest he frequently promotes that of the society more effectually than when he really intends to promote it.[20]

In reply to Aristotle, Aquinas, and other philosophers and theologians who feared the free exercise of self-interest, Smith was confident that competitive forces would protect the consumers. If one butcher, brewer, or baker charged exorbitant prices, the consumers would buy their meat, ale, or bread from another. Indeed, Smith believed that a competitive system

---

[17]Quoted in Sombart, *Quintessence*, 84.

[18]Adam Smith, *An Inquiry into the Nature and Causes of the Wealth of Nations*, vol. 2 (Oxford: Clarendon Press, 1976), 660.

[19]Ibid., 26–27.

[20]Ibid., 456.

would establish itself—with little need for antitrust legislation—if the government-sponsored monopolistic practices of the mercantilists were abandoned:

All systems either of preference or of restraint, therefore, being thus completely taken away, the obvious and simple system of natural liberty establishes itself of its own accord. Every man, as long as he does not violate the laws of justice, is left perfectly free to promote his own interest in his own way, and to bring both his industry and capital into competition with those of any other man, or order of men.[21]

Adam Smith contributed far more, of course, than assertions in favor of his system of natural liberty. He also provided a rather sophisticated—for his day—explanation of the laws of supply and demand that guide the "invisible hand" of the market. If the quantity of a product available for sale on any given day is insufficient to meet the "effectual demand," the price of the product will rise, and the self-interests of producers will encourage them to supply more of the product in the future. In the long run, production will gravitate toward effectual demand, and the price should be sufficient to provide for normal payments of wages, profit, and rent.

According to Smith, the government has only three duties in his system of natural liberty, although they are duties of great importance—to provide for national defense, to administer justice, and to provide public goods ("certain public works . . . which it can never be for the interest of any individual or small number of individuals to erect and maintain").[22] Efficient management of the production system, he believed, was far beyond the capacity of any system of central planning:

The sovereign is completely discharged from a duty, in the attempting to perform which he must always be exposed to innumerable delusions, and for the proper performance of which no human wisdom or knowledge could ever be sufficient, the duty of superintending the industry of private people, and of directing it towards the employments most suitable to the interest of the society.[23]

These declamations against central planning and excessive governmental control have new relevance in the transitional economies of Eastern Europe. According to Vaclav Klaus, the prime minister of the Czech Republic, "I am convinced that Adam Smith supplies us with a vision of where to go that needs no correction. . . . It may be trivial to you, but it is not trivial in our part of the world."[24]

Adam Smith's arguments were refined and extended by successive members of the classical school. Jean-Baptiste Say (1767–1832), Smith's French disciple, continued the campaign against those latter-day mercantilists who

---

[21]Ibid.

[22]Ibid., 687–688.

[23]Ibid.

[24]Vaclav Klaus, "Adam Smith's Legacy and Economic Transformation of Czechoslovakia," *Business Economics* 28 (January 1993): 7.

argued that a large stock of monetary gold was needed to support the demand for products. With an insufficient supply of money, they contended, the economy would suffer recession or depression. Say's reply was quite simple: The quantity of money in a nation is not terribly important because commodities are ultimately purchased with other commodities. Money is a useful medium of exchange, but it is not the ultimate source of demand for goods:

Sales cannot be said to be dull because money is scarce, but because other products are so. . . . A product is no sooner created, than it, from that instant, affords a market for other products to the full extent of its own value. When the producer has put the finishing hand to his product, he is most anxious to sell it immediately, lest its value should diminish in his hands. Nor is he less anxious to dispose of the money he may get for it; for the value of money is also perishable. . . . Thus, the mere circumstance of the creation of one product immediately opens a vent for other products.[25]

Thus, **Say's Law**, as Keynes stated it over a century later, holds that supply creates its own demand. The government need only create a healthy environment for production and trade, and the free play of the market will ensure that the nation's output is sold. "It is the aim of good government to stimulate production," Say concluded, "and of bad government to encourage consumption."[26] This, in a nutshell, is the idea behind what is now called **supply-side economics**.

Say's Law was a controversial proposition from the very beginning, even among members of the classical school. Thomas Malthus (1766–1834), for one, was skeptical: "I by no means think that the power to purchase necessarily involves a proportionate will to purchase, and I cannot agree . . . that in reference to a nation, supply can never exceed demand."[27]

Of course, Malthus was pessimistic about far more than the ability of the market system to generate a demand for goods. He was more concerned about the ability of the system to generate a sufficient supply of food. It was Malthus who suggested that mankind was destined to endure wars, famine, and plagues because "the power of population is indefinitely greater than the power in the earth to produce subsistence for man."[28] Foreshadowing the arguments of modern-day conservatives, Malthus argued that governmental programs to help the poor would only exacerbate the population problem. Little wonder that Thomas Carlyle, after he read Malthus, called economics "the dismal science."

Say's Law was accepted uncritically by Malthus's contemporary and close friend, David Ricardo (1772–1823). According to Ricardo, the prospective problems of capitalist society would not stem from an insufficient demand

---

[25]Jean-Baptiste Say, "Of the Demand or Market for Products," in *Classics of Economics*, ed. Charles W. Needy (Oak Park, Ill.: Moore Publishing, 1980), 58.

[26]Ibid., 61.

[27]In a letter to David Ricardo. See David Ricardo, *The Works and Correspondence of David Ricardo*, ed. Piero Sraffa, vol. 6 (London: Cambridge University Press, 1951–1955), 132.

[28]Thomas Robert Malthus, *An Essay on the Principle of Population* (New York: W. W. Norton, 1976), 20.

for products or from an insufficient supply of food, but from an undesirable trend in the distribution of national income between laborers, capitalists, and landlords.

Like other classical economists, Ricardo believed that productive invest-ment, undertaken by the emerging capitalist class, was the driving force be-hind economic growth and development. Economic growth would increase the demand for labor, but any resulting increase in real wages would usually cause an acceleration of population growth. Thus, in the long run, real wages would tend to remain at a level allowing only the physical subsistence of the working class.

In the meanwhile, population growth would stimulate the demand for food and shelter, allowing landlords to collect larger rents for agricultural and residential land. Rising food prices would require the capitalists to pay their employees higher *money* wages in order to maintain *real* wages at a bare subsistence level. Caught between rising money wage costs and land rental costs, the profits retained by capitalists would tend to diminish. As profits continued their decline, Ricardo believed that capitalists would eventually refuse to invest in additional production, and economic growth would come to a halt.

Fortunately, however, Ricardo believed that England could postpone or avoid this chain of events by adopting a policy of free international trade. If mercantilist restrictions on the importation of grain—the Corn Laws—were lifted, Ricardo predicted that food prices, money wages, and land rents would fall and profits would rise.

At any rate, Ricardo believed that England should import more grain be-cause its "comparative advantage" (another concept contributed by Ri-cardo) lay in industrial production, not in agriculture. Put differently, he believed that the opportunity cost of agricultural production, measured in terms of forgone industrial production, was higher in England than in Eu-rope or America.

Twenty-three years after his death, Ricardo's arguments finally carried the day (with support from the Anti-Corn Law League and food shortages caused by the Irish potato blight of 1845) and the Corn Law was repealed in 1846. England adopted a policy of free trade that persisted until the outbreak of World War I. Between the decades of the 1820s and the 1860s, British im-ports of wheat multiplied sixteen times and British exports of coal increased by a multiple of twenty-nine.

John Stuart Mill (1806–1873), who is usually considered the last of the great classical economists, perceived still another set of problems in capital-ist society. Mill accepted Say's Law, and was not terribly worried about the macroeconomic stability of capitalism. He accepted Ricardo's argument that a falling rate of profit would eventually lead to a cessation of economic growth, but he did not consider this to be a problem:

I cannot . . . regard the stationary state of capital and wealth with the unaffected aversion so generally manifested towards it by political economists of the old school. I am inclined to believe it would be, on the whole, a very considerable improvement of our condition. I confess I am not charmed with the ideal of life held out by those who think that the normal state of human beings is that of struggling to get on; that the trampling, crushing, elbowing, and treading on each other's heels, which form the existing type of social life, are the most desirable lot of human kind, or anything but the disagreeable symptoms of one of the phases of industrial progress.[29]

Whereas Smith and Say took it as a foregone conclusion that the benefits of economic growth and industrialization would filter down to the working class, nearly a century after the advent of the Industrial Revolution, Mill concluded that "it is questionable if all of the mechanical inventions yet made have lightened the day's toil of any human being."[30] To Mill, therefore, what was lacking in nineteenth-century capitalism was not an ample supply of gold, food, or profits, but an adequate code of social justice. Charles Dickens, Mill's contemporary, wrote in *Hard Times* and *Oliver Twist* of the overcrowded, disease-ridden cities created by the Industrial Revolution and of the Poor Law that required the children of paupers to labor in mines and factories for 14-hour workdays, often under horrendous conditions.

The situation was so desperate, Mill lamented, that "if this, or Communism, were the alternative, all the difficulties, great or small, of Communism, would be but as dust in the balance."[31] Nevertheless, Mill believed that other alternatives were available. He advocated the reform, rather than the outright elimination, of capitalism, through governmental taxation of large inheritances, redistribution of income to the poor, and provision of public education, health, and sanitation services. Thus, Mill may be considered an early advocate of welfare capitalism, but an advocate who was concerned with maintenance of work incentives:

Relief must be given; no one must be allowed to starve; the necessaries of life and health must be tendered to all who apply for them; but to all who are capable of work they must be tendered on such terms, as shall make the necessity of accepting them be regarded as a misfortune. . . . To this end, relief must be given only in exchange for labour, and labour at least as irksome and severe as that of the least fortunate among independent labourers.[32]

KARL MARX: THE SOCIALIST CRITIQUE

We have seen that Adam Smith and his followers were not blind to the economic problems of their day. Smith was concerned about the spread of monopolistic privileges, Ricardo was worried about the prospects for continued economic growth, Malthus was fearful of population growth, and Mill was

---

[29]John Stuart Mill, *Principles of Political Economy,* in *Masterworks of Economics,* vol. 2, ed. Leonard D. Abbott (New York: McGraw-Hill, 1973), 163–164.

[30]Ibid., 166.

[31]Ibid., 138.

[32]John Stuart Mill, "The Proposed Reform of the Poor Laws," cited in Robert Ekelund and Robert Hebert, *A History of Economic Theory and Method* (New York: McGraw-Hill, 1983), 182.

disturbed by the living conditions of the lower classes. Nevertheless, none of the classical economists suggested that conditions would deteriorate so severely that the entire capitalist system would be overthrown. Indeed, most of them believed that more extensive application of laissez-faire and free-trade principles would alleviate the remaining problems. Even Mill called only for the legislative reform of capitalism, not for its overthrow.

A very different picture of the history, nature, and future of capitalist society was painted by Karl Marx (1818–1883) and his collaborator, Friedrich Engels (1820–1895). In keeping with their materialist conception of history, Marx and Engels argued that each society spontaneously adopts an economic system that is appropriate for its current stage of economic development. As Engels put it:

The materialist conception of history starts from the proposition that the production of the means to support human life and, next to production, the exchange of things produced, is the basis of all social structure; that in every society that has appeared in history, the manner in which wealth is distributed and society divided into classes or orders is dependent upon what is produced, how it is produced, and how the products are exchanged.[33]

Accordingly, it is natural for simple primitive societies to adopt a simple tribal or communal form of organization. At a higher level of economic development, slavery and feudal institutions are introduced to extract surplus production for the use of the upper class. As society continues to advance, technological improvements make it possible for a single producer to supply a large market area, and workers need to be free to move from agriculture to industry. Enter capitalism. Nevertheless, Marx maintained that the freedom of the working class in capitalist society is illusory: "The worker, whose sole source of livelihood is the sale of his labor power . . . belongs not to this or that capitalist, but to the capitalist class."[34] In other words, laborers are enslaved to the capitalist class because they cannot work for themselves. They cannot work for themselves because all the means of production are owned by the capitalists. Thus, laborers are exploited in capitalist society in very nearly the same sense that they were exploited in feudal or slave societies, but their status is obscured by the apparent freedom of the labor market—by their ability to move from one capitalist employer to another.

Interestingly, although Marx emphasized the sinister and exploitive aspects of capitalism, he believed these to be necessary evils—necessary for the eventual attainment of socialism:

Fanatically bent on making value expand itself, [the capitalist] ruthlessly forces the human race to produce for production's sake; he thus forces the development of the productive powers of society, and creates those material conditions, which alone

---

[33]Friedrich Engels, *Socialism: Utopian and Scientific,* in *The Marx-Engels Reader,* ed. Robert Tucker (New York: W. W. Norton, 1978), 700–701.

[34]Karl Marx, *Wage Labour and Capital,* in *The Marx-Engels Reader,* 205.

can form the real basis of a higher form of society, a society in which the full and free development of every individual forms the ruling principle.[35]

In other words, Marx and Engels believed that the socialist system was appropriate only for countries that had achieved high levels of economic development, and that market capitalism, with its high rate of investment and its heavy-handed treatment of the labor force, was the *only* system capable of driving society to the level of economic development necessary for the transition to socialism.

A large part of Marx's writing was devoted to the forces that would, in his view, *inevitably* lead to the downfall of capitalism. The root problem is the capitalist himself and his continual accumulation of wealth. The capitalist lives to accumulate, according to Marx, for he derives his enjoyment from amassing wealth rather than from consumption: "He shares with the miser the passion for wealth as wealth."[36] Furthermore, the capitalist must accumulate in order to live—he must invest in machinery and equipment that reduces his costs of production in order to remain competitive.

Driven by desire and necessity, the capitalists' exploitation of labor and accumulation of wealth eventually would cause several other economic and social problems, according to Marx. First, they would combine to cause a chronic underconsumption of goods—a state of excess aggregate supply. The rapid growth of the capital stock and harsh treatment of the labor force would create a fertile environment for the production of goods, but not for their sale. The ability of the working class to purchase the flood of new goods is limited by low income levels, while the capitalist class has a strong preference for saving over consumption. In a word, Marx did not accept Say's Law. Insufficient demand for final products would inevitably lead to a series of business depressions.

Second, Marx believed that the process of capital accumulation would cause the general rate of profit to trend downward. In the long run, he argued, the source of all profits is exploitation of live labor. Investment in machinery and equipment may provide the capitalist with a short-term windfall profit if it reduces his costs of production below those of his competitors, but in the long run his rivals will also invest in the new technology and the price of the final product will fall to a level consistent with the lower industrywide costs of production. In the end, all the capitalists will invest in the new technology, but none will gain a lasting profit from it. As the capitalists are forced by competition to devote more of their investment to machinery and equipment that does not provide an enduring profit, the rate of profit will fall.

The falling rate of profit, Marx predicted, would encourage capitalists to further exploit their laborers by lengthening the working day and reducing wage rates. Furthermore, the profit squeeze would drive the smaller and weaker capitalists out of business as their companies are "gobbled up" by the

---

[35]Karl Marx, *Capital*, vol. 1 (New York: International Publishers, 1967), 592.
[36]Ibid.

larger capitalists; the small capitalists themselves would be cast into the growing "reserve army of the unemployed." In the end, the capitalist system would self-destruct:

Along with the constantly diminishing number of the magnates of capital . . . grows the mass of misery, oppression, slavery, degradation, exploitation; but with this too grows the revolt of the working class. . . . The knell of capitalist private property sounds. The expropriators are expropriated.[37]

In retrospect, many of the predictions made by Marx and Engels were no more, and no less, accurate than the predictions made by Adam Smith, David Ricardo, Thomas Malthus, and John Stuart Mill. For example, the notion that the rate of profit would tend to drift downward in capitalist countries was not originated by Marx, but by Adam Smith. Smith believed that profits would fall as markets grew more competitive, and as economic growth increased the demand for labor and increased real wages. He believed, in other words, that a falling rate of profit was a sign of economic health. Ricardo believed that profits would decline as money wages were driven up by rising food prices. He predicted that the falling rate of profit would eventually cause investment to cease and would lead to a dismal, no-growth, "stationary state." On the other hand, Marx viewed the falling rate of profit as one of the factors that would cause the breakdown of capitalist society. The actual historical trend in the rate of profit is still a subject of considerable controversy.

Critics of Marx can point to several failed predictions. The long-term trend in the living conditions of the working class in industrial countries has been toward improvement, rather than toward greater "misery, oppression, slavery, and degradation."[38] The first socialist revolution did not occur in one of the most developed capitalist countries, as Marx's analysis suggested, but in relatively backward Russia.

On the other hand, Marx was one of the first economists to formally challenge Say's Law and to present an analysis of business cycles. Furthermore, in a day when small businesses were still the norm, Marx foresaw the emergence of the giant business enterprises. Finally, with respect to his prediction of the eventual breakdown of capitalism, orthodox Marxists would suggest that the final chapter is yet to be written.

THE GREAT DEPRESSION AND J. M. KEYNES

If there was ever a time when the Marxian "death knell of capitalism" seemed to toll loudly, it was in 1933. Between 1929 and 1933, some 85,000 American businesses were forced to close their doors, causing national income to drop by 30 percent and the unemployment rate to climb to nearly 25 percent. Literally millions of Americans who had never known poverty

---

[37]Ibid., 763.

[38]For an opposing view, see Xenophon Zolotas, *Economic Growth and Declining Social Welfare* (New York: New York University Press, 1981).

were faced with the threat of starvation. The nightmare of the depression quickly spread to all the other major industrial capitalist countries and many Americans and Europeans turned to the Communist Party for leadership and inspiration.

Among those who were not convinced by the Marxian interpretation of the depression, we find the eminent British economist, John Maynard Keynes (1883–1946). In 1931, Keynes made his opinion of Marxian economics quite clear:

> How can I accept a doctrine which sets up as its bible, above and beyond criticism, an obsolete economic textbook which I know to be not only scientifically erroneous but without interest or application for the modern world? How can I adopt a creed which, preferring the mud to the fish, exalts the boorish proletariat above the bourgeois and intelligentsia who, with all their faults, are the quality of life and surely carry the seeds of human advancement.[39]

Whereas many Marxists believed that the capitalist system was doomed to extinction, Keynes suggested that the system could and should be preserved by appropriate governmental action. In late 1933, Keynes prescribed a program of expansionary fiscal and monetary policies to the new American president, Franklin D. Roosevelt, in an open letter published in the *New York Times*. The influence that this letter, and a meeting between Keynes and Roosevelt in the summer of 1934, may have had on the formulation of the New Deal policies of the 1930s is uncertain. The Roosevelt program, though revolutionary in its own right, was not designed to draw the nation out of the depression through fiscal and monetary stimulus, but only to provide a minimum level of relief for those in the greatest need.[40] It would require the fiscal stimulus of World War II to prove Keynes's point once and for all.

Although his proposals may not have been fully implemented during the depression, Keynes was certainly correct (if immodest) when, in 1935, he wrote to his socialist friend, George Bernard Shaw, that he was writing a book that would eventually "revolutionize . . . the way the world thinks about economic problems." His *General Theory of Employment, Interest, and Money*, first published in 1936, has done exactly that. In effect, Keynes rejected elements of both the classical and Marxian views of capitalism and formed his own middle ground.

Keynes broke with his classical heritage most fundamentally on the subject of Say's Law. As we noted earlier, the classical economists (with the notable exception of Malthus) believed that a market economy would spontaneously generate enough demand to purchase all the goods produced by a fully employed work force. Production creates income, they reasoned, and income creates demand. If some individuals choose to save their income rather than spend it, their savings will ordinarily be transferred to borrowers

---

[39]J. M. Keynes, *Essays in Persuasion* (New York: Harcourt, Brace, and Company, 1932), 300.

[40]For a full discussion of this point, see Herbert Stein, *The Fiscal Revolution in America* (Chicago: University of Chicago Press, 1969), Chapter 4.

who will, in turn, purchase investment goods. On this last point, Keynes was not convinced:

Those who think in this way are deceived . . . by an optical illusion, which makes two essentially different activities appear to be the same. They are fallaciously supposing that there is a nexus which unites decisions to abstain from current consumption with decisions to provide for future consumption, whereas the motives which determine the latter are not linked in any simple way with the motives which determine the former.[41]

If the market could not be trusted to automatically generate investment demand sufficient to absorb the savings of a fully employed labor force, the government must take action to fill the void: "I conceive, therefore, that a somewhat comprehensive socialization of investment will prove the only means of securing an approximation to full employment; though this need not exclude all manner of compromises and of devices by which public authority will cooperate with private initiative."[42]

Although Keynes agreed with Marx on the invalidity of Say's Law, he disagreed on a number of equally important issues. As we have seen, Marx believed that, regardless of any governmental action, the internal contradictions of capitalism would inevitably lead to: (1) a violent overthrow of the system, (2) establishment of social ownership of the means of production, and (3) social control of the allocation of resources and the distribution of income. In contrast, Keynes believed: (1) that the measures needed to restore and maintain full employment "can be introduced gradually and without a break in the general traditions of society"; (2) that "it is not the ownership of the instruments of production which it is important for the State to assume," but control of the aggregate level of demand for goods; and (3) that the allocation and distribution of goods and resources should be left to private, rather than social, initiative:

If our central controls succeed in establishing . . . full employment as nearly as is practicable, the classical theory comes into its own again from this point onwards. If we assume the volume of output to be given, . . . then there is no objection to be raised against the classical analysis of the manner in which private self-interest will determine what in particular is produced, in what proportions the factors of production will be combined to produce it, and how the final product will be distributed between them.[43]

In the end, Keynes seemed to be confident that the capitalist system could survive into the distant future if his proposals were accepted. With a "right analysis of the problem," he suggested that it would be possible to "cure the disease [of unemployment] whilst preserving efficiency and freedom."[44]

---

[41]John Maynard Keynes, *The General Theory of Employment, Interest, and Money* (New York: Harcourt, Brace, and World, 1964), 21.

[42]Ibid., 378.

[43]Ibid., 378–379.

[44]Ibid., 381.

SCHUMPETER AND "CREATIVE DESTRUCTION"

The publication of Keynes's *General Theory* was a major event in the economics profession, and the book immediately drew strong praise and harsh criticism. Among the most notable critics, Joseph Schumpeter (1883–1950) and Friedrich A. Hayek (1899–1992) were two Austrian economists who emigrated in the early 1930s to avoid Hitler's onslaught. Both were influenced by an intellectual tradition at the University of Vienna that emphasized methodological individualism and dismissed macroeconomic analysis.

A former Austrian minister of finance, Schumpeter came to the United States in 1931 and served for many years on the faculty at Harvard University. He claimed that Keynes's theory was based on a simplistic view of production; an increase in output requires a proportional increase in employment. "The outstanding feature of capitalism," though, is that production functions "are being incessantly revolutionized." Thus, Keynes has devised "the theory of another world" that is "out of all contact with modern industrial fact, unemployment included."[45]

In 1942, Schumpeter advanced his own analysis of economic and social development in *Capitalism, Socialism, and Democracy*. The driving force behind capitalism, he said, is the entrepreneur, who continually revolutionizes production with new products, technologies, and systems of industrial organization. To make room for new economic structures, the old must be removed. Thus, the process of **creative destruction** is "the essential fact about capitalism."[46] Many of the apparent failures of capitalism are necessary for its subsequent achievements.

Applied at the macroeconomic level, Schumpeter's doctrine suggests that business recessions are a necessary component of capitalist economic development; they clear away the wreckage of old enterprises, products, and technologies to make way for the new. Thus, Keynesian policies designed to stabilize the economy and prevent unemployment are likely to kill the capitalist goose that lays the golden eggs. "The real tragedy," said Schumpeter, "is not unemployment *per se*, but unemployment plus the impossibility of providing adequately for the unemployed without impairing the conditions of further economic development."[47]

At the microeconomic level, Schumpeter rejected the notion that large monopolistic firms are likely to exploit their market power and operate inefficiently. To provide for their future survival, monopolists must search for new products and technologies today; "the businessman feels himself to be in a competitive situation even if he is alone in his field." In their race against creative destruction, large corporations attract the best financial, physical, and

---

[45]Joseph Schumpeter, Review of *The General Theory of Employment, Interest, and Money* by John Maynard Keynes, in *Journal of the American Statistical Association* (December 1936): 793.

[46]Joseph A. Schumpeter, *Capitalism, Socialism, and Democracy*, 3rd ed. (New York: Harper and Brothers, 1950), 82–83.

[47]Ibid., 70.

human resources; they are "the most powerful engine of progress" in capitalist society.[48]

In the long run, Schumpeter believed that capitalism itself would fall victim to creative destruction. Unlike Marx, who believed that capitalism would be overthrown by economic instability and class warfare, Schumpeter argued that the system would be undermined by its own achievements. Capitalist industrialization and financial analysis would have a "rationalizing" influence on society. Business management and innovation would become routine, practiced by salaried professionals rather than profit-seeking entrepreneurs. In the end, capitalist enterprises would be transformed peacefully into nationalized industries. Schumpeter asked, "Can capitalism survive?" and answered, "No. I do not think it can."[49]

In retrospect, it seems that Schumpeter underestimated the staying power of capitalism. After a wave of industrial nationalization in Europe after World War II, the past decade has witnessed an equally dramatic wave of privatization. In recent years, private enterprise has been winning new converts around the world. The entrepreneur, once considered an endangered species, has continued to generate new products, technologies, and modes of organization.

On the other hand, Schumpeter's concept of "creative destruction" still provides a useful framework to analyze the dynamics of capitalist development. Consider, for example, the failures of financial institutions in the United States during the 1980s and the recent collapse of production in the transitional economies of Russia and Eastern Europe. "Failures" such as these are usually ascribed to shortcomings in private management, public regulation, or macroeconomic policy. From a Schumpeterian perspective, they may serve a positive purpose. They may leave behind leaner, more efficient institutions, better able to withstand the competitive pressures of the world economy.

HAYEK AND THE ECONOMICS OF INFORMATION

Friedrich Hayek, who taught at the London School of Economics and the University of Chicago, was more adamantly opposed to Keynesian policy than Schumpeter. In 1944, Hayek warned that the United States and England were embarking on a catastrophic "road to serfdom." Drawing on the experience of Nazi Germany, Hayek feared that macroeconomic management would lead to central planning, and central planning would lead to despotism:

> *In Germany it was largely people of good will, men who were admired and held up as models in the democratic countries, who prepared the way for . . . everything they detest. Yet our chance of averting a similar fate depends on our facing the danger and*

---

[48]Ibid., 85 and 106.

[49]Ibid., 61. Empirical studies provide some support for Schumpeter's analysis of the entrepreneurial behavior of large corporations. See Zoltan J. Acs and David B. Audretsch, "Testing the Schumpeterian Hypothesis," *Eastern Economic Journal* 14 (April-June 1988): 129–140.

on our being prepared to revise even our most cherished hopes and ambitions if they should prove to be the source of the danger.[50]

Against those who claimed the inevitability of more macroeconomic management and planning, Hayek argued that central authorities could not utilize information as efficiently as the market economy. "The most significant fact" about the market system, he suggested, "is the economy of knowledge with which it operates, or how little the individual participants need to know in order to be able to make the right action." Individual consumers and businesses have detailed information about their own circumstances, and the other information they need is distilled in market prices. The proper goal of economic policy should be to "dispense with the need of conscious control" and provide incentives for individuals to exhibit desirable behavior "without anyone having to tell them what to do."[51] Direct governmental intervention is likely to distort relative prices and disturb the operation of markets.

In a letter to Hayek, Keynes insisted that the dangers of economic planning would be ameliorated in an enlightened democratic society. "We almost certainly want more" planning, not less, "but the planning should take place in a community in which as many people as possible, both leaders and followers, wholly share your own moral position. Moderate planning will be safe if those who carry it out are rightly oriented in their own minds and hearts to the moral issue."[52] Hayek may have been flattered, but he was not convinced.

NEW TWISTS ON OLD IDEAS

Despite the reservations of his critics, Keynes's theory of macroeconomic management gained prominence after World War II. The theory was supported by Simon Kuznets's pioneering work during the war on national income accounts, and it was popularized by Paul Samuelson's landmark textbook, *Economics* (first published in 1948).

The first explicit exercise of Keynesian policy on American soil was undertaken when the Kennedy administration took office in 1961. Faced by a rising rate of unemployment in that year, Walter Heller, the president's unabashedly Keynesian economic advisor, called for a major program of tax cuts, despite the fact that the federal budget was already in deficit.

The tax cut was finally enacted in 1964, during the first year of the Johnson administration. Soon thereafter, Johnson laid on two additional programs of fiscal stimulus. First, under the Great Society program, federal expenditures on social welfare were more than doubled between 1965 and 1970. Second, as U.S. participation in the Vietnam War escalated, defense spending increased by about 56 percent between 1965 and 1968. The result? The federal budget

---

[50]Friedrich A. Hayek, *The Road to Serfdom* (Chicago: University of Chicago Press, 1944), 3.

[51]Friedrich A. Hayek, "The Use of Knowledge in Society," *American Economic Review* 35 (September 1935): 519–530.

[52]John Maynard Keynes, *The Collected Writings of John Maynard Keynes* 27 (London: Macmillan, 1973), 387.

deficit, which stood at $1.6 billion in 1965, ballooned to over $25 billion in 1968. The unemployment rate, which stood at 6.5 percent when the Kennedy administration took office in 1961, steadily fell to 3.4 percent in 1969.

The Keynesian policies had worked, but at a heavy cost (in addition to the human cost of the Vietnam War). Fueled by rising fiscal deficits, financed by the creation of new money, consumer price inflation accelerated. Efforts by the Nixon and Ford administrations to control inflation and unemployment through a combination of monetary and fiscal policies and price controls seemed only to make the situation worse. In 1975 the unthinkable happened—the inflation rate, at 9 percent, and the unemployment rate, at 8.5 percent, both hit new postwar record levels *in the same year*. Keynesian demand management policies came under attack from several quarters. "By about 1980," says Alan Blinder, "it was hard to find an American academic macroeconomist under the age of 40 who professed to be a Keynesian."[53]

MONETARISM

The monetarist school, led by Milton Friedman, initiated a conservative resurgence in macroeconomic policy in the 1970s. Reaffirming Say's Law, monetarists believe that the market system will spontaneously achieve full employment (or, as Friedman puts it, the unemployment rate will adjust to its "natural" level) if two basic requirements are met. First, the government must allow the market system to operate with a great deal of freedom. Thus, monetarists are generally opposed to minimum wage laws, agricultural price supports, exchange rate restrictions, wage and price controls, or other measures that limit market flexibility.

Second, the monetary authorities must maintain a slow but steady growth of the nation's money supply. Between 1929 and 1933, when the Federal Reserve allowed the money supply to shrink by about 25 percent, unemployment ravaged the United States. Thus, according to Friedman, the Great Depression did not demonstrate the instability of capitalism; it only proved the importance of a stable monetary policy.

Beginning in the late 1970s, a number of countries—including the United States, France, the United Kingdom, and Chile—experimented with monetarist policies to cure inflationary problems. More recently, monetarist "shock treatments" have been administered in several of the transitional economies of Eastern Europe. These programs generally have been effective against inflation, but often at the cost of mass unemployment.

SUPPLY-SIDE ECONOMICS

Disillusionment with monetarism in recent years has set the stage for new strands of economic thought at the conservative end of the political spectrum. Perhaps the most influential of these is the supply-side movement, which declares that Keynesians and monetarists have overemphasized the

---

[53]Alan S. Blinder, "The Fall and Rise of Keynesian Economics," *Economic Record* 64 (December 1988): 278.

importance of the demand for goods and have paid too little attention to the factors that influence productivity.[54] Supply-siders agree with monetarists on the veracity of Say's Law, and they agree that the economic role of the government should be strictly limited, but they generally disagree with monetarists on the desirability of a fixed monetary growth rule.

Supply-siders can be divided into two camps. The traditional wing advocates low marginal tax rates, deregulation of industry, and a flexible anti-inflationary monetary policy. These policies, they believe, will contribute to high levels of capital investment, economic efficiency, and economic growth.

The "new" supply-siders can be distinguished from the traditional camp by their support of a monetary gold standard or some other form of commodity-money standard, and by their more extravagant claims. Reductions in marginal tax *rates*, they say, will stimulate work incentives and economic growth to such an extent that *total* tax revenues will increase. According to Martin Feldstein, a traditionalist, the claims of these supply-side "extremists" were disproved by the budget deficits that arose from the tax cuts of the 1980s.[55]

New-Keynesians and Post-Keynesians

On the liberal reformist wing of the political spectrum, we find a diverse group of economists who are attempting to extend Keynesian theory and adapt it to new conditions. The New Keynesians (NKs) have attempted to build a microeconomic foundation for the theory of unemployment. Generally, NK theories are meant to explain inflexibilities of prices and wages that prevent markets from clearing.[56]

The Post-Keynesians (PKs) are an even more diverse group, including American institutionalists, Keynes's followers at Cambridge, and a broad array of other critics of neoclassical economics.

According to Alfred Eichner, five essential elements distinguish PK theory from the neoclassical orthodoxy. First, PK theory is usually concerned with economic growth, where neoclassical theory (including the textbook version of Keynesian theory) emphasizes static equilibrium. Second, the key determinant of growth is taken to be the rate of investment and the rate of growth is directly related to the distribution of income. Third, the money supply is believed to play an important role in long-term economic growth, where the neoclassical model would say that it only determines the general price level. Fourth, the competitive assumptions of neoclassical theory are replaced with an explicit treatment of the influence of multinational corporations and labor

[54]Supply-side analysis has been influential in the policy sphere, but the "new classical" and "rational expectations" schools have made important contributions in the intellectual sphere. For a useful survey, see N. Gregory Mankiw, "A Quick Refresher Course in Macroeconomics," *Journal of Economic Literature* 28 (December 1990): 1645–1660.

[55]Martin Feldstein, "Supply Side Economics: Old Truths and New Claims," *American Economic Review* 76 (May 1986): 26–30.

[56]Robert J. Gordon, "What Is New-Keynesian Economics?" *Journal of Economic Literature* 28 (September 1990): 1115–1171.

"If a bank lends you $1,000, the bank controls you. If a bank lends you $1 million, you control the bank." A few years ago, when the international banking crisis became the lead story in the daily news, a *Wall Street Journal* reporter attempted to find the origin of this saying and learned an important lesson about the history of ideas.

After several false starts, the reporter was directed to Donald Moggridge, a professor at the University of Toronto, who is a joint managing editor of the collected works of J. M. Keynes. In volume 24 (of 30 volumes), Moggridge located the following passage from a paper that Keynes sent to the British Cabinet in 1945: "The old saying holds: Owe your banker 1,000 pounds and you are at his mercy. Owe him one million pounds and the position is reversed."

Now all that remains is to find out whom Keynes was quoting.

Source: Lawrence Rout, "Keynes (or Maybe Publius) Speaks on the International Banking Crisis," *The Wall Street Journal*, February 24, 1983, 29.

---

unions. And fifth, PK analysis aspires to include treatment of nonmarket forms of resource allocation—including the operation of the government.[57]

A more concise definition is offered by Joan Robinson: "To me, the expression *post-Keynesian* has a definite meaning; it applies to an economic theory or method of analysis which takes account of the difference between the future and the past."[58] Like their namesake, the Post Keynesians recognize that the future is uncertain and they believe that speculative behavior lends instability to the capitalist system. Unlike Keynes, who believed that the government should primarily involve itself in macroeconomic stabilization, many of the PKs support an active public role in the distribution and allocation of income and resources.

RADICAL ECONOMICS

Finally, somewhere to the left of the average PK, we find a group of neo-Marxists and other radicals who continue to believe that the capitalist system is beyond reform—it must be replaced. The radicals have their own professional journals and their own cast of prominent authors, including Paul Sweezy, Samuel Bowles, Richard Edwards, Herbert Gintis, Michael Reich, and Thomas Weisskopf.

With some updating and revisions, the radicals generally accept the Marxian analysis of exploitation and class struggle in capitalist society. The

---

[57] Alfred Eichner, "Post-Keynesian Theory: An Introduction," *Challenge* 21 (May-June 1978): 4–17.
[58] Joan Robinson, "Keynes and Ricardo," *Journal of Post-Keynesian Economics* 1 (Fall 1978): 12.

present stage of capitalism, they say, is distinguished by at least three characteristics: (1) the ascendance of large, "monopolistic" enterprises; (2) the leadership of multinational corporations in the internationalization of capital; and (3) the absence of a strong socialist opposition. Under these conditions, capitalism is free to "intensify exploitation, inequality, polarization, and susceptibility to crises both within and between countries." Left unchecked, the "rule of capital promises nothing but disaster for the human species." In the long run, our only hope for survival "lies in the rebirth of a powerful revolutionary opposition."[59]

TRENDS IN GLOBAL CAPITALISM

Regardless of their ideologies, economists generally agree that capitalism is now a global phenomenon. Technological revolutions in the fields of international transportation and communication have reduced the importance of political boundaries and have enhanced every aspect of international cooperation and competition:

- *Internationalization of Trade.* World exports grew from 14 percent of global production in 1970 to 22 percent in 1995.[60] Growing trade relations are supported by an expanding web of international and regional free-trade organizations and agreements.

- *Internationalization of Investment, Production, and Employment.* In a world of multinational corporations and mobile international employees, it grows ever more difficult to draw clear lines between the economies of individual countries. What, for example, is an American product? Is it something produced in the United States by American workers, or is it something produced by American-owned companies, located in the United States or abroad? By the first definition, which is the conventional one, the United States had a $28 billion trade *deficit* in 1991. By the second definition, incorporating the sales of American-owned foreign affiliates, the United States recorded a $24 billion trade *surplus* in the same year.[61] In 1960, all of Motorola's employees were in the United States; in 1993, 44 percent were outside the country.[62]

- *Internationalization of Finance.* With increasingly integrated international capital markets, investors are able to search the world for the

---

[59] Paul M. Sweezy, "Monthly Review in Historical Perspective; Marxist Analysis of the 20th Century," *Monthly Review* 45 (January 1994).

[60] According to World Bank, *World Development Report 1994* (New York: Oxford University Press, 1994), 179; and *World Development Report 1997*, 239.

[61] J. Steven Landefeld, Obie Whichard, and Jeffrey Lowe, "Alternative Frameworks for U.S. International Transactions," *Survey of Current Business* 73 (December 1993): 57–61.

[62] Ray Marshall, "Internationalization: Implications for Workers," *Journal of International Affairs* 48 (Summer 1994): 60.

highest rates of return on their savings. Mutual funds make it possible for even small investors to dabble in the international capital markets. The volume of international issues increased from less than $10 billion in 1990 to nearly $54 billion in 1994.[63] International capital flows can have a major impact on the distribution of global economic activity. For example, developing countries saved 22 percent of GDP in 1995, but capital inflows made it possible for them to finance investments equal to 27 percent of GDP.

■ *Internationalization of Information.* International exchanges of information, says Peter Drucker, "are probably growing faster than any category of transactions in history."[64] In a world of Internet, CNN, cellular phones, satellites, fiber-optics, and videoconferences, ubiquitous information is both product and propeller of the globalization process.

Is all this internationalization a good thing? Will it contribute to the wealth and security of the participating nations? Most radical economists would answer these questions with an emphatic no. Expansion of the world capitalist system through international trade, investment, and employment will, in their opinions, exacerbate the exploitation of labor and natural resources, widen the gulf between the rich and the poor, and elevate the levels of conflict within and between nations.

Based on the doctrines of Adam Smith and David Ricardo, the large majority of mainstream economists (including monetarists, supply-siders, many New-Keynesians and Post-Keynesians, and others) seem to agree that internationalization of *trade* is a good thing. Thus, in a 1990 survey, 71 percent of U.S. economists said they "generally agree" with the statement, "Tariffs and import quotas usually reduce general economic welfare," and another 21 percent said they "agree with provisos."[65]

Many mainstream economists also believe that trade encourages international communication and understanding, contributing to peace and goodwill. John Stuart Mill may have been a bit naive in his belief that "commerce . . . is rapidly rendering war obsolete," but it is difficult to imagine a peaceful world without healthy diplomatic, cultural, and trade relationships.[66]

Although mainstream economists generally believe that commodity trade is beneficial to all participating countries, they are less certain about the benefits derived from international investment, employment, and fi-

[63]Euromoney Bondware estimates, published in *Financial Times*, January 23, 1995, 13.

[64]Peter F. Drucker, "Trade Lessons from the World Economy," *Foreign Affairs* 73 (January/February 1995): 100.

[65]Richard M. Alston, J. R. Kearl, and Michael B. Vaughan, "Is There a Consensus Among Economists in the 1990s?" *American Economic Review* 82 (May 1992): 204.

[66]John Stuart Mill, *Principles of Political Economy*, vol. 2 (New York: Hill and Company, 1904), 95.

nance. Classical theory suggests that free mobility of capital and labor should lead to *global* improvements in efficiency and productivity, strengthening the overall performance of the world economy. Unlike international commodity trade, though, which is thought to benefit each of the participating countries, international factor movements may cause gains for some countries and losses for others.

Internationalization of employment, for example, is beneficial to workers who are willing and able to search the world for attractive opportunities, and it may contribute to the dynamism and efficiency of the global economy, but it may threaten the long-term economic health of individual nations. In 1993 alone, Russia lost some 70,000–90,000 of its most talented scientists and intellectuals, and 80 percent of Russian scientists said they would like to emigrate.[67] China sent 230,000 of its brightest students abroad for higher education between 1978 and 1994, but less than one-third returned home; the return rate from the United States was less than 10 percent.[68] The United States itself is not immune to the international brain drain. According to a recent survey, about 25 percent of college-educated Americans and those who earn at least $50,000 a year have considered moving abroad.[69]

If a country is injured by loss of its talented workers, what of its capital resources? Would the economies of the capital-exporting countries be healthier if they built more factories, farms, and highways at home, rather than abroad (Table 3.1)? Adam Smith and the other classical economists anticipated this issue, but doubted its significance. An investor, Smith reasoned, will ordinarily "employ his capital as near home as he can, and consequently as much as he can in the support of domestic industry." The investor naturally prefers domestic operations because "his capital is never so long out of his sight," he can "know better the character and situation" of his business associates, and he "knows better the laws of the country."[70]

These "natural" barriers to international investment may have been effective in the eighteenth century, but they have little relevance in a world of multinational corporations, global investment funds, fax machines, and videoconferences. Once again, these developments may hold great promise for the global economy, but their significance for individual nations is unclear. What would Adam Smith, the nationalist, say about all this? We can only wonder.[71]

---

[67]Dmitry Chelyshev, "Brain Drain Threatens Nation's Scientific Heritage," Inter Press Service, November 21, 1994.

[68]Rone Tempest, "China Tries to Lure Its Best Back Home," *Los Angeles Times*, January 3, 1995, A1.

[69]Gary Belsky, "Escape from America," *Money*, July 1994, 60.

[70]Smith, *Wealth of Nations*, vol. 1, 454.

[71]See Joseph Persky, "Adam Smith's Invisible Hands," *Journal of Economic Perspectives* 3 (Fall 1989): 195–201. For a more optimistic assessment, suggesting that "investment abroad creates jobs at home," see Drucker, "Trade Lessons from the World Economy," 99–108.

■ **TABLE 3.1**

GLOBAL PATTERN OF DIRECT INVESTMENT, 1976–1994
(BILLION DOLLARS, ANNUAL AVERAGES)

	1976–80	1981–85	1986–90	1991–94
Outflows				
Industrial Countries	39.0	41.4	158.6	176.3
United States	16.9	7.6	25.3	47.2
Japan	2.3	5.1	32.1	19.9
United Kingdom	7.8	9.2	28.1	22.9
Other Europe	10.0	15.1	63.9	78.7
Developing Countries	0.8	1.8	9.1	23.4
Asia	0.1	1.1	7.8	19.8
Latin America	0.2	0.2	0.6	1.8
Total	39.7	43.2	167.7	199.8
Inflows				
Industrial Countries	25.3	36.2	126.8	108.9
United States	9.0	18.6	53.4	29.4
Japan	0.1	0.3	0.3	1.3
United Kingdom	5.6	4.3	21.7	14.5
Other Europe	8.7	9.9	38.8	54.3
Developing Countries	6.4	19.1	25.6	71.7
Asia	2.1	5.6	15.2	45.2
Eastern Europe	neg.	neg.	0.2	4.4
Latin America	3.6	5.6	6.6	16.5
Total	31.8	55.3	152.4	180.6

Source: Bank for International Settlements, *65th Annual Report* (Basle: 1995), 66; and International Monetary Fund, *World Economic Outlook*, May 1997, 107.

THE EVOLVING FRAMEWORK OF WORLD CAPITALISM

At the end of World War II, many people feared a repetition of the events that followed the previous war, when an economic slump led to a destructive round of protectionism and "beggar thy neighbor" trade policies, culminating in a protracted economic depression. Hoping to prevent these developments, delegates from 44 countries met in Bretton Woods, New Hampshire, for the International Monetary and Financial Conference of 1944. After three weeks of meetings, the delegates agreed to create two important organizations: the International Monetary Fund (IMF) and the International Bank for Reconstruction and Development (IBRD or World Bank).

Under the original design of the **Bretton Woods system**, the IMF would promote international monetary stability by helping member countries with short-term balance-of-payments problems and by supporting a system of fixed, but adjustable, currency exchange rates. The World Bank would assist the European countries in their reconstruction from the war by facilitating the flow of investment capital. By most accounts, the IMF and the World Bank performed their original functions rather well. Western Europe recovered quickly from the war, and a broad system of stable exchange rates was maintained for more than twenty years.

In the mid–1950s, the World Bank shifted its focus from Europe to the developing countries, where it initially provided financing for public sector infrastructure projects. Since that time, the Bank and its affiliates have broadened the functional and geographic scope of their activities.[72] Functionally, they have provided funding for educational, environmental, and public health programs, provided dispute settlement and risk insurance services, and provided support for economic reform, private sector development, and privatization programs. Geographically, they now provide support to the vast majority of developing countries in the world, including most of the former communist countries.

The original mission of the IMF virtually disappeared in the early 1970s, when the major industrial countries abandoned the system of fixed exchange rates. The institution was able to redefine itself, however, when rising oil prices in the 1970s led to the world debt crisis of the 1980s. The IMF played a prominent role in the negotiation of debt restructuring agreements, and worked with the debtor countries to design policies for financial stabilization and economic reform. More recently, the IMF has provided financial and technical support to countries passing through the transition from central planning to the market system.

In addition to the World Bank and the IMF, delegates to the 1944 Bretton Woods conference also discussed the creation of an International Trade Organization (ITO), a powerful body that would be responsible for removal and prevention of international trade barriers. An ambitious charter for the ITO was formulated at a series of conferences in London, Geneva, and Havana, but, in the end, was unacceptable to U.S. business interests, and failed to gain approval from the U.S. Senate. Without U.S. participation and leadership, the ITO charter became a dead letter.

In 1947, in the wake of the ITO failure, twenty-three countries agreed to establish a less powerful organization, known as the General Agreement on Tariffs and Trade (GATT), which the United States could join without

---

[72]Today, the World Bank Group is comprised of five institutions: The original International Bank for Reconstruction and Development (IBRD), established in 1946, makes market-based loans, primarily to governments; the International Finance Corporation (IFC), 1956, makes market-based loans to the private sector; the International Development Association (IDA), 1960, makes concessional loans to governments in low-income countries, funded primarily from grants; the International Center for Settlement of Investment Disputes (ICSID), 1966, resolves disputes between foreign investors and host governments; and the Multilateral Investment Guarantee Agency (MIGA), 1988, provides risk insurance to promote investment.

congressional approval. Each member, or "contracting party," of the GATT agreed to: (1) participate in multinational negotiations to reduce tariffs and other trade barriers; (2) reduce the number of import quotas; and (3) extend **most-favored nation (MFN)** treatment to all other members (that is, if country X grants a tariff reduction to one country, it automatically grants the same reduction to all other member countries). The agreement provided an important exception to the MFN rule for countries joining customs unions and free-trade areas.

Under the GATT umbrella, eight major rounds of multilateral tariff negotiations have been completed, yielding reductions of average tariffs on industrial products in the major industrial countries from about 40 percent of product value in 1947 to less than 4 percent today. The number of participants increased from 23 countries in the first round of GATT negotiations to 117 in the eighth round. If tariff reduction was the focus of the first six rounds of negotiations, removal of non-tariff barriers has gained prominence since 1973, when the seventh, or Tokyo Round, commenced.

The eighth round of GATT negotiations began in 1986 in Punta del Este, Uruguay, and was concluded in 1993. This was clearly the most ambitious GATT negotiation ever undertaken. Among its important provisions are the following:

- *World Trade Organization.* In memory of the unbegotten ITO, a new World Trade Organization (WTO) was created to replace the GATT organization. Unlike GATT, the WTO has a powerful system of dispute-resolution panels, whose decisions cannot be vetoed by members.

- *Industrial Tariffs.* Average tariff rates on imports were scheduled to decline by about 38 percent in the developed countries and 20 percent in the developing countries (Table 3.2). The developed countries agreed to completely eliminate tariffs for several sectors that account for about 40 percent of their imports, including steel, paper, furniture, pharmaceuticals, and medical, construction, and farm equipment.

- *Agriculture.* Trade-distorting subsidies and other import barriers were scheduled for cuts over a period of six years. Subsidized agricultural exports were cut by 21 percent. Japan and South Korea agreed to end bans on rice imports. All quantitative restrictions were to be replaced by tariffs, which would be scheduled for reductions.

- *Intellectual Property.* Countries joining the WTO must accept an extensive system of intellectual property rights protection, including seven years of protection for trademarks, twenty years for patents, and up to fifty years for copyrights.

- *Services.* A General Agreement on Trade in Services (GATS) was adopted, providing the first legally enforceable and multilateral framework for liberalization of trade and investment in services. Few specific commitments were made during the Uruguay Round

■ **TABLE 3.2**

**EFFECT OF THE URUGUAY ROUND ON INDUSTRIAL TARIFFS AND ON
WELFARE GAINS FROM TRADE IN GOODS AND SERVICES**

Country or Group	Pre-Uruguay Average Tariff (%)	Post-Uruguay Average Tariff (%)	Average Tariff Reduction (%)	Range of Predicted Gains (billion dollars)
Developed Countries	6.3	3.9	38	$139–394
Canada	9.0	4.8	47	4–12
European Union	5.7	3.6	37	61–164
Japan	3.9	1.7	56	27–42
United States	4.6	3.0	34	28–122
Developing Countries	15.3	12.3	20	36–78
Economies in Transition	8.6	6.0	30	37

Sources: *Financial Times*, November 2, 1994, 3; International Monetary Fund, *World Economic Outlook*, May 1994, Table 18; "The $510 Billion Question," *The Economist*, November 12, 1994, 82.

(some countries agreed to open their markets to legal services, accounting, and software), but negotiations are continuing under the GATS.

Estimates from computable general equilibrium models suggest that full implementation of the Uruguay Round agreement should contribute $510 billion (or about 2 percent) to world GDP, but the actual contribution may be much larger. All regions of the world are expected to benefit from the agreement, but the European Union is expected to capture the largest gains (Table 3.2). European countries should benefit from removal of costly distortions in agriculture and from increased access to foreign markets for high-technology goods and services.[73]

GLOBALISM AND REGIONALISM

As we noted earlier, the 1947 GATT accord required nondiscriminatory trade among its members, based on the unconditional most-favored-nation principle. Successive rounds of GATT negotiations have led to global and multilateral

[73]See "The Uruguay Round: Results and Implications," in International Monetary Fund, *World Economic Outlook*, May 1994, Annex 1; and Trien Nguyen, Carlo Perroni, and Randall Wigle, "An Evaluation of the Final Act of the Uruguay Round," *Economic Journal* 103 (November 1993): 1540–1549.

reductions of trade barriers. At the same time, the original GATT included an important exception to the doctrine of nondiscrimination, allowing members to form exclusive free-trade areas when: (1) trade barriers are virtually eliminated within the area; (2) trade barriers against nonmembers do not grow more restrictive; and (3) interim arrangements leading to the free-trade area are reasonably brief.

The nations of Western Europe quickly took advantage of this exception to the GATT, and created the European Economic Community (now the European Union) in 1957 and the European Free-Trade Association in 1960. In recent years, preferential trade has accelerated with the creation of the Asia Pacific Economic Cooperation Association (APEC), the North American Free-Trade Association (NAFTA), the Southern Cone Common Market (MERCOSUR), and other regional institutions. These take several different forms. In a basic **free-trade area**, the members agree to eliminate tariffs among themselves, but each maintains the right to set its own tariffs against nonmember nations. A higher level of integration may be attained by a **customs union**, a free-trade association in which all the member countries adopt a common set of tariffs against nonmembers. Higher still is a **common market**—a customs union with the additional removal of barriers to factor movements between members. Finally, a group of countries may advance to an **economic union**, in which all economic policies—monetary, fiscal, labor, antitrust, and others—are integrated.

From the standpoint of global economic efficiency, any of these preferential trading areas may yield a mixture of benefits and costs. On the positive side of the ledger, reduction of regional trade barriers should encourage members to import goods that were previously produced at home, and increase export production to pay for the imports. This process of **trade creation** should encourage members to specialize in their fields of comparative advantage and benefit from economies of large-scale production.

On the negative side of the ledger, creation of a free-trade area may interfere with efficient trading relationships between members and nonmembers. Suppose, for example, that country X traditionally has imported widgets from country Y, a low-cost producer. Also suppose that X forms a free-trade area with country Z. To avoid paying tariffs to their own government, consumers in X may decide to purchase their widgets duty-free from Z, even if Y offers a better pre-tariff price. Thus, country X diverts its purchases from country Y to country Z, and pays a higher external price for its imports. Rather than encouraging a larger volume of international trade, this free-trade area causes an inefficient rearrangement of the existing volume of trade, known as **trade diversion**.[74]

---

[74]The distinction between trade creation and trade diversion was discussed first by Jacob Viner in his book, *The Customs Union Issue* (New York: Carnegie Endowment for International Peace, 1950). For a more recent discussion of the topic, see Beth Yarbrough and Robert Yarbrough, *The World Economy: Trade and Finance*, 2d ed. (Chicago: The Dryden Press, 1991), 378–381.

The foregoing analysis raises two important questions. First, what is the net effect of regional free-trade associations on the volume and efficiency of international trade? Do they cause more trade creation or more trade diversion? The specter of a "Fortress Europe," raised in many journalistic and academic accounts, seems to imply that the European Union is predominantly a trade-diverting institution. Indeed, according to Lester Thurow of MIT, "history tells us that an economic union has to keep outsiders out, since this is the glue that holds the disparate insiders together."[75] On the other hand, statistical analyses of the European Union and other regional organizations have usually found that their trade-creating effects are significantly larger than their trade-diverting effects.

The second question is related to the first: Will the development of regional trading organizations support or hinder the development of a global system of free trade? A few years ago, Thurow suggested that the next fifty years would be characterized by "head-to-head" competition and managed trade between strong trading blocs in Europe, Asia, and the Americas. At about the same time, a study for the International Monetary Fund concluded that "beyond a certain threshold an undue emphasis on regionalism would undercut the multilateral trading system and render it inoperative."[76] Fortunately, though, fears of excessive regionalism have subsided since the successful conclusion of the Uruguay Round of GATT negotiations and the creation of the World Trade Organization. Even Lester Thurow acknowledges that "free trade within regions and managed trade between regions may well be the long-run route to freer world trade."[77] These liberalizing trends could give way to protectionism, of course, if the world slips into a serious recession. On the other hand, if systems of regional free trade eventually merge into a system of global free trade, we may witness the ultimate victory of laissez-faire capitalism.

SUMMARY

Several historical preconditions had to be fulfilled before the capitalist economic system could develop. Growth of market exchange required the development of monetary institutions and a relatively safe area of travel. In the political and legal spheres, capitalism requires the development of a system of property rights and a reasonable measure of political freedom for a large segment of society. In the areas of religion and philosophy, capitalism requires the relaxation of taboos against individualism and accumulation of wealth. Finally, it requires the formation of a class of people (capitalists) who

---

[75]Lester Thurow, *Head to Head* (New York: William Morrow and Company, 1992), 77.

[76]Augusto de la Torre and Margaret R. Kelly, *Regional Trade Arrangements*, Occasional Paper 93 (Washington, D.C.: International Monetary Fund, March 1992).

[77]Thurow, *Head to Head*, 82.

direct savings into productive investment rather than into the erection of monuments.

The mercantilists were among the first to call for an active governmental role in the market economy, particularly in the regulation of foreign trade. Adam Smith argued that the mercantilist controls were counterproductive and he proposed a system of "natural liberty" regulated by the competitive market mechanism. Smith's followers in the classical school supported his recommendations, but they foresaw problems in the operation of capitalism. Malthus feared overproduction of goods and population crises. Ricardo predicted a trend toward a no-growth, "stationary state." Mill decried the social injustice of capitalism.

According to Karl Marx, capitalism is an exploitive system and its eventual replacement by socialism is an inevitable law of history. During the Great Depression, when it seemed that the Marxian prediction was becoming reality, J. M. Keynes argued that the capitalist system could be saved through macroeconomic stabilization. Keynes's critics, though, claimed that his cure would be worse than the disease of unemployment. Schumpeter claimed that Keynesian policy would interfere with the progressive force of "creative destruction," and Hayek warned that governmental activism would lead us down a dangerous "road to serfdom." The popularity of Keynesian ideas peaked in the 1960s and then declined during the stagflation of the 1970s.

At the current time, the capitalist system is interpreted in many different ways by different groups of economists. Monetarists and supply-siders draw their inspiration from Adam Smith and his classical school. They generally believe in the stability of the capitalist system and advocate a limited role for the government. New-Keynesians and Post-Keynesians question the stability, competitiveness, and equity of modern capitalism and many of them favor broad programs of macroeconomic stabilization and social reform. Radical economists expand on Marx in their analysis of domestic and international capitalist exploitation and argue that growing frictions between democracy and capitalism require the adoption of democratic socialism.

Rapid developments in transportation and communication technologies have reduced the importance of national boundaries, encouraging the internationalization of trade, investment, production, employment, finance, and information. Mainstream economists generally support the internationalization of trade, but they have reservations concerning international investment, employment, and finance.

The institutional framework of international capitalism took new form at the end of World War II, with the creation of such organizations as the International Monetary Fund, the World Bank, and the General Agreement on Tariffs and Trade, and has continued to develop with the recent establishment of the World Trade Organization. Development of these global institutions has been accompanied by regional free-trade institutions, such as the EU, EFTA, APEC, and NAFTA. The relationship between global trade liberalization and development of regional trading blocks is a matter of continuing controversy.

DISCUSSION AND REVIEW QUESTIONS

1. What basic preconditions had to be fulfilled for the development of capitalism? What role was played by the enclosure movement? The Renaissance? The Protestant Reformation?

2. What was the mercantilist argument in favor of governmental control in a market economy? How did Adam Smith respond?

3. What is Say's Law? Which economists accepted and rejected it? On what grounds?

4. What, according to Ricardo, would cause economic growth to cease in a capitalist country? What was Mill's attitude toward the "stationary state"?

5. Based on the analyses of Marx and Schumpeter, interpret Robert Heilbroner's contention that "the economic enemy of capitalism has always been its own self-generated dynamics."

6. How does Keynesianism differ from Marxism? How does supply-side economics differ from monetarism?

7. What is the relationship, if any, between capitalism and democracy?

8. How will the role of the nation-state be affected by the growing internationalization of information and capitalist institutions?

9. How do regional trade agreements contribute to, and how do they interfere with, a free and efficient system of world trade?

SUGGESTED READINGS

Buchholz, Todd G. *New Ideas from Dead Economists.* New York: Plume, 1989. *Written from a relatively conservative perspective, this book provides a lively account of the history of economic thought.*

Cameron, Rondo. *A Concise Economic History of the World: From Paleolithic Times to the Present.* New York: Oxford University Press, 1989. *Drawing on the historical experience of industrial and developing economies, Cameron grapples with the question: Why are some nations rich and others poor?*

Cherry, Robert, et al., eds. *The Imperiled Economy.* New York: The Union for Radical Political Economics, 1987. *This two-volume collection of essays presents a radical perspective on current issues in American and international capitalism.*

Drucker, Peter F. *Post-Capitalist Society.* New York: HarperCollins, 1993. *How will the transition from industrial capitalism to a knowledge-based society affect the economic, political, and international systems? A leading management guru offers his insights.*

Gottlieb, Manuel. *Comparative Economic Systems: Preindustrial and Modern Case Studies.* Ames: Iowa State University Press, 1988. *Focusing on the historical development of modern mixed economies, this book includes chapters on imperial, medieval, mercantilist, and early capitalist economic systems.*

Heilbroner, Robert L. *The Making of Economic Society.* 8th ed. Englewood Cliffs, N.J.: Prentice-Hall, 1989. *By the author of* The Worldly Philosophers, *this may be the most accessible introduction to the history of capitalism.*

O'Brien, Richard. *Global Financial Integration: The End of Geography.* London: Royal Institute of International Affairs, 1992. *The chief economist of American Express Bank, Ltd., discusses the impact of global communications on the financial markets, and issues involved in creating a global framework for cooperation and regulation.*

Smith, Adam. *An Inquiry into the Nature and Causes of the Wealth of Nations.* Oxford: Clarendon Press, 1976. *If you intend to study the history and theories of capitalism from original texts, this is a good place to begin.*

Sweezy, Paul. *The Theory of Capitalist Development.* New York: Monthly Review Press, 1968. *A classic, and readable, introduction to Marxism.*

Thurow, Lester C. *Head to Head: The Coming Economic Battle among Japan, Europe, and America.* New York: William Morrow and Company, 1992. *Written by the dean of business at MIT, this is a provocative analysis of the changing nature of capitalist competition.*

Viljoen, Stephan. *Economic Systems in World History.* London: Longman, 1974. *Provides a particularly strong discussion of pre-capitalist economic systems.*

INTERNET RESOURCES

Adam Smith
http://www.efr.hw.ac.uk/EDC/edinburghers/adam-smith.html

Cato Institute
http://www.cato.org/

Free-Market
http://www.free-market.com/

Hoover Institution
http://hoover.stanford.edu/www/welcome.html

International Trade Law Project (including GATT and establishment of WTO)
http://ananse.irv.uit.no/trade_law/

Libertarianism
http://www.libertarianism.com/

Right Side of the Web
http://www.rtside.com/

Wealth of Nations
gopher://gopher.vt.edu:10010/02/141/1

World Trade Organization
http://www.wto.org/

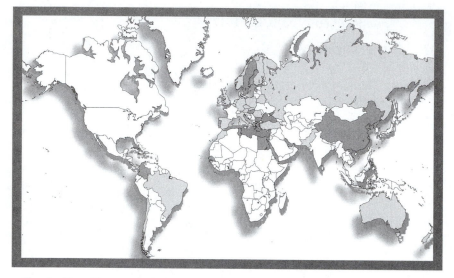

Socialist Representation in World Parliaments

 51% – 100%

21% – 50%

0% – 20% or Data Unavailable

Source: Table 4.2 of this chapter.

4

History and Theories of Socialism

People speak of socialism. We should speak of socialisms.
There is an amnesia about the socialist tradition that
abandons entire definitions of that ideal made by serious
mass movements. . . . What is needed, if socialism is to
find a new relevance for the twenty-first century, is some
sense of its enormous diversity and complexity.

—Michael Harrington
Socialism: Past and Future, 1989

hy should we concern ourselves with the ideologies and institutions of socialism? Is socialism
dead? Does it have a future? Has the entire socialist movement been discredited by the totalitarian excesses and economic failures of
Marxism-Leninism-Stalinism-Maoism in the former Soviet Union, Eastern Europe, and China? Is
it true, once and for all, that "the contest between
capitalism and socialism is over: capitalism has
won"?[1]

Similar questions have been asked before. Late
in the nineteenth century, when revolutionary movements were defeated
throughout Europe and socialist experiments were abandoned in Europe
and America, Karl Marx reported that "all party organizations and party
journals of the working classes" had been "crushed by the iron hand of
force . . . and the short-lived dreams of emancipation vanished before an
epoch of industrial fever, moral morasme, and political reaction."[2] In 1921, an
English noble made the following entry in her diary: "Nansen was here to tea
and gave me the reassuring news that our troubles with Russia are over.

---

[1]Robert Heilbroner, "The Triumph of Capitalism," *The New Yorker*, January 23, 1989, 98.

[2]Karl Marx, "Inaugural Address of the Working Men's International Association," in *The Marx-Engels Reader*, 2d ed., ed. Robert C. Tucker (New York: W. W. Norton, 1978), 516.

Lenin is introducing a New Economic Policy which restores a free market and represents a return to capitalist exchange of goods in Russia."[3]

Today, it seems most unlikely that any country will launch another Soviet-style program of nationalized industry, collectivized agriculture, and detailed central planning. That system, in fact, has been thoroughly discredited. In the eyes of many observers, however, the collapse of Soviet Stalinism represented a victory over totalitarianism, not a failure of socialism.[4] Indeed, many socialists consistently opposed the Soviet-style system because it gave most members of society "no control over the economy they theoretically own."[5]

The leading voices of contemporary socialism are reformers rather than revolutionaries, democrats rather than centralists. They follow democratic socialist traditions that were prominent in the historic campaigns for women's suffrage, progressive taxation, universal public education, abolition of child labor, and protection of labor unions. Today, their agenda has grown to include support for workplace democracy, universal health care, and environmental protection. They control large voting blocs in the parliaments of countries as diverse as Australia, Colombia, Egypt, Greece, Hungary, Pakistan, Portugal, Sweden, and Tunisia. Thus, it may be premature to declare the death of socialism.

In this chapter, we shall explore the history and diversity of socialist thought and practice. Many of the earliest disagreements among socialists concerned the proper system of ownership. Should private ownership remain unrestricted, or should society regulate and exercise ownership rights? Should social ownership be exercised at the level of the national government (that is, state socialism), or should it be limited to local cooperative and communal arrangements?

If the government is drawn into the operation of socialism, how should this be accomplished? Is it possible to develop socialist institutions through a gradual process of legislative reform, or is it necessary to overthrow the existing governmental and social system? If a revolution is necessary, how should it be initiated, and by whom? And finally, if the society assumes ownership of the means of production, how should they be administered? Should the activities of factories be coordinated by a central plan or a decentralized market? Can a socialist economy operate as efficiently as a capitalist economy? These and other questions have animated the socialist debate through the centuries. Some have been answered by experience, but others seem to defy resolution.

SOCIALISM IN THE ANCIENT WORLD

In their study of primitive cultures, anthropologists have found evidence of both market exchange and socialist cooperation. Many of these cultures prac-

---

[3]Lady Kennet of Deane, quoted in Bertram Wolfe, "A Historian Looks at the Convergence Theory," in *Sidney Hook and the Contemporary World*, ed. Paul Kurtz (New York: John Day, 1968), 55.

[4]See Amanda Bennett, "U.S. Marxists Thrive Despite Communism's Demise," *The Wall Street Journal*, September 6, 1994, B1.

[5]Michael Harrington, *Socialism: Past and Future* (New York: Arcade Publishing, 1989), 61.

ticed a primitive form of communism, whereby the tribe owned productive goods and food was distributed by the chief.[6] Adam Smith, the father of classical economics, spoke of "that rude state of society which precedes both the accumulation of stock and the appropriation of land," when "the whole produce of labour belongs to the labourer."[7] Primitive communism was not the product of any ideal philosophical system; it was little more than a pragmatic response to the challenge of survival in the "rude state of society."

In ancient Greece, the birthplace of formal utopian philosophy, we find a lively discussion of socialist ideas. According to Aristotle, the first scholar to argue that "the citizens of a state ought to have equal possessions" was Phaleas of Chalcedon, who believed this arrangement would prevent social disputes and revolutionary movements.[8] In *Republic*, Plato advocated a system of social ownership and communal living arrangements, but only for members of the ruling class of philosophers and soldiers. The purpose was to prevent conflicts of interest, not to promote egalitarianism. In order to maintain work incentives, Plato favored individual ownership of property among members of the lower classes. Democritus and Aristotle defended the right of all social classes to own private property.

One of the earliest recorded collectivist experiments was performed by the early Christians in Jerusalem, for whom "all things were common property," and "there was not a needy person among them, for all who were owners of land or houses would sell them . . . and they would be distributed to each, as they had need."[9] This seems to have been a voluntary response to a situation of extreme need, not to a governmental or religious edict; the Christians outside of Jerusalem maintained ownership of their property.[10] Lacking political or economic power, the early Christians directed their message to individual people and churches, not to the Roman government.[11]

EARLY CRITICS OF CAPITALISM

To trace the origins of socialism as a mass movement, we must leap forward to the late 1700s, when the political revolutions in America and France and the Industrial Revolution in England were laying fertile ground for a new social movement. The rebels in America and France supported private property rights, but they also demonstrated the feasibility of revolutionary action and demanded political equality, the forerunner of economic equality. The Industrial Revolution generated, among other things, a Dickensian world of

---

[6] See, for example, Manning Nash, "The Organization of Economic Life," in *Tribal and Peasant Economics*, ed. George Dalton (Garden City, N.Y.: The Natural History Press, 1967), 3–4.

[7] Adam Smith, *An Inquiry into the Nature and Causes of the Wealth of Nations* (Oxford: Clarendon Press, 1976, originally published in 1776), 82.

[8] Aristotle, *Politics* 2.7.1266a35.

[9] Acts 4:32–35.

[10] Rom. 16:3–5; Col. 4:15; and Philem. 2.

[11] For an extended discussion of socialist ideas in ancient Greece, Asia, South America, and in the early Christian church, see Igor Shafarevich, *The Socialist Phenomenon* (New York: Harper & Row, 1980), Chapters 1, 2, 4, and 5.

urban blight and child labor and a vast sum of new wealth to be redistributed.

As early as 1755, the French philosopher Jean Jacques Rousseau (1712–1778) declared his belief in the superiority of the lowly savage over modern society. "How many crimes, wars, murders, sufferings, and horrors mankind would have been spared, if, when the first man enclosed a plot of land and said, `This is mine,' someone would have torn down the fence and cried: `Don't listen to this impostor; you are lost if you forget that the earth belongs to no one, and that the fruits are for all!'"[12] Although Rousseau did not propose the abolition of private property, he inspired others to take that next step.

Also in 1755, a French philosopher named Morelly outlined several "sacred and fundamental laws that would tear out the roots of vice and of all the evils of society." His first proposal was that "nothing in society will belong to anyone, either as a personal possession or as capital goods, except the things for which the person has immediate use."[13] In Morelly's ideal society, production and distribution of goods, choice of occupations, location and arrangement of cities, rites of marriage, communal housing and training of children (including religious training), and many other activities would be regulated by governmental bodies. In order to "prevent all tyrannical domination," governmental leadership would be rotated and every head of a family would become a senator at the age of 50.

UTOPIAN SOCIALISM

In the 1790s, William Godwin (1756–1836) in England and the Marquis de Condorcet (1743–1794) in France predicted that the advance of human knowledge and reasoning would lead to improvements in virtue—they believed in human **perfectibility**. Based on this premise, they also predicted that people would share property more equally in the future, and that governmental institutions designed to protect the population from force and fraud would no longer be necessary.[14]

Early in the nineteenth century, the philosophy of perfectionism led naturally to the development of **utopian socialism**. Most of the utopian socialists would have agreed with the environmentalist slogan, "Think globally, act locally."[15] They had a broad, global, perfectionist view of human potential, but they designed and advocated local, communitarian schemes for social re-

---

[12]Jean Jacques Rousseau, "Discourse on the Origin of Inequality among Men," in *Socialist Thought: A Documentary History*, ed. Albert Fried and Ronald Sanders (Garden City, N.Y.: Doubleday and Company, 1964), 33.

[13]Morelly, "Code of Nature," in *Socialist Thought: A Documentary History*, 20.

[14]Malthus wrote his essay on population growth, mentioned in the previous chapter, to debunk the optimistic scenario presented by Godwin and Condorcet.

[15]This slogan has been attributed to Ed Sanders, an American democratic socialist poet who was a member of the counterculture of the 1960s. The slogan grew in popularity after it was the theme of the 1980 meeting of the World Future Society in Toronto.

form. Generally, they believed that commercial and public institutions should be placed under the control of associations of workers. This could be accomplished gradually, they thought, without resort to violence.

HENRI DE SAINT-SIMON

The first important utopian socialist may have been Henri de Saint-Simon (1760–1825), a member of the French nobility. He did not object to private ownership of property, but believed that economic and political power should be transferred from the old privileged class of aristocrats, landlords, clergymen, and other "idlers" to the productive class, which he defined broadly to include bankers, industrialists, artists, scientists, and laborers.

If France lost its 30,000 most privileged people, the nation "would grieve them for purely sentimental reasons," but their loss "would result in no political evil for the State." On the other hand, if France lost its 3,000 leading scientists and artisans, "the nation would become a lifeless corpse," and would "immediately fall into a position of inferiority."[16] Thus, the followers of Saint-Simon were the first to advocate a society organized around "associations of workers."[17]

To facilitate worker participation in social issues, Saint-Simon proposed an interesting system of economic planning for public works expenditures. According to his scheme, planning would be handled by a three-chamber industrial parliament. A Chamber of Invention, composed of engineers, poets, artists, architects, and musicians, would generate ideas for public works and prioritize them. Next, a Chamber of Examination, composed primarily of mathematicians and physical scientists, would evaluate the feasibility of the projects. Finally, a Chamber of Execution, composed of industrialists, would exercise veto power over the projects in the plan and develop a program to finance and implement them. Although his ideas were not adopted during his life, Saint-Simon is considered by many to be an inspirational force behind French indicative planning.

ROBERT OWEN

In the year 1800, a prosperous Manchester businessman named Robert Owen (1771–1859) acquired the New Lanark factory in Scotland. Espousing ideas unusual at the time, Owen believed that environmental factors, rather than heredity or sinfulness, held back the progress of the lower classes. With the proper environment, "*any* habits and sentiments can be given to mankind," and "every individual may be trained to produce far more than he can consume."[18] Furthermore, he argued that an improvement in the educational and cultural level of the poor would benefit everyone, including the rich.

---

[16]Henri de Saint-Simon, *Social Organization, The Science of Man, and Other Writings* (New York: Harper Torchbooks, 1964), 72–73.

[17]Harrington, *Socialism: Past and Future*, 30–32.

[18]Robert Owen, "An Address to the Inhabitants of New Lanark," in *Socialist Thought: A Documentary History*, 173.

Based on this philosophy, Owen transformed New Lanark into a model community. He took young children out of the factories and established one of the first systems of universal education. He raised wages, shortened working hours, and provided good housing, sanitation, and nonprofit stores. To the amazement of his fellow industrialists, New Lanark continued to earn substantial profits after the reforms were introduced. Owen contented himself with a 5 percent return on his investment, and used the remaining profits for the welfare of his workers.

After succeeding at New Lanark, Owen solicited the aid of the British government to establish a number of "villages of cooperation." When his proposals were spurned in England and on the Continent, he emigrated to the United States and established a cooperative society in New Harmony, Indiana, in 1826. Unfortunately, Owen was bilked by an associate and by 1828 the New Harmony experiment failed. Owen lost most of his fortune and returned to England to spend the rest of his days working for the trade union movement.

CHARLES FOURIER

Another important exponent of utopian cooperation was Charles Fourier (1772–1837), a businessman and writer in Lyons. Fourier, we should note, was either eccentric or slightly insane. He believed, for instance, that the world would eventually reach a state of harmony, in which six new moons would replace the one in existence and all the violent and repulsive beasts would be replaced by their opposites—lions by anti-lions, rats by anti-rats, and so on. For some reason, this part of his theory was never taken seriously.

Fourier developed a detailed proposal for a system of producer cooperatives called *phalansteries.* Each of these would include about 1,600 people, all of whom would live and work in one large building with adjoining farmland. Like Saint-Simon, Fourier had no objection to private ownership; shareholders who invested in a phalanstery would receive one-third of its profits. The remaining profits would be divided between labor (five-twelfths) and management (one-quarter). In order to avoid the monotony of the factory system, participants would rotate job assignments every few hours and competitive games would be organized around the work process.

Fourier never was able to finance his experiment in France, but more than 40 phalansteries were established in the United States. The most famous of these was Brook Farm in Massachusetts, whose members included Nathaniel Hawthorne and Ralph Waldo Emerson. Brook Farm was reasonably successful until it burned to the ground in 1846. Another phalanstery, La Reunion, played a significant role in the early history of Dallas, Texas. One of its residents, an immigrant from Switzerland, later served twice as mayor of Dallas.[19] Almost all the American phalansteries disappeared by the mid–1850s.

---

[19]Steve Blow, "Socialists? In Dallas? Indeed," *Dallas Morning News*, July 24, 1994, 33A.

PIERRE JOSEPH PROUDHON

The most radical utopians were the **anarchists,** led by Pierre Joseph Proud-hon (1809–1865), a Parisian, and Mikhail Bakunin (1814–1876), a violent Russian exile.[20] The anarchists declared that all governmental power is corrupt—even if it is wielded by the workers. Thus, they rejected all proposals to seize governmental power or to promote governmental reform. Earlier, Godwin, Condorcet, and Saint-Simon predicted a gradual "withering away of the state," but the anarchists called for its immediate replacement with a system of voluntary cooperatives and contracts. As Proudhon explained:

> *It is industrial organization that we will put in place of government. . . . In place of laws, we will put contracts. . . . In place of political power, we will put economic forces. . . . In place of standing armies, we will put industrial associations. In place of police, we will put identity of interests.*[21]

Indeed, this is radical utopianism. How, we might ask, will contracts replace laws when the latter are needed to enforce the former? To their credit, however, Proudhon and Bakunin anticipated the critical danger in state socialism: Governmental ownership of the means of production could become the basis of a new form of oppression.

REVOLUTIONARY SOCIALISM

One of the first socialists to call for the violent overthrow of the existing system was Francois "Gracchus" Babeuf (1760–1797), a journalist who led the Society of the Pantheon. This group was organized in 1795 to denounce the decline of the French Revolution and to advance the cause of communist egalitarianism. According to Babeuf and his followers, the promise of political equality was empty and insufficient:

> *We are speaking of something more sublime and more equitable, the COMMON GOOD, or the COMMUNITY OF GOODS! No more individual ownership of the land: the land belongs to no one. We are demanding, we desire, communal enjoyment of the fruits of the earth: the fruits belong to all.*[22]

Babeuf was executed in 1797 for plotting to overthrow the government, but his name became a rallying cry for later revolutionaries.

Auguste Blanqui (1805–1885) advocated the forceful expropriation of large estates, control over factories, and establishment of free education and a progressive income tax. He did not believe that the workers would ever organize their own revolution or that socialist measures would be adopted in a

---

[20]In the words of Joseph Schumpeter, "Anarchism was utopianism with a vengeance." See his *Capitalism, Socialism, and Democracy* (New York: Harper and Brothers, 1950), 307.

[21]Pierre Joseph Proudhon, "General Idea of the Revolution in the Nineteenth Century," in *French Utopias: An Anthology of Ideal Societies*, ed. F. E. Manuel and F. P. Manuel (New York: Free Press, 1966), 371.

[22]"Manifesto of the Equals," in *Socialist Thought: A Documentary History*, 53.

democratic society, even if the poor were allowed to vote. The poor, he said, did not know the source of their miseries. Thus, he believed that a revolutionary coup must be initiated by a small, well-organized minority—a concept that was rejected by Marx and Engels, but later adopted by Lenin. Blanqui devoted himself to several insurrectionist causes and spent much of his adult life in jail.

KARL MARX AND FRIEDRICH ENGELS

As we have seen, Karl Marx (1818–1883) and his associate Friedrich Engels (1820–1895) spent much of their time exposing the "true nature of capitalism" and the forces leading to its destruction; they spent little time preparing a blueprint for socialist society. Nevertheless, their ideas have been so influential that some people use the words *socialism* and *Marxism* interchangeably. Marx and Engels drew together many elements of earlier socialist philosophies and added many of their own. Their socialism was revolutionary and pragmatic in the short run, evolutionary and utopian in the long run. They established a mainstream of socialism that drew many adherents on the Continent, while reformism prevailed in England.

Marx and Engels dismissed the utopian program of voluntary cooperation as a quaint and naïve dream and proposed their own system of **scientific socialism**. In opposition to those who believed that socialism could be attained by peaceful means, Marx and Engels believed that the capitalist class would not surrender control of society without a fight. In countries where the capitalist class structure is firmly established, "the lever of our revolution must be force."[23] In opposition to those like Blanqui (and eventually Lenin), "who openly state that the workers are too uneducated to emancipate themselves," Marx countered that "the emancipation of the working class must be the work of the working class itself."[24]

After the revolution, Marx and Engels believed that socialism would proceed through several stages. First, control of society would pass from the capitalist class to a new **dictatorship of the proletariat**. Despite the dreams of anarchists, forceful measures would be necessary during this stage of history to protect the new socialist regime from lingering reactionary forces at home and abroad. "The class domination of workers over the resisting strata of the old world" must continue, Marx said, "until the economic foundations of the existence of classes are destroyed."[25]

Marx maintained that several of the defects of capitalist society must continue during the early stages of socialism, because socialism is "still stamped with the birth marks of the old society from whose womb it emerges."[26] Thus,

---

[23]Karl Marx, "On the Possibility of Non-Violent Revolution," in *The Marx-Engels Reader*, 523. Interestingly, Marx believed that nonviolent revolutions could possibly occur in America and England because of the institutions, mores, and traditions in those countries.

[24]Karl Marx, "The Manifesto of the Three Zurichers," in *The Marx-Engels Reader*, 555.

[25]Karl Marx, "After the Revolution," in *The Marx-Engels Reader*, 547.

[26]Karl Marx, "Critique of the Gotha Program," in *The Marx-Engels Reader*, 529.

■ **TABLE 4.1**

NINETEENTH-CENTURY SOCIALISTS: A TYPOLOGY

		Preferred Form of Social Ownership	
		State	Cooperative, Communal
Expected Method of Transition to Socialism	*Gradual Reform*	Blanc S. and B. Webb	Fourier, Owen Mill
	Revolution	Blanqui Marx (short run)	Proudhon, Bakunin Marx (long run)

it is not possible to immediately dispense with coercive governmental institutions. In addition, some income inequality must continue in order to maintain work incentives and to make the new system politically acceptable. Goods must be distributed according to the rule, "To each according to his work."

Marx believed that several preconditions must be satisfied in the early stages of socialism before communism, the final utopian stage, can be attained. First, society must reach a high stage of economic development. Second, an unselfish "new man" for whom "labour has become not only a means of life but life's prime want" must evolve.[27] And third, Marx apparently believed (as did Trotsky after him) that the socialist revolution must spread to all countries before communism can emerge in any country. The working class in a single nation cannot put an end to class struggle because the defenders of capitalism in that country are "linked up in a brotherhood . . . with the bourgeois of all other countries."[28]

After these conditions are fulfilled, the other features of communism would naturally follow. The victory of the dictatorship of the proletariat and the gradual improvement of social consciousness would give rise to a classless society. With an abundance of goods and an unselfish, hard-working population, it finally would become possible to distribute consumer goods according to the rule, "To each according to his needs."

Marx believed that many of the institutions of the old society would become obsolete under full communism. The use of money, for example, would pass away when goods are abundant and people are unselfish. The state, as we presently know it, would "wither away" because the cessation of domestic and international class conflict would reduce or eliminate the need for many of the legislative, law enforcement, and military functions of the government. Thus, Marx rejected the anarchist vision of a stateless society in the short run (during the dictatorship of the proletariat), but he embraced it in the utopian long run (Table 4.1).

---

[27]Ibid., 531.
[28]Ibid., 533.

Marx believed that the socialist economy would operate according to a plan that "distributes labour-power and means of production to the different branches of production," but he did not explain how the plan was to be formulated.[29] What agency would prepare the plan, especially after the "withering away" of the state? How often should the plans be prepared? How should the central planners take account of the interdependence of the economy, and how should they control implementation of the plans? Marx and Engels, who devoted most of their writing to the capitalist system, were silent on these and many other questions about socialism.

After 1848, the pivotal year when Marx and Engels wrote their *Communist Manifesto* and when workers' revolts were crushed in several countries, the socialist movement fell into disarray. The utopian experiments inspired by Owen, Fourier, and others continued through the 1840s, but most of them disappeared by the mid–1850s.

THE FIRST INTERNATIONAL AND THE PARIS COMMUNE

In 1864, Marx played an important role in establishing the Working Men's International Association (or the First International, as it was more commonly known). Although the First International marked an important stage in the development of the trade union movement, it did very little to advance Marx's dream of a national socialist movement. Specifically, the International succeeded in coordinating the activities of trade unionists in several countries, preventing strike-breaking activities by workers in adjoining countries, and preventing the British government from supporting the South in the American Civil War. It lost much of its influence, however, because of tactical disputes between the Marxist and Bakuninist wings of the association.

Rivalry within the First International was further intensified by the formation of the Paris Commune in 1871. In that year, the National Guard of Paris led a revolt against the national government; socialists of all stripes were elected to a majority of the seats on the new Commune Assembly. The Commune attempted to institute a number of social reforms, but it was crushed within a few weeks by the national government.

The Commune had little lasting impact on French history, but it was extolled by Marx, Engels, and Lenin as the first realistic attempt to establish a dictatorship of the proletariat.[30] This, in turn, intensified the debate in the First International between the Marxists, who believed in the necessity of a revolutionary dictatorship of the proletariat, and the anarchists, who rejected any proposal to take over the government. Marx had Bakunin and his supporters expelled from the International in 1872 and the organization collapsed over the next 4 years.

---

[29]Karl Marx, *Capital*, vol. 2 (Moscow: Progress Publishers, 1956, originally published in 1893), 362.

[30]See Edward S. Mason, *The Paris Commune: An Episode in the History of the Socialist Movement* (New York: The Macmillan Co., 1930), Chapters 5, 6, and 7.

V. I. Lenin and the Russian Revolution

The late 1800s witnessed the death of Marx (in 1883) and Engels (in 1895), the birth of an ineffectual Second International (in 1889), and the formation of socialist parties in several European countries. From the very beginning, one of the prime movers among the Russian Social Democrats was a young lawyer named Vladimir I. Lenin (1870–1924). Lenin became a radical at the age of 16, when his older brother was executed for participating in a plot to assassinate Tsar Alexander III. He studied Marxian theory at home and abroad, and in 1902 published a pamphlet, titled *What Is to Be Done?*, which echoed Blanqui in saying that the revolution must be led by an elite vanguard of professionals:

I assert: (1) that no movement can be durable without a stable organization of leaders to maintain continuity; (2) that the more widely the masses are spontaneously drawn into the struggle and form the basis of the movement and participate in it, the more necessary it is to have such an organization . . . ; (3) that the organization must consist chiefly of persons engaged in revolutionary activities as a profession; (4) that in a country with an autocratic government, the more we restrict *the membership of this organization to persons who are engaged in revolutionary activities as a profession . . . ; and (5) the* wider *will be the circle of men and women of the working class . . . able to join the movement and perform active work in it.*[31]

When the Russian Social Democrats held their first congress in 1903, the followers of Lenin commanded a temporary majority and called themselves the **Bolsheviks** (from *bol'shinstvo*, majority). Their opponents, who rejected the idea of an authoritarian vanguard style of leadership, came to be known as the **Mensheviks** (minority). The names stuck, even when the Bolsheviks constituted a minority of the Social Democratic Party.

Initially, Lenin faced stiff resistance *within* the Bolshevik faction because he seemed to be violating the Marxian belief that the proletarian revolution would first occur in the most advanced capitalist countries. To this charge, Lenin answered that the Russian revolution could proceed "in a different way from that of the West-European countries," because the Russian proletariat had already demonstrated their revolutionary zeal and because the imperialist policies of the advanced countries had shifted the focus of capitalist exploitation to Russia and other developing countries:

If a definite level of culture is required for the building of Socialism (although nobody can say just what that definite "level of culture" is, for it differs in every West-European country), why cannot we begin by first achieving the prerequisites for that definite level of culture in a revolutionary way, and then, *with the aid of the workers' and peasants' government and the Soviet system, proceed to overtake the other nations?*[32]

---

[31]V. I. Lenin, "What Is to Be Done?" in *Essential Works of Lenin*, ed. Henry M. Christman (New York: Bantam Books, 1966), 147–148.

[32]V. I. Lenin, "Our Revolution," in *A Documentary History of Communism*, ed. Robert V. Daniels (New York: Random House, 1960), 229.

Lenin's arguments, supported by Leon Trotsky's (1879–1940) theory that a revolution in Russia would be supported by the encouragement of a "permanent revolution" in other countries, carried the day. As we shall consider at length in later chapters, the Bolsheviks took control of the government in November 1917 and the Soviet state was born. After experimenting with market socialism in the 1920s, the government eventually adopted a centralized system of economic planning and administration.

Under central planning, individual enterprise managers in Irkutsk, Minsk, and Pinsk made few important decisions. In principle, the planners in Moscow would tell the enterprise what to produce, where to obtain raw materials, where to sell the final products, what prices to charge, and a host of other requirements. The manager and his employees were paid to carry out orders. Hence, the Soviet system was sometimes called a **command economy.**

DEMOCRATIC SOCIALISM

While Blanqui, Marx, Engels, Lenin, and others were organizing revolutionary socialist movements, another cast of characters remained dedicated to the idea that socialist goals could be accomplished through evolutionary, nonviolent, democratic programs of reform. They rejected the Marxian notion that existing governments—including democratic governments—had to be overthrown because they were irredeemable tools of the ruling capitalist class. Democratic socialists believed, as they do today, that governments can play a progressive role in society.

LOUIS BLANC

In 1848, long before the creation of the Paris Commune, Louis Blanc (1811–1882) gained a position in the French Provisional Government. Blanc was already known as a socialist theoretician, having formulated the slogan, "From each according to his abilities, to each according to his needs." To address the problem of unemployment, Blanc believed the state should use its power to guarantee each person a "right to work." Thus, he used his own governmental power to support the creation of a system of "national workshops." According to Blanc's design, the workshops should be owned by the state, but they should be governed, in large part, by the workers.

A few months after Blanc joined the government, labor unrest and governmental budgetary problems mounted, and the workshops were closed. Thousands of workers and soldiers were killed in the riots that ensued, and Blanc fled to England. Nevertheless, he is remembered for his advocacy of public ownership and his belief that socialist reforms could be adopted by the democratic machinery of the existing government.

FERDINAND LASALLE

In Germany, the revolutionary doctrine of Karl Marx stood in direct opposition to the more democratic notions of Ferdinand Lasalle (1825–1864). The state can be an agent of socialist reform, Lasalle argued, if it operates on a democratic basis with universal suffrage. Unlike most of the utopian socialists, who advocated the creation of small-scale producer cooperatives, Lasalle believed that the workers, with legal and financial assistance from the state, should gain control of large-scale factories with their "enormous advantage in productivity."

Known as a great orator, Lasalle organized the first German socialist party in 1863, and its membership grew rapidly. Lasalle was killed in a duel one year later, but his party survived and his followers perpetuated his ideas. Their democratic hopes were encouraged in 1871 when Bismarck, the German emperor, established a new parliament whose lower house, the *Reichstag*, was elected by a popular vote. From the beginning, socialists were able to win seats in the new parliament.

Hoping to increase their voting strength, the followers of Marx and Lasalle agreed to meet in 1875 in the town of Gotha to discuss the merger of their parties into a single German Social Democratic Party. The draft of the party program, prepared for the meeting, had a strong Lasallean tone: "The working class strives for its emancipation first of all within the framework of the present-day national state. . . ." The new party "demands the establishment of producers' cooperative societies with state aid under the democratic control of the toiling people."

Marx objected strongly to this language, arguing that the "present-day national state" cannot be reformed; it must be overthrown.[33] Nevertheless, in their desire to unite with the Lasalleans, Marx's followers ignored his objections. The Gotha Congress adopted the draft program with minor alterations, and the German Social Democratic Party became a parliamentary party, striving for political power and social reform by constitutional means.

Confronted by a united Social Democratic Party, Bismarck was forced to enact the first comprehensive social security system in Europe, helping those afflicted by unemployment, accidents, sickness, and old age. In 1895, twelve years after Marx's death, even Friedrich Engels had to acknowledge the electoral success of the German Democratic Socialist Party: "The two million voters whom it sends to the ballot box . . . form the most numerous, most compact mass, the decisive `shock force' of the international proletarian army. . . . We are thriving far better on legal methods than on illegal methods and overthrow."[34]

The German Social Democratic Party quickly became the model for similar parties in most of the other European countries. Socialist parties were organized in Denmark (1879), Spain (1879), France (1880), Russia (1883), Belgium (1885), Norway (1887), Sweden (1889), Italy (1892), Poland (1892), Netherlands (1893), and Finland (1899). In some countries, such as Russia and Poland, the new parties were not able to participate in parliamentary democracy; they were driven underground into revolutionary activities. In most of the other countries, they became an important force in the democratic system, and they remain active today.

---

[33]See his "Critique of the Gotha Program," 525–541.

[34]Friedrich Engels, "The Tactics of Social Democracy," in *The Marx-Engels Reader*, 571.

JOHN STUART MILL

In Great Britain, the socialist movement developed with particularly strong democratic and libertarian roots. John Stuart Mill (1806–1873) may have been the author of *On Liberty* and an advocate of the laissez-faire principles of Adam Smith, but he also lived to see the darker side of the Industrial Revolution and was profoundly influenced by the utopian socialists.

Putting together these strands of thought, Mill came to believe that capitalism would gradually and spontaneously evolve into socialist cooperation. "If mankind continues to improve," Mill said, production eventually will be dominated by "the association of the labourers themselves on terms of equality, collectively owning the capital with which they carry on their operations, and working under managers elected and removable by themselves."[35]

Mill looked forward to a system of democratic labor-managed cooperatives. He was an early supporter of governmental involvement in health, education, and welfare reform, and he believed that socialist aims could and should be attained with a minimum of revolutionary fervor, governmental interference, expropriation of property, or central planning.

THE FABIAN SOCIETY

In 1884, three socialist organizations were established in England. Two of them, the Social Democratic Federation and the Socialist League, had Marxist roots and never attracted large followings. The third, the Fabian Society, was also small, but was far more influential. Led by Sidney and Beatrice Webb and George Bernard Shaw, and inspired by the ideas of John Stuart Mill, the Fabians supported an evolutionary program of social reforms:

We who call ourselves Socialists today in England, largely through Mill's teaching and example, find a confirmation of this hope in social history and economics, and see already in the distance the glad vision of a brighter day, when, practically, the whole product of labor will be the worker's and the worker's alone, and at last the social arrangements will be deliberately based on the Apostolic rule ignored by so many Christians, that if a man does not work, neither shall he eat.[36]

Like Mill, the Fabians believed that workers' organizations, local governments, and national governments would gradually gain ownership and control of business enterprises, and would turn the existing state into a "welfare state." This could be accomplished, they believed, "with little more dislocation of industry than is caused by the daily purchase of shares on the Stock Exchange."[37]

Unlike Marx, who was a materialist, the Fabians believed that the power of the socialist *idea* was sufficient to alter the course of history: "Socialists do

---

[35]John Stuart Mill, *Principles of Political Economy*, ed. W. J. Ashley (New York: Augustus M. Kelley, 1965, originally published in 1848), 772–773.

[36]Sidney Webb, "English Progress toward Social Democracy," in *Socialist Thought: A Documentary History*, 398–399.

[37]Ibid., 400.

but foretell the probable direction of English social evolution; and it needs nothing but a general recognition of that development, and a clear determination not to allow the selfish interests of any class to hinder or hamper it, for Socialism to secure universal assent." In fact, they believed that this process of democratic socialization had begun long before the establishment of any socialist party, and that England, not Germany, "is already the most Socialist of all European communities."[38]

The evolutionary socialist ideas of the Fabian Society were incorporated into the platforms of the Independent Labour Party, organized in 1893, and the Labour Party, reorganized in 1918. In 1945, Labour gained its first strong parliamentary majority, and pursued a program of nationalization of industry and social welfare legislation.

THE EFFICIENCY OF SOCIALISM

The early socialists directed attention to the "inherent flaws" of capitalism: exploitation, inequality, worker alienation, economic instability, unemployment, militarism, and many others. Socialism, they thought, would be more equitable and also more efficient. According to L.V. Kantorovich, the Russian recipient of a Nobel Prize in economics: "Socialist society . . . is *by its nature* capable of securing a more complete and rational use of productive resources for the better satisfaction of the needs of society [emphasis added]."[39]

Since their inception, however, socialist proposals have encountered criticism. Aristotle warned that public property would be employed and maintained inefficiently because "that which is common to the greatest number has the least care bestowed upon it."[40] Long before any specific schemes were devised for socialist economic planning, Adam Smith warned that "no human wisdom or knowledge could ever be sufficient" to devise a scheme for "superintending the industry of private people, and . . . directing it towards the employments most suitable to the interest of the society."[41]

John Stuart Mill generally sympathized with the aims of socialists, but he opposed wholesale nationalization of industry and agreed with Smith's condemnation of national economic planning. Specifically, Mill rejected any scheme "which aims at taking possession of the whole land and capital of the country, and beginning at once to administer it on the public account." Aside from the injustice of expropriation, "the very idea of conducting the whole industry of a country by direction from a single center is so obviously chimerical that nobody ventures to propose any mode in which it should be done."[42]

---

[38]Ibid., 401.

[39]L.V. Kantorovich, "Mathematical Formulation of the Problem of Optimal Planning," in *Socialist Economics*, ed. Alec Nove and D. M. Nuti (Baltimore: Penguin, 1972, first published in 1955), 464.

[40]Aristotle *Politics* 2.3.1261b34.

[41]Smith, *Wealth of Nations*, 687.

[42]Mill, *Principles of Political Economy*, 988.

Mill also rejected the ideas of Fourier and other socialists who supported rotation of work assignments, "an arrangement which by putting an end to the division of employments would sacrifice . . . the productiveness of labor."[43] He also disagreed with socialists who blamed market competition for "all of the economical evils which at present exist." We may dislike the dehumanizing aspects of competition, which may be a "source of jealousy and hostility among those of the same occupation," but we must not forget "that wherever competition is not, monopoly is; and that monopoly in all of its forms is the taxation of the industrious for the support of indolence, if not of plunder."[44] Mill believed a socialist system could be devised that would preserve the benefits of competition and deliver an adequate standard of living.

In the end, Mill believed that the choice between capitalism and socialism would not hinge on narrow questions of economic efficiency, but "mainly on one consideration, viz. which of the two systems is consistent with the greatest amount of human liberty and spontaneity. . . . It remains to be discovered how far the preservation of this characteristic would be found compatible with the communistic organization of society."[45]

LUDWIG VON MISES AND THE CALCULATION DEBATE

After the Bolsheviks gained power in Russia, socialism was no longer a utopian abstraction. A protracted debate began, involving economists from several countries, concerning the possibility (or impossibility) of efficient management of a socialist economy.

The debate began in earnest in 1920, when Austrian economist Ludwig von Mises (1881–1973) argued that efficient planning is impossible in a system of state socialism.[46] According to Mises, market exchange of producer goods cannot occur under state socialism because all producer goods are held by a single owner—the state. If producer goods are not exchanged, then it will be impossible to determine their market prices. If there are no market prices for producer goods, it will be impossible to perform the calculations that are necessary to make rational decisions.

If a steel mill is to be built, for example, where should it be located, and what technology should be employed? What energy source should be used, and what mix of raw materials? To answer these questions in a way that will minimize the social cost of building the steel mill, the cost of land, equipment, and raw materials must somehow be measured and added. Under

---

[43]Ibid., 207.

[44]Ibid., 792.

[45]Ibid., 210.

[46]Ludwig von Mises, "Economic Calculation in the Socialist Commonwealth," in *Socialist Economics* (first published in 1920), 75–91. The title of this essay is most important; Mises is concerned with economic calculation in a socialist *commonwealth*, that is, in a system of state socialism in which "all the means of production are the property of the community." His arguments do not seem to apply with equal force to a system of cooperative socialism or syndicalism, in which the factories and farms are owned by smaller groups of workers.

state socialism, Mises argued, it may be possible to make vague estimates of cost, but no reliable yardstick will exist.

LANGE'S THEORY OF MARKET SOCIALISM

The challenge presented by Mises elicited a number of responses. In the Soviet Union, economists and officials maintained that the inefficiencies of centrally planned socialism were trivial in comparison to the monopolistic distortions, business cycles, and unemployment inherent in capitalism. Some Soviet economists suggested that the problem of valuation, emphasized by Mises, could be solved with linear programming models and other mathematical techniques.

Outside of the Soviet Union, few supporters of socialism defended the efficiency of Soviet-style central planning. Instead, they argued for alternative forms of socialism, based on market principles and cooperative ownership. These, they argued, would equal or surpass the efficiency of the capitalist system.

Although John Stuart Mill proposed a system of **market socialism** as early as 1848, the first to answer Mises with such a system was Fred M. Taylor, in his 1928 presidential address to the American Economic Association. His arguments were extended and amplified by Oskar Lange (a Polish economist), H. D. Dickinson (British), Abba Lerner (British-American), Joseph Schumpeter (Austro-American), and Burnham Beckwith (American) between 1936 and 1949.[47] Their analyses were similar, but the version offered by Lange attracted the largest audience.

According to Lange, a decentralized system could be devised to operate state socialism in a way "quite analogous to that in a competitive market."[48] The pattern of production would be set by consumer sovereignty, and freedom of occupational choice would be maintained. The allocative efficiency of the economy would be greater than that of a capitalist economy, Lange believed, because it would be free of the distortions caused by monopolies and externalities.

According to Lange's scheme, enterprise managers should be required to follow two rules. First, in order to minimize the average cost of production, they should attempt to equalize the marginal products derived from the last unit of money spent on each of the factors of production. Second, in order to operate at optimal levels of production, they should expand production at their enterprises until marginal costs are equal to the prices of their final products. These are precisely the rules that are followed by a "perfectly competitive" producer in a theoretical capitalist economy.

The Central Planning Board (CPB) in Lange's model takes the place of the market. If a shortage or surplus of any commodity or productive resource

---

[47]For an annotated bibliography of these and other works on market socialism, see Burnham P. Beckwith, *Liberal Socialism*, 2d ed. (Jericho, N.Y.: Exposition Press, 1974), 445–455.

[48]Oskar Lange, "On the Economic Theory of Socialism," in *On the Economic System of Socialism*, ed. Benjamin E. Lippincott (Minneapolis: University of Minnesota Press, 1938), 82.

exists at the end of the accounting period, the CPB raises or reduces its price. Lange argued that this trial-and-error procedure would generate a set of equilibrium prices more rapidly than a competitive market because "the Central Planning Board has a much wider knowledge of what is going on in the whole economic system than any private entrepreneur can ever have."[49]

Lange claimed several additional advantages of market socialism over capitalism.[50] First, because the means of production are owned by the public, there are no property incomes; thus the distribution of income would be more even. Second, the managers of socialist factories would be willing to take fuller account of the social costs of production (including the cost of pollution, etc.) than the managers of profit-seeking capitalist enterprises.

Third, unlike the situation in capitalist society, where monopolists may restrict production in an effort to inflate their prices and profits, managers of socialist enterprises would be instructed to produce to the efficient level where price equals marginal cost.[51] Finally, a socialist economy would avoid business cycle fluctuations because the planners would be able to keep a downturn in one sector of the economy from adversely affecting the others.

LANGE'S CRITICS

As one might expect, Lange's response to Mises drew both praise and criticism.[52] According to his critics, Lange underestimated the difficulty of the price-setting job of the CPB. Millions of prices must be set in a modern economy, and these must be changed continuously to maintain equilibrium. To obtain the necessary information on shortages and surpluses, and to adjust all of the prices in a timely manner, the CPB would require a huge bureaucracy.

Even if Lange's planners and managers could match the performance of a market economy in static equilibrium, his critics say that the dynamic efficiency of his theoretical system is dubious. In a world where decisions are based not only on our knowledge of the present, but also on our conjecture of the future, Lange's two operating rules may be insufficient to guide the actions of enterprise managers. Prices set in a capitalist market are influenced by current conditions and by expectations; it is unlikely that the prices set by Lange's central planners would incorporate all of that information.

---

[49]Ibid., 89.

[50]Ibid., 98–108.

[51]Recall that the profit-maximizing level of output for a monopolist is lower than the equilibrium level of output for a competitive industry.

[52]For critical evaluations of Lange's model, see Friedrich Hayek, "Socialist Calculation: The Competitive `Solution'," *Economica* 7 (May 1940): 125–149; Abram Bergson, "Market Socialism Revisited," *Journal of Political Economy* 75 (October 1967): 655–673; Peter Murrell, "Did the Theory of Market Socialism Answer the Challenge of Ludwig von Mises? A Reinterpretation of the Socialist Controversy," *History of Political Economy* 15 (1983): 92–105; and Don Lavoie, *Rivalry and Central Planning: The Socialist Calculation Debate* (New York: Cambridge University Press, 1985).

Another objection concerns Lange's failure to describe the methods used to monitor performance of enterprise managers and how they would be motivated to run their operations efficiently. Should profits be used as a measure of success? Should a share of profits be given to the manager? If this is done, some of the purported advantages of socialism may be lost. Profit-earning managers would have an incentive to take advantage of monopoly power, possibly causing them to ignore social costs (for example, of pollution) in order to reduce their private costs. If profits are not used to measure the success of the enterprise and to reward its manager, what will take their place?

OTHER MARKET SOCIALIST MODELS

In the 1950s and 1960s, Yugoslavia and a number of Eastern European countries began to experiment with market socialism. We will consider these experiments in the chapters that follow. In addition to their operational importance, the Eastern European systems also inspired the creation of several new theoretical models of market socialism.

Ben Ward initiated a new round of theorizing in 1958 with his theory of **labor-managed socialism,** based on an abstraction of the Yugoslav system.[53] In his model of the idealized nation of Illyria, the state owns the means of production but entrusts management to the workers in each enterprise. Commodities are exchanged in actual markets, where their prices are determined by supply and demand. Aside from taxes and rental fees paid to the government and funds retained for enterprise investment, any profits earned by the enterprise are divided among the workers.

Given these conditions, Ward assumes that the enterprise manager, who is elected by the workers, attempts to maximize the income of the average worker in the enterprise. Unlike the manager of a capitalist enterprise, who, according to the usual assumption, attempts to maximize total profits, the Illyrian manager attempts to maximize profits per worker. As we shall discuss in a later chapter, the behavior of the Illyrian manager may be quite different from that of a capitalist manager. Unlike Lange's model, prices in Ward's model are set by market forces rather than by central planners, and the motivation system of the enterprise (retention of profits) is clearly defined.

In recent years, and particularly since the collapse of command socialism in the Soviet Union and Eastern Europe, several authors have designed new models of market socialism. Designed to meet the needs of transitional societies that are unwilling or unable to move "all the way" to unfettered capitalism, these proposals have several elements in common. To distinguish them from utopian, radical, centrally planned, and totalitarian models of socialism, their authors describe them as *pragmatic, feasible, market-oriented*, and

---

[53]Benjamin Ward, "The Firm in Illyria: Market Syndicalism," *American Economic Review* 48 (September 1958): 566–589.

democratic systems of socialism. They are predicated on the development or maintenance of democratic institutions, and, unlike the Lange model, they rely on a profit motive and on market determination of prices.[54] Furthermore, most of these models would allow private or cooperative ownership of small and entrepreneurial firms.

Recent socialist proposals differ widely in their arrangements for ownership and management of large enterprises. James Yunker and Alec Nove have developed blueprints for **market-oriented state socialism,** based on direct state ownership, which would allow broad enterprise autonomy.[55] In particular, Yunker would nationalize large corporations under a Bureau of Public Ownership (BPO), authorized to hire, fire, and evaluate the work of enterprise executives. The BPO would have veto power over executive compensation plans, which would be strongly dependent on profitability, but the BPO would be prohibited from interfering in the day-to-day enterprise management. After deductions for managerial pay and administrative costs of the BPO, the bulk of profits would be paid to the public as a social dividend. The dividend would be divided between households in proportion to their earned incomes.

Contingent on its existing financial institutions, Pranab Bardhan and John Roemer would have a country choose between two variants of market socialism.[56] A country that already has a well-organized stock market would adopt a system of **voucher socialism**. Initially, all adults would be given vouchers, allowing them to purchase stock in large and formerly state-owned enterprises. Afterwards, citizens would be free to exchange their holdings for other stocks or mutual funds, but they would not be allowed to liquidate their holdings for money or other assets.[57] Thus, it would be impossible for ownership of industry to become concentrated in the hands of a small capitalist class, and enterprise profits would be distributed rather evenly to the population in the form of stock dividends. Enterprise managers would be free to conduct business in roughly the same way as managers under conventional corporate capitalism, and they would respond to a similar system of oversight and incentives from shareholders.

---

[54]Indeed, several of its proponents claim that market socialism will remedy the problems caused by separation of corporate ownership and control under modern capitalism, yielding a stronger profit motive and a higher level of economic efficiency. Although most of these proposals rely on market pricing, some authors would employ selective price controls to curb abuses of monopoly power. Similar controls are used in many capitalist systems.

[55]Alec Nove, *The Economics of Feasible Socialism* (London: George Allen and Unwin, 1983); and James A. Yunker, *Socialism Revised and Modernized* (New York: Praeger, 1992).

[56]Pranab Bardhan and John Roemer, "Market Socialism: A Case for Rejuvenation," *Journal of Economic Perspectives* 6 (Summer 1992): 101–116. Also, see *Market Socialism: The Current Debate*, ed. by Pranab Bardhan and John Roemer (New York: Oxford University Press, 1993).

[57]According to Bardhan and Roemer, the prohibition against liquidation of ownership rights in their system of economic democracy is analogous to the prohibition against selling of voting rights in a system of political democracy.

In countries without well-organized stock markets, Bardhan and Roemer recommend a system of **bank-centric socialism,** based on an adaptation of the Japanese economic system. In Japan, diversified groups of companies (*keiretsu* organizations) are organized under the leadership and partial ownership of large investment banks. The banks, which are owned privately in Japan, would be majority-owned by the state in the Bardhan-Roemer proposal, but their intended role would be the same: to provide broad oversight and financial support and discipline for companies in their financial groups.

Aside from the investment banks, other large companies would not be owned directly by the state. Instead, their shares would be owned by workers within the company, by other public firms (including their workers) in the same financial group, and by the group's investment bank and its subsidiaries. According to its authors, this system would encourage efficiency and accountability, and, like the Japanese system, would encourage companies to consider a long time horizon in their investments, but it would provide a relatively egalitarian distribution of ownership, control, and income.

Many of the most recent socialist proposals are promoted under the banner of **economic democracy**. According to Alan Charney, director of the Democratic Socialists of America: *By economic democracy we mean, in the most general terms, the direct ownership and control of much of the economic resources of society by the great majority of wage and income earners. The centerpieces of this movement are alternative economic institutions such as cooperatives and worker-owned facilities, but this movement also encompasses existing financial arrangements, such as pension funds and employee stock ownership plans (ESOPs) that can, through legal and political contestation, be fashioned into devices that also enrich and expand the movement for economic democracy.*[58]

Even if it is politically impossible to introduce any broad system of state, cooperative, or worker ownership, Robin Archer suggests that socialists can still work toward a meaningful program of economic democracy.[59] Under Archer's proposal, people who are not employees could continue to own shares in a firm, and they could derive dividend income from those shares, but they would have limited control over management of the firm. Instead, in the "ideal" case, managers would be elected by and accountable to their workers. Workers may direct their managers to seek outside capital investment, just as they may seek customers for the company's products, but they would no more relinquish managerial control of the firm to investors than to

---

[58] Alan Charney, "Back to the Beginning," October 8, 1994, on the Internet server, Democratic Socialists of America (http://ccme-mac4.bsd.uchicago.edu/DSA.html).

[59] Robin Archer, *Economic Democracy: The Politics of Feasible Socialism* (Oxford: Clarendon Press, 1995); and Robin Archer, "One Democratic Goal Remains in Labour's Works," *The Guardian,* May 8, 1995, 14.

customers. Recalling that full political democracy did not materialize in Britain until nearly a century after the Reform Act of 1832, Archer acknowledges that full economic democracy may develop slowly. A good first step, he says, would be establishment of German-style works councils in all large and medium-sized firms.[60]

The market socialist proposals of Lange and his followers have attracted criticism from both the left and the right. According to orthodox Marxists, the competitive rivalry and macroeconomic instability of the market system are inconsistent with socialist aspirations. According to libertarians, socialist restriction of property rights is the first step down Hayek's "road to serfdom." Based on more than twenty years of experimentation in Hungary, Janos Kornai suggests that we abandon the cause of market socialism:

> It is futile to expect that the state unit will behave as if it were privately owned and will spontaneously act as if it were a market-oriented agent. It is time to let go of this vain hope once and for all. Never, no more.[61]

SOCIALISM SINCE WORLD WAR II

THE GROWTH AND DECLINE OF COMMAND SOCIALISM

Until the latter years of World War II, the Soviet Union and Mongolia were the only strongholds of command socialism in the world.[62] Beginning in 1944, the Red Army installed Communist governments in the countries of Eastern Europe and North Korea, liberating them from fascist and Japanese domination. Mock elections were held in Bulgaria, East Germany, Hungary, Poland, and Romania because the indigenous Marxist movements were rather weak in those countries.

The situation was somewhat different in Albania, Czechoslovakia, Yugoslavia, and Vietnam. In Czechoslovakia, the Communists won a rightful place on a coalition government in a free election in 1946. Within 2 years, though, they edged all non-Communists out of power. Albania, Yugoslavia, and Vietnam drove out the Axis powers with little outside help. They all had relatively strong indigenous Marxist movements and none of them shared a common border with the Soviet Union. Furthermore, the Yugoslav and Vietnamese Communist leaders, Marshall Tito and Ho Chi Minh, were war heroes. Albania, Yugoslavia, and Vietnam were closely allied with the Soviet

---

[60]For a description and discussion of German works councils, see Chapter 11.

[61]Janos Kornai, *The Road to a Free Economy* (New York: W. W. Norton, 1990), 58. A similar line of criticism against market socialism may be found in Andrei Schleifer and Robert W. Vishny, "The Politics of Market Socialism," *Journal of Economic Perspectives* 8 (Spring 1994): 165–176.

[62]Mongolia fell under Communist control in 1921, resulting from its involvement as a staging ground in the Russian civil war.

Union immediately after the war, but they were in a political and geographic position to act independently of Moscow.

Under the leadership of Mao Zedong, the Chinese Communists came to power in 1949 by defeating the Kuomintang in a long civil war. The Chinese Communists received little help, and some hindrance, from the Soviet Union during the war, but afterwards the Soviet Union provided aid, equipment, and advisors to install Soviet-style socialism in China.

The Communist movement spread to Latin America in 1960, when Fidel Castro gained power in Cuba, and to Africa in the 1960s and 1970s, when European colonialism began to crumble. The leaders of national liberation movements in many of the African countries were attracted to the Leninist theories of revolution and nationalization. With aid from the Soviet Union and its allies, Marxist regimes came to power in Angola, Mozambique, Madagascar, the Congo, Benin, and Ethiopia, and self-styled socialist regimes controlled several other countries.

Thus, the Communist world grew rapidly after World War II, but, in true dialectical fashion, its growth was fraught with conflicts and contradictions. Disagreements between Tito and Stalin led in 1948 to the expulsion of Yugoslavia from the Cominform, the international organization of the Soviet bloc. A few years later, Yugoslavia began to organize its unique system of labor-managed market socialism.

World communism was shaken by Stalin's death in 1953 and by Khrushchev's denunciation of Stalin's terror at the 1956 Party Congress. The Albanian leaders criticized Khrushchev for his blasphemy, and dropped out of the Soviet bloc to preserve their variety of Stalinism. The Poles and Hungarians were heartened by Khrushchev's remarks, and workers' groups demanded democratic reforms, higher wages, privatization of agriculture, and Yugoslav-style worker self-management. When Hungary attempted to leave the Warsaw Pact, the effort was crushed by Soviet troops and tanks.

In China, Mao Zedong was troubled by Khrushchev's de-Stalinization campaign, by his policy of peaceful co-existence with the West, and by his shift toward consumer goods production at a time when China was attempting to establish an industrial base. Mao ignored his Soviet advisors in 1958 and initiated his ill-fated Great Leap Forward program of rural communes and small-scale industrial production. A war of words ensued between Moscow and Beijing, and Soviet advisors were withdrawn from China in 1960.

In the mid–1960s, Soviet economic performance began to deteriorate, and Soviet economists gained more freedom to discuss programs of reform. Again, the Eastern Europeans were encouraged by these developments, and initiated new reform programs of their own. This time it was Czechoslovakia that pressed the Soviet leaders beyond their limits, calling for the creation of democratic institutions and independent trade unions. In 1968, the so-called Prague Spring was terminated by a quarter of a million Warsaw Pact troops.

A decade after the invasion of Czechoslovakia, the Communist world was shaken again when the Catholic church chose a prelate from Poland to serve as its first non-Italian Pope in 450 years. With support from John Paul II, the church grew stronger in Poland, and it played an important role in the formation of Solidarity, the first independent trade union in the Communist bloc. After a series of strikes and political demands in 1980 and 1981, the Communist leadership attempted to regain control by imposing martial law. Nevertheless, the events in Poland exposed the deep chasm between the Communist leadership and the working class; the seeds of an anti-Communist revolution had been sewn in Eastern Europe.

The dissolution of authoritarian socialism accelerated after 1985, when Mikhail Gorbachev came to power in the Soviet Union. His policy of *glasnost* (openness) made it possible to openly discuss the deterioration of economic performance, the crimes of Stalinism, the cost of the war in Afghanistan, and hundreds of other subjects that had been suppressed. His policy of *perestroika* (restructuring) made it possible to start working toward a more market-oriented economic system and a more democratic political system.

Equally important for the rest of the Communist world, Gorbachev abandoned the so-called Brezhnev Doctrine, which committed the Soviet Union to preserve Communism in other countries. In July 1989, Gorbachev cautioned the Eastern European leaders not to count on the Red Army for support: "Each people determines the future of its own country and chooses its own form of society. There must be no interference from outside, no matter what the pretext." Within a few months of this announcement, a Solidarity member became prime minister of Poland, the Hungarian parliament changed their country's name to Republic of Hungary, shedding Marxian terminology, and Communist regimes began to topple throughout Eastern Europe. In August 1991, responding to an abortive coup attempt against Gorbachev's government, Russian President Boris Yeltsin suspended the activities of the Communist Party and Gorbachev agreed to dissolve the Soviet Union.

With less fanfare, the collapse of authoritarian socialism spread quickly to the Third World. During the 1980s, the Soviet Union, Eastern Europe, and China could offer only one-tenth as much economic aid to developing countries as the Western industrial countries. Troubled by domestic problems, the Soviet Union and China cut their economic aid programs by 74 percent and 68 percent, respectively, in 1989.[63] A year later, new democratic constitutions were adopted in Benin, Mozambique, and the Congo, and the Sandinistas were voted out of power in Nicaragua. The governments in these and many other developing countries initiated privatization programs in agriculture and industry.

---

[63]U.S. Central Intelligence Agency, *Handbook of Economic Statistics*, 1990 (CPAS 90–10001, September 1990), 180–187.

DEMOCRATIC SOCIALISM IN TRANSITION

After World War II, as in earlier years, the focus of democratic socialist activity was in Western Europe. Communist parties and other radical socialist organizations continued to operate in many European nations, but their activities were moderated and inhibited by Western European participation in NATO, and by the public reactions to the Berlin blockade, the revelation of Stalin's crimes, the invasions of Hungary and Czechoslovakia, and the ultimate collapse of Soviet communism.

In Great Britain, the Labour party was victorious in the first postwar election in 1945, and it quickly launched a program to nationalize the "commanding heights" of industry and to create an extensive welfare state. The Labour party was formally committed to public ownership in clause four of its constitution, reproduced on party membership cards: "to secure for the workers . . . the full fruits of their industry . . . upon the basis of the common ownership of the means of production."

Programs of nationalization were also conducted in France and Italy after World War II, where Socialist and Communist parties participated in coalition governments. On the other hand, the ruling Social Democratic party in Sweden dropped its plans for postwar nationalization to secure the cooperation of employers in a program of centralized collective bargaining. The division of Germany after the war led to a strong spirit of anticommunism in the West. Thus, the German Social Democratic Party moved away from its Marxist heritage, and it adopted a new program in 1959, declaring that the "fundamental values of socialism" are not revolution and public ownership, but "freedom, justice, and solidarity."[64]

In 1982, a socialist government in France initiated the largest postwar nationalization program in the Western world. Nevertheless, the recent trend in democratic (as well as autocratic) countries has been away from nationalization, and toward privatization, of industry. This movement began in the early 1980s in England, under the Conservative leadership of Margaret Thatcher, and it spread quickly throughout the world. In 1995, the British Labour party formally amended clause four of its constitution; references to "common ownership" were replaced with a commitment to the values of "freedom, equality, and solidarity."

If socialism is defined in terms of governmental policies to promote economic equality, the democratic socialist movement still seems to be robust. According to an international poll conducted by the Times Mirror organization in 1991, large majorities of the populations in twelve nations of Eastern and Western Europe agreed that "the state has a responsibility to take care of people who cannot take care of themselves." Only in the United States and West Germany did the majority disagree.[65] Transfer payments to households

---

[64]M. Donald Hancock, *West Germany: The Politics of Democratic Corporatism* (Chatham, N.J.: Chatham House, 1989), 83.

[65]"What Europeans Think," *Los Angeles Times*, September 17, 1991, special edition, H/B.

■ TABLE 4.2

SOCIALIST REPRESENTATION IN WORLD PARLIAMENTS, 1995

Country	Last Election	Socialist % of Parliament	Country	Last Election	Socialist % of Parliament
Albania	2/92	32	Ireland	11/92	23
Australia	3/96	33	Israel	6/92	37
Austria	12/95	39	Italy	3/94	27
Belarus	5/95	30	Jamaica	3/93	100
Belgium	5/95	27	Japan	10/96	8
Brazil	10/94	21	Morocco	6/93	20
Bulgaria	12/94	52	Netherlands	5/94	13
Canada	10/93	3	New Zealand	10/96	31
Chile	12/93	25	Nicaragua	10/96	42
China	3/93	100	North Korea	4/90	100
Colombia	3/94	57	Norway	9/93	48
Costa Rica	2/94	49	Pakistan	10/93	40
Cuba	2/93	100	Poland	9/93	37
Czech Rep.	5/96	42	Portugal	1/96	93
Denmark	9/94	35	Romania	10/92	38
Dominican Rep.	5/94	48	Russia	12/95	40
Ecuador	5/96	5	Senegal	5/93	72
Egypt	11/95	70	Slovakia	9/94	7
Finland	3/95	43	Ukraine	3/94	32
France	3/93	16	Spain	3/96	46
Germany	10/94	38	Sweden	9/94	52
Greece	9/96	61	Tunisia	3/94	96
Hungary	5/94	54	Turkey	12/95	22
India	7/92	9	United Kingdom	4/92	41

Note: Here, a parliamentarian is considered to be a socialist if she/he is affiliated with a party that is a full member, consultative party, or observer party in the Socialist International (for a list of these parties, see http://ccme-mac4.bsd.uchicago.edu/DSASI.html on the World Wide Web), or another party that identifies itself as "socialist," "social democratic," "communist," "labor," "left," or, in the case of Russia, "agrarian." In countries with bicameral systems, the data in this table refer only to the lower house of parliament. Information on parliamentary representation was assembled from reports of IBC Political Risk Service and from media accounts.

have grown steadily as a percentage of GNP in most of the Western democracies since World War II. Transfer payments are generally highest, and incomes are distributed most equally, in countries such as Sweden where Social Democratic parties have maintained parliamentary majorities.

If socialism is defined in terms of "economic democracy" and worker participation in management, the democratic socialist movement again seems to be robust. Worker participation takes many forms. In the United States, legislation encouraging the formation of employee stock ownership plans (ESOPs) has allowed more workers to gain a share of ownership in their businesses. In Germany, workers have a legally protected voice in management through their representatives on works councils and on corporate management boards. Implementation of the European Social Charter should lead to the development of a similar system of worker participation in the other countries of the European Union.

Finally, if we measure the strength of socialism by its representation in world parliaments, we find that the movement is far from dead (Table 4.2). Democratic socialist parties, alone or in coalitions, are playing active roles in the governments of countries in Africa, Asia, Europe, and Latin America. Like every other political movement, the socialists are attempting to redefine their role in a rapidly changing world. In the end, they will be judged by their ability to address the challenges of social justice, economic security, and environmental disruption in a setting of intense global competition.

SUMMARY

In the primitive world, a form of communal ownership was sometimes practiced within the tribe, and communal systems were sometimes advocated or practiced in Greek and biblical times. These, however, were usually voluntary responses to special circumstances. Revolutionary proposals for socialism as a mass movement began in the late 1700s, encouraged by the political revolutions in America and France and the Industrial Revolution in England. The French philosopher, Rousseau, criticized the system of capitalist ownership, and Morelly called for its abolition.

William Godwin and the Marquis de Condorcet predicted that the advance of reasoning would lead to improvements in virtue, an approach that encouraged the development of utopian socialism and anarchism. Saint-Simon, perhaps the first utopian socialist, championed the cause of working people in decision making, and devised a system of national economic planning based on this principle. Robert Owen operated a successful model community, and attempted to organize several other cooperative communities. A similar proposal for a communal society, including provisions to reduce the monotony of work, was developed by Charles Fourier; several of his communities were established in America. The anarchists Proudhon and Bakunin took utopianism a step farther, and wished to replace the state altogether with a system of cooperatives.

Francois Babeuf was among the first to be executed for the cause of revolutionary socialism, and Auguste Blanqui argued that a socialist revolution would require the leadership of a small, well-organized minority.

Marx and Engels defined a mainstream of socialism that prescribed revolutionary tactics, state ownership, and a dictatorship of the proletariat in the short run, asserting that the state and monetary exchange would "wither away" in the long run. Their description of socialist society was not particularly detailed. The socialist movement was weakened by internal rivalries and revolutionary failures during the second half of the nineteenth century.

Early in the twentieth century, Lenin followed Blanqui in saying that the revolution must be initiated and led by an elite vanguard of professionals; he provided a justification for beginning the revolution in Russia, a relatively poor country.

Louis Blanc helped to initiate the democratic socialist movement when he supported a gradual program of socialist reform in France. In Germany, Ferdinand Lasalle argued that electoral reforms would lead to the adoption of socialism, with worker control of large efficient factories; his followers established the German Social Democratic party, which successfully campaigned for a broad program of social reforms, and created a model for social democracy in other European countries.

In England, John Stuart Mill believed that society would eventually adopt labor ownership and management, and that it should do so without revolution or excessive governmental involvement. His ideas inspired the Fabian Socialist movement, which championed an evolutionary program of social reforms, and contributed to the establishment of the British Labour party.

After the Bolshevik victory in the Russian Revolution, the feasibility of efficient socialist planning became a subject of extensive debate. Ludwig von Mises argued that efficient planning was impossible because the absence of a market to set prices for producer goods would make it impossible to calculate accurate costs and benefits. Oskar Lange, among others, argued that a system of market socialism could equal or exceed the efficiency of the capitalist system.

After systems of market socialism were actually adopted in Yugoslavia and Hungary, theoretical analysis of these systems was initiated by Ben Ward, calling their efficiency into question. In recent years, a number of new blueprints for market-oriented state socialism, voucher socialism, bank-centric socialism, and economic democracy have been developed to remedy the problems of existing systems.

From 1917 until the close of World War II, the Soviet Union and Mongolia had the only socialist command economies in the world. After the war, they were joined by China, North Korea, the nations of Eastern Europe, and later by a host of developing countries. World communism was shaken by Stalin's death in 1953, followed by revolt in Eastern Europe and the Sino-Soviet split. The Soviet Union was able to hold the Communist movement together in the 1960s and 1970s, but an amazing progression of economic, political, and social events led to the collapse of command socialism in the 1980s and early 1990s.

The focus of democratic socialism after World War II was in Western Europe, where nationalization programs were conducted in several countries, but the recent trend has been toward privatization. If democratic socialism is defined as a system to promote equality of opportunity, full employment, distributive equity, and worker participation in management, and if its strength is measured by parliamentary representation, the movement seems to be quite alive.

DISCUSSION AND REVIEW QUESTIONS

1. According to the broad conceptual framework suggested by people like Michael Harrington, what countries have come closest to fulfilling the ideals of socialism?

2. What role did the French and American revolutions play in the early history of socialism?

3. Describe and critically evaluate Saint-Simon's scheme for planning of public works.

4. What was the philosophy that prompted Owen's experiments in social reform? Why was it revolutionary at the time?

5. In what sense were Mill's socialist proposals consistent with the doctrines of Adam Smith and the classical school?

6. According to Marx and Engels, how would the early stages of socialist society differ from the later stages?

7. Explain the Mises critique of the efficiency of socialism. Do the market socialist proposals of Lange, Nove, and Yunker answer his criticisms?

8. What are some of the philosophical differences and historical events that have created and maintained the split between revolutionary and democratic socialists?

9. According to Robin Archer, how should the managerial control of an enterprise be divided between its owners, its workers, and its customers? Do you agree? Why or why not?

SUGGESTED READINGS

Buber, Martin. *Paths in Utopia*. New York: Macmillan, 1950. *A thoughtful polemic in favor of voluntary socialist cooperation by a noted theologian, with a particularly good discussion of Proudhon.*

Eatwell, John; Murray Milgate and Peter Newman, eds. *The New Palgrave: Problems of the Planned Economy*. New York: W. W. Norton, 1990. *Includes cogent essays on "Socialism" by Alec Nove, "Command Economy" by Gregory Grossman, and "Market Socialism" by W. Brus, to name a few.*

Freedman, Robert. *The Marxist System: Economic, Political, and Social Perspectives*. Chatham, N.J.: Chatham House Publishers, 1990. *Perhaps the most concise, readable, and reliable introduction to Marxian economic theories in their political and social context.*

Fried, Albert, and Ronald Sanders, eds. *Socialist Thought: A Documentary History*. Garden City, N.Y.: Doubleday, 1964. *Selections from many of the prominent socialists from Morelly in the eighteenth century through Crosland in the twentieth century.*

Harrington, Michael. *Socialism: Past and Future*. New York: Arcade Publishing, 1989. *The last major work by a well-regarded American socialist, this book surveys the history of socialism and suggests how the movement can be renewed in the future.*

Nove, Alec, and D. M. Nuti, eds. *Socialist Economics*. Harmondsworth, Eng.: Penguin, 1972. *A book of readings, most from the twentieth century, including the Mises and Lange contributions and other articles on socialist growth, planning, and reform.*

Tucker, Robert C., ed. *The Marx-Engels Reader*. 2d ed. New York: W. W. Norton, 1978. *Includes a good sampling of their work and several readings that are difficult to find elsewhere.*

Wild, Lawrence. *Modern European Socialism*. Aldershot: Dartmouth Publishing, 1994. *This thoroughly documented study reviews the modern socialist movements in several countries of Western and Eastern Europe, and discusses the prospects for socialist internationalism in a more unified Europe.*

Yunker, James A. *Socialism Revised and Modernized*. New York: Praeger, 1992. *Written during the collapse of the Soviet empire, this may be the most detailed recent proposal for a system of democratic market socialism, including an extended defense of its workability and relative efficiency.*

INTERNET RESOURCES

Anarchy Home Page
http://www.duke.edu/~eagle/anarchy/

Committees of Correspondence
gopher://garnet.berkeley.edu:2000/

Democratic Socialists of America
http://ccme-mac4.bsd.uchicago.edu/DSA.html

Economic Democracy Web
http://garnet.berkeley.edu:3333/

Fundamentally Green
http://www.csv.warwick.ac.uk/~esrhi/fundi.html

Intentional Communities
http://www.well.com/www/cmty

Left Side of the Web
http://paul.spu.edu/~sinnfein/progressive.html

Little Red Web Page
http://www.gold.net/users/ad31/index.html

Marxism Page
http://www.anu.edu.au/polsci/marx/marx.html

The Seed
http://web.cs.cty.ac.uk/homes/louise/seed2.html

The World: Infant Mortality per 1,000 Live Births, 1995

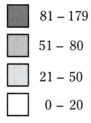

81 – 179

51 – 80

21 – 50

0 – 20

Source: World Bank, *World Development Report 1997.*

5

ECONOMICS OF THE DEVELOPING WORLD

> Most of the people in the world are poor, so if we knew
> the Economics of being poor we would know much of the
> Economics that really matters.
>
> —THEODORE W. SCHULTZ
> NOBEL LECTURE
> *JOURNAL OF POLITICAL ECONOMY*, AUGUST 1980

wo centuries after the Industrial Revolution, more than 1.3 billion people still live in **absolute poverty**—a condition of life "so characterized by malnutrition, illiteracy, and disease" that the World Bank finds it "beneath any reasonable definition of human decency."[1] These people and 3 billion others live in a collection of countries we know optimistically as the "developing world." They invade our consciousness when we hear of another civil war in Africa, another famine in South Asia, another financial crisis in Latin America, or another reversal of world commodity prices.

Who are the poor? Why do they remain poor? What can be done about it? Why hasn't it been done? These are important, difficult, and immortal questions; they extend far beyond the scope of comparative economic systems. For our present purposes, we will survey only a few of the relevant issues and hope that these will inspire additional study.

WHO ARE THE POOR?

A general profile of population, income, health, and education in the developing world is presented in Table 5.1. By nearly any yardstick, the poorest and most underprivileged people in the world are found in Sub-Saharan Africa, India, and the other countries of South Asia. China has a higher average level of income and human development than the average for other developing countries (although many regions of China are still desperately poor), and the other nations of East Asia have achieved exceptional levels of economic and social development. Income and literacy rates are relatively

---

[1] This description is taken from World Bank, *Poverty and Human Development* (New York: Oxford University Press, 1980), v. The numerical estimate is from "Richest Nations Turn Backs on Poorest," Reuters News Service, June 13, 1995. See the discussion of poverty estimates in Chapter 2.

■ TABLE 5.1

DEVELOPING COUNTRIES: POPULATION, INCOME, AND DEVELOPMENT

	1992 Population (millions)	1992 Population per km² of arable land	1991 GDP per capita ($ at PPP)	1980–90 Absolute Poverty (%)	1992 Adult Literacy (%)	1992 Infant Mortality (per 1,000)	1992 Human Developme Index
Industrial Countries	1,210	171	14,860	—	—	13	.92
Developing Countries	4,240	551	2,730	31	69	69	.54
Sub-Saharan Africa	560	355	1,250	54	51	101	.36
Middle East & North Africa	260	511	4,420	25	57	54	.63
India	880	482	1,150	40	50	89	.38
Other South Asia	300	726	1,600	52	39	106	.36
China	1,187	1,204	2,946	9	80	27	.64
Other East Asia	80	1,448	7,190	6	97	24	.86
Southeast Asia	470	762	3,420	35	86	55	.61
Latin America & Caribbean	450	344	5,360	40	86	47	.76

Source: United Nations Development Programme, *Human Development Report 1994*, 207–218.

high in Latin America, but poverty rates are also high because incomes are distributed unevenly.

Growth rates for income and human development are recorded in Table 5.2. As a group, the developing countries had higher rates of income growth than the industrial countries before 1973, but they had lower rates after 1980. At the same time, because of improvements in their health and educational programs, the developing countries consistently attained larger increments in the human development index (HDI) than did the industrial countries. Even in Africa and the Middle East, where income levels deteriorated after 1980, progress continued according to the HDI. Thus, according to the United Nations, the proportion of the world's population living in conditions of "low human development" fell from 73 percent in 1960 to 35 percent in 1992.[2]

Still, there is no room for complacency. Although the *proportion* of humankind living in absolute poverty has fallen, population growth has caused the *number* of poor to increase from about 1.1 billion in 1985 to 1.3 billion in 1994, and perhaps to 1.5 billion by 2000.[3] Infant mortality is still five times higher in the developing world than in the industrial countries, maternal mortality is 17 times higher, literacy is 30 percent lower, real income per capita is only one-fifth as large, and life expectancy is 11 years shorter. Much

[2]United Nations Development Programme, *Human Development Report 1994* (New York: Oxford University Press, 1994), 95.

[3]Robin Wright, "Foreign Aid Hits Lowest Level in Two Decades," *Los Angeles Times*, June 13, 1995, 1.

■ **TABLE 5.2**

DEVELOPING COUNTRIES: INCOME GROWTH AND HUMAN DEVELOPMENT

	Growth of GDP per capita (% per year)				Growth of Human Development (absolute increase of HDI)		
	1965–1973	1973–1980	1980–1990	1990–1992	1960–1970	1970–1980	1980–1992
Industrial Countries	3.7	2.1	2.3	5.9	0.060	0.030	0.029
Developing Countries	4.3	2.6	1.2	2.8	0.087	0.081	0.113
Middle-income countries	4.5	2.4	0.5	3.0	—	—	—
Low-income countries	2.5	2.7	4.0	2.7	—	—	—
Sub-Saharan Africa	1.7	0.6	–1.3	–2.8	0.055	0.051	0.051
Middle East & North Africa	6.0	1.0	–2.5	–1.0	0.086	0.117	0.151
South Asia	1.2	1.8	3.2	2.0	0.046	0.042	0.086
East Asia & Pacific	5.0	4.8	6.2	9.4	0.124	0.105	0.169
Latin America & Caribbean	4.6	2.3	–0.4	10.0	0.101	0.114	0.075

Sources: World Bank, *World Development Report 1992*, 196; *1993*, 199; and *1994*, 163; World Bank, *World Tables* 1994, 2–9; and UNDP, *Human Development Report 1994*, 95. For an explanation of the Human Development Index (HDI), see Chapter 2 of this text.

progress has been made, but the challenge of economic and social development has never been greater.

OBSTACLES TO DEVELOPMENT

Although social scientists do not agree on the causes of persistent poverty, few would dispute the basic issues. First, if a country wishes for sustained economic growth, it must somehow increase its stock of physical and/or human capital (factories, machinery, equipment, health, and education). If this is to be done without massive foreign assistance, the country must be able to produce an output that exceeds the subsistence needs of the population. Furthermore, some group of people, whether they be private entrepreneurs, government leaders, or foreign colonialists, must mobilize that surplus toward productive ends (building factories, schools, roads, and so forth) rather than allowing it to dissipate on extravagant consumption, military adventures, civic monuments, or capital flight.

Speaking very generally, countries that remain poor are those that fail to generate a sufficient investable surplus or those that fail to invest it in productive activities. Within this framework, the various camps of economists differ on the causes of the low saving and investment rates. Traditional theories usually stress environmental and institutional barriers and the "vicious circles of poverty." Radical economists believe that the surplus of the poor countries is transferred to the rich by an exploitive system of investment and trade.

ENVIRONMENT AND CULTURE

In their search for the underlying causes of poverty, some social scientists have argued that the developing countries are accursed by geographic, environmental, and cultural conditions that are difficult to overcome. The average developing country, for example, must use each square kilometer of its arable land to feed more than three times as many people as the average industrial country (Table 5.1). Accordingly, it is difficult to generate an investable surplus of output above the subsistence needs of the population.

Most of the developing world, and very little of the industrial world, is located in a band around the equator that stretches from the Tropic of Capricorn to the Tropic of Cancer. Most of this region receives heavy rain all year (within 1,000 miles of the equator) or heavy monsoon rains for half of the year and no rain for the rest of the year (1,000 to 1,500 miles from the equator), or has turned to desert. Except in high-altitude areas, temperatures range from hot to very hot, placing a strain on human bodies, electronic equipment, and automotive radiators.

Through much of the region that is not covered by jungle, desert, or volcanic or alluvial soil, excessive heat has burned away the organic matter of the soil and excessive rain has washed away its nutrients. The tropical climate and poor sanitation foster the reproduction of insects, parasites, and pests that attack people, plants, and animals. Winter, the great exterminator, never comes.[4]

The impact of cultural and religious factors on economic development is more speculative and controversial. With the exception of Japan, all high-income industrial countries are predominantly Christian and all Protestant countries have high incomes. Few Islamic countries have advanced beyond the lower-middle income level without the help of petroleum exports.[5] According to cultural determinists, patterns such as these can be explained by religious and cultural attitudes toward freedom, conformity, competition, equality, honesty, work, science, education, birth control, and wealth accumulation.[6]

A cultural determinist would say, for example, that Latin America is relatively poor and North America is relatively rich because of differences between their Spanish and British colonial heritages. Spain was overpowered by the Moors (or Muslims) in the eighth century and, despite centuries of civil war, did not fully regain its independence until 1492, the year of Columbus's voyage. Thus, some would say that Spain inherited an authoritarian culture from the Moors and the long process of reconquest created an

---

[4]Andrew Karmarck, *The Tropics and Economic Development* (Baltimore: The Johns Hopkins University Press, 1976).

[5]Everett Hagen, *The Economics of Development*, 4th ed. (Homewood, Ill.: Irwin, 1986), 44. In the 1994 edition of the World Bank's *World Development Report*, Malaysia became the first Islamic country to achieve "upper-middle-income" status with a relatively diversified export base (which still includes petroleum). Turkey probably will be the first to achieve that rank with a relatively limited raw materials base.

[6]See Mark Casson, "Cultural Determinants of Economic Performance," *Journal of Comparative Economics* 17 (June 1993): 418–442.

extremely orthodox and intolerant brand of Roman Catholicism. This intolerance led Spain to launch its Inquisition in 1480 and to expel all Jews from its territory in 1492. Spanish corruption, authoritarianism, inequality, and intolerance were allegedly transplanted in Latin America, where they have stood in the way of economic development.[7]

In Asia, rough cultural lines can be drawn between the Muslim countries of the Middle East and Pakistan, the Hindu countries of the south (India, Bangladesh, and Nepal), and the Confucian and Buddhist countries of the east. Many believe that the Confucian work ethic has contributed to the successful growth of Japan and the East Asian Gang of Four—Hong Kong, Singapore, South Korea, and Taiwan. Conversely, certain aspects of Hinduism have allegedly retarded development in South Asia. The caste system, for example, places limits on labor mobility, income equality, and work incentives. The law of *karma*, which says that one's fate in this life is a reward or punishment for actions in a previous life, supposedly evokes a fatalistic acceptance of the status quo.

Like other single-factor theories of economic development, geographic and cultural determinism leave many questions unanswered. Why were the ancient civilizations of Egypt, Mesopotamia, China, and the Mayas able to flourish under the curse of tropical geography? Why has it taken so long for the Confucian work ethic to take its place beside (or ahead of) the Protestant ethic? The links between geography, culture, and development are indisputable, but they are not well understood.

THE ECONOMIC SYSTEM

Quite often, economic growth and development is fettered by the backwardness of economic institutions. The specific problems vary tremendously from one country to another, but a few are rather common.

LAND TENURE. Several different systems of land ownership are used in the developing countries; few of them promote economic development. In much of Africa and Asia, particularly in nomadic areas, the land is held in common with no identifiable owner or controlled by a village, tribe, or extended family. In order to ensure equity, the right to use the best land is rotated among families. Thus, an individual family has little incentive or opportunity to engage in long-term projects to irrigate and improve the land. If such efforts are undertaken, they usually require the cooperation of an entire community.

In most of the countries of Latin America, the land is held privately, but its distribution is very uneven. With the exception of countries that have implemented major land reforms (Mexico, Bolivia, Cuba, and Nicaragua), the *latifundios* (very large farms) usually constitute less than 5 percent of the farms while holding more than 50 percent of the land. The sharecroppers on the

---

[7]For an extended discussion of Latin American development by a cultural determinist, see Lawrence E. Harrison, *Development Is a State of Mind: The Latin American Case* (Lanham, Md.: University Press of America, 1985).

latifundios have little incentive to improve land that they do not own and the landlords have a poor record of investment. The small farms are barely able to provide a living for their owners.

MARKET STRUCTURE.   In some countries, the market mechanism is still operating at a primitive level, with limited ability to coordinate and guide the development of the economy. In Africa, for example, about 25 percent of all economic activity was based on barter in the 1970s, and roughly 10 percent is still conducted outside the monetized sector.[8] In countries with poor transportation and communication systems, markets are disconnected from one another and from those in the outside world. Price controls and state monopolies, which cripple the operation of the market system, are still common in the developing world.

LABOR MARKETS.   A wide gulf usually exists between the modern sector of a developing economy, which typically involves capital-intensive industrial production in the cities, and the traditional sector of labor-intensive agricultural production and crafts. Thus, many countries have a **dual labor market** in which urban wages are two or three times larger than rural incomes. It is difficult to explain these differences in terms of skill or productivity; several other factors are apparently involved. The urban workers are more likely to be unionized, more likely to work for nationalized companies, and more likely to have the protection of a legal minimum wage. Business firms in the modern sector may be willing to pay relatively high wages to maintain a stable force of experienced workers. Whatever the cause, the dual wage structure promotes income inequality and attracts large numbers of people into the cities, contributing to urban unemployment.

FINANCIAL MARKETS.   The limited quantity and quality of financial intermediation is a serious problem in many developing countries. The entire financial system is usually organized around a few banks, which are heavily regulated because they have excessive market power. Securities markets are rudimentary or nonexistent, making it difficult to raise money through stock or bond issues. Few people channel their savings through life insurance companies. Governmental taxation and control of interest rates frequently reduce the incentive to save.

Vicious Circles of Poverty

If environmental, cultural, and institutional factors explain some of the initial causes of poverty, a number of vicious circles help to explain why the poor remain poor.

SAVING AND INVESTMENT.   It is difficult for a destitute country to generate the savings that are needed to finance investment. The investment

---

[8]Anand G. Chandavarkar, "Monetization of Developing Countries," *International Monetary Fund Staff Papers* 24 (November 1977): 678–679; and author's estimate, based on money/GDP ratios for 1970 and 1992, found in World Bank, *World Development Report 1994* (New York: Oxford University Press, 1994), 184.

rate of low-income countries is lower than that of any other group of countries. Their low rate of investment, in turn, contributes to their low rate of economic growth.

HEALTH AND EDUCATION. Similarly, it is difficult for a poor country to set aside the resources that are needed to provide health and education services to the population, and it is difficult for the children of the poor to take time off from work for their education. Thus, poverty begets disease and illiteracy, which cause the continuation of poverty.

MARKET SIZE. Low income levels and primitive transportation systems restrict the market demand for any given commodity in a developing country. With limited demand, it is difficult to increase efficiency through mass production. A low level of efficiency leads to a continuation of poverty.

POLITICAL INSTABILITY. Poverty also regenerates itself by provoking political instability, often in a senseless series of coups d'etat. Since 1948, the average developing country has had at least one coup attempt every five years.[9] Between 1825, when it gained independence, and 1985, when it established a stable democratic system, Bolivia had more than 150 governments. After the Communists were deposed in 1989, Poland had five governments in five years. Short terms of office encourage rulers to undertake short-sighted economic policies, such as inflationary creation of money. Political instability discourages foreign investment, and encourages the flight of domestic capital. According to one comprehensive study, economic growth has usually begun in Latin American countries with "the emergence at long last of a stable government able to exercise effective control of the country for an extended period."[10]

POPULATION GROWTH. In comparison to the industrial countries, percentage rates of population growth are more than twice as high in middle-income developing countries, more than three times as high in low-income countries of South Asia, and almost four times as high in low-income countries of Africa.[11] The populations of poor countries tend to grow rapidly because of their rural lifestyles and their inability or unwillingness (for religious and other reasons) to practice birth control. Rapid population growth, in turn, makes it difficult for a society to expand and maintain a sufficient stock of housing, productive capital, natural resources, educational services, medical facilities, and other elements of social infrastructure. The poorest countries also tend to have the highest **dependency ratios**—that is, the percentage of the population that is not of working age. In 1992 the dependency ratio was 33 percent in the industrial countries, 38 percent in the middle-income developing countries, and 43 percent in the low-income countries (excluding China, where

[9]World Bank, *World Development Report 1991*, 128.

[10]Lloyd G. Reynolds, "The Spread of Economic Growth to the Third World: 1850–1980," *Journal of Economic Literature* 21 (September 1983): 964.

[11]Based on growth rates for 1990–1995 in World Bank, *World Development Report 1997*, 221.

strict policies have reduced population growth and dependency ratios to the levels of middle-income countries).[12]

INCOME INEQUALITY. Poor countries tend to experience greater income inequality than high-income countries, and efforts to promote economic development may cause inequality to grow worse before it improves. This pattern, known as Kuznets's Law, is illustrated by the data in Table 5.3. On average, income inequality is greatest in the upper-middle-income countries, and lowest in high-income countries. By implication, as a country grows out of the low-income category, it may take a long time for the benefits of economic growth to trickle down to the lower classes of society. Economic growth accompanied by increasing income inequality may contribute to political instability, which may put an end to economic growth.[13]

IMPERIALISM AND DEPENDENCY

Marxists and many others do not accept the environmental and vicious-circle explanations of poverty. The industrial countries, they say, have employed a number of methods to extract the investable surpluses of the developing countries. The rich have grown richer by causing the poor to remain poor.

Most observers would agree that the developing countries were exploited during the colonial era. For example, the American Revolution was fought to end the burden of British colonial taxation. Spanish colonial rule in Latin America was more harsh and covered a longer period. Colonialism continued in India, the Middle East, and the Philippines until the end of World War II and in much of Africa and Indochina until the 1960s.

The impact of colonial rule was not entirely negative, particularly under the British and the Japanese. The rulers generally built schools, ports, railways, electric power systems, and other utilities. Karl Marx gave the British credit for breaking the power of the village communities in India, which "had always been the solid foundation of Oriental despotism," and he attributed great importance to the building of railways: "Modern industry, resulting from the railway system, will dissolve the hereditary divisions of labor, upon which rest the Indian castes, those decisive impediments to Indian progress and Indian power."[14]

Now that overt colonialism is largely a thing of the past, Marxists and so-called **dependency theorists** believe that the industrial countries have continued their exploitation of the developing countries through foreign trade and investment. Multinational corporations (MNCs) are said to play an

---

[12]Ibid.

[13]For a more optimistic assessment, which proposes that the Kuznets effect is too small to negate the welfare effects of economic growth, see Gustav Papanek and Oldrich Kyn, "The Effect on Income Distribution of Development, the Rate of Growth, and Economic Strategy," *Journal of Development Economics* 23 (September 1986): 55–65.

[14]Marx in the *New York Daily Tribune*, June 25, 1853, quoted in H. A. Reitsma and J. M. G. Kleinpenning, *The Third World in Perspective* (Assen, Neth.: Van Gorcum, 1985), 217.

■ **TABLE 5.3**

THE KUZNETS HYPOTHESIS: INCOME AND INEQUALITY

	1995 GDP Per Capita Range (dollars)	Average Share of Poorest 40 Percent of Households in Total Income
25 Low-income countries	80–730	16.3
31 Lower-middle-income countries	770–3,020	17.1
7 Upper-middle-income countries	3,160–8,210	15.2
20 High-income countries	9,700–40,630	18.2

Source: World Bank, *World Development Report 1997*, 214–215, 222–223; and author's calculations.

important role in this process. Critics say that the MNCs extract excessive profits from the host countries and that they fund some of their operations out of local credit markets, crowding out domestic borrowers. Because of their foreign orientation, they introduce products and technologies that are inappropriate for the needs of the developing countries. They create low-skill jobs in the developing countries and shift the high-skill jobs elsewhere. Most important, they encourage governmental corruption and manipulate policies to the detriment of the local populations.[15]

Defenders of the MNCs say that they provide jobs, training, capital, technology, and tax revenues to the host countries. Juscelino Kubitschek, the Brazilian president who opened the country to foreign investment during the 1960s, said at the time that it was senseless to argue about industries that did not exist; the first priority is to get the industries established, with or without foreign help.[16] Evidence from Cote d'Ivoire and Venezuela suggests that foreign-owned manufacturing firms are more efficient than locally owned firms, even after capital intensity and firm size are taken into account.[17] For these and other reasons, the World Bank argues that "equity forms of investment can clearly be beneficial to developing countries, and it is desirable that they be increased."[18]

Marxists found it difficult to build a strong quantitative case for the link between foreign investment and world poverty. The profits that are taken out of the developing countries by the MNCs are relatively small as a proportion of national income, particularly for countries such as India. Thus, the dependency theorists shifted attention from investment to international trade and

---

[15]See, for example, John Madeley, *Trade and the Poor* (New York: St. Martin's Press, 1993), 87–118.

[16]Robert J. Alexander, "Import Substitution in Latin America in Retrospect," in *Progress Toward Development in Latin America*, eds. James L. Dietz and Dilmus D. James (Boulder: Lynne Rienner, 1990), 24.

[17]World Bank, *World Development Report 1991*, 94.

[18]World Bank, *World Development Report 1985*, 134.

specialization. In their view, the core (industrial) economies have manipulated the patterns of trade to their own advantage and to the detriment of the peripheral (developing) economies.

Dependency theory grew out of the writings of Raul Prebisch, an Argentine economist, who argued in the 1950s that the developing countries are victimized by their specialization in primary-goods production. The international terms of trade tend to deteriorate for the developing countries, he said, because growth in world income increases the demand for manufactured goods more rapidly than the demand for primary products. Prebisch attempted to support his theory with statistical evidence, but subsequent research has cast doubt over the declining-terms-of-trade hypothesis.[19]

Subsequently, the French economist Arghiri Emmanuel argued that, regardless of their historical trends, the export prices received by the developing world are simply too low; poor countries are forced to surrender their primary goods in an **unequal exchange** for high-priced industrial goods. The prices of primary goods are low, he says, because they incorporate the low labor costs of the poor countries. Thus, poverty begets low prices and low prices beget poverty.[20]

According to traditional analysis, the unequal exchange hypothesis is just as invalid as the cheap-foreign-labor argument of protectionists in the industrial countries. International trade based on comparative advantage, according to theory, is mutually beneficial to the rich and the poor countries. However, the traditional theory says nothing about the equity with which the gains from trade are distributed between the rich and the poor.

Dependency theorists argue that the developing countries are crippled in many other ways by their peripheral role in the world capitalist system. Their product markets are jolted by broad swings in world commodity prices. Their financial systems are destabilized by erratic inflows and outflows of international capital.[21] The international arms race, allegedly manipulated by the arms merchants in the industrial countries, forces the developing countries to squander much of their investable surplus. More generally, dependent development means that "some countries can expand through self-impulsion while others . . . can only expand as a reflection of the dominant countries, which may have positive or negative effects on their immediate development."[22]

---

[19]For a review of the evidence, see John Spraos, "The Statistical Debate on the Net Barter Terms of Trade between Primary Commodities and Manufactures," *Economic Journal* 90 (March 1980): 107–128.

[20]For a discussion of Emmanuel's theory and other radical perspectives on development, see Keith Griffin and John Gurley, "Radical Analyses of Imperialism, the Third World, and the Transition to Socialism: A Survey Article," *Journal of Economic Literature* 23 (September 1985): 1089–1143.

[21]According to a recent study by Goldman, Sachs, & Co., 80 percent of the turbulence in Mexico's financial markets in 1994 was caused by "a retrenchment of liquidity that was taking place around the world" rather than by domestic economic or political events. See Tim Carrington, "Private-Capital Flows Can Hurt Poor Countries," *The Wall Street Journal*, January 30, 1995, A1.

[22]Theotonio Dos Santos, "The Structure of Dependence," *American Economic Review* 60 (May 1970): 289–290.

DEVELOPMENT STRATEGIES

If explanations of poverty differ among countries and economists, proposals to alleviate it are equally diverse. A person persuaded by geographic or cultural determinism, by vicious-circle theories, by theories of imperialism and dependency, or by some combination of these may conclude that the future of the developing world is hopeless, or that it merely requires the removal of a few obstacles, or that it requires the adoption of a system of national planning, or that it requires the creation of a so-called new international economic order. A few of the more prominent strategies are surveyed here.

Smith, Ricardo, and Surplus Labor

Always the optimist, Adam Smith declared in 1755 that "little else is requisite to carry a state to the highest degree of opulence, but peace, easy taxes, and a tolerable administration of justice; all the rest being brought about by the natural course of things." Twenty-one years later, in his *Wealth of Nations*, Smith explained that economic development is rooted in the "uniform, constant, and uninterrupted effort of every man to better his condition." The efforts of individuals, coordinated by markets, are "frequently powerful enough to maintain the natural progress of things toward improvement, in spite of the extravagance of government, and of the greatest errors of administration."[23] Thus, Adam Smith advanced the "growth is natural" school of thought; little is needed from the government to promote it, and little can be done by the government to stop it.

David Ricardo, one of Smith's disciples, believed that British growth was threatened by restrictions on agricultural imports under the Corn Laws. The restrictions, he said, kept an artificially large labor force in the agricultural sector, working at very low marginal productivity. If the Corn Laws were repealed, market forces would move these excess workers into industry, where their productivity would be greater. The rise in productivity would create a surplus of output over the subsistence needs of the population, which would open the door to investment and economic growth.

In 1954, W. Arthur Lewis revived the idea that a surplus population of underemployed rural labor could be shifted into industry to increase productivity, generate savings, and fuel economic growth.[24] Lewis said that rapid population growth had created a rural **labor surplus** in the poor countries—a surplus that could be mobilized:

The [developing countries] have within themselves all that is required for growth. They have surpluses of fuel and the principal minerals. They have enough land to feed themselves, if they cultivate it properly. They are capable of learning the skills of manufacturing, and of saving the capital required for modernization. Their development does not in the long run depend on the existence of the developed countries, and

---

[23] Adam Smith, *An Inquiry into the Nature and Causes of the Wealth of Nations* (Oxford: Clarendon Press, 1976), 343.

[24] W. A. Lewis, "Economic Development with Unlimited Supplies of Labor," *The Manchester School* (May 1954): 139–191.

their potential for growth would be unaffected even if all the developed countries were to sink under the sea.[25]

Although Lewis believes that economic planning and governmental action may be needed to move the surplus agricultural workers into industry, his description of planning is reminiscent of Smith: "The economics of development is not very complicated; the secret of successful planning lies more in sensible politics and good public administration."[26]

ROSENSTEIN-RODAN, NURSKE, AND BALANCED GROWTH

As the world faced recovery from World War II, several economists agreed that industrialization could be launched by mobilizing the underemployed rural population, but few of them shared Lewis's view that development was "not very complicated." Writing as early as 1943, Paul Rosenstein-Rodan emphasized the obstacles to development and believed that industrialization would require a **big push:**

> *Launching a country into self-sustaining growth is a little like getting an airplane off the ground. There is a critical ground speed which must be passed before the craft can become airborne. . . . A big push seems to be required to jump over the economic obstacles to development. . . . An atmosphere of development may only arise with a minimum speed or size of investment.*[27]

Supporting Rosenstein-Rodan's call for a big push, in 1953 Ragnar Nurske popularized the idea that economic progress is not a spontaneous or automatic affair because vicious circles of poverty, limited investment, malnutrition, and limited market size have stunted economic growth and development. Industrialization requires a comprehensive policy of **balanced growth,** accomplished by a wave of capital investments in a number of different industries. No single industry can go it alone, he says, because of the operation of Say's Law—the demand for one product is generated by the production of other goods.

ROSTOW, HIRSCHMAN, AND UNBALANCED GROWTH

Nurske's strategy of balanced growth was a counsel of despair in many of the poor countries: it implied that one must somehow support a wide range of industries or do nothing at all. Walt Rostow, also writing in 1953, struck a more responsive chord when he said that development could be initiated by launching a few **leading sectors.**[28] Based on his reading of European and

---

[25]W. A. Lewis quoted in Gerald Meier, *Emerging from Poverty: The Economics that Really Matters* (New York: Oxford University Press, 1984), 207.

[26]Ibid., 208.

[27]Rosenstein-Rodan quoted in Meier, *Emerging from Poverty,* 138. Note the apparent influence of Rosenstein-Rodan on Rostow's conception of a "take-off into self-sustained growth," discussed in the following section.

[28]Rostow's theory of leading sectors, which first appeared in a 1953 essay, was popularized in his book, *The Stages of Economic Growth* (London: Cambridge University Press, 1960).

American history, Rostow concluded that societies pass through several distinct stages on their way to affluence.

According to Rostow's theory, societies emerge from the backward traditional stage as they fulfill the "preconditions for take-off." During the preconditions stage, attitudes toward economic and scientific progress begin to change, an entrepreneurial class is formed, and an infrastructure of transport and communications facilities is built. When the "old blocks and resistances to steady growth are finally overcome," the nation can begin its "take-off into self-sustained growth." The trends in social change, production, and scientific progress that were initiated during the preconditions stage will begin to accelerate, and the rate of investment will roughly double. A few leading sectors will grow most rapidly and will serve as a locomotive for the rest of the economy. The leading sector that launched the British Industrial Revolution, for example, was the cotton industry; the railroads led the way in the United States. After take-off, Rostow's stereotypical society progresses to "technological maturity," then to "mass consumption," and finally to the "search for quality."

In the eyes of its critics, Rostow's theory is too neat, clean, and deterministic to serve as a description of the development path of all societies. The same criticism has been applied to the Marxian stage theory, which Rostow hoped to displace. The leaders of many developing countries have adopted Rostow's analysis as a how-to guide for growth; the take-off and leading sector concepts have entered the vernacular of economic development.

If a country wishes to develop a few leading sectors, which sectors should it choose? In his theory of **unbalanced growth,** Albert Hirschman suggests that special attention should be directed to industries that have strong **linkages** to other industries. These linkages may take several forms. Industries such as automotive manufacturing that create a strong demand for inputs from other industries are said to have strong **backward linkages.** Those that produce important inputs for other industries are said to have **forward linkages.**

IMPORT SUBSTITUTION, EXPORT PROMOTION, AND THE WASHINGTON CONSENSUS

As Nurske emphasized, one of the dangers of an unbalanced growth strategy is that the domestic market will not be able to provide sufficient demand for the output of an isolated industry. One way to get around this problem is through a policy of **import substitution.** If an industrial product is being imported, then a domestic demand for that product obviously exists. All that must be done is to develop an indigenous industry and protect it from foreign competition.

From the 1930s to the 1980s, import substitution was employed extensively in Latin America and Africa. Dependency theorists favor this approach because it attempts to shift the developing countries to more advanced lines of production, to reduce their vulnerability to fluctuations in the world market, and to alleviate their balance of payments problems.

Critics of import substitution say that it distorts the allocation of re-sources, reducing the benefits gained from international trade according to comparative advantage. It requires that the government decide which sec-tors to protect from foreign competition; these decisions invite governmental bribery and corruption. Reduction of imports causes a reduction in the de-mand for foreign exchange, which causes the exchange rate of the local cur-rency to rise, which makes it more difficult to sell the country's exports. Thus, the balance of payments may not improve. Maintenance of high import bar-riers will often require an enormous system of controls to prevent smug-gling. Infant industries that are created by the program will often fail to mature. Finally, the strategy is self-limiting, in that it must stop when all of the nation's imports have been replaced.

Based on the disappointing results of import substitution and the cele-brated successes of countries such as Hong Kong, South Korea, and Singa-pore, many countries have shifted to a policy of **export promotion.** This approach suggests that a country should base its development efforts on leading sectors that can compete quickly on the world market; industries that can compete only on a protected domestic market should receive little prior-ity. Instead of imposing heavy tariffs and quantitative restrictions on im-ports, the government should support emerging export industries with an appropriate legal and regulatory environment, education and training pro-grams, infrastructure for transportation and communications, and moderate levels of tax relief, import duty rebates, subsidies, and low-interest credit.

Advocates of export promotion say that it keeps the country open to for-eign trade and competition, deriving benefits from international specializa-tion. Production for the large and competitive world market rather than a small and monopolized domestic market forces companies to maintain high quality standards and low production costs and allows them to fully exploit economies of scale. An outward orientation forces the government to resist inflationary policies and overvalued exchange rates. Generally, export pro-motion is accomplished through positive incentives rather than a bureau-cratic system of direct controls, so it seems to invite less political corruption.[29]

Export promotion is the centerpiece of the so-called **Washington Con-sensus,** a market-oriented development strategy supported by agencies of the U.S. government, the World Bank, the International Monetary Fund, and the regional development banks. In addition to an export promoting, or "outward-oriented," trade policy, the consensus suggests that governments in developing countries should focus on their core functions, including public health, education, public infrastructure, and administration of justice; they should privatize many state-owned industries, remove controls on prices and interest rates, reduce budget deficits and excessive monetary growth, and dismantle regulations that stifle entrepreneurship and foreign investment.

The data in Table 5.4 were compiled by the International Monetary Fund to confirm the efficacy of a market-oriented development policy. Countries

---

[29]Anne O. Krueger, "Import Substitution versus Export Promotion," *Finance and Development* 22 (June 1985): 20–23.

■ TABLE 5.4

HIGH-GROWTH AND LOW-GROWTH DEVELOPING COUNTRIES, 1984–1993

	All Developing Countries	42 High-Growth Countries	42 Low-Growth Countries
Annual percentage changes:			
GDP	5.1	7.4	1.4
Consumer prices	43.5	11.5	53.5
Export volume	7.6	10.4	3.4
Terms of trade	−1.1	0.1	−3.0
Real effective exchange rate	−3.1	−5.9	1.6
Total factor productivity	1.7	3.4	−1.1
Percent of GDP:			
Investment	25.6	30.1	20.9
Saving	24.3	29.3	18.8
Fiscal deficit	−4.3	−3.2	−5.3
External debt	39.6	29.4	51.2
Real interest rate	0.02	2.89	−2.81

Note: Generally, the data in this table encompass 126 developing countries, the 42 countries with highest GDP growth, and the 42 countries with lowest GDP growth. Data for total productivity growth and real interest rates are based on smaller samples of countries for which data are available. The real interest rate is defined as the short-term nominal interest rate minus the rate of inflation.

Source: International Monetary Fund, *World Economic Outlook*, May 1994, 55–57.

that have achieved high rates of economic growth seem to be those that have maintained low rates of inflation, small fiscal deficits, low levels of foreign debt, and high levels of export growth. Their regulatory environments do not cause exchange rates to become overvalued, which would inhibit export growth, or cause real interest rates to become negative, which would inhibit saving. Lawrence Summers, whose work at the World Bank and the U.S. Treasury helped to establish the Washington Consensus, says that the evidence is clear: "National development failures are the fault of national policies—they cannot be blamed on a hostile international environment or on physical limits to growth."[30]

Despite its growing acceptance in the developing world, the Washington Consensus has many critics. The successful economies in East Asia, they say, have relied on a variety of protectionist tools to develop their industrial base, and programs of export promotion have been most successful in countries that inherited an industrial base from a prior program of import substitution. Excessive reliance on export promotion and financial deregulation will

---

[30]Lawrence H. Summers, "The Challenges of Development: Some Lessons of History for Sub-Saharan Africa," *Finance and Development* 29 (March 1992): 6.

expose developing countries to gyrations of the world market; they will create enclaves of export-oriented companies and financial institutions with weak linkages to the rest of the economy. Reliance on foreign investment and management will lead to labor exploitation, environmental degradation, and disruption of indigenous cultures. If all developing countries were to adopt policies of export promotion simultaneously, causing heavy job losses in the industrial countries, politicians would respond quickly with new import barriers.[31] Even if deregulation provides benefits in the long run, critics say that the transition from a tariff-ridden system of import substitution to a more market-oriented allocation of resources will yield unacceptable unemployment and income inequality in the medium term.[32]

DEVELOPMENT PLANNING AND THE MARKET

In order to pursue the kinds of growth strategies considered above—balanced or unbalanced growth, import substitution or export promotion—the leaders of the developing countries have prepared hundreds of economic plans. These can be divided into three broad categories.[33] First, Soviet-style central plans were prepared in all the Communist countries; less comprehensive versions were attempted in India, Pakistan, and Turkey in the 1950s and 1960s, and in Bangladesh, Sri Lanka, and Ethiopia in the 1970s. In developing countries, these 5-year plans generally included targets for all the major sectors of the economy, but a large part of economic activity in these countries was always controlled by markets and by hand-to-mouth subsistence sectors. Adherence to the plans was controlled through nationalized companies and through licensing and production quotas.

Second, the eastern Asian countries of Japan, Korea, and Singapore developed their own style of indicative planning, based on Confucian traditions and influenced by French planning. The plans are comprehensive in scope—they cover all major sectors—and they are prepared cooperatively by the public and private sectors. According to the World Bank, eastern Asian plans are "characterized not by technical sophistication or strict adherence to targets, but by consultations and flexibility."[34] Because of the export orientation of these countries, plan fulfillment is encouraged through positive incentives rather than direct controls.

In most of the other developing countries, including many in Latin America, Africa, and Southeast Asia, planning was introduced to satisfy the de-

---

[31] According to Paul Bairoch, if the entire developing world exported manufactured goods at the same per-capita rate as the Four Dragons—Hong Kong, South Korea, Singapore, and Taiwan—this would be nearly equivalent to the current consumption of manufactures in the Western industrial countries. See his *Economics and World History* (Chicago: University of Chicago Press, 1993), 168.

[32] For a sophisticated critique of the Washington Consensus and a discussion of alternatives, see Lance Taylor, "Stabilization, Adjustment, and Reform," in *The Rocky Road to Reform: Adjustment, Income Distribution, and Growth in the Developing World,* ed. by Lance Taylor (Cambridge, Mass.: The MIT Press, 1993), 39–94.

[33] Ramgopal Agarwala, "Planning in Developing Countries," *Finance and Development* 22 (March 1985): 13–16.

[34] Ibid., 14.

mands of colonial powers and international aid agencies. After World War II, for example, the socialist government in Britain required planning in its territories under the Colonial Development and Welfare Act of 1945. Some Latin American countries prepared development plans in the 1930s to organize their programs of import substitution, and they prepared plans with the United States during the 1940s to support the war effort. After the war, they returned to import-substitution planning under the influence of the U.N. Economic Commission for Latin America, and they expanded these efforts in the 1960s with help from the United States under the Alliance for Progress. Since the 1980s, under the influence of the World Bank, the International Monetary Fund, and the U.S. government, the focus of development planning—in Latin America and elsewhere—has turned to trade liberalization, privatization, encouragement of foreign investment, and other elements of the Washington Consensus.

The developing countries use their plans to support applications for project loans and grants from development banks and for rescheduling of debt with the International Monetary Fund and the major commercial banks. Thus, the plans give special attention to projects and macroeconomic variables that interest the foreign audience. Targets for the private sector are usually indicative rather than coercive and are often exercises in wishful thinking. On the domestic level, development plans are used to announce policy changes, to share information, to promote cooperation and consultation, and to build consensus between the private and public sectors.

PROSPECTS AND CHALLENGES

What does the future hold for the developing world? To be honest, we simply do not know. Mainstream economists, who are encouraged by large capital flows, by the successful outcome of the Uruguay Round of trade negotiations, and by growing acceptance of market-oriented development strategies, have never been more optimistic.[35] Thus, according to the World Bank, if developing countries will stick to their reforms and maintain political stability, they presently have the best chance in decades of achieving rapid and stable economic growth (Table 5.5). According to their forecast, the share of the developing world and the former Soviet Union in world output will rise from about 44 percent in 1993 to more than 50 percent by the end of the decade. Based on this and other evidence, editors of The Economist foresee a fundamental realignment of the international balance of economic power:

Over the next 25 years, the world will see the biggest shift in economic strength for more than a century. Today, the so-called industrial economies dominate the globe, as they have for the past 150 years or so. Yet within a generation several are

---

[35]The flow of foreign direct investment to developing countries grew steadily from $14 billion in 1985 to more than $80 billion in 1994. See *Financial Times*, April 10, 1995, 15. On the other hand, tight budgets caused the industrial countries to cut their real flow of official development aid in 1994 to the lowest level in two decades. See *Los Angeles Times*, June 13, 1995, 1.

■ **TABLE 5.5**

WORLD ECONOMIC GROWTH, 1965–2005
(annual percentage change in real GDP)

Region	1965–1973	1973–1980	1980–1990	1990–1995	Forecast 1996–2005
World Total	5.0	3.3	3.1	2.0	3.5
Industrial Countries	4.8	3.1	3.2	2.0	2.9
Developing Countries	6.5	4.7	2.8	2.1	5.3
East Asia and Pacific	8.1	6.6	7.6	10.3	7.9
South Asia	3.6	4.2	5.7	4.6	5.4
Sub-Saharan Africa	4.8	3.2	1.7	1.4	3.8
Latin America and the Caribbean	6.5	5.0	1.7	3.2	3.8
Europe and Central Asia	4.2*	2.8**	2.3	−6.5	4.3
Middle East and North Africa	7.7	3.9	0.2	2.3	2.9

*1960–1970 **1970–1980

Sources: Historical data are from World Bank, *World Development Report 1991*, 186, and World Bank, *World Development Report 1997*, 234–235; forecasts are from World Bank, *Global Economic Prospects and the Developing Countries 1996*, 10. Growth rates for Europe and Central Asia between 1960 and 1980 are based on rate for the USSR and Eastern Europe in Central Intelligence Agency, *Handbook of Economic Statistics 1990* (CPAS 90-10001 September 1990), 37.

likely to be dwarfed by newly emerging economic giants. History suggests, alas, that such shifts in economic power are rarely smooth.[36]

Many historians and heterodox economists, who have less faith in the free-trade policies of the Washington Consensus, are less sanguine about the prospects for the developing world. According to Paul Bairoch, an economic historian at the University of Geneva, "there is no doubt" that industrialization was delayed in India, Latin America, and other low-income countries during the nineteenth century when they were forced to open their markets to manufactured goods from Europe and the United States; "the liberal trade experience in the Third World was a complete failure."[37] Although Bairoch concedes that evidence from the nineteenth century may have little relevance in the twenty-first, he expresses little cause for optimism in the developing world.

Paul Kennedy, a Yale University historian, is not convinced that the economic balance of power will soon shift toward the South: "In sum," he says, "as we move into the next century the developed economies appear to have all of the trump cards in their hands—capital, technology, control of communications, surplus foodstuffs, powerful multinational companies—and, if

---

[36]"War of the Worlds: Survey of the Global Economy," *The Economist*, October 1, 1994, S1.

[37]Bairoch, *Economics and World History*, 53–54 and 171.

[38]Paul Kennedy, *Preparing for the Twenty-First Century* (New York: Random House, 1993), 225.

anything, their advantages are growing because technology is eroding the value of labor and materials, the chief assets of developing countries."[38] According to Kennedy, the developing countries should avoid extreme strategies of socialism or free-market liberalism, and should imitate East Asia's mixture of official controls and private enterprise.

If barriers to trade, transportation, and communication continue to fall, causing world markets to grow more open and integrated, all countries, including the developing countries, will face greater competitive risks and broader opportunities. Nations, regions, and individual people who acquire the latest skills and tools will, in general, have tremendous opportunities. Nations, regions, and individual people who do not acquire these skills will, in general, compete for jobs and incomes with the least privileged people in the world. The challenge of economic and social development continues for each of us.

SUMMARY

The least privileged people in the world live in Sub-Saharan Africa and South Asia. The nations of East Asia have achieved exceptional levels of economic development. The record is mixed in Latin America.

Very generally, countries that remain poor are those that fail to generate a sufficient investable surplus or those that fail to invest it in productive activities. In many countries, the effort to produce an investable surplus is complicated by such environmental factors as geography, soil, and climate, and the utilization of this surplus is influenced by religion and other aspects of culture. Institutional factors that stand in the way of economic development include inefficient and inequitable systems of land tenure, primitive market structures, dualism in labor markets, and limitations in the quantity and quality of financial intermediation. Poverty sustains itself through the operation of several vicious circles. Although people with low incomes find it difficult to save, saving is needed to finance investment. Likewise, poverty places limits on educational opportunity, health, and market size, and it promotes rapid population growth, income inequality, and political instability.

Marxists and dependency theorists believe that the industrial countries, with their imperialist policies, shoulder much of the blame for world poverty. This form of exploitation was clear enough during the colonial era; they believe that it continues today through the operations of multinational corporations and through an unfair system of international prices.

Adam Smith and his followers believed that economic development is the natural order of things and that little is needed to promote it. In the 1950s, Arthur Lewis argued that independent development could be promoted by shifting rural surplus labor into industry. Rosenstein-Rodan agreed that this was possible, but added that it would require a big push to begin. Nurske proposed that such a push should be made simultaneously in several sectors, while Rostow argued for confining the initial push to leading sectors and Hirschman recommended that growth be encouraged in sectors with strong linkages. In many cases, particularly in Latin America, unbalanced growth was linked with a policy of import substitution. In the 1980s, though, import substitution policies were abandoned in many countries, and a Washington Consensus formed around policies of export promotion, privatization, and free markets.

Economic plans in the developing world have fallen into three categories: Soviet-style central plans, Japanese-style indicative plans, and project plans encouraged by aid agencies. In recent years, the plans have shifted toward a stronger market orientation.

Based on recent capital flows, trade negotiations, and liberalization policies, many mainstream economists are optimistic about prospects for the developing world. Historians seem to find less cause for optimism, but, in the end, economic development will depend on exploitation of opportunities by individual people, regions, and nations.

DISCUSSION AND REVIEW QUESTIONS

1. Do you believe that cultural and religious traditions can have an important impact on economic development? Is it possible to study these influences in a scientific way?

2. How do traditional systems of land tenure influence economic development? What kinds of forces stand in the way of land reform?

3. What is a dual labor market? What are its causes and effects?

4. What kinds of vicious circles were discussed in the chapter? Can you think of others? What kinds of policies would be necessary to break them?

5. What is dependency theory? How does it explain the problems of the developing world? What policy recommendations are derived from the theory?

6. What are the relative advantages of import substitution and export promotion strategies of economic development?

7. Describe the different kinds of economic plans that are prepared in developing countries. What factors would influence a country's choice of a particular style of planning?

8. During the early years of the twenty-first century, what will be the balance of economic power between the industrial countries and the current list of developing countries?

SUGGESTED READINGS

Dutt, Amitava Krishna, and Kenneth P. Jameson eds. *New Directions in Development Economics.* Aldershot: Edward Elgar, 1992. *Essays by six authors, most of whom are critical of the Washington Consensus.*

Harrison, Lawrence E. *Development Is a State of Mind: The Latin American Case.* Lanham, Md.: University Press of America, 1985. *Presents an interesting example for cultural determinism.*

Karmarck, Andrew. *The Tropics and Economic Development*. Baltimore: The Johns Hopkins University Press, 1976. *Presents an interesting case for environmental determinism.*

Landes, David S. "Why Are We So Rich and They So Poor?" *American Economic Review* 80 (May 1990): 1–13. *A cogent lecture on the subject, presented to an annual meeting of the American Economic Association by a respected Harvard historian.*

United Nations Development Programme, *Human Development Report.* New York: Oxford University Press, annual. *Similar in some respects to its older cousin at the World Bank (below), this annual report takes a strong stance on demilitarization and a basic-needs approach to poverty reduction.*

The World Bank, *World Development Report.* New York: Oxford University Press, annual. *Provides a wealth of authoritative statistical information, analysis, and policy guidance. Each year, the report follows a different theme, such as infrastructure (1994), health (1993), environment (1992), development strategy (1991), and poverty (1990). Taken together, these volumes provide a comprehensive mainstream analysis of the subject.*

INTERNET RESOURCES

Asian Development Bank
http://www.asiandevbank.org/

Canadian International Development Agency
http://gsro.carleton.ca/npsia/cida/cidindex.html

HungerWeb (Brown University)
http://www.netspace.org/hungerweb/

Institute of Development Studies
University of Sussex
http://www.ids.ac.uk/

Inter-American Development Bank
http://www.iadb.org/

International Development Center
Queen Elizabeth House Library
http://info.ox.ac.uk:80/~qehlib/

International Development Research Center (IDRC)
http://www.idrc.ca/

International Institute for Sustainable Development
http://iisd1.iisd.ca/

ReliefNet
http://www.reliefnet.org:2805/reliefnet.html

U.N. Conference on Trade and Development
http://gatekeeper.unicc.org/unctad/

U.N. Development Programme
http://www.undp.org/undp_data.html

U.S. Agency for International Development
http://www.info.usaid.gov/

World Health Organization
http://www.who.ch/

III

THE AMERICAS

Western Hemisphere Regional Trade Organizations

6

THE WESTERN HEMISPHERE: AN INTRODUCTION

> These new regions which we found and explored with the
> fleet . . . we may rightly call a New World . . . a continent
> more densely peopled and abounding in animals than our
> Europe or Asia or Africa; and, in addition, a climate milder
> than in any other region known to us.
>
> —AMERIGO VESPUCCI, *MUNDUS NOVUS*, 1503

 ive hundred years after its discovery by Europeans, the Western Hemisphere is still, in many ways, a New World. The region has only 13 percent of the world's population, but covers about 33 percent of its arable land. The United States receives as many immigrants each year as all other countries in the world combined.[1] Vast areas of South America are still unexplored and thinly populated. Argentina, which accepted more than a million European refugees at the end of World War II, is again hoping to attract a wave of skilled immigrants from Eastern Europe. "We have room for lots of people," says an Argentine official, "and we welcome them."[2]

The hemisphere also seems to be a New World in the field of market liberalization. The North American Free Trade Agreement, linking the economies of Canada, Mexico, and the United States into the world's largest trading area, has captured worldwide attention. Equally important, but less reported, are the programs of market liberalization spreading across Latin America. The possibility of merging the entire hemisphere into a vast free trade area, proposed more than a century ago, is now a subject of serious discussion.

This chapter will provide a brief introduction to the Western Hemisphere and assess its position in the world economy. We will explore the broad economic and social forces that have molded economic systems in the region,

---

[1]Fred Arnold, "International Migration: Who Goes Where?" *Finance and Development*, 27 (June 1990): 46.

[2]Gary Marx, "South America Beckons Workers Fleeing the Former East Bloc," *Chicago Tribune*, February 16, 1992, C19.

devoting special attention to trade, investment, labor, and financial relations. Finally, we will consider the prospects for broader hemispheric cooperation.

DIVERSITY AND COMMUNITY

The role of the Western Hemisphere in the world economy is summarized statistically in Table 6.1. The region's share of world GDP is more than double its share of world population. That may be explained partially by the large endowment of arable land in the region, and partially by the higher literacy of years of schooling available to its inhabitants. The share of the hemisphere in world exports is somewhat smaller than its share in world GDP. Why? Primarily because a large proportion of hemispheric trade is conducted *within* the United States. Deliveries of cheese from Wisconsin to California, for example, are counted in GDP, but not in exports.

The United States is, of course, the dominant country in the Western Hemisphere, accounting for one-third of its population and two-thirds of its GDP. The United States provides almost half of the goods imported by Latin America and three-quarters of the goods imported by Canada (Table 6.2). Based in part on its economic leverage, the United States has long considered the entire hemisphere to be its sphere of influence. This has certainly been true since 1823, when the Monroe Doctrine outlawed European interference in "any portion of this hemisphere." Under this umbrella, even Henry Kissinger concedes that the United States has pursued policies "not all that different from the dreams of any European king."[3]

The other countries in the hemisphere are, in many ways, a heterogeneous lot. They include expansive countries like Canada and Brazil, either of which is geographically larger than the European Community, and dots on the Caribbean, such as Grenada and Antigua, comparable to midsized cities in the United States or Europe. The hemisphere includes relatively rich coun-

---

■ TABLE 6.1

THE WESTERN HEMISPHERE AND THE WORLD, 1995

	Western Hemisphere	World	W.H. as % of World
Population (mil.)	771	5,673	13.6
Arable land (1,000 sq. kil.)	3,986	12,244	32.6
GDP (billion $)	9,209	27,846	33.1
GDP/capita ($)	11,944	4,909	243.3
Exports (bil. $)	998	5,145	19.4
Adult Literacy (percent)	92	76	121.1

Sources: World Bank, *World Development Report 1997.*

---

[3]Henry Kissinger, *Diplomacy* (New York: Simon and Schuster, 1994), 36.

■ **TABLE 6.2**

THE WESTERN HEMISPHERE IN WORLD TRADE

Exports To:	World	Western Hemisphere	United States	Canada	Latin America
Exports From:					
World					
1980	2000.9	417.1	240.3	50.7	126.1
1995	4879.0	1212.5	793.6	164.6	254.3
W. Hemisphere					
1980	389.4	177.3	76.1	36.9	64.3
1995	971.3	537.2	258.9	128.7	149.6
United States					
1980	216.6	72.1	—	34.1	38.0
1995	583.9	233.0	—	125.6	107.4
Canada					
1980	64.9	44.5	41.2	—	3.3
1995	191.3	160.2	156.4	—	3.8
Latin America					
1980	107.9	60.7	34.9	2.8	23.0
1995	196.1	144.0	102.5	3.1	38.4

Source: United Nations, *Monthly Bulletin of Statistics*, (June 1994 and June 1996).

tries, such as Argentina, the Bahamas, and Barbados, and some of the poorest countries in the world, such as Bolivia, Haiti, and Honduras. Within the space of a short boat ride, we find Cuba, which was once the staging ground for Marxism in the Western Hemisphere, and Grand Cayman, which is now a center of offshore international banking and a symbol of unrestrained capitalism.

The countries of the Western Hemisphere also have much in common. They share, with obvious variations, a dominant culture grounded in European Judeo-Christianity. They conduct government and commerce in only four major languages: English, Spanish, Portuguese, and French. Europe, in contrast, is divided between more than 20 official languages.[4] Nearly all of the Western Hemispheric countries were, for a century or more, colonies of England, Spain, France, or Portugal. By 1824, nearly all gained their independence, but the legacies of colonialism are still evident today.

The social structures in the Western Hemisphere were molded by colonial contacts and conflicts between three important populations: natives of the

---

[4]European languages used by 15 million people or more include Dutch, English, French, German, Italian, Polish, Portuguese, Romanian, Russian, Serbo-Croatian, Spanish, and Ukrainian.

Western Hemisphere, immigrants from Europe (free colonists and indentured servants), and slaves from Africa. In the United States and the British West Indies, the native populations were expelled from their homelands and partially exterminated; plantation work was performed by imported slaves. In the Spanish colonies of Central and South America, few Africans were imported, but the natives were sometimes pressed into slavery. In Brazil, the Portuguese colonists imposed slavery on the natives and also imported large numbers of Africans. Intermarriage of the three populations became more common in Latin America than in North America. Today, nearly half of Brazilians have a mixture of native, European, and African ancestries.

Most countries in the Western Hemisphere had to fight for independence from colonialism. The spirit of nationalism in each country was molded and strengthened during this struggle. Simon Bolivar, George Washington, and many of the other cultural heroes were leaders of colonial rebellions. In most countries, Independence Day is the major national holiday. We should not be surprised, therefore, that most countries in the hemisphere have jealously guarded their economic independence. At various times in their histories, most have followed strict programs of protectionism against foreign trade and investment. Quite often, protectionism has been the economic expression of political independence.

THE UNITED STATES: FROM PROTECTIONISM TO LIBERALISM

Protectionist and isolationist sentiments were expressed in the United States soon after its independence from colonialism. John Adams declared that foreign commerce was "incompatible with Republicanism." Thomas Jefferson said he sometimes wished the Atlantic were "an ocean of fire between the new and the old world."[5] Alexander Hamilton, treasury secretary in the first U.S. government, provided a formal rationale for protectionism in his famous *Report on Manufactures*, presented to Congress in 1791. A nation must be able to produce its own "means of subsistence, habitation, clothing, and defense" to guarantee the safety and welfare of its citizens. The nation's "infant industries" must be protected from foreign competition, he argued, until they grow to maturity and reach an efficient scale of operations.

Despite these opinions and proposals, the United States did not immediately adopt a protectionist policy. Instead, it took advantage of its neutrality during the Napoleonic Wars, and expanded its trade with Europe. Protectionist barriers were built after 1806, to retaliate against European naval blockades, after 1812, to protect industries established during the Napoleonic Wars, after 1828, when a coalition of protectionist forces in Congress passed the infamous Tariff of Abominations, and after the outbreak of the Civil War, when the political balance shifted in favor of industrial protec-

---

[5]Arthur M. Schlesinger, Jr., *The Cycles of American History* (Boston: Houghton Mifflin, 1986), 131.

tionists in the North. By 1875, when tariffs on manufactured goods had been eliminated in Great Britain and were about 10 percent in continental Europe, they were about 45 percent in the United States.[6]

Beginning in 1913, President Wilson pressed for a more liberal trade policy, and tariff rates were reduced substantially during the 1920s. Protectionist sentiments reached a new extreme, though, during the onset of the Great Depression; the Smoot-Hawley Act of 1930 raised average tariff rates on manufactured goods to nearly 50 percent. Within two years, 60 countries retaliated with large tariff hikes and U.S. trade fell to less than one-third of its 1929 level. Thus, the depression encouraged protectionism, and protectionism added depth to the depression.

The United States' Trade Agreements Act of 1934 called a truce. It shifted some tariff-setting authority from the legislature, which is particularly vulnerable to special interest groups, to the executive branch. In particular, it authorized the president to negotiate bilateral agreements with other countries to reduce tariffs by up to 50 percent in exchange for similar reductions. Furthermore, the 1934 act provided for **most-favored-nation clauses** in the agreements. If country X is given MFN status by the United States, then any tariff reduction that is granted to another country is automatically granted to country X. By the outbreak of World War II, the United States had reached 21 agreements with other nations and the level of protection was substantially reduced. After the war, the United States played a leading role in trade liberalization, and U.S. tariffs continued to decline (Table 6.3).

■ TABLE 6.3

AVERAGE U.S. TARIFF RATES 1821–1995
(TOTAL DUTIES AS A PERCENTAGE OF TOTAL DUTIABLE IMPORTS)

Year	Average Tariff	Year	Average Tariff
1821	45	1925	38
1830	62	1932	59
1835	40	1940	36
1850	27	1950	13
1861	19	1960	12
1865	48	1970	10
1893	50	1980	6
1900	49	1985	6
1910	42	1990	5
1920	16	1995	5

Sources: U.S. Department of Commerce, Bureau of the Census, *Historical Statistics of the United States* (Washington, D.C.: 1985); and U.S. Department of Commerce, Bureau of the Census, *Statistical Abstract of the United States 1996* (Washington, D.C.: 1996), 806.

---

[6]Paul Bairoch, *Economics and World History: Myths and Paradoxes* (Chicago: University of Chicago Press, 1993), 24, 35.

LATIN AMERICA: FROM LIBERALISM TO PROTECTIONISM AND BACK AGAIN

In Latin America, the end of colonialism initially led to a liberalization of trade. Freed from vassalage to Spain and Portugal during the first quarter of the nineteenth century, the independent nations sought a wider circle of partners. England, after assisting several of the countries in their independence movements, moved quickly to conclude trade agreements in Latin America. Some of the region's most influential thinkers, including Manuel Belgrano in Argentina and Jose Bonifacio in Brazil, were advocates of trade liberalization.[7] In Argentina, total exports increased sevenfold between 1853 and 1873, doubled again by 1893, and doubled still again by 1903.

Early in the twentieth century, external conditions deteriorated, and Latin American leaders grew disenchanted with the international market. Many were offended by the neocolonial "big stick" posture of President Theodore Roosevelt, dramatized by his seizure of the Panama Canal Zone in 1904. They faced new competition from African and Asian producers of coffee, cacao, and rubber. Shipping disruptions during World War I and international price movements during the 1920s caused their export earnings to fluctuate wildly. The last straw was the Great Depression, which caused export earnings to collapse. For Latin America as a whole, the capacity to purchase imports dropped about 31 percent during 1930–1934, and for Brazil, Chile, and Mexico it fell more than 45 percent.[8]

The collapse of the international market strengthened the position of an emerging class of Latin American industrialists who demanded tariff protection. Repeating the arguments of Alexander Hamilton, they insisted that economic growth based on domestic sales would be more stable than export-led growth. Protected development of "infant industries" would reduce Latin American dependence on imported industrial goods, would relieve balance of payments pressures, and would contribute to economic and social modernization. Accordingly, the Latin American countries adopted programs of import-substituting industrialization (ISI) during the early 1930s. Several countries returned to export promotion during the late 1930s, but their efforts were confounded by disruption of shipping during World War II.[9]

After the war, the ISI strategy became widely accepted and firmly entrenched in Latin America. Its strongest advocates were a team of analysts at the United Nations Economic Commission for Latin America (ECLA), led by

[7]For a discussion of these and other currents of economic thought in Latin America during the nineteenth century, see Wendell C. Gordon, *The Economy of Latin America* (New York: Columbia University Press, 1950), 7–19.

[8]Celso Furtado, *Economic Development of Latin America* (Cambridge, Mass.: Cambridge University Press, 1970), 40–41. For a fuller discussion of the factors leading to a policy change, see Roberto Cortes Conde, "Export-Led Growth in Latin America: 1870–1930," *Journal of Latin American Studies* 24 (Quincentenary Supplement, 1992): 163–179.

[9]Rosemary Thorp, "A Reappraisal of the Origins of Import-Substitution Industrialization, 1930–1950," *Journal of Latin American Studies* 24 (Supplement, 1992).

Argentine economist, Raul Prebisch. In their first major report, they found "no reason to hope" that export growth would reassert itself, and declared that "these countries no longer have an alternative" to "internal expansion through industrialization."[10]

Prebisch acknowledged, however, that two major dangers were inherent in the ISI strategy. First, if protection from foreign competition was excessive, domestic efficiency would suffer, and infant industries would remain immature. Therefore, tariff barriers should be moderate, covering a limited number of products for a limited number of years. Second, if each Latin American nation attempted to produce a broad range of industrial products, their markets would be too small to support efficient, large-scale production. Therefore, Prebisch believed the ISI strategy should be implemented on a *regional* basis, within a new Latin American common market, to avoid excessive duplication of production.[11]

Unfortunately, Prebisch's worst fears were realized. During the early 1960s, Latin American tariff rates became the highest in the world, sometimes exceeding 500 percent. A Latin American Free Trade Association (LAFTA) was formed in 1960, but it was a toothless organization, unable to prevent duplication of production. Prebisch found that the protected industries "deprived the Latin American countries of the advantages of specialization and economies of scale," so that "a healthy form of internal competition has failed to develop, to the detriment of efficient production."[12]

The situation grew even worse during the 1970s, when the world was shaken by two oil price shocks, and during the 1980s, when Latin America was devastated by a major debt crisis. The annual growth of GDP per capita in the region decelerated from 4.6 percent in 1965–1973 to 2.2 percent in 1973–1980; there was no growth at all during the 1980s.

In 1973, when General Pinochet seized power in Chile, he entrusted economic policy to a team of young U.S.-trained economists. Instead of the protectionist ideas of Alexander Hamilton, these young "Chicago Boys" had been schooled in the free-market philosophies of Adam Smith and Milton Friedman. They were impressed by the economic successes of East Asian countries that mixed political authoritarianism with economic freedom and export promotion. Thus, the "Chicago Boys" introduced a radical program of tight money, privatization, trade liberalization, and export promotion in Chile that attracted international attention. Building on the Chilean experience and responding to pressure from the International Monetary Fund and the World Bank, other Latin American countries introduced programs of neoliberal reform. The return to trade liberalization and the establishment of

---

[10]*The Economic Development of Latin America and Its Principle Problems* (New York: United Nations, 1950), 6.

[11]For a discussion of Prebisch's integration proposals, see Jose Manuel Salazar-Xirinacha, "The Integration Revival: A Return to Prebisch's Policy Prescriptions?" *CEPAL Review* 50 (August 1993): 21–40.

[12]*Towards a Dynamic Development Policy for Latin America* (New York: United Nations, 1963), 71.

■ **TABLE 6.4**

WESTERN HEMISPHERE INTEGRATION
ORGANIZATIONS: CHRONOLOGY

1890	International Union of American Republics
1948	U.N. Economic Commission for Latin America
1948	Organization of American States
1959	Inter-American Development Bank
1960	Central American Common Market
1960	Latin American Free Trade Association (LAFTA)
1961	Alliance for Progress
1971	Andean Common Market
1973	Caribbean Community and Common Market
1980	LAFTA becomes Latin American Integration Association (LAIA)
1989	Canada-United States Free Trade Agreement
1990	Enterprise for the Americas Initiative
1991	Common Market of the South (MERCOSUR)
1992	Colombia-Venezuela Customs Union
1994	North American Free Trade Association
1994	Mexico agrees to enter Colombia-Venezuela Customs Union
1994	Association of Caribbean States
1995	Andean Free Trade Zone

the North American Free Trade Agreement, in turn, sparked new interest in economic integration within Latin America and across the entire Western Hemisphere.

ECONOMIC INTEGRATION IN THE WESTERN HEMISPHERE

Despite the atmosphere of protectionism that emerged in the United States during the nineteenth century and in Latin America during the 1930s, proposals for regional integration have been circulating in the Western Hemisphere for more than a century (Table 6.4). In the past, these schemes were seldom successful. Today, in the face of competitive challenges from Asia and Europe, the Americas seem to be entering a new era of cooperation.

HEMISPHERIC INTEGRATION: BEGINNINGS

The first major advocate of integration in the hemisphere was James G. Blaine, a nominee for the United States presidency in 1884 and Secretary of State under Presidents Garfield and Harrison. Blaine hoped that a hemispheric customs union would allow the United States to capture the Latin American market from European exporters of manufactured goods, cultivating "friendly, commercial relations with all American countries," and leading to a "large increase in the export trade of the United States."[13] Stronger economic ties, he hoped, would also reduce hostilities between Latin American nations and reduce European military interference in the hemisphere.

Blaine, as secretary of state, made the customs union proposal a centerpiece of his First International Conference of the American States. Held in Washington during the winter of 1889–90, the conference was attended by all the independent republics of Latin America except the Dominican Republic. Many of the delegates were offended by Blaine's assertiveness and alarmed by the growing power of their northern neighbor. Argentina adamantly opposed the customs union proposal, fearing it would disrupt trade relations with Europe.

In the end, Blaine's customs union was rejected by Latin America. Still, the delegates to the 1890 conference agreed to create an International Union of American Republics (IUAR). Through its permanent office in Washington, the IUAR provided a forum for members to negotiate agreements on international transportation, banking, trade documentation, and other commercial issues.[14]

Latin American leaders grew even more cautious in their relations with the United States after 1904, when President Theodore Roosevelt announced his "corollary" to the Monroe Doctrine, claiming that the United States had a right to intervene in the hemisphere when "wrongdoing, or an impotence . . . results in a general lessening of the ties of civilized society." During the next decade, the United States wielded its "big stick" in the affairs of Haiti, Nicaragua, the Dominican Republic, Cuba, Panama, and Mexico. In Latin America, "Yankee imperialism" seemed to fill the vacuum left by European colonialism.

When Franklin D. Roosevelt became president in 1933, he dedicated the United States to the policy of the "good neighbor" who "resolutely respects himself, and because he does so, respects the rights of others." Under the **good neighbor policy,** the United States renounced its unilateral right of intervention, and pledged to cooperate with other countries in the hemisphere on a basis of consultation and legal equality. This new relationship yielded immediate diplomatic dividends, but it could provide little economic benefit; protectionist forces gained strength throughout the hemisphere during the Great Depression.

---

[13]Blaine quoted in Joseph Grunwald, Miguel Wionczec, and Martin Carnoy, *Latin American Economic Integration and U.S. Policy* (Washington, D.C.: Brookings Institution, 1972), 67.

[14]In 1910, the IUAR was reorganized to become the Pan American Union, and in 1948 it became the Organization of American States.

LATIN AMERICAN INTEGRATION: THE TROUBLED 1960S

Latin American leaders began to express interest in regional integration in the late 1930s. Their objective, though, was to promote industrialization through import substitution; they intentionally excluded the United States and Canada from their common market proposals.

Initially, the United States opposed the creation of an exclusively Latin American common market. Leaders in Washington feared that Latin American countries would replace low-cost imports of manufactured goods from the United States and Europe with high-cost imports from other countries in Latin America, causing costly trade diversion. The United States tried to resurrect Blaine's 1889 proposal for a hemispheric common market, but the idea was rejected again.[15]

In mid–1959, a few months after Fidel Castro assumed power in Cuba, the United States announced that it now favored the creation of common markets in Latin America, and it agreed to provide $350 million for a new Inter-American Development Bank. During 1960, a Central American Common Market (CACM) and a Latin American Free Trade Association (LAFTA) were both created.[16] The CACM received substantial support from the United States, and it was highly successful for several years. It immediately eliminated about 75 percent of tariff barriers in the region; trade among CACM countries grew at an annual rate of 36 percent between 1962 and 1966. Beginning in 1969, though, the CACM fell victim to the "soccer war" between Honduras and El Salvador, the civil war in Nicaragua, and political violence within and between several of the other member states.

The LAFTA never was terribly successful. The members initially agreed to phase out all intra-regional tariff barriers over a period of fifteen years, but they were not able to agree on a strategy to accomplish that goal. The organization received little financial support from abroad, and protectionist forces in the individual countries gained control of the process. Within a few years, the LAFTA became dormant.

THE ALLIANCE FOR PROGRESS

Early in 1961, in an effort to accelerate economic growth in Latin America and prevent the spread of Castro's revolution, President Kennedy launched an ambitious Alliance for Progress. This, he said, would be a "vast cooperative effort, unparalleled in magnitude and nobility of purpose, to satisfy the basic needs of the American people for homes, work and land, health and schools—*techo, trabajo y tierra, salud y escuela.*"[17] A few months later, represen-

---

[15]Carnoy, *Latin American Economic Integration*, 70–74.

[16]The CACM included Costa Rica, Nicaragua, Honduras, El Salvador, and Guatemala. The LAFTA was founded by Argentina, Brazil, Chile, Colombia, Ecuador, Mexico, Peru, Paraguay, and Uruguay, and later joined by Bolivia and Venezuela.

[17]Quoted in Harvey S. Perloff, *Alliance for Progress: A Social Invention in the Making* (Baltimore: Johns Hopkins Press, 1969), 21.

tatives from the United States and all of the Latin American countries except Cuba met at Punta del Este, Uruguay, and prepared a Charter that set the following goals for 1961–1971:

Accelerate the growth of GDP per capita to an average annual rate of 2.5 percent *in every Latin American nation*. The average annual rate for the entire region had been 1.8 percent during 1955–1960.

Based on the additional economic growth, raise living standards of the poor and increase the proportion of national income devoted to investment.

Eliminate adult illiteracy and provide six years of primary education to all children.

Increase life expectancy at birth by a minimum of five years and cut child mortality rates in half.

Carry out programs of land reform and tax reform to promote social justice and improve economic efficiency.

All of these actions were to be carried out, according to the charter, "within the framework of personal dignity and political liberty . . . in democratic societies adapted to their own needs and desires."[18]

Each country was expected to devise its own economic development plan, specifying targets, strategies, lines of administrative responsibility, and resources needed to execute the program. Based on these plans and estimates, the United States committed itself to provide about $1 billion of assistance each year to support Alliance programs. It would also support programs of regional cooperation through the CACM, the LAFTA, and through organizations established by the Alliance.

In the end, most of the goals of the Alliance were not fulfilled. The average Latin American country met the economic growth target, but several countries, including Colombia, Paraguay, and Uruguay, fell far short. Illiteracy in the region fell from about 30 percent in 1960 to about 25 percent in 1970 (and to 15 percent in 1990), but it certainly was not eliminated. Likewise, significant progress was made in the fields of health and education, but below the ambitious goals set in Punta del Este. Little progress was made in the areas of income distribution, land reform, or tax reform. Military dictators thrived in Latin America during the 1960s, and their countries received about two-thirds of the financial support distributed by the United States to the Alliance.

Still, we should not pronounce the Alliance a failure because of the ambitiousness of its goals. It did not perform miracles, but the Alliance provided support for moderate economic and social progress in Latin America, and, for a time, it promoted a more cooperative relationship between the United

---

[18]Ibid., 27.

States and its neighbors. In 1962, during the Cuban missile crisis, that spirit of cooperation was critically important.

ANCOM, CARICOM, AND LAIA

In the mid–1960s, the United States became preoccupied with its own War on Poverty and its growing involvement in Vietnam. Relations with the Western Hemisphere attracted little interest or support. In 1967, when President Johnson attended a hemispheric summit conference in Punta del Este, he wanted to offer a five-year, $1.5 billion aid commitment to the Latin American leaders; he was not able to gain approval, though, from the United States Congress.

Left to fend for themselves, the Latin American leaders tried to reinvigorate programs of regional integration. In 1968, most of the Caribbean countries formed a free-trade area, which was reorganized in 1973 as the Caribbean Community and Common Market (CARICOM). In 1969, five members of the Andean Pact (Bolivia, Colombia, Chile, Ecuador, and Peru, but not Venezuela), agreed to form an Andean common market (ANCOM), which commenced operations in 1971. Their efforts were interrupted, though, in 1973, when the new government of General Pinochet in Chile decided to withdraw from the Andean Pact. More generally, the 1973 oil shock and the subsequent debt crisis created a division between Latin American exporters and importers of oil.

In 1980, the full membership of LAFTA decided to revive the organization under a new treaty, and transform it into the Latin American Integration Association (LAIA). This time, LAIA was designed to function as an umbrella organization for negotiation of other bilateral, multilateral, and "partial multilateral" trade and cooperation agreements. Again, though, it was launched under most difficult circumstances. Latin America was shaken during 1980–82 by falling commodity prices, by rising interest rates and indebtedness, and by a brief war between the United Kingdom and Argentina over control of the Falkland/Malvinas islands.

THE BAKER AND BRADY DEBT PLANS

Latin America's external debts, which amounted to less than 20 percent of the region's GDP in 1975, grew to more than 30 percent in 1980 and 40 percent in 1982.[19] A genuine crisis erupted in August 1982, when the Mexican finance minister declared his country was unable to meet its payment obligations. After negotiations with its creditors, Mexico agreed to maintain current interest payments, and its debt repayment was rescheduled over a longer period of time. This procedure quickly spread to the other debtor countries in the region. Between 1983 and 1985, international banks and Latin American countries negotiated 28 rescheduling agreements.

A new stage of debt adjustment began in 1985, when the U.S. Treasury secretary, James Baker, proposed that countries undertaking market-oriented re-

---

[19]Sebastian Edwards, *Latin America and the Caribbean: A Decade After the Debt Crisis* (Washington, D.C.: World Bank, 1993), 7–8.

forms should have access to new lending from banks and official agencies, allowing them to sustain economic growth while repaying their debts. Of the fifteen countries Baker recommended for this treatment, ten were in Latin America. In the end, the multinational lending institutions (such as the World Bank) supported Baker's plan, but commercial banks refused to participate.

The third phase of Latin American adjustment began in 1989, when another U.S. Treasury secretary, Nicholas Brady, announced a new plan for voluntary debt reduction. Countries that demonstrated a commitment to macroeconomic stabilization and economic reform could acquire long-term credit at low interest rates by issuing bonds, with payment guaranteed by the IMF and the World Bank. The proceeds from these bond sales could be used to repay old debts, often at a deep discount. Costa Rica, for example, was able to retire $991 million of old debt with payments of only $159 million. For Latin America as a whole, external debt declined from 54 percent of GDP in 1987 to 36 percent in 1996.[20]

ENTERPRISE FOR THE AMERICAS

In June 1990, U.S. President George Bush launched the Enterprise for the Americas Initiative (EAI), designed "to reinforce Latin America's growing recognition that free market reform is the key to sustained growth and political stability."[21] The EAI would be built on three pillars:

Free Trade. The United States would liberalize its trade with nations in the region through the General Agreement on Tariffs and Trade and would work toward the long-term goal of a free trade zone encompassing the entire hemisphere—"from the port of Anchorage to the Tierra del Fuego." The first step would be negotiation of a North American Free Trade Agreement.

Investment. A new Multilateral Investment Fund, administered by the Inter-American Development Bank (IDB), would be created to finance privatization programs and other market-oriented investments. The United States would, in the space of five years, contribute $500 million to the fund, and it would encourage Japan and the European Community to do the same.

Debt and the Environment. In addition to the actions taken under the Brady Plan, the United States would cancel some of the $7 billion of debt associated with U.S. aid programs, and would encourage the use of debt-for-nature swaps to reduce Latin American debt burdens and protect the environment. The United States also would allow countries to make interest payments on some of their debts in local currency. These payments would accumulate in trust accounts, which would be used to fund environmental projects.

---

[20]International Monetary Fund, *World Economic Outlook* (May 1994, and May 1997).

[21]"Policy Address by President Bush Concerning the Economies of Latin America," Federal News Service, June 27, 1990.

Like the Alliance for Progress in the 1960s, the EAI has not been able to meet all its goals and schedules, but it has inspired and supported a great deal of activity. Negotiations on NAFTA, for example, began in 1991, but the treaty between the United States, Canada, and Mexico did not become effective until 1994. Meanwhile, the United States negotiated 16 framework agreements on trade and investment with 31 countries in the region, paving the way for a broader system of cooperation.

After numerous delays, the Multilateral Investment Fund (MIF) was established in 1992 and began operations at the end of 1993 with total pledges of $1.25 billion from 21 countries.[22] The fund includes a Human Resources Facility, supporting training programs for displaced workers; an Enterprise Development Facility, providing start-up capital and loans for small businesses; and a Technical Assistance Facility, providing grants for privatization programs and development of financial institutions.[23] In 1994, for example, the Technical Assistance Facility provided $4.9 million to modernize the clearance and settlement systems of stock exchanges in Central America and the Caribbean.[24]

The debt reduction objectives of the EAI have been particularly difficult to fulfill. Faced with tight domestic budgets and new challenges in Russia and Eastern Europe, the U.S. Congress has reduced or denied most presidential requests for aid to Latin America. Still, during 1991–1993, Congress approved cancellation of $875 million of debt owed to the United States government by Argentina, Bolivia, Chile, Colombia, El Salvador, Jamaica, and Uruguay.

THE CANADA-U.S. FREE TRADE AGREEMENT (CUFTA)

In 1986, several years before the EAI, Canada expressed interest in forming a free trade area with the United States. The Canadian leaders wanted to prevent the U.S. Congress, which was concerned about rising trade deficits, from passing protectionist legislation that would jeopardize Canada's largest export market. A Canada-U.S. Free Trade Agreement (CUFTA) was negotiated in 1987 and signed in 1988, but it was hotly contested in the Canadian federal election of November 1988. Critics of the agreement argued that Canada, confronted with U.S. competition, would be forced to abandon its distinctive features, such as its system of national health care. In the end, supporters of the pact won a surprising victory in the 1988 Canadian election, and implementation of the CUFTA began in 1989.

The United States and Canada already had the world's largest trading relationship before the CUFTA, and their tariff barriers were already relatively

---

[22]As intended, the United States and Japan eventually pledged $500 million each, but relatively small commitments from Europe (Spain, $50 million, and Germany and Italy, $30 million) were offset by commitments from Canada and from several Latin American countries.

[23]"IDB Launches Latin American Investment Fund," *Euromoney Trade Finance and Banker International* (February 1993), 18.

[24]Will Acworth, "Central American Bolsas Seek to Upgrade Standards," *LDC Debt Report/Latin American Markets* 7 (September 5, 1994), 5.

low. Under the agreement, the two countries vowed to remove all remaining tariff barriers by 1999 and reduce or eliminate non-tariff barriers in the energy, agricultural, and service sectors. When fully implemented, the agreement would account for a net increase of roughly $3.3 billion per year in American imports and $2.4 billion per year in Canadian imports.[25]

The CUFTA also established a Canada-United States Trade Commission, responsible for monitoring implementation and resolving disputes. Despite efforts of the negotiators, the CUFTA did not establish a unified regulatory system for price subsidies and other unfair pricing policies. Instead, each country maintained its own regulatory laws and institutions, but agreed to submit these to judicial review by a new network of binational panels.

Implementation of the CUFTA proceeded rather smoothly. Tariff barriers were removed ahead of schedule. The physical volume of trade between the United States and Canada, which grew at an average annual rate of 6 percent during 1980–1987, accelerated to a 7 percent growth rate during 1988–1993.[26] Investment barriers were also dismantled, and the new system of binational panels for review of pricing policies was found to work "extremely well."[27] Still, the United States and Canada were unable to resolve disputes over price subsidies for wheat and lumber.

FROM CUFTA TO NAFTA

In June 1990, the presidents of the United States and Mexico agreed to negotiate a bilateral free trade accord as a first step in the Enterprise for the Americas Initiative. A few months later the Canadian government decided to join the negotiations and work toward creation of a North American Free Trade Agreement (NAFTA). Negotiations began in June 1991, and the three heads of state initialed a preliminary agreement in August 1992.

Ratification of NAFTA became a central issue in the 1992 U.S. election. George Bush, the incumbent, supported the existing agreement. Ross Perot opposed NAFTA, arguing its adoption would cause a "giant sucking sound" of American jobs leaving the country. Bill Clinton supported NAFTA, but called for supplemental negotiations on labor and environmental issues. When Clinton won the election, these additional negotiations began. The final agreement was approved narrowly by the Canadian and U.S. legislatures, and overwhelmingly by the Mexican Senate. Implementation of NAFTA began in 1994.

---

[25]These estimates account for both the trade "created" between the United States and Canada and the trade "diverted" from other countries. See David Karemera and Won W. Koo, "Trade Creation and Trade Diversion Effects of the U.S.-Canadian Free Trade Agreement," *Contemporary Economic Policy* 12 (January 1994): 12–23.

[26]Calculations of the author, based on trade data and price indices provided by the U.S. Department of Commerce.

[27]Murray G. Smith, "The Future Evolution of the Canada-U.S. Free Trade Agreement: Opportunities and Risks," in *Implications of a North American Free Trade Region: Multidisciplinary Perspectives*, ed. by Joseph A. McKinney and M. Rebecca Sharpless (Waco, Tex.: Baylor University Press, 1992), 34.

The text of the free trade agreement runs more than 2,000 pages, replete with diplomatic and legal language. What follows are a few of its most important provisions.

Tariffs. The three nations agreed to eliminate all internal tariffs—some immediately and others over periods of five, ten, and fifteen years. For example, in the case of motor vehicles, where U.S.–Canada trade was already duty free, the United States agreed to remove its tariffs against Mexico immediately. Mexico would cut its tariff in half, and phase out the remainder over five years for light trucks and ten years for cars. Negotiations for accelerated tariff elimination began in 1994.

Rules of Origin. Unlike the European Union, which has a unified schedule of external tariffs, each of the NAFTA members has its own set of tariffs for nonmembers. If nothing were done to stop them, nonmembers would be able to ship each of their products into the member country with the lowest tariff on that product, and then transfer the goods duty-free to other member countries. Thus, to move duty-free between NAFTA members, products must meet specific **rules of origin**. In general, at least half the value of a qualified product must be derived from North American production. Stricter rules of origin apply to sensitive sectors, such as automobiles, textiles, and apparel.

Investment. Mexico agreed to remove all export and domestic content requirements on foreign investments within ten years, and to allow free repatriation of profits. Despite a constitutional ban, Mexico would allow investments in its petrochemicals sector. Property owned by foreigners would not be taken without fair compensation.

Financial Services. U.S. and Canadian banks, securities firms, and insurance companies would be allowed to establish wholly owned subsidiaries in Mexico under restrictions that would be phased out by January 2000.

Transportation. U.S. trucking companies could carry freight in the contiguous states of Mexico in 1995 and in all of Mexico by the end of 1999.

Dispute Settlement. Building on the experience of the CUFTA, the NAFTA established a North American Free Trade Commission, composed of cabinet-level officials, to adjudicate broad disputes. Narrower issues are handled by five-member panels of private-sector experts. Noncompliance can result in trade sanctions.

The Environment. Side agreements established a cabinet-level Environmental Council and a professional Environmental Secretariat, but Canada and Mexico refused to grant supranational enforcement powers to these agencies. Instead, the agencies are able to monitor compliance, offer advice, and enlist the aid of dispute resolution panels created by NAFTA. A Border Environmental Cooperation Commission (BECC) and a North American Development Bank (NADBank) were created to coordinate and finance environmental projects along the U.S.-Mexico border. By 1998, the lending capacity of NADBank would be more than $2 billion.

Labor Issues. A Labor Council was created to monitor compliance with local laws, resolve disputes, and promote cooperation in occupational safety and health, human resource development, labor statistics, and worker benefits and compensation. Again, voluntary compliance is the primary means of enforcement, but dispute resolution panels can ultimately impose fines or trade sanctions. The staff of the Labor Secretariat performs research and prepares reports on a similar range of labor issues.

Its supporters claim that NAFTA, the world's largest free trade area, provides benefits to all its members by encouraging regional cooperation, specialization, and large-scale production, by supporting economic development and democratization in Mexico, and by countervailing the power of regional trading blocs in Europe and Asia. Formal statistical studies generally have found that NAFTA will confer net welfare gains on all three participants; the main beneficiary should be Mexico, where cooperation with its northern neighbors could cause GNP to increase by as much as 11 percent by the year 2000.[28]

According to its critics, NAFTA encourages American and Canadian companies to move their factories to Mexico, where they pay lower wages, provide fewer benefits, and avoid regulations on employee safety, environmental disruption, and product safety and quality. The AFL-CIO predicted that about 500,000 U.S. jobs would be lost during the first few years of the agreement.[29] Ross Perot brought national attention to an estimate, considered absurd by others, that up to 5.9 million U.S. jobs would move to Mexico.[30]

Defenders of NAFTA can point to independent studies indicating that full implementation of the agreement will cause U.S. employment to increase by 60,000 to 170,000; average U.S. wages also will increase by a small amount.[31] They say that critics fail to consider several key points:

Just before NAFTA was adopted, the average Mexican tariff on U.S. goods (10.7 percent) was significantly higher than the average U.S. tariff on Mexican goods (3.5 percent). Thus, other things equal, elimination of tariffs should strengthen the relative competitive position of the United States.[32]

---

[28]Drusilla K. Brown, Alan V. Deardorff, and Robert M. Stern, "North American Integration," *Economic Journal* 102 (November 1992): 1507–1518.

[29]"A NAFTA Primer," *The Dallas Morning News*, November 10, 1993, 13A.

[30]This estimate is based on the extreme assumption that the United States would lose all jobs that pay more than $6 per hour in industries in which labor accounts for more than 20 percent of costs. See Alan Reynolds, "Ross, Get a New Brain Trust," *International Economy*, July/August 1993, 6–7.

[31]See Alan Madian, "A Free Trade Area with Mexico: Will U.S. Workers Lose?" *Annals of the American Academy of Political and Social Sciences* 526 (March 1993): 81–91; and Gary Hufbauer, "Mass Distortion," *International Economy*, July/August 1993, 8–10.

[32]Madian, "A Free Trade Area with Mexico," 83.

Hourly compensation of manufacturing workers was 4.7 times higher in the United States than in Mexico in 1991, but U.S. manufacturing productivity was 4.6 times higher. Thus, labor costs per unit of output were similar in the two countries.[33]

In some cases, U.S. firms have opened production facilities in Mexico to avoid payment of Mexican import tariffs. NAFTA will reduce or eliminate the need for this kind of investment, reducing the outflow of U.S. jobs and capital.

With or without NAFTA, many low-wage jobs will probably move from the United States and Canada to Latin America, Asia, Southern Europe, or Africa during the next decade. If those jobs move to Latin America, a relatively large proportion of the resulting income will be spent in North America.

The Mexican economy is less than 5 percent of the size of the U.S. economy, and U.S. direct investment in Mexico amounts to only about 1 percent of annual business investment in the United States. Any positive or negative impact of NAFTA on the United States is likely to be small.

Labor and environmental concerns are addressed, more or less adequately, in side agreements. U.S. labor unions are using new institutions created by NAFTA to press for tighter enforcement of Mexican labor laws.[34] The U.S. Labor Department also created a NAFTA Transitional Adjustment Assistance Program to pay for retraining, job counseling, job search, and relocation expenses for workers who directly or indirectly lose their jobs during the first two years of implementation of NAFTA. During the first year of its operation, about 10,000 workers from 20 states were approved for assistance under this program.[35]

Total U.S. exports to Mexico tripled between 1987 and 1993. During the first half of 1994, immediately after the adoption of NAFTA, U.S. exports to Mexico increased 16 percent, with the largest increases in high-wage sectors, such as automobiles, electronic components, and jet engines.[36] By stimulating the Mexican economy and reducing trade barriers, NAFTA should generate U.S. exports and jobs.

Have the critics of NAFTA been silenced by these arguments? Of course not! Nevertheless, the early results of NAFTA have raised the level of interest in regional cooperation; the battle against trade barriers is spreading across the Western Hemisphere.

---

[33]Reynolds, "Ross, Get a New Brain Trust," 7.

[34]Nancy Dunne, "U.S. Unions Bring First Charges under NAFTA," *Financial Times*, August 5, 1994, 4.

[35]Raju Narisetti, "Not Everybody Wins," *The Wall Street Journal*, October 28, 1994, R10.

[36]See "NAFTA's First Six Months Show Good Results, Brown Says," *BNA International Trade Daily*, August 22, 1994; and "So Far, So Good," *The Wall Street Journal*, October 28, 1994, R1.

NEW LIFE FOR LATIN AMERICAN INTEGRATION

As we have seen, programs of economic integration in Latin America achieved little during the 1960s and 1970s, and little was even attempted during the 1980s. The efforts of LAFTA, CACM, ANCOM, and CARICOM were frustrated by economic and political instabilities within the member countries, and by civil wars and trade disputes between members. More fundamentally, these organizations found it difficult to promote free trade within a framework of import substitution and regional protectionism.

In recent years, under the influence of international lending agencies, the Latin American countries have shifted from policies of import substitution to export promotion. Prompted by the examples of Europe and North America, and encouraged by the Enterprise for the Americas Initiative, Latin America has made remarkable progress toward the elusive goal of regional integration (Table 6.5).

In 1991, as negotiations were beginning on NAFTA, the leaders of Argentina, Brazil, Paraguay, and Uruguay agreed to create a Common Market of the South (*Mercado Comun del Sur, or MERCOSUR*). The pact among these four countries, accounting for more than half of Latin American GDP, was the most ambitious attempt that had ever been made toward regional integration in Latin America.[37] They agreed to quickly remove barriers against movement of goods, capital, and people, and to coordinate their macroeconomic policies, establish a common external tariff, and create institutions for policy review and dispute resolution. By mid–1993, tariffs among members already had been reduced 75 percent; by 1995, tariffs on 85 percent of intra-MERCOSUR trade were scheduled for complete elimination. Negotiations over establishment of a common external tariff were long and difficult, but agreement was finally reached in 1994 on a set of tariffs ranging from 0–20 percent.[38] In 1994, Chile and Bolivia signed protocols to become associate members of MERCOSUR.

In 1992, Colombia and Venezuela — two countries that nearly went to war in 1987 — formed a customs union and quickly dropped tariffs to zero. Trade between the two countries doubled in one year. According to a Venezuelan paper manufacturer, "When we sell to Colombia, we don't even feel as if we are exporting. We are the same market."[39] In 1994, Colombia and Venezuela enlarged their free trade area to include Mexico, and offered to accept additional members.

In 1993, the Central American Common Market (CACM) was reorganized under a new agreement; Panama was accepted into the group, and the Triangle of the North—El Salvador, Guatemala, and Honduras—launched a common external tariff ranging from 5–20 percent. Trade relations are developing rapidly among these northern members of CACM, and travel is

---

[37]Luigi Manzetti, "The Political Economy of MERCOSUR," *Journal of Interamerican Studies and World Affairs* 35 (Winter 1993–94), 102.

[38]John Barham and Patrick McCurry, "MERCOSUR Four Limp to Customs Union Signing," *Financial Times*, August 5, 1994, 4.

[39]James Brooke, "In Latin America, a Free Trade Rush," *The New York Times*, June 13, 1994, D1.

■ TABLE 6.5

WESTERN HEMISPHERE INTEGRATION
ORGANIZATIONS: MEMBERSHIP

	ACS	AFTZ	CACM	CARICOM	LAIA	MERCOSUR	NAFTA
Antigua/Barbuda	M			M			
Argentina					M	M	
Bahamas	M			M			
Barbados	M			M			
Belize	M			M			
Bolivia		M			M	O	
Brazil					M	M	
Canada							M
Chile		*			M	A	
Colombia		M			M		
Costa Rica	M		M		O		
Cuba	M			O	O		
Dominica	M			M			
Dominican Republic	M			O	O		
Ecuador		M			M		
El Salvador	M		M		O		
Grenada	M			M			
Guatemala			M		O		
Guyana	M			M			
Haiti	M			O			
Honduras	M		M		O		
Jamaica	M			M			
Mexico	M				M		M
Montserrat	M			M			
Nicaragua	M		M		O		

passport-free. Also in 1994, members of the Andean Pact agreed to create an Andean Free Trade Zone, and, on Simon Bolivar's birthday, the thirteen members of the Caribbean Community and Common Market (CARICOM) joined forces with twelve other countries in Latin America and the Caribbean to form the Association of Caribbean States (ACS). The ACS was the first regional organization to accept Cuba as a full member since the 1960s, when Cuba was expelled from the Organization of American States. According to its founding documents, ACS initially will promote social, political, and economic cooperation among its members; eventually it will work toward creation of a free trade area.

This new wave of economic integration in Latin America is not designed to build a fortress of regional import substitution. Indeed, regional integra-

■ **TABLE 6.5 CONTINUED**

WESTERN HEMISPHERE INTEGRATION ORGANIZATIONS: MEMBERSHIP

	ACS	AFTZ	CACM	CARICOM	LAIA	MERCOSUR	NAFTA
Panama	M	A	M		O		
Paraguay					M	M	
Peru		M			M		
St. Kitts-Nevis	M			M			
St. Lucia	M			M			
St. Vincent & Grenadines	M			M			
Suriname	M			O			
Trinidad & Tobago	M			M			
United States	O						M
Uruguay					M	M	
Venezuela	M	M			M		

ACS – Association of Caribbean States

AFTZ – Andean Free Trade Zone

CACM – Central American Common Market

CARICOM – Caribbean Community and Common Market

LAIA – Latin American Integration Association. Before 1981, LAFTA.

MERCOSUR – Southern Cone Common Market

NAFTA – North American Free Trade Association

A – Associate Member

M – Member

O – Observer

*Resigned in 1976

Sources: U.S. Central Intelligence Agency, *The World Factbook 1996*; G. Pope Atkins, "Institutional Arrangements for Hemispheric Free Trade," *Annals of the American Academy of Political and Social Science* 526 (March 1993): 186; and news reports.

tion has been combined with external liberalization. The average Latin American tariff on goods entering from outside the region, which was about 56 percent a decade ago, was about 12 percent in 1994.[40] Latin American integration has caused a great deal of trade creation; external tariff reductions presumably have prevented inefficient trade diversion.

A FREE TRADE AREA FOR THE WESTERN HEMISPHERE?

Earlier, we noted the efforts of James G. Blaine, secretary of state under Presidents Garfield and Harrison, to establish a hemispheric customs union. These proposals were rejected by Latin American leaders who were hesitant to subject their newly independent nations to the "big stick" of the United

---

[40]Ibid.

States. Early in the 1960s, the U.S. National Planning Association resurrected Blaine's proposal, but it was rejected again; free trade with the United States would interrupt Latin American programs of import substitution.

In 1990, President Bush announced that the United States was ready to ne-gotiate free trade agreements with countries in Latin America and the Caribbean, leading eventually to the creation of a free trade area reaching "from the port of Anchorage to the Tierra del Fuego." This time, he found a much more receptive audience in Latin America. Within two years, the United States had signed framework agreements—preliminary commit-ments to hold future talks—with the MERCOSUR group (four nations), the CARICOM group (thirteen nations), and fourteen other individual nations. Why were the Latin American leaders ready to talk? Several reasons have been suggested:

> After the Vietnam War, the United States withdrew from its active role as a "global policeman." Despite U.S. adventures in Iraq, Nicaragua, Grenada, Panama, Somalia, and Haiti, fears of Yankee imperialism subsided in Latin America.

> After the collapse of communism, Latin American leaders were concerned that U.S. trade, aid, and investment would be diverted to Eastern Eu-rope and the former Soviet Union. They were pleased to hear a state-ment of U.S. commitment to the Western Hemisphere.[41]

> After rejecting import substitution and adopting export promotion, Latin American leaders realized that they needed free access to the United States, their largest export market.

> When Mexico entered NAFTA, it gained closer access to U.S. and Cana-dian markets, and it also gained a new image of economic and politi-cal maturity. Both of these factors attracted investment resources to Mexico. Leaders of other Latin American countries have taken notice.

If progress continues toward creation of a Western Hemisphere Free Trade Agreement (WHFTA), several issues will have to be resolved:

What Level of Integration? Aside from eventual elimination of tariffs, what other barriers to the movement of goods, services, capital, and labor will be removed? Will the hemisphere move toward a customs union arrangement, with a common external tariff? The wide disparities between income levels and macroeconomic policies in the hemisphere will probably preclude, for the time being, any movement toward a common monetary system.

What Countries Can Be Members? Should membership in the organization be restricted to countries in the Western Hemisphere ("closed regionalism"), or should it be open to countries in other parts of the world ("open regional-ism")? The European Union is organized on the former principle; the Asia-Pacific Economic Cooperation (APEC) organization is based on the latter. An

---

[41]Peter Hakim, "Western Hemisphere Free Trade: Why Should Latin America Be Interested?" *Annals of the American Academy of Political and Social Sciences* 526 (March 1993): 121–125.

agreement based on open regionalism is less likely to cause trade diversion or to provoke retaliation from outsiders.[42]

What Are the Entrance Requirements? What criteria should determine the *order* in which countries, or groups of countries, are admitted into the WHFTA? If the WHFTA follows the precedent of the European Union, countries will be required to meet standards of "readiness" *before* they enter the organization. Thus, researchers at the Institute of International Economics have devised a "readiness" index for Latin American and Caribbean countries, based on criteria such as price and exchange rate stability, budget discipline, and level of democracy. According to their index, Chile, Trinidad, and Tobago (with equal scores of 4.4 on a 5-point scale) are best prepared for economic integration with the United States and Canada, followed by Mexico and Venezuela (3.9), Colombia, Bolivia, Paraguay, and Uruguay (3.7), Argentina (2.6), and Brazil (2.3).[43]

According to another point of view, membership in the WHFTA should be open to any country that commits to remove all tariff and nontariff restrictions on the movement of goods, services, and investment capital before a fixed date in the future. Thus, countries that have not already achieved a specified level of "readiness" would be able to participate in the WHFTA if they are willing to move toward free trade. According to its adherents, this approach will allow the WHFTA to expand more rapidly, will reduce the probability of trade diversion in the WHFTA, and will support the development of market institutions in the countries that need them most.[44] This open-door policy would not be workable if the WHFTA had a short-term objective of monetary or political union, but nobody has suggested that level of integration.

What Structure for the WHFTA? One option for the WHFTA is a **hub-and-spoke structure,** requiring a single country (probably the United States) to negotiate separate agreements with each of the new members. Alternatively, the WHFTA can have a **plurilateral structure,** with a unified system of rules and negotiations for the entire group.

A hub-and-spoke arrangement has at least two possible advantages: (1) negotiations can begin immediately without the creation of any new regional institutions; and (2) agreements between the "hub" country and the other nations and subregional groups (such as MERCOSUR) can be adapted to special circumstances and needs; there is no need to create a "one-size-fits-all" agreement. On the other hand, this structure has several serious disadvantages: (1) only the hub country is involved in broad hemispheric relations; the other countries and groups have little new contact with one another;

---

[42]Albert Fishlow has suggested, for example, that Taiwan or Korea could be the next country, after the United States, Canada, Mexico, and Chile, to join the WHFTA. See his "Latin America Transformed: An Accounting," *New Perspectives* 10 (Fall 1993), 25–26.

[43]Study by Gary Clyde Hufbauer and Jeffrey Schott, described in Paul Kelash, "So, Barbados Is Better? Economists Say Caribbean Should Be Next into NAFTA," *LDC Debt Report/Latin American Markets* 7 (July 11, 1994): 1.

[44]Rudiger Dornbusch, "2005: A Trade Odyssey," *The International Economy* 7 (September/October 1993), 59–61.

(2) preferential arrangements with the hub country may cause trade diversion; and (3) the hub country will be burdened with endless negotiations and disputes; for example, the host may be criticized for granting concessions to one country or group that it does not grant to others.

Based on these considerations, economists are nearly unanimous in their preference for a plurilateral rather than a hub-and-spoke structure.[45] This could be accomplished, for example, by adding an accession clause to NAFTA, providing open membership to countries that have fulfilled, or commit to fulfill, certain requirements. A new member could quickly gain free access to the markets of all the other members, not only the market of a hub country.

The size and distribution of gains and losses arising from a WHFTA would depend, among other things, on the scale and structure of the organization, and on the degree of trade and investment liberalization. The specific arguments for and against a WHFTA are quite similar to the arguments that surrounded the adoption of NAFTA. According to researchers at the Institute for International Economics, expanding NAFTA to include the entire Western Hemisphere would cause hemispheric GDP to grow by an additional 18 percent over a twelve-year period. In the United States, they estimate that exports would expand by an additional $36 billion, the trade surplus would increase, and about 60,000 new jobs would be created.[46]

Will progress continue toward the creation of a WHFTA? That will depend, in large part, on two considerations — one economic and one political. First, progress will be more likely to continue if we experience steady economic growth. A deep recession could rekindle protectionist sentiments and make trade negotiations very difficult. Second, continued progress will require all of the countries in the hemisphere, including the United States, to engage in a "redefinition of sovereignty."[47] New lines of authority will have to be drawn between national governments, international agencies, and the free flow of market forces. In the words of that very American poet, Robert Frost, "Good fences make good neighbors." Americans, like others around the world, must learn how to be good neighbors in a world with fewer fences.

SUMMARY

The Western Hemisphere is still a New World with a relatively low population density and high rate of immigration, currently experiencing a new wave of market liberalization. The hemispheric level of income is relatively high, but foreign trade dependency is relatively low. The United States is the

---

[45]See, for example, Fishlow, "Latin America Transformed," 25; Dornbusch, "2005: A Trade Odyssey," 61; and the views of Hufbauer and Schott in Kelash, "So, Barbados Is Better," 1.

[46]Lia Richwine, "U.S. Exports Would Jump $36 Billion with Expanded NAFTA, Study Says," States News Service, July 6, 1994.

[47]Sidney Weintraub, "Western Hemisphere Free Trade: Probability or Pipe Dream?" *Annals of the American Academy of Political and Social Sciences* 526 (March 1993): 19.

dominant power; other countries have many differences, but share a dominant culture grounded in European Judeo-Christianity and post-colonialism.

In the United States, the end of colonialism led to chronic economic protectionism, based on the doctrines of Alexander Hamilton. U.S. trade barriers trended downward after 1934, with passage of the Trade Agreements Act. Latin American countries adopted protectionist policies of import substitution during the early 1930s. These continued until the 1970s, when the "Chicago Boys" gained influence in Chile, and the 1980s, when the debt crisis caused many other Latin American countries to switch from policies of import substitution to export promotion.

Proposals for economic integration in the Western Hemisphere have been circulating since the 1880s, when James Blaine's plan for a hemispheric customs union was rejected by Latin America. During the 1960s, Latin American countries tried to create free trade areas, intentionally excluding the United States and Canada, to support their policies of import substitution. These schemes, including the CACM, LAFTA (later LAIA), CARICOM, and ANCOM were generally unsuccessful; they fell prey to regional disputes and protectionist philosophies.

Also during the 1960s, the United States extended a major program of aid and cooperation to Latin America through the Alliance for Progress. The Alliance fell short of its lofty goals, but provided support for moderate economic and social progress in Latin America.

Latin American external indebtedness grew rapidly in the late 1970s, and reached a crisis stage in 1982. Beginning in 1985, countries undertaking market-oriented reforms were able to obtain new lending from international agencies under the Baker and Brady Plans. These programs of economic reform and financial relief have substantially reduced the debt burden in Latin America.

Announced in 1990, the Enterprise for the Americas Initiative called for liberalization of trade and investment, creation of new facilities for investment finance, and promotion of continued progress on the debt problem, including the use of debt-for-nature swaps. Some progress has been made in all of these areas, but the financial and debt reduction goals have been particularly difficult to meet.

Progress toward broad Western Hemispheric integration began with the Canada-U.S. Free Trade Agreement (CUFTA, which became effective in 1989), and took a major step forward with the implementation of the North American Free Trade Agreement (NAFTA), beginning in 1994. NAFTA calls for eventual elimination of all tariff barriers between the United States, Canada, and Mexico, liberalization of external investment, financial services, and transport, and creation of institutions to resolve trade, environmental, and labor disputes. Despite enormous disagreement and controversy on the subject, formal economic studies generally suggest that NAFTA will raise income levels, wages, and employment in all three of the member countries, but the largest gains will go to Mexico.

Since the adoption of NAFTA, new regional organizations have been created in Latin America, such as MERCOSUR, and some of the old organizations have been reorganized and energized. Trade barriers within Latin America have been substantially reduced. Furthermore, many of these countries are now receptive to a broad free trade agreement for the Western Hemisphere. If progress continues toward an agreement of this kind, its success or failure will depend on the resolution of several issues: What level of integration will be attempted? Which countries will be allowed to join, and under what conditions? How will the organization be structured, and exactly how will countries become members? According to one estimate, a broad free trade agreement would increase hemispheric GDP by about 18 percent over twelve years. Movement toward this goal will require political ingenuity and courage.

DISCUSSION AND REVIEW QUESTIONS

1. What do the countries of the Western Hemisphere have in common? How do they differ? Based on these similarities and differences, should economic integration in the Western Hemisphere be more or less difficult than in Europe?

2. At various times in their histories, what has caused the countries of the Western Hemisphere to adopt protectionist and liberal trade policies? How long do you think the current stage of liberalism will continue?

3. Why were early U.S. proposals for Western Hemispheric integration rejected by Latin American leaders? Why are they more receptive today?

4. Compare and contrast the Alliance for Progress and Enterprise for the Americas programs. Why were they introduced? What were their objectives? Were they successful?

5. Based on the experience of the European Union, CUFTA, and NAFTA, what issues will need to be resolved to move forward with creation of a free trade area for the Western Hemisphere? Is this a reasonable objective? How long will it take?

SUGGESTED READINGS

Grunwald, Joseph, et al. *Latin American Economic Integration and U.S. Policy.* Washington, D.C.: Brookings Institution, 1972. *Based on a background study for the 1967 meeting of Western Hemisphere heads of state, this book encouraged U.S. leaders to support Latin American regional integration. It also provides an early discussion of prospects for broader cooperation in the hemisphere.*

McKinney, Joseph A., and M. Rebecca Sharpless, eds. *Implications of a North American Free Trade Region: Multidisciplinary Perspectives.* Waco, Tex.: Baylor University Press, 1992. *Separate chapters by eighteen authors analyze the economic, political, legal, social, and cultural implications of the North American Free Trade Agreement from Canadian, Mexican, and U.S. perspectives.*

Perloff, Harvey S. *Alliance for Progress: A Social Invention in the Making*. Baltimore: Johns Hopkins Press, 1969. *Written by one of its architects, this book provides an inside account of the Alliance for Progress, from its roots in the Good Neighbor Policy to an assessment of its initial results.*

Rosenberg, Jerry M. *The New American Community*. New York: Praeger, 1992. *Argues that the Western Hemisphere should borrow heavily from the European experience and move quickly to a high level of political and economic integration. Includes proposals for a New American Community Treaty, a standards policy, a social charter, and a formal structure for the Community, including a parliamentary body.*

Weintraub, Sidney, special editor. *Free Trade in the Western Hemisphere*. Special issue of *Annals of the American Academy of Political and Social Sciences*, 526 (March 1993). *Chapters by separate authors discuss the possibilities for a broad free trade area in the Western Hemisphere, and explore its historical, strategic, economic, and institutional implications.*

INTERNET RESOURCES

Americas
Florida International University
http://americas.fiu.edu/

Center for the Study of Western Hemispheric Trade
University of Texas at El Paso
http://www.borderbase.utep.edu/cswht/

Market of the South (MERCOSUR)
gopher://gopher.cr-df.rnp.br:70/11/assunto/mercosul

NAFTAnet (electronic commerce)
http://www.nafta.net/

NAFTA & Inter-American Trade Monitor
gopher://gopher.etext.org:70/00/Politics/NAFTA.Monitor/

NAFTA Implementation Resource Guide
gopher://una.hh.lib.umich.edu:70/00/ebb/general/nafta.tel

North American Free Trade Agreement (NAFTA)
http://the-tech.mit.edu/Bulletins/nafta.html

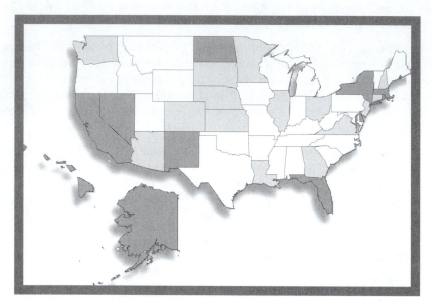

United States: Share of Services in Employment, 1996

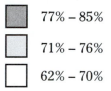

77% – 85%

71% – 76%

62% – 70%

Source: U.S. Bureau of Labor Statistics.

7

THE UNITED STATES: THE SERVICE ECONOMY

Here individuals of all nations are melted into a new race of men, whose labors will one day cause great changes in the world.

—J. H. ST. JOHN DE CRÉVECOEUR
LETTERS FROM AN AMERICAN FARMER, 1782

In the United States a man builds a house in which to spend his old age, and he sells it before the roof is on; . . . he brings a field into tillage and leaves other men to gather the crops; he embraces a profession and gives it up; he settles in a place, which he soon afterward leaves to carry his changeable longings elsewhere.

—ALEXIS DE TOCQUEVILLE
DEMOCRACY IN AMERICA, 1840

any readers of this book—including those who are not Americans—will already be familiar with the economic system of the United States. However, a quick review of the subject is warranted for at least two reasons. First, the comparative perspective of this book should allow us to gain new insights into the nature of the American system. We will ask, what is it about the U.S. economy that is truly unique? In later chapters, it will sometimes be helpful to use the United States as a basis of comparison.

Second, the United States produces more goods and services—valued at eight trillion dollars in 1997—than any other country in the world. Despite spectacular growth in many other countries since World War II, the American economy is still twice as large as the Japanese, and nearly as large as the *combined* economies of the fifteen members of the European community.[1] Clearly, our analysis of world economic systems would be incomplete without consideration of the United States.

THE ENVIRONMENT

A significant part of American economic growth and prosperity can be attributed to the richness of its natural resources. The United States claims only 5 percent of the world's population, but approximately 7 percent of its land area, over 15 percent of its copper and cadmium reserves, and over 20 percent of its reserves of coal, lead, silver, and zinc.[2] American croplands are among the most fertile in the world and benefit from an exceptionally mild climate. According to recent research, resource abundance played a key role in the development of America's industrial sector, particularly during the period between 1890 and 1940.[3]

Nonetheless, the prosperity of the United States is only partially explained by its rich natural endowment. Russia, for example, has 80 percent more land area and larger reserves of fossil fuels, gold, diamonds, manganese, and platinum-group metals. Some of the world's poorest countries, including many in Africa, are more favorably endowed (on a per capita basis) with land and minerals.[4]

The American labor force descended from a multinational assortment of religious and political dissidents, opportunists, and slaves. In many cases, the experiences of these groups instilled a disdain for higher authority. Thus, America is known as a "melting pot" nation and the home of "rugged individualism." These two aspects of American society have left a lasting imprint on the economy.

The philosophy of individualism, for example, is the basis of the so-called American Dream—the idea that anyone can "pull himself up by his bootstraps" to a higher standard of living through frugality and hard work. The dream was personified by such men as Andrew Carnegie, the son of poor Scottish immigrants. Carnegie started work at the age of thirteen as a bobbin boy in a Pennsylvania cloth mill and eventually built a steel empire that he sold in 1900 for over $400 million. He argued that individual freedom and competition are "best for the race" because they ensure "the survival of the fittest in every department."[5]

---

[1]Total GDP was about $2.5 trillion in Japan, $6.1 trillion in the United States, and $6.5 trillion in the 15 current members of the European Union in 1992, according to estimates of population and GDP per capita at purchasing power parity in the United Nations Development Programme, *Human Development Report 1994* (New York: Oxford University Press, 1995), 203, 208.

[2]U.S. Bureau of Mines estimates reported in D. Hargreaves and S. Fromson, *World Index of Strategic Minerals* (New York: Facts on File, 1983), 31ff.

[3]Gavin Wright, "The Origins of American Industrial Success, 1879–1940," *American Economic Review* 80 (September 1990): 651–668.

[4]For a ranking of nations in terms of their potential organic and mineral production, see S. R. Eyre, *The Real Wealth of Nations* (New York: St. Martin's Press, 1978), 116–129.

[5]*The North American Review* of 1889, quoted in Daniel Fusfeld's *The Age of the Economist* (Glenview, Ill.: Scott, Foresman and Co., 1972), 82.

Americans generally believe that individual wealth is the reward for hard work and frugality; Europeans are more likely to attribute large accumulations of wealth to inheritance. As a result, Americans are relatively uncomfortable with governmental schemes to redistribute income. Opinion surveys have found little support for major redistribution schemes, even among the poorest Americans. According to an international poll by the Times Mirror organization, only 23 percent of Americans believe "the state has a responsibility to take care of poor people who can't take care of themselves," compared to 50 percent of Germans, 62 percent of the French and British, 66 percent of Italians, and 71 percent of Spaniards.[6] Accordingly, the U.S. government allocates a smaller share of national income to social security and welfare programs than the governments of most European countries.[7]

The philosophy of individualism may also help to explain the American preoccupation with higher education. In 1991, about 66 percent of Americans in their early twenties were full-time students in colleges and universities, compared to about 39 percent of young people in Japan and 30 percent in the European Union.[8]

The "melting pot" also has its economic ramifications. On the positive side of the ledger, the United States benefits from the diversity of skills and talents that its ethnic groups have mastered.[9] On the other hand, some economic problems are obviously caused by racial discrimination and by the fact that millions of Americans have serious difficulty with spoken English.

Furthermore, the "melting pot" may provide another explanation for the relatively low level of U.S. welfare spending. In France, Italy, West Germany, and Sweden, each population is relatively homogeneous in terms of race and religion. As a result, there is little perception in these countries that welfare payments represent a transfer of income from one identifiable segment of society to another. In the United States, despite the fact that two-thirds of the people living below the poverty line are white, the perception persists that welfare payments only serve to redistribute income from whites to other races. Not too surprisingly, this perception provokes an unusual amount of political opposition.

THE CHANGING STRUCTURE OF THE ECONOMY

Compared with the nations of Western Europe, America is a relative latecomer to industrialization. In 1840, when only 23 percent of the British labor force was working in agriculture, about 69 percent of American laborers

---

[6]"What Europeans Think," *Los Angeles Times*, September 17, 1991, special edition, H/B.

[7]In 1992, the United States devoted 7 percent of GDP to social security benefits; the average for the European Union was 13 percent. See United Nations Development Programme, *Human Development Report 1995*, 203.

[8]United Nations Development Programme, *Human Development Report 1995*, 200.

[9]For a provocative assessment of the role of ethnicity in U.S. economic development, see Thomas Sowell, *The Economics and Politics of Race* (New York: William Morrow, 1983), Chapter 6.

continued to farm. As late as 1900, more Americans were employed in agriculture than in the industrial or service sectors (Table 7.1).

According to Adam Smith, writing in the 1770s, America's commitment to agriculture was extremely beneficial:

It has been the principal cause of the rapid progress of our American colonies towards wealth and greatness, that almost their whole capitals have hitherto been employed in agriculture. They have no manufactures, those household and coarser manufactures excepted which necessarily accompany the progress of agriculture, and which are the work of women and children in every private family.[10]

In this, Smith undoubtedly was influenced by his French acquaintances, the Physiocrats, who believed that agricultural workers are always more productive than industrial workers. According to Smith, "As a marriage which affords three children is certainly more productive than one which affords only two; so the labor of farmers and country laborers is certainly more productive than that of merchants, artificers, and manufacturers."[11] In addition, Smith undoubtedly realized that American soil and climate were perfect for agriculture.

The French Revolution and the Napoleonic Wars (1785–1815) further enhanced the benefits of American agriculture. As a neutral power, America was able to export agricultural goods to all sides and foreign demand was so great that U.S. export prices more than doubled between 1794 and 1799.[12]

■ TABLE 7.1

UNITED STATES: PERCENTAGE DISTRIBUTION OF EMPLOYMENT, 1870–2005

Year	Agriculture	Industry	Services
1870	47	27	26
1900	35	34	31
1920	24	41	35
1940	19	35	46
1960	8	41	51
1980	4	32	64
1990	3	27	70
1995	3	20	77
2005	3	17	80

Sources: 1870–1940: Victor Fuchs, *The Service Economy* (New York: National Bureau of Economic Research, 1968), 24, 30; 1960–1990: *Economic Report of the President* (Washington, D.C.: USGPO, 1997), Tables B33 and B44. The forecasts for the year 2005 are baseline projections of the U.S. Department of Labor, reported in James C. Franklin, "Industry Output and Employment Projections to 2005," *Monthly Labor Review* 118 (November 1995): 47.

[10]Adam Smith, *An Inquiry into the Nature and Causes of the Wealth of Nations* (New York: P. F. Collier, 1909 [1776]), 308.

[11]Ibid., 460.

[12]D. C. North, *The Economic Growth of the United States* (Englewood Cliffs, N.J.: Prentice-Hall, 1961), 25–26.

The resulting agricultural boom frustrated Alexander Hamilton's desire to launch America into an early industrialization.

INDUSTRIAL GROWTH

Led by the creation of national transportation and communication networks, America finally embarked on a stage of industrial growth during the first half of the nineteenth century. The successful completion of the Erie Canal in 1825, linking New York City with the agricultural regions in western New York, reduced transportation costs in that region by 90 percent. A boom in canal-building resulted and by 1859 some 1.6 billion ton-miles of cargo were being transported on canals. In 1828, the first steam railway in America, the Baltimore and Ohio, commenced operations. By 1840, America had a rail network of over 3,000 miles of track; by 1860 it exceeded 30,000 miles. Samuel Morse invented a practical telegraph in 1837 and the telegraph lines of Western Union reached the Pacific by 1861.

These rapid advances in transportation and communication formed a national market. Coal could now be moved from the rich fields in Pennsylvania to the industrial centers of the East. Large factories could be built with the assurance that their output could be sold throughout the country and overseas. Industrialization had begun and it was sustained by two distinctively American production technologies—the system of interchangeable parts (introduced by Eli Whitney in 1801) and the moving assembly line (introduced at Ford Motors in 1913). By the 1880s, many of the classic American industrial giants were well established—Standard Oil, Westinghouse, Edison General Electric, Western Electric, Singer, John Deere, and National Cash Register, to name a few. By the mid–1880s, America had bypassed Great Britain to become the world's leading producer of industrial goods. It still holds that position today.[13]

THE RISE OF THE SERVICE SECTOR

Although the United States is still the largest industrial power in the world, the dominance of the industrial sector *within* the American economy was relatively short-lived. Industry employed more laborers than agriculture and the service sector for less than 30 years—from the early 1900s to the mid–1920s (Table 7.1). In contrast, the plurality of British workers was involved in industrial production for over 100 years—from the 1840s until the late 1960s.[14]

By 1960, over half the U.S. labor force was employed in the service sector, and that proportion has continued to rise. In other words, the majority of

---

[13]W. W. Rostow, *The World Economy: History and Prospect* (Austin: University of Texas Press, 1978), 52–53.

[14]Simon Kuznets, *Modern Economic Growth* (New Haven: Yale University Press, 1966), 106; and Organization for Economic Cooperation and Development, *National Accounts: 1964–1981*, vol. 2 (Paris, 1983), 275. Here, as elsewhere, I have adopted the method of aggregating detailed sectors into agriculture, industry, and services as described in Victor Fuchs, *The Service Economy* (New York: National Bureau of Economic Research, 1968), 16–17. In particular, transportation, communications, and utilities are included in industry rather than services.

American workers are what Adam Smith called "unproductive laborers"—people who do not produce a physical, tangible commodity.[15] Although the labor force has shifted from industry to services in all the advanced countries, the shift was more rapid and complete in the United States than in any other major country.

The first phase of service growth, between the end of the Civil War and the beginning of the Great Depression, was based on expansion of wholesale and retail trade. Growth in the trade network was a natural concomitant of the industrial growth that occurred during that era and was made possible by the improvements in transportation and communication noted earlier. Thus, the second half of the 1800s ushered in the large chain stores—A&P, Kroger, J. C. Penney, Woolworth, and Walgreen—and the giant mail-order houses—Montgomery Ward and Sears, Roebuck.

The second stage of growth in service employment was launched by the expansion of public services during the Great Depression. Government employment, which absorbed only 9 percent of the nation's labor force in 1929, encompassed 17 percent of the labor force in 1939. Since that time, the governmental share of employment has remained relatively stable.[16]

The causes of rapid growth in service employment since World War II have been a subject of extensive research, speculation, and controversy. Most cheerful is the **income elasticity hypothesis,** which suggests that the American people, having fulfilled their basic needs for food, clothing, and shelter, are able to devote much of their affluence to health, educational, recreational, and personal services. Thus, the growth of service employment is driven by rising domestic demand.

Least cheerful, perhaps, is the **deindustrialization hypothesis,** which suggests that the United States is losing the international competition for industrial jobs. Due to poor maintenance of American product quality, sluggish growth of manufacturing productivity, loss of technological leadership, and unfair foreign competitive practices, the hypothesis says that Americans are losing high-paying factory jobs, forcing them to accept "hamburger-flipping" service jobs.[17]

The deindustrialization thesis may describe the experiences of millions of Americans, but it can explain only a small part of service sector growth. Compared to its peak in 1979, employment in the goods-producing sector declined by about 2 million in 1996, but the service sector created more than 36 million jobs.[18] During the same years, the American share of world exports of manufactured goods actually increased by a small amount.[19] Furthermore,

---

[15]Smith, *Wealth of Nations,* 270–271.

[16]Thomas M. Stanback, Jr., et al., *Services: The New Economy* (Totowa, N.J.: Allanheld, Osmun, & Co., 1981), 12–13.

[17]See Barry Bluestone and Bennett Harrison, *The Deindustrialization of America* (New York: Basic Books, 1982), passim.

[18]*Economic Report of the President 1997* (Washington, D.C.: USGPO, 1997), 350–351.

[19]From 16.8 percent in 1979 to 17.4 percent in 1993 according to the *Statistical Abstract of the United States 1994* (Washington, D.C.: USGPO, 1994), Table 1243.

if America's service sector expanded because of lost manufacturing jobs, why did America's trade partners also experience growth of service employment?

Official data seem to be more consistent with the **cost disease hypothesis,** which is quite different from the demand elasticity and deindustrialization approaches.[20] According to this interpretation, the demand for services has grown at roughly the same rate as the demand for products, but labor productivity has grown much more slowly in the service sector (see Table 7.2). Thus, service employment has grown rapidly to compensate for the lower rate of productivity growth. Slow productivity growth has also raised production costs and prices in the service sector. Thus, the share of the service sector in GDP has been stable if measured in constant prices, but it has increased if measured in current (rising) prices.[21]

Two other supply-oriented hypotheses may also help to explain the growth of service employment. According to the **economies of scale hypothesis,** growth of the service sector arose from efforts to improve organizational efficiency. Many business tasks, such as accounting, computer programming, mailing, and printing, may be performed more efficiently if they are moved from small offices in industrial firms into specialized firms in the service sector.

The **labor supply hypothesis** emphasizes the changing structure of the labor force. In particular, the proportion of women in the American labor

---

■ **TABLE 7.2**

UNITED STATES: AVERAGE ANNUAL GROWTH OF OUTPUT PER WORKER, 1950–1994

Years	Total Production	Goods Production	Service Production
1950–1960	2.1	2.8	1.7
1960–1970	2.0	3.1	1.1
1970–1980	0.4	1.9	0.0
1980–1990	0.9	3.0	0.1
1990–1994	1.1	4.0	0.3

Sources: Author's calculations based on U.S. Department of Commerce, Bureau of the Census, *Historical Statistics of the United States, Colonial Times to 1970*, Part 2 (Washington, D.C.: USGPO, 1975), Series F32–56; and *Economic Report of the President* (Washington, D.C.: USGPO, 1997), Tables B–8, B–33, and B–44.

---

[20] William J. Baumol, Sue Anne Batey Blackman, and Edward N. Wolff, *Productivity and American Leadership: The Long View* (Cambridge: The MIT Press, 1989), Chapter 6; and Jeffrey G. Williamson, "Productivity and American Leadership: A Review Article," *Journal of Economic Literature* 29 (March 1991): 59–60.

[21] Between 1980 and 1995, the share of services in constant-price GDP increased by only 0.3 percentage points (from 52.9 percent to 53.2 percent); the share of services in current-price GDP increased by 8.3 percentage points (from 45.8 percent to 54.1 percent). See *Economic Report of the President 1997*, 308–309.

force increased from about 28 percent in 1950 to 46 percent in 1995, and many women have found employment in the service sector. Women account for less than 30 percent of employment in agriculture and industry, but they hold more than half the service jobs.

SIGNIFICANCE OF THE SHIFT TO SERVICES

The shift to services has profoundly influenced the structure and performance of the American economy. First, and most clearly, it has changed the nature of work and employment. More Americans are now engaged in sales (wholesale and retail) than in manufacturing. College students who may have prepared for engineering professions in the 1950s and 1960s are now more likely to specialize in business, legal, computer, health, educational, or recreational services. Compared with their industrial colleagues, service workers are more likely to be self-employed, to work at home, and to work part-time, but they are less likely to join labor unions.

Recent evidence suggests that growth of the service sector has contributed to greater income inequality in the United States. As the proportion of employment in manufacturing has declined, gains in service employment have been divided between low-income sectors, such as personal services and retail trade, and high-income sectors, such as financial and professional services. Furthermore, according to the Gini ratios reported in Table 7.3, incomes are distributed more unevenly *within* each of the service sectors than within manufacturing.

Still, the growth of service employment explains a relatively small part—maybe 10 or 20 percent—of the recent increase in American income inequality. More of the rise seems to be explained by a growing gap between the incomes of skilled and unskilled workers (caused in part by technological changes and foreign competition that reduce the relative demand for unskilled labor), by declining union membership, by growth in the number of single-income families, and by an increase in the proportion of part-time jobs.[22]

As we already noted, measured labor productivity has grown more slowly in the service sector than in the goods-producing sectors (Table 7.2). In fact, productivity improvements are inherently slow in many service activities; it takes four people just as long to perform a string quartet composition today as it did when the piece was written, perhaps hundreds of years ago.[23] The shift toward service employment has caused overall productivity growth to decelerate in the United States.

---

[22]Paul Ryscavage and Peter Henle, "Earnings Inequality Accelerates in the 1980s," *Monthly Labor Review* (December 1990): 3–16; Richard B. Freeman, "How Much Has DeUnionization Contributed to the Rise in Male Earnings Inequality?" in Sheldon Danziger and Peter Gottschalk, eds., *Uneven Tides: Rising Inequality in America* (New York: Russell Sage Foundation, 1993), 133–163; George J. Boorjas and Valerie A. Ramey, "Time Series Evidence on the Sources of Trends in Wage Inequality," *American Economic Review* 84 (May 1994): 10–16; and Gary Burtless, "International Trade and the Rise in Earnings Inequality," *Journal of Economic Literature* 33 (June 1995): 800–816.

[23]Baumol et al., *Productivity and American Leadership: The Long View,* 124–140.

■ **TABLE 7.3**

UNITED STATES: DISTRIBUTION OF EMPLOYMENT AND EARNINGS OF
MEN WORKING FULL TIME, 1978 AND 1987

	Percentage of Full-Time Employment		Average Earnings (dollars)		Gini Ratios	
	1978	1987	1978	1987	1978	1987
Agriculture	4.2	3.4	10,896	17,199	.448	.432
Industry:						
Manufacturing	30.0	25.5	17,692	30,619	.247	.286
Mining	1.2	1.0	20,899	35,738	.258	.282
Construction	7.8	8.8	16,730	25,994	.302	.306
TCPU*	9.1	10.1	18,233	31,407	.224	.252
Services:						
Wholesale trade	5.4	5.8	18,682	30,242	.296	.325
Retail trade	9.6	12.3	14,194	23,496	.314	.351
FIRE**	4.7	5.3	22,187	40,394	.344	.376
Business services	4.0	6.1	16,423	28,787	.347	.379
Personal services	1.5	1.6	12,420	20,295	.339	.357
Entertainment	0.7	1.0	14,601	26,705	.331	.360
Professional services	12.0	13.0	20,777	36,187	.350	.365
Public administration	7.4	6.1	18,233	29,966	.209	.229
Total	100.0	100.0	17,526	29,866	.296	.332

* TCPU—transportation, communications, and public utilities

** FIRE—finance, insurance, and real estate

Source: Paul Ryscavage and Peter Henle, "Earnings Inequality Accelerates in the 1980s," *Monthly Labor Review* (December 1990): Table 5.

Of course, part of this deterioration in productivity growth may be a statistical illusion; the output of service workers is very difficult to measure. How can the governmental statisticians know, for example, whether a college professor has performed her duties more effectively this year than she did last year? A lawyer? A social worker? How can we balance the life-saving improvements in medical technology against the unwillingness of doctors to make house calls?[24] Whatever its rate of growth, studies by the McKinsey Global Institute have found that the level of productivity in the American

---

[24]See Alfred L. Malabre, Jr., and Lindley H. Clark, Jr., "Productivity Statistics for the Service Sector May Understate Gains," *The Wall Street Journal*, August 12, 1992, A1.

service sector is substantially higher than the levels in Europe and Japan, particularly in the fields of banking, retail sales, and airline transportation.[25]

Possibly because of the slow growth of service productivity (emphasized in the cost-disease hypothesis), and possibly because the service sector faces little foreign competition, the rate of price inflation in the service sector is relatively high. Between 1970 and 1996, while the average annual rate of inflation for commodities was about 5 percent, the inflation rate for services was nearly 7 percent.[26] Price increases for medical services and college tuition have been particularly steep.

Even if service productivity has grown slowly in the past, retarding economic growth and fueling inflation, these trends may not continue in the future. If the technological achievements of the past were oriented toward goods production, recent advances in computer hardware and software and telecommunications technology are particularly useful for accounting firms, banks, educational institutions, and other services. Many service companies are attempting to improve labor productivity by strengthening their programs of employee training and benefits.[27]

Regardless of its effects on productivity and inflation, growth of the service sector has clearly increased the *stability* of employment and output. Except for small dips in 1958 and 1991, service employment grew every year between 1948 and 1996. Industrial employment drifted up and down with waves of the business cycle.[28]

Several factors may account for the apparent immunity of the service sector to recessions. First, many people in service occupations are self-employed, including more than 33 percent of lawyers, realtors, artists, barbers, and child-care workers; in contrast, less than 10 percent of industrial mechanics, technicians, and machine operators are self-employed.[29] Many service employees, including salespeople, waiters and waitresses, barbers and beauticians, realtors, and insurance agents, are paid on a commission or piecework basis. In all these cases, a drop in the market demand for services is likely to reduce the incomes of service workers, but it is not likely to cause them to lose their jobs. In industry, where wages are less flexible, a reduction in demand is more likely to result in unemployment.

---

[25]David Wessel, "U.S. Excels in Service Productivity Poll," *The Wall Street Journal*, October 13, 1992, A2; and Martin Dickson, Tony Jackson, and Louise Kehoe, "American Way of Serving Leads to Success," *Financial Times*, February 15, 1994, 4.

[26]*Economic Report of the President 1997*, 368. Again, this may be little more than a statistical illusion. Can we be sure, for example, how much the increased cost of health care was caused by higher prices per unit of care, and how much it was caused by an improvement in the quantity and quality of care?

[27]David Wessel, "With Labor Scarce, Service Firms Strive to Increase Productivity," *The Wall Street Journal*, June 1, 1989, 1.

[28]For a contrary view, suggesting that the stability of service employment is beginning to weaken, see Henry F. Myers, "Some Service Jobs May Get Less Stable," *The Wall Street Journal*, February 25, 1991, 1.

[29]See George Silvestri and John Lukasiewicz, "Occupational Employment Projections," *Monthly Labor Review* 114 (November 1991): 85–86.

Second, unlike manufactured goods, the output of the service sector usually cannot be stored in inventories. It is unlikely, therefore, that a surplus of services (which must be sold before production can resume) will be produced. The standard Keynesian theory of unemployment, based on an assumption of inflexible wages and an inventory adjustment mechanism, may have lost some of its relevance in an economy dominated by services.

A third reason for the stability of service employment is that governmental services usually are not reduced during recessions. In fact, new government workers may be hired to process the expanded load of claims for unemployment and welfare benefits.

Finally, in addition to its beneficial influence on the growth and stability of employment, the service sector also has contributed positively to the American balance of international payments. In 1993, when exports of merchandise fell short of imports by $133 billion, this deficit was partially offset by a $57 billion surplus on service transactions.[30] One of the major objectives of the United States in recent rounds of international trade negotiations has been to reduce barriers to trade in services.

INDUSTRIAL ORGANIZATION

Before the Civil War, the U.S. economy approximated the textbook model of perfect competition. Over half the labor force worked on small, owner-managed farms. In manufacturing, no single plant was known to control as much as 10 percent of the output of any product in the early 1800s. As late as 1870, the average firm in the iron and steel industry employed fewer than 100 people. Each firm produced a relatively homogeneous product, and the government played a very limited role in the economy.

The nationwide network of transportation and communication, in place by the end of the Civil War, enabled the age of Big Business to begin, led by the so-called captains of industry. By 1879, the Standard Oil trust (controlled by John D. Rockefeller) controlled about 90 percent of American oil refining, and by 1900 the Carnegie empire produced nearly half of the nation's steel.

The trend toward bigness accelerated after 1889 when the New Jersey legislature legalized the formation of holding companies. The resulting merger movement, which lasted until 1904, created the largest private corporations the world had known. In 1901, for example, J. P. Morgan formed America's first billion-dollar company, U.S. Steel, by merging the old Carnegie company with its eight largest competitors. By 1904, one or two giant firms controlled at least half of the output of 78 different industries. Just as significant, the age of the owner-managers—the captains of industry—began to give way to an age in which large corporations were run by professional managers who often had little stake in ownership.

---

[30] According to national income and product accounts. Also, see Ralph T. King, Jr., "U.S. Service Exports Are Growing Rapidly, But Almost Unnoticed," *The Wall Street Journal*, April 21, 1993, A1.

THE ANTITRUST MOVEMENT

A backlash against monopoly began in 1887 when the Interstate Commerce Commission was established to regulate railroad rates. The Sherman Antitrust Act, passed in 1890, prohibited any contract, combination, or conspiracy "in restraint of trade" or any attempt to monopolize "any part of the trade or commerce among the several States." Filling in more detail, the Clayton Antitrust Act of 1914 declared four specific practices to be illegal if their "effect was to substantially lessen competition or tend to create a monopoly":

Merger of competing companies

Price discrimination—charging different prices to different customers for the same product

Tying contracts—requiring a buyer to purchase goods from one seller

Interlocking directorates—directors of one company sitting on the boards of directors of competing companies

By international standards, the Sherman and Clayton acts established a strict American tradition of antitrust policy. They were enacted at a time when the European and Japanese governments were encouraging the formation of large enterprises, conglomerates, and cartels to compete on the battlefield of international trade. The governments in those countries were willing to sacrifice domestic competition for international competitiveness. The United States, with its enormous domestic market, was relatively independent of the foreign market, so public attention centered on domestic competition. Monopolies and cartels were perceived as a threat to domestic consumers.

In recent years, American antitrust policy has grown more permissive, while remaining strict by international standards. With the growing challenge of foreign competition, the American fear of domestic monopolies has been replaced gradually by a fear of foreign encroachment. New guidelines were issued in 1982 and 1984, liberalizing the Clayton Act to allow corporate mergers that reduce production and transportation costs. In 1984, Congress loosened the rules for companies to engage in joint research, clearing the way for alliances between such companies as IBM and Apple Computer. During the 1980s, with the White House under Republican control, the antitrust enforcement staffs of the Justice Department and the Federal Trade Commission were cut in half, and few actions were taken to prevent mergers or monopolization. The number and value of merger transactions increased rapidly after 1980, and they continued to grow after Democrats regained the White House in 1992 (Table 7.4).[31]

During the 1980s, the most significant American antitrust action was the breakup and deregulation of the world's largest corporation—the American Telephone & Telegraph Company. After a long court battle with the Justice

---

[31]For more information on the merger guidelines of 1968, 1982, 1984, 1987, and 1992, see Stephen Martin, *Industrial Economics*, 2d ed. (New York: McMillan, 1994), 317–323.

■ TABLE 7.4

UNITED STATES: MERGERS AND ACQUISITIONS, 1965–1996

Year	Number	Value (billion dollars)
1965	1,893	n.a.
1970	1,318	n.a.
1975	981	n.a.
1980	1,558	32.8
1982	2,298	60.7
1984	3,175	126.1
1986	2,523	220.8
1988	3,011	291.3
1990	4,312	206.8
1992	3,752	125.3
1994	4,962	276.5
1996	6,828	550.7

Source: MLR Publishing Company, *Mergers and Acquisitions*, March/April 1990, 95; September/October 1990, 88; March/April 1991, 103; and March/April 1997, 41.

Department, AT&T agreed in 1982 to divest itself of 22 local telephone companies, reducing its assets from $155 billion to about $43 billion. In return, the company gained greater freedom to set prices and to enter new areas of telecommunications and computing. At the same time, technological advances made it possible for new competitors to enter the long-distance business, and the AT&T share of the long-distance market fell from 84 percent in 1984 to 63 percent in 1991. Surprisingly, though, the new competition apparently did not lead to lower prices in the long-distance market.[32]

More recently, the U.S. Justice Department has kept a watchful eye on Microsoft Corporation, whose Windows operating system is installed in about 90 percent of all new personal computers worldwide. In 1994, the department accused Microsoft of using its market power to force PC manufacturers to accept anticompetitive licensing terms, and in 1995 it blocked Microsoft's acquisition of Intuit, another leading software company, and investigated its plans to enter the market for online information services. Microsoft accused the Justice Department of a "campaign of harassment."[33]

TRENDS IN BUSINESS SIZE AND CONCENTRATION

Although it is fairly clear that big businesses became more influential in America between 1860 and 1900, the more recent trends are difficult to assess. It is debatable whether large corporations play a more dominant role in

---

[32]William E. Taylor and Lester D. Taylor, "Postdivestiture Long-Distance Competition in the United States," *American Economic Review* 83 (May 1993): 185–190.

[33]Louise Kehoe, "Giant Snaps at Oppressors," *Financial Times*, June 30, 1995, 4.

the United States than they do in other countries, and whether their influence has grown in recent years.

Trends and levels of industrial concentration are measured in several ways. The most familiar yardstick is the **four-firm concentration ratio**—the percentage of total sales of the four largest firms in an industry. Concentration ratios for several American industries are presented in Table 7.5. According to these data, the levels of concentration range from very high (aluminum and automobiles) to very low (sporting goods and jewelry). The share of the four largest firms has risen in some industries (men's suits) and fallen in others (steel mills and audio/video equipment).

In international perspective, comparisons conducted by F. M. Scherer and Frederic Pryor indicate that the average level of industrial concentration in America is less than or roughly equal to levels in France, West Germany, Italy, Japan, and the United Kingdom. Concentration seems to be highest in such countries as Belgium, Canada, Sweden, and Switzerland, where the domestic markets (measured by population or GNP) are too small to accommodate a large number of competitors.[34]

In his classic study of trends in American industrial organization, Warren Nutter defined an industry to be effectively monopolistic if its four-firm concentration ratio exceeded 50 percent. Applying that criterion to the period between 1899 and 1937, he detected only a very slight increase—from 19 to

■ TABLE 7.5

UNITED STATES: FOUR-FIRM CONCENTRATION RATIOS IN SELECTED INDUSTRIES, 1947–1987 (PERCENTAGES)

	1947	1958	1967	1977	1987
Motor Vehicles	n.a.	n.a.	92	93	90
Aircraft	n.a.	83	69	59	72
Aluminum	100	n.a.	n.a.	76	74
Synthetic Rubber	n.a.	60	61	60	50
Steel Mills	50	53	48	45	44
Elevators	63	62	55	52	52
Men's Suits	9	11	17	21	34
Home Audio/Video Equipment	n.a.	n.a.	49	51	39
Sporting Goods	24	41	27	21	13
Jewelry	13	18	23	18	12

Source: U.S. Department of Commerce, Bureau of the Census, *1987 Census of Manufactures: Concentration Ratios in Manufacturing*, MC87-S-6 (Washington, D.C.: USGPO, 1992), Table 4.

---

[34]Frederic L. Pryor, *Property and Industrial Organization in Communist and Capitalist Nations* (Bloomington, Ind.: Indiana University Press, 1973), 199–205; F. M. Scherer and others, *The Economics of Multi-Plant Operation: An International Comparisons Study* (Cambridge: Harvard University Press, 1975), 218–219, 426–428.

20 percent—in the fraction of private production originating in monopolistic industries.[35] Likewise, for the 1947–1972 period, estimates by Scherer indicate a very small rise (about 2 percentage points) in the average concentration ratio for manufacturing industries.[36]

A more comprehensive assessment of recent trends (including those in agriculture and services) has been assembled by William Shepherd.[37] In Shepherd's study, each industry or sector of the economy is assigned to one of four categories:

Pure Monopoly—Market share near 100 percent, effective barriers to entry, control of prices.

Dominant Firm—A market share of 50 to 90 percent, no close rival, high entry barriers, control of prices.

Tight Oligopoly—Four-firm concentration ratio above 60 percent, stable market shares, medium or high entry barriers, rigid prices.

Effective Competition—Four-firm ratio below 40 percent, unstable market shares, flexible pricing.

Obviously, Shepherd was forced to make many judgment calls in his assignment of industries. In the end, he found that the market structure of the U.S. economy was rather stable between 1939 and 1958, but he detected a "remarkable" growth in competitiveness after 1958. According to his estimates, the share of national income originating in industries that are effectively competitive rose from 56 percent in 1958 to 77 percent in 1980 (Table 7.6).

■ **TABLE 7.6**

UNITED STATES: COMPETITIVE STRUCTURE OF THE ECONOMY, 1939–1980

Percentage share of national income originating in:

Year	Pure Monopoly	Domnant Firm	Tight Oligopoly	Effective Competition
1939	6.2	5.0	36.4	52.4
1958	3.1	5.0	35.6	56.3
1980	2.5	2.8	18.0	76.7

Source: William G. Shepherd, "Causes of Increased Competition in the U.S. Economy, 1939–1980," *Review of Economics and Statistics*, 64 (November 1982): 618.

---

[35]G. Warren Nutter and Henry A. Einhorn, *Enterprise Monopoly in the United States: 1899–1958* (New York: Columbia University Press, 1969), 50.

[36]F. M. Scherer, *Industrial Market Structure and Economic Performance*, 2d ed. (Chicago: Rand-Mc-Nally, 1980), Table 3.7.

[37]William G. Shepherd, "Causes of Increased Competition in the U.S. Economy, 1939–1980," *Review of Economics and Statistics* 64 (November 1982): 613–626.

In Shepherd's opinion, over half the increase in American competition during the years before 1980 was caused directly or indirectly by stricter enforcement of antitrust laws. In addition, he notes the importance of rising import competition and deregulation of the transport, communications, and banking industries.

As we noted earlier, lenient enforcement of antitrust laws allowed a huge wave of corporate mergers after 1980. For several reasons, though, the merger boom may not have reversed the trend toward competition. First, many of these mergers were of the *conglomerate* variety, uniting noncompeting firms in different industries. Thus, some American companies grew larger and more diversified, but concentration ratios did not necessarily increase for individual product lines.[38] Second, continued growth of the service sector increased the number of small, entrepreneurial firms. The proportion of the labor force working in small establishments (those with less than 100 employees) actually increased from 54 percent in 1980 to 56 percent in 1991.[39] And third, domestic firms were exposed to an increasing volume of foreign competition. Measured in constant prices, the share of imports in GNP increased from 7 percent in 1980 to 13 percent in 1995.[40]

THE SOCIAL COSTS OF INDUSTRIAL CONCENTRATION

Although large corporations may not dominate the U.S. economy, they certainly control a number of important markets. For several reasons, the American public has long been concerned about the economic and political power of concentrated industries. First, opinion surveys indicate that Americans simply do not trust corporate executives. The public has more confidence in the military, the church, the police, the presidency, and the news media; among major institutions, only the Congress and the criminal justice system inspire a lower level of confidence than big business.[41] Although 64 percent of Americans believe the moral and ethical standards of small business owners are "excellent" or "good," only 31 percent trust the ethics of corporate executives.[42]

---

[38]Conglomerates seem to operate with lower administrative, marketing, and interest costs than other firms in their industries, and they earn higher profit margins on revenues, but they do not, on average, earn a higher rate of return on stockholders' equity. See Winson B. Lee and Elizabeth S. Cooperman, "Conglomerates in the 1980s: A Performance Appraisal," *Financial Management* 18 (Spring 1989): 45–54.

[39]*Statistical Abstract of the United States 1989*, Table 859; and *Statistical Abstract of the United States 1994*, Table 845.

[40]*Economic Report of the President 1997*, 302–303. For evidence that import competition significantly tightened profit margins during 1976–1986, see Michelle M. Katics and Bruce C. Petersen, "The Effect of Rising Import Competition on Market Power: A Panel Study of U.S. Manufacturing," *Journal of Industrial Economics* 42 (September 1994): 277–285. For an opposing view, see M. M. Saghafi and M. Attaran, "Is This the Beginning of the End in the Competitive Trend?" *Eastern Economic Journal* 16 (April-June 1990): 125–132.

[41]Frank Newport and Lydia Saad, "Confidence in Institutions," *The Gallup Poll Monthly*, April 1994, 5.

[42]A 1992 Harris poll, reported in Karlyn H. Bowman and others, "How's Business?" *The Public Perspective* 5 (November/December 1993): 83.

Second, many Americans believe that the profits of large corporations are excessive, contributing to an unequal distribution of income and wealth, and about 62 percent of Americans believe that businesses have "lost sight of human values in the pursuit of profits."[43] Indeed, a number of studies have found that profit rates tend to be above average in industries that have four-firm concentration ratios above 50 or 60 percent.[44] On the other hand, another study has found that the incomes of the most affluent households would fall by less than 1.5 percent and the remaining income groups would experience gains of less than 1 percent if the four-firm concentration ratios of all American manufacturing industries were reduced to a maximum of 40 percent.[45]

Questions have also been raised about the efficiency of large corporations. Traditional economic theory suggests that monopolistic firms will restrict their level of production below the competitive level, reducing the allocative efficiency of the economy. In the American context, estimates of this efficiency loss range from paltry (0.1 percent of GNP) to significant (4 to 7 percent of GNP).[46]

According to Harvey Leibenstein, monopolistic corporations may also be guilty of what he calls **x-inefficiency**—that is, without the discipline of competition they may make little effort to fully minimize their costs of production. Adam Smith noted two centuries ago, "monopoly . . . is a great enemy to good management." Although most of the evidence is anecdotal, this problem is undoubtedly a real one. In several cases, when former monopolists have been confronted by the pressure of competition, they have been able to cut their unit costs by 10 to 20 percent and more.[47] On the other hand, a decade of corporate restructuring may have reduced this problem in sectors exposed to foreign competition.

Some economists believe that large corporations pose a threat to the macroeconomic stability of the American economy. In recent years, the federal government has concluded that failures of large industrial corporations would have such a detrimental effect on the entire economy that it has sometimes stepped in to bail them out. If large corporations are reasonably sure that the government will not allow them to fail, they may be even more prone to x-inefficiency.

Moreover, it is often alleged that the corporate giants contribute to macroeconomic instability through their handling of capital investment. About half of all capital expenditures in manufacturing are controlled by the 200 largest firms. If a relatively small number of corporate executives become pessimistic about the business outlook, a significant downturn in investment

---

[43] A 1991 Roper survey, reported in Bowman and others, "How's Business," 1.

[44] This literature is reviewed in Martin, *Industrial Economics,* Chapter 7; and Michael Salinger, "The Concentration-Margins Relationship Reconsidered," *Brookings Papers on Economic Activity: Microeconomics* (1990): 287–335.

[45] Irene Powell, "The Effect of Reductions in Concentration on Income Distribution," *Review of Economics and Statistics* 69 (February 1987): 75–82.

[46] Scherer, *Industrial Market Structure and Economic Performance,* 459–464.

[47] Ibid., 464–466.

spending may occur, possibly resulting in a business recession. According to John Kenneth Galbraith, recessionary trends in competitive industries are self-limiting and self-correcting, but concentrated industries are "inherently unstable."[48]

BIG BUSINESS DEFENDED

In defense of the large corporations, many economists believe that the standard measures of market power (for example, the four-firm concentration ratio) significantly overstate the extent of monopoly. They point to several sources of competition that are commonly ignored. For example, the ratios seldom take account of competition from imports or from substitutes that are produced by other industries (for example, competition between aluminum foil, plastic wrap, and waxed paper producers).

William Baumol argues that monopoly profits are constrained by the threat of potential competition. Concentrated markets operate very much like competitive markets, he says, as long as they are "contestable"—that is, as long as other companies are free to enter.[49] Unfortunately, according to Stephen Martin, "no real-world industry has yet been shown to be contestable."[50]

John Kenneth Galbraith contends that the power of monopolistic sellers is often withstood by the **countervailing power** of monopolistic buyers. Large steel producers, for example, are faced by large, powerful purchasers of steel in the automobile industry, and large producers of consumer goods are faced by Sears and the other large retail chains.

Even if it can be shown that the exercise of monopoly power results in various forms of allocative and x-inefficiencies, these costs must be balanced against the savings that accrue from large-scale research, production, and marketing. Indeed, according to the **efficiency hypothesis,** formulated and tested by Harold Demsetz of UCLA and the University of Chicago, the high profit rates of corporations in highly concentrated industries are explained, not by abuses of market power, but by superior efficiency and low production costs.[51] According to Yale Brozen, also from the University of Chicago:

Concentration occurs and persists where it is the efficient structure for producing and distributing a product and for adapting to changing technical possibilities, shifting demand, and increasing regulatory requirements. . . . Where centralization is not efficient, industries do not become concentrated.[52]

---

[48]On the macroeconomic stability of competitive and concentrated industries, see John Kenneth Galbraith, *Economics and the Public Purpose* (Boston: Houghton Mifflin, 1973), 179.

[49]William J. Baumol, "Contestable Markets, Antitrust, and Regulation," *The Wharton Magazine* 7 (Fall 1982): 24.

[50]Martin, *Industrial Economics*, 224.

[51]Harold Demsetz, "Industry Structure, Market Rivalry, and Public Policy," *Journal of Law and Economics* 16 (April 1973):1–10. For recent support of the efficiency hypothesis, see E. Woodrow Eckard, "A Note on the Profit-Concentration Relation," *Applied Economics* 27 (February 1995): 219–223.

[52]Yale Brozen, *Concentration, Mergers, and Public Policy* (New York: Macmillan, 1982), 56–57.

THE LABOR MARKET

Neoclassical theory suggests that employment and wages are determined by the supply and demand of labor if labor markets are sufficiently competitive. In comparison with many other industrial capitalist countries, the U.S. labor market seems to be relatively competitive, and it may be growing more competitive through time.

On the employers' side of the market, there is little evidence of widespread monopsonistic power of the kind that would depress wages below their competitive levels. Studies of local labor markets have found that a very small percentage of American workers live in towns where the ten largest firms employ over half the labor force. Furthermore, the average American manufacturing establishment had a smaller number of employees (implying a lower level of market power) in 1992 than in 1947.[53]

From the employees' perspective, labor unions are the most important expressions of market power, but only 15.5 percent of American workers are presently enrolled in unions. That proportion has been falling since the mid–1950s, when it peaked at about 27 percent. Union membership rates are much higher in Western Europe than in the United States, with the exceptions of France and Switzerland.

Thus, the American labor market seems to be relatively competitive, but this raises another question. Neoclassical theory suggests that unregulated competitive markets should adjust to a supply-demand equilibrium, leaving no surplus or shortage of the commodity in question. However, the United States and other capitalist countries have experienced a persistent labor surplus, or unemployment. How can this be explained?

A full discussion of unemployment would take us far afield, but a few words are in order. Neoclassical theory suggests that unemployment is caused by downward inflexibility of nominal wages, stemming from long-term labor contracts, minimum wage laws, unemployment compensation, and the like. Keynesians would say that a reduction in nominal wage rates may not reduce unemployment; it may only reduce labor income and the aggregate demand for goods.

According to comparative data, although unemployment rates increased in all major capitalist countries between 1973 and 1995, the rate increased by a smaller amount in the United States than in most other countries. Thus, the American unemployment rate was higher than the average for members of the European Union before 1979, but it has been significantly lower since 1983 (Figure 7.1). Equally important, the incidence of long-term unemployment (one year or more of joblessness) is much lower in the United States than in Japan or most of Europe (refer to Table 2.8).

How did the United States improve its relative employment performance during the 1980s? This is a complex question that cannot be treated

---

[53]U.S. Department of Commerce, Bureau of the Census, *1987 Census of Manufacturers*, MC87-S-5 (Washington, D.C.: USGPO, 1991), 5–3; and *Statistical Abstract of the United States 1996*, Table 1210.

■ FIGURE 7.1

UNITED STATES AND EUROPEAN UNION: UNEMPLOYMENT RATES, 1973–1995 (PERCENT)

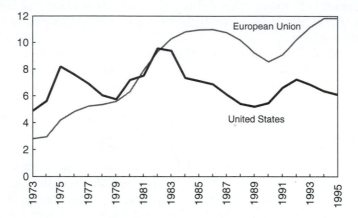

adequately here. In a nutshell, it seems that Americans held or regained their jobs by accepting relatively small wage increases. Between 1970 and 1993, real compensation per employee increased by about 77 percent in the average country of Western Europe, but by only 8 percent in the United States.[54] Why were American workers willing to settle for much smaller wage increases than their European counterparts? Some analysts base their explanations on the low level of union membership and militancy in the United States. Others point to the relatively modest program of unemployment benefits in the United States, and to the rising percentages of young, unskilled, and immigrant workers in the labor force.[55]

REASONS FOR DECLINING UNIONIZATION

Earlier, we noted that American union membership declined from 27 percent of the labor force in the mid–1950s to about 15 percent today. Approximately one-fifth of this decline can be attributed to the growth of the service economy.[56] As we have seen, firms in the service sector tend to be smaller than industrial firms, and many service workers are self-employed. Thus, the service sector is less susceptible than industry to union activity. In 1994, union members accounted for less than 14 percent of service employment

---

[54]Author's calculations, based on annual growth rates of compensation per employee and on consumer price inflation rates in *OECD Economic Outlook* 56 (December 1994), Annex Tables 11 and 15.

[55]For a full discussion of these issues, see Richard R. Freeman, "Evaluating the European View that the United States Has No Unemployment Problem," *American Economic Review* 78 (May 1988): 294–299; Charles R. Bean, "European Unemployment: A Survey," *Journal of Economic Literature* 32 (June 1994): 573–619; and George J. Borjas, "The Economics of Immigration," *Journal of Economic Literature* 32 (December 1994): 1667–1717.

[56]This is the estimate given in Henry S. Farber, "The Decline of Unionization in the United States: What Can Be Learned from Recent Experience?" *Journal of Labor Economics* 8 (January 1990): S79. Some early estimates of the impact of service growth on union membership were much larger.

(and only 6 percent of private service employment), compared to 23 percent in industry (Table 7.7).

The other factors that have caused a decline in unionism are more difficult to distinguish. According to the *job satisfaction hypothesis*, fewer workers are demanding union representation because they are happy with their jobs. In fact, public opinion polls indicate that a large and increasing proportion of Americans are satisfied with their jobs.[57] According to the *employer resistance*

■ TABLE 7.7

UNITED STATES: UNION MEMBERSHIP AND MEDIAN WEEKLY
EARNINGS OF UNIONIZED AND NONUNIONIZED FULL-TIME
WAGE AND SALARY WORKERS, 1994

	Union Members as % of Total Employment	Earnings of Union Members	Earnings of Nonunion	Union/ Nonunion Earnings Ratio
All workers	15.5	$592	$432	1.37
Occupations:				
Managerial/Professional	14.4	729	672	1.08
Craft and repair	23.9	672	458	1.47
Technicians	11.4	629	521	1.21
Transport workers	26.0	600	410	1.46
Administrative support	13.8	511	372	1.37
Machine operators	24.4	492	322	1.53
Handlers and helpers	21.9	478	288	1.66
Service occupations	14.3	483	268	1.80
Sales occupations	4.9	483	448	1.08
Sectors:				
Agriculture	2.3	n.a.	279	n.a.
Industry:				
Mining	15.7	664	634	1.05
Construction	18.8	696	425	1.64
Manufacturing	18.2	533	464	1.15
TCPU*	28.4	665	531	1.25
Services:				
Wholesale/Retail trade	6.2	453	352	1.29
FIRE**	2.3	471	485	0.97
Personal services	6.2	485	420	1.15
Government	38.7	623	493	1.26

* TCPU-transportation, communications, and public utilities

** FIRE-finance, insurance, and real estate

Source: U.S. Department of Labor, *Employment and Earnings* (January 1995): 214–217.

[57]Farber, "The Decline of Unionization in the United States," S99.

hypothesis, foreign competition and domestic deregulation have encouraged employers to oppose union activities more forcefully. To this end, employers may attempt to influence union elections directly, or they may offer higher wages and fringe benefits to strengthen worker loyalty. The *government substitution hypothesis* says that many of the functions of labor unions have been taken over by public agencies. Guarantees that were once embedded in union contracts—unemployment insurance, retirement benefits, health and safety requirements—are now objects of legislation. Accordingly, within the United States, unionism has declined most rapidly in states that have done the most to uphold workers' rights.[58] In international perspective, though, union membership is generally largest in such countries as Sweden, where governmental spending on social security and welfare are high in relation to national income.

LABOR LEGISLATION

One reason for the low level of union membership in the United States (by international standards) is that pro-labor legislation came late to America. In Sweden, for example, the major employers agreed in 1906 that they would not attempt to disrupt unionizing activities. In America, these guarantees were not extended until the passage of the Norris-LaGuardia Act of 1932 and the National Labor Relations Act of 1935. In 1938, the Fair Labor Standards Act enacted a minimum wage rate (25 cents per hour!) and a maximum workweek (44 hours) for labor engaged in interstate commerce.

Public opinion turned against the labor unions at the end of World War II when a long series of strikes disrupted the coal, steel, telephone, automobile, and meat-packing industries. In 1946, approximately 116 million man-hours were lost due to labor disputes. In the aftermath, the Labor-Management (Taft-Hartley) Act of 1947 was enacted to exercise control over the unions. Under the act, the **closed shop,** which requires job applicants to join the union before they may be hired, was outlawed. The **union shop,** which requires employees to join the union within a specified period after they are hired, was not prohibited by the act, but the individual states were permitted to pass **right-to-work laws** that prohibit union shops. Twenty states, most of them in the South and West, presently have right-to-work laws.

The Taft-Hartley Act also placed restrictions on the right of unions to call strikes. If the government feels that a strike is likely to create a national emergency, it can require an 80-day cooling-off period and intervention by the Federal Mediation and Conciliation Service.

THE ECONOMIC IMPACT OF LABOR UNIONS

The most important goal of labor unions traditionally has been to raise and maintain the wages of their members. They pursue this goal by bargaining collectively with management (with the threat of a strike if bargaining fails),

---

[58]George R. Neumann and Ellen R. Rissman, "Where Have All the Union Members Gone?" *Journal of Labor Economics* 2 (April 1984): 175–192.

by restricting the supply of union labor, by increasing the demand for their labor through featherbedding (creation of new, and sometimes useless, jobs), and through efforts to increase the demand for their final product (for example, "Look for the union label" and "Buy American" slogans).

The actual impact of unions on wage levels can be estimated in a number of different ways, and economists disagree on the methods that should be used. Nevertheless, few economists would question the proposition that union members receive higher wages, on average, than nonmembers. Historically, union wages have exceeded nonunion wages by about 20–25 percent in the United States. Nonunion wages seem to draw closer to union wages during periods of price inflation, and fall behind during periods of price stability. During the early years of the Great Depression, when the price level was falling, the wage advantage of union members grew to about 50 percent.[59] In 1994, median weekly earnings of union members were 37 percent higher than those of nonmembers. Managerial and sales personnel gained little from union membership, but union members in service occupations had earnings 80 percent larger than those of nonmembers (Table 7.7).

Although labor unions apparently have succeeded in raising the wages of their members, this does not necessarily imply that they have raised the average level of wages for all workers. A number of economists believe that the gains of union laborers have been won at the expense of nonunion laborers rather than at the expense of corporate stockholders. If high wages cause unemployment in the unionized sector and the unemployed spill over into the nonunion sector, then competition for jobs may reduce the wages of nonmembers.

In fact, the share of U.S. national income received by all laborers (union and nonunion) has been remarkably stable for more than 50 years. In 1933, when only 7 percent of the labor force was unionized, laborers received about 73 percent of national income. In 1954, when the unionized share of the labor force peaked at 27 percent, labor's share of national income was 69 percent. In 1993, unions claimed about 16 percent of the labor force and labor received about 74 percent of national income.[60]

THE FINANCIAL SECTOR

Financial institutions—including banks, securities firms, insurance companies, and others—perform a number of important functions in market economies. They provide efficient and safe methods for payment between

[59]John Pencavel and Catherine E. Hartsog, "A Reconsideration of the Effects of Unionism on Relative Wages and Employment in the United States, 1920–1980," *Journal of Labor Economics* 2 (April 1984): 206. For a discussion of the voluminous literature on this subject, see H. Gregg Lewis, *Union Relative Wage Effects: A Survey* (Chicago: University of Chicago Press, 1986); Kay E. Anderson, Philip M. Doyle, and Albert E. Schwenk, "Measuring Union-Nonunion Earnings Differences," *Monthly Labor Review* (June 1990): 26–38; and George Jakubson, "Estimation and Testing of the Union Wage Effect Using Panel Data," *Review of Economic Studies* 88 (October 1991): 971–991.

[60]Here, I take compensation of employees to represent labor's share of national income. Labor's share is even more stable if we include proprietors' income. These data are taken from *Economic Report of the President 1991*, 312; and *Economic Report of the President 1994*, 302.

buyers and sellers (checking accounts, letters of credit, bankers' acceptances, and so on); they provide for safe storage of financial wealth (savings accounts, etc.); they extend credit (bank loans, bond sales, etc.); they allow individuals to share their risks with larger numbers of people (insurance policies); and they facilitate efficient transfers of ownership of businesses, housing, and other capital goods (stock market and real estate transactions).

In the United States, the finance, insurance, real estate, and business service sectors account for about 27 percent of GDP and 15 percent of total employment. These are the largest proportions found in any OECD country, with the possible exception of Italy.[61]

TRENDS IN AMERICAN BANK REGULATION

Before 1863, the U.S. banking system was almost wholly unregulated by the national government. With the exception of the First and Second Banks of the United States, which were chartered by the U.S. Congress, the 2,500 banks established between 1781 and 1861 were all chartered by authorities at the state level. Many of these banks were unsound and nearly two-fifths of them were forced to close within tens years after they opened. To make matters worse, each bank was able to issue its own banknotes, which were used as currency. In the mid–1800s, literally thousands of different kinds of currency were in circulation in the United States, making it very difficult to detect counterfeit notes.

The National Banking Acts of 1863 and 1864 put the state banks out of the business of issuing currency and established a uniform and safe currency system. Furthermore, the acts established the office of the Comptroller of the Currency in the Treasury Department and empowered it to charter and supervise a system of national banks. Hence, a unique (by international standards) system of **dual banking** was created, with national banks chartered by the comptroller and state banks chartered by state banking authorities.

Although the national banking system established a uniform currency, it did not provide an efficient national system for clearing checks—that is, for moving funds from one bank to another. Likewise, the system did not provide an efficient means for banks that were short of funds to borrow from banks with excess reserves. Most important, the National Banking Acts did not establish a central bank that could adjust the supply of money to meet the needs of the economy. The establishment of a central bank was resisted strongly by conservative Democrats who feared encroachment on states' rights.

The Federal Reserve Act of 1913 struck a compromise between the demands for state autonomy and the need for a central bank. The act established 12 Federal Reserve district banks, each of which is owned by the member banks in its district. To this day, the district banks are the only central banks in the world that are wholly owned by commercial banks. Furthermore, each district bank is controlled by a board of nine directors, six of whom are elected by the member banks in the district.

---

[61]But Italian statistics include some community, social, and personal services in this category. See *OECD in Figures 1997*, published with the *OECD Observer* (June-July 1997), 38–39.

A seven-member board of governors, appointed by the president, was placed at the head of the Federal Reserve system. All national banks were required to become members of the system and state banks were invited to join. Member banks were allowed to borrow money at the discount window of the Federal Reserve and could use its check-clearing facilities, but they were regulated more tightly (for example, larger reserve and capital requirements) than many of the state banks that did not choose to join the system.

In response to the speculative boom of the 1920s and the financial collapse of the 1930s, Congress enacted several new laws to stabilize the banking industry. The Glass-Steagall Act of 1933 imposed the separation of commercial banking (accepting deposits) from investment banking (securities transactions and underwriting). Thus, the United States developed a unique system of specialized banks that stand in stark contrast to the "universal" banks in Germany. The Glass-Steagall Act also created the Federal Deposit Insurance Corporation (FDIC), and required all national banks to carry FDIC insurance. The Banking Act of 1935 shifted more authority from the district Federal Reserve banks to the Board of Governors in Washington, making it possible to pursue a more deliberate monetary policy.

The authority of the Federal Reserve began to decline after World War II as a growing number of banks dropped out of the Federal Reserve system to escape stringent reserve requirements. This exodus allegedly threatened the safety of the banking system and crippled the Federal Reserve's efforts to control the growth of the money supply. To deal with these and other problems, Congress passed the Depository Institutions Deregulation and Monetary Control Act of 1980. Among the important provisions of the act were the following:

> The Federal Reserve was given authority to set reserve requirements on checking accounts at *all* federally insured depository institutions—member banks, nonmember banks, savings and loan associations, credit unions, and so forth.

> Federal Reserve loans and other Federal Reserve services (for example, check collection) were made available at a fee to *all* depository institutions.

> All depository institutions were given the authority to offer interest-earning checking accounts.

> A phaseout of interest rate ceilings on deposits and other accounts was initiated.

The 1980 legislation was meant to reassert the authority of the Federal Reserve and to place all depository institutions—member and nonmember banks, savings and loan associations, and others—on an equal footing. Deregulation of deposit interest rates under the 1980 act contributed to the efficiency of the financial system, but it also caused problems for many banks and thrift institutions. In order to compete, many of them were forced to pay higher interest rates on deposits than the average yield on their investment portfolios. For this reason and others (including recession, declining property values, fraud, mismanagement, and nonpayment of debt by oil companies and Third World borrowers), hundreds of banks and thrift institutions have been forced to close their doors. The average number of bank failures jumped from 5 per year in 1945–1980 to 114 per year in 1981–1993.[62]

For several years, the U.S. Congress has been considering a new program of bank reforms, aimed at increasing the efficiency and international competitiveness of the system, and minimizing the cost of potential taxpayer bailouts. Proposals under consideration include the following:

Restore competitiveness by allowing banks to open branches nationwide and offer new services, such as investment banking and insurance, through subsidiaries. The Treasury estimates that branch banking alone could reduce the operating costs of the banking industry by about $10 billion per year.

Reduce the scope of deposit insurance coverage, and regulate banks more tightly to reduce risk of failure.

Streamline the regulatory structure, with national banks supervised by the Treasury and state banks by the Federal Reserve.

Exempt most banks from the 1977 Community Reinvestment Act, which requires that banks lend in the communities where they take deposits.[63]

The American banking system continues to be unique from an international perspective. The Federal Reserve remains a *federal* system, with its network of locally owned district banks, and banking authorities in the individual states still have the authority to establish regulations on a wide range of issues. Nevertheless, domestic budgetary problems and international competition seem to be pushing the system toward more centralization, consistent with practice in the rest of the world.[64]

THE GOVERNMENTAL SECTOR

By international standards, the activities of the U.S. government are rather limited. Taken as a percentage of GNP, for example, government expenditures are smaller in the United States than in any other major industrial nation, with the possible exception of Japan.[65]

From historical and international perspectives, the United States was slow to adopt a strong central government. In keeping with the philosophy of fed-

---

[62]Federal Deposit Insurance Corporation, *Annual Report 1993* (Washington, D.C., 1994), 135.

[63]David Lascelles, "Last Chance for a Sweeping Overhaul," *Financial Times*, April 4, 1991, 12; Kenneth H. Bacon, "Banking Panel Approves Plan on Branches," *The Wall Street Journal*, June 26, 1991, A3; John R. Wilke, "Sweeping Reforms of Banking Laws Appear Unlikely to Pass in Congress," *The Wall Street Journal*, May 5, 1995, A5; and John R. Wilke, "Deregulation for Banks Nears Panel Approval," *The Wall Street Journal*, June 28, 1995, A3.

[64]See Anthony M. Santomero, "European Banking Post–1992: Lessons from the United States," in *European Banking in the 1990s*, ed. by Jean Dermine (London: Basil Blackwell, 1990), 437–457.

[65]According to OECD estimates, total outlays of the general government have been a smaller fraction of GDP in Japan than in the United States in the past, but this is no longer true. See *OECD Economic Outlook* 61 (June 1997), Annex Table 28.

eralism, the focus of governmental power was kept close to the electorate—at the state and local levels. After independence was won from the British, the Articles of Confederation denied the central government the power to collect taxes. When the Constitution was adopted in 1789, it gave a broad range of economic powers to the Congress, but these were used sparingly.

Probably the most significant economic contribution of the government in the early years was in launching the systems of transportation and communication. In 1806, Congress committed the federal government to build the Cumberland National Road, linking farmers of the Ohio valley to Eastern markets. The Erie Canal, completed in 1825, was built, owned, and operated by the state of New York. Unlike the British, who built most of their transportation system with private capital, the early American governments were responsible for about 70 percent of investment in canals and 30 percent of investment in railroads.[66]

For the first 140 years, over half of all U.S. governmental spending was carried out at the local level (Table 7.8). It took nothing less than the Great Depression and World War II to elevate the central government to a position

■ TABLE 7.8

UNITED STATES: DISTRIBUTION OF FEDERAL, STATE, AND LOCAL DIRECT GOVERNMENTAL EXPENDITURES, 1902–1993

Year	Federal	State	Local	Total
1902	34	8	58	100
1913	30	9	61	100
1922	39	12	49	100
1927	30	13	57	100
1936	49	15	36	100
1944	90	3	7	100
1950	60	15	25	100
1960	60	15	25	100
1970	56	17	27	100
1980	55	18	27	100
1990	56	18	26	100
1993	53	20	27	100

Sources: U.S. Department of Commerce, Bureau of the Census, *Historical Statistics of the United States, Colonial Times to 1970*, Part 2 (Washington, D.C.: USGPO, 1975), Series Y 613, Y 757, and Y 785; and U.S. Department of Commerce, Bureau of the Census, *Statistical Abstract of the United States 1996* (Washington, D.C.: USGPO, 1996), 297.

---

[66]Estimates of Carter Goodrich, cited in Arthur M. Schlesinger, Jr., *The Cycles of American History* (Boston: Houghton Mifflin, 1986), 224. For an extended discussion of the activist aspects of early American economic policy, see Frank Bourgin, *The Great Challenge: The Myth of Laissez-Faire in the Early Republic* (New York: George Braziller, 1989), passim.

of dominance. Along with the shift toward centralization of government, the postwar generations also witnessed a dramatic shift in the functional distribution of governmental spending.

Before World War II, the government spent more money on the postal and transportation systems than it spent on national defense, social security, and welfare, combined (Table 7.9). During the war, the military absorbed over three-fourths of all governmental expenditures. The military share dropped again after the war, but not to the prewar level. At the same time, the governmental commitment to social security and welfare, which began during the Depression, grew rapidly after the war. Taken together, the share of national defense, social security, and welfare in U.S. governmental spending increased from 8 percent in 1927 to 45 percent in 1991.

REGULATION OF THE ECONOMY

We already noted the important role of the American government in regulating product, labor, and financial markets. Regulation of banking began in earnest in the 1860s, antitrust action began in the 1890s, and guidance of labor relations began in the 1930s.

Governmental concern for public health and safety began with the passage of the Pure Food and Drug Act of 1906, prompted by the publication of Upton Sinclair's novel, *The Jungle*, that same year. In later years, the regulatory umbrella was expanded to cover consumer and occupational safety, environmental protection, energy production, transportation, communication, and a number of other concerns. Most recently, new environmental

■ TABLE 7.9

UNITED STATES: FUNCTIONAL DISTRIBUTION OF FEDERAL, STATE, AND LOCAL GOVERNMENTAL EXPENDITURES, 1902–1991

	1902	1936	1944	1950	1970	1991
Defense, Foreign Relations	9.9	5.6	77.8	26.1	25.3	15.9
Education	15.5	14.1	2.6	13.7	16.7	14.3
Postal,Transport	19.5	17.7	6.4	9.6	8.5	5.5
Social Security, Welfare	2.5	7.3	1.8	14.0	19.8	29.1
Health	6.9	4.7	1.0	5.0	5.1	4.5
Police, Fire	5.4	3.2	0.7	1.9	2.1	3.8
Interest on Debt	5.8	8.7	2.4	6.9	5.5	10.8
Other	34.5	38.7	7.3	22.8	17.0	15.9
Total	100.0	100.0	100.0	100.0	100.0	100.0

Sources: U.S. Department of Commerce, Bureau of the Census, *Historical Statistics of the United States, Colonial Times to 1970*, Part 1 (Washington, D.C.: USGPO, 1975), Series Y 533–566; U.S. Department of Commerce, Bureau of the Census, *Government Finances: 1990–91* (Washington, D.C.: USGPO, 1993), Table 1.

regulations have been prompted by research revealing deterioration of the earth's protective ozone layer.

Most of the regulatory agencies were established to deal with important national problems; very few economists or politicians would advocate abolishing the entire governmental rulebook. Nevertheless, the regulatory process has fallen under broad criticism in recent years.

First, many would say that governmental regulations are too expensive. In addition to the billions of dollars spent to operate regulatory agencies, private businesses must spend additional billions to comply with regulations, and these costs are passed to consumers in higher taxes and prices. Between 1970 and 1992, for example, the cost to businesses of complying with pollution abatement regulations increased by nearly 90 percent in constant prices, from $60 billion to $113 billion. Estimates of the annual total cost of regulation to the U.S. economy range all the way from $200 billion to $500 billion.[67]

Another criticism of governmental control is suggested by the **regulatory capture** theory, which states that, in time, and sometimes quite innocently, regulators become tools of the industries they are supposed to regulate. For example, governmental agencies barred the entry of new competitors into the trucking and airline industries for many years, granting monopoly power to the existing companies. Officials of the Federal Reserve often lobby in Congress for legislation that favors the banking industry.

Partially reversing the earlier trend, a wave of deregulation has swept the United States since the early 1970s. New legislation and revised guidelines from regulatory agencies have reduced restrictions on entry, exit, and pricing in domestic satellite operations (1972 and 1979), railroads (1976), air cargo and transportation (1978 and 1980), petroleum products (1981), cable television (1980 and 1984), and telecommunications (1995).

Programs of deregulation may inject new competitiveness and flexibility into the economy, but they also carry risks. According to survey data, only 16 percent of Americans wish to postpone stronger standards for air and water pollution.[68] Under more permissive guidelines, airlines have canceled service to some small cities.[69] The epidemic of bank failures during the late 1980s and early 1990s may have been connected with deregulation of that industry. When the government was forced to bail out the Continental Illinois banking corporation, Federal Reserve Chairman Volcker admitted to Congress that, "in hindsight, it's an unassailable argument that the central bank should have been tougher with Continental."[70]

---

[67]U.S. General Accounting Office, *Regulatory Reform—Information on Costs, Cost-Effectiveness, and Mandated Deadlines for Regulations* (GAO/PEMD–95–18BR, March 8, 1995), passim; and John M. Berry, "Rising Cost of Rules Leads to a Rising Tide against Them," *Washington Post*, January 19, 1995, D9.

[68]Survey by the Roper Organization, reported in "How's Business?" *The Public Perspective* 5 (November/December 1993): 83.

[69]For an account of "the folly of deregulation" of the airlines, see Hobart Rowen, *Self-Inflicted Wounds: From LBJs Guns and Butter to Reagan's Voodoo Economics* (New York: Random House, 1994), Chapter 12.

[70]G. Christian Hill and Edwin Finn, "Big Depositors' Runs on Beleaguered Banks Speed the Failure Rate," *The Wall Street Journal*, August 23, 1984, 12.

FISCAL AND MONETARY POLICY

Superficially, the institutional machinery that sets fiscal and monetary policy in the United States is quite simple. On the fiscal side, the national budget is prepared by the executive branch under the coordination of the Office of Management and Budget. It is sent to Congress for amendment, debate, and approval, and then it is returned to the president to be signed into law. At each step, the formation of fiscal policy is influenced by the actions of lobbyists and by the demands of the electorate.

Monetary policy is set by the governors of the Federal Reserve System, each of whom is appointed by the president of the United States for a 14-year term. Because of these long terms of office, and because the Federal Reserve is able to cover its operating expenses without appropriations from Congress, the board of governors is insulated from political pressure.

During the Great Depression, the U.S. government enacted programs to help the poor, but it did not attempt to stimulate employment with active programs of fiscal and monetary policy. Indeed, in 1937 the government reduced its expenditures, and the Federal Reserve acted to reduce the size of the money supply. In the end, the World War II experience confirmed the Keynesian proposition that unemployment could be reduced by a program of governmental spending. Indeed, wartime spending successfully reduced the rate of unemployment in America from 17 percent in 1939 to 2 percent in 1945.

After the war, a new attitude toward fiscal policy was reflected in the Employment Act of 1946, which declared that the federal government had an obligation to promote maximum employment, production, and purchasing power. The president was authorized to appoint a new Council of Economic Advisors, and, for several years, the objectives of the Employment Act were attained rather effectively. One major study found that between 1955 and 1965 the American government used fiscal policy more successfully than any of the major European governments to stabilize the growth of national income.[71]

Since the 1960s, American fiscal policy has been slipping out of control. Due to expenditures on the Vietnam War and social programs in the 1960s and 1970s and tax cuts in the early 1980s, the budget has followed a steady trend toward larger deficits.[72] At the same time, the macroeconomic performance of the American economy has been mixed, with relatively high inflation during the 1970s, high unemployment during the 1980s, and slow growth of GDP during the 1990s (Table 7.10).

The federal budget distinguishes between two categories of expenditures: mandatory and discretionary. **Mandatory expenditures** include interest on the national debt and **entitlements,** such as Medicare and Social Security,

---

[71] Bent Hansen, *Fiscal Policy in Seven Countries: 1955–1965* (Paris: Organization for Economic Cooperation and Development, 1969), 69–73.

[72] Actually, the rise in the official budget deficit may be overestimated because federal accounts do not distinguish between current expenses and investment. See Robert Eisner, "Budget Deficits: Rhetoric and Reality," *Journal of Economic Perspectives* 3 (Spring 1989): 73–93.

■ **TABLE 7.10**

**UNITED STATES: MACROECONOMIC PERFORMANCE BY DECADES,
1950–1990**

	1950–1959	1960–1969	1970–1979	1980–1989	1990–1996
Unemployment Rate (percent)	4.4	4.7	6.1	7.3	6.3
Consumer Price Inflation (annual average percentage)	2.0	2.3	7.1	5.6	3.4
Real GDP Growth (annual average percentage)	3.9	4.1	2.9	2.5	1.9
Federal Government Budget Balance as Percent of GNP	–0.4	–0.8	–2.0	–4.0	–3.4

Source: *Economic Report of the President 1977*, Appendix B.

that are relatively difficult to control because they provide legally prescribed benefits to anyone who meets eligibility requirements. **Discretionary expenditures,** including those on national defense, transportation, energy, and a wide range of other programs, are generally controlled on a year-to-year basis. Since the 1960s, the share of mandatory expenditures in total outlays of the U.S. government has increased steadily as follows:[73]

1962	26%	
1970	31	
1980	45	
1990	45	
1995	49	
2002	57	(forecast)

In an effort to regain fiscal control, Congress passed the Gramm-Rudman-Hollings Act (GRH) in 1985, establishing a series of targets that were meant to balance the budget by 1991. If the targets were not met in each year's budget negotiations, GRH called for automatic cuts in discretionary expenditures. Congress and the Reagan administration were not able to meet these targets, and loopholes in the law allowed them to avoid large automatic cuts. The Budget Enforcement Act (BEA) of 1990 filled some of these loopholes and established legally binding caps (adjusted for inflation and technical factors) that imposed a "flexible freeze" on discretionary expenditures. The BEA was temporarily suspended to pay for the Persian Gulf War, but then the federal budget deficit declined during 1993, 1994, and 1995—the first three-year reduction since the mid–1970s.[74]

In 1995, the Republican Party gained control of both houses of Congress, and its leadership promised to balance the budget by the year 2002 while reducing taxes by $245 billion. This will be done, they say, by cutting federal expenditures by $958 billion over seven years, including reductions of $270

[73]Office of Management and Budget, *Budget of the United States Government, Fiscal Year 1996: Historical Tables* (Washington, D.C.: USGPO, 1995), 95.

[74]Ibid., 14. For a fuller discussion of the implications of the Budget Enforcement Act, see *Economic Report of the President 1993*, 111–113.

billion and $182 billion, respectively, in the growth of Medicare and Medicaid spending. According to the Republican plan, a number of federal agencies will be closed, and the funding and administration of many programs will be turned over to the state governments. In the end, of course, a compromise will have to be struck between Republicans and Democrats, but a consensus seems to be forming around the need to balance the budget.[75]

Aside from the use of fiscal and monetary policy to stabilize employment and the price level, the U.S. government has made little use of indicative planning or industrial policy to influence the structure of the economy. There is no American counterpart to the Japanese Ministry of International Trade and Industry, which uses subsidies and other means to encourage the development of favored industries. Generally, Republican administrations have been opposed to industrial targeting: "Attempts to second-guess the market and to direct government support to particular firms, industries, or technologies in the name of promoting growth are inevitably counterproductive."[76] In recent years, Democratic leaders have advocated a "uniquely American model" of business-government cooperation. This approach includes stronger financial support for basic research in scientific fields that are important to industry, greater cooperation between federal laboratories and commercial interests, and regulatory reform targeted at biotechnology, telecommunications, and other vital industries.[77]

REDISTRIBUTION OF INCOME AND WEALTH

America, according to the slogan, is a "land of opportunity." Indeed, the American economic and social systems have given immigrants from many countries the opportunity to amass significant fortunes. Most Americans believe that rich people gain their wealth from a "strong effort to succeed" rather than from "luck or circumstances beyond their control"; most believe that a person who works hard has a "good chance" of becoming rich; and a large majority say that they "admire people who get rich by working hard." On the other hand, very few believe that the present distribution of income and wealth is fair, and two-thirds of Americans believe that riches should be distributed more evenly.[78]

Thus, Americans support moderate programs of redistribution, but they are more conservative in this regard than most Europeans. The United States

---

[75]David Hage, "New Budget Harmony?" *U.S. News & World Report*, June 26, 1995, 46.

[76]Position of the Bush administration, stated in *Economic Report of the President 1991*, 6. This position, however, was not implemented strictly. See Bob Davis, "White House, Reversing Policy under Pressure, Begins to Pick High-Tech Winners and Losers," *The Wall Street Journal*, May 13, 1991, A16.

[77]Michael Borrus, "Industrial Policy American Style," *International Economic Insights* (March-April 1993): 10–13; and Gerald Seib and Jeffrey Birnbaum, "Clinton Industrial Policy Stressing Cooperation Can Clash with Administration's Populist Bent," *The Wall Street Journal*, March 21, 1994, A14.

[78]George Gallup, Jr., and Frank Newport, "Americans Widely Disagree on What Constitutes `Rich,'" *The Gallup Poll Monthly*, July 1990, 28–36; "Haves and Have Nots," *The American Enterprise* 4 (May-June 1993): 85; and Princeton Survey Research Associates, "People, the Press, and Politics: New Political Landscape," reported in Roper Center, *Public Opinion Online*, October 7, 1994, Accession 0222636, Question 7.

■ TABLE 7.11

UNITED STATES: INFLUENCE OF TRANSFER PAYMENTS AND TAXES ON
THE DISTRIBUTION OF INCOME, 1995

	Percentage of total income received by:					
	Poorest 20%	Second 20%	Third 20%	Fourth 20%	Richest 20%	Gini Ratio
Income before Taxes and Transfers	0.9	7.2	14.7	24.2	52.9	.509
Income after Federal and State Income and Payroll Taxes	1.1	8.4	15.9	24.9	49.7	.481
Income after Taxes and All Transfers	5.0	10.8	16.3	23.3	44.5	.394

Source: U.S. Department of Commerce, Bureau of the Census, *Money Income in the United States: 1995* (Current Population Report P–60–193, 1996), Table E.

devotes a smaller proportion of national income to social protection expenditures than any other OECD country, and is the only major industrial country without a family allowance system to help parents provide for their children.[79] The limited role of government, together with a range of demographic factors, may help to explain why the United States has a relatively unequal distribution of income and a high rate of child poverty.[80]

An assessment of the impact of taxes and governmental transfer payments on the U.S. distribution of income is presented in Table 7.11. According to these estimates, the system of income taxation has a rather minor impact on the income distribution, reducing the Gini inequality ratio by only 6. This may seem surprising, since the United States has a progressive income tax, but its progressivity is reduced considerably by treatment of deductions and capital gains.[81] According to survey data, most Americans believe that the current income tax system is "basically unfair," and two-thirds believe that the rich are paying too little.[82]

Transfer payments, such as Social Security, aid to families with dependent children, and unemployment compensation, seem to have a stronger equalizing effect on the distribution of income than the tax system. According to Table 7.11, transfers reduce the Gini inequality ratio by about 18 percent. On

[79]*OECD Employment Outlook*, July 1994, 151. Regarding family allowance systems, see Margaret S. Gordon, *Social Security Policies in Industrial Countries: A Comparative Analysis* (Cambridge: Cambridge University Press, 1988), Chapter 13.

[80]See Timothy Smeeding, Barbara Boyle Torrey, and Martin Rein, "Patterns of Income and Poverty: Economic Status of Children and the Elderly in Eight Countries," in J. Palmer, T. Smeeding, and B. Torrey, eds., *The Vulnerable* (Washington, D.C.: Urban Institute Press, 1988), Table 5.3.

[81]The effect of taxation would appear even less progressive if adjustments were made for regressive state and local sales and property taxes. For estimates of this kind, see Joseph A. Pechman, *Who Paid the Taxes, 1966–1985?* (Washington, D.C.: The Brookings Institution, 1985).

[82]NBC/Wall Street Journal poll reported in Roper Center, *Public Opinion Online*, May 4, 1995, Accession 0235513, Question 54; and Gallup Poll reported in Roper Center, *Public Opinion Online*, May 5, 1994, Accession 0214806, Question 45.

■ TABLE 7.12

UNITED STATES: DISTRIBUTION OF INCOME AND POVERTY RATES,
1950–1995

Percentage of total family income received by:

	Poorest 20%	Second 20%	Third 20%	Fourth 20%	Richest 20%	Gini Ratio	Poverty Rate (%)
1950	4.5	12.0	17.4	23.4	42.7	.379	n.a.
1960	4.8	12.2	17.8	24.0	41.3	.364	22.2
1970	5.4	12.2	17.6	23.8	40.9	.353	12.6
1980	5.1	11.6	17.5	24.3	41.6	.365	13.0
1990	4.6	10.8	16.6	23.8	44.3	.396	13.5
1995	4.4	10.1	15.8	23.2	46.5	.425	13.8

Source: U.S. Department of Commerce, Bureau of the Census, *Current Population Reports*, P60-191, P60-193, and P60-194, 1996.

the other hand, when Americans are asked, "Do you think most of the spending done by the federal government goes to help rich people, or middle income people, or poor people?" only 25 percent answer "poor people," while 48 percent say "rich people."[83] Even if Americans acknowledge the progressive effects of transfer payments, they apparently believe that the rich are the main beneficiaries of military spending and other government purchases.

The data in Table 7.12 indicate that the American income distribution became more equal and the poverty rate fell during 1950–1970, but income inequality and poverty increased during 1970–1995.[84] In a similar way, the distribution of household wealth (net worth) apparently trended toward equality before 1979 and toward inequality afterward.[85] Despite these movements, the underlying stability of the income and wealth distributions seem remarkable when we consider the changes that have occurred in the American economy since World War II: the rising participation of women in the

[83] According to a national poll administered by the Los Angeles Times, reported in Roper Center, *Public Opinion Online*, March 21, 1995, Accession 0232704, Question 16.

[84] If the data in Table 7.12 were adjusted for the effects of taxation, the trend toward inequality after 1970 apparently would be greater because the progressivity of the tax system deteriorated. See Pechman, *Who Paid the Taxes, 1966–1985?*, Chapter 5. For measurements disaggregated by family size and composition, see Lynn A. Karoly, "The Trend in Inequality among Families, Individuals, and Workers in the United States," in Danziger and Gottschalk, eds., *Uneven Tides: Rising Inequality in America*, 19–97. For more information on trends and causes of poverty, see Isabel V. Sawhill, "Poverty in the United States: Why Is It So Persistent?" *Journal of Economic Literature* 26 (September 1988): 1073–1119; and Robert Haveman, "Who Are the Nation's Truly Poor?" *The Brookings Review* (Winter 1993): 24–27.

[85] Edward N. Wolff, "Estimates of Household Wealth Inequality in the U.S., 1962–1983," *Review of Income and Wealth* 33 (September 1987): 231–256; and Edward N. Wolff, "Trends in Household Wealth in the United States, 1962–83 and 1983–89," *Review of Income and Wealth* 40 (June 1994): 143–174.

paid labor force, the general improvement in educational levels, the establishment of affirmative action programs to counteract the effects of racial and sexual discrimination, the continuing series of technological revolutions, and the rising influence of international trade and investment. Transfer payments, which have a progressive effect on the income distribution, represented a rising proportion of personal income:[86]

1950	6.7%
1960	7.0
1970	10.1
1980	14.2
1990	14.7
1995	16.7

How do we reconcile the rising significance of transfer payments with the relative stability of the distribution of income? Apparently, the distribution of market (nontransfer) income grew less equal over time, and this trend was partially offset by the growth of governmental transfer payments.[87]

What has caused the rising inequality of market incomes? Here, one will find little agreement. Many conservatives believe that the growing system of transfer payments has seriously reduced work incentives among the poor and created an underclass of permanent welfare recipients.[88] Thus, the distribution of total income has been relatively stable in the United States because governmental transfer programs are both cause and cure.

Others place the blame for rising inequality of market incomes on the growth of service employment, educational inequality, part-time employment, declining union membership, deterioration (in real terms) of the legal minimum wage, and rising international competition for low-wage jobs.[89] Some conservatives believe that these inequalities of income are rooted in natural inequalities of intelligence, which cannot be ameliorated by governmental programs.[90] Centrists and liberals reject this view, and call for active

---

[86]*Economic Report of the President 1987*, 272–73; and *Economic Report of the President 1997*, 330–331.

[87]This was the conclusion reached for the 1950–1970 period by Morgan Reynolds and Eugene Smolensky in their *Public Expenditures, Taxes, and the Distribution of Income* (New York: Academic Press, 1977); and by Edward Gramlich, Richard Kasten, and Frank Sammartino for 1980–1990 in their "Growing Inequality in the 1980s: The Role of Federal Taxes and Cash Transfers," in Danziger and Gottschalk, eds., *Uneven Tides: Rising Inequality in America*, 225–249. Likewise, research by Joseph Hastag and Lori Taylor indicates that the distribution of earned income (excluding transfers) trended toward inequality from 1952 to 1989. See their "A Look at Long-Term Developments in the Distribution of Income," *Economic Review of the Federal Reserve Bank of Dallas* (First Quarter 1993): 19–30.

[88]See, for example, Charles Murray, *Losing Ground: America's Social Policy, 1950–1980* (New York: Basic Books, 1984), passim; and Lawrence Mead, *The New Politics of Poverty: The Nonworking Poor in America* (New York: Basic Books, 1992), passim.

[89]Andrew J. Winnick, *Toward Two Societies: The Changing Distributions of Income and Wealth in the U.S. since 1960* (New York: Praeger, 1989); and Ronald B. Mincy, "Raising the Minimum Wage: Effects on Family Poverty," *Monthly Labor Review* (July 1990): 18–25.

[90]Richard J. Herrnstein and Charles Murray, *The Bell Curve: Intelligence and Class Structure in American Life* (New York: Free Press, 1994), passim.

public policies to promote equality and international competitiveness.[91] The United States, they say, must not resign itself to "cognitive inequality," but must live up to its promise—a nation where all people are understood to be "created equal."

SUMMARY

The United States has built the largest system of production in the world on the basis of an excellent endowment of natural resources and a labor force dedicated to the philosophy of individualism. The plurality of the workers remained in agriculture until the twentieth century and then, after a brief period of industrial dominance, moved rapidly into services. The growth of the service sector in recent years is variously explained by the income elasticity, deindustrialization, cost disease, economies of scale, and labor supply hypotheses. The growth of the service sector has contributed to a growth in self-employment and weakened the role of the labor unions. It may have retarded the overall rate of economic growth, exacerbated the problem of price inflation, and contributed to income inequality, but it apparently stabilized the growth of employment and output.

A relatively competitive system gave way to rising industrial concentration after the Civil War, leading to the adoption of antitrust legislation around the turn of the century at a time when merger and concentration were encouraged in other countries. Partly for this reason, the United States has an average or relatively low level of industrial concentration (by international standards), and the level of concentration has been fairly stable or diminishing during most of the twentieth century. Lenient regulation since the early 1980s has allowed a new wave of merger activity.

In the labor market, trade unions play a relatively limited role (in comparison to their role in other industrial countries) and their share of the labor force has declined. Reasons for the decline in membership may include rising job satisfaction, employer resistance, and governmental assumption of responsibilities for worker protection. The relative competitiveness of the U.S. labor market is also suggested by the record of employment and wage flexibility.

In the financial sector, American federalism led to the creation of a dual system of state and national banks and a unique central banking system with elements of local ownership and control. Current proposals for deregulation in banking, including the establishment of a system of nationwide branch banking, are intended to increase the efficiency and international competitiveness of the system. Likewise, the focus of governmental authority was maintained at the state and local levels until the Great Depression and World War II. Governmental regulation of the economy expanded through most of

---

[91] Arthur S. Goldberger and Charles S. Maski, "Review: *The Bell Curve* by Herrnstein and Murray," *Journal of Economic Literature* 33 (June 1995): 762–776; Martin Neil Baily, Gary Burtless, and Robert E. Litan, *Growth with Equity: Economic Policy Making for the Next Century* (Washington, D.C.: The Brookings Institution, 1993), passim; and essays in Danziger and Gottschalk, eds., *Uneven Tides: Rising Inequality in America*, passim.

the twentieth century, but a trend toward deregulation has received bipartisan support in recent years.

Monetary and fiscal tools of macroeconomic management were employed in the 1960s and 1970s, but in recent years the government has attempted to regain control of inflation and fiscal deficits. A formal system of indicative planning and industrial policy has never been established. Despite the influence of the progressive national income tax and the growing program of transfer payments, the distribution of income has been remarkably stable.

DISCUSSION AND REVIEW QUESTIONS

1. How is the econoxmic system in the United States affected by the large size of its market and the heterogeneity of its population?

2. How can we explain the fact that employment is more stable in the service sector than in the industrial sector?

3. What explains the decline in American unemployment in recent years relative to European unemployment? Will American unemployment rates remain below European levels?

4. How has American federalism influenced the system of financial regulation? What are the arguments for and against moving toward a system of nationwide branch banking?

5. What have been the strengths and weaknesses of American budgetary processes in recent years? Have they been successful?

6. How can we explain the fact that the American distribution of income has remained relatively stable, despite the progressive income tax system and the growth of governmental transfer payments?

SUGGESTED READINGS

Baily, Martin Neil, Gary Burtless, and Robert E. Litan. *Growth with Equity: Economic Policy Making for the Next Century*. Washington, D.C.: The Brookings Institution, 1993. *Reviews the evidence on the productivity slowdown and the growth of inequality in the United States, and prescribes an investment-oriented strategy to attack both problems.*

Balk, Alfred. *The Myth of American Eclipse*. New Brunswick, N.J.: Transaction Books, 1990. *The editor of the* World Press Review *argues that the United States is outperforming Japan in many areas, but he also argues for restructuring of priorities away from military production and toward education and social programs.*

Baumol, William J., Sue Anne Batey Blackman, and Edward N. Wolff. *Productivity and American Leadership*: The Long View. Cambridge, Mass.: The MIT Press, 1989. *A careful review of the evidence finds no clear long-run trend toward slower productivity growth, and little support for the deindustrialization thesis. Proposes a long-run strategy to strengthen productivity.*

Bergsten, C. Fred. *America in the World Economy: A Strategy for the 1990s.* Washington, D.C.: Institute for International Economics, 1988. *The author, a highly regarded Washington economist and former Treasury official, argues for a policy of trade liberalization, deficit reduction, exchange rate stabilization, export-oriented growth, and assistance to indebted Third World countries.*

Bourgin, Frank. *The Great Challenge: The Myth of Laissez-Faire in the Early Republic.* New York: George Braziller, 1989. *A fascinating reexamination of the economic and social philosophies of the Founding Fathers. Be sure to read the foreword by Arthur Schlesinger, Jr., explaining the controversial events at the University of Chicago over a 50-year period that led to publication of this book.*

Economic Report of the President. Washington, D.C.: USGPO, annual. *Includes an annual review of macroeconomic policy and a wealth of statistical material.*

Feldstein, Martin, ed. *American Economic Policy in the 1980s.* Chicago: University of Chicago Press, 1994. *A team of 39 leading economists and policymakers survey the lessons of the 1980s in 11 broad areas of policy for the National Bureau of Economic Research.*

Minarik, Joseph J. *Making America's Budget Policy.* Armonk, N.Y.: Sharpe, 1990. *Written by the executive director of the Joint Economic Committee of the U.S. Congress, this book provides a clear explanation of the fiscal policy process and chronological account of the controversies over tax reform, budget policy, and deficits.*

Papers and proceedings of the meetings of the American Economic Association, *The American Economic Review,* May issues, annual. *The record of the annual convocation of the nation's largest economics association, these volumes include accessible essays (quite unlike the technical reports that are found in the other issues of this journal) on a broad range of issues concerning the American economy.*

Rowen, Hobart. *Self-Inflicted Wounds: From LBJs Guns and Butter to Reagan's Voodoo Economics.* New York: Random House, 1994. *Written by a veteran journalist, this is an entertaining account of reversals in American economic policy.*

Tocqueville, Alexis de. *Democracy in America.* New York: Harper, 1966. *A penetrating analysis of the roots of American individualism, based on his visit in the 1830s.*

INTERNET RESOURCES

The American Prospect
http://epn.org/prospect.html

Congressional Quarterly
gopher://gopher.cqalert.com/

National Review
gopher://gopher.enews.com/11/magazines/alphabetic/all/national_re-
view

Research Seminar in Quantitative Economics
Department of Economics, University of Michigan
(Current forecasts for U.S. economy)
http://mqem.econ.lsa.umich.edu/

U.S. Department of Commerce:
Bureau of the Census
http://www.census.gov

U.S. Department of Commerce:
Bureau of Economic Analysis
http://www.doc.gov/resources/beahome.html

U.S. Department of Commerce:
Economic Bulletin Board
gopher://una.hh.lib.umich.edu/11/ebb

U.S. Department of Commerce:
Stat-USA
http://www.stat-usa.gov:80/

U.S. House of Representatives
http://www.house.gov/

U.S. Department of Labor

Bureau of Labor Statistics
http://stats.bls.gov/blshome.html

U.S. Senate
gopher://gopher.senate.gov:70/

Weekly Economic Memorandum
First Fidelity Bancorporation
Economics Department
http://www.netaxs.com/~econ/

White House
http://www.whitehouse.gov/

Latin America and the Caribbean Area

8

LATIN AMERICA: THE JAGUARS AWAKEN

What, then, must have been the emotions of the Spaniards, when, after working their toilsome way into the upper air, the cloudy tabernacle parted before their eyes, and they beheld these fair scenes in all their pristine magnificence and beauty! It was like the spectacle which greeted the eyes of Moses from the summit of Pisgah, and in the warm glow of their feelings, they cried out, "It is the promised land!"

—WILLIAM HICKLING PRESCOTT
THE CONQUEST OF MEXICO, 1843

One of the most truly remarkable events of the last decade has been the political and economic democratization of Latin America. . . . If the 1980s were the decade of the Asian tigers, then the 1990s will be the decade of the South American jaguars.

—RON BROWN, U.S. SECRETARY OF COMMERCE
REUTERS BUSINESS REPORT, JULY 20, 1994

he nations of Latin America and the Caribbean are engaged in programs of political and economic liberalization that may prove as historic as their struggles for independence from Spain and Portugal. After decades of political instability, corruption, and military dictatorship, many countries in the region seem to be developing stable democracies. Markets long protected from competition are opening to foreign trade, foreign investment, and regional cooperation.

In this chapter, we will briefly survey the history, environment, and institutional structures of Latin America, and we will evaluate the economic and social reforms transforming the region today. The transitional economies of Eastern Europe and Asia may have much to learn from the Latin American experience.

ENVIRONMENT AND HISTORY

The Latin American region, encompassing a land area somewhat larger than the combined areas of Canada and the United States, may be usefully divided into three subregions: Middle America (Mexico and the 6 nations of Central America), South America (12 independent nations and French Guiana), and the Caribbean area (24 nations and territories, many of which are not "Latin").[1] The narrow Isthmus of Panama and the waters of the Caribbean have traditionally restricted interaction between these three subregions. Within South America, the northern nations (Colombia, Ecuador, Guyana, Venezuela, and Suriname) are separated from the so-called southern cone (Argentina, Bolivia, Brazil, Chile, Paraguay, and Peru) by the thinly populated rain forests of the Amazon River basin. The western rim of South America (including all of Chile) is divided from the remainder of the continent by the Andes Mountains, which extend more than 5,000 miles—the entire length of the continent—and are exceeded in average height only by the Himalayas.

INDIGENOUS CULTURES

In contrast to North America, which had a relatively small, migratory, and primitive native population, Middle and South America had large and advanced aboriginal civilizations. About two thousand years ago, the Mayas settled in the lowland tropics of Middle America, where steady cultivation of corn allowed them to end their migratory existence. The Mayas have been called the Greeks of Latin America because their culture emphasized intellectual, artistic, and athletic values. Their civilization dominated in present-day Guatemala between the third and tenth centuries A.D., with a population of perhaps two million. Skilled Mayan artists and technicians built magnificent pyramids and palaces, and their astronomers developed a calendar more accurate than the one that was used in Europe.

The Aztecs, who organized a powerful society in the Valley of Mexico early in the fourteenth century, used advanced agricultural techniques, including controlled irrigation, and built an integrated system of canals for water transportation. Beginning in the fifteenth century, Montezuma I and his followers used ruthless military force to extract taxes and tribute from a large part of Middle America; thousands of captives were taken to Tenochtitlán and the other Aztec treasure cities for rituals of human sacrifice. When Hernán Cortés arrived in 1519 with only 508 Spanish soldiers, he was able to conquer the mighty Aztecs by leading the native people of the region in a revolt against their oppressors.

The largest and most highly organized empire in all of the Americas was led by the Incas, who began their ascendancy late in the twelfth century. When the Spaniards arrived in 1531, the Incas controlled an area with perhaps 20 million inhabitants (Spain then had a population of about 10 mil-

---

[1]We follow the convention of counting Belize among the Caribbean nations, despite its location on the Central American mainland.

lion), stretching about 2,000 miles from southern Colombia to central Chile. From their headquarters in Cuzco Basin of the Peruvian Andes, the Incas organized a large administrative bureaucracy, a rigidly controlled society, and a centrally planned economy. The population was divided into groups of ten, each with a squad leader, to perform communal agricultural labor. The land was divided into sections used for the Inca rulers, for the priestly class, and for the local community. Marriages were officially arranged, and families could live only where permitted. The Incas organized the construction of magnificent temples, long roads, suspension bridges, and terraced fields on the sides of mountains, supported by stone walls, and they operated a regular postal service. The empire was divided into two units early in the sixteenth century, and the resulting dissension made it possible for Francisco Pizarro, with 183 Spanish soldiers and two dozen horses, to gain victory over the Inca leadership in 1533.

In summary, the natives of Middle and South America had experience with social, economic, and political development, authoritarian organization, and colonial exploitation long before the Europeans arrived. The Spanish and Portuguese colonialists imported their European systems of political, economic, and religious organization into the Americas, but they preserved some aspects of the indigenous cultures. Together with later waves of European, African, and Asian immigrants (Peru has a large and influential Japanese community), the nations of Middle and South America have developed a wide variety of "Latin American" cultures and institutions.

THE COLONIAL PERIOD

During the years just before their expeditions to the Americas, the Spaniards were engaged in a long struggle to free their country from the Moors (or Muslims) who had dominated most of Spain since the eighth century. Thus, the military commanders who traveled to the New World had extensive experience in conquest, looting, strict public administration, and forceful imposition of orthodox Catholicism. According to Lawrence Harrison, a well-known cultural determinist, "Latin America—and Spain until the last few decades—has suffered the consequences of a traditional Iberian culture that is anti-democratic, anti-social, anti-work, and anti-innovation."[2]

A full analysis of the colonial economic systems in Latin America would carry us far afield. Suffice it to say that the motives of the Spanish and Portuguese adventurers, like the Aztecs and Incas before them, were primarily extractive. That is, they had little interest in the broad economic development of the conquered areas; they demanded quick extraction of wealth, particularly of precious metals, and its secure passage to the colonial headquarters. Initially, this involved the looting and enslavement of native empires and populations, with little attention to agricultural development. One observer in the area that is now Peru described the payment of tribute to the Spaniards:

---

[2]Lawrence Harrison, "Latin America: Democracy and the Market Are Not Enough," *World Affairs* 155 (Spring 1993): 170.

The Indians of Parinacocha have to carry their tribute over two hundred miles to Cuzco: wheat, maize, cloth, bars of silver, etc. Indian men are loaded with it, and so are the women, the pregnant ones with their heads on their swollen bellies. . . . [They] climb with their loads up slopes that a horse could not climb.3

The native populations suffered not only from the wars of conquest, from looting, and from slave labor, but, perhaps worst of all, from their lack of immunity to smallpox, malaria, yellow fever, and a score of other diseases introduced by Europeans and their African slaves. If roughly 20 million natives lived in Middle America when the Spaniards arrived, only 2.5 million remained a century later.[4]

The transportation systems in Latin America were initially developed to facilitate the growth of one-way extraction. To ensure that their bounty was not diverted to other countries, the colonial powers allowed the operation of only a small number of seaports, where they maintained tight control over shipping. Radiating outward from the major production and collection centers to the seaports, the colonialists built roads (and, later, railroads), but they built few of the internal transportation links needed for broader economic development. The systems of unilateral extraction and controlled shipping made it impossible for the colonies to gain the benefits of multilateral trade.

As the colonial period continued, a growing number of administrators were needed for positions in local government and the military, and to manage mining, road construction, and commercial activities. The highest of these positions were reserved for *gachupines* (Spaniards born in Europe), but secondary posts were also held by *criollos* (American-born settlers with pure Spanish ancestry). Positions as overseers and foremen were often held by *mestizos* (American-born settlers with mixed native and Spanish ancestry). Thus, the seventeenth century witnessed the rise of a secondary aristocracy and a middle class whose ties to the New World were stronger than their ties to the Old.

When the looting of the Aztecs and Incas was complete, the best mining deposits were depleted, and a growing immigrant population demanded more food, the focus of economic activity in Latin America shifted toward farming and ranching. A dualistic system of *latifundios* and *minifundios* (very large and small farms) emerged, with the *criollos* controlling many of the former and the *mestizos* and native populations controlling the latter. As the masters of the agricultural sector, the *criollos* were able to exercise strict authoritarian rule over their farm workers, and they eventually were able to challenge the authority of European-born colonial leaders.

INDEPENDENCE

A number of forces converged in the closing years of the eighteenth century to fan the flames of Latin American independence. As we have just seen, a

---

[3]Quoted in Peter Worsley, *The Three Worlds: Culture and World Development* (Chicago: The University of Chicago Press, 1984), 8.

[4]H. J. Blij and Peter O. Muller, *Geography: Regions and Concepts*, 6th ed. (New York: John Wiley and Sons, 1991), 255.

new domestic aristocracy arose to defy European rule. In 1776, the Declaration of Independence of the North American colonies provided a clear precedent for Latin American revolutionaries. Following the lead of Adam Smith's *Wealth of Nations*, also written in 1776, a number of Latin American authors established an intellectual basis for free trade, and called attention to the costs imposed by European commercial regulations.[5] Before the end of the colonial period, Britain forced Spain to open some of its ports to British ships, weakening the system of colonial control.

In 1804, Haiti became the first country in the region to win its independence; most of the others were free within 20 years. The most important leader of the revolutionary era was Simón Bolivar, a Venezuelan *criollo* who dedicated his military talents, aristocratic position, and substantial wealth to the cause of independence. Bolivar led revolutions in his native Venezuela and in Colombia, Ecuador, Panama, Peru, and Bolivia. All these countries officially invested him with the title *Libertador*, and he served as president of Bolivia, the country that adopted his name.

Thus, the Latin American nations gained the benefits of independence about 40 years later than the United States, but about a century earlier than much of Africa and Asia. Freedom from colonial controls allowed Latin America to expand and diversify its international trade linkages, but it caused few internal structural reforms. For example, the large agricultural estates were not divided into smaller, more equitable and manageable units. The new aristocracy preserved many of the inefficiencies of the colonial era after independence. Native populations, whose ancestors had been enslaved by the Aztecs, Incas, Spaniards, and Portuguese, were now subjugated to the *criollos*. These inequities eventually led to new revolutionary movements and major land reforms.

IMPORT SUBSTITUTION, STATE CONTROL, AND REVOLUTION

As we noted in previous chapters, independence from colonialism allowed Latin American countries to seek new markets for their exports, launching an economic boom in the 1830s. Initially, the newly independent states avoided interference in domestic and international trade, but beginning in the 1870s they followed the lead of the United States, introducing tariffs to protect their "infant industries." According to the architect of the Brazilian tariff of 1879, "protective measures are never wrong for new countries like ours, where industry is not strong enough to face foreign competition."[6]

The era of export-led growth continued until the 1930s, when the Great Depression caused foreign export demand to collapse. Under pressure from industrialists and labor leaders, governments throughout Latin America

---

[5]These writings are discussed in Wendell C. Gordon, *The Economy of Latin America* (New York: Colombia University Press, 1950), 7–9.

[6]A. Bandeira de Mello, quoted in Paul Bairoch, *Economics and World History* (Chicago: University of Chicago Press, 1993), 91.

strengthened their programs of trade protectionism and import-substituting industrialization (ISI). After World War II, the ISI strategy gained legitimacy and support from the well-known Argentine economist Raul Prebisch and his colleagues at the United Nations Economic Commission for Latin America (ECLA). The ECLA argued that Latin American countries would suffer from deterioration of their international terms of trade (the export/import price ratio) if they continued to rely on exports of primary goods.[7] Thus, the governments needed to take active measures to encourage and protect new industries. The ECLA advanced these ideas in its publications, press releases, meetings with government officials, and training programs for civil servants.

Under the broad banner of ISI, Latin American governments experimented with a wide range of interventionist programs during the 1950s and 1960s. The details vary from one country to another, but many of them established national planning offices, erected import barriers, created new public enterprises (sometimes by expropriating foreign companies), introduced programs of agrarian reform, and encouraged the development of workers' participation schemes and cooperative enterprises.

When these programs were introduced in a moderate way, without causing great social and financial instability, they were generally successful. Thus, real incomes nearly doubled in Latin America between 1950 and 1973, during the glory days of ISI (Table 8.1). On the other hand, in previous chapters we have discussed some of the weaknesses of this strategy: its reliance on small domestic markets and large regulatory bureaucracies; its tendency to cause overvaluation of exchange rates and to stifle the efficiencies of competition.

Perhaps the most serious deficiency of the ISI strategy was its failure to clearly specify the limits of state intervention. The strategy tended to encourage and legitimize the latent authoritarianism in Latin American culture, rooted in its colonial and precolonial heritage. Thus, the leaders of many Latin American countries introduced programs of state intervention and personal aggrandizement that extended far beyond the basic design of ISI. These took many forms.

In Argentina, Juan Domingo Perón won the 1946 presidential election as a Labour party candidate, having served as labor minister in a wartime military government. With support from industrialists and labor unions, Perón established an economic and political system modeled after Italian fascism. Attempting to expand industry at the expense of agriculture, he paid large subsidies to favored sectors, imposed strict controls on exports and imports, and placed commercial banks under direct control of the central bank. In addition, he nationalized the railways and other foreign-owned industries, and established a liberal system of social insurance and labor benefits.

Perón's policies, together with a drop in world food prices, caused Argentine agricultural production to collapse. The balance of international pay-

[7]The ECLAC continues to emphasize this issue today. See Economic Commission for Latin America and the Caribbean, *Economic Survey of Latin America and the Caribbean 1992*, vol. 1 (Santiago: United Nations, 1994), 138–139.

■ TABLE 8.1

GDP PER CAPITA IN SELECTED COUNTRIES OF LATIN AMERICA AND THE CARIBBEAN, 1870–1995 (1995 DOLLARS AT PURCHASING POWER PARITY)

	1870	1913	1950	1973	1980	1990	1995
Latin America & Caribbean	992*	1,597*	2,576	5,053	6,039	5,331	5,741
Caribbean							
Dominican Republic	—	—	1,547	3,174	3,411	3,505	3,870
Haiti	—	—	971	1,508	1,862	1,420	910
Middle America							
El Salvador	—	—	1,887	2,771	2,771	2.136	2,610
Guatemala	—	—	2,247	3,577	4,029	3,163	3,340
Honduras	—	—	1,562	1,833	2,070	1,854	1,900
Mexico	1,449	1,884	2,679	5,383	7,201	6,667	6,400
South America							
Argentina	2,091	4,004	5,257	8,400	8,876	6,702	8,310
Bolivia	—	—	2,352	2,874	3,302	2,369	2,540
Brazil	539	901	1,857	4,333	5,508	5,090	5,400
Chile	—	2,047	3,832	5,396	6,167	7,179	9,520
Colombia	—	1,408	2,452	4,075	5,058	5,340	6,130
Ecuador	—	—	1,516	3,251	5,009	3,977	4,220
Paraguay	—	—	2,041	2,683	4,257	3,578	3,650
Peru	—	1,588	2,616	4,570	4,673	3,206	3,770
Uruguay	—	—	5,983	6,163	7,396	5,609	6,630
Venezuela	—	—	4,680	8,956	10,016	7,861	7,900

*Very rough approximations based on available data.

Sources: Author's calculations based on real GDP per capita data for 1995 in World Bank, *World Development Report 1997*, 214–215. These are moved backward in time with data from Angus Maddison, *The World Economy in the 20th Century* (Paris: OECD, 1989), 19; Angus Maddison, "A Comparison of Levels of GDP per Capita in Developed and Developing Countries, 1700–1980," *Journal of Economic History* 43 (March 1993): 30; B. R. Mitchell, *International Historical Statistics: The Americas 1750–1988* (New York: Stockton Press, 1993); and International Monetary Fund, *International Financial Statistics*.

ments, which had been in surplus, fell steeply into deficit in the early 1950s. With the country tilting toward bankruptcy, Perón was ousted from office by a military coup in 1955.[8]

A few years after the fall of Perón in Argentina, another charismatic autocrat ascended to power in Cuba. The revolutionaries who supported Fidel

---

[8]The ouster of Perón was made possible by a number of factors, including the death in 1952 of his popular wife, Eva Duarte, or Evita, still known by audiences of the musical theater. He returned to power in 1973, but died ten months later, and his second wife, Isabel, who had been elected as his vice-president, became the first female head of state in the western hemisphere. The military removed Isabel Perón in 1976, and initiated its "dirty war" against leftists; about 20,000 people lost their lives. Democracy was restored in 1983, after the military lost its war against Britain for control of the Falklands/Malvinas Islands.

Castro in 1959 hoped to end the wanton terror, corruption, large-scale organized crime, and undemocratic practices that characterized the Batista
regime. Castro quickly moved to consolidate power and to set up his own
authoritarian government. Many leaders of the opposition to Batista were
executed or imprisoned for opposing Castro's policies; hundreds of thousands of Cubans fled the island.

The centerpiece of Castro's economic policy was the agrarian reform of
1959, which expropriated all landholdings exceeding 1,000 acres and eventually converted them to state farms. The regime also nationalized urban land,
banks, transport, and industry. Seizures of property from the United States
alone were valued at about $1.8 billion. Other governmental programs es-
tablished rent controls, infant care and charity clinics, dining rooms for
schoolchildren and indigents, and an expanded program of social security
benefits.

Early in 1961, the United States ended diplomatic relations with Cuba and
imposed a partial trade embargo; by the end of that year diplomatic relations
were dissolved between Cuba and 13 countries in the Western Hemisphere,
and relations were established with all of the Warsaw Pact Countries. In May,
two weeks after the abortive "Bay of Pigs" invasion, Castro praised the Soviet leadership and proclaimed Cuba to be a socialist state. A year later, the
Cold War reached its most critical stage during the Cuban missile crisis. The
United States tightened and extended its trade embargo, depriving Cuba of
about $35 million of annual export revenues.

Programs of import substitution and efforts to reduce Cuba's dependence
on sugar exports have not been terribly successful. Sugar continues to account for about 75 percent of export earnings, although sugar production
and exports have declined during recent years. For many years, weaknesses
in Cuba's economy and the effects of the U.S. economic embargo were offset
by heavy subsidies from the former Soviet Union and its allies. Those subsidies ended abruptly with the decline and dissolution of the Soviet system in
the late 1980s and early 1990s. According to official statistics, Cuban national
income increased by nearly 75 percent between 1975 and 1985, and then declined by roughly 55 percent between 1985 and 1993.[9]

If Perón was a fascist and Castro an orthodox communist, the most prominent representative of democratic socialism in Latin America was Dr. Salvador Allende of Chile. Supported by an alliance of socialist, communist,
and other radical groups, Allende took advantage of divisions between cen-
trist and conservative parties in 1970 to become the first democratically
elected socialist president in Latin America.

---

[9]*Historically Planned Economies: A Guide to the Data*, 1993 edition (Washington, D.C.: World Bank,
1993), 104–105; and Prensa Latina news agency, Havana, November 21, 1994, as transmitted by
BBC Monitoring Service, November 29, 1994. Measurement of economic growth in Cuba is a
matter of heated debate. See the interchange between Claes Brunendius and Andrew Zimbalist,
on one side, and Carmelo Mesa-Lago and Jorge Perez-Lopez, on the other, in the Spring 1995
and Winter 1995 issues of *Comparative Economic Studies*.

Lacking a parliamentary majority, Allende's government bypassed Congress in its efforts to implement a broad socialist program of agrarian reform, nationalization, import protection, and wage increases. Some of Allende's ministers and high officials had previously worked for ECLA and other United Nations agencies, and they saw these policies as an extension of the basic ISI strategy.[10]

Allende financed his programs with rapid monetary growth, which caused a ninefold increase in the general price level between 1970 and 1973. Efforts to slow the rate of inflation with price controls only created widespread shortages and a vast black market. Allende's policies also caused a reduction of unemployment, helping his alliance to gain voting strength in the parliamentary elections of March 1973. Nevertheless, in the face of accelerating inflation, a balance of payments crisis, a rash of disruptive government-supported strikes, and rising militancy from his opposition, Allende died (perhaps at his own hand) during a military coup d'etat in September 1973.

EXPORT PROMOTION AND MARKET REFORM

The first major challenge to the ISI strategy arose from another coup, this one in 1964, overthrowing the populist alliance in Brazil. The military leaders adopted an export-oriented development strategy and an open door to foreign investment. For several years, this strategy seemed rather successful. Growth of real GDP, which had been proceeding at an annual rate of 4.5 percent between 1960 and 1965, doubled to 9.3 percent between 1965 and 1975. Between the same time periods, the annual inflation rate fell from 64 percent to 24 percent. Furthermore, Brazil received more direct foreign investment than any other developing country during the 1970s. By the end of 1983, the stock of foreign holdings was more than $22 billion—twice the amount in Mexico, the second largest recipient. Nearly 75 percent of these investments were made in the manufacturing sector.[11] For all these reasons, economists spoke of a "Brazilian economic miracle" during the late 1960s and early 1970s.

Although the Brazilian leaders made an early shift from import substitution to export promotion, they did not adopt the other elements of a market-oriented or neoliberal development policy. The government continued to play a dominant economic role, with generous subsidy and tax incentive programs, broad reliance on wage, price, and credit controls, and continued support for nationalized companies. Perhaps "the biggest mistake in Brazil's modern history," according to a former finance minister, was the decision to build Brasilia, the ultramodern capital city that provides a comfortable staging ground for one of the world's most entrenched bureaucracies.[12] Fiscal

---

[10]Cristobal Kay, *Latin American Theories of Development and Underdevelopment* (London: Routledge, 1989), 199–200.

[11]World Bank, *World Development Report 1985* (New York: Oxford University Press, 1985), 127.

[12]See Matt Moffett, "Brazil's New President Has Monster to Tame: Bureaucracy in Brasilia," *The Wall Street Journal*, October 5, 1994, A1.

imbalances, together with the oil price shocks of the 1970s, eventually led to rapid inflation and a debt crisis of the 1980s, and to an interruption of Brazilian growth. Programs of privatization and trade liberalization began in 1990, but despite several highly publicized plans, Brazil has been slow to implement programs of fiscal and monetary reform.

In Chile, a controversial step toward market reform began in 1973, when the ruthless regime of General Augosto Pinochet overturned the socialist government of Salvador Allende.[13] Pinochet, who had no personal blueprint for economic policy, appointed a cadre of young, U.S.-trained technocrats—the so-called Chicago Boys.[14] They designed market-oriented reforms for virtually every sector of the Chilean economy. In the face of galloping inflation, they removed existing wage and price controls, attacking the inflation problem with strict fiscal and monetary policies. In the face of a large balance of payments deficit, they reduced tariffs and removed other import barriers, attacking the payments problem instead with a large devaluation of the exchange rate. The Chicago Boys also implemented major programs of deregulation, privatization, and social security reform. These actions were widely criticized when they were implemented by a despotic military regime, but they gained acceptability throughout Latin America after 1989, when the reforms were extended by a civilian government.

In many countries of Latin America, the decisive shift toward market reform began in the late-1980s and early-1990s when escalating inflation and the international debt crisis forced them to consider drastic measures (Tables 8.2 and 8.3). The apparent exhaustion of the ISI strategy, the accomplishments of the East Asian countries and Chile, the rise of a new cadre of leaders, pressure from the international lending institutions, led by the "Washington Consensus," and the desire to enter regional trade groups, such as NAFTA, all encouraged a revolution in Latin American economic policy.[15] Major programs of fiscal adjustment and trade liberalization began in 1985 in Mexico and Bolivia, and spread to most of the other countries in the region during the early 1990s.[16]

---

[13]Humanitarian organizations estimate that more than 3,000 people died from human rights violations during Pinochet's rule, according to *The World Almanac and Book of Facts 1995* (Mahwah, N.J.: Funk & Wagnalls, 1994), 755.

[14]This heavy reliance on economists with U.S. training continued after 1989, when civilian democratic rule was restored. Of 23 ministers and senior members of the Aylwin administration, 18 had undertaken postgraduate work in the United States. See David E. Hojman, "The Political Economy of Recent Conversions to Market Economics in Latin America," *Journal of Latin American Studies* 26 (February 1994): 191–219.

[15]Like the Chicago Boys in Chile, many of the officials who designed reforms in other Latin American countries were graduates of top universities in the United States. See Matt Moffett, "Key Finance Ministers in Latin America Are Old Harvard-MIT Pals," *The Wall Street Journal*, August 1, 1994, A1.

[16]For a useful summary of the timing of these reforms, see Sebastian Edwards, *Latin America and the Caribbean: A Decade after the Debt Crisis* (Washington, D.C.: World Bank, 1993), Table 3.1.

■ TABLE 8.2

CONSUMER PRICE INFLATION RATES IN SELECTED COUNTRIES OF LATIN AMERICA AND THE CARIBBEAN, 1950–1996 (AVERAGE ANNUAL PERCENTAGE RATES)

	1951–1960	1961–1970	1971–1980	1981–1990	1991–1996
Latin America & Caribbean	—	22.9	35.1	176.6	127.6
Caribbean					
Dominican Republic	0.6	1.9	10.5	25.9	12.8
Haiti	—	3.1	10.9	7.0	23.4
Trinidad/Tobago	—	3.1	13.1	11.1	3.0
Middle America					
El Salvador	3.0	0.8	10.9	19.2	12.4
Guatemala	0.9	0.7	9.7	15.1	13.9
Honduras	—	2.2	7.9	7.9	21.1
Mexico	7.4	2.6	16.8	69.1	20.2
Nicaragua	4.9	1.9	15.1	3,259.6	35.0
South America					
Argentina	28.2	22.8	141.5	787.0	26.3
Bolivia	60.7	5.7	20.2	1,364.6	11.9
Brazil	—	47.3	48.0	605.1	558.3
Chile	25.9	27.5	174.2	20.5	12.7
Colombia	6.8	12.0	21.3	23.7	24.1
Ecuador	—	4.2	12.7	374.9	36.6
Paraguay	30.2	2.6	13.4	22.0	16.8
Peru	7.8	10.1	31.9	1,223.6	65.0
Uruguay	—	51.0	64.0	65.6	55.0
Venezuela	1.8	1.2	8.5	25.0	52.4

Sources: World Bank, *World Tables;* and International Monetary Fund, *International Financial Statistics*, various issues.

AGRICULTURE

In Latin America as a whole, the proportion of the labor force working in agriculture dropped sharply between the 1960s and 1990s, with a large number moving into the service sector (Table 8.4). Still, at 25 percent, the agricultural share of the work force is nearly three times larger in Latin America than in the industrial countries of North America and Europe. Furthermore, in countries such as Benin, Bolivia, Dominican Republic, Haiti, Nicaragua, and Paraguay, agriculture employs 40 percent or more of the working populations. Among indigenous populations, more than 70 percent are still engaged in farming.

■ TABLE 8.3

EXTERNAL DEBT AS PERCENTAGE OF GDP IN SELECTED COUNTRIES OF LATIN AMERICA AND THE CARIBBEAN, 1970–1992

	1970	1975	1980	1985	1990	1995
Latin America & Caribbean	11	19	36	39	42	38
Caribbean						
Dominican Republic	16	19	30	62	63	37
Haiti	10	10	21	36	36	40
Trinidad/Tobago	13	6	13	n.a.	51	54
Middle America						
El Salvador	9	23	26	43	40	27
Guatemala	6	7	15	21	38	22
Honduras	13	34	58	73	141	125
Mexico	9	17	30	53	42	70
Nicaragua	20	39	105	185	n.a.	590
South America						
Argentina	9	15	35	56	62	33
Bolivia	48	50	88	137	101	91
Brazil	8	19	30	44	25	24
Chile	26	66	44	124	74	43
Colombia	19	21	21	33	45	28
Ecuador	12	16	51	62	121	84
Paraguay	19	15	21	60	41	29
Peru	12	31	45	75	59	54
Uruguay	11	22	17	58	47	32
Venezuela	6	5	42	46	71	49

Sources: Sebastian Edwards, *Latin America and the Caribbean: A Decade after the Debt Crisis* (Washington, D.C.: World Bank, 1993), Table 1.2; World Bank, *World Debt Tables;* and International Monetary Fund, *World Economic Outlook.*

■ TABLE 8.4

LATIN AMERICA AND THE CARIBBEAN: SECTORAL COMPOSITION OF THE LABOR FORCE, 1965–1990 (PERCENTAGES OF TOTAL LABOR FORCE)

	1960	1980	1990
Agriculture	49	34	25
Industry	20	25	24
Services	30	41	51

Source: United Nations Development Programme, *Human Development Report 1996,* 211; and World Bank, *World Development Report 1997,* 221.

PLANTATION AND HACIENDA

After independence from Spain and Portugal, many native people continued to practice traditional subsistence agriculture in remote areas, and to work communally on village-owned lands, known as *ejidos* in Mexico. These native holdings were gradually absorbed by two major systems of land tenure developed during the colonial era. On the Caribbean islands and in the coastal regions of Brazil, Venezuela, Colombia, Guyana, Suriname, and Central America, agriculture was organized on large **plantations**. Generally, each plantation was oriented toward production of one or two cash crops for export, such as sugar or bananas. Thus, earnings were unstable, fluctuating with the prices of a few commodities, and production was highly seasonal, often requiring migration of workers. On the other hand, economies of large-scale production and extensive mechanization often provided a high level of efficiency and productivity on plantations.

On the mainland of Latin America, with less access to international markets, the Spaniards and *criollos* organized agriculture on self-sufficient *haciendas*, as they were known in Mexico and Chile, or *estancias* in Argentina. A single *hacienda* community would include a large farm, or *latifundio*, and the surrounding small farms, or *minifundios*. The details differed from one country to another, but the *latifundio* often covered thousands of acres and was inhabited by the lord, or *patrón*, of the *hacienda*, his family and servants, and a resident staff of managers, foremen, and tenant workers. Unlike the plantation, which was characteristically organized to earn profits for its owners, the *hacienda* was dedicated to local self-sufficiency and to the power and prestige of the *patrón* and his family. Thus, it often operated inefficiently.

The *minifundio* was often little more than a garden plot, too small to support a family, so the owners were forced to seek work at the neighboring *latifundios*. Many countries had a system of *debt peonage*, preventing peasants from leaving the *hacienda* if they were indebted to the *patrón*. After World War II, Peru still had a feudal system that prevented workers from freely leaving the land, and they were transferred with the land when it was sold.[17]

REVOLUTION AND LAND REFORM

Each in their own way, the plantation and hacienda systems became symbols of all that was considered wrong in Latin America. The plantations symbolized foreign ownership and exploitation, and excessive dependence on foreign markets and single crops. The *haciendas* symbolized the old system of social class, privilege, strong-man leadership, debt peonage, income inequality, and inefficient production. Many of the major social movements in Latin America, from the Mexican revolution of 1910–1915 to the Cuban revolution of 1959, were supported by people who wished to overturn these systems of land tenure.

In Mexico, a presidential decree in 1890 expropriated the communal lands of the native villages, the *ejidos*, and transferred them to the *haciendas*. By

---

[17]Gordon, *The Economy of Latin America*, 36–37.

1910, 834 landowners controlled two-thirds of the country's area. Nearly 97 percent of rural heads of households owned no land at all. Popular resentment led to a series of political intrigues and violent conflicts, culminating in a 1915 presidential decree and a 1917 Constitution providing for a major program of land reform. Land that had been seized from the *ejidos* was restored to them. More important, the new Constitution called for the government to expropriate land holdings larger than 100 hectares (247 acres) from the *haciendas*, and redistribute them to the *ejidos*. Residents of the *ejidos* would be allowed to transfer ownership rights to their children as an inheritance, but to avoid new concentrations of land ownership, they would not be allowed to rent, sell, or mortgage the property.

The program of land expropriation began slowly in Mexico, but more than 60 million acres were redistributed by the end of 1939, and nearly half the cultivated land was redistributed by 1950. The *hacienda* system and the *latifundios* were virtually eliminated in many regions of Mexico, but they survived or resurfaced in other regions, including the poor southern state of Chiápas.

In most other countries of Latin America, land reforms did not begin until the late 1950s and 1960s, encouraged by the Alliance for Progress as a means to improve productivity and the distribution of income. Programs of land expropriation and redistribution were initiated, for example, in Bolivia in 1953, Venezuela in 1958, Cuba in 1959, Chile in 1964, and Peru in 1968. Nevertheless, in the 1970s more than 70 percent of the land under cultivation in Latin America was still held by less than 2 percent of landowners.[18]

When General Pinochet and his Chicago Boys came to power in Chile, land reform was one of many issues that received a new examination. In 1973, in connection with a broader program of privatization, the regime decided to return farms that had been seized by the Allende government to their original owners. Furthermore, the new government decided to halt any further expropriation of farms, and to privatize the lands that were under state ownership. By 1979, when the process was nearly complete, 30 percent of expropriated lands had been returned to previous owners, 44 percent had been transferred or sold to private owners, and 18 percent had been transferred to nonprofit institutions.[19]

Following the Chilean example, the legislature in Peru recently removed all limits on land ownership. Peruvian leaders have apparently concluded that large concentrations of land are needed to attract the investments needed for modernization of agriculture. They express little concern about the possible return of *latifundios*, and they risk retaliation from the notorious Shining Path guerrillas, who adhere to a Maoist ideology.[20]

---

[18]Michael Todaro, *Economic Development in the Third World*, 2d ed. (New York: Longman, 1981), 260.

[19]Eduardo Bitran and Raúl E. Saez, "Privatization and Regulation in Chile," in Barry Bosworth, Rudiger Dornbusch, and Raúl Labán, eds., *The Chilean Economy: Policy Lessons and Challenges* (Washington, D.C.: The Brookings Institution, 1994), 335.

[20]Sally Bowen, "Peru Set to Sweep Away 27-Year-Old Land Reform Laws," *Financial Times*, July 18, 1995, 23; and Orin Starn, "Maoism in the Andes," *Journal of Latin American Studies* 27 (May 1995): 399–421.

Back in Mexico, the market-oriented government of President Salinas hoped in 1992 to end expropriation of land and to reform the *ejido* system of communal land ownership. Claiming that concentrations of land ownership were no longer a problem, Salinas led the Mexican Congress to approve amendments to the 1917 Constitution that (1) formally ended the land redistribution program; (2) gave members of *ejidos* the right to become owners of their plots; and (3) allowed *ejido* members to buy land, rent their plots, and conclude contracts or joint venture agreements with domestic and foreign partners. The amendments did not remove the 100-hectare constitutional limit on individual holdings, but implied that no effort would be made to enforce the limit.

The new agrarian policy, together with other social inequities, led to a violent peasant uprising in Chiápas, beginning in January 1994. The peasants claimed that many illegal estates, some dating back to the Spanish conquest, were never redistributed. Indigenous customs and autonomy would be threatened, they said, if the *ejidos* were allowed to fragment. Early in 1995, President Zedillo departed from the policy of his predecessor, and initiated a new program of redistribution, beginning with more than 25,000 hectares of land in Chiápas.[21]

INDUSTRIAL ORGANIZATION

Latin American countries have a full spectrum of institutional arrangements in industry, including companies that are public or private, formal or informal, large or small, competitive or monopolistic, corporate or individual, and local or multinational. These structures were influenced profoundly by the import-substitution model of industrialization, which caused a major migration from rural areas to the cities, raising the urban share of the Latin American population from 48 percent in 1960 to 74 percent in 1995.

Most of the companies in Latin America are **microenterprises**, employing 15 employees or less; larger companies account for most of employment and sales. In Mexico, for example, 97 percent of the companies operating in the early 1990s were microenterprises, but these accounted for only 11 percent of total employment.[22]

THE INFORMAL ECONOMY

The microenterprises, together with self-employed workers, unpaid family workers, and domestic servants, comprise most of the so-called **informal sector**, which has consistently accounted for about one-third of Latin American urban employment since the 1960s (Table 8.5). Much of the attention now given to the informal sector has arisen from the work of Hernando de Soto,

---

[21]See Andrew Reding, "Chiápas Is Mexico," *World Policy Journal* 11 (Spring 1994): 11–25; and Natalya Johnson, "Rural Reforms Fail to Take Root," *Business Mexico*, March 1995, 1.

[22]Leticia Rodriguez, "Helping Out Micro-, Small- and Medium-Sized Business Financing to Secure the Future," *Business Mexico*, September 1994, 1; and Guillermo Rosenbluth, "The Informal Sector and Poverty in Latin America," *CEPAL Review* 52 (April 1994): 168.

■ TABLE 8.5

LATIN AMERICA: URBAN INFORMAL EMPLOYMENT AS A
PERCENTAGE OF THE URBAN ECONOMICALLY ACTIVE POPULATION,
1960–1990

	1960	1970	1980	1990
Argentina	21	19	39	40
Bolivia	62	56	57	27
Brazil	27	28	43	46
Chile	35	24	27	30
Colombia	39	31	34	27
Costa Rica	29	23	20	22
Ecuador	35	58	53	—
El Salvador	43	40	40	—
Guatemala	52	44	40	54
Mexico	37	35	36	36
Panama	25	27	36	39
Peru	47	41	41	39
Uruguay	19	21	32	35
Venezuela	32	31	30	33
Latin America	31	30	30	31

Source: Estimates of the Regional Employment Program of the International Labor Office (known by the Spanish acronym, PREALC), compiled in Alejandro Portes and Richard Schauffler, "Competing Perspectives on the Latin American Informal Sector," *Population and Development Review* 19 (March 1993): 42; and Guillermo Rosenbluth, "The Informal Sector and Poverty in Latin America," *CEPAL Review* 52 (April 1994): 168.

director of the Institute for Liberty and Democracy (ILD) in Lima, Peru.[23] According to de Soto, the formal sectors in Latin America are based on a mercantilist system, rooted in national cultures and the regulatory structures of import substitution, that reserves monopoly privileges for a chosen few.

In particular, monopoly privileges have been protected by complex and costly registration procedures that make it difficult to create legal business enterprises. In 1983, researchers for de Soto's ILD attempted to obtain eleven permits from eight governmental agencies to establish a fictitious clothing

[23]Keith Hart, an anthropologist, was the first to speak of an "informal sector" in 1971, and important empirical research on informality was performed by the Regional Employment Program of the International Labor Office, but de Soto's market-oriented approach to the subject, calling for elimination of state regulatory barriers, gained a receptive audience in the Washington-based international development agencies. See Alejandro Portes and Richard Schauffler, "Competing Perspectives on the Latin American Informal Sector," *Population and Development Review* 19 (March 1993): 40.

factory as a single proprietorship (incorporation would have been much more difficult). The registration process required 289 days of full-time labor and $1,231 of fees, expenses, lost income, and bribes (they paid two of the ten bribes solicited)—the equivalent of 32 minimum monthly wages. Legal establishment of a small store required negotiations with three agencies, lasting 43 days, and costing $590 (15 minimum monthly wages).[24]

According to de Soto, when industrialization drew millions of rural Latin Americans into the cities, they encountered a hostile reception from the elite urban populations. Unable to find jobs, and unable to pay the prices of formality, they created informal enterprises. To the extent possible, they also created informal systems of governance, property rights, contractual relationships, and financial institutions. De Soto estimates that 30 informal banking systems were established in Peru.

De Soto considers informal enterprises to be productive and entrepreneurial, but severely disadvantaged by their legal status. To avoid detection and punishment, their operations must be kept small and mobile; they cannot freely advertise their product, operate in the best locations, maintain complete financial records, or benefit from the formal systems of civil and criminal justice. On the other hand, they must pay bribes and fines to officials and usurious interest rates to lenders.

To remedy these problems, de Soto has led a campaign to simplify procedures and reduce fees for companies to join the formal sector. In the simplest cases, it is now possible for Peruvian entrepreneurs to register their businesses in a single day. The number of businesses completing registration in Peru increased from a monthly average of about 2,000 in 1990 to 11,000 in 1993.[25] Similar reforms have been undertaken in other Latin American countries.

BIG BUSINESS AND THE MULTINATIONALS

There are millions of business organizations in Latin America, but the 500 largest companies account for about one-third of the gross product of the entire region (Table 8.6). Brazil, which has about one-third of the Latin American population, has more than half the region's largest companies. Mexico has less than 20 percent of the population in the region, and less than 20 percent of the large companies, but it accounts for nearly 30 percent of large company sales.

---

[24]Hernando de Soto, *The Other Path: The Invisible Revolution in the Third World* (New York: Harper & Row, 1989), 132–143. The title of this book refers to the contrast between de Soto's free market ideas and those of Shining Path, the Peruvian Maoist group. In 1992, an unsuccessful attempt on de Soto's life with a 400kg car bomb was attributed to Shining Path. See Stephen Fidler, "Practical Visionary," *The Financial Times*, September 29, 1993, supplement, 8.

[25]Ibid.

■ TABLE 8.6

LATIN AMERICA: 500 LARGEST COMPANIES, 1992

	Number of Companies	Sales (US$ Mill.)	Sales as % of GDP*
Location:			
Brazil	255	165,552	43
Mexico	86	113,458	34
Argentina	64	37,119	16
Venezuela	24	31,579	14
Chile	30	16,423	40
Colombia	25	9,572	20
Peru	9	4,075	18
Panama	1	3,213	54
Ecuador	1	1,880	15
Uruguay	4	1,414	12
Bolivia	1	645	12
Ownership:			
Private	268	143,314	12
Foreign	140	105,166	9
State	92	136,451	12
Total	500	384,931	33

*Sales for each country taken as percentage of national GDP; sales by ownership are taken as percentage of total GDP for the countries listed.
Sources: *America Economia* (Special issue, 1993/1994), 72; World Bank, *World Development Report 1994*, 166–167; and author's calculations.

More than half the large companies in Latin America are owned domestically by private individuals and corporations. They generally dominate in such fields as construction, communications, retail distribution, and steel production. Less than one-fifth of the large companies are state-owned, but these account for more than one-third of large-company sales. Despite major programs of privatization, the three largest companies in Latin America in 1992 were PDVSA, Pemex, and Petrobras, the state-owned petroleum monopolies of Venezuela, Mexico, and Brazil; in many countries, the public sector continues to dominate in electricity generation and mining.

About one-quarter of the large companies are owned by foreigners, and they account for about one-fourth of large-company sales, or 9 percent of Latin American GDP. The sales of a single multinational corporation, McDermott International, amount to more than half the GDP of Panama, its host country. Multinationals dominate in production of automobiles, office equipment, pharmaceuticals, beverages, and electronics.

In recent years, a particular group of foreign enterprises, the *maquiladoras*, have attracted a great deal of attention. These began to appear after 1966, when a treaty between Mexico and the United States created special zones in northern Mexico where U.S. raw materials and components could be imported duty-free, assembled into final products, and imported back into the United States with a tariff levied only on the value added by Mexican labor. Between 1982 and 1995, the number of *maquiladora* factories increased dramatically, from 588 to more than 2,000; employment in the factories increased from 122,000 to more than 600,000.[26] In the meanwhile, *maquiladoras* have been established in several other countries of Central America and the Caribbean.

The *maquiladoras* became a major issue during negotiation of the North American Free Trade Agreement (NAFTA). In the United States, they symbolized the flight of manufacturing jobs to factories in Latin America with low wages, unsafe working conditions, and weak environmental regulations. Side agreements to NAFTA were negotiated to ameliorate these problems. Under terms of the final agreement, the *maquiladora* regions will lose their special tariff status in the year 2001, and all of Mexico will, in effect, become a free-trade zone.

State Ownership and Privatization[27]

State participation in ownership and control of industry has a long history in Latin America. The Incas and the Aztecs had centrally planned economies, and the mercantile Spaniards pursued economic extraction in the name of the crown. In 1911, the president of Uruguay, José Battle y Ordóñez, outlined the economic role of the "modern state":

Modern conditions have increased the number of industries that fall under the heading of public services. . . . The modern state unhesitatingly accepts its status as an economic organization. It will enter industry when competition is not practicable, when control by private interests vests in them authority inconsistent with the welfare of the State, when a fiscal monopoly may serve as a great source of income to meet urgent tax problems, when the continued export of the national wealth is considered undesirable.28

During the 1930s, dissatisfaction with the practices of foreign owners and employers led to the expropriation and nationalization of energy companies, telephone systems, and a range of other public utilities. For example, a dispute over wages and benefits in 1938 led to seizure of the Mexican oil industry from 17 companies, and to the creation of a state-owned petroleum monopoly, Petróleos Mexicanos (PEMEX), which is still the largest company in Mexico.

---

[26]Kevin G. Hall, "Boom Goes On: Industry Still Pouring Development onto Mexican Border," *Chicago Tribune*, June 18, 1995, 7A.

[27]General sources of data and information for this section include Edwards, *Latin America and the Caribbean: A Decade after the Debt Crisis*, 77–92; Frank Sader, *Privatization and Foreign Investment in the Developing World*, 1988–92, WPS 1202, Debt and International Finance Division, International Economics Department, World Bank, Washington, D.C., October 1993, passim; and "1994 Privatization in Latin America," *LatinFinance* 55 (March 1994), supplement.

[28]Quoted in Simon G. Hanson, *Utopia in Uruguay* (New York: Oxford University Press, 1938), 24.

Also beginning in the 1930s, the program of import-substituting industrialization led to the establishment of many state-owned manufacturing companies. This process continued after World War II, and accelerated during the 1960s. Hundreds of domestic and foreign companies were nationalized by Marxist regimes in countries such as Cuba, Chile, and Nicaragua. In Chile, for example, the number of state-owned enterprises (SOEs) increased from 67 to 529 between 1970 and 1973.[29]

The first important wave of Latin American privatizations began in the mid–1970s, when Salvador Allende was overthrown in Chile and his socialist policies were repudiated by the Pinochet regime. Between 1973 and 1978, Pinochet and his Chicago Boys privatized nearly 500 enterprises. About half of these had been seized without compensation during the Allende years, and they were returned without compensation. The other half were sold, primarily to domestic companies and investors, for a total of nearly $1 billion.

A second wave of privatization began in the mid-1980s, when Latin American governments were trying to reduce their runaway budget deficits, their accelerating inflation rates, and their foreign debts. Privatization of money-losing SOEs would allow the governments to stop paying costly budget subsidies, and revenues from privatization could be used to repay international debts or to finance domestic budget deficits.

Once again, Chile led the way between 1984 and 1989 by selling about 80 large SOEs, including public utilities, the national airline, and the country's largest steel mill, for about $1.4 billion. This time, foreign investors were invited to participate, and many of the sales were structured as **debt-for-equity swaps**. That is, the government repaid a portion of its foreign debt by exchanging stock in its privatized companies for bonds and other debt instruments held by foreigners. To allay public fears of excessive foreign ownership, and to broaden the domestic base of capital ownership, the government offered special financial terms and discounts to individual Chilean investors under its programs of "popular capitalism" and "worker capitalism."[30] Nevertheless, the Chilean privatization program virtually ended in 1989 when the country returned to democratic rule. The country's largest company, Codelco, which is a huge copper mining enterprise, was still under state ownership.

In Mexico, the number of SOEs climbed from about 240 in 1960 to 391 in 1970, and then to a peak of 1,155 in 1982. When Mexico faced a debt crisis in 1982, President López Portillo followed tradition and nationalized most of the banks, compensating their owners with ten-year government bonds. Unsurprisingly, this action only worsened a horrible situation, causing a wild flight of capital from Mexico. A few months later, the new government led by President Miguel de la Madrid reversed the trend, and initiated programs of

---

[29]Bitran and Saez, "Privatization and Regulation in Chile," 332–333.

[30]William F. Maloney, "Privatization with Share Diffusion: Popular Capitalism in Chile, 1985–1988," in Werner Baer and Melissa Birch, eds., *Privatization in Latin America: New Roles for the Public and Private Sectors*, (Westport, Conn.: Praeger, 1994), 135–161.

macroeconomic stabilization and privatization. The government began with closure, liquidation, and merger of small and medium-sized companies. It delayed the sale of banks and larger enterprises, because their values were depressed by the continuing economic crisis. Still, by the end of the de la Madrid administration in 1988, the number of SOEs had been cut by nearly two-thirds, to 412 enterprises, and more than $2 billion of privatization proceeds had been collected.[31]

The Mexican program accelerated between 1988 and 1994, during the administration of President Carlos Salinas de Gortari. Some 360 state enterprises, many of them very large, including the national telephone company, the two airlines, a gigantic steel complex, and the 18 domestic banks that had been seized during the Portillo administration, were sold to the highest domestic or international bidders. The total proceeds for the sales were nearly $19 billion, most of which was derived from the sale of banks and the telephone company.[32] These revenues have been used exclusively to repay internal debts, not to finance new spending programs.

The Mexican program enjoyed substantial political support because it was designed in cooperation with labor unions and the private sector. Under Mexican law, the labor unions have the right of first refusal on any privatization; unions bought controlling interests in 16 companies and substantial shares of others. The government also extracted informal commitments from purchasers of SOEs that they would not lay off large numbers of workers. The Mexican constitution prohibits the sale of PEMEX, the petroleum monopoly, which is Latin America's largest employer, and Ferronales, the national railroad, which is Latin America's largest transport company.

The third wave of Latin American privatization began in the early 1990s, when domestic financial problems, pressure from international lending institutions, and the successful experiences of Chile and Mexico caused other countries to start or accelerate their programs. In Argentina, for example, the annual losses of SOEs imposed a drain on the public budget equal to 9 percent of GDP, or 64 percent larger than public expenditures on health and education.[33]

Argentine privatization began in 1990, and, unlike the programs in Chile and Mexico, it began with some of the largest and most controversial companies. During the first year, the government offered 60 percent of the national telephone company, which accounted for about one-third of the country's SOE deficit, and exchanged it for debt reduction with a market value of $1.3 billion.[34] Even more unlike the Chileans and Mexicans, who

[31]"Number of Unsold Mexican Firms at 222," *Reuters Financial Report*, September 18, 1992, 1.

[32]"Finance Secretary Provides Details on the Results of Privatization Programs since 1988," *SourceMex*, July 27, 1994, 1. These U.S. dollar figures should only be taken as rough approximations; the privatizations were performed during years of extreme exchange rate instability.

[33]These losses were larger, as a proportion of GDP, than those in most developing countries. See United Nations Development Programme, *Human Development Report 1993* (New York: Oxford University Press, 1993), Table 3.4.

[34]The retired government bonds had a face value of $5 billion. This was the largest debt-equity privatization ever undertaken.

have been unwilling or unable to sell their copper and petroleum monopolies, the Argentines quickly initiated sales of their state-owned petroleum producers, distributors, and refineries. They also sold national airlines, railroads, power utilities, television networks, and steel mills. By the end of 1993, after only a few years of work, the government completed privatizations with a market value of $8.9 billion, and used them to retire public debt with a face value of approximately $17 billion.

Brazil, the largest economic power in Latin America, was slow to begin its program of privatization, but it sold about $7 billion of SOE assets in the steel, petrochemical, and fertilizer industries between 1990 and 1994, and it announced plans in 1995 to sell assets worth another $15 billion. Privatizations have also been performed in Ecuador ($100 million), Honduras ($12 million), Peru ($3.1 billion), and Venezuela ($2.3 billion). Of the twenty largest privatizations transacted in the world between 1984 and 1993, ten took place in Latin America.[35]

To privatize six of its public utility companies, Bolivia has developed an interesting new model known as **capitalization**. According to the 1994 law that controls this system, a 50 percent share of each public utility is sold to a "strategic investor," who has managerial control of the enterprise. Unlike a traditional privatization, none of the proceeds from the strategic investor are paid to the government; the capital remains within the company where it can be used for investment and production. The other half of the shares held by the state are transferred to all Bolivian adults by crediting their individual "capitalization accounts," which are managed by private pension funds. This scheme is designed to attract new capital and managerial resources into the SOEs, to spread the system of capital ownership to the entire population, and to encourage the development of pension funds and other financial institutions.

THE LABOR MARKET

Before World War II, when the Latin American economies were predominantly agrarian, the labor market in each country was largely a reflection of its system of land tenure (*hacienda*, plantation, family farm) and the socioethnic composition of the population (native, European, African, *criollo*, *mestizo*). Extreme inequalities still exist in the agrarian sectors of Latin America; 61 percent of the rural population lives in absolute poverty, compared with 30 percent of the urban population.[36]

In industry, a number of historic influences have made it difficult to develop stable systems of collective bargaining. Before and during the colonial era, mining and manufacturing were often based on systems of slavery and other forms of forced labor. In the nineteenth century, legal codes in many

---

[35]Jorge F. Segura, "The Past, Present, and Future of Privatization," *LatinFinance* 53 (December 1993), S32.

[36]United Nations Development Programme, *Human Development Report 1994*, 210.

countries prohibited workers from signing binding contracts with their employers. These codes originally were meant to protect poor and illiterate workers from contracts they could not read, but they retarded the development of collective bargaining and long-term agreements.[37]

In most countries of Latin America, organization of labor unions was patently illegal until the early years of the twentieth century. The earliest unions, encouraged by the Catholic Church, were organized to allow workers to pool their resources in a social insurance system; they usually made no attempt to bargain with employers. Eventually, more militant unions began to organize in mining towns and textile mills. When they attempted to organize strikes, the governments often supported employers with military force.[38]

Relationships between labor and management began to change in many ways during the 1930s. The Great Depression undermined the old institutional structure of society, and an increasing number of countries adopted labor codes that protected rights of workers. At the same time, the import-substitution industrialization strategy encouraged migration from rural areas to the cities, which contributed to the development of the informal sector. Companies in the informal economy had little need for collective bargaining or long-term contracts, and they would seldom comply with the new minimum wage and labor laws.

The import competition system also created and legitimized a strong industrial role of the state, and encouraged the establishment of state-owned enterprises. Thus, the state had to deal directly with the labor unions. In some cases, this took the form of a paternalistic relationship, as in the Perón and Allende administrations; more often, the relationship was antagonistic or openly violent. This relationship could change radically from one day to the next, as it did when Allende was overthrown by General Pinochet:

In the wake of the coup, factory owners suddenly had absolute control over their workers and could fire any worker without cause. From 1973 through 1978, practically every labor right for organized and unorganized workers was suspended. All the tools of collective bargaining, including of course the right to strike, were outlawed.39

Together with other social and historic factors, the diverse and unstable relationships between governments and labor unions may explain why union membership levels are very low in some countries and very high in others. In Colombia, Guatemala, and Paraguay, less than 10 percent of the labor force is unionized; in Honduras, Peru, and Venezuela, membership rates are higher than 30 percent.[40]

---

[37]Gordon, *The Economy of Latin America*, 146.

[38]This was the case, for example, in Mexico, where the Diaz regime used military force to suppress strikes in 1906 and 1907.

[39]John Lear and Joseph Collins, "Working in Chile's Free Market," *Latin American Perspectives* 84 (Winter 1995): 13.

[40]Statistics on union membership are notoriously unreliable, but these data are taken from the country pages of U.S. Central Intelligence Agency, *The World Factbook 1992*, passim.

At any rate, Latin American governments have seldom been able to play the role of an impartial referee between independent businesses and labor unions. The establishment of stable civilian governments throughout Latin America, the shift to market-oriented development strategies, and the opening of the economies to import competition and free movement of labor seem to call for new relationships between public and private organizations.

As a first step toward a more cooperative relationship, the governments in some countries have begun to consult more closely with business and labor leaders on their stabilization and privatization programs. In Mexico, for example, the de la Madrid government signed an Economic Solidarity Pact in 1987 with representatives of organized labor, agricultural producers, and the business sector. The pact included macroeconomic targets, plans for privatization, trade liberalization, and, perhaps most important, a set of wage and price guidelines to break inflationary pressures and expectations. According to formal econometric studies, the wage-price guidelines play a significant role in explaining the rapid decline of Mexican inflation from 159 percent in 1987 to 52 percent in 1988 and 20 percent in 1989.[41] Thus, when President Salinas took power in 1988, he quickly announced a new Pact for Economic Stability and Growth to sustain progress; the agreements have been updated each year by subsequent administrations, in consultation with private sector representatives.

Based on its success in Mexico, the practice of negotiating public-private pacts has spread to other countries in the region. According to Luis Anderson, a Panamanian union leader, the pacts are useful, but they should not be allowed to perpetuate the paternalistic role of Latin American governments; instead, they should be "a product of understanding between the state, the business sector, unions and other bodies on an equal footing."[42]

In addition to the antagonistic system of collective bargaining, some economists believe that two other factors seriously reduce the flexibility and efficiency of Latin American labor markets. First, in international perspective, labor laws in these countries impose very high costs on formal-sector employers for dismissing their employees. Laws prohibiting temporary employment and requiring large severance payments for "unjust" dismissals are meant to promote stability of employment, but they may also discourage the creation of new jobs. Latin American severance payments are larger than similar payments in Germany, Spain, and the United Kingdom.[43]

The other factor reducing the efficiency of Latin American labor markets is the relatively high level of social security payroll taxes. In the early 1990s, these ranged from 14 percent in Venezuela to 46 percent in Argentina, with an average of about 23 percent. These are designed, of course, to fund the so-

---

[41]Nora Lustig, *Mexico: The Remaking of an Economy* (Washington, D.C.: The Brookings Institution, 1992), 52.

[42]Humberto Marquez, "Latin America: Unions Respond to Changing Winds," Inter Press Wire Service, April 27, 1995.

[43]Edwards, *Latin America and the Caribbean: A Decade after the Debt Crisis*, 93–95.

cial security systems, but they are thought to discourage job formation and distort the labor market more severely than other forms of taxation and financing.[44] Chile, for example, has shifted to a system based on personal saving, rather than on taxation.[45]

INFLATION AND THE FINANCIAL SECTOR

Through much of recent history, the financial markets in Latin American countries have been crippled and distorted by the direct and indirect effects of rapid inflation. During the period between 1965 and 1996, the average annual rate of inflation was about 8 percent in developing countries of East Asia and South Asia, 16 percent in Sub-Saharan Africa, and 120 percent in Latin America.[46] Furthermore, the Latin American inflation rate (which places a large weight on Brazil, the largest country) has accelerated during each decade between the 1960s and the 1980s (Table 8.2).

Why have the Latin American countries been plagued with so much inflation for so many years? To a monetarist, the answer is simple: Central banks in the region have allowed the creation of too many pesos, cruzeiros, reais, soles, and córdobas. Although this is undoubtedly true, it only raises another question: Why are central bankers in Latin America more inclined to print money than their colleagues in Africa and Asia?

A different explanation of chronic inflation is offered by **structuralism**, a school of economic thought developed in Latin America, and "the first original body of development theory to emanate from the Third World."[47] Instead of concentrating their attention on the excess creation of money, structuralists emphasize the importance of inefficient land tenure systems, limited industrial capacities, and structural imbalances between agriculture and industry that restrict the growth of productivity. The most serious problem, they say, is not excessive growth of the monetary demand for goods, but deficient growth of the material supply. The solution, therefore, is structural reform, including land reform and development of the industrial base. Programs of financial austerity that interfere with these structural reforms may slow the rate of inflation in the short run, but they will exacerbate the problem in the long run.[48]

The structuralist position provides a useful counterweight to simplistic applications of monetarism, but the questions remain: Why have average

---

[44]Ibid., 95–96.

[45]See G. A. Mackenzie, "Reforming Latin America's Old-Age Pension Systems," *Finance & Development* 32 (March 1995): 10–13.

[46]Calculations from data in Appendix Table 1 of the 1989 and 1992 editions of World Bank, *World Development Report*, and from International Monetary Fund, *World Economic Outlook*, May 1997, 145.

[47]Kay, *Latin American Theories of Development and Underdevelopment*, 10.

[48]Ibid., 47–57; and Raymond F. Mikesell, "Inflation in Latin America," in Charles T. Nisbet, ed. *Latin America: Problems in Economic Development* (New York: The Free Press, 1969), 143–189.

inflation rates persisted at higher levels in Latin America than in other developing countries? Are the problems of land tenure and industrial capacity more serious in Latin America than in Africa or South Asia? Can supply limitations explain chronic inflation rates above 100 percent?

Aside from the general messages of monetarism and structuralism, three other considerations may help to explain the Latin American inflation problem. First, political regimes in the region have been notoriously unstable, causing political leaders to seek short-run solutions, such as the printing of money, for long-run development problems. With 150 regimes in 160 years, Bolivia was, until recently, the standard against which unstable countries were measured. After a stable democratic government was established in 1985, the Bolivian inflation rate fell dramatically (Table 8.2). The political situation in Latin America has improved profoundly in recent years, but as recently as 1990, the president of Venezuela predicted a resurgence of instability: "Latin America is a volcano," he said, "that is about to erupt."[49] In 1994, international bankers still considered Honduras, Peru, and Bolivia to be greater credit risks than Lebanon, Bangladesh, Kenya, and Ghana.[50]

A second consideration: Strong dependence on the import-substitution industrialization strategy, which was promoted by many of the structuralists, may have reduced the level of financial discipline in Latin America, and contributed to chronic inflation. In countries that emphasize market-oriented export promotion, the governments face greater pressure to maintain stable prices, which are needed to maintain export competitiveness. Under a regime of import substitution, with high protective tariffs and nontariff barriers, competitiveness on world markets is not a major policy concern.[51] Thus, writing in the 1960s, Mikesell noted that an inward orientation encourages inflation, and inflation reinforces the inward orientation: "Inflation coupled with overvalued exchange rates and a variety of governmental controls and import restrictions has created in Latin America closed economies whose level and structure of internal prices and costs bears little relationship to that of the outside world, including those of other Latin American economies."[52]

A third consideration: Inflation became institutionalized in Latin America through extensive use of **indexation**. In Chile, indexation of wages began as early as the 1940s, and by 1959 the official consumer price index determined the legal wage adjustment for all public sector workers and for private workers not covered by collective bargaining. In Brazil, indexation began in the

---

[49]Anthony Boadle, "Latin America's Democracy Threatened by Social Powder Keg," Reuters News Service, March 13, 1990.

[50]Ratings reported in Harvey D. Shapiro, "Wages of Virtue; Sovereign Creditworthiness," *Institutional Investor* 28 (March 1994), 87.

[51]Anne O. Krueger, "Import Substitution versus Export Promotion," *Finance & Development* 22 (June 1985): 23; and Ching-yuan Lin, "East Asia and Latin America as Contrasting Models," *Economic Development and Cultural Change* 36 (April 1988, Supplement): S160–S165.

[52]Mikesell, "Inflation in Latin America," 175.

1960s and continued for 30 years, eventually covering nearly every transaction in the economy. Brazilian workers, landlords, and retired people were protected from inflation by indexation of wages, rents, and pensions, with adjustments sometimes made on a monthly basis. Sellers and savers were protected by indexation of contract prices, interest rates on bank accounts, and yields on other securities. The government protected itself by indexing tax rates.

With so many interest groups protected from the direct effects of inflation, Latin American governments fell under little pressure to tighten their monetary policies. Indexation perpetuated and sometimes accelerated the inflation problem by driving up wage costs and raw material prices. When countries in the region shifted to an export orientation, and realized that inflation was an obstacle to competitiveness, they began to dismantle their programs of indexation. This process began in Chile in 1979, in Mexico in 1983, and in Brazil in 1995.[53]

FINANCIAL REPRESSION AND LIBERALIZATION

Aside from its influence on the internal distribution of income and on external competitiveness, inflation also tends to distort the operation of financial markets. If the inflation rate is extremely high, as it was in Nicaragua, Bolivia, and Peru during the 1980s, money begins to lose its usefulness as a medium of exchange, as a unit of account, and as a store of value, threatening the entire financial system with collapse. At lower rates of inflation, a number of other serious problems may arise.

If nominal interest rates are left uncontrolled by the government, they will usually hover a few points above the anticipated inflation rate. Thus, when inflation accelerates, market interest rates tend to rise. High interest rates, though, have been scorned by philosophers and regulated by public authorities since ancient times. In Latin America, interest rate controls were already in place at the end of World War II.[54]

If nominal interest rates are controlled while inflation accelerates, real interest rates may become negative. This was the situation in Bolivia and Peru during all the years between 1980 and 1986, and it was the situation in the average Latin American country during 1979 and 1980.[55] When real interest rates become negative, credit markets and market-oriented financial institutions cannot play their normal role in the market economy: They cannot stimulate savings or efficiently allocate financial resources to their most profitable uses. Thus, the government generally increases its intervention: Credit

---

[53]Alejandra Mizala and Pilar Romaguera, "Testing for Wage Leadership Processes in the Chilean Economy," *Applied Economics* 27 (March 1995): 303; Lustig, *Mexico: The Remaking of an Economy*, 29; and "Brazil: Kicking the Habit," *Business Latin America*, July 24, 1995, 1.

[54]Gordon, *The Economy of Latin America*, 242.

[55]In Bolivia, the real interest rate sank as low as –97.5 percent in 1985. See Edwards, *Latin America and the Caribbean: A Decade after the Debt Crisis*, 101.

is rationed to borrowers who are favored by the government, foreign exchange markets are heavily regulated; and barriers are erected against the creation of new financial markets, such as securities markets, that may circumvent the system of governmental controls.

The debt crisis of the 1980s and the accompanying acceleration of inflation made all these problems much more serious. When Latin American countries no longer had access to foreign credit, it became clear that they would have to develop pools of domestic savings. To do this, they needed to restore positive real interest rates, and develop a wider range of financial institutions. Thus, interest rate controls were removed in Chile in the mid–1970s, in Bolivia in 1985, in Mexico in 1988–89, and in most of the other countries in the early 1990s. By 1995, real interest rates were still negative in only two countries: Venezuela and Uruguay.[56]

At the same time, entry barriers were removed, allowing the operation of new domestic and foreign banks, investment companies, and securities firms. To date, these institutional reforms, together with lower inflation rates, have led to disappointing increases in domestic saving, but they have supported a huge influx of foreign capital. After a dry period during the 1980s, capital inflows to Latin America grew to $13 billion in 1990, and then surged to $57 billion in 1994.[57] According to the United Nations Economic Commission for Latin America and the Caribbean, these capital inflows have played a most constructive role in the region:

New capital inflows have financed imports, investments, and speculative operations, have helped to cover fiscal deficits. . . . have fueled a non-inflationary expansion of credit for private-sector investment and consumption, and have added to the region's international reserves.[58]

The dangers inherent in huge flows of international portfolio investment became clear, however, in December 1994, when a currency devaluation in Mexico led to a massive outflow of capital. All the benefits listed in the previous paragraph reversed themselves, and Mexico plunged into a serious recession. During the first six months after the financial panic, some 18,000 people lost their jobs.[59] Nevertheless, the continuing reforms and the underlying potential of the Latin American economies give us reason to believe that Mexico and her neighbors will return again from the financial ashes: "The realization that Latin America is neither the promised land described in the promotional brochures of the early 1990s nor the wasteland depicted in scathing articles prompted by the crisis will eventually sink in."[60]

---

[56]Based on nominal deposit interest rates in World Bank, *World Development Report 1997*, 216–217, and consumer price inflation rates for 1992.

[57]Moisés Naim, "Latin America the Morning After," *Foreign Affairs* 74 (July/August 1995): 48.

[58]United Nations Economic Commission for Latin America and the Caribbean, *Economic Survey of Latin America and the Caribbean 1992*, vol. 1 (Santiago: United Nations, 1994), 9–10.

[59]Leslie Crawford, "Mexico's Vigil of Woe," *Financial Times*, June 2, 1995, 12.

[60]Naim, "Latin America the Morning After," 59.

THE CHURCH, THE STATE, AND THE POOR

In other chapters of this book, this space would be reserved for a general discussion of the role of government in the economy. However, we have already discussed the changing role of Latin American governments, shifting from interventionist programs of import substitution to market-oriented programs of export promotion. We noted the rise and fall of state-owned enterprises, the evolution of land reform, and the causes and effects of rapid price inflation. We have not, however, discussed governmental programs to alleviate income inequality and poverty. We will close the chapter with that discussion, and broaden our focus to consider the economic role of another major institution in Latin America: the Roman Catholic Church.

Basic information on Latin American poverty and income inequality is presented in Table 8.7 (also, refer to Table 2.7). The incidence of absolute poverty is lower in Latin America than in Africa or South Asia, but much higher than in East Asia. Poverty rates were no higher than 20 percent in six of the listed countries, but no less than 40 percent in Guatemala, Honduras, Nicaragua, and Peru. The average poverty rate for the region fell from about 39 percent in 1970 to 35 percent in 1980, but then returned to 39 percent in 1990.[61]

The resurgence of poverty during the 1980s can be broken into two components. First, the international debt crisis precipitated a prolonged recession, causing the real income of the average Latin American to drop by 12 percent between 1980 and 1990 (Table 8.1). Second, the regional distribution of income, which was already the most unequal in the world, grew even more uneven. This is indicated by rising Gini coefficients in ten of thirteen countries in Table 8.7.

Why did inequality increase during the 1980s? Evidence from Mexico suggests that the richest 10 percent of the population took advantage of capital mobility, high interest rates, and opportunities presented by the economic reforms to sustain or increase their incomes.[62] Thus, when President Salinas took power in 1988, Mexico had one known billionaire; by 1993 it reportedly had fourteen.[63] Of the other 90 percent of the population, a large proportion suffered falling wages or unemployment, or, in agriculture, falling food prices.

THE ROLE OF THE CHURCH

About 90 percent of Latin Americans are nominally associated with the Roman Catholic church. The number of "practicing" Catholics is much smaller, perhaps no more than 20 percent, and the number of Protestants is

---

[61]Edwards, *Latin America and the Caribbean: A Decade after the Debt Crisis*, 4; and Oscar Altimir, "Income Distribution and Poverty through Crisis and Adjustment," *CEPAL Review* 32 (April 1994): 12.

[62]Organization for Economic Cooperation and Development, *OECD Economic Surveys: Mexico 1991/1992* (Paris: OECD, 1992), 110.

[63]Arthur Jones, "Gap between Rich, Poor Expands in Mexico," *National Catholic Reporter* 29 (August 13, 1993): 11.

■ TABLE 8.7

LATIN AMERICA AND THE CARIBBEAN: POVERTY, INEQUALITY, AND EDUCATIONAL EXPENDITURES, 1980–1995

	Absolute Poverty Rate 1981–1995 (%)	Gini Coefficients			Education Expenditure % of GDP 1990
		Early 1980s	Late 1980s	Early 1990s	
Caribbean					
Dominican Republic	20	—	0.51	—	1.6
Haiti	—	—	—		1.8
Middle America					
Costa Rica	19	0.48	0.42	0.46	4.4
El Salvador	—	—	—	—	1.6
Guatemala	53	0.48	0.59	0.60	1.5
Honduras	47	—	—	0.53	4.1
Mexico	15	0.43	0.47	0.50	4.9
Nicaragua	44	—	—	0.50	—
Panama	26	0.49	0.57	—	5.5
South America					
Argentina	—	0.41	0.44	—	3.1
Bolivia	7	0.48	0.52	0.42	—
Brazil	29	0.59	0.63	—	4.6
Chile	15	0.52	0.53	0.57	2.9
Colombia	7	0.58	0.53	0.51	3.1
Ecuador	30	—	—	0.47	2.7
Paraguay	—	0.45	0.40	—	2.6
Peru	49	0.43	0.44	0.45	—
Uruguay	—	0.44	0.45	—	2.8
Venezuela	12	0.43	0.44	0.54	5.3

Sources: Marcio Marcel and Andrés Solimano, "The Distribution of Income and Economic Adjustment," in *The Chilean Economy*, ed. by Barry Bosworth, Rudiger Dornbusch, and Raúl Labán (Washington, D.C.: Brookings Institution, 1994), 247; Sebastian Edwards, *Latin America and the Caribbean: A Decade after the Debt Crisis* (Washington, D.C.: World Bank, 1993), 120; Organization for Economic Cooperation and Development, *OECD Economic Surveys: Mexico 1991/92* (Paris: OECD, 1992), 110; United Nations Development Program, *Human Development Report 1996*, 164–165; and World Bank, *World Development Report 1997*, 214–215 and 222–223.

growing rapidly, perhaps by 3 million per year.[64] Still, in many countries, the church has more political power than any other nongovernmental institution.

Since colonial times, the church has played a controversial role in the economic development of Latin America. An early missionary was often the pawn of a conquistador, who governed a region of the New World as a

---

[64]Penny Lernoux, "Latin America Is Converting to Fundamentalism," *Newsday*, July 12, 1988, 49.

"trust," or *encomienda*, from the Spanish crown. The *encomienda* allowed the conquistador to extract riches for himself and for the crown, which often involved a system of forced labor, but also made the conquistador responsible for religious training of the native people. Thus, the local priests became accomplices in a system of paternalism, discipline, and gross exploitation. The church eventually accumulated its own large holdings of land, and its leaders gained positions of privilege.

On the other hand, the priests attempted to help the native people in many ways: They established educational systems, introduced new farming methods and medical services, provided the only significant source of agricultural credit, and played an important role in the early formation of social security systems and labor unions. As early as the sixteenth century, Bartolome de las Casas, the bishop of Chiápas, campaigned against cruel treatment of the indigenous people in Mexico, gaining them some relief from the Spanish crown. In the seventeenth and eighteenth centuries, priests established an independent Jesuit republic in South America to protect the Guarani people from Portuguese slavers.

Two members of the lower clergy, Father Miguel Hidalgo y Costilla and Father Morelos y Payon, led the Mexican revolution against Spain in 1810, demanding human rights for the natives and *mestizos*.[65] A century later, though, when Mexico experienced civil war and land reform, the church was identified with the rich and the landowners. In "some of the worst repression against Catholics anywhere in history," churches were closed, property was confiscated, priests were banned, and many of them were executed, together with their protectors.[66]

During the 1960s, two developments began to change the political face of the church in Latin America. One was an institutional reform, initiated by Pope John XXIII, that ended the monopoly of European-blooded clerics, and led to the appointment of indigenous bishops. The other was an ideological movement, known as "liberation theology," that developed concurrently with other leftist intellectual currents in Latin America, including dependency theory, structuralism, and Castroism. Camilo Torres, a Colombian priest killed by government troops in 1966, put it this way:

> *Under the present circumstances in Latin America we see that we cannot feed, or clothe, or house the majorities. . . . The power must be taken for the majorities' part so that structural, economic, social, and political reforms benefiting these majorities may be realized. This is called revolution and if it is necessary in order to fulfill love for one's neighbor, then it is necessary for a Christian to be a revolutionary.67*

Liberation theology reached a wider audience in 1971, when Gustavo Gutierrez, a Peruvian priest, published *The Theology of Revolution*. The book

---

[65]Richard O'Mara, "Aristide's Lineage: Latin America's Radical Priesthood," *The Sun* (Baltimore), September 25, 1994, 1E.

[66]Jones, "Gap between Rich, Poor Expands in Mexico," 11.

[67]Quoted in Jeanine Swift, *Economic Development in Latin America* (New York: St. Martin's Press, 1978), 10.

encouraged a new activism that caused one confrontation after another with military dictators. In 1973, several members of Christians for Socialism lost their lives during the military takeover in Chile. In Argentina, Priests for the Third World were among those killed during the so-called Dirty War, which began in 1976. Two well-known Sandinista priests, Miguel D'Escoto and Ernesto Cardenal, fought in the 1979 revolution to remove the Somoza dictatorship in Nicaragua. Archbishop Oscar Romero, an opponent of the military in El Salvador, was assassinated in 1980, and in Haiti, the assassination of one priest, Jean-Marie Vincent, contributed to the collapse of military rule in 1994, and the return of another priest, Jean-Bertrand Aristide, to serve as president.

The 1995 annual meeting of Latin American bishops in Mexico City demonstrated again the impact of Catholic institutional reforms, leftist ideologies, and social concerns. In a document titled "Latin America: Stand Up and Walk," the bishops scolded national leaders for their reckless programs of market-oriented reform, and decried public indifference to the poor. The ruling neoliberal orthodoxy, they said, is "unnatural and inhuman," and eventually "will fall by itself, perhaps more rapidly than communism." The bishops claimed that "the absolutization of market forces and the power of money" are the most important causes of inequality and poverty in the region. These views are alarming to national leaders, and to market-oriented international aid agencies. They also disturb the Catholic hierarchy in Rome, where the Pope is a veteran critic of communism and liberation theology.[68]

PUBLIC PROGRAMS TO REDUCE POVERTY

For many years, Latin American governments and the Washington-based aid agencies believed that economic growth and industrialization would solve the poverty problem in the region in a reasonable period of time. Thus, problems of macroeconomic stabilization and the relative merits of import substitution and export promotion dominated economic policy discussions. Little attention was given to programs of public health, education, and social security that are specifically targeted at reduction of poverty.

Recently, for a number of reasons, poverty reduction has moved to a higher place on the policy agenda. Removal of military dictatorships and restoration of democracy has fundamentally changed the political landscape of Latin America. Liberal priests and politicians, who were once in hiding, now have access to legislative seats and, in the case of Haiti, the presidency. The demands of the unemployed in Bogotá and the peasants in Chiápas can no longer be silenced and ignored.

The regional governments and the aid agencies also have come to a new realization that broad-brush policies of economic growth and industrialization are not sufficient to attack the problems of poverty. "Higher growth is

[68]"Bishops Predict Collapse of 'Inhuman' Neoliberalism," InterPress News Service, May 8, 1995.

important," says a recent World Bank report, "but not enough."[69] The real income of the *average* Latin American tripled between the 1950s and the 1990s, but the percentage of the population living in poverty declined slowly (and increased during the 1980s) because of growing income inequality. Furthermore, because of continuing population growth, the World Bank believes that the *number* of people living in absolute poverty has not declined since the 1950s. To reduce the number of poor the region must maintain an annual growth rate of 3.2 percent, roughly equal to the rate that prevailed between 1991 and 1993. Like Alice's Wonderland, the World Bank says that, in Latin America, "It takes all of the running you can do to stay in the same place."[70]

Thus, the need for policies designed to reduce income inequality and policy. According to statistical investigations, the most important determinant of income inequality seems to be education. The probability of a person with less than five years of schooling being in the poorest quintile of the population is 83 percent in Panama, 69 percent in Argentina, and 42 percent in Brazil.[71] In 1992, the average adult in Latin America had only 5.4 years of schooling, compared with 8.1 years in East Asia (excluding China).[72] Countries that devote small percentages of GDP to educational expenditure, such as Guatemala and Haiti, tend to have the highest rates of absolute poverty (Table 8.7). According to a World Bank analysis, if the macroeconomic environment is stable, two-thirds of the absolute poverty in Latin America could be eliminated by improving educational facilities and increasing average schooling levels to nine years.[73]

Latin America also has a poor record of performance in the field of public health. Compared to East Asia, the infant mortality rate, the proportion of the population without access to safe water, and the proportion of the population without access to sanitation services are all twice as high.

Social security systems exist in most Latin American countries that provide pension and health benefits, and they were among the few social services that received expenditure increases during the 1980s. Still, most of the programs are underfunded, actuarially unsound, and inefficient, and they do not reach the poorest segments of society. In Brazil, only 18 percent of people in the poorest 40 percent of the population are covered by social security, and they receive only 3 percent of the benefits.[74] Despite chronic unemployment problems, most countries (including relatively high-income countries such as Mexico) do not have an unemployment compensation program.

As we noted earlier, health, education, and social security, together with land reform and other policies that affect the poor, are beginning to attract

---

[69]Stephen Fidler, "Latin America Shakes Off Crisis but Flaws Remain," *Financial Post*, June 28, 1995, 50.

[70]"Latin America Must Rebuild State, Exports," Inter-Press News Service, June 12, 1995.

[71]Edwards, *Latin America and the Caribbean: A Decade after the Debt Crisis*, 120–121.

[72]United Nations Development Programme, *Human Development Report 1994*, 207.

[73]"Latin American Nations Must Invest in Education—World Bank," Reuters News Service, June 13, 1995.

[74]Edwards, *Latin America and the Caribbean: A Decade after the Debt Crisis*, 127.

more attention from politicians and international aid agencies. In Chile, a major shift in social policy began in 1990 when democracy was restored under the Aylwin administration. The minimum wage was quickly increased by 36 percent, and pensions and social subsidies were raised. Between 1990 and 1995, real social expenditures increased by about 50 percent.[75]

In Mexico, President Zedillo announced in 1995 that his government would invest 9 billion new pesos during the second half of the 1990s in programs to help the educationally disadvantaged. This is the largest commitment Mexico has ever made to education of the poor, with special attention to the indigenous people. It will be supported by a $500 million loan to Mexico from the World Bank, aimed at development of public education, health, nutrition, and employment.[76] A similar program is being launched in Argentina, where a $300 million credit from the Inter-American Development Bank will support a $600 million project to improve primary education.[77]

SUMMARY

Latin America includes three diverse subregions: Middle America, South America, and the Caribbean area. The indigenous cultures, including the great Mayan, Aztec, and Inca civilizations, had experience with economic development, authoritarian organization, and colonial exploitation before Europeans arrived. Long-term developments in the region were influenced by the authoritarian culture and extractive motives of the Europeans.

Latin American independence movements were encouraged by a mixture of internal and external economic motives, intellectual currents, and political leaders. Independence allowed a new era of trade expansion to begin, but it did not quickly lead to an equitable system of land tenure. The Great Depression ended the era of trade expansion and prompted a system of import substituting industrialization (ISI), which continued after World War II. Applied moderately, ISI provided impressive results, but it invited excesses, contributing to the rise of authoritarian regimes. Brazil shifted toward export promotion during the 1960s, and Chile made a broader shift toward market liberalization and fiscal austerity during the 1970s. Prompted by the debt crisis of the 1980s, the Chilean experience, and pressure from international institutions, market liberalization spread to other countries in the 1980s and 1990s.

Latin American agricultural institutions are derived from the colonial plantation and *hacienda* systems, from programs of land reform, and from recent programs of land privatization. Industrial structures include the microenterprises of the informal sector, the large domestic enterprises in the formal sector, state-owned enterprises (SOEs), and multinationals, which in-

---

[75]Howard LaFranchi, "Progress Has Come at a High Cost," *The Christian Science Monitor*, July 25, 1995, 2.

[76]"Mexico to Spend 9 bln New Pesos on Education," Reuters News Service, July 6, 1995.

[77]"IADB, Argentina Sign Contract for $300 Million Loan," Reuters News Service, April 2, 1995.

clude the *maquiladoras*. The number of SOEs increased dramatically during the ISI years, but it declined in Chile beginning in the 1970s, and elsewhere beginning in the 1980s. Several models of privatization have been developed, including the Bolivian system of capitalization.

In the rural sector, labor markets have been characterized by continuing inequities. In industry, the dominant state and the growth of the informal sector have made it difficult to develop a stable and evenhanded system of collective bargaining. Public–private pacts, negotiated in recent years, may contribute to a more balanced relationship between labor, industry, and the state. Latin America has experienced high rates of chronic inflation, eliciting a number of monetarist, structural, and political explanations. Rapid inflation, in turn, led to interest controls, credit rationing, barriers to entry of new financial institutions, and other symptoms of financial repression. Control of inflation and financial liberalization has been a major focus of reform in recent years, leading to large inflows and outflows of international capital.

Latin American countries have high levels of income inequality, which continued to increase during the 1980s. The Roman Catholic church has a long and controversial record in its relations with the poor, including the development of liberation theology since the 1960s. The governments have traditionally relied on economic growth to aid the poor, but now they are shifting to targeted policies of poverty reduction.

DISCUSSION AND REVIEW QUESTIONS

1. How are Latin American economies influenced today by their colonial and precolonial heritage? How do these differ between Latin America and the United States?

2. What have been the objectives of land reform in Latin America? Have these been met satisfactorily?

3. "Without the dictatorial measures of the Pinochet regime, Chile could not have a stable economic and political system today." Do you agree with this statement?

4. What is the role of the informal sector in the urban economies of Latin America? To the individual business owner, what are the costs and benefits of operating in the informal sector?

5. Why has Latin America experienced rapid and persistent inflation? Do you believe the cycle of inflation has been broken in the region?

6. What are the benefits and costs of receiving large inflows of international capital? Should Latin American countries control these capital flows?

7. How should Latin American countries allocate educational expenditures to reduce poverty? How should expenditures be divided between primary, secondary, and higher education? Between liberal and vocational education? Between rural and urban education?

SUGGESTED READINGS

Baer, Werner, and Melissa Birch, eds. *Privatization in Latin America: New Roles for the Public and Private Sectors*. Westport, Conn.: Praeger Publishers, 1994. *Nine essays survey the different methods and styles of privatization in Latin America and Spain, and analyze their impact on public policy and on domestic business interests and foreign investors.*

Bosworth, Barry P., Rudiger Dornbusch, and Rául Labán, eds. *The Chilean Economy: Policy Lessons and Challenges*. Washington, D.C.: The Brookings Institution, 1994. *An excellent conference volume with nine essays and sixteen comments by a team of forty economists from Chile and the United States, analyzing shifts in Chilean policy since the 1950s.*

Casanova, Pablo Gonzalez, ed. *Latin America Today*. Tokyo: United Nations University Press, 1993. *Described as "the culmination of one of the largest studies ever undertaken in Latin America," this volume is primarily concerned with political and social issues, but it also includes an analysis of "economy and crisis" from a left-leaning Latin American perspective.*

de Soto, Hernando. *The Other Path: The Invisible Revolution in the Third World*. New York: Harper & Row, 1989. *Based on the experience in Peru, this is an eye-opening account of the regulatory causes and economic consequences of informal sector growth.*

Dietz, James L., and Dilmus D. James, eds. *Progress toward Development in Latin America: From Prebisch to Technological Autonomy*. Boulder: Lynne Rienner Publishers, 1990. *In eleven essays by eight authors, this volume considers the Latin American experience from structuralist and institutionalist perspectives.*

Edwards, Sebastian. *Latin America and the Caribbean: A Decade after the Debt Crisis*. Washington, D.C.: World Bank, Latin America and the Caribbean Regional Office, 1993. *A comprehensive, authoritative, and concise (159 pages) evaluation of Latin American adjustments programs, and their impact on macroeconomic performance, income distribution, and poverty.*

Lustig, Nora. *Mexico: The Remaking of an Economy*. Washington, D.C.: The Brookings Institution, 1992. *An evaluation of the benefits and costs of the transformation of the Mexican economy since the 1982 debt crisis.*

INTERNET RESOURCES

Consejo Latinamericano de Ciensias Sociales
gopher://lanic.utexas.edu:70/11/la/region/clacso

Environment and Latin America Network (ELAN)
Colorado State University
http://csf.colorado.edu/hypermail/elan/index.html

Hemisphere
http://www.fiu.edu:80/~lacc/hemisphere/

Latin America Development Archive (LADARK)
Johns Hopkins University
http://www.jhu.edu/~soc/ladark.html

Latin American and Caribbean Center
Florida International University
http://www.fiu.edu:80/~lacc/

Latin American and Caribbean Economic and Social Data
U.S. Agency for International Development
http://lanic.utexas.edu:80/la/region/aid/

Latin American Historical Economic Data
http://milkman.cac.psu.edu/~rlg7/hist/proj/garner.html

Latin American Newsletters
http://www.softopt.co.uk/latin/

Latin American Studies
University of Texas at Austin
http://lanic.utexas.edu/las.html

IV

WESTERN EUROPE

Western Europe

9

THE EUROPEAN ECONOMY: AN INTRODUCTION

No man is an island, entire of itself; every man is a piece of the continent, a part of the main; if a clod be washed away by the sea, Europe is the less, as well as if a promontory were, as well as if a manor of thy friends or of thine own were; any man's death diminishes me, because I am involved in all mankind; and therefore never send to know for whom the bell tolls; it tolls for thee.

—JOHN DONNE
DEVOTIONS UPON EMERGENT OCCASIONS, 1624

Have I said clearly enough that the Community we have created is not an end in itself? It is a process of change, continuing that same process which in an earlier period of history produced our national forms of life. Like our provinces in the past, our nations today must learn to live together under common rules and institutions freely arrived at. The sovereign nations of the past can no longer solve the problems of the present; they cannot ensure their own progress and control their own future. And the Community itself is only a stage on the way to the organized world of tomorrow.

—JEAN MONNET, *MEMOIRS*, 1978

ince the 1980s, two revolutions in Europe have dramatically changed the political and economic shape of the world. In Russia and Eastern Europe, the overthrow of communism and central planning has turned the tide elsewhere against Marxism, and has supported a global trend toward market-oriented economic policies. In Western Europe, national leaders have regained the vision of Jean Monnet and other postwar

founders of the European Community; they have taken important steps toward the creation of a unified market and a stronger European system of political institutions. The liberated nations of Eastern Europe have lined up at the door of the new European Union, and the trend toward regional economic integration has spread to every corner of the world.

In this chapter, to provide a backdrop for our discussions of individual countries, we will survey the development of economic and political cooperation in Western Europe (Table 9.1). Here, we consider the problems of Eastern European nations only in the context of their efforts to enter the European Union. We will turn to a broader discussion of the economic transition of Eastern Europe in the next section of this book.

THE HISTORY OF EUROPEAN INTEGRATION

Unification of Europe has been a dream of tyrants, poets, diplomats, and technocrats since time immemorial. To the Roman and Holy Roman Emperors, the Habsburgs, Napoleon, and Hitler, the objective of European unification was simple—to augment the wealth, power, and security of their imperial systems. To European and American leaders after World War II, the objective again was simple—to prevent a third world war. Economic cooperation, they hoped, would speed recovery and reconstruction, laying a groundwork for peace and stability.

The postwar era was not the first time in European history that an economic union was created to serve a political purpose. In 1834, Prussia took its first step toward unification of Germany by establishing a customs union, the *Zollverein*, with its neighboring states. In 1897, the Austrian foreign minister, Count Guluchowski, called on European leaders to retaliate against American monopolistic practices and protectionist policies by establishing what nowadays would be called a Fortress Europe:

> *The disastrous competition which, in all domains of human activity, we have to submit to from over the seas, and which we will also have to encounter in the future, must be resisted if the vital interests of Europe are not to suffer, and if Europe is not to fall into gradual decay . . . The nations of Europe must unite in order to defend our very means of existence.*[1]

World War I interrupted the dream of European unity, but also underlined the need for cooperation. Soon after the war, an agreement was drafted to organize a United Europe, governed by a European Council consisting of delegates of the various states, a parliament consisting of delegates from the national parliaments, and a high court. In 1929, the French statesman Aristide Briand proposed the establishment of a "federal link" between the peoples of Europe, but one that would not affect the sovereign rights of nations; a year later he proposed the formation of a European "common market,"

---

[1]Count Guluchowski, in a report to the Austro-Hungarian parliament, from Jacob Viner, The Customs Union Issue (Washington, D.C.: Anderson Kramer Associates, 1961), 23–24.

■ TABLE 9.1 WESTERN EUROPE: BASIC ECONOMIC STATISTICS, 1995

	Population (millions)	GDP per Capita ($ at PPP)	GDP ($ at market exchange rates)	Unemployment Rate (% total labor force)	Long-Term Unemployment (% of total unemployment)	Consumer Price Inflation (%)
European Union	372.0	18,608	8415.1	11.3	48.6	3.2
Austria	8.0	20,772	233.3	3.6	17.4	2.3
Belgium	10.1	20,792	269.2	12.0	62.4	1.5
Denmark	5.2	21,529	173.3	8.0	27.9	2.1
Finland	5.1	17,788	125.0	18.2	32.3	1.0
France	58.1	19,939	1,537.6	11.6	45.6	1.8
Germany	81.7	20,497	2,412.5	8.4	48.3	1.8
Greece	10.5	12,174	114.3	9.6	50.9	8.9
Ireland	3.6	17,228	64.3	14.7	61.4	2.5
Italy	57.3	19,464	1,082.2	11.9	62.9	5.2
Luxembourg	0.4	31,303	17.3	2.3	22.4	1.9
Netherlands	15.5	19,782	395.5	6.8	43.2	1.9
Portugal	9.9	12,457	99.8	6.9	48.7	4.1
Spain	39.2	14,226	559.6	23.8	56.5	4.7
Sweden	8.8	18,673	230.6	8.0	15.7	2.5
United Kingdom	58.6	17,756	1,100.6	9.6	43.5	3.4
EFTA	11.8	23,939	459.2	4.3	29.6	2.1
Iceland	0.3	21,938	7.0	5.3	12.2	1.7
Norway	4.4	22,672	146.1	5.4	26.5	2.5
Switzerland	7.1	24,809	306.1	3.6	32.3	1.8
For Comparison						
Japan	125.3	21,795	5,114.0	2.9	18.1	-0.1
United States	263.1	26,438	6,954.8	6.0	9.7	2.8

Sources: OECD in Figures, 1997, a supplement to The OECD Observer, July 1997; International Monetary Fund, International Financial Statistics, June 1997; and author's calculations.

supported by political structures and institutions.[2] Unfortunately, Briand's plans did not materialize. The consequences of that failure were noted in 1950 by another French statesman: "Europe was not built, and we had war."[3]

FROM 1945 TO 1950: GAULLISTS, FEDERALISTS, AND THE MARSHALL PLAN

A broad consensus for European unity developed after World War II. In 1944, before the war was even over, the Benelux countries (Belgium, Netherlands, and Luxembourg) established a successful customs union, and made rapid progress toward free movement of goods, labor, and capital. Elsewhere, European and American leaders agreed that cooperation was needed to speed economic recovery, and to prevent another war. They disagreed, however, on the proper limits of cooperation. The opinions of European leaders were influenced by a range of political and economic factors, by their attitudes toward each other, and by their relations with the United States.

Like Count Guluchowski in the nineteenth century, a few of the postwar European leaders harbored a deep distrust of the United States. Most notably, President Charles de Gaulle of France believed that American economic and military strength represented a grave danger to French sovereignty.[4] Thus, despite his intense nationalism, de Gaulle was willing to abide by the rules of a European common market if it would "do battle abroad" against American competition. Even so, de Gaulle would commit France only to a "Europe of sovereign states"; he opposed any supranational scheme of political unification.[5]

The so-called "Europeans" or "federalists," who supported creation of a strong economic and political union, were generally people who admired the United States. In the eighteenth century, George Washington had predicted that "some day" a new generation of leaders would create a United States of Europe, "taking its pattern from the United States."[6] Likewise, during the nineteenth century, Victor Hugo foretold the creation of "first the United States of Europe, then the United States of the World."[7]

Chief among the federalists was Jean Monnet, de Gaulle's director of economic planning, who played a leading role in the creation of the European

---

[2]Jean Monnet, *Memoirs* (Garden City, N.Y.: Doubleday and Company, 1978), 283; and Françoise de la Sierre, "The European Economic Community: Economic and Political Union," in *Modern Political Systems: Europe*, 7th ed., ed. by Roy C. Macridis (Englewood Cliffs, N.J.: Prentice Hall, 1990), 330–332.

[3]Monnet, *Memoirs*, 300.

[4]The distrust between de Gaulle and American leaders was mutual, and "troubled Franco-American relations for . . . thirty years." See Monnet, *Memoirs*, 220.

[5]Robert Marjolin, *Architect of European Unity: Memoirs 1911–1986* (London: Weidenfeld and Nicolson, 1989), 258.

[6]Cited in "Political union; The Vision Recedes," *The Economist*, April 26, 1975, 40.

[7]Found in 1885 on the wall of the room in which Hugo (best known today for his novel-made-musical, *Les Misérables*) died. Cited in John Bartlett, *Familiar Quotations*, 16th ed. (Boston: Little, Brown and Company, 1992), 428.

Community. Monnet first visited the United States in 1906, when he was eighteen, and found "in contrast to the static balance of the old Europe, this was the dynamism of a world on the move."[8] During subsequent years, as a businessman and a diplomat, Monnet made many trips across the Atlantic. In 1948, during one of his visits, Monnet learned that a new **Organization for European Economic Cooperation (OEEC)** had been created in Paris. Concerned by the contrast between the OEEC, which could govern only by unanimous consent of the members, and the USA, a strong federation, Monnet sent the following message to Robert Schuman, the French foreign affairs minister:

I cannot but be struck by the relationship that threatens to develop between this great and dynamic nation and the countries of Europe. . . . Everything I have seen and reflected on here leads me to a conclusion which is now my profound conviction: that to tackle the present situation, to face the dangers that threaten us, and to match the American effort, the countries of Western Europe must turn their national efforts into a truly European effort. This will be possible only through a federation of the West.[9]

Another important federalist was Robert Marjolin, one of Monnet's colleagues in France and another frequent visitor to the United States. According to Marjolin, in the postwar years America became "the ideal." The aim of European economic development was to "catch up with the United States, or at any rate, to come as close as possible," and the strategy was to "adopt American methods of production and organization, duplicate American economies of scale," and create "a vast European market, comparable to the American market."[10]

As secretary-general of the OEEC, Marjolin was responsible for administration of aid from the United States under the **Marshall Plan**. The Plan provided about $14 billion ($180 billion in 1995 prices) of American support for European reconstruction between 1948 and 1952. To ensure that this money would not be wasted, the United States required Europe to develop a cooperative plan for economic recovery, and encouraged creation of a supranational European organization for this purpose. Largely because of British resistance, though, the OEEC was able to rule only by unanimous consent. In the context of the Marshall Plan, the United States also supported the creation of a European customs union and a European defense community. According to Robert Marjolin, the idea of a united Europe was "expressed most forcefully" by the United States in the years after the war. The Marshall Plan, in his estimation, was "the most dazzling political and economic success in the history of the western world since 1914."[11]

---

[8]Monnet, *Memoirs*, 46.

[9]Ibid., 272–273.

[10]Marjolin, *Architect of European Unity*, 278.

[11]Ibid., 175, 212, and 278.

FROM 1950 TO 1955: COAL, STEEL, AND THE FAILURE OF POLITICAL UNION

After World War II, German coalfields were placed under the control of American, French, and British occupation forces. The French, unable to obtain enough German coal to support recovery of their own steel industry, grew unhappy with this shared system of control. The Germans, of course, were unhappy with the continuing system of Allied external control.

In 1950 French foreign minister Schuman devised a plan that would be mutually beneficial to the French and the Germans. With permission from the Allies, control of the French and German coal and steel industries would be pooled under an independent and supranational "High Authority," consisting of nine officials chosen by the French and German governments. Other European countries would be invited to participate, but they would have a voice in the High Authority only if their steel and coal industries were included in the pool. Thus, Germany would regain some control over its own industries, and France felt that it would benefit from better access to German resources. The German chancellor, Konrad Adenauer, publicly expressed his satisfaction with the "generous" French proposal; he recognized its economic benefits and also those that were "highly political":

> *There was still a fear in France that when Germany had recovered she would attack France. It could also be imagined that in Germany, on the other hand, there was a corresponding desire for greater security. Rearmament would have to begin by increasing coal, iron, and steel production. If an organization such as Schuman envisaged were set up, enabling both countries to discern the first signs of any such rearmament, this new possibility would bring great relief to France.*[12]

In addition to France and Germany, Italy and the Benelux countries (Belgium, Netherlands, and Luxembourg) accepted the Schuman proposal and ratified the 1951 Treaty of Paris to create the **European Coal and Steel Community (ECSC)**. These founding countries were known as the Six; their cooperative relationship in coal and steel would lead them, a few years later, to create the Common Market.

The United States enthusiastically supported creation of the ECSC and encouraged the United Kingdom, which produced about half of Europe's coal and a third of its steel, to participate. The Labor government in London refused because it had recently nationalized the British coal and steel industries, and it had little interest in placing them under supranational control. Furthermore, the British feared that a strong link to Europe through the ECSC would disrupt its reliable and traditional relations with the USA and members of its Commonwealth.

The ECSC was governed by a network of institutions, including the High Authority; an Assembly, composed of representatives from the national parliaments; a Council of Ministers; and a Court of Justice. These had supranational power over production, pricing, research and development, invest-

---

[12]Translated from Adenauer's memoirs in Monnet, *Memoirs*, 303.

ment, cartels and mergers, and labor conditions in the coal and steel industries. Tariffs and quotas were removed to create a single market for these products, and the distribution system for coal supplies was reorganized. Between 1952 and 1958, the ECSC members increased their steel production by 50 percent and more than doubled their trade in steel.

Prompted by the successes of the ECSC and the Benelux economic union, the Six explored new opportunities for cooperation. In 1952, they signed treaties to establish a Political Community and a European Defense Community. These were ratified by five of the countries, but fears of German rearmament led to a veto in the French National Assembly in 1954. Without French participation, the dreams of the federalists were temporarily dashed: "One could no longer mention the subject of European defense, nor that of supranationality, European constitution, relinquishment or delegation of sovereignty, or even European institutions."[13]

FROM 1955 TO 1985: TREATIES OF ROME, THE EFTA, AND EUROPESSIMISM

After the defeat of political integration, the Benelux countries, led by Paul-Henri Spaak, a Belgian statesman, suggested that efforts for European integration should be redoubled in the economic area. Negotiations began at a major conference of the Six in Messina, Italy, led by Spaak in 1955. The British were invited to participate, but declined. The negotiations culminated in the 1957 Treaties of Rome, establishing the **European Economic Community (EEC)**, and the European Atomic Energy Community (Euratom). Like the ECSC, each of these had its own Commission (similar to the High Authority), Assembly (representatives of national parliaments), Council of Ministers, and Court of Justice.

According to the treaty, the EEC (or Common Market, as it was commonly known) would develop a customs union for industrial products: Internal trade restrictions would be phased out and a **common external tariff (CET)** would be phased in between 1961 and 1968. Furthermore, the EEC would develop a **Common Agricultural Policy (CAP)** for farm products and would foster the free movement of labor and capital.

Again, the United Kingdom was unwilling to join the EEC; it did not want to cede control of its tariff policy to the CET, and participation in the CAP would deprive the UK of cheap agricultural imports from members of its Commonwealth. In 1958, the UK proposed creation of a free trade area encompassing itself, the EEC, and any other European countries that wished to join. Under the plan, trade would be free through all of Western Europe, and each country or group of countries would be free to set its own tariffs or CET against non-European countries. This arrangement would have allowed the UK to gain free access to the European markets without sacrificing its system of Commonwealth preferences. On the other hand, it threatened to undermine the operation of the CET and the CAP in the EEC. Each product would

---

[13]Marjolin, *Architect of European Unity*, 276.

tend to be imported into Europe through the country with the lowest external trade barrier, and then would be shipped duty-free to other European countries.

When the proposal for a pan-European free trade area was rejected by the EEC, the UK persuaded Austria, Denmark, Norway, Portugal, Sweden, and Switzerland in 1960 (and later Finland and Iceland) to establish a **European Free Trade Association (EFTA)**. The members of the EFTA abolished their mutual tariff barriers on nonagricultural goods, but they did not create a CET, a CAP, powerful supranational institutions, or any other threats to national sovereignty. This suited the UK, of course, because it was able to preserve its special relationships with former colonies, and it suited Austria and Finland, which had special relationships with the Soviet Union and Eastern Europe. The Scandinavian countries were able to join the EFTA with little threat to their policies of neutrality or their unique social welfare systems.

During the early 1960s, the EEC was preoccupied with the practical work of creating a customs union and a CAP: removing internal tariffs, negotiating a CET, and resolving disputes over access to agricultural markets. In 1967, the governing institutions of the three European Communities were merged to form a single European Commission (replacing the ECSC High Authority and the EEC and Euratom Commissions), a European Parliament (replacing the Assemblies), and a European Court of Justice.

As the EEC grew stronger, and as British ties to its Commonwealth grew weaker, the UK grew more interested in joining the EEC. Proposals for British accession were vetoed in 1963 and 1968 by General de Gaulle, who doubted British commitment to Europe, and continued to harbor resentment toward the Anglo-American world for his treatment by Churchill and Roosevelt during World War II.

After de Gaulle resigned from the French Presidency in 1969, new progress was made toward enlargement of the EEC. In 1971, a compromise was struck between the British and French leaders, whereby, among other things, the UK would accept the existing treaties and would make heavy contributions to the EEC budget in exchange for permission to continue low-cost imports of dairy products and sugar cane from Commonwealth producers. The UK, together with Denmark and Ireland, enlarged the EEC from the Six to the Nine in 1973. Successive rounds of enlargement created the Ten in 1981, the Twelve in 1986, and the Fifteen in 1995 (Table 9.2).

As the Community grew larger, it became clear that its institutions needed additional strength to maintain cohesion. In 1974, at a summit conference in Paris, the heads of state decided to form themselves into a European Council (or "Summit," as it is known informally), that would meet about three times each year. They also decided to raise the profile of the European Parliament, previously appointed by national parliaments, by organizing direct European elections; the first election was held in 1979. Also in 1979, the Council launched a new European Monetary System (EMS), based on the European Currency Unit and a stronger set of institutions to stabilize exchange rates.

Despite these efforts, the late 1970s and the early 1980s were a period of growing "Europessimism." The Community did not respond effectively to

■ TABLE 9.2

THE EUROPEAN UNION AND BEYOND, 1958–1997

The Six (members of the European Economic Community since 1958)	Belgium, France, Germany, Italy, Luxembourg, and the Netherlands
The Nine (members of the European Community since 1973)	The Six plus Denmark, Ireland, and the United Kingdom
The Ten (members of the European Community since 1981)	The Nine plus Greece
The Twelve (members of the European Community since 1986)	The Ten plus Portugal and Spain
The Fifteen (members of the European Union since 1995)	The Twelve plus Austria, Finland, and Sweden
Countries that have formally applied for membership in the European Union	Cyprus, Hungary, Malta, Poland, Turkey
Other countries negotiating preliminary agreements for membership in or association with the European Union	Albania, Bulgaria, Czech Republic, Estonia, Latvia, Lithuania, Romania, Slovakia, and Slovenia
Members of the European Free Trade Association (in 1995, after departures of Austria, Denmark, Finland, Portugal, Sweden, and the United Kingdom)	Iceland, Norway, Liechtenstein, and Switzerland
Other members of the Council of Europe (in addition to all countries above)	Macedonia, Moldova, Russia, San Marino, and Ukraine
Applicants for Council of Europe membership	Armenia, Azerbaijan, Belarus, Croatia, Georgia, and Serbia
Other European countries	Bosnia/Herzegovina, and Serbia

the oil price shock of 1973, and quarreling continued for more than a decade when the UK tried to renegotiate its contributions to the Community budget. The unemployment rate of the region climbed from 2.6 percent in 1970 to 4.3 percent in 1975, and then to 6.4 percent in 1980 and 11.9 percent in 1985.[14] The natural result was rising internal protectionism, with rising production subsidies, stiff quality standards on imported goods, and other nontariff barriers to trade.[15]

AFTER 1985: THE ROAD TO ECONOMIC, MONETARY, AND POLITICAL UNION

The tide began to turn against Europessimism in 1984 and 1985 when French President François Mitterrand, an old "European," became president of the European Council, and his former finance minister, Jacques Delors, began a

---

[14]*OECD Economic Outlook* 40 (December 1986), Table R12.

[15]Not all was lost during these years by the federalists. In 1979, the European Court of Justice established an important precedent for mutual recognition of technical standards. In the early 1980s, the European Commission successfully ended enormous subsidies in the synthetic fibers industry.

long term as president of the European Commission. In March 1985, the European Council, meeting in Brussels, issued instructions to the Commission to "draw up a detailed program with a specific timetable" that would "achieve a single large market by 1992, thereby creating a more favorable environment for stimulating enterprise, competition, and trade."[16] The Commission responded three months later with a White Paper, entitled "Completing the Internal Market," listing some 300 actions needed to remove physical, technical, and fiscal barriers to trade before the end of 1992.

Soon after publication of the White Paper, the Commission initiated a massive economic research project, directed by Paolo Cecchini, to measure "the costs of non-Europe," or the potential economic benefits of European unification. The **Cecchini Report**, which was cited widely after its publication in 1988, estimated that creation of a unified market would strengthen European efficiency and competitiveness, causing GDP to increase by about 5 percent, or adding about $800 to the annual income of every European.[17]

If the White Paper and the Cecchini Report popularized the vision of a united "Europe 1992," the **Single European Act (SEA)**, which came into effect in 1987, made the vision politically plausible. Drawing on proposals in the White Paper, the SEA called for implementation of 282 directives by the end of 1992, removing physical, technical, and fiscal trade barriers. Most important, the SEA amended the Treaty of Rome to increase the range of Community decisions made by a "qualified majority vote," rather than by unanimous consent. The SEA also established procedures for cooperation in foreign policy and endorsed the objective of monetary union.

The White Paper and the SEA provided a strong assault against physical, technical, and fiscal barriers to trade, but they suggested few concrete measures to remove monetary barriers. If Europe wished to have a true "single market," it would seem to need a single currency. The time, trouble, and financial cost of exchanging currencies is a substantial barrier to trade that is not present, for example, within the United States market. In 1989, a special Committee for the Study of Economic and Monetary Union—better known as the Delors Committee—recommended a series of steps, including creation of a European System of Central Banks, that would eventually lead to irrevocably fixed exchange rates between European currencies. The Delors Report did not specifically call for a single currency (although it discussed the advantages), and it suggested few specific implementation dates, but it prompted a spirited debate on monetary unification.

At the end of 1991 in Maastricht, Netherlands, members of the Community agreed on historic amendments to the treaties of Rome and Paris, pro-

[16]Communique of the Council, quoted in European Commission, "Completing the Internal Market," White Paper from the Commission to the European Council (Brussels, 1985), 1.

[17]The Report was released in three publications. For a popular audience, there was Paolo Cecchini, *1992 The European Challenge: Benefits of a Single Market* (Aldershot: Wildwood House, 1988). For economists, the full analytical report to the Economic Commission was released as Michael Emerson and others, *The Economics of 1992*, published under the same title in the journal *European Economy* 35 (March 1988), and in book form by the Oxford University Press, 1988. Citations here are to the Emerson book.

viding for accelerated economic, monetary, and political union, for free movement of people and capital, for recognition of European citizenship and passports, and for shared social, environmental, and technological policies. In the area of monetary unification, for example, the **Maastricht Treaty** adopted the general recommendations of the Delors Report, established a timetable for implementation, and specifically called for adoption of a single currency. In November 1993, after all the Community members ratified the treaty, the **European Union (EU)** was officially established.

According to the Maastricht Treaty, the EU stands on three "pillars": (1) economic and social cooperation, administered on a supranational basis by the three European Communities;[18] (2) cooperation in foreign policy and regional security, handled on an intergovernmental basis; and (3) cooperation in the fields of justice and home affairs, also administered intergovernmentally. When the British government decided not to participate in cooperation on social matters (part of the first pillar), the other members decided to formulate a separate Social Chapter of the Maastricht Treaty, not applicable to the UK. This area is sometimes considered a fourth pillar.

Since the SEA and the Maastricht Treaty were adopted, the EU has made substantial progress toward implementation of their goals. Community officials have been forced, however, to divide their time between internal and external challenges. After communist regimes began to collapse in Eastern Europe in 1989, the Community concluded "association agreements" with the new governments, providing for economic cooperation, political dialogue, and the possibility of granting full membership to these countries at some time in the future. In 1992, the EU and the EFTA agreed to create a **European Economic Area (EEA)**, liberating the movement of goods, services, capital, and labor throughout Western Europe. The membership of the EU climbed to fifteen in 1995, and more countries were standing at the door. At the same time, hostilities in Bosnia and other areas of former Yugoslavia severely tested the limits and effectiveness of a European foreign policy.

EUROPEAN INSTITUTIONS AND POLICY FORMATION

As we have seen, the institutions of the EU have gradually gained strength since the 1950s. Today, the most important central institutions are as follows:

European Council:[19] Composed of the president of the European Commission and a president or prime minister from each member country, assisted by foreign ministers and European Commission representatives. Meets at least twice a year, the Maastricht Treaty says, to "provide the Union with

---

[18]A note on terminology: The Maastricht Treaty changed the name of the European Economic Community (EEC) to the European Community (EC). The three European Communities (plural) are the EC, ECSC, and Euratom.

[19]The European Council must not be confused with the Council of Europe, an intergovernmental organization established in 1949 that encourages cooperation among democratically oriented countries, particularly in the field of human rights.

■ TABLE 9.3

NATIONAL REPRESENTATION IN EUROPEAN UNION INSTITUTIONS, 1995 (NUMBER OF REPRESENTATIVES OR VOTES)

	European Commission (members)	European Council of Ministers (votes)	European Parliament (members)	ESC and CoR* (members)
Austria	1	4	21	12
Belgium	1	5	25	12
Denmark	1	3	16	9
Finland	1	3	16	9
France	2	10	87	24
Germany	2	10	99	24
Greece	1	5	25	12
Ireland	1	3	15	9
Italy	2	10	87	24
Luxembourg	1	2	6	6
Netherlands	1	5	31	12
Portugal	1	5	25	12
Spain	2	8	64	21
Sweden	1	4	22	12
United Kingdom	2	10	87	24
Total	**20**	**87**	**626**	**222**

*EU Economic and Social Committee and EU Committee of Regions, which have the same structures of representation.

Source: *European Report*, March 5, 1994, 1; *Agra Europe* 1627 (January 13, 1995), E8; and *European Report*, February 16, 1995, 1.

the necessary impetus for its development," and to "define the general political guidelines" of its evolution. Decisions are usually based on consensus.

European Commission: Twenty members, nominated by national governments for four-year terms, approved by leaders of all member countries, and confirmed by the European Parliament. Five large countries are represented by two commissioners, the others have one (Table 9.3). As the executive branch of the EU, the Commission initiates and implements policy in areas that fall under EU treaties, and leads the work of its 24 directorates-general (specializing in such fields as industry, agriculture, transport, telecommunications, and education).

EU Council of Ministers: Ruling on recommendations from the Commission and/or from **COREPER,** this is the principal decision-making body of the EU. Each country has a fixed number of "qualified" votes, but it chooses ministers or other officials to attend each meeting according to the subject under discussion.

EU Committee of Permanent Representatives: Known by its French acronym, **COREPER,** this is a powerful, but unofficial, organization, composed of the 15 ambassadors from the member states to the EU. It lays the groundwork for meetings of the EU Council of Ministers.

European Parliament: The 626 Members of the European Parliament (MEPs), elected by popular vote in each country, are primarily a consultative and advisory body, but they have significant power over budgetary matters and can amend or reject some actions of the European Commission and the EU Council of Ministers. Unlike voting in the Council of Ministers, where each country acts as a single block, MEPs from a country may be divided among several political alliances (Socialists, Christian Democrats, Greens, and so forth).

EU Court of Justice: The so-called supreme court of the EU is led by one judge from each member state, assisted by nine advocates-general who make preliminary recommendations. It has final authority in the interpretation of EU treaties and laws, but has no general jurisdiction over the courts and laws of the member states.

EU Court of Auditors: With one judge from each member state and a permanent staff of some 335, this court attempts to ensure the accuracy of financial accounts kept by EU agencies, and to guard against improper expenditures, fraud, and waste.

EU Economic and Social Committee: With 222 members drawn from a broad array of interest groups, including industry, trade unions, farmers, and consumers, this is a purely advisory group that must be consulted (but is often ignored) before decisions are taken by other EU institutions.

EU Committee of Regions: Also with 222 members, appointed by national (not regional) governments, this is another advisory body, established by the Maastricht Treaty to advance the views of regional and local governments. It was created as a frail response to powerful regions in countries such as Germany that have long demanded a voice in European affairs.

In most of the European institutions, a compromise has been struck between the principles of equal representation for each country and equal representation for each citizen. Countries with large populations have more representatives than small countries, but not in full proportion to their size. Thus, Germany, with a population of 81 million, has more votes than any one of the Benelux countries, which have a combined population of only 26 million. Taken together, however, the Benelux countries have more votes on the European Commission, the Council of Ministers, the Economic and Social Committee, and the Committee of Regions than Germany.

Any attempt to summarize the processes of policy formation, decision making, and legislation in the EU will require simplification and generalization. With that in mind, we can say the following:

Policy Initiation: Major initiatives, such as the Single Market program or the Monetary Union program, are usually launched at a meeting of the European Council. Support from the national leaders in the European Council is especially important when a program will require approval of new treaties or legislation in the member countries. Other policy initiatives and proposals for new legislation may originate in the European Commission.

Policy Analysis and Preparation of Legislation: For important new initiatives, the Commission may appoint a special committee (such as the Delors Committee for the Study of Economic and Monetary Union) to study the problem, and may draft a white paper with initial recommendations for public discussion. It will invite comment from the Economic and Social Committee, the Committee on Regions, and other interest groups. It may also solicit technical analysis from its directorates-general and from task forces of external experts (such as the team for the Cecchini Report, which included personnel from academia and from OECD). Based on this analysis and consultation, the Commission prepares new legislative proposals, usually in the form of a "draft directive."

Amendment and Approval of Legislation: A draft directive is sent initially to the European Parliament, which accepts or rejects its general concept on "first reading." In principle, the Parliament does not propose amendments at this stage, but in fact, having gained new powers under the Maastricht Treaty, the Parliament often requires changes before initial approval.[20]

After passage on first reading, the proposal moves to the EU Council of Ministers, which may call for further analysis through its own directorates-general, and may delegate part of its intergovernmental deliberative task to COREPER. In practice, the Council attempts to base its decisions on unanimous consent, but the SEA increased the range of issues that can be settled by a "qualified majority vote" (approval by 62 of the 87 votes, with more votes allocated to the larger countries).

After approval by the Council, the proposal returns to the Parliament for a "second reading." At this point, the parliament may give final approval to the proposal, making it an official directive, or it may reject the proposal or propose amendments. If the proposal is rejected by the Parliament, it may still be approved by a unanimous vote of the Council; otherwise, the proposal fails. If the Parliament proposes amendments, the proposal is returned to the Commission for redrafting, and then returned to the Council for final decision. The Council can disregard the amendments and approve the original proposal by a unanimous vote, or it can approve the amended proposal by a qualified majority vote; otherwise, the proposal fails.

This is a complex legislative process, but one thing is clear: The EU Council of Ministers, which is constructed to represent individual national interests rather than broad European interests or ideologies, still holds the strongest hand in the legislative process. Proposals from the Commission and amendments from the Parliament cannot gain final approval without assent of the Council. On the other hand, proposals that are rejected or amended by the Parliament can still be approved without amendment by unanimous assent of the Council. Because of the strong position of the Council, EU policy formation is still based on de Gaulle's model of a "Europe of sovereign states."

The rights of the individual nations in the EU are also protected by the so-called principle of **subsidiarity**, which limits the powers of the EU institutions in roughly the same way that the U.S. Constitution limits the powers of the central government over the states. According to the Maastricht Treaty:

---

[20]This was true, for example, when the Parliament recently required the Commission to accelerate its proposed schedule for automotive safety standards. In another case, the Parliament insisted that a program to simplify cross-border payment transfers should apply only to small payments (less than Ecu10,000) by consumers and small firms. See *EuroWatch*, July 28, 1995, 1; and *International Trade Finance*, June 30, 1995, 1.

> ### HOW BENDS THE EURO BANANA?
>
> In 1994, the European Commission incited anger from German fruit lovers and derision from British tabloids when it declared that a banana cannot be sold in the EU if it is "abnormally bent," shorter than 5.5 inches, or thinner than 1.06 inches. In Brussels, a spokesman for the Commission explained, "If we are going to pay subsidies to banana producers, then of course we are going to ensure that we are not paying out for rubbish." In London, the *Sun* asked its readers to report offending grocers to its "banana hotline," and offered to have its "banana spies" investigate the crimes.

Sources: "Just How Bent Must a Bent Banana Be?" *Evening Standard*, September 21, 1994, 23; and Lance Gay, "Eurocrats' Rules Cover Everything from Sex to Snails," *Rocky Mountain News*, December 22, 1994, 68A.

The Community shall act within the limit of the powers conferred upon it by this Treaty and of the objectives assigned to it therein. In areas which do not fall within its exclusive competence, the Community shall take action, in accordance with the principle of subsidiarity, only if and in so far as the objectives of the proposed action cannot be sufficiently achieved by the Member States and can therefore, by reason of the scale or effects of the proposed action, be better achieved by the Community. Any action by the Community shall not go beyond what is necessary to achieve the objectives of this Treaty.[21]

Policy Implementation: After an EU directive gains final approval, the details of its implementation are overseen by the European Commission and its directorates-general. The Commission issues specific interpretations, instructions, and regulations to make the directive operational, and works with agencies of member governments to monitor compliance with directives and other treaty obligations. Disputes are settled by the EU Court of Justice.

It is during this implementation phase that many complain about the "meddling army of unelected Eurocrats in Brussels." Their instructions attempt to regulate everything from competitive conditions in the telecommunications industry to the depth of snow necessary on ski slopes (See box, "How Bends the Euro Banana?").

THE ECONOMICS OF THE SINGLE EUROPEAN MARKET

As we noted earlier, the EEC was created by the 1957 Treaty of Rome, and its customs union was completed in 1968, with total elimination of internal tariffs and adoption of a common external tariff. Formation of the EEC, together

---

[21]Title II, Article G of the Maastricht Treaty, which calls for these words to be inserted as Article 3b in the Treaty of Rome that created the EEC.

with other sources of postwar economic growth, caused the real volume of intra-EEC trade to expand ninefold between 1958 and 1986.[22]

During its early years, the EEC apparently caused little trade diversion (disruption of trade with nonmembers); external tariffs were relatively low, and they became even lower during the so-called Kennedy Round of GATT negotiations (1963–1968).[23] The average external tariff of EEC members fell from 13 percent in 1958 to 6.6 percent at the end of the Kennedy Round.[24] Indeed, according to Hufbauer, "without the prior formation of the EEC, there would not have been a Kennedy Round at all."[25] The real volume of EEC trade with external countries grew more slowly than internal trade, but it still quadrupled between 1958 and 1986. In 1987, EEC imports from external countries amounted to 9.3 percent of regional GDP, indicating greater openness than in North America (7.8 percent) or Japan (6.2 percent).[26]

Economists have devised many statistical techniques to measure trade creation and trade diversion during the early stages of EEC integration, and they have calculated a wide range of estimates. Nearly all the studies, though, have found that the beneficial effects of trade creation exceeded the harmful effects of trade diversion. Several researchers have found that the EEC created about $10 billion of trade and diverted about $1 billion during its early years. Trade creation was concentrated in manufacturing; trade diversion was primarily caused by the Common Agricultural Policy. Furthermore, the growth of European trade during the 1960s and 1970s was concentrated in intraindustry trade and specialization (such as trading Mercedes automobiles for Fiats), rather than interindustry trade (cars for clothing). This was important because intraindustry specialization did not require the closing of entire national industries; adjustment costs were relatively low.[27]

PHYSICAL BARRIERS

The so-called 1992 Program or Single Market Program, introduced in the 1985 White Paper, attempted to remove three categories of nontariff trade barriers: physical, technical, and fiscal. The most conspicuous physical barriers in Europe are checkpoints at borders, maintained to support law enforcement, to prevent evasion of taxes and agricultural price controls, and to allow collection of statistical data. The Cecchini Report found that border de-

---

[22]According to Gary Hufbauer (who cites a study by Arthur Andersen and Co.), the nominal dollar value of internal EU trade increased by a factor of 16. According to the U.S. national income accounts, the average of import and export price indexes increased by a factor of 4. See Gary C. Hufbauer, "An Overview," in *Europe 1992: An American Perspective*, ed. Gary C. Hufbauer (Washington, D.C.: The Brookings Institution, 1990), 22; and *Economic Report of the President* (Washington, D.C.: USGPO, 1994), 273.

[23]Recall the discussion of trade creation, trade diversion, and the GATT in Chapter 3.

[24]André Sapir, "Regional Integration in Europe," *The Economic Journal* 102 (November 1992): 1500.

[25]Hufbauer, "An Overview," 5.

[26]Ibid., 22.

[27]Jeffrey Harrop, *The Political Economy of Integration in the European Community* (Aldershot: Edward Elgar, 1989), 51; and Sapir, "Regional Integration in Europe," 1495–1499.

lays and paperwork impose a direct cost of some $10 billion every year on Europeans.[28] The 1985 White Paper called for cooperation between national law enforcement agencies, development of new statistical reporting systems, harmonization of tax codes and visa policies, and a range of other measures to enable free movement of people and products within the entire Community by 1992.

Also in 1985, representatives from the Benelux countries, France, and Germany met in Schengen, a village in Luxembourg, where they agreed to accelerate the removal of border controls between their countries. The so-called Schengen Group was expanded to include Italy in 1990, Spain and Portugal in 1991, Greece in 1992, and Austria in 1994.[29] Their original goal was free movement of people within "Schengenland" (the region covered by the Schengen Agreement) by the beginning of 1990.

Implementation of the Schengen Agreement has been slow and difficult. Germany called for postponement in 1989 when the fall of communist regimes in Eastern Europe led to large refugee movements. In subsequent years, progress moved slowly on creation of a Schengen Information System to share law-enforcement information, and on establishment of a coordinated immigration policy. On January 1, 1993, when the Single Market officially came into existence, most border controls on the movement of goods were lifted, but controls were maintained on the movement of people.

In March 1995, the Schengen Agreement finally entered full implementation in seven of the member countries.[30] People of all nationalities were now free to travel from one country to another within Schengenland without passport or visa controls. At the same time, controls on some of the external borders of Schengenland were tightened considerably.[31] In July 1995, the EU Commission called for extension of the Schengen "testing ground" to all of the EU. These plans were immediately thwarted when the British threatened a veto in the EU Council of Ministers, and when France, reacting to a series of terrorist bombings, announced that it would continue passport controls in 1996.[32]

TECHNICAL BARRIERS

According to the Cecchini Report, more than 100,000 different sets of technical regulations were operating in the EC in 1988, many conflicting with one another, and their number was growing rapidly with technological

---

[28]Emerson and others, *The Economics of 1992*, 38.

[29]Austria joined as an observer in 1994 and gained full membership in 1995. Also in 1995, negotiations proceeded on membership for Denmark, Finland, and Sweden. These three were looking for a way to preserve the Nordic passport union with Norway and Iceland, which are not eligible for Schengen membership because they are not members of the EU.

[30]Belgium, France, Germany, Luxembourg, Netherlands, Portugal, and Spain. Details are described in "The Implementation of the Convention Applying the Schengen Agreement," *European Community Press Release*, Memo 95/57, March 24, 1995.

[31]Rick Atkinson, "Europe's Two Worlds Divided by More than a River," *The Washington Post*, August 2, 1995, A1.

[32]Janet McEvoy, "Europe's Border Free Plans Hit Setbacks," Reuters World Service, August 15, 1995; and "France to Seek Schengen Delay," *Financial Times*, September 20, 1995.

developments and concern for health, safety, and consumer protection. These, according to the report, were the most pervasive, complex, and insidious barriers to nonagricultural trade in Europe. European manufacturers could not compete effectively with one another or fully exploit economies of large-scale production if they could not legally sell their products throughout Europe.

The problem of technical barriers had been recognized long before 1985, and efforts had been made to reduce these barriers through **harmonization of standards**. That is, the EC would attempt to formulate communitywide standards for each product, and the Council of Ministers would pass directives, requiring all countries to adopt these standards. Progress was made toward harmonization of standards for some products, but it was slow, because rulings of the Council required unanimity, and individual countries were rapidly producing new conflicting standards.

The 1985 White Paper called for a "new approach" to removal of technical barriers, based on the understanding that health and safety interests are "more often than not identical" in all member countries. Thus, the EC would no longer attempt to harmonize every specification for every product, but would strive for agreement on "essential health and safety requirements which will be obligatory in all Member States."[33]

In sectors that do not have a uniform code of Community standards, the White Paper recommended that products should move across national borders on the basis of **mutual recognition** of technical standards. That is, unless it can present a strong case for exclusion, country A should allow products to enter its market from country B on the presumption that standards in country B will protect the "essential health and safety" of citizens in country A. An important precedent for the principle of mutual recognition had been established in 1979, in the Cassis de Dijon case, when the European Court of Justice required Germany to allow importation of a French liqueur that did not meet German quality standards.

Using this "new approach," and using powers bestowed by the 1987 SEA, allowing the EU Council of Ministers to adopt uniform standards on the basis of a qualified majority vote, important progress has been made on removal of technical barriers, but many still exist. In 1994, a survey by the Danish government found that about half the nation's exporters still faced obstacles inside Europe, particularly in the form of German and French technical standards. Of those who encountered obstacles, more than 60 percent said that the competitive situation in Europe had changed little since 1992; only 25 percent believed the barriers were falling; about 10 percent said the technical barriers were growing.[34]

FISCAL BARRIERS

Ideally, firms in a unified market should compete on a "level playing field"; government(s) should avoid creation of false competitive advantages that

---

[33]European Commission, "Completing the Internal Market," paragraphs 58 and 65.

[34]Peter Gumbel, "Customs of the Countries," *The Wall Street Journal*, September 30, 1994, R10.

distort the allocation of resources. Unfortunately, governments usually fall short of this ideal in their management of fiscal (expenditure and taxation) policy.

On the expenditure side, governments have an understandable tendency to purchase products and services from their domestic companies, even when a foreign supplier can offer a lower price and a higher level of quality. According to the Cecchini Report, governments in the EC kept more than 98 percent of their procurement expenditures at home during the 1980s. The report found that open competition would reduce procurement costs by about $25 billion each year, an amount equal to 0.6 percent of Community GDP.[35] Thus, the 1985 White Paper and the 1987 SEA called for adoption of seven EC Directives requiring all countries to establish coordinated systems of competitive bidding by 1992.

According to the EU Commission, the countries that have done most to open their procurement markets during the past decade are the Netherlands, Luxembourg, and Denmark; Germany, Belgium, the UK, and Italy have done little to implement Commission directives, and Spain, Portugal, and Greece have been granted exemptions from most of the directives.[36] The Commission is "not satisfied at all" with progress in this area, and the economic effects are said to be "huge."[37]

Also on the expenditure side of fiscal policy, market distortions are caused by production subsidies and other forms of state aid to producers. In a 1988 White Paper, the EC Commission found that member states had been spending about 100 billion ECU annually on state subsidies, representing 3 percent of the GDP of the Community or more than $2,000 for each person engaged in manufacturing.[38] The subsidies were reduced to a Community average of about 2 percent of GDP during 1988–1990, but they remained at higher levels in Italy, Belgium, and Greece.[39] In 1994, critics charged that the EU Commission was faltering in its campaign to reduce subsidies. During that year, the Commission allowed the French government to provide more than $2 billion of support to Cie des Machines Bull, a computer manufacturer, and nearly $4 billion to Air France, and allowed the Greek government to bail out Olympic Airways with an expenditure of more than $2 billion. The Commission claimed that these payments were allowed for the companies in question to ease their transition to a more open competitive environment.[40]

On the revenue side of fiscal policy, European countries rely more heavily than other OECD countries on indirect taxation (taxes on purchases) rather than on direct taxation (taxes on income). Taxes on goods and services

[35]Emerson and others, *The Economics of 1992*, 48, 52, and 55.

[36]"Public Procurement: EU Rules Not Always So Well Applied," *Europe Energy* 442 (March 9, 1995), 1.

[37]"Action Urged to Remove EU Market Barriers," *The Irish Times*, June 6, 1995, 12.

[38]Douglas E. Rosenthal, "Competition Policy," in *Europe 1992: An American Perspective*, 332.

[39]Peter Hoeller and Marie-Odile Louppe, "The EC's Internal Market: Implementation and Economic Effects," *OECD Economic Studies* 23 (Winter 1994): 64.

[40]James Pressley, "EU Commission Gives In on Subsidies, Undermining Free-Market Crusaders," *The Wall Street Journal*, October 12, 1994, A12.

account for nearly one-third of total tax receipts in EU and EFTA countries, but for less than one-fifth in Japan and the United States (Table 9.4). This is important, because indirect taxes, which affect the sale prices of goods and services, may affect the operation of the internal market.

The most important form of indirect taxation in the EU is the *value added tax (VAT)*, which has been used since 1954 in France and since 1973 in all other member countries. VAT is a sales tax, paid through the entire production and distribution process. Intermediate producers and distributors (but not the final consumer) are able to reduce their tax liabilities by presenting

■ TABLE 9.4

INDIRECT TAXATION IN WESTERN EUROPE

	Total Tax Receipts as % of GDP 1994	Taxes on Goods and Services as % of Total Receipts 1994	Basic Rates of Value Added Tax April 1987	Basic Rates of Value Added Tax July 1997
European Union				
Austria	42.8	30.9	—	20.0
Belgium	46.6	26.7	19.0	20.5
Denmark	51.6	32.0	22.0	25.0
Finland	47.3	30.8	—	22.0
France	44.1	27.1	18.6	20.6
Germany	39.3	28.7	14.0	15.0
Greece	42.5	41.0	18.0	18.0
Ireland	37.5	39.1	25.0	21.0
Italy	41.7	28.3	18.0	19.0
Luxembourg	45.0	27.4	12.0	15.0
Netherlands	45.9	25.8	20.0	17.5
Portugal	33.0	44.6	16.0	17.0
Spain	35.8	27.9	12.0	15.0
Sweden	51.0	25.8	—	25.0
United Kingdom	34.1	35.3	15.0	17.5
EFTA				
Iceland	30.9	49.2	—	—
Norway	41.2	38.4	—	23.0
Switzerland	33.9	16.3	—	6.5
For Comparison				
Australia	29.9	29.7	—	—
Canada	36.1	26.3	—	—
Japan	27.8	15.5	—	—
United States	27.6	17.9		

Sources: Michael Emerson and others, *The Economics of 1992*, *European Economy* 35 (March 1988): 59; "Oh Drat, the VAT!" *USA Today*, August 25, 1995, 9D; and *OECD in Figures 1997*, a supplement to *The OECD Observer*, July 1997, 46–47.

purchase invoices to the tax authorities, indicating that taxes have already been paid on the earlier stages of production. Thus, in the end, a VAT is formally equivalent to a retail sales tax, levied only on the sale to a final consumer (the major form of taxation at the state level in the United States). The VAT is harder to avoid, however, because: (1) the tax authorities are able to compare invoices received from intermediate buyers and sellers, and (2) the entire burden of collecting the tax does not fall on the final seller. Thus, VAT systems have been adopted throughout Latin America and Eastern Europe to strengthen tax compliance.

A major goal of the Single Market Program is to draw the VAT systems of the EU countries into harmony with one another. This is important for several reasons. Suppose, hypothetically, that Germany is able to produce ball bearings at lower cost than France, but also suppose that the sales tax on bearings is much higher in Germany than in France. In the absence of trade barriers, tax considerations may cause German and French consumers to purchase their bearings from France, the higher-cost producer.[41]Thus, neither country will reap the full benefits of efficient trade, and Germany may be tempted to maintain physical and technical trade barriers to prevent the loss of production and sales to France. Furthermore, companies that conduct business in both countries must endure the complexities and administrative costs of complying with more than one VAT system in the so-called single market.

As the data in Table 9.4 indicate, the record on harmonization of VAT rates in the EU has been slow and uneven. In 1987, basic VAT rates ranged from 12 percent (Spain) to 25 percent (Ireland)—a 13-point spread. In 1997, rates ranged from 15 percent (in Germany, Spain, and Luxembourg) to 25 percent (Denmark and Sweden)—still a 10-point spread. Most EU countries moved their rates toward the group average, but a few (Denmark, Germany, and Portugal) were farther from the group average in 1997 than in 1987.

Furthermore, the basic VAT rates in Table 9.4 tell only part of the story. Many of the EU countries have reduced rates of VAT for food, children's clothing, books, newspapers, and other concessional items. In the United Kingdom and Ireland, products such as these are exempted from VAT altogether. The EU Council has ruled, however, that all exemptions should end by 1997, and a minimum rate of 5 percent shall be levied on all items.

Despite persistent differences in national VAT rates, structures, and coverages, the EU Commission claims that these no longer cause any "significant distortions of competition," and there is "no justification" for immediate reform of the underlying system.[42] European companies, however, would like to see further simplification and harmonization of the system to reduce their administrative costs.

---

[41]In principle, this problem should correct itself if (1) each country has a single rate of VAT on all goods and services and (2) the exchange rate between the German mark and French franc is allowed to float freely. Under these conditions, the high rate of VAT in Germany should raise the general price level in that country, causing the Mark to depreciate on the foreign exchange market, and restoring the competitive position of German widgets. In practice, though, each EU country does not have a single rate of VAT, and the EU is attempting to form a monetary union—the countries are attempting to establish fixed exchange rates among their currencies.

[42]"Getting VAT Right in the EU," *Business Europe*, July 10, 1995, 1.

BENEFITS AND COSTS OF A SINGLE MARKET

In every area, we see that important progress has been made toward creation of single market, but obstacles remain. Physical, technical, and fiscal barriers have been reduced, but not eliminated. What benefits and costs should emerge if the European market is fully unified?

As previously noted, the Cecchini Report, published in 1988, suggested that removal of internal nontariff barriers would cause European GDP to increase by about 5 percent in the medium term. The authors predicted that these benefits will take several forms and emerge in several stages. First, consumers, producers, and government procurement officers will realize **direct cost reductions** from improved access to low-cost suppliers in the single European market, and from lower administrative costs at border crossings and tax offices. As the market grows more unified, and as producers lose their local monopolies, the latter will be forced to reduce overstaffing, increase product quality and production efficiency, and seek other forms of **competitive cost reduction.** As European companies compete more effectively on the world market, and as production is rationalized in larger, more efficient factories, the European economy will benefit from substantial **economies of scale.**

Because of its broad scope and authoritative authorship, the Cecchini Report quickly became the centerpiece of economic debate on the Single Market Program; its results were considered pessimistic by some, and excessively optimistic by others. According to Euro-optimists, the gains from removal of nontariff barriers should be reinforced by monetary union, by a post–cold war "peace dividend," and by successful conclusion of the Uruguay Round of GATT negotiations, but none of these were reflected in the Cecchini Report. Furthermore, according to Richard Baldwin, the unified market should permanently improve the EU investment climate, causing long-term economic growth in the region to accelerate by about one-half a percentage point. Thus, Baldwin suggests that the long-term gains from unification could be more than double those in the Cecchini Report.[43]

Europessimists emphasize the difficulties of fully implementing the Single Market Program. Border controls are needed, they say, to control crime, terrorism, and drug trafficking. Each country should be free to establish health and safety standards without the intrusion of Eurocrats in Brussels. Differences among national systems of taxation, product distribution, and monopoly regulation cannot be harmonized quickly. Political pressures will continue to influence public procurement, and national brand loyalties will influence consumer demand. The outcome of the Single Market Program will vary from one product to another, influenced by the patterns of competitive and oligopolistic interaction that arise in each market.[44]

---

[43]Richard E. Baldwin, "The Growth Effects of 1992," *Economic Policy* 9 (October 1989): 248–281, summarized in "The Lure of 1992," *The Economist*, November 18, 1989, 77.

[44]On this last point, see Carmen Matutes, "Some Considerations about 1992," *Atlantic Economic Journal* 17 (September 1989): 1–11.

The Cecchini Report said much about the potential gains from unification, but little about the transitional unemployment and other adjustment costs that would inevitably emerge from a major restructuring of the European economy. When the report acknowledged the possibility of transitional problems, it assumed that they would disappear quickly, and would be justified by subsequent economic gains.[45] The report also said little about the regional redistribution of production and income that would occur in a single market. Subsequent studies have been divided on this issue. Some suggest that unification will favor Germany, the dominant economy in Europe; others suggest that the biggest winners will be the lower-income countries of southern Europe, benefiting from access to the markets of high-income northern countries.[46]

Another issue that arouses controversy is the influence of the Single Market Program on external countries. What, for example, will be its effect on European-American economic relations? In the late 1980s, soon after the program was launched, many Americans feared the creation of a discriminatory "Fortress Europe." In particular, Americans feared that technical standards for European goods would be purposefully designed to exclude American products. According to Lester Thurow, "Outsiders have to face the fact that European integration will hurt them. It wouldn't work if it didn't."[47]

On the other hand, we should recall that the EEC was created with the support and encouragement of the United States, and the weight of evidence suggests that the EEC has been a trade-creating organization, particularly outside of agriculture. Trade liberalization within Europe has usually been complementary with multilateral trade liberalization in the GATT framework. American and other "outside" companies have been able to participate in the EU standards-setting process through their European subsidiaries. More generally, if the EU successfully creates a large, integrated, border-free market, that will be a most familiar environment for American, Canadian, and Japanese firms. Instead of developing different products and distribution systems for each of the European countries, outside companies will be able to develop a broad strategy for all of Europe. It should be easier to attack a single "fortress" than to fight one battle after another in the walled cities of Europe.

COMMON AGRICULTURAL POLICY

During the mid–1950s, when creation of the European common market was under negotiation, the interests of the major countries were quite different. The industrial exporters—West Germany, Belgium, and Luxembourg—favored an industrial customs union, but feared that liberalization of agricultural trade would drive their inefficient farmers out of business. The

---

[45]See, for example, Emerson and others, *The Economics of 1992*, 212–221.

[46]On the German hypothesis, see Tony Cutler and others, *1992—The Struggle for Europe* (New York: Berg Publishers, 1989), 9–43. On the southern Europe hypothesis, see Damien J. Neven, "EEC Integration towards 1992: Some Distributional Aspects," *Economic Policy* 10 (April 1990): 14–46.

[47]Lester Thurow, *Head to Head* (New York: William Morrow and Company, 1992), 69.

food exporters—France, Italy, and the Netherlands—wanted to gain preferential access to German and other European agricultural markets, shielded from American and other non-European competition. In exchange, they would be willing to join an industrial customs union.

At the Messina conference in 1955, the Six agreed to negotiate a **Common Agricultural Policy (CAP).** After years of discussion and analysis, they adopted a CAP in 1962, and began its implementation in 1964. Since its inception, the CAP always has been a matter of bewildering complexity, with its own vocabulary of green currencies, mini-switch-overs and switch-unders, set-asides, and monetary compensation amounts, and a welter of exceptions and variations for different commodities, years, and monetary systems. Reforms of the system seldom have contributed to simplicity or transparency.

Reduced to essentials, the CAP initially had four major components. First, it provided for the economic viability of farmers in Germany and other high-cost countries by fixing EU agricultural prices at high levels. Second, it met the demands of France and other agricultural exporters by opening internal markets and by maintaining uniform internal prices. Third, it protected the European agricultural market from import competition with a system of variable levies. Fourth, it established a system of export subsidies to ensure that European farmers could compete on external markets. The import levies and export subsidies had to be large enough to counteract the inflated levels of internal agricultural prices.

To maintain target prices, the European Agricultural Guarantee and Guidance Fund stands ready to buy any qualified products not purchased by consumers at target price levels. During the mid-1980s, these purchases kept European prices two times higher than world prices for wheat, three times higher for sugar and butter, and nine times higher for skimmed milk powder.[48] High prices and guaranteed EU purchases encourage surplus production of commodities, which must be stored or destroyed at taxpayer expense. More generally, these "rivers" of surplus wine and olive oil and "mountains" of cheese and butter have long served as symbols of the wastefulness of the CAP.

A special problem arises from the fact that farm prices are intended to be uniform throughout the EU, but the region does not yet have a single currency. A partial solution to this difficulty became available in 1979, when a new accounting unit was created, the so-called European Currency Unit (ECU). Each spring, the EU farm ministers agree on a target price in ECUs for each of the agricultural products. The price of the commodity in a particular country is determined by applying the agreed ECU price to the exchange rate between the ECU and the national currency.

The CAP, we have seen, is designed to support farm production with high and stable agricultural prices. Under the system just described, however, an increase in the value of, say, the German D-mark relative to the ECU should cause the prices of agricultural goods in Germany to fall. To prevent this from happening, the EC decided in 1969 to establish a separate set of "green exchange rates" for agricultural transactions that are more stable than market exchange rates; values calculated according to these rates are known as **green currencies.** From time to time, however, it has been necessary to realign the green rates to keep them from diverging too far from market exchange rates. When this has happened, the target commodity prices, measured in ECUs, have been increased to ensure that domestic prices remain stable in countries with appreciating currencies. This practice of increasing ECU prices to counteract exchange rate appreciation is known as the **switch-over.**

With each year, the EU faces greater pressure to thoroughly reform the CAP. This pressure arises, first, from the massive budgetary cost of the program. Price support payments and other agricultural subsidies have absorbed as much as 80 percent of the EU budget in some years; in 1995 they accounted for about $35 billion, or about half the EU budget.[49] Furthermore, the budgetary cost of the CAP is only the tip of the iceberg. The system requires European consumers to pay a larger fraction of their monthly budget on food than American consumers, but they get less food for their money. Subsidies to agricultural producers from the EU budget were $85 billion in 1996, compared with about $24 billion in the United States.[50]

Pressure for reform of the CAP also comes from the United States, and from commitments made during the Uruguay Round of GATT negotiations. The EU agreed to steeply reduce its agricultural export subsidies. This, in turn, means that the EU must reduce its support prices if it wishes to compete on world agricultural markets.

Finally, the CAP must be reformed before the EU can extend full membership to the countries of Central and Eastern Europe. An enormous increase in price support purchases would have to be added to the EU budget to boost agricultural prices in Eastern Europe to Western European levels. And if that were done, low-income consumers in Eastern Europe would not be able to afford the high-priced European goods.

For these and other reasons, the EC began in 1992 to introduce major changes in the CAP. Price supports were reduced, and some farmers were required to set aside part of their land to reduce surplus production. Farmers were compensated for these price and quantity reductions with direct income subsidies. In 1995, the switch-over procedure was discontinued, because it led to higher support prices and larger subsidies. These reforms have not reduced the total subsidization of European agriculture, but they have yielded important results. In 1995, the EU prices of many products, including cereals, were roughly equal to world market prices, and the rivers and mountains of surplus food were substantially smaller. Reserves of cereals, which stood at 33 million tons in 1993, fell to about 6 million tons in 1995.[51]

---

[49]"Europe Ploughs an Even More Erratic Furrow on CAP," *The Daily Telegraph,* August 30, 1995, 25.

[50]*OECD in Figures, 1997 Edition,* supplement to *OECD Observer,* July 1997, 35.

[51]John Palmer, "Reforms Eat into Europe's Food Mountains," *The Guardian,* August 2, 1995, 9.

Based on these achievements, the British government called in 1995 for a new wave of CAP reform, with deep reductions of subsidies and quantitative restrictions. The European Commission has demonstrated little interest.

MONETARY UNIFICATION

The operation of the CAP, with its green currencies and switch-overs, illustrates how difficult it is to create a truly unified market in a region with several independent national currencies. Furthermore, anyone who has traveled in Europe, accumulating pockets full of pounds, pence, punts, pfennigs, and other paper and metal currencies, can appreciate the reduction in accounting and other transactions costs that a unified European monetary system would afford. These costs represent a major barrier to expansion of European trade. On the other hand, creation of a common currency requires each country to relinquish its separate monetary policy and a portion of its national sovereignty.

Jean Monnet, the architect of European economic unity, proposed, in 1958, the creation of a European Bank and Reserve Fund that would steer the development of a "common financial policy."[52] The EC formed a Monetary Committee in that same year, and organized a Committee of Governors of Central Banks in 1964. Nevertheless, little progress was made toward financial cooperation until the late 1960s, when unstable exchange rates threatened to disrupt European trade and investment. In 1969, the heads of state asked the EC Commission to prepare a plan for economic and monetary union. The resulting document, known as the Werner Report, called for gradual reduction of exchange rate fluctuations among member countries, leading toward full monetary union.

In 1972, the EC nations concluded a **Joint Float Agreement,** whereby the exchange rates of their currencies would float broadly against the dollar and other external currencies, but would be held within 2.25 percent bands of fluctuation against one another. The Joint Float was also known as the **European Snake,** because the U.S. dollar exchange rates of the EC currencies, when plotted together, outlined a curving pattern on a time-series chart that looked like the narrow body of a snake. Unfortunately, the Joint Float provided EC members with few tools to fulfill its objectives. Faced with the financial instabilities of the mid–1970s, five EC members withdrew from the system within two years.

The **European Monetary System (EMS),** which replaced the Joint Float, became operational in 1979. The EMS initially retained the basic objective of the Joint Float—to hold internal EC exchange rates within 2.25 percent bands of fluctuation—but it introduced several operational innovations. First, the members created a new **European Currency Unit (ECU),** which became the benchmark or unit of account for measurement of EC exchange rates, budgets, national incomes, foreign transactions, and other financial accounts. An ECU is worth a fixed "basket" of EC currencies, each weighted according to shares of regional GDP and trade.

---

[52]Monnet, *Memoirs,* 428.

Second, the EMS created a coordinated system of intervention, known as the **Exchange Rate Mechanism (ERM),** to enable its members to fulfill the region's monetary goals. Under the ERM, a permissible range of fluctuation is established between each pair of currencies in the system, and a band is established for each currency around its "central rate" with the ECU. According to an organized procedure, member countries are required to purchase or sell currencies that move outside of their prescribed ranges.

In principle, all EC countries are members of the EMS, but they are not required to participate in the ERM. When it was established in 1979, eight countries joined the ERM: France, Denmark, Ireland, Italy, West Germany, and the Benelux nations. While the stronger countries maintained 2.25 percent bands for their currencies, Italy was allowed to regulate its relatively unstable lira within a 6 percent band. During the first eight years of its operation, the central exchange rates in the ERM were realigned eleven times, often involving revaluation of the German mark and the Dutch guilder against the ECU, and devaluation of the Italian lira and the French franc.[53] Beginning in 1987, the ERM members grew more determined to move toward full monetary union; they avoided realignments of their currencies, even when underlying economic forces made it difficult to defend the existing exchange rates.

In 1989, 1990, and 1992, respectively, Spain, the United Kingdom, and Portugal joined the ERM, and all three were allowed to adopt 6 percent margins for their currencies. The addition of these three weak currencies to the system, the policy of avoiding realignments, and uncertainties over ratification of the Maastricht Treaty led to a major exchange crisis in September 1992, causing the United Kingdom and Italy to withdraw from the ERM. The crisis reached a new crescendo in August 1993, when it became necessary to expand all the 2.25 and 6 percent bands of fluctuation to 15 percent.[54]

In 1995, when three new members joined the EU, only Austria immediately joined the ERM. Finland and Sweden announced no specific schedule, but indicated they would attempt to enter the ERM in 1996. Greece, which joined the EC in 1981, intends, at long last, to enter the ERM in 1996, and Italy plans to reenter during that same year. As this is written, the United Kingdom is most uncertain about its future role in the ERM or in any successor organization promoting monetary union.

All in all, how well has the EMS performed? During its early years, it usually received good marks. The currencies were realigned frequently enough to maintain the viability of the system, but infrequently enough to stabilize exchange rates. The volatility of intra-EMS exchange rates declined sharply after 1979, while foreign exchange markets grew more volatile outside the EMS. Because of the dominance of Germany in the EMS, there was a tendency for monetary growth rates and inflation rates to converge toward the low German levels, and to become less variable.[55]

---

[53]For details of these realignments, see Harrop, *The Political Economy of Integration*, 140.

[54]By informal agreement, Germany and the Netherlands maintained a 2.25 percent band between the mark and the guilder. For analysis of the crises of 1992 and 1993, see Joseph A. Whitt, Jr., "Monetary Union in Europe," *Economic Review*, Federal Reserve Bank of Atlanta 79 (January/February 1994): 17–23.

■ FIGURE 9.1

UNEMPLOYMENT AND INFLATION IN THE
EUROPEAN UNION, 1970–1994

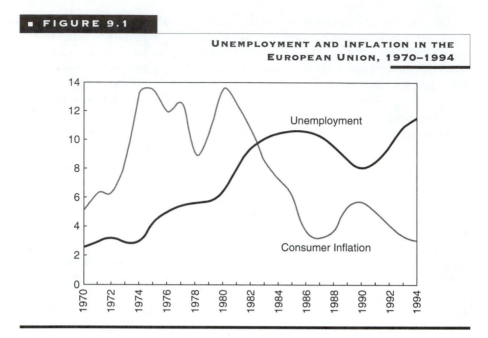

On the other hand, the benefits derived from the EMS have not been cost-free. Between 1980 and 1986, while austerity programs induced by the EMS supported a ten-percentage-point reduction in the EU inflation rate, they also contributed to a five-percentage-point increase in the EU unemployment rate (Figure 9.1). Since that time, inflation has remained under control, but unemployment has persisted at high levels. Why has high unemployment been so persistent in Western Europe? Some economists, including the staff of the OECD, lay the blame on rules and regulations in Europe that reduce the flexibility of labor markets. Others, including Nobel laureate Robert Solow, believe that Europe is suffering from continued insufficiency of aggregate demand, stemming from a German-dominated EMS.[56]

THE BUMPY ROAD TO A SINGLE CURRENCY

In 1988, the European Council asked the Commission to develop a step-by-step strategy for full unification of the European monetary system. Jacques Delors, who was chairman of the European Commission, convened a special Committee for the Study of Economic and Monetary Union, whose members included the twelve central bank governors, two members of the European Commission (including Delors as chair), and three independent experts.

The Delors Committee recommended a three-stage program for monetary union. Stage one, it said, would begin in 1990, and would include three major

---

[55]Frank McDonald and George Zis, "The European Monetary System: Towards 1992 and Beyond," *Journal of Common Market Studies* 27 (March 1989): 184–191.

[56]Robert Taylor, "Faced by More Job Losses, EU States Look to U.S. Flexibility," *Financial Times*, August 22, 1995, 2; and Robert Solow, "Europe's Unnecessary Unemployment," *International Economic Insights* (March/April 1994): 10–11. For a more general discussion of these issues, see Charles R. Bean, "European Unemployment: A Survey," *Journal of Economic Literature* 32 (June 1994): 573–619.

objectives: (1) efforts would be made to include all the Community currencies in the ERM, (2) EU members would remove all restrictions on international movements of capital, and (3) central bank governors would play a more active role in coordination of economic policies, devoting special attention to harmonization of inflation rates.[57]

The Maastricht Treaty was negotiated in 1991, when stage one had already begun. The treaty adopted the three-stage structure of the Delors report, but added many new details. Stage two, it said, would begin in 1994, and during its tenure the member states would be expected to (1) give independence to their individual central banks, and (2) create a **European Monetary Institute (EMI).** The EMI would be responsible for administration of the EMS, for coordination of monetary policies, and for laying the groundwork of a monetary union. Recommendations of the EMI to the member states would have no binding force.

The third and final stage of monetary unification, according to the treaty, would include the following provisions: (1) the EMS would be transformed into a **European Monetary Union (EMU),** based on irrevocably fixed exchange rates and eventual adoption of a single currency; and (2) the EMI would be transformed into a **European Central Bank (ECB),** with supranational powers. The timing of stage three and the eligibility of each EMS member for membership in the EMU would depend on the following **convergence criteria:**

- ■ Sustainable price performance and an average rate of consumer price inflation for one year that does not exceed that of the best three performers by more than 1.5 percentage points.

- ■ A budget deficit no more than 3 percent of GDP and an outstanding debt no larger than 60 percent of GDP.

- ■ Participation in the narrow (2.25 percent) bands of the ERM for at least two years "without severe tensions" and without realignment of bilateral exchange rates.

- ■ Long-term interest rates, averaged for one year, no more than two percentage points higher than those of the best three performers.

According to the treaty, stage three would begin in 1997 if the majority of EMS members were able to meet these convergence criteria. In any event, the treaty provided that stage three should begin no later than 1999, even if only a minority of countries could meet the convergence criteria to form the initial membership of the EMU.

As we have seen, the timing of the Maastricht Treaty was unfortunate. In 1992, one year after the treaty was negotiated, a major currency crisis caused the United Kingdom and Italy to withdraw from the ERM. In August 1993, a few months before the treaty was ratified, it became necessary to expand the bands of exchange rate fluctuation in the ERM to 15 percent. Early in 1995, when Austria, Sweden, and Finland joined the EU, only Austria was prepared immediately to join the ERM.

---

[57]Niels Thygesen, "The Delors Report and European Economic and Monetary Union," *International Affairs* 65 (Autumn 1989): 637–652.

In mid-1995, the Commission reported that only three of the fifteen EU members—Germany, Ireland, and Luxembourg—already met the government debt and deficit criteria required for the EMU. Budget deficits in Greece, Italy, Spain, and Sweden were more than double the targets of the Maastricht Treaty.[58] Of the three countries that met the budgetary targets, only Germany and Luxembourg had maintained stable exchange rates during the previous two years.[59] Thus, in June 1995, at a summit meeting in Cannes, the EU leaders acknowledged that it would be impossible to launch a new currency in 1997; they agreed to work toward the 1999 deadline established in the Maastricht Treaty.[60]

A few months after the Cannes summit, when the EU leaders met again on the Spanish island of Majorca, the 1999 goal was called into question. The German finance minister expressed doubt that several countries, including Italy (one of the original Six), would be able to meet the convergence criteria by 1999. Nevertheless, he said, the criteria must not be relaxed. British prime minister John Major predicted that convergence will grow even more difficult as new members are added to the EU. It is "simply not economically and politically credible," he said, to build an EMU with only a few members within an EU that may grow to include 25 or 30 members. Lamberto Dini, the Italian prime minister, suggested that the EMU should be delayed by a year or two to allow more countries to qualify. On the other hand, Jacques Santer, president of the European Commission, warned that any deviation from the Maastricht Treaty could cause the entire structure to collapse.[61]

EU ENLARGEMENT AND THE FUTURE OF EUROPE

Each time the EC has accepted new members, the nature of the community has changed. The 1973 enlargement, which added Denmark, Ireland, and the United Kingdom, strengthened the trade liberalization camp of the EC and created a closer link to the United States through its "special relationship" with the UK. The enlargements of 1981 and 1986, adding Greece, Portugal, and Spain, created a so-called Club Med within the EC that strengthened the leadership role of France, tilted the EC back toward protectionism, and absorbed a large share of agricultural and regional aid. The 1995 enlargement, adding Austria, Finland, and Sweden, is expected to restore the "northern" balance of liberalism over protectionism, draw attention to environmental dangers from the former Soviet Union, and encourage development of a European social policy.

Today, at least 14 nations in Central and Eastern Europe and the Mediterranean area are standing at the entry door of the EU, and several have initi-

---

[58]Lionel Barber, "1997 Is Dead—But EMU Is Far from Buried," *Financial Times*, June 21, 1995, 2.

[59]Martin Wolf, "Cracks in the Single Market," *Financial Times*, May 2, 1995, 13.

[60]Lionel Barber, "EU Leaders Plan 1999 Launch Date of Single Currency," *Financial Times*, June 27, 1995, 1.

[61]"European Leaders Hold Summit," AP News Service, September 23, 1995; Philip Gawith, "Dollar Will Point the Way after Majorca," *Financial Times*, September 25, 1995, 2; and "EU's Santer Says No Deviation from EMU Path," Reuter News Service, October 2, 1995.

ated formal application processes (the sixth and seventh categories in Table 9.1). The current leadership of the EU has decided, though, that none of these countries will be able to gain membership until several things happen. First, the internal governmental structures of the EU (the Commission, Council, Parliament, and so on), which were originally designed for a smaller group of countries, must be reformed to accommodate a larger union. This is a major objective of an intergovernmental conference (IGC) in 1996–1997. Negotiations on the memberships of Cyprus, Malta, Hungary, Poland, the Czech Republic, and Slovakia are expected to begin about six months after conclusion of the IGC.[62]

It is also clear that enlargement cannot proceed until the EU has completed additional reforms of its agricultural and regional policies. Without reform, the budgetary cost of incorporating four relatively successful countries—Poland, Hungary, the Czech Republic, and Slovakia—into the CAP and the regional development program would be about ECU 36 billion ($46.8 billion).[63]

A number of other issues are less clear. How carefully, for example, will the EU examine the human rights records of its applicants? Formulation of a new Bill of Rights may be on the IGC agenda, and may call for suspension or expulsion of countries that use the death penalty, and countries that fail to protect their citizens from racism, xenophobia, or other abuses.[64] According to Jacques Santer, president of the European Commission, "We often tend to forget that the success of our Community is based on the fact that it is a community of law, established with the cooperation of the national governments and independent judiciaries. Reaching a comparable stage in the candidate countries will not be achieved overnight."[65]

How will Russia react to EU encroachment into Central and Eastern Europe and the Baltic states—in countries that previously fell under the Soviet sphere of influence? How quickly will European economic cooperation develop into political and military cooperation, and how actively will European countries participate in the Atlantic alliance? Will closer political and military cooperation allow Europe to respond more effectively to future Bosnia-style conflicts?

Finally, what will be the new architecture of Europe? On this subject, metaphors are mixed freely. Some leaders favor a Europe of "variable geometry" or "concentric circles." Germany and a few other countries in the "hard inner core" of Europe should, they say, charge ahead on EMU and other projects, laying groundwork for other countries to follow in later years. Others favor a "single-track" approach to European integration, arguing that a variable approach will weaken regional unity, leading to eventual disintegration of the EU. European integration, they say, must proceed at a pace that allows

---

[62]"Splits Likely to Delay Enlargement to the East," AFX News Service, September 25, 1995.

[63]Jonathan Clayton, "EU Leaders Reflect on What Expansion Means," Reuter News Service: European Community Report, September 23, 1995.

[64]Lionel Barber, "EU Seeks Human Rights Censure," *Financial Times*, September 5, 1995, 2.

[65]"EU Enlargement: Determined Attitude from Commission," *Euro-East* 36 (September 26, 1995), 1.

the majority of member countries to participate fully.[66] Enlargement of the EU raises a host of questions about the future of Europe; the answers seem to change with each new generation.

SUMMARY

Efforts have been made for hundreds of years to unify the economic and political systems of Europe, leading to a broad consensus for cooperation after World War II. Postwar integration was encouraged in many ways by the United States. Some Europeans supported a strong European federation to emulate the performance of the unified American economy; others supported a weaker confederation to protect Europe from American hegemony. The United States also supported European unification through the Marshall Plan and encouraged formation of the European Coal and Steel Community and the European Economic Community. These institutions were created in the late 1950s and operated with some success during the 1960s, but were overtaken by "Europessimism" during the economic crises of the 1970s.

Progress toward European unity resumed with publication of the 1985 White Paper, the 1988 Cecchini Report, and the 1987 Single European Act, which provided analytical and institutional support for creation of a European Single Market by the end of 1992, and by the 1989 report of the Delors Committee, providing a partial blueprint for European Monetary Union. The Maastricht Treaty, negotiated in 1991 and ratified in 1993, provided fuller detail and a specific timetable for monetary union, and transformed the European Community into a European Union.

The "general political guidelines" of the European Union are determined by the European Council. The Commission is the executive branch of the EU, and it, together with the Committee of Permanent Representatives, the Economic and Social Committee, Committee of Regions, and other advisory groups, provides recommendations to the Council of Ministers, the principal decision-making body. Under the Single European Act and the Maastricht Treaty, more actions can be taken on the basis of qualified majority voting, without full unanimity, and new powers have been gained by the European Parliament and the Court of Justice.

Statistical studies of postwar European integration have usually found that the beneficial effects of trade creation exceeded the harmful effects of trade diversion, and that growth was concentrated on intraindustry trade, which imposes smaller adjustment costs than interindustry trade.

The Single Market Program has attempted to remove physical barriers, such as border controls; technical barriers, such as conflicting product safety standards; and fiscal barriers, such as national subsidies and conflicting systems of taxation. Progress has been made in all these areas, but much remains to be done. Some observers believe that the Single Market will become a protective "Fortress Europe," but the evidence does not seem to support these fears.

By far, the most expensive and protective program of the European Union

---

[66]"Back to the Drawing Board," *The Economist*, September 10, 1994, 21–23.

is its Common Agricultural Policy. The CAP includes systems of price supports and income subsidies to provide for the economic survival of high-cost European farmers, export subsidies to make the high-priced agricultural goods salable on foreign markets, and a system of "green" exchange rates to neutralize the short-term effects of foreign exchange markets on relative agricultural prices. Presently, the CAP is being reformed to reduce its budgetary cost, to conform to requirements of the GATT, and to make way for accession of new EU members from Central and Eastern Europe.

Monetary unification of Europe is supported by those economists who believe that monetary transaction costs are an important barrier to trade, and by those politicians who support the broader unification of Europe. It is opposed by economists who believe that each country needs to have firm control of its own monetary policy, and by politicians who fear loss of national sovereignty. Concrete steps toward unification began in 1972 with the Joint Float Agreement. In 1979, the European Monetary System created a new European Currency Unit and established a coordinated system of exchange rate intervention. The Delors Committee and the Maastricht Treaty established a three-stage program for European Monetary Union, with the last stage beginning sometime between 1997 and 1999. So far, few prospective members have been able to fulfill the convergence criteria for entry into the EMU.

Enlargements in 1973, 1981, 1986, and 1995 have all changed the policy orientation and internal political alliances in the EC. Presently, some 14 countries in Central and Eastern Europe and the Mediterranean area are working toward membership in the EU. Again, their application will require reform of EU governmental structures, reforms of the Common Agricultural Policy, and clarification of human rights, national security, and organizational issues.

DISCUSSION AND REVIEW QUESTIONS

1. How do the opinions of Gaullists and federalists differ on the subject of European economic and political integration? How are they similar?

2. The United States and other outside countries seem to be less supportive of European unification today than they were during the 1950s and 1960s. Do you agree? If so, why might this be true?

3. How does the governmental structure of the EU resemble that of a national government, and how does it differ? How will it need to change to accommodate a large number of new members?

4. How did formation of the EEC affect the volume of trade among its members? How did it affect trade between members and nonmembers?

5. What kinds of trade barriers were attacked by the Single Market Program? Which ones were most important? How have they been removed, and how successfully?

6. Why has the EC handled agricultural policy separately from industrial policy? How does the system of agricultural intervention differ from a common external tariff? What forces have led to reform of the Common Agricultural Policy?

7. What would be the advantages and disadvantages of a single currency in Europe? If you were the leader of Poland, would you wish to gain eventual entry in the EMU?

8. Suppose that you are a delegate from Germany to the intergovernmental conference of the EU. What conditions and procedures would you wish to set for countries of Central and Eastern Europe to join the EU?

Suggested Readings

Cutler, Tony, and others. *1992—The Struggle for Europe*. New York: Berg Publishers, 1989. *According to the authors of this provocative critique of the Cecchini Report, the Single Market Program will perpetuate German domination of European manufacturing and trade. Their objective, they say, is to redefine and broaden the issues in the debate.*

Emerson, Michael, and others. *The Economics of 1992*. Oxford: Oxford University Press, 1988. *This is the more technical version of the so-called Cecchini Report, including a full discussion of the economics of integration and an extended presentation of statistical studies measuring the expected benefits of a single European market.*

Harrop, Jeffrey. *The Political Economy of Integration in the European Community*. Aldershot: Edward Elgar, 1989. *Written as a textbook for undergraduate courses on the European economy, this is a concise and scholarly analysis of the subject from a very British perspective.*

Hufbauer, Gary C., ed. *Europe 1992: An American Perspective*. Washington, D.C.: The Brookings Institution, 1990. *After an excellent 50-page overview of the subject by the editor, the other six chapters of this volume take an American (or other outsider) view of the impact of a Single Market on the European banking, automotive, telecommunications, and semiconductor sectors, and on European competition policies and negotiating strategies.*

Marjolin, Robert. *Architect of European Unity: Memoirs 1911–1986*. London: Weidenfeld and Nicolson, 1989. *Written by the first secretary-general of the Organization for European Economic Cooperation, the forerunner of the OECD, this is a well-written and wideranging record of the people and events involved in European integration.*

Monnet, Jean. *Memoirs*. Garden City, N.Y.: Doubleday and Company, 1978. *Written by the "father" of the European Community, this is a life story, an account of world events, and a passionate argument for political as well as economic unification of Europe.*

Internet Resources

ECHO
European Commission Host Organization
http://www.echo.lu/echo/en/menuecho.html

ERCOMER
European Research Centre on Migration and Ethnic Relations

http://www.ruu.nl/ercomer/

EURODATA Research Archive
Mannheim Centre for European Social Research
http://www.sowi.uni-mannheim.de/eurodata/eurodata.html

EuroDocs: Primary Historical Documents
From Western Europe
http://library.byu.edu/~rdh/eurodocs/

EUROPA
European Commission
http://www.cec.lu/Welcome.html

European Journalism
http://www.demon.co.uk/eurojournalism/

European Union and Internet
http://shiva.di.uminho.pt/~jmv/htmls/ueuropeia.html

European Union Basics FAQ
http://www.vub.ac.be/SMIT/eubasics/index.html
or
gopher://gopher.vub.ac.be:70/00/LocalProjects/CSMINC/extern/euba-
sics.txt

Eurostat
The Statistical Office of the European Communities
http://www.cec.lu/en/comm/eurostat/eurostat.html

Fact Sheet: The European Union
U.S. Department of State
gopher://dosfan.lib.uic.edu:70/0F–1%3A3539%3A95/05/20%20Fact%20Sh
eet

Historical Archives of the European Communities
http://wwwarc.iue.it/

Information Society Project Office
http://www.ispo.cec.be/

Maastricht Treaty
gopher://wiretap.Spies.COM:70/11/Gov/Maast

New Europe
http://www.new-europe.gr/

OneEurope Magazine
http://www.informatik.rwth-aachen.de/AEGEE/oneEurope/

Treaty of Rome
http://www.tufts.edu/departments/fletcher/multi/texts/BH343.txt

What's New in Europe
http://www.ukshops.co.uk:8000/whatsnew/thisweek.html

The United Kingdom

10

THE UNITED KINGDOM: DECLINING CAPITALISM

Men of England, Heirs of Glory, Heroes of unwritten story,

Nurslings of one mighty mother,

Hope of her, and one another,

Rise, like lions after slumber, In unvanquished number,

Shake your chains to earth like dew,

Which in sleep had fall'n on you.

—PERCY BYSSHE SHELLEY
THE MASQUE OF ANARCHY, 1819

reat Britain, the cardle of the Industrial Revolution, was the political, military, and economic superpower of the nineteenth century.[1] Today, despite decades of relative decline, the United Kingdom continues to play a pivotal role in the world economy. London is still a most important financial and commercial center. Conservative prime ministers Margaret Thatcher and John Major led the world in programs of privatization, deregulation, and labor market reform, and Labour prime minister Tony Blair is preparing a radical program of welfare reform. In the European Union, British leaders are among the strongest champions of national sovereignty; they seldom support programs of political, social, or military unification.

Why did the United Kingdom lose its historic superpower status? Why were British industries nationalized in previous decades, and why have they been privatized more recently? Why is the UK such a reluctant member of the European Union? Will the British pound be replaced by a European currency? We will explore these and many other questions in this chapter.

---

[1]Great Britain was formed in 1707 by uniting England, Scotland, and Wales. The United Kingdom was formed in 1801 by the union of Great Britain and Ireland. The Irish Free State withdrew from the United Kingdom in 1922, but Northern Ireland was retained.

THE ECONOMICS OF DECLINE

During the nineteenth century, Britannia ruled the waves and established an empire on which the sun never set. Wellington's victory over Napoleon in 1815 silenced any doubt of British military superiority raised by the American Revolution. By the end of the century, Britain controlled over one-fifth of the world's land surface and governed one-quarter of the world's population.

British military power during the nineteenth century was only a reflection of her economic power. In 1870, the British were only 2 percent of the world's population, but they accounted for nearly a third of its industrial production and a quarter of its trade.[2] British average incomes were 10 percent larger than those of the Americans or the French, and twice as large as those of the Germans or the Swedes. London was the dominant financial center of the entire world, and the pound sterling was the key currency in the international monetary system.

Today, some seventeen countries, including four of England's former colonies, have higher per capita incomes than the United Kingdom.[3] The British share of world industrial production has fallen from 32 percent in 1870 to about 2 percent in 1997. During the past century, the relative economic position of Britain has declined more dramatically than that of any other country.

REASONS FOR DECLINE: AN OVERVIEW

What went wrong: Why did British dominance come to an end? That question has been debated for years by social scientists. Most of their explanations revolve around the British failure to maintain its technological lead after the Industrial Revolution.

Although the British quickly adopted the first generation of new technologies in the textile, iron, and steel industries, they were slow to install the second generation of technologies. In 1870, the average open-hearth furnace in the British steel industry was roughly the same size as a furnace in Germany. Twenty years later, the German furnaces were 50 percent larger and total production was 65 percent greater. The method of continuous rolling of steel was invented in England in the 1860s, but it was first employed on a large scale in the United States in the 1890s.

The British were not only slow to adopt new techniques in the old staple industries (iron, coal, steel, and textiles), but also slow to develop production capacities in the electrical, chemical, and automobile industries—the growth sectors of the early twentieth century. To understand the relative economic decline of the British, it seems that we must explore the factors that

---

[2]W. W. Rostow, *The World Economy: History and Prospect* (Austin: University of Texas Press, 1978), 52, 70.

[3]World Bank, *World Development Report 1997* (New York: Oxford University Press, 1997), 215.

prevented them from maintaining technological leadership. These issues have been widely debated in recent years; they are particularly interesting in light of recent claims that the United States is losing its technological and competitive edge.

DISADVANTAGES OF A HEAD START

It may seem that Britain, the first country to pass through the Industrial Revolution, should have been able to establish and maintain a technological advantage over its competitors. On the other hand, because England was the first country to build a network of large, capital-intensive industries, it was also the first country to be saddled with a large, outdated capital stock. According to one interpretation, the small, owner-managed companies that launched British industrialization created a vested interest against a modern system of corporate capitalism.[4]

The latecomers to industrialization were able to learn from the British experience. They had the advantage of starting afresh with the newest technologies in the most progressive industries. They could sell their products on a growing British market that was free from import barriers. They also benefited from huge infusions of British capital investment. In 1913, over 80 percent of the issues in the London capital market were directed toward investment overseas: "No country, before or since, has invested as high a proportion of its resources abroad over such a sustained period."[5]

PUBLIC POLICY AND RELATIVE DECLINE

Analysts of all persuasions tend to lay a considerable amount of blame on the British government, but they disagree on the policies that should have been pursued. Scholars who lean to the political left believe that the British government should have conducted a more active industrial policy to promote the adoption of advanced technologies and the production of advanced industrial goods. Proponents of this view claim that governments played an active role in the economies of England's major competitors—in France, Germany, Russia, Japan, and the United States—while the British government held to a policy of *laissez faire*. Hence, England was the only industrial country in which the government neither built nor financed any part of the railway system. The average German tariff on British industrial products was 25 percent in 1904 and the average American tariff was 73 percent, but no tariff was charged on manufactured goods entering Britain.

Cut off from the fast-growing markets enjoyed by their competitors, British manufacturers didn't stand a chance. . . . The [Great Depression] was the culmination of

---

[4]Bernard Elbaum and William Lazonick, "An Institutional Perspective on British Decline," in *The Decline of the British Economy*, ed. Bernard Elbaum and William Lazonick (Oxford: Clarendon Press, 1986), 1–17.

[5]M. W. Kirby, *The Decline of British Economic Power since 1870* (London: George Allen and Unwin, 1981), 14.

a bitter competitive struggle [of] British laissez faire *against the continental weapon of state-protected, bank-financed industrialization.* Laissez faire *lost.6*

At the right end of the political spectrum, supply-side economists blame the British government for wasteful management of nationalized companies, and for creating a poor system of investment and work incentives. Until the Thatcher administration adjusted the tax system in 1979–1980, the United Kingdom had the highest marginal tax rates in the capitalist world, aside from the welfare states of northern Europe. To a strict supply-side economists, this alone is sufficient to explain the slow growth of labor productivity that stunted the British economy.

According to another viewpoint, the British government has routinely sacrificed its domestic policy goals to its foreign policy.[7] Unwilling to accept the declining role of the pound sterling in the world economy, the British government made a fetish of defending its international value. This prompted a destabilizing "stop-and-go" pattern of fiscal and monetary policy.

Conspicuously absent from most of the literature is any discussion of the relationship between British economic decline and the loss of her far-flung empire. Was the loss of empire an important cause of economic decline, or was it only a symptom? Despite their diminished international role, the British have continued to devote a larger proportion of their national income to military production than any other Western country, aside from the United States. According to W. B. Walker, two other legacies from the colonial era have contributed to British decline:

Firstly, the cultural, institutional, and economic protection prevailing in Empire markets discouraged risk-taking and removed much of the pressure to improve international competitiveness. . . . Secondly, the Empire reinforced many of the features of British society and institutions that stood in the way of change: it encouraged Englishmen to believe in their everlasting superiority over other races; administering the Empire provided large numbers of remunerative and prestigious jobs for the educated elite.8

SOCIOLOGICAL REASONS FOR DECLINE

Another group of observers holds the British social structure responsible for the relative decline of the economy. The industrial Revolution, they argue, was created by the entrepreneurial spirit of the lower-middle class. By the final quarter of the nineteenth century, however, the symptoms of third-generation decline began to appear: "a growing antipathy towards the conduct of their businesses which manifested itself in an increasing proclivity to squander the hard-won wealth of their forebears in ostentatious and

---

[6]John Eatwell, *Whatever Happened to Britain?* (New York: Oxford University Press, 1982), 66–67.

[7]Andrew Shonfield, *British Economic Policy since the War* (Middlesex: Penguin, 1958).

[8]Quoted in David Coates, *The Question of UK Decline* (New York: Harvester Wheatsheaf, 1994), 270–271.

extravagant living."[9] In the lower ranks of society, labor productivity was stifled by an antiquated and militant trade-union establishment. Simply put, according to one Labour party official, "For generations this country has not earned an honest living."[10]

An elitist educational system was established to serve the upper classes and the humanities were stressed in the curriculum to the exclusion of the natural sciences, engineering, and business. During the 1970s, a study by the British Department of Industry found that "attitudes toward industry . . . are less favorable in Britain than in other major industrialized countries, and are reflected in our educational system."[11]

Until recent years, few British universities offered a business degree. Oxford announced only in 1994 that its long-awaited MBA program would be open for business in 1996. Only 37 percent of the college-aged population is engaged in any form of higher education (compared to 36 percent in Germany, 50 percent in France, and 81 percent in the United States).[12] Lured by higher pay, better research facilities, and more progressive attitudes, many of Britain's best and brightest have left the country for greener pastures. According to the National Science Foundation, British scientists and engineers moved to America during the 1980s at a rate of about 1,000 per year—a greater "brain drain" than the total for other European countries.[13] One-fifth of the fellows elected in 1991 to the prestigious Royal Society of Medicine were working in the United States, up from 13 percent in 1985 and 4 percent in 1960.[14]

According to another sociological perspective, the entire notion of British decline is a statistical artifact. Walter Neale, for one, believes that the British have willingly sacrificed economic growth to form a decent society—"a society which puts more emphasis on kindliness than on efficiency, more emphasis on considerateness than on productivity—a society that puts more emphasis on the pleasant enjoyment of the even tenor of one's way than rapidly increasing material wealth."[15] In other words, the British may have experienced an improvement in social welfare that is not reflected in the standard income and growth statistics. Indeed, international survey data suggest that the British enjoy higher levels of "happiness" and "life satisfaction" than residents of many countries with higher average incomes.[16]

---

[9]Kirby, *The Decline of British Economic Power*, 9.

[10]Ray Gunter, Minister of Labor, 1964–1968, quoted in Andrew Gamble, *Britain in Decline* (Boston: Beacon Press, 1981) 23.

[11]Quoted in *The Managed Economy*, ed. Charles Feinstein (Oxford: Oxford University Press, 1983), 224.

[12]World Bank, *World Development Report 1997*, 227.

[13]"Britain's Brains Go Down the Drain," *The Economist* 302 (March 28, 1987): 59.

[14]Annabel Ferriman, "Scientist Brain Drain—Latest Victim of the British Disease," *Observer*, January 5, 1992, 35.

[15]Walter C. Neale, *The British Economy: Toward a Decent Society* (Columbus: Grid Publishing, 1980), 209.

[16]Ronald Inglehart and Jaques-Rene Rabier, "If You're Unhappy, This Must Be Belgium," *Public Opinion* 8 (April/May, 1985): 10–15.

INDUSTRIAL ORGANIZATION

British governments traditionally have displayed a permissive attitude toward industrial concentration and monopoly. In the eighteenth century, Adam Smith criticized cozy relationships between government and industry that interfered with foreign and domestic competition. In the nineteenth century, when the United States initiated legislation to prevent price-fixing and other collusive arrangements between firms, England continued to ignore the problem; no regulatory structure existed until 1948, when the Monopolies Commission was established, and no specific list of monopolistic practices was prohibited until 1956.

Today, according to its critics, the British system of monopoly regulation is "cumbersome, confusing, and toothless," and out of step with standards approved by the European Union.[17] The oversight and regulatory tasks are divided among several agencies. A preliminary investigation is conducted by the Office of Fair Trading (OFT) when an unfair competitive practice or a corporate merger threatens to restrict competition. If it finds evidence of a problem, the OFT refers the case to the Minister of Trade and Industry, who may dismiss the case, or seek an administrative remedy, or instruct the Monopolies and Mergers Commission (MMC) to conduct a more extensive investigation. In response to a recommendation from the MMC, the Minister may once again dismiss the case, or prohibit the anticompetitive practice or merger, or impose other conditions on the companies involved.

The British courts play a limited role in this process, and they generally have authority only to make it more permissive. If, for example, the Minister of Trade and Industry and other administrative authorities find that a group of companies is engaged in an illegal price-fixing agreement, the companies may appeal the decision to a special Restrictive Practices Court. The court may approve the cartel arrangement if it protects employment, promotes exports, or serves some other public purpose. Thus, for many years, book prices were supported by a court-approved Net Book Agreement.

According to critics of the British system, the political discretion of the Minister of Trade and Industry is much too broad. In 1995, for example, Minister Michael Heseltine ignored a preliminary ruling of the OFT, and approved a merger that gave Hasbro more than 50 percent of the British market for board games.[18] Two months later, Heseltine ignored a recommendation of the MMC, and allowed General Electric Co PLC, which already owned a major shipyard, to bid for ownership of VSEL PLC, the only submarine builder in the UK.[19] In an extraordinary effort to prevent meddling from the EU competition directorate, the British government invoked Article 223 of

---

[17]David Nicholson-Lord, "Consumers 'Cheated' by Competition Law," *The Independent*, May, 2, 1995, 6.

[18]By Pennington, "No Monopoly in Monopoly," *The Times*, March 1, 1995, 1.

[19]Michael Harrison, "VSEL Battle Continues," *The Evening Standard*, May 23, 1995, 1.

the Treaty of Rome, and ordered GEC not to notify Brussels of the merger on grounds of national security.[20]

To prevent political abuses, to expedite and strengthen antitrust investigations, and to prevent duplication of effort, British reformers believe that the OFT and MMC should be merged into a single agency with powers of enforcement. Furthermore, to comply with the Treaty of Rome, they believe that the UK should replace its discretionary competition policy with a **prohibition approach.** In other words, the law should prohibit specific anti-competitive practices, and should prescribe specific remedies, including payment of substantial fines. Penalties should be imposed even for first offenses, and victims of anticompetitive practices should be able to sue for damages. The conservative party and the Confederation of British Industry argue that broad prohibitions would be inherently unfair, would be difficult to supervise, and would impose heavy legal expenses on companies.[21]

How have permissive competition policies influenced the British industrial structure? In the 1970s, a major study found that the largest British firms in an industry were usually twice as large as their German competitors and three times larger than the leading French firms. The authors attributed these results to differences in national merger laws and regulations.[22] In 1994, the United Kingdom accounted for less than one-seventh of European economic activity, but it was still the home of more than one-third of the largest companies in Europe.[23]

If the UK has a bias toward industrial concentration, is that a good or a bad thing for the economy and the general population? This is, of course, a controversial question. According to Michael Heseltine, the former Minister of Trade and Industry, the UK needs to encourage the development of large companies that can serve as "national champions" in the international market. Conversely, the National Consumer Council claims that "time and again our competition regulators have failed consumers," allowing concentrated industries to practice predatory pricing. The council argues that archaic regulatory practices, far from creating industrial champions, are more likely to isolate Britain from Europe and the industrial world.[24]

THE LABOR MARKET AND LABOR RELATIONS

The triangular relationship between organized labor, private business, and governmental institutions (including nationalized companies) has played a most important role in British economic history. This is indicated by the very

---

[20]Richard House, "Europe's Competition Watchdogs Begin to Bite," *Institutional Investor,* November 1995, 139.

[21]Stefan Wagstyl, "Heavyweights Still in the Fight," *Financial Times,* January 3, 1996, 13.

[22]Kenneth G. George and T. S. Ward, *The Structure of Industry in the EEC* (Cambridge: Cambridge University Press, 1975), 23–26.

[23]Ranked by market capitalization, 180 of the 500 largest companies in Europe were based in the UK in 1994. See *Financial Times,* January 20, 1995, supplement.

[24]Nicholson-Lord, "Consumers 'Cheated' by Competition Law," 6.

fact that a *Labour* party and a *Conservative* party are the leading political contestants. Changes in the political power structure have affected, and have been affected by, the relationships between organized labor and management.

During the eighteenth century, public policy leaned heavily in favor of employers; formation of trade unions and other worker organizations was heavily restricted. Thus, Adam Smith reported in 1776, "We have no acts of parliament against combining to lower the price of work; but many against combining to raise it."[25] In 1799, the Combination Acts placed additional limits on organizing activities, and the home secretary warned that labor unions would be "a most dangerous instrument to disturb the public tranquillity."[26]

The pendulum began to swing in 1825, when a new parliament repealed the Combination Acts and trade unions began to form in the Manchester cotton factories. The unions could now represent labor in wage negotiations, but could not engage in picketing, strikes, or other forms of confrontation. During the 1830s and 1840s, organized labor participated in a political movement known as Chartism, which attempted to gain suffrage and other political rights for the working class. The movement attracted considerable support in factory towns, but encountered strong opposition in Parliament. Eventually, the Chartists split into moderate and radical factions, and the movement gradually fizzled.

In the 1850s, the so-called New Model unions dominated the labor movement. Beginning with the Amalgamated Society of Engineers, each New Model union limited its membership to skilled workers in a specific craft. By attracting an elite class of workers, the unions gained influence, and by avoiding political intrigue and confrontational tactics, they gained acceptance. Because of their exclusiveness, however, union membership grew slowly. Most factory workers and unskilled laborers remained unorganized.

The New Model unions also contributed to a complex system of multiple representation. Even today, with the exception of the National Union of Mineworkers, British unions are not organized according to industry. Instead, skilled workers are organized according to craft, and unions that represent unskilled and semiskilled workers attempt to recruit workers from all industries. Thus, workers in a given company may be represented by as many as twenty different unions, making it difficult to organize industrywide, or even companywide, collective bargaining.[27] Wage negotiations are often long and complex.

In 1868, at a conference in Manchester, a group of union leaders established a new coordinating agency known as the **Trades Union Congress (TUC).** Since that time, the TUC has enjoyed continuous existence, and has counted all the major British unions among its members. The closest equivalent in the United States, the AFL-CIO, does not include the United Automobile Workers, the United Mine Workers, or the Teamsters. Because of its size,

---

[25]Adam Smith, *An Inquiry into the Nature and Causes of the Wealth of Nations* (Oxford: Clarendon Press, 1976), 84.

[26]Albert Tucker, *A History of English Civilization* (New York: Harper and Row, 1972), 563.

[27]Thomas Kennedy, *European Labor Relations* (Lexington, Mass.: Lexington Books, 1980), 3.

the TUC has been able to play a prominent role in British politics, labor mediation, and public education. However, unlike the labor confederations in some European countries, the TUC does not engage directly in collective bargaining.

British unions won the right to picket in 1871, and in 1893 they gained political strength by joining in the formation of an Independent Labour party (reorganized in 1918 as the Labour party). In 1906, union leaders gained legal immunity for acts performed by their members while picketing, and in 1911 the trade unions gained the right to sell insurance. Strengthened by developments such as these, and by widespread support for strikes conducted between 1910 and 1920, the unions increased their membership from 13 percent of the labor force in 1906 to 45 percent in 1920.

In 1926, several trade unions joined in a general strike to support the coal miners, whose incomes were threatened by a reduction of public subsidies. When the general strike failed to sway the government, the labor movement was seriously damaged. Union membership fell, and it continued to decline during the Great Depression.

The trade unions regained stature and strength during World War II, when they provided vital support to the war effort. During 1945–1951, the Labour party gained its first strong parliamentary majority, and Prime Minister Clement Attlee appointed union leaders to many public positions. The same was true during 1964–1970 and 1974–1979, when Labour was again the ruling party. When James Callaghan was prime minister between 1976 and 1979, fully two-thirds of his cabinet were former union officials.

In 1971, the Conservative government led by Edward Heath passed an Industrial Relations Act, designed to reduce the power of the trade unions. The act was repealed three years later, however, when Labour returned to power. Beginning in 1979, during a sustained period of Conservative leadership, Prime Ministers Margaret Thatcher and John Major waged a successful campaign against the political and economic influence of the trade unions. According to new provisions of British labor law enacted by the Conservatives:[28]

- Workers have the right to join the union of their choice unless membership is limited to an occupation or skill. Unions cannot agree among themselves to exclude individuals through "no poaching" agreements.

- Dismissal of an employee for refusing to join a trade union is, in all cases, an "unfair practice."

- Industrial action (such as strikes) must be approved in advance by a secret ballot of members. Unions must give employers seven days written notice of intention to ballot on industrial action.

- Unions and their leaders may be held responsible for damages caused during unlawful industrial actions.

---

[28]See Brian Trowers, "Running the Gauntlet: British Trade Unions under Thatcher, 1979–1988," *Industrial and Labor Relations Review* 42 (January 1989): 163–188; and Diane Summers, "A–Z of the New Law for Employers, Workers," *Financial Times*, June 22, 1993, 9.

■ FIGURE 10.1

**UNITED STATES AND UNITED KINGDOM: TRADE UNION MEMBERSHIP
AS A PERCENTAGE OF CIVILIAN LABOR FORCE, 1900–1993**

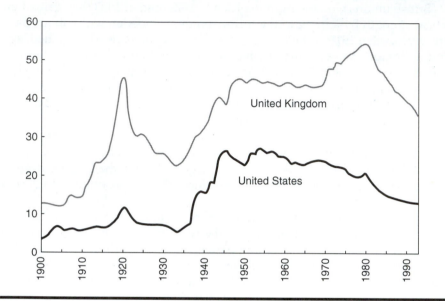

SOURCES: U.K. Department of Employment and U.S. Bureau of Labour Statistics.

■ Executive committees of unions must be elected or reelected by secret ballot at least once in every five years.

The new regulations clearly changed the balance of power between labor and management. On numerous occasions, when union executives attempted to call strikes, workers rejected their proposals by secret ballot.

TRENDS IN UNION MEMBERSHIP

Between 1920 and 1970, the forces that influenced British union growth seem to have been very similar to those that influenced American growth (Figure 10.1). Statistical analysis by Bain and Elsheikh suggests that union growth in both countries is affected by the inflation rate, the unemployment rate, and the rate of change of money wages.[29]

---

[29]George S. Bain and Farouk Elsheikh, *Union Growth and the Business Cycle: An Econometric Analysis* (Oxford: Basil Blackwell, 1976); and Farouk Elsheikh and George S. Bain, "American Trade Union Growth: An Alternative Model," *Industrial Relations* 17 (February 1978): 75–79. For a comparison of Bain's model to other models of union growth, see B. Mason and P. Bain, "Determinants of Trade Union Membership in Britain: A Survey of the Literature," *Industrial Labor Relations Review* 46 (January 1993): 332–351.

Inflation encourages union growth because it strengthens the need for institutions that can bargain for wage increases. Unemployment discourages union growth because jobless workers are likely to drop their union membership, and those who remain employed are less likely to demand wage increases. Wage increases seem to encourage union growth, perhaps because they demonstrate the benefits of union membership.

During the 1970s, the close correlation between American and British union growth temporarily disappeared. While unions continued their downward slide in the United States, membership grew rapidly in the United Kingdom. Public policy was relatively favorable to the unions under the Labour governments of Harold Wilson and James Callaghan (1974–1979), and a relatively high inflation rate (about 14 percent annually during the 1970s, compared to 7 percent in the United States) may have increased the demand for union services.

Reacting to dramatic changes in the political and legal environments, trade union membership fell from more than half the labor force in 1979 to about one-third in 1993. As membership declined, a smaller number of business establishments found it necessary to recognize unions as collective bargaining partners. Among establishments employing manual workers, the union recognition rate fell from 61 percent in 1980 to 48 percent in 1990.[30]

LABOR MARKET FLEXIBILITY

The British government adopted a relatively tight monetary policy in 1979, when the Conservative party gained power, and the need for an antiinflationary monetary policy is accepted now by leaders of both major parties. Unfortunately, we know that efforts to reduce inflation may also cause rising unemployment. Is it possible to cure one economic illness without causing another? Many economists believe that employment will be more stable and more quick to recover from a recession if the labor market is relatively flexible.

In a **flexible labor market,** wages are free to rise and fall in response to market forces, relatively unrestricted by minimum wage laws and long-term contracts. Workers are free to move from one job to another, relatively unrestricted by professional licensing procedures, residency permits, and union membership requirements. Employers are free to hire and fire workers with relatively few limits on union status, working hours, or other conditions of employment. Quite clearly, efforts to increase labor market flexibility may conflict with other social and institutional objectives.

The campaigns against trade unions waged by Prime Ministers Thatcher and Major were part of political agenda to weaken the base of the Labour

[30]Richard Disney, Amanda Gosling, and Stephen Machin, "British Unions in Decline: Determinants of the 1980s Fall in Union Recognition," *Industrial and Labor Relations Review* 48 (April 1995): 405.

party, but they were also part of an economic program to increase the flexibility of the British labor market. By reducing the number of closed shops, where union membership is necessary for employment, the Conservatives hoped to increase the flexibility of the high-income labor market. At the lower end of the pay scale, the Conservatives sought to increase market flexibility by introducing a system of Work Trials (see "British Work Trials: The Cost of Flexibility"), and by eliminating minimum wages set by the **wages councils.**

Although efforts were made as early as 1795, the first successful piece of British minimum wage legislation was the Trade Boards Act of 1909. Modeled on Australian practice, each trade board consisted of equal numbers of workers and employers, led by an impartial chairman, who were responsible for setting a single wage floor for workers in one of the "sweated" (low-skill) trades. In 1945, the boards were renamed under the Wages Councils Act, and were given authority to set a range of minimum wage rates for workers at different levels of skill.

When Margaret Thatcher took power in 1979, the wages councils fixed minimum rates for about 2.5 million low-income workers in restaurants, hotels, retail stores, and other service establishments. In legislation adopted by the Conservatives in 1986, the councils lost their authority to set minimum wages for people under age 21 or to fix more than a single rate for all people in a sector of the economy. In 1993, the wages councils were abolished altogether, making the United Kingdom the only high-income country in Europe or North America without a mandatory minimum wage.[31] In 1997, the new Labour government announced its intention to restore the minimum wage.

THE FINANCIAL SECTOR

Although it no longer occupies the dominant position it enjoyed in the nineteenth century, London is still among the most important financial centers in the world. In an area of one square mile, the City of London hosts more than 400 foreign banks, 200 stockbroking firms, and a range of other financial services. The City handles more than $450 billion of foreign exchange transactions per day, more than the United States and Japan combined. The Eurobond capital of the world, London has a 70 percent share of the market. It is the world's most important center for international lending, insurance, shipping contracts, and trading of gold bullion.[32] Its stock exchange is the world's third largest, following only New York and Tokyo.[33]

---

[31]For information on minimum wage systems in high-income countries, see Organization for Economic Cooperation and Development, *Employment Outlook* (July 1994), 148–149.

[32]"Maintaining the City's Competitive Edge," Press Release, Cabinet Office, Canada (February 6, 1996).

[33]"Global Stock Exchange Directory," *Institutional Investor,* October 1994, 137.

BRITISH WORK TRIALS: THE COST OF FLEXIBILITY

As part of its strategy to address the problem of long-term unemployment, the Conservative government introduced a Work Trials scheme in 1995. Individuals unemployed for more than six months may work for up to three weeks on a trial basis, without pay, while continuing to receive their unemployment benefits and a small allowance to cover travel and food expenses. Employers are supposed to satisfy certain criteria to participate in the program: They must have a permanent vacancy for more than 16 hours a week; and the Employment Service must be allowed to carry out a health and safety inspection.

The program initially supported 20,000 positions, and was slated to provide 40,000 positions in 1997. The employment minister quickly found the program to be an "outstanding success," and reported that nearly two-thirds of the participants were ending their trial periods with permanent jobs.

A very different account was offered by Sally Asher, a journalist who participated in a work trial. She, together with eight others, accepted a one-week trial for the position of "temporary operative" in the toiletries department of a packaging plant. After the unpaid trial, each of the workers was offered an eight-week paying job. After five weeks of paid work, though, two of the participants (both of whom happened to be pregnent women) were terminated because "there is just not enough work." Within days, they were replaced by other temporary workers.

Asher is skeptical of governmental claims that the scheme is moving people into "permanent" jobs:

> But for how long? Four weeks in the case of my two colleagues. And how many temporary jobs make up the Chancellor's "impressive record," allowing the long-term unemployed to work for a few weeks after which they are returned to the dole-queue? The clock is then reset at zero: the long-term unemployed have been successfully converted into short-term unemployed. Are work trials just another way for the Government to fiddle its figures?

SOURCES: "Work Trials Expanded—High Success Rate," *Press Release*, U.K. Employment Department, March 31, 1995; Sally Asher, "Work Trials—Short Cuts in Status," *The Guardian*, February 8, 1995, 2.

BANKING

British commercial banks are all privately owned, and are dominated by the "big four": Barclays, National Westminster, Midland, and Lloyds. Together, these account for about 75 percent of all domestic deposits. Thus, the British banking sector is far more concentrated than the American (where the ten largest banks account for less than 20 percent of deposits).

Regulation of the banking system is primarily a responsibility of the **Bank of England,** which was founded in 1694 to finance a war with France. Among the world's central banks, only the Riksbank in Sweden is older. The Bank was nationalized in 1946, making it the only state-owned bank in the United Kingdom. Its governors and directors are all nominated by the prime minister and appointed by the queen.

The Chancellor of the Exchequer is authorized to issue directions to the Bank, after consultation with the governor. Thus, the Bank is not quite as independent as the U.S. Federal Reserve or the German Bundesbank. This may help to explain the chronically high inflation rates in Britain between 1945 and 1979.

The broader responsibilities of the Bank are similar to those of the Federal Reserve system in the United States. Since a major restructuring in 1994, the Bank has been organized in two policy "wings" and a central service area. The monetary stability wing conducts economic research, makes recommendations to the government on monetary policy, and implements monetary policy in the financial markets. The financial stability wing is responsible for regulating depository institutions and developing programs to strengthen the efficiency and competitiveness of the British financial system. The central services area handles the Bank's own finances and personnel, and operates a school of central banking. An international division, which existed before 1994, was merged into the other wings, reflecting the growing interdependence of foreign and domestic policy.

Regulation of British banking traditionally has been permissive, contributing to rapid growth of the system, but it has fallen under increasing criticism since the high-profile failures of Johnson Matthey Bankers in 1984, the Bank of Credit and Commerce International (BCCI) in 1991, and the Barings Group in 1995. Still, the Bank of England has resisted changing to a strict American style of supervision. According to a leading British bank regulator, "We are still nothing like the armies of OCC [Office of the Comptroller of the Currency] investigators who pretty well live in some of the big U.S. banks."[34]

SECURITIES MARKETS

For more than 200 years, the British Stock Exchange had a monopoly on domestic securities transactions and faced little European competition. British stockbrokers, insurers, and other financial groups were allowed to police themselves through their own trade groups. The United Kingdom had no counterpart, for example, to the U.S. Securities and Exchange Commission, established in 1934.

In 1985, after a number of securities scandals, the Secretary of Trade and Industry called for a radical reform of existing law to protect the public

---

[34]John Gapper, "Survey of the Bank of England," *Financial Times,* July 27, 1994, II.

against fraud, negligence, and monopolistic practices. The first and most radical reform was introduced in October 1986, when the so-called **Big Bang** shook the London Stock Exchange. Trading in stocks and government bonds, previously the exclusive domain of 19 British firms, was opened to foreign competition. Barriers that protected brokers from other kinds of financial firms were removed. Fixed commissions, which had been established by collusive arrangements, were abolished. In the new competitive environment, commissions fell by 53 percent in the first four months.[35]

Also in 1986, a **Securities and Investments Board (SIB)** was established to regulate stock and commodity traders, overseeing the work of the so-called **self-regulatory organizations (SROs).** Today, there are 22 SROs, such as the Securities and Futures Authority, each led by a practitioner-elected board. Unlike the powerful Securities and Exchange commission in the United States, the SIB has very limited judicial powers, a small enforcement division, and little direct access to corporate information, and is financed by the industry it is supposed to regulate.[36] Recently, the Labour party has suggested that the SIB should have more power over the SROs, and the regulatory powers of the Bank of England should be shifted to the SIB.[37]

Together with changes in its regulatory framework, the London Stock Exchange (LSE) is also facing changes in its competitive environment. In 1995, the Tradepoint Investment Exchange became the first major domestic competitor, offering an order-driven trading system that promises to settle transactions more efficiently than the old quote-driven system of the LSE. Internationally, an EU Investment Services Directive entered force in 1996 that encourages equity trading across borders. Thus, the LSE may find it difficult to maintain its dominant role in the European financial markets.[38]

THE GOVERNMENTAL SECTOR

By all accounts, the role of the government in the British economy was relatively small before World War II. Great Britian embraced the writings of Adam Smith in the eighteenth century and a policy of free trade in the nineteenth. Some observers believe that England's present problems are a legacy of past governmental inactivity. The British were slow to impose regulations on monopolies, banks, and other financial institutions. Very few industries

---

[35]Gary Putka and Matthew Winkler, "Gloom Prevails 110 Days after Big Bang," *The Wall Street Journal*, February 18, 1987, 28.

[36]Gary Putka, "London's Exchange Braces for Big Bang Set to Occur Monday," *The Wall Street Journal*, October 24, 1986, 18.

[37]"Top UK Regulator Aims for Greater Efficiency," Reuter News Service, January 5, 1996.

[38]David Fairlamb, "Reinventing the City," *Institutional Investor*, November 1995, 126–136; and "London Stock Exchange Faces Tough Year in 1996," Reuter News Service, January 3, 1996.

were nationalized before the war, and government purchases were a relatively small proportion of GDP.

During World WAR II, the governments of many countries were given emergency powers; England was no exception. The airlines were nationalized in 1939 by a Conservative government, food and clothing were rationed, prices were controlled, and men were conscripted into the service—all contributing to the notion that individual freedom could be subordinated to the national welfare.

In 1941, as the war raged on, Parliament formed the Beverigade Committee to formulate recommendations for a system of social services to heal British society at the end of the war. The Committee called for creation of a national system of health and unemployment insurance, family allowances, old-age pensions, and funeral benefits—that is, it called for the establishment of a comprehensive welfare state. This sounded quite promising to a generation of Britons who feared that the end of the war would mean a return to the Depression. When the war ended in 1945, Winston Churchill shrugged the Beveridge Report aside as little more than "a cloud of pledges and promises," and his Conservatives were soundly defeated by the Labour party under Clement Attlee.

The Attlee government (1945–1951) moved quickly to implement the most important provisions of the Beveridge Report, establish the National Health Service, and nationalize the "commanding heights" of the economy—the Bank of England; the steel, coal, electricity, and gas industries; the railroads; trucking; and civil aviation.[39] Nondefense governmental expenditures jumped from 6 percent of GNP in 1946 to 1 percent in 1951.[40] Furthermore, the wartime systems of wage and price controls and rationing were phased out very slowly. Altogether, the government began to play an unprecedented role in the British economy.

More significantly, a succession of Conservative governments between 1951 and 1964 did not dismantle the essential elements of the welfare state. The National Health Service was preserved and nondefense governmental expenditures declined only slightly as a percentage of GNP—to 14 percent in 1965.[41] Of the industries that were nationalized by Labour, only steel and

---

[39]The notion that a socialist government can exercise sufficient control over the economy by nationalizing only the commanding heights of industry was introduced by V.I. Lenin, the Soviet leader, during the 1920s to explain his decision to return several industries to private ownership during his New Economic Policy.

[40]B. R. Mitchell and H. G. Jones, *Second Abstract of British Historical Statistics* (Cambridge: Cambridge University Press, 1971), 151, 161.

[41]Governmental outlays on social services actually increased during this period, from 13 percent of GNP in 1950 to 17 percent in 1965. See William G. Shepherd, "Alternatives for Public Expenditure," in *Britain's Economic Prospects,* ed. Richard E. Caves (Washington, D.C.: The Brookings Institution, 1968), 383.

trucking were returned to private ownership by the Conservatives. Further-more, it was a Conservative government that set up a limited program of na-tional economic planning in 1961.

Much has changed, of course, since Margaret Thatcher and John Major began a long period of Conservative leadership in 1979. Many of the nation-alized industries were privatized, and significant reforms were introduced in the social security and pension programs. On the other hand, the Conserva-tives did not attempt to dismantle the National Health Service, and many welfare-state programs were trimmed, but few were abandoned. Central government expenditures on health, education, and welfare increased signif-icantly between 1980 and 1993, from 18 percent of GDP to 22 percent.[42] Clearly, the Conservative party found it difficult to reverse the momentum of governmental growth.

THE NATIONALIZED INDUSTRIES

A list of the principal British nationalized industries is presented in Ta-ble 10.1. As the data show, the companies were nationalized over a long span of years and in a fairly wide range of industries. Why were these par-ticular companies nationalized? We can isolate several different motivations that help to explain the pattern.

First, there was an ideological motive. Many of the industries were na-tionalized as the end of World War II by a socialist Labour government that wished to exercise greater control over the economy. Thus, they chose the Bank of England and the commanding heights of industry as takeover tar-gets. The National Health Service was the centerpiece of their social welfare program.

Second, a number of industries were nationalized for purposes of na-tional security. This was the case when the postal service, the petroleum in-dustry (at the beginning of World War I), and the airlines (at the beginning of World War II) were acquired. Interestingly, in a number of ancient despotic societies the postmaster general was simultaneously the director of internal security.[43]

Third, failing companies were sometimes nationalized to maintain em-ployment. In the 1970s, for example, when Rolls Royce and British Leyland

---

[42]World Bank, *World Development Report 1995*, 181.

[43]Frederic L. Pryor, *Property and Industrial Organization* in Communist and Capitalist Nations (Bloomington, Ind.: Indiana University Press, 1973), 40.

■ TABLE 10.1

PRINCIPAL NATIONALIZATION AND PRIVATIZATION OF BRITISH ENTERPRISES

	Year initially Nationalized	Privatized during 1979–1997? (Year)	Proceeds of Privatization ($ million)
Communications			
Post Office	Before 1850	No	—
British Telecom	Before 1900	1984	21,990
Cable and Wireless	Before 1900	1983, 1985	1,466
British Broadcasting	1927	No	—
Transportation			
British Railways	1948	1996	3,185
British Waterways	1948	No	—
British Airways	1939, 1946	1987	1,400
National Freight	1969	1982	9
Associated British Ports	1963	1983, 1985	139
British Airports Authority	1966	1987	1,590
Energy			
Regional Electricity Boards	1948	1990	n.a.
British Gas	1949	1986	12,930
British Coal	1947	1995	1,280
British Petroleum	1913	1979, 1981 1983, 1987	8, 570
British Nuclear Fuels	1971	No	
Britoil	1976	1982, 1985	1,513
Enterprise Oil	n.a.	1984	543
Other Industrial			
Royal Ordnance	Before 1800	1986	305
New Town Development	1946	No	
Commonwealth Development	1948	No	
British Steel	1951, 1967	1988	4,150
Rolls Royce	1971	1987	1,770
Jaguar Cars	1975	1984	425
British Aerospace	1977	1981	556
Amershan International	n.a.	1982	92
Water Authorities	1983	1989	7,150

Continued

■ **TABLE 10.1**

CONTINUED

	Year initially Nationalized	Privatized during 1979–1995? (Year)	Proceeds of Privatization ($ million)
Financial			
Bank of England	1946	No	
Social			
National Health Service	1948	No	

SOURCES: William G. Shepherd, *Public Enterprise: Economic Analysis of Theory and Practice* (Lexington, Mass.: Lexington Books, 1976), 106–107; Matthew R. Bishop and John A. Kay, "Privatization in the United Kingdom: Lessons from Experience," *World Development* 17 (1989): 648–649; Amanda Hughes, "Employment in the Public and Private Sectors," *Economic Trends* (January 1995): 14–22; *The Wall Street Journal*, October 2, 1995, R13; and other media reports.

were facing bankruptcy, they were taken over by the government to keep them alive. In contrast, when the American government was faced with the imminent collapse of Chrysler Corporation in 1980, nationalization never was seriously considered. Instead, the company was left in private hands and bailed out with a package of governmental loan guarantees and union wage concessions.

Fourth, natural monopolies were often nationalized to prevent abuses of market power. These primarily included the network industries—postal services, electricity, gas, and telephone—that are difficult to divide between several competitors. By contrast, the usual American practice was to leave natural monopolies in private hands, but to regulate them heavily.

Fifth, economic theory suggests that a market economy will tend to allocate too few resources to industries that provide external benefits—benefits that are received by someone other than the buyer of the product. Health care, for example, provides direct benefits to those who received treatment, but also provides indirect benefits to those who are spared from contracting infectious diseases. Therefore, an economic argument can be made for public support of the health-care industry. In the British case, that support is provided through the National Health Service. In the United States, the governmental subsidy is more limited and much of it is provided to doctors in the private sector through such programs as Medicare and Medicaid.

A final motive for nationalization—eliminating foreign ownership and control—did not play a prominent role in the United Kingdom. In countries such as the former Soviet Union and Cuba, overthrow of foreign imperialism was one of the primary objectives of their socialist revolutions. In the 1980s, President Mitterrand of France claimed that reduction of foreign control was one of his reasons for nationalizing several industrial groups.

PROBLEMS AND PRIVATIZATION

The performance of the nationalized industries has been a subject of debate in Britain throughout the postwar era. When a company is taken over by the government, it is inevitably transformed into a political creature. Interest groups of all kinds attempt to determine how the enterprise is run. There is an old saying in England: The private sector is the part of the economy that the government controls; and the public sector is the part that nobody controls.

Compounding the problem, there is no consensus on how one should judge the performance of the nationalized industries. The industries are often criticized, for example, because many of them fail to operate at a profit, requiring that they be subsidized by the government. This criterion may be less than fair; many of the industries were nationalized precisely in order to pursue some objective other than profit maximization. Some were intended to provide public goods, others to maintain employment. British Airways flew several unprofitable routes to provide service to outlying communities. On a number of occasions, public enterprises have been required to lead in the government's fight against inflation by holding their prices steady in the face of rising labor costs.

All things considered, it is not surprising that many of the nationalized industries require governmental subsidies to fulfill their many objectives. Despite some evidence to the contrary, their losses are often ascribed to excessive union pressure and poor, bureaucratic management.[44]

Accordingly, when Thatcher took office, she quickly set about the task of privatizing as many of the nationalized industries as possible. Between 1979 and 1991, the share of state-owned firms in British GDP declined from 6 percent to 2 percent.[45] By mid-1995, 48 major businesses were sold to private stockholders, raising about $95 billion for the Treasury (Table 10.1).[46] In addition, the government has signed contracts with private companies to provide a host of services, such as garbage collection, that were formerly handled by the government.

---

[44]Richard Pryke, *Public Enterprise in Practice: The British Experience of Nationalization over Two Decades* (New York: St. Martin's Press, 1972); and J.A. Kay and D.J. Thompson, "Privatization: A Policy in Search of a Rationale," *The Economic Journal* 96 (March 1986): 18–32.

[45]World Bank, *Bureaucrats in Business: The Economics and Politics of Government Ownership* (New York: Oxford University Press, 1995), 270–271

[46]Dana Milbank, "Backlash: Britain Embraced Privatization before It was the Thing to Do. Was It Worth It?" *The Wall Street Journal*, October 2, 1995, R17.

The British privatization program has attracted worldwide attention, emulation, praise, and criticism. Supporters of the program emphasize the gains to the Treasury from sale of company stock and elimination of subsidies. They point to several companies that have become profitable since they were placed in private hands.

Its supporters also claim that privatization has turned workers into owners of capital, reducing the class divisions in British society. The National Freight Consortium, for example, was sold to its 12,000 workers; and over 90 percent of the employees of British Telecom bought stock in their company when it was sold. Another 750,000 families purchased the houses they previously rented from the government. All this, they say, has improved efficiency and given the public a greater pride of ownership. The best proof may be the fact that the Labour party amended its constitution in 1995 to drop its historic commitment to nationalization.

Critics of privatization claim the government "sold the family silver"—sometimes at cut-rate prices—to handle its budgetary problems. After holding their stock for one week, the traders who purchased such companies as Amersham International, British Telecom, and Associated British Ports were able to sell their shares on the open market for 35 percent to 98 percent more than they paid the government.[47]

Critics also point back to the original purposes of nationalization. Monopolies, such as British Telecom and British Airways, should not be allowed to exercise their market power. In noncompetitive industries, there is no clear evidence to suggest that private ownership enhances productivity.[48] The water companies were privatized in 1989, despite 83 percent opposition from the public. By 1995, the average family's water bill had increased by 74 percent, and pretax profits of the private companies had increased by 150 percent.[49]

Some would argue that firms playing a vital national security role, such as British Aerospace and Royal Ordnance factories, should be controlled by the government. Employment of coal miners and other workers should be maintained without strict adherence to profitability criteria.

MACROECONOMIC POLICY

Ironically, the home of John Maynard Keynes has a relatively poor reputation for handling fiscal and monetary policy. According to a classic study of seven industrialized countries in the 1950s and 1960s, the United Kingdom was the only country whose government actually destabilized the economy through

---

[47]Kay and Thompson, "Privatization: A Policy in Search of a Rationale," 28.

[48]John Vickers and George Yarrow, "Economic Perspectives on Privatization," *Journal of Economic Perspectives* 5 (Spring 1991): 117–118.

[49]Milbank, "Backlash," R17.

■ TABLE 10.2

RELATIVE PERORMANCE OF THE BRITISH
ECONOMY, 1951–1996

	1951–1960	1961–1970	1971–1980	1981–1990	1991–1996
Average annual growth of real GDP (%)					
United Kingdom	2.8	2.9	1.9	2.7	1.3
OECD Average	4.2	5.1	3.2	2.8	2.0
Average annual consumer price inflation (%)					
United Kingdom	4.1	3.9	13.8	6.6	3.3
OECD Average	3.3	3.9	9.1	8.1	4.9
Unemployment rate (%)					
United Kingdom	2.5	2.8	4.7	10.1	8.8
OECD Average	3.6*	2.8*	4.5	7.3	7.5

*Based on data for Canada, France, Germany, Italy, Japan, Sweden, the United Kingdom, and the United States.
SOURCES: World Bank, *World Tables*, 1980 and 1995; Irving Kravis, Alan Heston, and Robert Summers, *World Product and Income* (Baltimore: Johns Hopkins University Press, 1982), 343; Angus Maddison, *Phases of Capitalist Development* (Oxford: Oxford University Press, 1982), appendicies A, C, and E; *OECD Economic Outlook*, December 1986 and June 1997; and International Monetary Fund, *World Economic Outlook*, May 1997.

its use of fiscal policy.[50] During the 1960s and 1970s, the UK simultaneously had a lower rate of economic growth and a higher rate of inflation than the averages for OECD countries (Table 10.2).

Traditionally, a **stop-go** style of policy implementation has contributed to British instability. The problem is rooted in a conflict between labor's demand for full employment and the financial community's demand for a strong balance of payments. When the unemployment rate rises, the government usually switches to an overly expansionary macroeconomic policy. This reduces the unemployment rate, but it also increases the inflation rate, stimulates the demand for imported goods, and often leads to a balance-of-payments crisis. To deal with this problem, the government switches to the stop phase of contractionary fiscal and monetary policies. The unemployment rate rises and the cycle repeats itself. This process can be found in many countries, but it seems to be reinforced in the United Kingdom by a unique balance of power between the labor and financial communities.

The British "stop-go" cycle is illustrated by Table 10.3. On average, there has been a five-year cycle from the end of one balance-of-payments crisis to

[50]Bent Hansen, *Fiscal Policy in Seven Countries 1955–1965* (Paris: Organization for Economic Cooperation and Development, 1969), 69–71. For a less negative appraisal of British fiscal policy, see John Bispham and Andrea Boltho, "Demand Management," in *The European Economy*, ed. *Andrea Boltho* (Oxford: Oxford University Press, 1982), 306–308.

the beginning of the next one. In each case, the crisis has led to fiscal contraction, followed by rising unemployment, fiscal stimulus, and another balance of payments crisis.

The stance of British macroeconomic policy changed dramatically in 1979, when Margaret Thatcher initiated a long period of Conservative leadership. As her Chancellor of the Exchequer, Nigel Lawson, said at the time: "It is the conquest of inflation, and not the pursuit of growth and employment, which is, or should be, the objective of macroeconomic policy."[51] Surely, Lord Keynes was spinning in his grave.

Since 1980, the Conservative governments have adopted a series of **Medium Term Financial Strategies (MTFS)** to formalize their efforts to reduce inflation and to provide a more stable framework for macroeconomic policy. Each MTFS establishes a four- or five-year program, with goals for monetary growth, reduction of the public-sector borrowing requirement (PSBR, a measure of the budget deficit), exchange rate policy, and a range of other policy instruments.

During the first half of the 1980s, the MTFS called for a strict regimen of monetarism, with rapid deceleration of the growth of sterling M3, a broad measure of the money supply. when unemployment climbed upward in the mid-1980s, the government continued its fight against inflation, but in a more gradual and balanced way, providing more room for economic growth. No longer devoting themselves exclusively to monetary aggregates (such as sterling M3), the authorities shifted attention toward stabilization of exchange rates. A solid international value of the currency, they hoped, would attract foreign investment to the UK, making it easier to maintain low interest rates. This was the line of reasoning that led, in 1990, to British entry into the European exchange rate mechanism (ERM).

In 1992, when a massive wave of currency speculation caused the UK and Italy to suspend participation in the ERM, the British authorities were forced to seek a new anchor for monetary policy. They adopted a policy that has three important elements. First, they decided that the central target should be the inflation rate itself, rather than monetary growth or some other indirect indicator. Second, they decided that monetary policy must be *forward looking*, because it takes one or two years for a policy change to have a significant impact on economic activity and inflation. Thus, monetary policy today should not be based on market conditions today, but on a forecast of conditions, say, two years rom now. Third, they decide that monetary policy should be *transparent* and *credible*. Thus, the minutes of monthly discussions between the Chancellor of the Exchequer and the Governor of the Bank of England are now published within two weeks of their meetings.[52]

---

[51]In his Mais Lecture, June 18, 1994, quoted in Peter Riddell, *The Thatcher Decade* (Oxford: Basil Blackwell, 1989), 14.

[52]Organization for Economic Cooperation and Development, *OECD Economic Surveys: United Kingdom, 1994–1995*, 33–34.

■ TABLE 10.3

THE STOP-GO CYCLE IN THE UNITED
KINGDOM, 1955–1997

Balance of Payments Problems in:	Followed by Fiscal Tightening in:	Followed by Rising Unemployment in:	Followed by Fiscal Stimulus in:
1955	1955	1956–1959	1959–1960
1960	1961–1962	1962–1963	1963
1964–1965	1966	1966–1972	1972
1973–1976	1977	1977	1978
1979	1979	1980–1983	1983
1986–1987	1988	1991–1992	1992–1993
1995	1996–1997		

NOTES: The balance of payments is measured by the current account balance in U.S. dollars. Fiscal stimulus is indicated by changes in the central government budget balance as a percentage of GDP. Author's calculations based on OECD and IMF data.

Based on more stable policies, the UK has been able to reduce its inflation rate below the OECD average during the years since 1980. Unfortunately, the cost, until very recently, has been a relatively high rate of unemployment and a low rate of economic growth (Table 10.2). As we noted earlier, enhanced flexibility of the British labor market has led to recent reductions of unemployment, but it has also caused stagnation of wages.[53]

Together with tight monetary policies, the Conservative governments have introduced major changes in the British tax system to improve the climate for economic growth and to draw the UK into compliance with EU tax policies. Top income tax rates were reduced from 98 percent to 75 percent in 1979, and to 40 percent in 1988. Corporate income tax rates have also been reduced, but by much smaller amounts. Revenue losses were replaced by raising the rate of the value added tax (VAT, the national sales tax), by broadening the VAT to include fuel and energy, and by increasing required contributions for National Insurance. Ideally, the shift from taxes on income to taxes on sales should give the public a stronger incentive to produce and earn income, and a stronger incentive to save and invest, rather than spend on goods that are taxed.

---

[53]See Dana Milbank, "Unlike Rest of Europe, Britain Is Creating Jobs, but They Pay Poorly," *The Wall Street Journal*, March 28, 1994, A1.

REDISTRIBUTION OF INCOME AND WEALTH

The British government has concerned itself with the distribution of income in one way or another since 1723, when the Poor Law made it possible for rural parishes to build workhouses for the able poor. Even this limited form of help was controversial at the time: Thomas Malthus argued that the Poor Laws would exacerbate the problem of population growth. In the years before World War II, the British government fell far behind the other governments of Western Europe in social welfare spending.

The postwar government, prodded by the memory of the Great Depression and guided by the report of the Beveridge Commission, made the establishment of a welfare state one of its top priorities. This objective has been pursued to a greater or lesser extent, respectively, by subsequent Labour and Conservative administrations. Even the Thatcher government claimed that the "charge that we want to dismantle the welfare state" is "totally unfounded."[54]

The distribution of British income trended toward greater equality from the 1950s until the mid-1970s, and has subsequently trended toward greater inequality. The latter trend is associated with a number of factors, including changes in earnings inequality, the structure of employment, unemployment, and levels of icome from capital.[55] Since 1977, the Gini coefficients in Table 10.4 seem to indicate that the deterioration of income equality has been rooted in original market incomes, and has been affected relatively little by changes in governmental systems of benefits or taxes.

THE UNITED KINGDOM IN THE EUROPEAN UNION

The United Kingdom is a member of the European Union, but it is, in many respects, a reluctant member. This reluctance is grounded in several basic differences between the UK and its European neighbors. First, the UK does not want to sacrifice its network of special relationships with the United States, Canada, Australia, and other former colonies and Commonwealth members. Second, the UK has only 2 percent of its labor force working in agriculture, compared to an EU average of 6 percent. Thus, it has little to gain, and much to lose, from price supports and other subsidies under the Common Agricultural Policy. Third, as a former superpower, it is particularly unwilling to surrender any aspect of its national sovereignty. And fourth, as the descendants of Adam Smith and the other patriarchs of classical economics, British leaders are often the strongest critics of restrictive rules and regulations issued by the Eurocrats in Brussels.

---

[54]*The Wall Street Journal,* May 19, 1983, 32.

[55]Stephen Jenkins, "Accounting for Inequality Trends: Decomposition Analysis for the UK, 1971–86," *Economica* 62 (February 1995): 29–63.

■ **TABLE 10.4**

UNITED KINGDOM: INFLUENCE OF BENEFITS AND TAXES
ON THE DISTRIBUTION OF INCOME, 1977–1993
(GINI COEFFICIENTS)

Year	1977	1979	1983	1988	1993
Original Income	43	44	48	51	53
Gross Income (after benefits)	29	30	32	37	38
Disposable Income (after direct taxes)	27	27	28	35	35
Post-Tax Income (after indirect taxes)	29	29	31	39	38

SOURCE: *Economic Trends*, March 1991 and December 1994.

In 1951, when the European nations strengthened their economic ties under the Treaty of Paris, the British initially chose not to participate. In the view of the ruling Labour party, the UK had little to gain from trade with war-ravaged Europe, and membership in a free trade organization would weaken their control of the domestic economy.

During the 1950s, a heated debate continued in the UK over the EC question. Its supporters argued that membership would provide a larger trading area, allowing efficient producers to exploit economies of scale, and would place inefficient producers under competitive pressure. Representatives of the Conservative party spoke of an additional benefit: Competitive pressure in the labor market would keep the country's powerful trade unions in line.

In 1961, the Conservative government of Prime Minister Harold Macmillan offered Britain's first application for admission to the EC. It was vetoed two years later by the French president, General de Gaulle, who feared that Britain would serve as a vehicle for U.S. influence in the Communities. A second application was filed in 1967 by the moderate Labour government of Harold Wilson and was negotiated and debated for five years. This time, the most serious opposition came not from abroad (de Gaulle resigned the French presidency in 1969), but from the left wing of the Labour party at home. Eventually, the European Communities bill was passed in the House of Commons by a majority of only eight votes and the United Kingdom became a member in 1973.

The impact of EC membership on British foreign trade was clear and immediate. Between 1973 and 1981, British exports to EC countries increased by 27 percent per year, compared with a 19 percent average for exports to the rest of the world. It is impossible to say how much additional trade was created by British membership in the Common Market and how much trade was diverted from the United States and other nonmembers. To the extent that Britain was encouraged to expand its overall levels of trade and specialization, the impact of membership presumably was beneficial. On the other hand, to the extent that tariffs on imports from nonmember countries caused Britain to replace low-cost agricultural imports from the Commonwealth and America with more expensive food from Europe, EC membership was costly.

A new chapter in UK relations with the EU began in 1979 when Prime Minister Margaret Thatcher came to power. From that point forward, the strongest critics of European institutions were members of Thatcher's nationalist wing of the Conservative party. As they were certainly aware, in the early 1980s the number of Britons who believed that EC membership was harmful to their country outnumbered those who considered it beneficial by a 2-to-1 margin.[56] Ignoring her top advisors, Thatcher refused to have the UK join the ERM throughout the 1980s, and she was criticized by other national leaders for her behavior at a series of meetings between 1979 and 1984 where she insisted that British contributions to the EC budget should be reduced. The UK joined in the Maastricht Treaty for European Union, but only after establishing its right to opt out of the monetary union and the unified social policies of the EU.

SUMMARY

Great Britain, the economic and political superpower of the nineteenth century, has suffered a long and deep decline in its relative world standing. According to one explanation, the countries that experienced later industrial revolutions were able to adopt newer technologies and benefit from British financing. Another says that the laissez faire policies of the nineteenth-century British government allowed foreign producers to invade the British market, and that the economic and political costs of superpower status outweighed the benefits. Other explanations lay blame on the peculiarities of British fiscal policy, the decline of entrepreneurial spirit, the elitist educational system, and the inordinate power of trade unions.

Governmental policies toward industrial concentration usually have been permissive and have encouraged the merger of small enterprises into larger ones. British financial markets are also relatively unregulated and are among the most important in the world. In the labor market, British trade unions differ from their American counterparts in their broader membership, stronger

---

[56]N. Webb and R. Wybrow, *The Gallup Report: Your Views in 1981* (London: Shere Books, 1982), 99.

political role, strong socialist tradition, organization by craft rather than industry, and local autonomy.

The role of the government expanded during the Labour government after World War II, with broad programs of nationalization, national health insurance, and social welfare reform. Arguments for nationalization included ideology, national security, maintenance of employment, control of natural monopolies, and provision of other public goods. The evidence seems to indicate that the social welfare system contributed to a significant reduction in inequality of income and wealth. Since 1979, the government has returned many of the nationalized companies to private ownership, employed tight money policies to reduce the inflation rate at the expense of higher unemployment, and exerted stronger legal and economic authority over the trade unions.

Great Britain was a latecomer to the EC in 1973, and has been reluctant to participate in European Monetary Union. Britain has been required to finance a heavy share of the EC budget.

DISCUSSION AND REVIEW QUESTIONS

1. Of the suggested reasons for British economic decline, which ones seem to be applicable in the United States today? Which ones are likely to trouble Japan in the future?

2. Why is it difficult to organize industrywide and factorywide collective bargaining in Great Britain?

3. How can we explain the correlation between fluctuations in American and British labor union membership?

4. What were the motivations for nationalizing British industries? What are the arguments for and against privatization?

5. How does the UK differ from other national members of the EU? Should the UK participate in European programs of monetary union and social reform?

SUGGESTED READINGS

Batstone, Eric, and Stephen Gourlay. *Unions, Unemployment, and Innovation.* Oxford: Basil Blackwell, 1986. *Based on case studies and a survey of over 1,000 shop stewards, this study provides a micro view of the organization and operation of British trade unions and their impact on technological innovation.*

Caves, Richard E., and Lawrence B. Krause, eds. *Britain's Economic Performance.* Washington, D.C.: The Brookings Institution, 1980. *An extremely useful compendium of studies by American authors on subjects ranging from trade union growth and industrial productivity to fiscal and monetary policy and the impact of North Sea oil.*

Coats, David. *The Question of UK Decline: The Economy, State, and Society.* New York: Harvester Wheatsheaf, 1994. *An excellent and accessible review of the entire decline literature, and an attempt to relate each hypothesis to the available evidence.*

Curwen, Peter J. *Public Enterprise: A Modern Approach.* Brighton: Wheatsheaf Books, 1986. *Provides comprehensive coverage and useful case studies of the history and performance of nationalized companies and the impact of the program of privatization.*

Lloyd, T. O. *Empire, Welfare State, Europe: English History 1906–1992.* Oxford: Oxford University Press, 1993. *An authoritative account of political and economic decisions in a changing environment.*

Mack, Joanna, and Stewart Lansley. *Poor Britain.* London: George Allen and Unwin, 1985. *Based on interviews in the so-called Breadline Britain survey, this is a survey of changing public attitudes concerning poverty and an assessment of the living conditions of the poor.*

Riddell, Peter. *The Thatcher Decade.* Oxford: Basil Blackwell, 1989. *A concise account of the Conservative revolution, with chapters on labor, privatization, the welfare state, and the state of the nation.*

Rubenstein, W. D. *Capitalism, Culture, and Decline in Britain: 1750–1990.* London: Routledge, 1993. *Delves deeply into educational and sociological explanations of decline.*

INTERNET RESOURCES

Bank of England
http://www.coi.gov.uk/coi/depts/GBE/GBE.html

BBC Westminster
http://www.bbc.co.uk/westonline/

British Politics
Keele University Conservative Association
http://www.keele.ac.uk/socs/ks20/cwis/brit.htm

Central Office of Information
http://www.coi.gov.uk/coi/

Central Statistical Office
http://www.emap.com/cso/

Conservative Party
http://www.conservative-party.org.uk/

Department of Education and Employment
http://www.open.gov.uk/dfe/dfehome.htm

Department of Social Security
http://www.open.gov.uk/dssasd/dsshome.htm

Department of Trade and Industry
http://www.dti.gov.uk/

Economic and Social Research Council Data Archive
University of Essex
http://dawww.essex.ac.uk/

Electronic Telegraph
http://www.telegraph.co.uk/

Financial Times
http://www.ft.com/

The Guardian
http://www.cityscape.co.uk/guardian/

H.M. Treasury
http://www.hm-treasury.gov.uk/

Institute for Fiscal Studies
http://www1.ifs.org.uk/

Labour Party
http://www.poptel.org.uk/labour-party/

Liberal Democratic Party
http://www.libdems.org.uk/

London School of Economics
http://www.lse.ac.uk/

MIDAS
Manchester Information Datasets and Associated Services
University of Manchester
http://midas.ac.uk/

Money World UK
http://www.moneyworld.co.uk/moneyworld/

Portico: British Library
http://portico.bl.uk/

Sunday Times
http://www.sunday-times.co.uk/

Trade Union Congress
http://www.tuc.org.uk/

UK Today
http://www.kdtech.co.uk/reg/uktoday/uktintro.html

Welfare at Work
http://www.tecc.co.uk/workers/workers.html

Germany

11

Germany: Unifying the Social Market Economy

We in West Germany have resorted to anything but a secret
science. . . . I have merely attempted . . . to overcome the
age-old antithesis of an unbridled liberalism and a
soulless State control, to find a sound middle way between
out-and-out freedom and totalitarianism.

—Ludwig Erhard
Prosperity Through Competition, 1958

The phrase "we are a socially oriented nation" is often the
first one out of the mouths of Germans seeking to explain a
century-long commitment made by the strong to the weak.
. . . But Germany and indeed all the other West European
nations to whom it exported social democratic ideas can no
longer afford this notion. . . . The cradle-to-grave social
welfare system has yielded a particularly airless
environment that stifles energy and innovation.

—Amity Shlaes
Foreign Affairs, October 1994

he Berlin Wall was the central monument of the
Cold War, dividing East from West, capitalism
from socialism, and totalitarianism from freedom. In November 1989, when the wall began to
crumble, we knew something very important
was happening—the beginning of a new era. The
German states would begin to reunite their families, neighborhoods, and cities. They would combine their resources under a democratic system, a
market economy, and a strong currency. A united
Germany would attempt to reclaim its historic
position as the preeminent power in an undivided Europe.

None of this would be accomplished easily; the economic and political institutions of the East were distorted by decades of totalitarian control and
central planning. In July 1990, the German authorities moved decisively.

With a stroke, they merged the economic and monetary systems of the German states, initiating a massive social transformation.

THE HISTORICAL LEGACY

German unification is an ancient and recurring theme. Late in the Middle Ages, when strong, centralized national governments were advancing in England and France, Germany remained a disunited, feuding collection of states. Protective tariffs dividing the German states were actually higher than tariffs against foreign powers. **Friedrich List** (1789–1846), a professor of politics and administration at the University of Tübingen, was among the first to confront this issue. He founded an association of industrialists to work for the economic and political unification of Germany. Unfortunately, List was imprisoned for unauthorized political activities, and was released only when he agreed to leave the country. He traveled to America in 1825, where he gained citizenship and became a successful businessman and statesman. Influenced by the philosophies and policies of Alexander Hamilton, List concluded that American economic success was rooted in its free internal market, in its protective tariffs against foreign manufactured goods, and in the strong hand of its government in canal construction and other infrastructure projects.

In 1832, List returned to Germany as a United State consul, enabling him to resume efforts for national unification. Two years later, he played an important role in Prussia's decision to establish a customs union, the *Zollverein*, with its neighboring states. In 1841, List published his most important work, *The National System of Political Economy*, which argued that the German states should continue their efforts to form a unified national economy, with free *internal* trade, but they should protect their infant industries from *external* competition. A policy of free external trade was appropriate for Adam Smith's Great Britain, a strong industrial nation, but it was inappropriate, List argued, for the fledgling economy of Germany.[1]

Under the leadership of another Prussian, **Otto von Bismarck** (1815–1898), the nationalist dreams of Friedrich List were translated into reality. Serving as German chancellor between 1871 and 1890, Bismarck was the first political leader to successfully consolidate the German states into a great empire. He maintained popular support by granting concessions to a number of interest groups. For the agriculturists and upper-class businessmen, Bismarck enacted a protective tariff on imports in 1879. Behind this wall of protection, with support from governmental policy and new technologies, German industry began to form itself into a concentrated system of monopolies, cartels, and syndicates.

For the working class, Bismarck created the world's first comprehensive social security system. Built between 1881 and 1889, the system included

---

[1]Friedrich List, *The National System of Political Economy* (London: Longmans, Green, 1922). For a provocative discussion of the continuing importance of List's ideas, see James Fallows, "How the World Works," *The Atlantic Monthly* 272 (December 1993): 60–87.

coverage for work accidents, sickness, retirement, and death. In all of this, Bismarck acknowledged that his motive was to draw the workers away from the "siren song of the socialists," who formed a unified Social Democratic Party in Germany in 1875.

After Bismarck, Germany continued its program of colonial expansion until it suffered defeat in World War I. In that war, Germany lost about 3 million lives and all its overseas colonies. Wartime spending was financed by money creation, causing the worst round of postwar inflation in world history—prices multiplied some 15 trillion times between 1914 and 1923. The harsh terms of the Treaty of Versailles caused a continuation of national decline, contributing to political instability. These troubles were compounded by the Great Depression; by 1932, nearly one-third of German workers stood unemployed and nearly half of the country's production capacity lay unused. In despair, Germany turned to the promises of another empire builder—Adolf Hitler and his National Socialist (Nazi) Party.

GERMAN FASCISM

The fascist economy, established by the Nazis, was first and foremost a system of wartime mobilization. Military expenditures nearly quadrupled in 1933 during the first year of Nazi rule, and doubled again in 1934. Responding to fiscal and monetary stimulus, German national income grew more than 40 percent between 1932 and 1936, and unemployment was nearly eliminated. While economic depression continued in other countries, the Nazis were able to keep their promise of "bread and work," creating a base of popular support for their chauvinist and genocidal objectives.[2]

The fascist system was based on totalitarian state control within a framework of private property ownership—capitalism without free enterprise. The private sector was controlled by a comprehensive system of governmental regulatory agencies, headed by the Department of Economics, and by private trade groups subservient to the government. Production was controlled directly through quotas and rationing of raw materials and indirectly through price controls, taxes, and tariffs.

Formation of monopolies and cartels was not only condoned by the Nazis, it was encouraged. Large monopolies, they believed, could project German power overseas more effectively than thousands of small businesses and could be regulated more easily by the government. A 1933 statute gave the Department of Economics authority to force small businesses to join cartels if it was found to be "desirable from the point of view of the entire economy."[3]

In the labor sector, the Nazis dissolved all the independent labor unions (under the pretext that they were dominated by Jews) and replaced them with a puppet organization, the German Labor Front. Final authority over

---

[2]Avraham Barkai, *Nazi Economics: Ideology, Theory, and Policy* (New Haven: Yale University Press, 1990), 1, 250, and 251.

[3]Otto Nathan, *The Nazi Economic System: Germany's Mobilization for War* (Durham, N.C.: Duke University Press, 1944), 71.

the setting of wages, salaries, and work conditions was left in the hands of 20 regional government officials—the Trustees of Labor—whose decisions could not be appealed. The purpose was to ensure labor peace and reduce the share of national income going to labor so that more could be set aside for investment and the military.

After military victories in Eastern Europe, a rising proportion of work in Germany was performed by prisoners of war, filling positions vacated by German soldiers. In 1944, more than 7 million POWs were employed in Germany, accounting for more than 20 percent of the total labor force. These figures do not include concentration camp laborers in enterprises outside Germany or Jews working for substandard wages in Germany ghetto enterprises.[4]

The fascist economic system served the purposes of the Nazi leadership relatively well, and maintained broad popular support until the early 1940s, when the labor force and other unexploited reserves became fully employed. From that time forward, continuation of wartime mobilization led to progressively more serious conflicts between competing interests. "It can be stated with certainty," concludes Barkai, "that a continuation of the economic system introduced by the Nazis would have been possible only under a permanent and increasingly severe dictatorship."[5]

THE SOCIAL MARKET ECONOMY[6]

When the Third Reich was defeated in 1945, Germany was divided into three western occupation zones, controlled by the United States, Britain, and France, and an eastern zone, controlled by the Soviet Union. Ludwig Erhard, the new economics administrator in the British and American zones, set several requirements for a new economic system. First, given the excesses of the Nazi era, it was clear that the power of the central government and the business cartels must be limited. Second, it was important to reignite economic growth in order to speed recovery from the war. Third, economic growth and the release of price controls could not be allowed to rekindle the inflation that destroyed the German currency after World War I. And fourth, the efforts to control inflation must not be hampered by public fears to unemployment and income insecurity.

To meet these requirements, Erhard borrowed a number of ideas from the Freiburg School of neoliberalism, headed by Walter Eucken, and designed an economic system for Germany known as the **social market economy (SME).** As the opening quotation of this chapter indicates, the SME was based on a

---

[4]Barkai, *Nazi Economics,* 239.

[5]*Ibid.,* 249.

[6]For a lively discussion of the formation of the social market, written by its architect, see Ludwig Erhard, *Prosperity through Competition* (London: Thames and Hudson, 1958). For a comprehensive discussion of the nature and origins of the social market philosophy, its application in Germany, and its relationship to other schools of thought, see A. J. Nicholls, *Freedom with Responsibility: The Social Market in Germany, 1918–1963* (Oxford: Clarendon Press, 1994).

compromise between classical liberal (laissez-faire) and interventionist philosophies. From the classical liberals, the SME adopted the ideas that the market system is the best means for coordinating economic activity and that the proper role of government is to provide a healthy environment for the operation of the market. Economic planning and Keynesian efforts to fine-tune the economy through short-run fiscal and monetary measures were ruled out. Instead, a monetarist program for price stability would be mixed with a supply-side program of tax cuts and investment incentives to encourage economic growth.

Erhard took decisive action on this part of his program. On June 20, 1948, before West Germany had even established a government, and with limited support from occupation authorities, Erhard introduced a bold currency reform, released price controls, and abolished most of the rules, regulations, rations, and production controls that remained from the Nazi era. Every German man, woman, and child was given 40 new deutsche marks with which to begin a new life. Bank savings of old reichsmarks were converted to the new currency at 6.5 percent of face value, but otherwise the old currency was declared worthless. Public confidence in the new deutsche mark was immediately demonstrated by the "shop-window miracle"; products that had long been hoarded "under the counter" were again on open display.[7]

To limit the power of the central authorities, a federal form of government was established by the Basic Law of 1949. The 11 state (*Länder*) governments were given control of the police, education, and all other matters that were not designated expressly to the central government. A staunchly independent central bank (the Bundesbank) was created to carry out the monetarist program of slow and stable monetary growth without governmental interference. The powers of both government and business were counterbalanced by the revival of the independent labor unions and by the system of codetermination.

On the interventionist side of the ledger, the architects of the SME doubted that capitalist economies were inherently competitive and equitable. In contract with Adam Smith and his classical school, who believed that monopolies would naturally disappear if the role of the state were restricted, Eucken and Erhard argued that cartel arrangements were so firmly entrenched in the German economy that aggressive action would be necessary to break them. In the words of Eucken:

> *More or less state activity—this kind of question misses the point. . . . Far more essential is a positive policy which aims at bringing the market form of complete competition into being. . . . It is here that the policy of the competitive order differs completely from the policy of laissez faire which, according to its own basic principles, did not recognize the need for a positive economic policy.*[8]

In 1952, Erhard introduced a bill in the Bundestag to ban most cartels, but it attracted strong opposition from industrialists. When a Law Against

---

[7]Nicholls, *Freedom with Responsibility*, 216.

[8]Walter Eucken, quoted in Sima Lieberman, *The Growth of European Mixed Economies, 1945–1970* (New York: John Wiley and Sons, 1977), 198.

Limitations of Competition was finally adopted in 1957, it fell short of Erhard's intentions.

With respect to social welfare legislation, proponents of the SME wished to find a middle ground between extreme laissez-faire and a paternalistic welfare state. In the tradition of Bismarck, public support should be provided to the poor, but individual liberties and responsibilities should be respected. Workers should have access to pension and health service systems, but those systems should be funded by insurance policies, not by general public expenditure. Support for the poor should not take the form of price controls or broad market-distorting subsidies.[9]

During the 1950s, Erhard's programs of market liberalization yielded marvelous results. The West German economy grew at an annual rate of 8.5 percent—almost double the OECD average—but generated only half as much consumer price inflation. The unemployment rate fell rapidly from 8.2 percent in 1950 to 4.3 percent in 1955, and below 1 percent during the early 1960s (Table 11.1).

With the economy at full employment, growth decelerated and became less stable during the 1960s. When Erhard was followed by a series of more interventionist leaders, macroeconomic policy shifted in a Keynesian direction and social welfare expenditures increased rapidly. Nevertheless, the SME philosophy had a lasting influence on German economic policy and garnered much of the credit for the country's political stability, moderate growth, low inflation, labor peace, and capacity to absorb more than 13 million refugees from East Germany and Eastern Europe.

Since the 1970s, it has been progressively more difficult for Germany to conduct an independent monetary and fiscal policy, unaffected by the actions of other industrial nations. Monetary policy has been most clearly influenced by the processes of monetary coordination in the European Union and monetary unification in Germany. The gradual opening of the economy to foreign trade and investment, together with the challenge of East-West unification, have made it increasingly difficult for Germany, with its high industrial wages and generous social welfare programs, to remain internationally competitive.

GERMAN UNIFICATION

The opening of the Berlin Wall in November 1989 led to a rapid succession of economic and political events. In March 1990, a new East German government was elected; it decided to adopt the political and economic system of the West by unification and established Treuhandanstalt, an agency responsible for safeguarding and privatizing East German enterprises. In May, West Germany established a special "Fund for Germany Unity" to support Eastern development. In June, the Western government assumed control of Treuhandanstalt, and price controls were removed in the East. In July, the German monetary system was unified, and the Bundesbank became the cen-

---

[9]Nicholls, *Freedom with Responsibility*, 324–325.

■ TABLE 11.1

RELATIVE PERFORMANCE OF THE GERMAN
ECONOMY, 1951–1996

	1951–1960	1961–1970	1971–1980	1981–1990	1991–1996
Average annual growth of real GDP (%)					
Germany	8.5	4.4	2.7	2.3	1.7*
OECD Average	4.2	5.1	3.2	2.8	2.0
Average annual consumer price inflation (%)					
Germany	1.8	2.6	5.1	2.6	3.4
OECD Average	3.3	3.9	9.1	8.1	4.9
Unemployment rate (%)					
Germany	4.3	0.8	2.5	6.1	8.8
OECD Average**	3.6**	2.8**	4.5	7.3	7.5

*In all cases, data for 1951–1990 are for West Germany and those for 1991–1996 are for
united Germany.
**Based on data for Canada, France, Germany, Italy, Japan, Sweden, the United Kingdom, and
the United States.
SOURCES: World Bank, *World Tables*, 1980 and 1995; Irving Kravis, Alan Heston, and Robert Summers, *World Product and Income* (Baltimore: Johns Hopkins University Press, 1982), 343; Angus
Maddison, *Phases of Capitalist Development* (Oxford: Oxford University Press, 1982), appendices A, C, and E; *OECD Economic Outlook*, December 1986 and December 1997; and International Monetary Fund, *World Economic Outlook*, May 1997.

tral bank for all Germany. In October, political union followed, and the East
adopted the Western systems of law and regulation. In December, the first
all-German parliamentary elections were held, and in January 1991, a united
German tax code came into force. Two months later, union leaders and employer representatives in the metals industry agreed that wage levels in the
East should reach those in the West by April 1994.

As this chronology indicates, German unification has been a huge undertaking, affecting every aspect of social, political, and economic life. Few
major decisions have passed without controversy. Consider, for example, the
program of monetary union.

MONETARY UNION. When monetary integration of the two German
states became a viable option, several questions had to be answered. First,
should East and West maintain separate currencies, at least temporarily,
linked through a flexible exchange rate, or should Eastern Germany be
merged quickly into the Western monetary system? Economists at the Bundesbank, Treuhandanstalt, the Ministry of Economy, and the major research

institutes were almost unanimous in their preference for gradualism: an exchange-rate union in the short run and full monetary union only in the long run.[10] A transitional exchange-rate mechanism was needed, they argued, to maintain the competitiveness of Eastern products that would now be exposed to Western competition. This position was overruled, however, by Chancellor Kohl and other political leaders who believed a more dramatic leap toward unification was necessary to stop massive immigration from East to West.

When it was decided that the East would be quickly merged into the Western monetary system, another difficult question arose: At what rate(s) of exchange should currency holdings, savings accounts, wage contracts, and other assets be converted from East German ostmarks to deutsche marks? This question was hotly contested, and recommended exchange ratios ranged from 8:1 to 1:1. In the end, the Western government adopted a set of differential ratios, ranging from 1:1 on salaries and pensions to 3:1 on claims of individuals living outside Eastern Germany, yielding an average effective rate of about 1.8 ostmarks per deutsche mark.

Monetary conversion at these rates was considered a "disaster" by the Bundesbank president, who said the rates overvalued the ostmark, required an inflationary issue of deutsche marks, and established excessively high wages in Eastern Germany, causing the East to be "completely uncompetitive."[11] Many government and independent economists agreed with this assessment, and their worst fears were validated by the collapse of the Eastern economy during 1990 and 1991.[12] Again, the political leaders had broader concerns. A lower valuation of the ostmark would have offended the Eastern Germans, would have introduced them into the market system with few initial assets, and may have endangered the larger unification process.

PRIVATIZATION. Plans for privatization of East German property began in 1989, in discussions among the Eastern agitators who led the revolt against the Communist regime. An early proposal was formulated, for example, by Wolfgang Ullman, an East German theologian and a leader in the citizens movement. He called for creation of an independent holding company to take possession of state enterprises, farmland, and other state-owned property. The holding company would ensure that state resources were managed according to market principles, and eventually it would redistribute ownership rights to the East German population through a voucher program.[13] In March 1990, the newly reformist East German parliament established the Treuhan-

---

[10]See Rolf Hasse, "German-German Monetary Union: Main Options, Costs and Repercussions," in *The Economics of German Unification,* ed. A. Ghanie Ghaussy and Wolf Shäfer (London: Routledge, 1993), 28–29 and 56–57.

[11]David Buchan and David Marsh, "Pöhl Says German Monetary Union Is Proving a Disaster," *Financial Times,* March 20, 1991, 1.

[12]For an economic analysis more supportive of the adopted exchange ratios, see Gerlinde Sinn and Hans-Werner Sinn, *Jumpstart: The Economic Unification of Germany* (Cambridge, Mass.: The MIT Press, 1992), 51–79.

danstalt ("trustee agency") with a plan similar to Ullman's in mind. Treuhand was immediately the world's largest holding company, responsible for the management and disposition of nearly 14,000 industrial enterprises, 23,000 retail businesses, and 4 million acres of farmland.

One month after Treuhand was established, a new East German government was formed, and negotiations commenced on a unification treaty. The Western government demanded several important changes in the operation of Treuhand and in the Eastern system of privatization. First, instead of maintaining ownership of state properties for an extended time, Treuhand would need to privatize them as quickly as possible. Second, instead of distributing state property to citizens in the East, the West insisted on the principle of **restitution.** When possible, property seized by the Nazi and Communist regimes should be returned to former owners, many of whom lived in the West. Third, instead of distributing ownership through a voucher program, enterprises should be sold to **strategic investors** who could offer scarce managerial skills, who were able to pay a fair price in "real money" for the assets they received, and who were willing to make legal commitments to renovate their factories and/or to maintain employment.

Despite a slow start caused partly by the complexities of the restitution process and partly by the assassination of its first president, Treuhand managed to complete its operations by the end of 1994. Some 3,700 industrial enterprises were found beyond repair and were liquidated. The remainder were sold: 2,700 in management buy-outs, 855 to foreign investors, and nearly 4,500 to West Germany investors.[14]

Opinions are sharply divided on the German privatization program. According to its critics, the absence of a voucher system deprived the Eastern population of a stake in ownership. Furthermore, Treuhand hastily liquidated too many Eastern enterprises, causing about 60 percent of the workers under its control to lose their jobs. It sold other enterprises for bargain-basement prices, collecting a total of only DM 70 billion ($47 billion) from asset sales—a mere fraction of the DM 600 billion ($400 billion) of sales projected by Treuhand in 1990, and far below the DM 337 billion ($225 billion) spent on subsidies, assumptions of enterprise debt, and environmental clean-up expenses. Thus, in the end, Treuhand passed a debt of DM 264 billion ($178 billion) to the German government. In a 1994 poll, 91 percent of Eastern Germans said they had a low opinion of Treuhand.[15]

According to its supporters, the German privatization program, oriented toward strategic investors, is preferable to a voucher program because it has

---

[13]This is similar to the privatization scheme that was used in the Czech Republic and in Russia. On Ullman's plan, see Mary Williams Walsh, "Going Private—The Profit and the Pain," *Los Angeles Times,* January 10, 1995, 1.

[14]See Peter Gumbel, "West German Program to Salvage East Shows Signs of Paying Off," *The Wall Street Journal,* December 9, 1994, A1; Hans-Peter Brunner, "German Blitz-Privatization: Lessons for the Reforming Economies?" *Transition* 6 (April 1995): 13–14; and Eric von der Heyden, "Privatization in East Germany: The Delivery of an Economy," *Columbia Journal of World Business* (Fall 1995): 42–53.

[15]"Farewell, Sweet Treuhand," *The Economist,* January 6, 1995, 82.

■ TABLE 11.2

UNIFICATION OF GERMANY: GROWTH, UNEMPLOYMENT, AND INFLATION, 1990–1996

	Growth of GDP	Consumer Price Inflation	Unemployment Rate
Western Germany			
1990	5.7%	2.7%	6.2%
1991	5.0	3.5	5.5
1992	1.8	4.0	5.8
1993	−1.7	4.1	7.3
1994	2.3	3.0	8.3
1995	1.5	1.8	8.3
1996	1.3	1.5	9.1
Eastern Germany			
1990	−15.0	0.0	2.5
1991	−22.5	12.0	15.8
1992	6.8	10.9	15.5
1993	5.8	8.7	15.6
1994	9.2	3.8	15.4
1995	6.3	1.8	14.0
1996	2.0	1.5	15.7
United Germany			
1990	4.0	2.3	5.5
1991	2.8	4.6	6.6
1992	2.2	4.9	7.7
1993	−1.1	4.7	8.8
1994	2.9	3.1	9.6
1995	1.9	1.8	9.4
1996	1.4	1.5	10.4

SOURCES: Deutsches Institut für Wirtschaftsforschung, *Economic Bulletin* No. 5, 1995; and International Monetary Fund, *World Economic Outlook*, May 1997; and press reports.

attracted managerial skill and capital resources to the East—the new owners have agreed to invest DM 207 billion ($140 billion) in renovating their enterprises and to maintain 1.5 million jobs. Unemployment in the East is not rooted in the privatization program, but in the inefficiency and backwardness of old Communist enterprises that have been exposed to Western competition since the 1990 currency union. Between 1992 and 1995, the Eastern economy recovered rapidly, based on construction activity (40 percent of

GDP in the East), large inflows of foreign investment, and about $100 billion of annual support from the central government (Table 11.2).[16] The boom subsided, however, and unemployment climbed to a dangerous level.

In the West, unification initially stimulated the economy, as Easterners invaded Western shops with their new deutsche marks. When this process led to higher inflation, though, the Bundesbank characteristically responded with a tighter monetary policy. Tight money combined with a stiff "solidarity tax" has slowed Western growth and contributed to Western unemployment since 1992.

INDUSTRIAL ORGANIZATION

Germany is the most industrial of the major high-income countries. About 39 percent of the German labor force is employed in industry, compared with an average of 32 percent for all high-income countries.[17] Unlike the experiences of the United States and Britain, where industrial market power was exercised most commonly through oligopolies and monopolies, German enterprises have a long history of open collusion through cartels and other price-fixing agreements. A **cartel** is an association of legally independent enterprises that are contractually bound to control prices and other market conditions. A cartel would sometimes establish a unified sales organization to market the goods of all its members, but the participants would maintain their identity as independent producers.

The German cartel movement began early in the nineteenth century and accelerated during the Bismarck era. An 1897 law affirmed the legality of cartel agreements, and, in 1923, when price-fixing agreements were already prohibited in the United States, German law merely restricted abuses of monopoly power. The number of cartel agreements grew from 385 in 1905 to over 3,000 in 1930.[18] They accounted for 93 percent of sales in the mining sector, 96 percent in chemicals, 95 percent in steel, and 87 percent in electrical engineering.[19] More cartels were established by the Nazis to control prices and mobilize for war.

After World War II, the architects of the SME called for a general prohibition of cartels and dissolved existing agreements in the steel, coal, and chemicals industries. They introduced a draft law on cartels in 1951, but strong opposition forced the addition of a number of amendments and exceptions.

---

[16]See Ullrich Heilemann and Wolfgang Reinicke, "Together Again: The Fiscal Cost of German Unity," *Brookings Review* 13 (Spring 1995): 42–45.

[17]United Nations Development Programme, *Human Development Report 1995* (New York: Oxford University Press, 1995), 201.

[18]Nathan, *The Nazi Economic System*, 65; and Eric Owen-Smith, "Government Intervention in the Economy of the Federal Republic of Germany," in *Government Intervention in the Developed Economy*, ed. Peter Maunder (New York: Praeger, 1979), 163.

[19]Helmut Bohme, *An Introduction to the Social and Economic History of Germany* (New York: St. Martin's Press, 1978), 109.

By the time the Law Against Limitations of Competition was finally passed in 1957, it allowed the existence of cartels to promote exports, ease the adjustment problems of dying industries, reduce research and development costs, or deal with other exceptional circumstances. Amendments to the law in 1965 and 1973 added more loopholes. The law is weak by American or British standards and falls far short of the social market ideal.

On the other hand, German enforcement of its antitrust laws has traditionally been second only to that in the United States.[20] Unlike their counterparts in many countries, German antitrust authorities are armed with subpoena powers and are able to assess fines commensurate with the excess profits gained through violation of the law. According to several comparative studies, Germany has one of the lowest levels of industrial concentration in the industrial world.[21]

Further improvement of German competitiveness has been restricted by a preference among workers and investors for the stability of large, well-established corporations. Entrepreneurs have the reputation of gamblers in many societies, but they have a particularly negative reputation in conservative Germany. New and small companies are generally dependent on banks for financing, and the banks tend to have conservative lending policies. The number of venture capital firms, though increasing, remains small.[22] Apple Computer, which was born in a California garage, "would still be in the garage here," according to the head of a Munich underwriting company.[23]

According to Chancellor Helmut Kohl, a portion of responsibility for Germany's lackluster technological performance falls on the educational system, which channels 40 percent of its graduates into public service careers. "It engenders a mentality of safety first too much, and too little entrepreneurial risk taking." Some 700,000 small and medium-sized family companies will need new owners within the next decade, but surveys indicate that the children of their founders would prefer to work in stable, salaried positions.[24]

THE LABOR MARKET AND LABOR RELATIONS

Until the 1980s, the operation of the German labor market had been nothing short of phenomenal. The country maintained one of the world's lowest unemployment rates and lowest rates of labor unrest, while it has simultaneously held to one of the lowest rates of wage and price inflation (Table 11.1).

[20]F. M. Scherer, *Industrial Market Structure and Performance*, 2nd ed. (Chicago: Rand McNally, 1980), 508.

[21]For example, according to one set of estimates for major OECD countries, only the United States had a lower level of industrial concentration. See Organization for Economic Coorperation and Development, *Economic Surveys: Japan 1991/1992*, 83.

[22]Organization for Economic Cooperation and Development, *Economic Surveys: Germany 1995*, 103.

[23]Roger Thurow, "New Vigor Is Infusing Small-Business Sector of West Germany," *The Wall Street Journal*, August 28, 1984, 1.

[24]Peter Norman, "Kohl Calls on Germans to Become Risk Takers," *Financial Times*, October 17, 1995, 1.

Credit for this performance has variously been given to the German system of collective bargaining, to codetermination, to the apprenticeship program for youth, and to the flexible use of guest workers from other countries. Let us consider each of these briefly.

COLLECTIVE BARGAINING

Approximately 35 percent of the German labor force is unionized, a proportion that has been remarkably stable since World War II.[25] This percentage is higher than that in the United States and France, but lower than that in the United Kingdom and most of northern Europe. The closed shop, which requires employees to join a union, is illegal in Germany.

German unions, as reorganized after the war, represent workers in relatively broad groups of industries. For example, IG Metall, the nation's largest union with 2.5 million members, represents almost all the workers in the iron, steel, and automobile industries, and in several other industries that involve metalworking. About 90 percent of all union members belong to one of the 16 unions that form the German Confederation of Labour. As a result, there is little of the British-style trouble with interunion rivalry, and collective bargaining is easy to organize along industry lines. Although Germany has a lower rate of union membership than many European countries, nonmembers are usually included in collective bargaining agreements, so some 88 percent of private-sector workers are covered by these agreements—the highest rate of coverage in the industrial world.[26] Perhaps because nonmembers are usually covered by union agreements, the average wage differential of union members over nonmembers is only 5 percent in Germany, compared with differentials of 10 percent in the United Kingdom and 20 percent in the United States.[27]

Chastened by memories of hyperinflation during the 1920s and repressed inflation during the 1940s, the German unions traditionally had a reputation for moderation. The oil price shocks of the 1970s that set off inflationary wage-price spirals in most Western countries were absorbed by lower real incomes in Germany. In more recent years, labor relations in Germany have remained relatively peaceful, but the unions have lost their reputation for moderation.

During the 1980s and 1990s, while real wages have fallen, on average, in other OECD countries, they have trended upward in Germany.[28] During the

---

[25]George S. Bain and Robert Price, *Profiles of Union Growth* (Oxford: Basil Blackwell, 1980), 134; and Organization for Economic Cooperation and Development, *Employment Outlook* (July 1994), 184.

[26]Organization for Economic Cooperation and Development, *Employment Outlook* (July 1994), 181.

[27]World Bank, *World Development Report 1995* (Oxford University Press, 1995), 81.

[28]Based on comparisons of employee compensation and consumer prices, German real incomes increased at an annual rate of 1.2 percent during the 1980s and 1.3 percent during 1991–1994. OECD incomes fell, respectively, by 0.7 percent and 0.5 percent, annually. These are estimates by the author, based on Organization for Economic Cooperation and Development, *OECD Economic Outlook* 58 (December 1995), annex tables 12 and 16.

mid-1990s, hourly labor costs in Western Germany were the world's highest, more than 50 percent above those in France, Japan, the United Kingdom, or the United States.[29] German unemployment climbed above the U.S. level in 1987 for the first time since 1955, and has remained above or near the U.S. level during recent years. Furthermore, the German rate of long-term unemployment, accounting for about 48 percent of the jobless, is almost five times higher than the American rate.[30]

When the two Germanys were united, the unions insisted that wages in the East must be quickly raised to parity with the West, despite a much lower level of labor productivity in the East. Furthermore, Eastern workers are covered by the generosity of the German welfare state. When employers tried to cancel the parity agreement in 1993, the powerful unions were able to force them back into compliance.[31]

German labor peace is strengthened by the bargain that was struck after World War II, whereby labor accepted limitations on its right to strike in exchange for a voice in management (codetermination). Under German law and union rules, a strike may not be called until the current contract has expired, peaceful means of settlement have been exhausted, the strike has been authorized by the national union, and 75 percent of the workers approve it in a secret ballot. Employees who take part in an illegal strike may be fired by their employer, expelled by the national union, and fined by a labor court.[32]

CODETERMINATION

One of the most interesting aspects of the German economic system is the system of **codetermination,** wherein workers are given a voice in the management of their companies. German employees are able to participate in management through works councils and through representation on corporate supervisory boards.

German **works councils** date back to the safety legislation of 1891, when employers were required to consult with their employees before drafting shop rules. Under current law, councils of labor representatives are required in all factories having five or more employees. They have an equal voice with management on matters relating to (1) job evaluation; (2) overtime, breaks, and holiday schedules; (3) recruitment, selection, and dismissal; and (4) training and safety. Strikes over these matters are prohibited by law and disputes are usually resolved through binding arbitration.

Thus, the councils represent labor on most issues other than the wage contract, which is reserved for the unions. Union wage negotiations are generally held at the industrial level, while the works councils negotiate with

---

[29]According to estimates by Morgan Stanley and the Hanover Chamber of Commerce, cited in Amity Shlaes, "Germany's Chained Economy," *Foreign Affairs* 73 (September/October 1994): 112.

[30]Organization for Economic Cooperation and Development, *OECD in Figures 1997* (Supplement to *OECD Observer,* July 1997), 12–13.

[31]Wolfgang Munchau, "Heads Roll Over Wage Deal in Germany," *Financial Times,* November 10, 1995, 2.

[32]Thomas Kennedy, *European Labor Relations* (Lexington, Mass.: Lexington Books, 1980), 180.

management at the factory level. During the 1980s, a survey of automobile and metal workers in the Munich area found that works councils were considered more important than unions in advancing labor interests.[33] More recently, in a series of five case studies, Kirsten Wever found that German works councils were effectively articulating and representing the interests of employees, and, in some cases, they also contributed to effective management of the companies.[34]

The second form of codetermination involves labor representation on corporate supervisory boards. Each German company has two boards of directors—a supervisory board, which meets about four times per year to handle broad policy issues, and a management board, which is appointed by the supervisory board to handle the day-to-day operation of the firm. In 1951, in order to prevent a disastrous strike in the iron, coal, and steel industries, one-half the positions on supervisory boards in those industries were turned over to representatives of labor. The stockholders' representatives reserved the right to nominate the chairperson of the board, but the labor representatives were allowed to designate a neutral member to cast tie-breaking votes. In other industries, the Works Constitution of 1952 gave labor one-third representation on the supervisory boards.

In 1976, a new law gave equal representation to labor on the supervisory boards of all companies with over 2,000 employees (or 1,000 employees in the iron, coal, and steel industries). Companies outside iron, coal, and steel with 500 to 2,000 employees must provide one-third representation to labor. About one-quarter of the German labor force is affected by one of these forms of codetermination.[35]

How has labor participation on supervisory boards influenced corporate policy in Germany? This was the question posed to a bipartisan investigating committee appointed in the late 1960s. Codetermination, they found, had exerted very little influence on the overall direction of corporate policy. To those who claimed that employees with no ownership stake in the company were likely to take a short-run view of things, the committee responded that the "interest of the employees in the continued prosperity of the enterprise was never less than that of the shareholders or owners."[36] More recent studies have reached similar conclusions.[37]

In many cases, codetermination has strengthened cooperation between labor and management. When it has been necessary to close excess iron and

---

[33]Charles J. Hobson and James B. Dworkin, "West German Labor Unrest: Are Unions Losing Ground to Worker Councils?" *Monthly Labor Review* 109 (February 1986): 47.

[34]Kirsten Wever, "Learning from Works Councils: Five Unspectacular Cases from Germany," *Industrial Relations* 33 (October 1994): 467–481.

[35]Egon Overbeck, "Codetermination at Company Level," in *German Yearbook on Business History, 1983* (Berlin: Springer-Verlag, 1984), 11.

[36]The committee report, quoted in Z. Almanasreh, "Institutional Forms of Worker Participation in the Federal German Republic," in *The Economics of Codetermination*, ed. David F. Heathfield (London: Macmillan, 1977), 98.

[37]See studies reviewed in Peter Katzenstein, *Policy and Politics in West Germany* (Philadelphia: Temple University Press, 1987), 125–148.

coal mines with the danger of causing unemployment, the labor representatives have been able to bargain for long adjustment periods. After an agreement is reached with management, the representatives have helped to sell unpopular policies to the workers—without causing the strikes one might expect in many countries.

Critics of codetermination say that it threatens the institution of private property and gives too much power to the unions. They admit that worker participation may have contributed to labor peace in the booming 1950s and 1960s when unemployment was not a serious problem, but in the more difficult environment since the 1970s they say that it has exacerbated tensions between labor and management and slowed corporate decision making. Nonetheless, Germany has continued to have one of the lowest strike rates in the world.[38]

APPRENTICESHIPS

Germany has one of the lowest rates of youth unemployment in the world. In 1993, only 7.5 percent of Germans under age 25 were unable to find work, compared with 13 percent of Americans, 17 percent of British, 18 percent of Canadians, and 25 percent of French.[39] Much of the credit goes to an unusual system of vocational education and training that has operated for the past 150 years.

Full-time compulsory education ends at age 16 in Germany, and almost three-quarters of the young people quit their formal education at that age. Of those, about 90 percent enter a two- to four-year apprenticeship—a dual program of vocational education (usually two or three days per week) and on-the-job training (usually three days per week). Some 380 apprenticeship curricula have gained official recognition, providing the skills required to qualify for a position as an auto mechanic, electrician, glassblower, jeweler, cashier, furniture salesman, or any of 30,000 other job titles.

The state and local chambers of commerce oversee the apprenticeship programs. They establish curriculum, health, safety, and compensation standards, approve companies that wish to participate, and provide guidance to young people entering the programs. The federal and state governments provide a small amount of financing, but the bulk of the annual training costs are borne by the companies. Apprentices are paid relatively low wages during their training—about one-third of a normal income—but companies commit major resources to their educational programs, hoping to create and attract a pool of highly skilled and disciplined workers. At Mannesmann AG, for example, the company spends about $47,000 on wages and training costs over a three-and-a-half-year period on each apprentice. Less than half of that cost is recouped from the productivity of the apprentice.[40]

---

[38]See David Goodhart, "An Orderly Model That Enforces Restraint," *Financial Times*, May 3, 1991, 15.

[39]Organization for Economic Cooperation and Development, *OECD in Figures 1995*, 12–13.

[40]John von Brachel, "What Price Apprenticeships?" *Across the Board*, January 1994, 35.

Apprentices are not required to stay with the employers who train them, and employers are not required to retain their apprentices, but more than half of apprentices stay with the same employer when their training is over. At Mannesmann, only 16 percent leave at the end of their apprenticeships, and 20 percent of the remainder leave over a five-year period, but half of apprentices normally remain with the company until retirement.[41]

GUEST WORKERS AND REFUGEES

Guest workers (*Gastarbeiter*) from other countries have performed an important shock-absorbing role in the German economy. In the early 1960s, a serious labor shortage developed as economic growth continued and immigration from East Germany was halted by the building of the Berlin Wall. To alleviate the problem, German firms actively began to recruit workers from other countries. The number of foreigners working in Germany rose from less than 100,000 in 1956 to a peak of 2.6 million in 1973. Almost half of these came from Turkey and Yugoslavia and primarily worked in unskilled and semiskilled jobs.[42]

In 1973, when unemployment started to rise during the first oil crisis, Germany imposed a ban on further recruiting of labor from outside the Common Market. By 1983, the number of guest workers had fallen to about 1.8 million, two-thirds of whom had been living in Germany for over six years. Late in 1983, the parliament passed a new law offering foreign workers prepaid social security benefits—as much as $14,000—to go home. Few responded.

Despite rising unemployment, ethnic tension, and continuing political efforts to reduce the level of immigration, Germany still has a larger immigrant population than any other European country (Table 11.3). In recent years, hostilities in former Yugoslavia, the opening of eastern borders, and the relatively liberal German asylum law have attracted a steady stream of refugees. In 1995, nearly 128,000 petitions were filed for asylum, including 33,000 from former Yugoslavia and 25,000 from Turkey. German authorities processed over 200,000 applications (including part of the backlog from previous years), and asylum was offered to more than 18,000 applicants.[43]

What would happen to Germany if all the *Gastarbeiter* and refugees were to return home? Presumably there would be some reduction in native unemployment. On the other hand, a study commissioned several years ago by the city of Dusseldorf concluded that garbage collection, construction, hospital, and public transport services would collapse; a sizable number of German

---

[41]A wealth of information is available on German apprenticeships. See, for example, Margaret Hilton, "Shared Training: Learning from Germany," *Monthly Labor Review* (March 1991): 33–37; and Hilary Steedman, "The Economics of Youth Training in Germany," *The Economic Journal* 103 (September 1993): 1279–1291.

[42]Hermann Korte, "Labor Migration and the Employment of Foreigners in Federal Republic of Germany since 1950," in *Guests Come to Stay: The Effects of European Labor Migration on Sending and Receiving Countries*, ed. Rosemarie Rogers (Boulder, Colo.: Westview Press, 1985), 29–49.

[43]"Germany Received 128,000 Asylum Petitions in 1995," *The Week in Germany*, January 12, 1996, 1. Also, see Judy Dempsey, "Cracks Behind the Unity," *Financial Times*, November 16, 1992, 14.

■ TABLE 11.3

IMMIGRANT POPULATIONS IN SELECTED
EUROPEAN COUNTRIES, 1992

(Thousands)
Country of Residence

Citizenship in:	France	Germany	Luxembourg	Netherlands	Sweden	United Kingdom
Europe	1,662	4,856	120	426	334	859
Africa	1,633	236	1	198	23	195
America	73	161	2	46	38	278
Asia/Oceania	229	561	1	60	85	568
Total	3,597	5,814	124	730	480	1,900
Percent of Population	6.3	7.3	30.9	4.8	5.6	3.3

SOURCE: Eurostat, *Migration Statistics 1994.*

teachers would lose their jobs; and whole residential quarters of the city would become derelict.[44]

FINANCIAL MARKETS

The financial sector of the German economy is similar, in several respects, to the Japanese system. Households in both countries have high savings rates, encouraged in part by tax incentives. Stock markets are relatively underdeveloped in both countries; large commercial banks are the central financial institutions, supporting national programs of capital investment and export finance.

Leadership of the German financial system is provided by the nation's fiercely independent central bank, the Bundesbank. Founded in 1957, the Bundesbank is required by law to safeguard the currency as its first priority. The bank is directed by a Central Bank Council, which consists of the president, the vice-president, the other eight members of the bank directorate, and the presidents of the state (Länd) central banks. Members of the directorate are appointed by the federal president for eight-year terms; the presidents of the Länd central banks are chosen by the Bundesrat, the house of Parliament representing all the Länder.

In keeping with the social market philosophy, the German government has usually maintained strong incentives to encourage household saving. Interest rate controls, which were used in many industrial countries until the 1980s, were removed in Germany during the 1960s. Real interest rates, which sometimes fall negative in other countries, have usually remained positive in

[44]*The Economist,* February 4, 1984, 24.

Germany.[45] Workers can avoid taxation on part of their income by setting it aside in special accounts that cannot be touched for seven years.[46] Interest on the accounts, which are normally managed by employers, is subsidized by the government. Saving is also encouraged by the absence of a tax on long-term capital gains and by the relatively low rate of inflation. A withholding tax on interest income was introduced in 1993, but the first DM 6,000 ($3,700) per person of income is exempt.[47] The result of all this? West Germans saved more than 22 percent of their GDP in 1992, compared to less than 20 percent for all OECD countries.[48] Among the major capitalist countries, only Japan has been able to finance a more rapid growth in its capital stock.

THE BANKING SECTOR

Banks play a predominant role in the German financial system, accounting for about 70 percent of the funds raised by enterprises and households. The system includes commercial banks, savings banks, cooperatives, and other specialized financial institutions.

Among the commercial banks, over 40 percent of all business is handled by the Big Three—Deutsche Bank, Dresdner, and Commerzbank—and by their thousands of branch offices located throughout the country.[49] In contrast to the situation in the United States, where commercial banks are presently gaining the right to engage in some investment banking activities, the Big Three for many years have been allowed to broker securities, underwrite stock and bond issues, and provide investment counseling.

The powerful position of the large banks has long been a matter of controversy in Germany. In 1992, banks and their subsidiary investment funds controlled an average of 84 percent of the represented votes at stockholders' meetings of large firms that are not majority owned.[50] This raises questions about the independence of German corporations, and about their ability to take entrepreneurial risks. It also raises questions concerning the willingness of banks to make loans to new businesses that may compete against firms in which the banks have major shares of ownership.[51]

Working beside these three nationwide all-purpose banks, the system of state and regional commercial banks generally restricts itself to conventional

[45]Warren Tease, Andrew Dean, Jorgen Elmeskov, and Peter Hoeller, "Real Interest Rate Trends: The Influence of Saving and Other Factors," *OECD Economic Studies* 17 (Fall 1991): 107

[46]According to Christian Strenger, the head of a large pension fund, Germany needs to establish saving incentives for retirement accounts, similar to those in the United States and the United Kingdom. See Andrew Fisher, "German Call for Pension Tax Breaks," *Financial Times*, November 13, 1995, 2.

[47]See Mark H. Robson, "Taxation and Household Saving: Reflections on the OECD Report," *Fiscal Studies* 16 (February 1995): 38–57.

[48]*OECD Economic Outlook* 61 (June 1997), A27.

[49]Germany has six branch banks for every 10,000 people, compared with five in France, four in Japan and the United States, and three in Italy and the United Kingdom. See Peter Gumbel, "German Bankers Get Busy Catching Up," *The Wall Street Journal*, November 29, 1994, A20.

[50]Organization for Economic Cooperation and Development, *Economic Surveys: Germany 1995*, 95.

[51]For a discussion of these issues, see W. R. Smyser, *The Economy of United Germany: Colossus at the Crossroads* (New York: St. Martin's Press, 1992), 83–90.

deposit and commercial loan activities. The savings banks are mostly owned by local authorities and operate according to local regulations. They obtain most of their funds from household deposits and lend to households and small businesses. The cooperatives were originally established to meet financial needs in agriculture, but they now pursue a full range of banking activities.

SECURITIES MARKETS

In comparison to the role played by direct bank lending, the securities markets play a relatively small role in the German financial system. There are eight securities exchanges in Germany. The largest, in Frankfurt, accounts for more than half of all transactions and handles nearly all the open-market operations of the Bundesbank. Together, the eight exchanges trade stock in only 700 companies, compared with 1,700 in Tokyo, 1,900 in the United Kingdom, and 7,300 in the United States.[52] Because of the small scale of the securities market, German companies obtain a relatively large part of their financing through bank lending and a relatively small part through equity ownership.

THE GOVERNMENTAL SECTOR

As we have seen, the German government has a long tradition of active involvement in the economy. Under Bismarck, a progressive system of social welfare was established and tariff policy was used to promote industrialization. Under the Nazis, the power of government was pervasive. A significant proportion of authority was returned to the private sector after the war, but the government continued to play an important role in promoting economic growth, providing a system of social welfare, controlling monopolies and cartels, and establishing a legal framework for codetermination. During recent years, the government has taken decisive action to unite the monetary, fiscal, legal, and social systems of Germany.

FISCAL POLICY AND PLANNING

We noted earlier that the postwar architects of the social market economy explicitly rejected the use of economic planning or Keynesian demand management. Instead, they coupled an anti-inflationary monetary policy with a supply-side package of tax cuts and investment incentives. As Chancellor Konrad Adenauer told Parliament in 1949, "The primary function of the state is to encourage capital formation."[53] According to supply-side economists, Germany's success during the 1950s provided strong evidence for the effectiveness of investment-oriented tax reductions.[54]

---

[52] Organization for Economic Cooperation and Development, *Economic Surveys: Germany 1995,* 87. For more detail, see "Global Stock Exchange Directory," *Institutional Investor,* October 1994, 137.

[53] Quoted in Willi Semmler, "Economic Aspects of Model Germany," in *The Political Economy of West Germany: Modell Deutschland,* ed. Andrei Markovits (New York: Praeger, 1982), 28.

[54] See, for example, Bruce Bartlett, *Reaganomics: Supply-Side Economics in Action* (New York: Quill, 1982), 192.

During the 1960s German economic growth decelerated and became more unstable. In 1963, an independent Council of Economic Experts (loosely patterned after the Council of Economic Advisers in the United States) was established to study the problem and to submit annual reports to the government. The recommendations of the "Five Wise Men," as they are known, are not always followed by the government, but they have enhanced the visibility and sophistication of public policy discussions.

In 1967, when Germany experienced its first serious postwar recession, a new coalition government was formed that included the Social Democrats; economic policy began to shift in the Keynesian direction. The Stability and Growth Law, passed in 1967, set four overall goals for economic policy: stable prices, full employment, balance of payments equilibrium, and stable economic growth. To give the government greater short-run flexibility in fine-tuning the economy, the law allowed the use of some new policy instruments, such as temporary tax surcharges, without prior legislative approval.

The Stability and Growth Law also established a framework for medium-term fiscal policy, requiring the government to formulate its annual budget within a five-year financial plan that rolls forward each year. The financial plan is accompanied by five-year target projections, prepared by the Ministry of Economic Affairs, for aggregates such as GDP growth, unemployment, inflation, the balance of payments, and the shares of profits and wages in national income.

The 1967 law also created a discussion group known as Concerted Action, with representatives from the government, private business, the labor unions, the Bundesbank, and the Council of Economic Experts. The group met a few times a year to consider the state of the economy, to exchange information and to formulate coordinated strategies, particularly those involving wage increases. Concerted Action had no real authority, but it provided a forum for debate and compromise that resembled, in a small way, the French system of indicative planning. The system fell apart in 1977, in the aftermath of the international oil price shocks, when the trade unions withdrew from participation.

A more active macroeconomic policy after 1967, a shift to floating exchange rates in 1971, and oil price shocks in 1974 and 1979 sent the German economy through a succession of "stop-go" cycles. Then, in 1982 the major conservative parties—the Christian Democratic Union and the Christian Social Union—regained power under the leadership of Helmut Kohl, and fiscal policy returned to a conservative orientation. The share of governmental expenditures in GNP, which grew from 39 percent in 1967 to 50 percent in 1982, was cut by the Kohl government to less than 48 percent in 1985 and was budgeted to fall below 43 percent in 1995.

In recent years, of course, fiscal policy has been rocked by the German unification process. Each year since 1990, Western Germany has transferred about DM 150 billion ($100 billion), or 5 percent of its GDP, to the East. About 40 percent of these expenditures have been financed through debt accumulation, and the remainder have been paid through tax increases (25 percent), increased social security contributions (25 percent), and reductions of other expenditures (10 percent). During 1991 and since the beginning of 1995, a

7.5 percent "solidarity surcharge" has been added to the personal income tax. These special taxes and expenditures are expected to continue until the end of the century.[55]

MONETARY POLICY

Although German fiscal philosophies may have zigzagged since World War II, the policy of the Bundesbank has remained staunchly monetarist. As we noted earlier, the central bank is legislatively required to "safeguard the currency" as its first priority. It is also obliged to "support the general policy of the federal government," but it is legally "independent of instructions" from the government.[56]

If safeguarding the currency means total price stability, the German record has not been perfect. However, the German rate of consumer price inflation has consistently fallen below the average for OECD countries, even during the years of monetary and economic unification (Table 11.1) If the bank was supposed to safeguard the international value of the currency, its performance has been even better. A deutsche mark that was worth only 24 cents in 1957 could be exchanged for about 59 cents in 1997. During that same period, the values of the British, French, and Italian currencies fell precipitously against the dollar.

The Bundesbank was also one of the first central banks in the world to set annual targets for monetary growth—a practice eventually adopted by almost all OECD countries. The projections have been used to communicate central bank intentions, to impose discipline on the central bankers themselves, and to subdue inflationary expectations. Between 1975 and 1987, the bank announced annual growth targets for central bank money, a narrow measure of the monetary base that includes currency and required bank reserves, but excludes excess reserves. Since 1988, the targets have been based on M3, a broad monetary aggregate that includes currency, demand deposits, and selected time and savings deposits. As the data in Table 11.4 indicate, the Bundesbank consistently overshot its targets in 1975–1978, but faithfully stayed within the target ranges in 1979–1985. Since that time, monetary growth has usually exceeded targets. During the late 1980s, Germany responded to requests from other countries, including the United States, to stimulate the demand for their exports and to support the international values of their currencies. During the 1990s, monetary targeting has been complicated by the processes of European and German unification.

REDISTRIBUTION OF INCOME

Bismarck's Germany led the world in the enactment of social insurance legislation in the nineteenth century. Untouched by the laissez-faire philosophy that inhibited the British and the French, and alarmed by the inroads of the socialists, Bismarck and his successors established national insurance programs against sickness in 1883, against accidents in 1884, for the old and

---

[55]Heilemann and Reinicke, "Together Again," 42–44

[56]*Encyclopedia of Banking and Finance*, ed. F. L. Garcia (Boston: Bankers Publishing Co., 1973), 106.

■ **TABLE 11.4**

GERMAN MONETARY GROWTH TARGETS, 1975–1997

Percentage Growth of Central Bank Money **Percentage Growth of M3**

Year	Target Growth	Actual Growth	Year	Target Growth	Actual Growth
1975	8	9.9	1988	3–6	6.7
1976	8	9.3	1989	"about 5"	4.6
1977	8	9.0	1990	4–6	5.5
1978	8	11.4	1991	3–5	5.2
1979	6–9	6.4	1992	3.5–5.5	9.4
1980	5–8	4.8	1993	4.5–6.5	7.5
1981	4–7	3.5	1994	4–6	5.7
1982	4–7	6.1	1995	4–6	2.1
1983	4–7	7.1	1996	4–7	8.1
1984	4–6	4.6	1997	3.5–6.5	
1985	3–5	4.5			
1986	3.5–5.5	7.8			
1987	3–6	8.1			

NOTE: Data through 1990 are for West Germany. Data since 1991 are for united Germany. Central bank money includes currency in circulation and required reserves. M3 includes currency in circulation, demand deposits, time deposits with maturities up to four years, and savings deposits with a three-month period of notice.

SOURCES: Peter Isard and Liliana Rojas-Suarez, "Velocity of Money and the Practice of Monetary Targeting," *Staff Studies for the World Economic Outlook* (Washington, D.C.: International Monetary Fund, July 1986), 84; and reports of the U.S. Embassy, published in *International Marketing Insights*, June 24, 1994 and March 21, 1997.

disabled in 1891, and for widows and orphans in 1911. National unemployment insurance was not established until after World War I, but local programs were adopted in some cities as early as 1894.

Based on this tradition, coupled with German fears of unemployment and inflation after World War II, the conservative architects of the social market economy were forced to build an extensive system of social welfare programs—even though they believed that "economic freedom and compulsory insurance are not compatible."[57] During 1959–1960, West Germany devoted a larger share of its GDP to public health, welfare, and social security expenditures than any other capitalist country. During the 1970s, Germany more than doubled its social protection expenditures, but some countries escalated even more rapidly. By 1980, the Germans had been overtaken by the Belgians and Danes, and had been surpassed by the Dutch and Swedes. Growth of social expenditures was arrested, relative to GDP, in most industrial countries during the 1980s, and this was true in Germany (Table 11.5).

---

[57]Erhard, *Prosperity through Competition*, 186.

■ TABLE 11.5

PUBLIC EXPENDITURES ON SOCIAL PROTECTION, 1959–1990 (PERCENTAGE OF GDP)

	1959–1960	1980	1990
Austria	10.0	23.4	24.5
Belgium	10.1	25.4	25.2
Canada	8.1	—	18.8
Denmark	9.6	26.0	27.8
Finland	7.1	21.4	27.1
France	9.0	23.9	26.5
Germany	11.0	25.4	23.5
Ireland	7.7	20.6	19.7
Italy	8.4	19.8	24.6
Netherlands	8.8	27.2	28.8
Norway	7.5	21.4	28.7
Portugal	n.a.	13.6	15.3
Spain	n.a.	16.8	19.3
Sweden	10.0	32.4	33.1
United Kingdom	8.8	21.3	22.3
United States	4.8	14.1	14.6

SOURCES: For 1959–1960: Margaret S. Gordon, *Social Security Policies in Industrial Countries* (Cambridge: Cambridge University Press, 1988), 348–350. For 1980 and 1990: OECD, *Employment Outlook* (July 1994), 151.

During the 1990s, however, the German social welfare system has been spinning out of control. High rates of unemployment, incorporation of Eastern Germany into a unified system, and a demographic shift to an older population have all increased the cost of the system. After recording a DM 6 billion surplus in 1992, the statutory pension insurance system recorded a deficit of DM 10–12 billion in 1993. In the statutory health insurance system, runaway spending (up 13 percent in 1991) could only be checked by more government intervention. The deficit in the unemployment insurance scheme grew from DM 3 billion in 1992 to a record DM 24.4 billion in 1993.[58] All things considered, social expenditures grew to 30 percent of GDP in Western Germany in 1993, and to a staggering 70 percent of GDP in Eastern Germany.[59]

As is true in most of Europe, the German social security system includes a number of programs that are not found in the United States and Japan. New mothers are paid maternity grants and are guaranteed a paid vacation for 12 months after the birth of their children, with protection against dismissal.

---

[58]Dieter Braeuninger, "Reforming Germany's Welfare System," *Deutsche Bank Bulletin,* January 17, 1994, 1.

[59]"Highlights of the Government Social Report 1993," *Germany—Economic News* (U.S. Embassy, Bonn), in National Trade Data Bank, March 21, 1995.

Family allowances are paid to all households with school-age children, and, to those who qualify, the state provides a free university education. The German unemployment insurance system covers a number of occupational groups, such as agricultural employees and at-home workers, that are excluded by the American system. Pensions paid under the social security system are larger than those in the United States, and the government contributes toward funeral costs.[60]

According to its critics, the German social welfare system is too generous, too fragmented and complex (90 transfer programs administered by 40 governmental and quasi-governmental agencies), and too dependent on employer contributions. For every DM 100 of direct wage costs, a German company must pay an additional DM 37 on statutory social insurance contributions and DM 47 on mandated fringe benefits. Germany ranks fifth in the world in direct wage costs, but these additions cause it to be first in total labor costs.[61]

To address these concerns, the German government has adjusted several of the social insurance programs, and broader reforms are being prepared. In 1994, the Cabinet approved a recommendation from the Labor Ministry to limit unemployment compensation to two years. The Ministry hopes that a time limit will directly reduce the cost of the unemployment program, and will encourage the unemployed to find jobs.[62]

The Labor Ministry is also recommending fundamental reforms of the unemployment insurance system. Job training and job creation programs, which are presently administered by an independent social insurance agency, will come under the direct control of the federal government. Obligatory contributions and government matching grants to the unemployment insurance fund will be reduced, and budgetary expenditures on this program will be cut by almost one-third.[63]

In 1995, the Cabinet approved another set of initiatives to move the unemployed from welfare to work. An employer who hires a long-term unemployed individual will receive a subsidy for up to six months, which can be as large as the welfare payment that the individual has been receiving. Assistance will be reduced by "at least" 25 percent if an individual refuses an "acceptable" job.[64]

---

[60]For more detail, see Katzenstein, *Policy and Politics in West Germany*, 168–192; and Margaret S. Gordon, *Social Security Policies in Industrial Countries: A Comparative Analysis* (Cambridge: Cambridge University Press, 1988), passim.

[61]Braeuninger, "Reforming Germany's Welfare System," 1.

[62]According to a recent study, differences in unemployment compensation programs explain part, but not all, of the difference between German and American long-term unemployment. See Jennifer Hunt, "The Effect of Unemployment Compensation on Unemployment Duration in Germany," *Journal of Labor Economics* 13 (1995): 88–120.

[63]German Labor Minister Bluem Recommends Fundamental Reform of Germany's Unemployment Insurance System," *Germany—Economic News* (U.S. Embassy, Bonn), in National Trade Data Bank, March 21, 1995.

[64]"Unemployment Compensation Reform: Cabinet Approves 'Workfare' Proposal," *Germany—Economic News* (U.S. Embassy, Bonn), in National Trade Data Bank, July 24, 1995.

UNITED GERMANY IN THE EUROPEAN UNION

Germany is the central economic power of the European Union (EU), accounting for about 25 percent of income and production in the entire region. The formation of the EEC after World War II provided broader access to the large German market and its resources. Efforts to harmonize technical standards for European products have been based, by and large, on German technologies. The Common Agricultural Policy (CAP) was adopted, principally, to ensure the economic survival of high-cost German farms. In recent years, Germany has supported reform of the CAP to reduce large agricultural subsidies and to support negotiation of GATT agreements. The deutsche mark is the key currency in the European financial system, and the Bundesbank will play a leading role in any program of European Monetary Union.

The fall of communism gave Germany an opportunity not only to unify as a nation, but also to renew its historical sphere of influence in Central and Eastern Europe. Thus, Germany has quickly expanded its trade and investment in countries throughout the region, and it has insisted, against opposition from other new and prospective EU members in southern Europe, on the formulation of an "enlargement" policy for the EU that includes the entire region.

Germany has a unique opportunity to lead in the creation of a framework for peace and prosperity throughout the European continent. If it can rise to that challenge, Germany will establish itself as a true superpower among nations.

SUMMARY

Unification of Germany is one of the great events of the post–cold-war era. German national unity and social policies have their roots in the nineteenth-century initiatives of Friedrich List and in the leadership of Otto von Bismarck, and in a reaction against the totalitarianism of the Nazi era. Drawing on the German heritage, and determined to put away the hyperinflation, cartel power, and political repression of the war years, Ludwig Erhard and his associates fashioned the social market economy (SME). The SME model is based on a rejection of central planning and an affirmation of the market system, an active effort to abolish cartels and to establish competition, a supply-side fiscal policy, a monetary policy dedicated to price stability, and a balanced social welfare system.

The 1989 opening of the Berlin Wall led to a rapid succession of events. Among the most important of these, monetary unification was enacted, against the advice of economists, in a single leap, with an average exchange ratio of 1.8 ostmarks per deutsche mark. Against the original intentions of some Eastern reformers, privatization of assets in the East was also accomplished rapidly; property was restored to original owners or sold to strategic investors. The privatization program has attracted investment capital to the

East, but it also has been associated with declining production and high unemployment.

Germany is the most industrial of the high-income countries. During the early 1950s, political opposition prevented the framers of the SME from enacting a strict anticartel law. The 1957 Law Against Limitations of Competition includes a number of loopholes, but is firmly enforced. Germany's conservative financial and educational institutions are thought to be responsible, in part, for a lackluster record of technological progress.

German unions, despite their moderate reputations, have won very high wages and short working hours for their members. High labor costs, in turn, have contributed to rising unemployment, and particularly to rising long-term unemployment. Although not a part of the original SME model, labor participation in management (codetermination) is another important component of the German economic system. Codetermination is handled through works councils, which consult with management on working conditions, and labor representation on corporate supervisory boards. Together with well-organized systems of collective bargaining and youth apprenticeships, and flexible use of migrant guest workers, the system of codetermination contributed to labor peace, price stability, and relatively low unemployment until recent years.

The financial sector is characterized by a strong and independent central bank that has remained dedicated to price stability and by a pervasive banking system and limited stock market. Although a Keynesian approach to fiscal policy was adopted in the mid-1960s and the governmental share of the economy increased steadily during the 1970s, economic policy returned to a more conservative orientation in 1982. In recent years, though, German fiscal, monetary, and social welfare policies have been rocked by the German and European unification processes.

Germany is the central economic power in the European Union, accounting for 25 percent of its production. Institutions in the EU have been shaped by German requirements, and Germany is playing a leading role in the processes of monetary integration and enlargement of the EU.

DISCUSSION AND REVIEW QUESTIONS

1. What were the essential elements of the Nazi economic system? How did the Nazi legacy influence the postwar years?

2. How did the philosophies of Friedrich List and the founders of the social market economy differ from the classical liberalism of Adam Smith?

3. What are the specialized roles of the labor unions, works councils, and labor members on supervisory boards in representing the interests of German workers?

4. How do the relative roles of banking and securities markets differ in the American and German financial systems?

5. What are the essential elements of the social market economy? How faithfully does the German economy fit that model today?

6. What have been the major programs involved in German economic unification? How has this process served the different needs of Eastern Germans and Western Germans? How has German unification influenced the pace and structure of economic integration in the EU?

SUGGESTED READINGS

Barkai, Avraham. *Nazi Economics: Ideology, Theory, and Policy.* New Haven: Yale University Press, 1990. *As its name implies, this volume offer an account of Nazi institutions and economic policies, but its focus is on the underlying ideological and theoretical framework.*

Erhard, Ludwig. *Prosperity through Competition.* London: Thames and Hudson, 1958. *A fascinating, if somewhat self-serving, first-hand account of the German miracle in the making.*

Giersch, Herbert, Karl-Heinz, Pasque, and Holger Schmieding. *The Fading Miracle: Four Decades of Market Economy in Germany.* Cambridge: Cambridge University Press, 1992. *Surveys the period between 1945 and 1990 from a strongly pro-market perspective.*

Heathfield, David F., ed. *The Economics of Codetermination.* London: Macmillan, 1977. *A compendium of papers comparing German codetermination with similar systems in other countries.*

Markovits, Andrei S. *The Political Economy of West Germany: Modell Deutschland.* New York: Praeger, 1982. *Written by a team of economists, historians, and political scientists, several chapters analyze the role of the government in the German economic system and its applicability to other countries.*

Nathan, Otto. *The Nazi Economic System: Germany's Mobilization for War.* Durham, N.C.: Duke University Press, 1944. *Provides a clear and comprehensive description of the institutional structure of the Nazi system and its influence on the mobilization effort.*

Nicholls, A. J. *Freedom with Responsibility: The Social Market in Germany, 1918–1963.* Oxford: Clarendon Press, 1994. *An authoritative account of the intellectual and practical origins of social market policies. In the preface, the author briefly discusses the implications of the German experience after World War II for transitional economics today.*

Organization for Economics Cooperation and Development, *OECD Economic Surveys: Germany.* Paris, annual. *An annual survey of macroeconomic policy.*

Rogers, Rosemarie, ed. *Guests Come to Stay: The Effects of European Labor Migration on Sending and Receiving Countries.* Boulder, Colo.: Westview Press,

1985. *Includes three chapters on the role of guest workers in Germany, other chapters on France, Sweden, and Switzerland, and four chapters on the sending countries.*

Sinn, Gerlinde, and Hans-Werner Sinn. *Jumpstart: The Economic Unification of Germany.* Cambridge, Mass.: The MIT Press, 1992. *With an excellent blend of institutional information, advanced economic analysis, and good writing, this is one of the best books available on German unification.*

Smyser, W. R. *The Economy of United Germany: Colossus at the Crossroads.* New York: St. Martin's Press, 1992. *This may be the best general survey of the German economy available in English at the current moment.*

Thimm, Alfred L. *The False Promise of Codetermination.* Lexington, Mass.: Lexington Books, 1980. *Argues that the system of codetermination has contributed little to the German success and that the system has generated more discord than harmony.*

INTERNET RESOURCES

Basic Law of the Federal Republic of Germany
(Including 1990 amendments)
gopher://jurix.jura.uni-sb.de:70/00/jur.internet/const/gg.eng

The Berlin Bear
(Berlin and Brandenburg Information)
http://www.berlin-bear.de/

Der Spiegel
http://muenchen.bda.de/bda/int/spiegel/

Die Welt
http://www.welt.de/

Eastern German Studies Group
http://www.calvin.edu/cas/egsg/

Frankfurt Money Strategist
http://www.fmstrategist.com/fms/

German Institute for Economic Research (DIW)
(Including their Economic Bulletin)
http://www.diw-berlin.de/

Germany: Reference Page
http://www.chemie.fu-berlin.de/adressen/brd.html

International Community
http://www.berlin-bear.de/IC/

Social democratic Party of Germany (SPD)
http://www.spd.de/

France

12

FRANCE: PLANNING IN THE MARKET ECONOMY

> Our government is entirely arranged on a new system,
> which is the absolute will of the ministers in each
> department; everything that shared that authority has been
> abrogated. Thus, the court resembles all that the heart is in
> the human body; everything passes and re-passes through
> it several times before circulating to the body's extremities.
>
> —MARQUIS D'ARGENSON, *CONSIDERATIONS SUR LE*
> *GOUVERNEMENT DE LA FRANCE*, 1672

> France was always very different from other capitalist
> countries, so different indeed that it should perhaps never
> have been included in any list of them.
>
> —PETER WILES, *ECONOMIC INSTITUTIONS*
> *COMPARED*, 1977

rance is a land of paradox, conflict, and contradiction. Parisians are admired throughout the world for their charm and diplomacy, but derided for their arrogance. Since the time of Jean Monnet, French statesmen have been the most important architects of European economic unification, but in 1992 their countrymen nearly rejected the Maastricht treaty.

France produced many of the great champions of individual liberties and limited government, including Jean-Jacques Rousseau, François Quesnay, Jean-Baptiste Say, and other philosophers, revolutionaries, and economists. Their slogans are still familiar: *"laissez faire, laissez passer"* ("let it be, let it go") and *"liberté, égalité, fraternité!"* ("liberty, equality, fraternity!").

THE ENVIRONMENT

The actual practice of French leadership, however, created a very different vocabulary. Policies resembling those of a certain seventeenth-century finance minister, including mercantilist trade controls and creation of state enterprises, came to be known as *Colbertism*. During the nineteenth century, *Bonapartism* came to represent an elite form of military autocracy.

After World War II, *Gaullism* was the name given to a system of French nationalism and state intervention in a broader framework of private enterprise. "We absolutely reject the old *laissez faire, laissez passer,*" declared de Gaulle, "and we wish that in our century it should be the Republic that drives the economic functioning of France."[1] Thus, Gaullism was associated with a number of other French concepts, including, *étatisme* (state authority), *dirigisme* (direction, interventionism), and *elitisme.*

Struck by the contrast between libertarian rhetoric and authoritarian reality, Thomas Carlyle described France as "a long despotism, tempered by epigrams."[2] Carlyle's description was a bit harsh; French authoritarianism was also tempered by other considerations. First, the actions of the government were made more reasonable, less arbitrary, by its devotion to the rule of law. The French preoccupation with law found perhaps its highest expression in the Code Napoléon, enacted in 1804 (civil) and 1810 (criminal), which became a model for legal reform in many other countries. Unlike the Anglo-American systems of common law and case law, which allow judges to rule with greater flexibility, the French system of code law is designed to protect defendants from "diverse judicial temperaments."[3]

Authoritarianism was also tempered by the professionalism of the French bureaucracy. Generals Bonaparte and de Gaulle established elite educational institutions to identify and train civil servants, preparing them to operate a powerful state apparatus with relative efficiency (see "Educating the French Elite," p. 351). According to opinion polls, the French still consider their public servants to be "bureaucratic," but also "competent."[4]

Today, of course, France is an advanced democratic society whose citizens enjoy a full range of civil liberties. Centuries of economic and political reform, international competition, and European integration have modified the most extreme aspects of "French exceptionalism," but the legacies of autocracy and elitism have not entirely disappeared.

French authoritarianism evidently arose from efforts to preserve order in a divided country. Through much of its history, France was shaken by clashes between church, state, military, aristocracy, industrial elite, *bourgeoisie*

---

[1]De Gaulle's *Discours et Messages,* quoted in Andrew Knapp, *Gaullism Since De Gaulle* (Aldershot: Dartmouth, 1994), 425.

[2]In the opening of his *History of the French Revolution* (1837).

[3]William Safran, *The French Polity,* 4th ed. (White Plains, N.Y.: Longman, 1995), 277. The conflict between true justice and narrow application of the law is personified in the character of Inspector Javert in Victor Hugo's classic, *Les Misérables.*

[4]Survey by Brule Ville Associes, reported in *Index to International Public Opinion,* 1993–1994 (Westport, Conn.: Greenwood Press, 1995), 148.

Educating the French Elite

During his 1995 campaign for the French presidency, Jacques Chirac blamed many of the nation's problems on "an omnipotent caste" of bureaucrats "cut off from reality" who seem "more talented in flattery than decisionmaking." Lionel Jospin, the Socialist candidate, claimed that Chirac and his Gaullist comrades were opposed to new ideas because they were all "trained in the same school."

The French public scoffed at all these comments, knowing that Chirac and Jospin both were *énarques*—graduates of the prestigious École Nationale d'Administration (ENA). After winning the presidency, Chirac appointed *énarques* to fill the prime minister's office and to head nearly three-quarters of all cabinet-level ministries. The ranks of ENA alumni also include 33 members of the National Assembly, including its chairman, the governor of the central bank, former president Valery Giscard d'Estaing, and a dozen former prime ministers. In the business sector, more than 40 of the country's 200 largest companies are led by *énarques*, and a similar number are led by graduates of École Polytechnique, the other leading *grande école*.

This is an amazing network of elite dominance, far more powerful in France than the networks of Harvard graduates in the United States or Oxford-Cambridge alumni in the United Kingdom. All this, despite the fact that ENA has existed only 50 years, enrolls only 100 students each year, and has a total pool of only six thousand graduates.

General de Gaulle created ENA in 1945, immediately after the fall of the Vichy collaborationist regime, to select and train a new corps of skilled civil servants. The school offers a demanding 27-month postgraduate curriculum, including a mixture of academic studies, training in public protocol, etiquette, and at least two foreign languages, and a high-level internship. To support the system of indicative planning, *énarques* are trained to take a long view in their economic analyses.

During the 1950s, 1960s, and 1970s, when France maintained relatively high rates of economic growth and low rates of unemployment, the civil servants claimed their share of credit. Their administrative skills, their pragmatic, nonideological approach, and their collegial relationships provided a stable and professional framework for policy formation.

In recent years, as economic performance has deteriorated, the civil servants and their elite educational system have attracted criticism. The ENA, according to its detractors, produces graduates who are too white, too male, and too disconnected from the French population. The homogeneity of the student body, they say, breeds a narrow view of reality, discourages originality, and invites political corruption. Nevertheless, according to ENA director Raymond-Francois Le Bris, "An

Continued

CONTINUED

affirmative action program that set quotas for women or other minorities would be totally against our constitution."

According to its critics, ENA has adjusted slowly to an environment of market-oriented international competition; it still prepares its graduates to lead programs of state-regulated national development. Fearing the loss of their privileged status, *énarques* have sometimes slowed the privatization of industry, and have prevented foreign investments that jeopardized domestic ownership and control of French companies.

One thing is quite clear. The professional civil servants have provided stability (some would call it inertia) to the French political and economic system while nominal leadership of the country has passed between Gaullists and Socialists. According to survey data, members of the French elite believe there is no such thing as management of the Left or the Right, there is only good or bad management. The winds of politics may cause changes at the top of society, says Jean Grenier, director-general of Eutelsat, but "underneath, the rest remained the same, and there was no political pressure to change anything in management."

SOURCES: William Drozdiak, "Alumnus Chirac Leads Charge Against Elite Paris School," *The Washington Post*, October 14, 1995, A17; "The Soft-Shoe Shuffle," *The Economist*, November 25, 1995, S14; "France's School for the Elite Turns 50," Reuters, October 4, 1995; Thierry Leveque, "School for French Pols in Midlife Crisis," *Chicago Tribune*, October 1, 1995, C16; "France's Social Capitalism in Crisis," *Swiss Review of World Affairs*, January 3, 1996, 1; and Vivien A. Schmidt, "An End to French Exceptionalism? The Transformation of Business under Mitterrand," in *The Mitterrand Era: Policy Alternatives and Political Mobilization in France* (New York: New York University Press, 1996), 125–136.

(middle class), *prolétariat* (industrial working class), and agricultural peasantry. Between the beginning of the French Revolution in 1789 and the establishment of the Fifth Republic in 1958, no less than 16 constitutions were enacted, establishing nearly every conceivable type of regime. The Fourth Republic, established in 1946, had 20 cabinets in 12 years—a new government every eight months!

Greater stability was established in 1958, when a new constitution created the Fifth Republic. Written under the firm direction of General Charles de Gaulle, the constitution provides for a relatively centralized system of government. Unlike the American, German, and Canadian federations, in which power is geographically dispersed, the French central government exercises strong control over local authorities.[5] Unlike the Fourth Republic, which granted more authority to Parliament, the Fifth Republic has been said to

---

[5]Since 1981, a series of reforms have initiated a transfer of power from the central government to local authorities, but the significance of these reforms is still a matter of disagreement. See Safran, *The French Polity*, 260–268.

provide for an "elected monarchy."[6] The president is able to appoint the prime minister without submitting to parliamentary approval, and can dissolve the National Assembly (lower house of parliament) at any time and call for new elections. Furthermore, the president can submit legislative proposals directly to the public by referendum and, in cases of national emergency, can rule by decree.[7]

After 1958, France was governed for many years by coalitions of Gaullists and other relatively conservative parties; the cabinet was reshuffled only 11 times in 23 years. The Socialist Party, which participated in governing coalitions during the 1950s, was forced into opposition.

In 1981, a Socialist-Communist coalition led by François Mitterrand gained control of the presidency and the parliament, and introduced leftist programs of nationalization, regulation, taxation, and expenditure. When a balance of payments crisis forced Mitterrand to adopt an austerity program in 1983, the communists left his government in protest.

In 1986, a coalition of the centrists (UDF) and neo-Gaullists (RPR) regained control of the parliament, and socialist President Mitterrand was forced to share power in **cohabitation** with Prime Minister Jacques Chirac of the RPR. The socialists reclaimed the prime minister's office after the 1988 elections, but lost it again in 1993, forcing President Mitterrand into another cohabitation with RPR prime minister, Edouard Balladur. In 1995, Jacques Chirac won the French presidency, and his RPR-UDF coalition consolidated control of the Prime Minister's office, the Cabinet, the National Assembly, the Senate, and all but one of the 22 regional governments.

INDICATIVE PLANNING

During the first half of the twentieth century, France passed through a long period of economic stagnation and military disruption. Between 1913 and 1950, real GDP grew by an average rate of only 1 percent per year. After prewar stagnation and wartime destruction, France emerged from World War II in a state of economic and technological backwardness. National income per capita, which had amounted to more than 80 percent of the American level in 1933, fell to about half of the U.S. level by the end of the war. The average age of machine tools was 6 years in the United States and 9 years in England, but 25 years in France. There was one tractor for every 43 farmers in the United States, but only one for every 200 farmers in France.

Despite its legacy of backwardness and stagnation, France achieved one of the best records of economic growth in the industrialized world during the 1950s, 1960s, and 1970s (Table 12.1). Correctly or not, many observers attributed this turn-around to the system of indicative planning that was

---

[6]*Financial Times,* April 7, 1995, 2.

[7]The French presidency served as a model for the farmers of the 1993 Russian constitution, which extended strong powers to President Yeltsin.

■ **TABLE 12.1**

RELATIVE PERFORMANCE OF THE FRENCH ECONOMY, 1951–1996

	1951–1960	1961–1970	1971–1980	1981–1990	1991–1996
Average annual growth of real GDP (%)					
France	4.8	5.5	4.0	2.4	1.2
OECD Average	4.2	5.1	3.2	2.8	2.0
Average annual consumer price inflation (%)					
France	5.7	3.8	9.7	6.4	2.2
OECD Average	3.3	3.9	9.1	8.1	4.9
Unemployment rate (%)					
France	2.1	1.7	4.1	9.3	11.3
OECD Average*	3.6*	2.8*	4.5	7.3	7.5

*Based on data for Canada, France, Germany, Italy, Japan, Sweden, the United Kingdom, and the United States.

SOURCES: *OECD Economic Outlook,* December 1986 and June 1997; World Bank, *World Tables,* 1980 and 1995; Irving Kravis, Alan Heston, and Robert Summers, *World Product and Income* (Baltimore: Johns Hopkins University Press, 1982), 343; and Angus Maddison, *Phases of Capitalist Development* (Oxford: Oxford University Press, 1982), appendices A, C, and E.

established after World War II. Based on the French example, several other countries adopted similar planning programs.

Jean Monnet, director of the Commissariat for Armaments, Supplies, and Reconstruction during the final days of the war, concluded that a national plan was needed for modernization and that all segments of French society would have to make additional sacrifices to rebuild the capital stock. Thus, Monnet proposed the creation of a Planning Commissariat and insisted that planning must be a cooperative enterprise. As he told General de Gaulle in 1945:

The French economy can't be transformed unless the French people take part in its transformation. And when I say "the French people," I don't mean an abstract entity: I mean trade unionists, industrialists, and civil servants. Everyone must be associated in an investment and modernization plan.[8]

The **Planning Commissariat** was established in 1946 and Monnet was its first director. With his successors, Etienne Hirsch and Pierre Masse, Monnet established the basic principles of French planning. First and foremost, indicative planning was never meant to replace the market system, but to improve its operation. Planning was intended to improve the flow of information between participants in the market and to encourage risk-averse businesspeople to base their investment decisions on more optimistic assumptions.

---

[8]Jean Monnet, *Memoirs* (Garden City, N. Y.: Doubleday, 1978), 234–235.

Second, to emphasize the limited role of planning, the Planning Commissariat was never allowed to become a large organization. For its headquarters, Monnet selected a small building on Rue de Martignac, in the university district of Paris, that could not accommodate a large bureaucracy. The Commissariat has the same address today. Aside from a period between 1981 and 1983, when the Socialist government created a Ministry of Planning, the Commissariat has always operated directly under the Prime Minister's office. At its apparent peak in 1987, the Commissariat had a staff of about 180 economists, statisticians, and sociologists—a small number in comparison with a government ministry, and even smaller in comparison with the thousands who worked for the Soviet State Planning Commission.

A third characteristic of French economic plans: Compliance with plan targets is not mandatory, even for public enterprises. Unlike Soviet-style directive plans, French plans never include detailed production targets for individual companies. At most, they include quantitative projections for broad product and industrial groups.

Although not compulsory, compliance with French plans has been encouraged in several ways. The plan is supposed to be a self-fulfilling prophesy. That is, it ideally provides a consensus view, based on input from all segments of society, of the most probable and desirable path for the economy over the plan period (usually five years). Hence, it is ideally in everyone's self-interest to act in accordance with the plan.

The government also is able to encourage plan compliance through its influence over nationalized industries and through its monetary, fiscal, and regulatory powers. Since 1982 the central government has concluded enforceable "plan contracts" with regional governments and enterprises, providing financial aid or other support in exchange for performance of tasks included in the plan.

PLANNING INSTITUTIONS AND PROCEDURE

We noted that the Planning Commissariat, attached to the Prime Minister's office, is responsible for coordinating the planning process. Monnet preferred this arrangement because "no Ministerial post would have offered as much scope as the undefinable position of Planning Commissioner," and with a small staff "no one will be jealous, and we shall be left in peace . . . we'll get others to do the work."[9]

As Monnet proposed, much of the planning work was done outside of the Commissariat by the so-called **modernization commissions,** numbering between 25 and 30 during the 1950s and 1970s. These included "vertical" commissions, which prepared plans for individual sectors in agriculture and industry, and "horizontal" commissions, which studied problems that cut across all sectors, such as the balance of payments, human resources, and the input-output balance of the economy. Each commission included representatives from business, labor, and the government.

---

[9]Ibid., 241.

For the Fifth Plan (1966–1970), a group of Regional Development Commissions was created to represent the needs of the provinces, and for the Sixth Plan (1971–1975), several social commissions were created, dealing with such issues as health, education, and housing. In 1982, most of these institutions were reorganized into a National Planning Commission, with nine working committees (*commissions de travail*) and about 40 subcommittees, but still including representatives from business, labor, the central government, the regions, and other "social partners."

Several agencies perform support and advisory roles in the formulation of plans. Statistical research and support is provided by the National Institute of Statistics and Economic Research (INSEE) and the forecasting office of the Ministry of Finance. The Economic and Social Council, a constitutionally established advisory body with representatives from business, labor, government, and academia, reviews plan documents as they are formulated. Since the 1960s, an important role has been played by Delegations for Spatial Planning and Regional Action (DATARs), composed of civil servants appointed by the Prime Minister who work with local and regional agencies on matters related to land utilization, urban planning, and the environment. Taken together, as many as 5,000 people have been involved at a time in the planning commissions, councils, and study groups.

The procedure used to formulate and approve plans has changed continuously through the years, but works roughly as follows. First, the Planning Commissariat and statistical agencies prepare an options report, which outlines the macroeconomic strategies available to the government and their expected influences on economic growth, inflation, unemployment, and the balance of payments. The report is discussed and debated in the governmental ministries, the Economic and Social Council, and the National Planning Commission, and the options are adjusted and revised, until one is chosen and approved—sometimes by a vote in Parliament.

Based on the selected macroeconomic framework, the working groups of the National Planning Commission and the DATARs prepare output and investment programs for their individual industries and regions. These are checked and adjusted for consistency, and the final draft of the plan is compiled by the Planning Commissariat. In the end, Parliament may vote to accept the plan as a whole, but it must vote on the specific provisions of the plan that involve public expenditures.

THE PLANNING RECORD

The objectives stated in the French national plans and the role of the planning process have gradually changed during the postwar era. The Monnet Plan (1947–1951, extended to 1952–1953) was a rather simple program of economic reconstruction and modernization, with large shares of investment directed to six high-priority sectors: electricity, coal, steel, agricultural machinery, transport, and cement. In the spirit of postwar cooperation, everyone from the business community to the Communist-dominated labor unions worked together to formulate and execute the plan, and the government used its powers to encourage compliance. For these reasons, and with the help of Marshall Plan aid from the United States, the Monnet Plan was quite successful.

Beginning with the Second Plan (1954–1957), the scope of planning expanded to encompass all sectors of the economy. The Fourth Plan (1962–1965) was the first to address social and regional issues. A growing number of people were involved in the planning process, and econometric methods made the plans more technically sophisticated.

At the same time, the whole enterprise grew less consensual. Labor leaders and small businessmen complained of unequal treatment on the modernization commissions. They claimed the meetings were dominated by civil servants and executives of large companies, former schoolmates in the *grandes écoles*. According to one observer, "when a trade union representative arrives in a modernization commission he feels like an uninvited guest at a family reunion."[10] The CGT, a large labor confederation with ties to the Communist Party, participated in the First Plan, but withdrew when it became clear that indicative planning would not transform France into a socialist society.

After Monnet left the Planning Commissariat in 1950 to direct the European Coal and Steel Community, the government demonstrated little fidelity to the plans. In 1952, Prime Minister Antoine Pinay replaced the Monnet Plan in its final year with a program to slow inflation. In 1953–1954, the Second Plan was overshadowed by an Eighteen Month Plan for Economic Expansion, formulated by Finance Minister Edgar Faure. The Third Plan, originally programmed for 1958–1965, was quickly rendered obsolete by the Algerian War, a balance of payments crisis, and creation of the Fifth Republic; it was replaced with a contractionary Interim Plan for 1960–1961. The Fourth Plan (1962–1965) was effectively replaced by a 1963 Stabilization Plan, and the Sixth (1971–1975) and Seventh (1976–1980) Plans were disrupted by unexpected hikes of international oil prices.

When Mitterrand and his Socialists assumed power in 1981, they immediately abandoned the Eighth Plan (1981–1984) and replaced it with a more expansionary Interim Plan for 1982–1983. However, when a balance of payments crisis developed in 1983, work began on a Ninth Plan (1985–1988), based on more conservative assumptions (Table 12.2). Its implementation was disrupted, in turn, by the 1986 elections, which established the first "cohabitation" between Socialist President Mitterrand and RPR Prime Minister Chirac. The new planning minister, Herve de Charette, declared that the Ninth Plan was dead: "the Titanic without the orchestra."[11]

In 1986, former president Giscard d'Estaing declared that France "no longer has need of administrative planning," and Prime Minister Chirac considered closing the doors of the Planning Commissariat. In the end, Chirac decided that the country still needed the planning process to organize

---

[10]Stephen S. Cohen, *Modern Capitalist Planning: The French Model* (Cambridge: Harvard University Press, 1969), 66.

[11]David Housego, "French Planners Heave a Sigh of Relief," *Financial Times*, February 10, 1987, 3.

■ **TABLE 12.2**

FRANCE: ECONOMIC PLANS AND PERFORMANCE
(ANNUAL PERCENTAGE GROWTH OF GDP)

Plan	Years	Planned	Actual
First "Monnet"	1947–1953	*	7.1
Second	1954–1957	4.4	5.4
Third	1958–1961	4.7	3.8
Fourth	1962–1965	5.5	5.8
Fifth	1966–1970	5.7	5.9
Sixth	1971–1975	5.9	3.7
Seventh	1976–1980	5.7	3.3
Eighth	1981–1984	2.7–3.2	1.4
Ninth	1985–1988	1.6–2.2	2.8
Tenth	1989–1992	n.a.	2.2
Eleventh	1993–1997	1.8–2.8	1.5

*No specific growth target for GDP stated in the plan.

research and public discussion on important long-term issues such as social security reform and European unification. Still, Chirac trimmed the budget of the Commissariat, reduced its staff, and asked it to focus its attention on a smaller number of high-priority goals.

The Tenth Plan was prepared for a four-year time horizon (1989–1992) to focus attention and resources on projects that were needed to prepare France for implementation of the Maastricht Treaty, beginning in 1993. The Eleventh Plan returned to a five-year (1993–1997) format, and gave special attention to regional economic development, and its contribution to reduction of unemployment. Each of the nation's 22 regions prepared its own plan by the end of 1992, and these were used during the following year as a basis to prepare plan contracts and the national plan.[12]

HAS PLANNING HELPED?

Considering the unwillingness of the French government to stick to its plans, one begins to wonder if this is a useful exercise. An indicative plan is supposed to be a self-fulfilling prophesy, but why would a private corporation voluntarily comply with a plan that has lost its credibility? Although the plans provided fairly accurate forecasts of economic growth in the 1950s and 1960s, they have often provided little more than wishful thinking during the 1970s, 1980s, and 1990s.

---

[12]"Regions Prepare the 11th National Plan," *Les Echos,* July 21, 1992; and Veronique Maurus, "Le Plan Retrouve 1993–1997: La Cohesion Sociale ou le Chaos," *Le Monde,* April 20, 1993, 28–29.

Defenders of French planning admit that the forecasts have not been accurate, but claim they are better than the guesses of individual economists. A government study during the 1960s found that managers of large enterprises were usually aware of the plans' growth projections, and most reported that the plans significantly influenced their investment decisions.[13]

Many proponents would agree with Pierre Masse (a former director of the Planning Commissariat) that "the planning process is more meaningful than the plan itself."[14] In other words, the success or failure of economic planning should be judged not by the fulfillment of quantitative production forecasts, but by the value of communication and cooperation stimulated between representatives of business, labor, the national government, and the regional bodies.

In recent years, French planners have drawn attention to a number of emerging national issues, including the financial crisis of the social security system, and the need to establish a coordinated system of business intelligence.[15] Some have questioned the value of economic planning, but French presidents and prime ministers, conservative and socialist, have decided to preserve it. True, the planning bureaucracy has been streamlined in recent years, and has been instructed to concentrate on a few high-priority issues, but these actions only seem to reaffirm the original principles of indicative planning, formulated by Jean Monnet and his associates more than 50 years ago.

INDUSTRIAL ORGANIZATION

Traditionally, three features have characterized the French industrial structure: (1) companies in the private sector are relatively small; (2) the nationalized sector is extensive, and includes relatively large companies; and (3) the entire system is dominated by a managerial elite, and by networks of cross-shareholdings and stable investors.

THE PRIVATE SECTOR

French companies in the private sector are generally smaller than their competitors in other major industrial countries. About 80 percent of all manufacturing companies in France are "small" (have between 20 and 99 employees), compared with about 70 percent in the United States and Germany.[16] Elf

---

[13]The findings of J. J. Carre and associates, whose work is discussed in Martin Cave and Paul Hare, *Alternative Approaches to Economic Planning* (New York: St. Martin's Press, 1981), 81–82.

[14]Quoted in J. R. Hough, *The French Economy* (New York: Holmes and Meier, 1982), 123.

[15]France Sees 28 Billion Welfare Deficit in 1996," Reuter News Service, November 7, 1994; and "Economic War as Seen by France," *Intelligence Newsletter*, April 13, 1995.

[16]European Economic Community, *Structure and Activity of Industry: Data by Size of Enterprise—1988/1989/1990* (Paris, 1994), 146; and U.S. Department of Commerce, Bureau of the Census, *Statistical Abstract of the United States, 1994* (Washington, D.C.: USGPO, 1994), 546. Also, see Kenneth D. George and T. S. Ward, *The Structure of Industry in the EEC* (Cambridge: Cambridge University Press, 1975), 30.

Aquitane, the largest private company in France, was ranked forty-sixth among the world's largest corporations in 1995, falling behind companies in eight other countries.[17]

That French companies are usually smaller than their competitors in Japan, the United States, and Germany may be explained simply by the fact that France has a smaller domestic market.[18] To explain the fact that French companies are smaller in certain categories than their British, Dutch, Italian, Korean, and Swiss counterparts, we would need to consider differences in financial markets, regulatory systems, and other determinants of competitive advantage. Part of the French penchant for smaller size, though, seems to be cultural. President Chirac recently launched a crusade against supermarkets, praising small stores and neighborhood cafes for their contributions to "humane" living, and for maintaining jobs. A bill introduced by the Trade Ministry in 1996 would require the permission of a panel of town mayors and trade representatives before a food store can be opened with an area larger than 3,300 square feet (307 square meters).[19]

During the 1950s, 1960s, and early 1970s, the French government was concerned that its small firms would not be able to take full advantage of economies of scale and compete effectively on the world market. Thus, for a time, the government provided loans and tax incentives to facilitate mergers, and promoted development of one or two large firms in each industry, the so-called **national champions**.[20] Support for industrial concentration had a high priority in the Fifth (1966–1970) and Sixth (1971–1975) Plans.

After the oil price shocks and macroeconomic disturbances of the mid-1970s, the national champion policy was reexamined. The government decided that smaller firms were more flexible, more innovative, and better able to respond to structural shifts in the international economy. Thus, the preferential treatment of larger companies subsided.[21] The proportion of the industrial labor force working in establishments with over 500 employees, which increased rapidly between 1966 and 1975, has subsequently declined (Table 12.3).

---

[17]"The Global 500," *Fortune*, August 5, 1996, F1.

[18]The exceptions to this generalization are found in the building materials, metal products, engineering, and specialty retailing sectors, where French companies—Saint-Gobain, Péchiney, Cie Générale des Eaux, and Carrefour, respectively—are ranked first in the world. The first two of these companies, however, have spent much of their lives in the nationalized sector. See international rankings for 39 sectors in "The Global 500," F15–F26.

[19]"Small Stores Are Beautiful for France's Chirac," Reuter News Service, April 29, 1996.

[20]For information on the rising level of merger activity between the 1950s and 1970s, see François Caron, *An Economic History of Modern France* (New York: Columbia University Press, 1979), 301–303.

[21]William James Adams, *Restructuring the French Economy* (Washington, D.C.: The Brookings Institution, 1989), 54. The national champion policy surfaced again for a short time in 1992, during the administration of Prime Minister Edith Cresson. See Ronald Tiersky, *France in the New Europe* (Belmont, Calif.: Wadsworth Publishing, 1994), 183.

■ TABLE 12.3

FRANCE: DISTRIBUTION OF INDUSTRIAL EMPLOYEES BY
SIZE OF ESTABLISHMENT, 1906–1990

Percentage of Industrial Labor Force
Employed in Establishments with:

Year	1–10 Workers	11–500 Workers	Over 500 Workers	Total
1906	32	49	19	100
1931	20	53	27	100
1954	16	57	27	100
1966	13	61	26	100
1975	6	58	36	100
1983	8	60	32	100
1990	8	61	31	100

SOURCES: 1906–1966—Francois Caron, *An Economic History of Modern France* (New York: Columbia University Press, 1979), 280; and 1975–1990—*Annuaire Statistique de la France* (Paris: INSEE, various years).

NATIONALIZED INDUSTRIES

France has long and extensive experience with nationalized industries. Finance Minister Colbert made arrangements for state ownership of the Gobelins royal furnishings company in 1667, and the state tobacco monopoly was established during the rule of Napoleon. Other companies were taken over during the 1930s and after World War II, including half of the nation's banks. The largest nationalization program in the postwar Western world was carried out in 1982, when the socialist government led by President Mitterrand acquired 39 banks, two financial holding companies, and nine major industrial groups at a cost of some $8 billion. The state owned 13 of the 20 largest firms in France, and held a controlling share of many other companies. State holdings accounted for more than 29 percent of sales, 22 percent of employment, and 52 percent of investment in the industrial sector, and state-owned banks controlled about 90 percent of the nation's bank deposits[22] (Table 12.4).

To avoid any suggestion of a Bolshevik-style confiscation of property, the Mitterrand government paid considerably more than prevailing market prices to purchase shares of the nationalized companies. These expenditures, together with other socialist programs, caused a serious balance of payments crisis in 1982, preventing Mitterrand from pressing his nationalization program any farther.

---

[22]Estimates of the Ministry of Industry, reported in *OECD Economic Survey 1982/1983: France*, 50.

■ TABLE 12.4

PRINCIPAL NATIONALIZATIONS AND PRIVATIZATIONS OF FRENCH ENTERPRISES

Company	Sector	Year Nationalized	Year Privatized
Aerospatiale	Aerospace	1936	Pending
Air France	Airline	1933, 1945	Pending
Alcatel-Alsthom	Electrical Engineering	1982	1987
Banque Hervet	Bank	1982	Pending
Banque Nationale de Paris	Bank	1945	1993
Caisse Centrale de Reassurance	Insurance	1946	Pending
Caisse Nationale de Prevoyance	Insurance	1868	Pending
Cie Financiére de Suez	Diversified Financial	n.a.	1987
Cie Générale Maritime	Transport	1933	1996
Crédit Lyonnais	Bank	1945	Pending
Électricité de France	Electrical Power	1946	Not Pending
Elf-Aquitaine	Oil	1941	1994
France Telecom	Telecommunications	n.a.	Pending
Gaz de France	Gas	1946	Not Pending
Groupe Bull	Computers	1975, 1982	1995
Groupe des Assurances Nationales	Insurance	1968	Pending
Matra	Defense/Electronics	1982	1988
Péchiney	Aluminum/Packaging	1982	1995
Postes et Télécommunications	Postal Service	n.a.	Not Pending
Renault	Automobiles	1945	1994
Rhóne Poulenc	Chemicals	1982	1993
Saint-Gobain	Glass/Packaging	1982	1987
SEITA	Tobacco/Matches	1946	Pending
Société Marseilleise de Crédit	Bank	1982	Pending
SNCF	Railways	1937	Not Pending
SNECMA	Aerospace Engines	1945	Pending
Thomson	Electronics	1982	Pending
Union des Assurances de Paris	Insurance	1968	1994
Usinor Sacilor	Steel	1981	1995

SOURCES: William James Adams, *Restructuring the French Economy* (Washington, D.C.: Brookings Institution, 1989), 60–61; *Financial Times,* June 22, 1993, 4; *The Wall Street Journal,* October 2, 1995, R12; and recent press reports.

■ TABLE 12.5

SHARE OF STATE-OWNED ENTERPRISES
IN ECONOMIC ACTIVITY, 1978–1991

	Percentage of Gross Domestic Product		Percentage of Gross Domestic Investment	
	1978–1985	1986–1991	1978–1985	1986–1991
France	10.7	10.0	15.2	11.6
Germany	7.1	n.a.	11.6	n.a.
Japan	n.a.	n.a.	10.2	5.5
Italy	6.7	5.6	12.2	12.9
Spain	4.0	n.a.	11.7	8.6
Sweden	n.a.	n.a.	29.5	17.5
United Kingdom	5.9	3.0	15.1	5.6
United States	1.3	1.0	3.7	3.7

SOURCE: World Bank *Bureaucrats in Business: The Economics and Politics of Government Ownership* (Oxford: Oxford University Press, 1995), Tables A.1 and A.3.

Jacques Chirac gained control of the prime minister's office in 1986, creating the first RPR-Socialist "cohabitation" government. Chirac announced his intention to return 65 nationalized companies to private ownership over a five-year period, potentially raising $50 billion for the treasury.[23] Chirac moved quickly, and his program was initially quite successful; the sales of Alcatel-Alsthom, the Saint-Gobain group, and eight other companies attracted large numbers of investors. In October 1987, however, stock markets crashed throughout the industrial world, forcing Chirac to postpone the remainder of his program. Then, in 1988, Mitterrand won a new seven-year term as president on a compromise platform that became popularly known as "Ni-ni"—neither additional nationalization nor additional privatization. Thus, while other European countries continued their programs of privatization, the role of state enterprises in France remained relatively stable (Table 12.5).

Parliamentary elections in 1983 returned RPR leaders to power in a second "cohabitation" government, and Chirac's victory in the 1995 presidential election, together with RPR and UDF success in parliamentary elections, returned the country to unified conservative leadership for the first time since 1981. Thus, an impressive list of companies, including three of the country's four largest—Elf-Aquitaine, Union des Assurances de Paris, and Renault—were privatized between 1993 and 1995, and a long list of privatizations is pending.

It is difficult to make a general statement about the actual performance of French state-owned enterprises. Some have performed quite well, and others have been fiscal disasters. Let us consider two examples.

---

[23]OECD Economic Survey 1986/87: France, 35.

Société, Nationale des Chemins de Fer Français (SNCF). The French are justly proud of their state railway service, SNCF, which was created in 1937 by merging two public and five private railway companies. SNCF ties together an otherwise fragmented country, and serves many routes with sleek TGV high-speed trains. In the spirit of national unity, passengers pay the same fare per kilometer traveled, regardless of cost, and money-losing lines (about half of the routes in the system) are never closed. All of this comes at a high cost. SNCF loses more money than any other enterprise in France—more than $2 billion in 1995, despite $10 billion of subsidies. Its debts at the end of 1995 amounted to about $37 billion.[24]

France Telecom (FT). The fourth-largest company in the world in the technologically sophisticated industry, FT posted a profit in 1994 of $1.8 billion. Despite its nationalized status, FT has been active in foreign telecommunications markets for decades, and maintains offices in major cities throughout Europe, North America, Latin America, and the Asia-Pacific region. FT offered the first commercial ISDN (integrated services digital network) service in the world, and operates the world's largest data network. In 1996, FT joined with Sprint (United States) and Deutsche Telekom (Germany) to form Global One, which is designed to compete with other alliances in the dynamic market for global telecommunications.[25]

PUBLIC AND PRIVATE MANAGEMENT

The examples of SNCF and FT make it clear that the circumstances, fortunes, and prospects of French state-owned companies can differ considerably. Some of these enterprises can be privatized with little adjustment, and others require major restructuring before they can be exposed to external competition. In many cases, though, the organizational objectives and management styles of firms in the private and public sectors are quite similar. Thus, programs of nationalization and privatization have often caused little change in the behavior and performance of French companies.

As we have noted, France has an unusually homogeneous pool of managerial talent, trained in the same elite schools and following similar career paths. Managers of large private companies often have backgrounds in the civil service, and they customarily retain close links to the government throughout their professional lives. Managers of state enterprises are often allowed to work rather independently, with little pressure to support state policies or ideologies. According to a former official in Mitterrand's socialist administration, "At first, we had several priorities for nationalized companies, but now the priority is profits; it's the only way to get really efficient management."[26]

---

[24]Thomas Kamm and David Levin, "Strikes in France May Pose a Challenge for European Union," *The Wall Street Journal,* December 22, 1995, A6.

[25]See company briefings and news releases at the France Telecom Web site, <http://www.francetelecom.com>.

[26]*The Wall Street Journal,* April 18, 1985, 1, 22.

Cozy relationships between directors of state-owned and private companies are also promoted by networks of cross-holdings of corporate stock, organized around groups of **stable investors** *(noyaux dur)*. When French companies have been privatized, the government has frequently provided preferential access to large domestic corporations. Thus, when Elf-Aquitaine stock was sold in 1994, Union des Assurances de Paris, Banque Nationale de France, and Renault were among the largest purchasers. When the latter three companies were privatized, Elf-Aquitaine was ready to return the favor.[27]

Why should an oil company, a bank, an insurance company, and an auto company, all formerly state owned, exchange ownership stakes with one another, and why should the top executives of these companies ignore their core competencies to sit on the various boards of directors? Successful privatization of a large enterprise requires the accumulation of a large volume of capital, but France has relatively shallow financial markets. Thus, according to Elie Cohen, the head of an economic research center in Paris, the *noyaux dur* were created to fill a gap in the French system:

We have no heavy investors, such as pension funds, so we had to invent something, and we invented cross-shareholdings. It is the problem of developing capitalism without capital.[28]

According to critics of the system, the real purpose of the *noyaux dur* is not to attract investment capital, but to protect the system of privilege enjoyed by the managerial elite, and to protect their companies from changes that they consider disruptive. Plenty of capital would be available, they say, if the privatizations were more open to foreign investors. "From the international investor's point of view," says Gary Dugan, a strategist at J. P. Morgan in London, "France seems to be a closed club of chairmen and managers made up of cross-holdings of companies, banks, and family interests."[29] Their defenders claim that the *noyaux dur* contribute stability and order to the French industrial system, but their detractors call it inflexibility and inefficiency.

THE LABOR MARKET AND LABOR RELATIONS

At first glance, the French system of labor relations seems to have much in common with the American system. France and the United States, together with Spain, have the lowest rates of labor union membership in the industrial world. In 1990, union members constituted only 10 percent of the French, 11 percent of the Spanish, and 16 percent of the U.S. labor force, compared to an average of 45 percent in 21 other industrial countries.[30] Furthermore, the labor movements

---

[27]John Ridding, "Hard Core or Soft Centre," Financial Times, February 10, 1994, 15.

[28]Ibid.

[29]John Chalmers, "Old Pillars of French Industrial Establishment Show Cracks," Reuter News Service, March 22, 1995, 1.

[30]Organization for Economic Cooperation and Development, *Employment Outlook,* July 1994, 184.

are fragmented in France and the United States. In neither France nor the United States does one find a unified confederation of labor unions, similar to the British Trade Union Congress or the German Confederation of Labor. This, though, is where the resemblance ends.

First, the patterns of union membership and representation are quite different in France and the United States. French unions include more white-collar and public-sector workers; American unions are more heavily oriented toward blue-collar workers in the private sector. Although union membership is low in France, decrees from the Labor Ministry frequently extend the outcomes of collective bargaining agreements to nonaffiliated workers and employers. Thus, the vast majority of French workers are covered by collective bargaining agreements. This is not true in the United States.[31]

French union members are divided between five major confederations, each of which exercises strong control over its affiliate unions. The oldest and largest confederation, the CGT, was established in 1895 and has close ties to the French Communist Party. According to public opinion data, the French public is unhappy with the political activities of the unions—particularly those of the CGT—and this seems to be one reason for the low level of union membership.[32] The other four confederations were formed by various anti-Communist groups, including the Roman Catholic Church, as alternatives to the CGT. In general, each confederation has an affiliate union for each major industry. Hence, an employer may have to deal with five different unions in a collective bargaining situation.

Because they are small and fragmented, the French labor unions are relatively weak. Because they have very limited financial resources to aid striking workers, French strikes are usually of short duration. Even the socialist Mitterrand administration was able to withstand union influence, and enacted an austerity program that was bitterly opposed by organized labor. However, the unions can be pushed only so far. The French government almost collapsed in 1968, when nearly half the workers and nearly all the university students participated in a general strike. In December 1995, when the Chirac-Juppé administration announced its plan to scale back the social security system, public-sector workers and students staged huge demonstrations, and brought the nation's trains, buses, and subways to a halt for three weeks. The strike ended when Juppé agreed to preserve the pension program of railroad workers that allows them to retire as early as age 50.

WORKER PARTICIPATION IN MANAGEMENT

In order to quell the general strike of 1968, General de Gaulle promised to establish an ill-defined system of worker participation in management. In fact, a very limited participation law was passed in 1969, but it fell far short of the demands of the Left. When the Socialist and Communist Parties forged their

---

[31]Ibid., 178 and 183.

[32]In a 1994 comparative poll, 55 percent of the French "totally agreed" with the statement, "unions are too politicized," compared to 23 percent of the Germans. See *Index to International Public Opinion, 1993–1994* (Westport, Conn.: Greenwood Press, 1995), 622.

so-called Common Program in 1972, they included a proposal for *autogestion* (workers' consultation in management). According to the proposal, workers' representatives would not participate directly in management, but would be consulted on major decisions and would have the right to veto layoffs and dismissals of workers.

Legislation to that effect—known as the Auroux laws after the labor minister at that time—was adopted in 1982 by the ruling Socialist-Communist coalition. All state-owned enterprises and private companies with more than 50 employees were required to establish a consultative works council. Furthermore, state-owned companies were required to allot one-third of their board seats to staff representatives. When the RPR-UDF coalition gained the parliamentary advantage in 1986, they repealed the provisions that required employers to obtain authorization before they could lay off workers, but workers in private joint-stock companies gained the right to designate a representative on the management board.

According to amendments to the Employment Code adopted in 1989, before a company lays off a group of workers it must prepare a **social plan,** describing plans for early retirement offers, placement services, training programs, and the like, and must present it to the works council. If the council finds the plan unacceptable, it may continue negotiations with the company, or may contest the plan in court. Thus, in 1994, when Digital France decided to cut 446 people from its staff, the action was opposed by the company's works council, and annulled by the high court at Evry. The court said that Digital's plan made insufficient arrangements for redeployment of staff.[33]

Evidently, French labor organizations have gained some of the elements of participatory management that are found, for example, in the German system of codetermination. In 1991, during her brief tenure as a socialist prime minister, Edith Cresson attempted to introduce other elements of the German system.[34] In the end, though, these efforts were frustrated by the return of conservative leadership, and by the fact that French trade unions were too small and fragmented to support a German-style system of labor relations in France. Indeed, enterprise-level worker participation may have replaced some of the functions of the national labor confederations, contributing to their decline.[35]

THE FINANCIAL SECTOR

French financial institutions traditionally have been characterized by extensive governmental ownership and control. In recent years, these institutions have been shaken by a range of new challenges, including massive programs

---

[33]*Les Echos,*July 12, 1994, 11.

[34]William Dawkins, "Chill Wind Blows Through French State Boardrooms," *Financial Times,* November 21, 1991, 2.

[35]This argument is made by Chris Howell, "French Socialism and the Transformation of Industrial Relations since 1981," in *The Mitterrand Era,* ed. Anthony Daley (Washington Square, N.Y.: New York University Press, 1996), 141–160.

of nationalization and privatization, liberalization of domestic, European, and global financial markets, and steps taken toward unification of the European monetary system.

The Bank of France (the central bank) and the three largest commercial banks were nationalized in 1945. Thirty-nine other commercial and savings banks were acquired in 1982, placing more than 90 percent of all bank deposits under state control. The government also owns many of the major insurance firms and financial holding companies, and operates a number of specialized lending institutions. As we have seen, many of these institutions have been privatized in recent years, and others are slated for privatization.

Before the mid–1980s, when the French government engaged in a more heavy-handed form of indicative planning and industrial policy, the importance of state-controlled financial institutions in the French economic system was quite clear. Through its control over bank lending, the French government was able to operate a **selective monetary policy.** That is, the government was able to control both the growth of the money supply and its distribution to priority sectors. This was one of the most powerful tools available to the government to encourage fulfillment of its indicative plans.

In recent years, though, we have noted that one of the obstacles to privatization, and one of the justifications for cross-holdings of stock, has been the lack of flexibility and depth in domestic financial markets. The Paris Stock Exchange, like other exchanges in continental Europe, handles a much smaller volume of business than its counterparts in the United States, Japan, and the United Kingdom. France has few pension funds or other large institutional investors because most pensions are financed on a pay-as-you-go basis.

To make Paris more competitive with New York, London, and Tokyo as a financial center, the Socialist government initiated a program in 1985 to strengthen and liberalize the securities market. Trading hours at the Paris exchange were extended, bond issues were liberalized, foreign-exchange controls were loosened, and trading was approved in a wider range of financial instruments. These efforts have continued in recent years, and they are showing some signs of success; in 1994, foreign investors held more than 30 percent of the capital on the Paris exchange.[36]

THE GOVERNMENTAL SECTOR

We already have considered the rise and fall of French governmental involvement in economic planning, ownership of industries, and regulation of financial markets. The government has also made major adjustments though the years in its handling of fiscal and monetary policy, and in its efforts to redistribute income.

---

[36]Chalmers, "Old Pillars of French Industrial Establishment Show Cracks," 1.

FISCAL AND MONETARY POLICY

While Germany ended World War II with a legacy of hyperinflation, the new French leaders inherited a legacy of stagnation. At 1 percent per year, the French economy grew more slowly between 1913 and 1950 than any other country in the industrial West, with the exception of Austria.[37] Thus, while the Germans placed a higher priority during the postwar years on fighting inflation, the French were more interested in stimulating economic growth and modernization.

Given these objectives, both countries were quite successful. Until the 1980s, the French economy grew more rapidly than the average for other Western countries, and unemployment remained relatively low (Table 12.1). How much of this success was attributable to governmental policy? We cannot say with certainty, but one set of estimates for the period between 1955 and 1971 suggests that fiscal policy eliminated 50 percent of the cyclical variability of French GNP—the highest degree of stabilization achieved anywhere in Western Europe.[38]

On the other hand, the excellent French growth performance was achieved at the cost of relatively high rates of inflation during the 1950s and 1970s, and was punctuated by recurrent balance of payments crises. Between 1959 and 1973, France posted an annual average balance of payments deficit of $193 million; all other major Western European nations posted average surpluses.[39] This nagging problem became an emergency in 1974 and 1976 when rising oil prices lifted the annual payments deficits above $3 billion.

Raymond Barre, an academic economist who became prime minister in late 1976, attacked the balance of payments problems with a strong dose of monetarism. He established strict monetary growth targets, lifted price controls, and cut industrial subsidies. As hoped, these policies improved the balance of payments—including large surpluses in 1978 and 1979—but also contributed to a steep and durable escalation of unemployment. The jobless rate increased from 4 percent in 1975 to more than 6 percent in 1980.

The socialist government of François Mitterrand entered office in 1981 with reduction of unemployment as its top macroeconomic goal. Fiscal policy, which had been contractionary in 1979 and 1980, turned to expansion in 1981 and 1982.[40] The monetary growth target, which had been reduced steadily by Barre, was increased in 1982. Again, these measures produced good and bad news. Employment and output grew modestly in 1982 (too modestly to reduce the unemployment rate), but the balance of payments deficit ballooned to $12 billion in 1982, almost emptying the nation's foreign exchange reserves.

---

[37] Angus Maddison, *Phases of Capitalist Development*, (Oxford: Oxford University Press, 1982), 45.

[38] John Bispham and Andrea Boltho, "Demand Management," in *The European Economy*, ed. Andrea Boltho (Oxford: Oxford University Press, 1982), 305–307.

[39] John Llewellyn and Stephen Potter, "Competitiveness and the Current Account," in *The European Economy*, 141.

[40] As measured by the fiscal impulse index. See International Monetary Fund, *World Economic Outlook* (Washington, D.C., April 1986), 121–123, 196.

Breaking from its previous policies, the socialist government launched a program of austerity (or *rigueur*, as the French call it) in mid–1982, and toughened it in 1983. The program included new taxes, social security adjustments, several devaluations of the franc, and limitations on tourist spending abroad. Wage increases for government employees were restricted, monetary growth targets were reduced sharply, and fiscal policy returned to a contractionary stance.

After years of escalation, the inflation rate and the balance of payments deficit began to follow a downward trend. As *The Economist* noted at the time, "Against expectations, a socialist government, having seen its own mistakes, is correcting chronic weaknesses which its conservative predecessors failed to deal with."[41] During all the years since 1982, French monetary policy has remained relatively stable and conservative, despite changes of leadership under Socialist, RPR-UDF, and cohabitation governments. The consumer price inflation rate declined during ten of the thirteen years between 1982 and 1994, starting the period at 12 percent and ending at 2 percent.[42]

President Mitterrand, a long-time activist in the cause of European economic integration, was committed to French participation in the process of monetary unification.[43] Thus, in 1983, France adopted a monetary policy that came to be known as the **franc fort**—the authorities would maintain a strong currency by stabilizing the exchange rate between the Franc and the DMark.[44] As Figure 12.1 indicates, the Franc/DMark exchange rate has been relatively stable since 1983, and especially since the Mitterrand-Chirac cohabitation began in 1986.

In 1994, the long-term stability of monetary policy was placed on firmer grounding. In line with the Maastricht Treaty, a new statute granted independence to the Bank of France, instructing it to define and implement monetary policy "with the objective of maintaining price stability." The broad policies of the Bank are now governed by a Monetary Policy Council. Its nine members, who are appointed by the Council of Ministers for nine-year terms (six years in the cases of the Governor and two Deputy-Governors), cannot be dismissed by the government, and cannot accept instructions from the government or any other entity.[45]

Compared to monetary policy, French fiscal policies of the past 15 years have been rather inconsistent. Generally, public expenditures increased during years of unified Socialist rule and decreased (as a percentage of GDP)

---

[41]"France: A Survey," *The Economist*, February 9, 1985, 9.

[42]*OECD Economic Outlook*, December 1995, A19.

[43]Mitterrand participated in the 1948 Hague conference that created the Council of Europe, and Jean Monnet, the architect of the EEC, crossed party lines to support Mitterrand in his 1965 presidential challenge against de Gaulle. On these matters, see Monnet, *Memoirs*, 273 and 483–484. In 1984, Mitterrand became president of the European Council, and a year later his former finance minister, Jacques Delors, became president of the European Commission. Delors, in turn, was the principle architect and advocate of European Monetary Union, which is still under construction.

[44]The term *franc fort* is a pun on the name of the city, Frankfurt, where the German central bank is located. In other words, it says that French monetary policy is directed in Germany.

[45]*OECD Economic Survey France 1993/94*, 42–43.

■ **FIGURE 12.1**

BUILDING THE FRANC FORT:
THE FRANC/DMARK EXCHANGE RATE

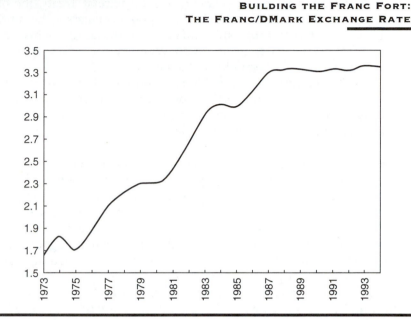

during years of cohabitation and RPR-UDF leadership. The tax system was a subject of constant revision and reform, but it extracted a stable 48–49 percent of GDP. The budget deficit climbed from less than 2 percent of GDP in 1981, when Mitterrand took office, to more than 6 percent in 1993, when the Mitterrand-Balladur cohabitation began.[46]

The Maastricht Treaty, which was narrowly approved by the French electorate in 1992, required each country to reduce its budget deficit to 3 percent of GDP by 1997 if it wished to participate in the first round of European Monetary Union. For French leaders, meeting that deadline became a matter of national pride. Every important economic decision was examined through the lens of the Maastricht convergence criteria. Thus, when the Chirac-Juppé administration endured three weeks of railroad strikes in 1995 to preserve reductions in social security and welfare expenditures, the headline was "French Stand Tough Against Strikers to Prove Readiness for Monetary Union."[47] The news media drew the same conclusion in 1996 when President Chirac and Prime Minister Juppé both used the word "draconian" to describe budget cuts that would be required during the next four or five years.[48]

---

[46]*OECD Economic Outlook,* December 1995, A31–A33.

[47]*The Wall Street Journal,* November 30, 1995, A18.

[48]See "France to Hold Spending Rise to Inflation," Reuter News Service, May 3, 1996; and "France Treads Warily in Battle to Cut Deficit," Reuter News Service, May 10, 1996. The word Chirac and Juppé used to describe their own policies is a bit surprising. *Draconian,* meaning "harsh" or "severe," is derived from *Draco,* the name of an Athenian lawmaker who, according to Plutarch, prescribed the death penalty for "almost all transgressions," including idleness and the theft of fruit. The code of Draco was eventually replaced by the more humane code of *Solon.* See Plutarch, *Solon* 17.1, which may be found at <http://www.perseus.tufts.edu/Texts.html>.

UNEMPLOYMENT POLICIES

Along with the financial requirements of the Maastricht Treaty, the other stark reality that must be addressed by French policymakers is the continuing problem of unemployment. While inflation was trending downward, the unemployment rate increased during every year between 1976 and 1987, rising from 4.4 percent at the beginning of the period to 10.5 percent at the end. After pausing for a few years, unemployment resumed its ascent in 1991, rising above 12 percent in 1996.[49] Furthermore, nearly half of the unemployed in France have been out of work for more than one year. This is a moderate proportion for a European country, but much higher than long-term rates in the United States, Canada, or Japan.[50]

What is the cause of high and persistent unemployment in France? At least two broad answers have been suggested. Economists with a Keynesian orientation are inclined to blame the problem on insufficient aggregate demand. In the French case, they believe that a tight monetary policy simultaneously caused declining inflation and rising unemployment.

True, the government often ran large budget deficits that might have provided Keynesian stimulation to the economy. Combined with a tight monetary policy, though, they only caused high interest rates, which "crowded out" the purchases of private consumers and investors. Among the major industrial countries, interest rates in France have recently been exceeded only by those in Canada and Italy; both of these countries also had high levels of unemployment.[51] Keynesians are usually in favor of relaxing the "franc fort" policy, allowing interest rates to drift downward as long as the resulting economic growth is not inflationary.[52]

Economists with a supply-side orientation are more inclined to blame unemployment on structural problems, including mismatches between skills and positions, trade-distorting taxes and subsidies, inflexible management of nationalized industries, payment of excessive unemployment benefits, high minimum wage rates, and large employer contributions to social security programs. Problems such as these cannot be solved with simple adjustments of fiscal or monetary policy; they require deeper institutional reforms.

During the Mitterrand era, governmental efforts to reduce unemployment were primarily focused on expansion of job training programs, on community work schemes, on providing tax incentives and subsidies to employers who created new jobs, and on a range of other "active" employment support programs. Expenditures on programs such as these increased from 27 billion francs in 1980 to 138 billion francs in 1993.[53]

---

[49]*OECD Economic Outlook,* June 1997, A24.

[50]*OECD in Figures 1997,* 12.

[51]For an international comparison of real interest rates, see *OECD Economic Survey France 1995,* 24.

[52]See, for example, Samuel Brittan, "The Need for a More Subtle Franc Fort," *Financial Times,* October 19, 1995, 14.

[53]*OECD Economic Survey France 1995,* 57.

When Jacques Chirac won the presidency in 1995, he emphasized the jobs issue in his victory statement: "Our principal battle has a name: the fight against unemployment. The classic remedies have failed. We need a new approach."[54] To date, however, the "new approach" is still unclear. One of the first acts of Chirac's government, for example, was to increase the minimum wage by 4 percent. This was done against advice from OECD and the International Monetary Fund, and despite the fact that France already had the highest minimum wage in the world, with the exception of the Netherlands. Other reforms have been proposed in the unemployment benefits program and the social security program, but little action has been taken.[55]

REDISTRIBUTION OF INCOME

Dating back to the excesses of Louis XIV, French social stratification and income inequality have been conspicuous. As recently as the 1970s, international comparisons of income distributions usually indicated that France had one of the highest levels of income inequality in the industrial world.[56]

Since the 1970s, however, France has employed a cradle-to-grave program of social benefits to redistribute income. Prenatal and maternity benefits cover most of a mother's earnings before and after a birth or adoption. Birth grants and monthly family allowances help defray the cost of raising children. Sickness benefits cover half of lost earnings, and national health insurance covers a large portion of doctor fees, hospital bills, and drugs. The system also includes generous unemployment and disability benefits, pensions, and survivor benefits.[57] In 1992, French expenditures on social protection programs of all kinds amounted to 29.2 percent of GDP—only the Scandinavian welfare states and the Netherlands dedicated larger proportions of their incomes to these purposes.[58]

What was the outcome of these programs? It is impossible to make definitive statements on such a complex issue. However, between the 1970s and the 1980s, while income inequality increased sharply in the United States, Germany, and the United Kingdom, the income distribution remained relatively stable in France.[59] Thus, in recent studies of income distribution and poverty, France is no longer found at the bottom of the list of industrial countries; it has climbed to the middle.

---

[54]*The Wall Street Journal*, May 8, 1995, A12.

[55]See *OECD Economic Survey France 1995*, 52–71; and "Structural Unemployment in France: Causes and Prescriptions," *IMF Survey*, October 31, 1994, 346–47.

[56]For example, see data for the 1970s in Malcolm Sawyer, "Income Distribution and the Welfare State," in *The European Economy*, 205–210; and Wouter van Ginnekin and Jong-goo Park, *Generating Internationally Comparable Income Distribution Statistics* (Geneva: International Labour Office, 1984), Tables 1 and A.1.

[57]U.S. Department of Health and Human Services, Social Security Administration, *Social Security around the World*, Research Report No. 58, 82–83; and Margaret S. Gordon, *Social Security Policies in Industrial Countries* (Cambridge: Cambridge University Press, 1988).

[58]Eurostat, *Yearbook 1995*, 230.

[59]This statement is based on comparisons of quintile ratios calculated from income distribution data in the 1988 edition (appendix table 26) and 1995 edition (appendix table 30) of the World Bank, *World Development Report*.

SUMMARY

France has a tradition of social discord, which encouraged the development of strong governmental institutions under Colbert, Napoleon, and de Gaulle to maintain order. Thus, although the French developed philosophies of liberty and equality, they developed traditions of governmental intervention in the economy and social elitism. One important form of intervention has been the system of indicative planning, established after World War II. Indicative planning is meant to improve the operation of the market mechanism through cooperation and exchange of information. Compliance with the plan is voluntary, but may be encouraged by governmental financial and regulatory actions and by the system of plan contracts. The record of plan fulfillment often has been poor, but the planning process has served as a useful forum for social discussion.

In the private sector, French firm sizes are relatively small for economic and cultural reasons. Mergers have sometimes been encouraged to create national champions. France has long and extensive experience with nationalized industries. A wide range of operations were nationalized by President Mitterrand in 1982, but many of these have been re-privatized since 1987. Some nationalized companies have performed well, with little interference from the government, and others have performed very poorly. Because of the cozy relations between elite managers and their companies, privatization sometimes makes little difference in the performance of a company.

Labor union membership is very small, and the unions are fragmented. Still, collective bargaining coverage is wider than union membership, and union membership is stronger and more influential in the nationalized sectors. Workers are also represented by company-level works councils.

French financial institutions traditionally have been characterized by extensive governmental ownership and control. Private financial institutions lack breadth and depth, providing a justification for cross-shareholdings between corporations.

During the postwar years, the general stance of fiscal and monetary policy has been pro-growth, with occasional austerity programs to handle balance of payments problems. The Mitterrand government was forced to adopt an austerity program in 1982–1983, and the stance of monetary policy—the so-called franc fort—has been more restrictive since that time. The Bank of France gained its independence in 1994.

Fiscal policy has been divided between the imperatives of meeting Maastricht convergence criteria and unemployment reduction. The high and persistent rates of unemployment can be explained from a demand-side or a supply-side perspective, each suggesting its own remedies.

DISCUSSION AND REVIEW QUESTIONS

1. Describe the organizational structure and procedure used to formulate an indicative plan in France. How should we evaluate its success or failure in France?

2. What would be the arguments for and against the adoption of indicative planning in a country making the transition from a centrally planned to a market economy?

3. Why are the organizational structures and management styles of French companies in the public and private sectors often quite similar? Is this situation likely to change?

4. How are the French and American labor markets similar? How are they different?

5. What is the "franc fort"? How has it affected the performance of the French economy?

6. What are some possible causes of French unemployment? Does a particular explanation seem most convincing to you? What policies would you support to alleviate the problem?

SUGGESTED READINGS

Adams, William James. *Restructuring the French Economy*. Washington, D.C.: The Brookings Institution, 1989. *A careful analysis of the impressive French record of economic growth since World War II, with special attention to the contributions of industrial policy and trade with the European Union.*

Bismut, C. J.; K. Habermeier; J. Levy; and P. R. Agenor. *France: Recent Economic Developments*. Washington, D.C.: International Monetary Fund, 1995. *A brief review of recent trends in fiscal, monetary, and labor policies, and of French participation in European economic integration.*

Caron, François. *An Economic History of Modern France*. New York: Columbia University Press, 1979. *Provides a wealth of statistical data and analysis on developments between 1815 and 1975.*

Estrin, Saul, and Peter Holmes. *French Planning in Theory and Practice*. Boston: Allyn and Unwin, 1983. *One of the few surveys of the theoretical literature on indicative planning, including its capacity to reduce uncertainty.*

Hayward, Jack. *The State and the Market Economy*. New York: New York University Press, 1986. *Particularly strong on the policies of the Mitterrand administration and the relationship between national and local economic authorities.*

Hough, J. R. *The French Economy*. New York: Holmes and Meier, 1982. *A brief overview of the system, with a particularly strong chapter on regional policy.*

Monnet, Jean. *Memoirs*. Garden City, N.Y.: Doubleday, 1978. *A fascinating firsthand account of the establishment of indicative planning, the founding of the European Community, and a broad range of other experiences.*

Safran, William. *The French Polity*. 4th Edition. White Plains, N.Y.: Longman, 1995. *An up-to-date survey of the French political system, with good discussions of economic policy formation and the political roles of trade unions and business organizations.*

Sutton, Michael. France to *2000: The Challenge of a Changing Europe*. London: Economist Intelligence Unit, 1992.

Tiersky, Ronald. *France in the New Europe*. Belmont, Calif.: Wadsworth Publishing, 1994. *An integrated and lively collection of essays on French political culture, emphasizing the challenge of European economic integration to French exceptionalism.*

INTERNET RESOURCES

AdmiNet – The French Connection
http://www.ensmp.fr/~scherer/adminet/

Agence France-Presse
http://www.afp.com/AFP_VA/afpaccueil_va.html

Commissariat Général du Plan
http://www.ensmp.fr:80/~scherer/adminet/min/pm/cgp

École Nationale d'Administration
http://www.ensmp.fr/~scherer/ING/fellow/ena.html

FranceScape
http://www.france.com/francescape/top.html

French Constitution
http://www.ensmp.fr/~scherer/adminet/constitution.html#french

French Economic Report
http://www.actufax.com/

French Economic Outlook
Ministry of Economics, Finance, and Planning
http://www.cri.ensmp.fr:80/dp/conj/
or
http://webhk.com/ftchk/corps/anglais/franceco/economie.html

French Economy
http://www.ftcsfo.org/english/franceco.htm

French Embassy in the United States
http://info-france.org/

French Political System
gopher://spartacus.univ-lyon2.fr/00/amb-wash.fr/profile/gover.txt

French Press Review
http://www.france.diplomatie.fr:80/www.interne/mae/revue/du_jour.html

Institut National de la Statistique et des Études Economiques (INSEE)
http://w3.ensae.fr/

Investing in France
http://www.webhk.com/ftchk/corps/anglais/7reasons/intro.html

Le Monde
http://www.lemonde.fr/

Le Monde Diplomatique
http://www.ina.fr/CP/MondeDiplo/index.fr.html

Paris Chamber of Commerce and Industry
http://www1.usa1.com/~ibnet/parccihp.html

Radio France Internationale
http://193.107.193.136/rfi1.html

Web Libération
http://www.liberation.fr/

Welcome to France
http://www.france.diplomatie.fr/index.gb.html

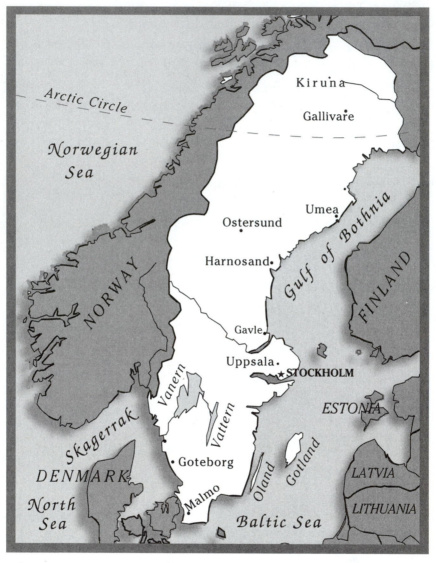

Sweden

13

SWEDEN:
WHITHER THE WELFARE STATE?

> Let us take the chance to build a new Swedish model.
> Human values are greater than market values, and these
> values are deeply anchored among us Swedes. . . . Social
> welfare will remain, we will pay for it, we will never
> desert the fundamental ideas behind it.
>
> —PRIME MINISTER GÖRAN PERSSON
> *AGENCE FRANCE PRESSE*, MARCH 15, 1996

> Despite all this rhetoric about how communism lost and
> capitalism won, the welfare state is very robust. It has
> weathered an economic hurricane and an ideological
> blizzard.
>
> —NICHOLAS BARR, *THE WALL STREET JOURNAL*
> JANUARY 30, 1995

ith fewer than nine million residents, Sweden is a small country—much smaller in population than Tokyo, Mexico City, New York City, or a dozen other cities. Nevertheless, Sweden merits attention as a social welfare state pushed to its limits. In recent years, Swedish leaders have made concessions to financial reality and European conformity, but they have maintained the core elements of a distinctive economic system.

During the century after 1870, Sweden posted the world's highest growth rates of GDP per capita and labor productivity.[1] Several factors made this possible. As a neutral country, Sweden avoided heavy military expenditures and physical destruction during the world wars. During the Great Depression, Sweden avoided massive unemployment and economic destruction by maintaining an active fiscal policy and an undervalued currency.

---

[1]Angus Maddison, *Phases of Capitalist Development* (Oxford: Oxford University Press, 1982), 45, 96. With higher rates of population growth, the United States and Canada had higher growth rates for total GDP.

■ **TABLE 13.1**

**RELATIVE PERFORMANCE OF THE SWEDISH
ECONOMY, 1951–1996**

	1951–1960	1961–1970	1971–1980	1981–1990	1991–1996
Average annual growth of real GDP (%)					
Sweden	3.4	4.4	2.0	2.0	0.6
OECD Average	4.2	5.1	3.2	2.8	2.0
Average annual consumer price inflation (%)					
Sweden	2.4	4.1	9.2	7.6	3.9
OECD Average	3.3	3.9	9.1	8.1	4.9
Unemployment rate (%)					
Sweden	1.8	1.7	2.1	2.7	7.9
OECD Average	3.6*	2.8*	4.5	7.3	7.5

*Based on data for Canada, France, Germany, Italy, Japan, Sweden, the United Kingdom, and the United States.

SOURCES: World Bank, *World Tables*, 1980 and 1995; Irving Kravis, Alan Heston, and Robert Summers, *World Product and Income* (Baltimore: Johns Hopkins University Press, 1982), 343; Angus Maddison, *Phases of Capitalist Development* (Oxford: Oxford University Press, 1982), appendices A, C, and E; *OECD Economic Outlook*, December 1986 and June 1997; and International Monetary Fund, *World Economic Outlook*, May 1997.

In 1936, Marquis Childs popularized the notion that Swedish economic success was grounded in a unique economic system, marking a "middle way" between the instability and inequality of free-enterprise capitalism and the inefficiency and repression of Soviet-style socialism.[2] The so-called Swedish model, with its mixture of social welfare, labor market, and macroeconomic institutions, continued to develop after World War II, and performed relatively well for several decades. Between the 1950s and 1980s, Swedish unemployment rates usually were less than half the OECD average, and Swedish inflation rates were moderate (Table 13.1). Sweden maintained one of the world's highest standards of living, with high levels of personal income, life expectancy, literacy, and income equality, and low levels of poverty, crime, and infant mortality. In 1970, Martin Schnitzer declared that Sweden had "perhaps the closest thing to a utopian society in existence."[3]

Swedish economic performance began to deteriorate during the 1970s, when rising oil prices led to higher inflation and unemployment rates, larger budget deficits, recurrent balance of payments crises, and depreciation of the currency, causing the Social Democratic Party to lose its monopolistic control of the political system. These difficulties were compounded during the 1980s, when Sweden's centralized system of collective bargaining ceased to function, and finally led to a crisis during the early 1990s, when a deep recession caused

[2]Marquis Childs, *Sweden: The Middle Way* (New Haven, Conn.: Yale University Press, 1936).
[3]Martin Schnitzer, *The Economy of Sweden* (New York: Praeger Publishers, 1970), 1.

unemployment to race beyond the record levels of the 1930s. The governmental budget, which recorded surpluses during the years between 1987 and 1990, plunged into a deficit in 1993 that exceeded 13 percent of GDP.

Late in 1994, while the economy was slowly recovering from recession, Swedish voters approved a proposal for their nation to join the European Union. Since that time, Swedish national leaders have been trying to strike a balance between the demands of the population, who support continuation of the welfare state, and the demands of full participation in the EU, which require continuation of deficit reduction. The government has been forced to reexamine the Swedish model, looking for opportunities to cut costs and maintain price stability, but to save the core of the welfare state.

THE ENVIRONMENT

Geography has been kind to Sweden. Richly endowed with natural resources, Sweden is the top producer of timber, wood pulp, and iron ore in Western Europe, and is second only to Germany in production of gold. Relatively isolated on the Scandinavian peninsula, the Swedes have not participated in a major war since they joined the fight against Napoleon in 1813. No foreign nation except neighboring Denmark has ever invaded or occupied Sweden. Spared the human and material devastation of war, the Swedes were able to devote a relatively small share of national income to the military.

Geographic isolation also explains why the Swedish population, like the Japanese, is ethnically and culturally homogeneous. About 85 percent of the Swedes are Germanic Scandinavians of the Lutheran faith.[4] These factors apparently contribute to a strong sense of solidarity and egalitarianism among the Swedish people. Even during the Middle Ages, feudalism and serfdom never took hold in Sweden; rural peasants maintained their freedom. Today, the Swedes, like the Japanese, still have a penchant for cooperation and consensus rather than conflict and litigation.

The culture of egalitarianism supported the development of a comprehensive welfare state. Unlike the situation in the United States and other "melting pot" societies, where the welfare system seems to redistribute income from one racial or cultural group to another, the "haves" in Sweden are difficult to distinguish from the "have nots." Thus, the politics of the welfare state are less divisive.

Another aspect of the political environment that has left its mark on the Swedish economic system is the traditional dominance of the **Social Democratic Party (SDP)**. Aside from periods during 1936, between 1976 and 1982, and between 1991 and 1994, the SDP has held power continuously since 1932, either alone or in a coalition. From its inception in 1889, the SDP was a socialist party, but one that believed socialism was best pursued through gradual reform of the capitalist system rather than through violent

---

[4]For a contrary view, arguing that "ethnic and cultural differences may have been even larger in Sweden during the 1970s than in the United States in the early years of the twentieth century," see Goran Rosenberg, "Sweden and Its Immigrants: Policies versus Opinions," *Daedalus* 124 (June 1995): 209.

revolution. Today, the SDP is split between two camps. The **traditionalists,** including many of the trade union officials, insist that the government must restore and preserve the social welfare benefits that were trimmed during recent financial crises. They generally oppose Swedish participation in the European Union, particularly when it threatens the independence of Swedish monetary, fiscal, and labor market policies. The **renewers,** including Göran Persson, who became prime minister in 1995, wish to preserve the "core" of the social welfare system, but believe that major reforms are needed to place the Swedish system on a stronger financial grounding.[5]

The coalition that governed Sweden between 1991 and 1994 was led by the **Moderate Party,** which is presently the strongest force of opposition to the SDP. Formerly known, perhaps more descriptively, as the Conservative Party, the Moderates call for major surgery on the social welfare system, and for full Swedish participation in the European Union. Led by former prime minister Carl Bildt, the Moderates argue that the family, not the state, should provide basic support to its members: "No other collective can replace the home as a base for human solidarity and cooperation."[6] The third important political force, the **Center Party,** appropriately stands between the SDP and the Moderate Party on most issues, but it has recently supported many of the reforms championed by the SDP renewers.

INDUSTRIAL ORGANIZATION

Unlike the British Labor Party, the SDP never promoted widespread nationalization of industry. The advocates of nationalization split from the SDP in 1921 to form the Communist Party (now known as the Left Party), which has played a minor role in Swedish politics. Hence, during most of the postwar era, more than 90 percent of industry has remained in private hands.

When companies have been nationalized, socialist ideology seldom has been the motive. For example, some of the major iron ore mines were purchased by the government in 1907, long before SDP rule, in order to oust foreign control of the nation's industry. During the recession of the late 1970s, a government led by the Center Party nationalized a number of financially troubled shipbuilding and commercial steel companies to save them from bankruptcy. Thus, the share of public enterprises in GDP and national investment increased to about 20 percent during the late 1970s and 1980s.[7]

When the SDP returned to power in 1982, they sold many of the recently nationalized firms back to private owners, reducing the public enterprise

---

[5]See, for example, Hugh Carnegy, "The Renewers Still Have Battles to Fight," *Financial Times,* December 15, 1995, supplement, 1.

[6]From the Web site of the Moderate Party: <http://www.moderat.se/Mod2.htm>.

[7]According to *The Wall Street Journal,* March 20, 1984, 31, the revenues of state-owned companies and utilities amounted to $16.7 billion, or 21 percent of GNP in 1982. According to World Bank estimates, the average share of state-owned enterprises in gross domestic investment was 22 percent between 1978 and 1985. See World Bank, *Bureaucrats in Business* (Oxford: Oxford University Press, 1995), 279.

■ **TABLE 13.2**

DISTRIBUTION OF EMPLOYMENT BY
COMPANY SIZE IN EUROPE, 1986

	Percentage of total employment in companies with:			
	1–9 employees	10–99 employees	100–499 employees	500+ employees
Denmark	16.8	42.4	23.2	17.6
France	15.1	28.6	16.7	39.6
Germany	18.2	27.3	18.7	35.8
Netherlands	14.0	27.7	17.1	41.3
Sweden	9.5	17.3	12.6	60.6
United Kingdom	23.2	23.9	22.9	30.0

SOURCE: Estimates of the Swedish Ministry of Public Administration (SOU) reported in Gregg M. Olsen, "Re-Modeling Sweden: The Rise and Demise of the Compromise in a Global Economy," *Social Problems* 43 (February 1996): 13.

share of the economy again to about 10 percent.[8] Another wave of privatizations was undertaken by the Moderate-led coalition government between 1992 and 1994, involving the sale of about 20 companies. The largest of these were stakes in Pharmacia, a pharmaceuticals company, for about $1.2 billion, and in Assidomaen, a pulp and paper company, for $985 million.[9] Thus, Anders Sundstrom, the current minister of industry, can truthfully say that the Swedish state "owns relatively little," but he seems less than candid when he says that "non-socialist governments have always extended the state's ownership." At any rate, as this is written, he seems to have few plans for further nationalization or privatization.[10]

The private sector of Swedish industry is dominated by a relatively small number of large, multinational companies. The largest of these are Volvo, an automotive company, Electrolux, a world leader in home appliances, and Ericsson, a telecommunications equipment company. More generally, the dominance of large companies is illustrated by the fact that companies with 500 or more employees account for a much larger share of employment in Sweden than in other European countries (Table 13.2).

Because of the dominance of large companies, and because Sweden is a small country with little room for competition in each market, Sweden has one of the highest levels of industrial concentration in the developed world. During the 1970s, the three largest firms in the average Swedish industry produced more than 80 percent of that industry's output. This was roughly

[8]According to World Bank, Bureaucrats in Business, 279, the investment share of public enterprises was 10.1 percent between 1986 and 1991.

[9]*The Wall Street Journal*, October 2, 1995, R13.

[10]Quoted in Trevor Datson, "Swedish Minister Neutral on Privatization," Reuter European Business Report, April 2, 1996.

double the American level of concentration.[11] Nothing has happened in recent years to reverse this pattern. In fact, the entire Nordic region recently has been experiencing a "merger mania." According to the vice-president of a Finnish firm that recently acquired a Swedish energy utility:

The bigger and more efficient companies eat the smaller ones. That is one reason why we want to be bigger and bigger.[12]

Despite the high level of market concentration, the power of Swedish companies on the domestic market is offset by a high level of import competition. Imports amounted to about 23 percent of GDP in 1992, which is equal to the European average and significantly higher than the 15 percent average for OECD countries.[13] The power of domestic manufacturers is also counterbalanced by the fact that Sweden has one of the world's most extensive systems of consumer cooperatives. Nearly half of the Swedes are members of Kooperativa Forbundet (KF), the national confederation of cooperatives. Organized in 1889, KF gained a reputation of strength during the early years of the twentieth century when it broke the cartels of margarine, footwear, and flour producers. Today, as Sweden's largest retail conglomerate, KF and its subsidiaries operate thousands of department stores, food stores, automobile dealerships, specialty shops, insurance companies, and other outlets for consumer goods and services. As the nation's largest purchaser of many consumer products, KF can bargain with manufacturers for cut-rate prices, passing the savings on to the consumers who own the organization.[14]

THE LABOR MARKET AND LABOR RELATIONS

One of the hallmarks of the Swedish welfare state is the smooth operation of its labor market. Although its reputation has tarnished in recent years, Sweden traditionally has maintained one of the lowest unemployment rates and one of the lowest levels of labor unrest (as measured by days lost to strikes) of any Western nation. In this respect, the Swedish and German economies both have been very successful. However, the Swedish and German formulas for harmonious labor relations are quite dissimilar.

COLLECTIVE BARGAINING

Swedish industrialization did not begin until the 1870s, but it caused unusually rapid growth of the number and size of labor unions. Several nation wide union organizations were established by the 1880s, and in 1898 they

---

[11]F. M. Scherer, *The Economics of Multi-Plant Operation: An International Comparisons Study* (Cambridge, Mass.: Harvard University Press, 1975), 218–219, 426–428.

[12]Jari Jaakkola of IVO, which recently acquired Gullspangs Kraft, quoted in Greg McIvor, "Deregulation Sparks Nordic Merger Frenzy," *Financial Times*, May 7, 1996, 23.

[13]United Nations Development Programme, *Human Development Report 1995* (Oxford: Oxford University Press, 1995), 212.

[14]Chua Mui Hoong, "Coops: Competing in the Business World," *The Straits Times*, October 29, 1995, 1.

combined to form the Swedish Confederation of Trade Unions (the LO), which has played a major role ever since. By 1929, when union members represented about 10 percent of the labor force in the United States and 25 percent in the United Kingdom, they already accounted for 33 percent in Sweden. This proportion grew to 68 percent in 1970, and then continued to grow—while union membership was declining in other industrial countries—to 82 percent in 1990.[15] Swedish unions now represent industrial and service workers, police officers and soldiers, schoolteachers, medical doctors, and even members of the clergy.

Although Swedish labor relations have been remarkably calm since World War II, they were not always so. At the beginning of this century Sweden and Norway had the highest levels of industrial conflict in the West.[16] In 1902, during one of the worst conflicts—a general strike in support of demands for universal suffrage—the Swedish Employers Association (SAF) was created to countervail the power of the LO.

After years of conflict and violence, faced with a governmental threat to pass laws limiting strikes and lockouts, the representatives of the LO and the SAF met in 1938 in the town of Saltsjöbaden to settle their differences. Under the terms of the **Basic Agreement of Saltsjöbaden,** as amended in 1947 and 1948, representatives of management agreed to recognize the unions as legitimate bargaining partners and to establish a system of general rules concerning layoffs and dismissals. Both sides pledged that they would no longer resort to strikes or lockouts without first holding direct negotiations and would not attempt to force the renegotiation of existing contracts. The Saltsjöbaden Agreement, reached and enforced with little governmental involvement, led to an immediate reduction in industrial unrest.

The rules of Swedish labor relations were refined further after World War II, when the employers pressed successfully for a system of **centralized collective bargaining.** Under this unique system, wage negotiations were first carried out at the national level between the labor union confederation (the LO) and the employers' confederation (the SAF), resulting in a binding framework agreement concerning average wage increases, working hours, and fringe benefits.[17]

Within the economywide guidelines established by the LO-SAF central agreement, industrywide and local negotiations were held between employers' groups and union affiliates. If the industrial and local negotiators did not abide by the provisions of the national framework agreement, they risked the loss of financial and administrative support from the LO and the SAF. Local

---

[15]*OECD Employment Outlook,* July 1994, 184.

[16]Walter Korpi, "Industrial Relations and Industrial Conflict: The Case of Sweden," in *Labor Relations in Advanced Industrial Societies,* ed. Benjamin Martin and Everett Kassalow (Washington, D.C.: Carnegie Endowment for International Peace, 1980), 93.

[17]Two labor groups are also involved. Whereas the LO (with 2.1 million members in 1981) primarily represents blue-collar workers, the Central Organization of Salaried Employees (TCO, with 1.1 million members) and the Swedish Confederation of Professional Associations and Federation of Government Employees (SACO-SR, with 234,000 members) were formed in the 1940s to represent the growing white-collar community.

union members, for example, could be deprived of financial aid from the LO during a strike or a lockout.

The employers initially pressed for centralized bargaining because they believed greater coordination and control of negotiations would reduce industrial conflict, and they believed centralization would strengthen their bargaining power. In a decentralized system, they reasoned, unions use the wage gains in early settlements as a basis for additional demands in later settlements. This leapfrogging process would add fuel to inflation and cause the unions to delay their negotiations.[18]

The unions agreed to the system of centralized bargaining in order to prevent governmental control of wages and to support their own policy of **wage solidarity.** Originally introduced in 1936, wage solidarity was the practice of granting the largest wage increases to the lowest-paid workers. In the beginning, its aim was simply to promote equity—equal pay for equal work.

In the 1950s, the equity motive for wage solidarity was buttressed by a productivity motive. Gösta Rehn, a prominent SDP economist, argued that equality of wage costs would force inefficient firms to either make improvements or close. Thus, the policy of wage solidarity would encourage a rapid adjustment to the long-run equilibrium structure of wages and employment.[19] To deal with transitory unemployment that would be caused by this structural adjustment, Rehn and his associate Rudolf Meidner designed an active labor market policy.

Between 1945 and 1970, the system of centralized collective bargaining seemed to work beautifully. Wage agreements were reached peacefully, without recourse to strikes or lockouts, and the demands of the LO and its union affiliates were modest, resulting in a moderate amount of inflation. The low rate of inflation contributed, in turn, to favorable balances of international payments.

The performance of the Swedish system of collective bargaining began to deteriorate after 1970. Heavy application of the wage solidarity principle led to an unsustainable compression of the wage structure. Between 1965 and 1975, wage dispersion declined by 74 percent among blue-collar workers and 40 percent among white-collar workers in the private sector. Between 1970 and 1982, wages were compressed by an additional 55 percent among blue-collar workers.[20] Distortions in the wage distribution eventually led to departures from the LO-SAF framework agreements, resulting in an inflationary **wage drift.** Between 1971 and 1984, unscheduled raises accounted for about one-third of the overall growth in industrial wages, and between 1985 and 1989 they accounted for about one-half of the total.[21]

---

[18]R. Bean, *Comparative Industrial Relations* (New York: St. Martin's Press, 1985), 83–84.

[19]Erik Lundberg, "The Rise and Fall of the Swedish Model," *Journal of Economic Literature* 23 (March 1985): 18–19.

[20]Gregg M. Olsen, "Re-Modeling Sweden: The Rise and Demise of the Compromise in a Global Economy," Social Problems 43 (February 1996): 4.

[21]Robert J. Flanagan, "Efficiency and Equality in Swedish Labor Markets," in *The Swedish Economy*, ed. Barry Bosworth and Alice Rivlin (Washington, D.C.: The Brookings Institution, 1987), 166–169; and Swedish Ministry of Finance, Sweden's Economy, April 1990, 43.

Rising wages and prices damaged the international competitiveness of Swedish industry.

Also during the years after 1970, the traditional tranquility of labor-management relations was interrupted by several instances of open conflict. During the so-called Luxury Strike of 1971, over 50,000 civil servants walked out, closing the railroads, courts, and schools. In 1980, efforts by the Center government to cut public spending provoked a massive conflict. Nearly half the industrial labor force was idle at some time during that year as public-sector strikes led to supportive strikes and lockouts in the private sector.

The system of centralized collective bargaining began to unravel in 1983, when the metalworkers union and the engineering industry's employers group broke away from the national talks to hold their own negotiations. The well-paid metalworkers were able to bargain for more generous pay increases than those allowed under the system of wage solidarity. During the years between 1984 and 1990, centralized bargaining was sometimes conducted between LO and SAF representatives, but they produced fewer specific directions for industry-level negotiators and more broad recommendations. In 1991, the SAF announced it would no longer take part in central negotiations and disbanded its wage bargaining staff. The task of initiating wage negotiations devolved to industry-level labor and employer associations.[22]

In recent years, the traditional peace between Swedish labor and management has deteriorated further, prompted by the collapse of centralized bargaining, by a series of governmental austerity programs, and by efforts to limit wage increases for public workers. In 1986, the SDP government successfully discontinued the 20-year-old practice of linking public-sector pay increases to those in the private sector, but provoked a strike that started with 14,000 health and welfare workers. Several thousand blue-collar workers quickly joined, and another 600,000 workers supported the strike by refusing to work overtime. Eventually the monthlong conflict included transport workers, teachers, postal employees, and thousands of other civil servants.

In 1990, the SDP government headed by Ingvar Carlsson was forced to resign temporarily and reorganize itself when parliament rejected its plan for a two-year freeze of wages, prices, rents, and strike activities. A strike that would have shut down public transport and other services in cities throughout the country was narrowly averted, but a three-week strike by 46,000 employees closed all the nation's banks. The bank employees eventually won a 13 percent pay increase.

In 1994, about 4,000 government doctors went on strike and 20,000 others refused to work overtime when the Moderate government reduced overtime pay and adopted a new system allowing patients to choose their physicians. Previously, patients who visited public clinics usually were required to accept the doctors on duty. The physician's union contended that the reform would cause about 3,200 doctors in local clinics to lose their jobs.

[22] Harry C. Katz, "The Decentralization of Collective Bargaining: A Literature Review and Comparative Analysis," *Industrial and Labor Relations Review* 47 (October 1993): 3; and Jonas Pontusson and Peter Swenson, "Labor Markets, Production Strategies, and Wage Bargaining Institutions," *Comparative Political Studies* 29 (April 1996): 223–247.

The collapse of systems of centralized collective bargaining and wage solidarity also reversed much of the wage compression that developed during the 1960s and 1970s. By 1990, the variance in wages already had returned to the level of the mid-1970s.[23] Reduction of wage compression apparently reduced market pressure for wage drift. Unscheduled wage increases, which accounted for half of all pay raises during the late 1980s, returned to one-third of the total in the early 1990s.[24]

ACTIVE AND PASSIVE LABOR MARKET POLICY

During most of the postwar era, the Swedish unemployment rate remained at extremely low levels despite the nation's rapid adjustment from a semi-industrial state to a modern technological economy, and despite the structural changes caused by the system of wage solidarity. A major share of credit for this accomplishment is usually extended to the **active labor market policy** pursued by the Swedish government. The policy is based on the premise that it is better for the government to *actively* promote reduction of unemployment rather than *passively* compensating those who are unemployed.

According to Gösta Rehn, a major architect of the Swedish system, an active labor market policy includes three components. **Demand-oriented programs,** which account for more than half of all expenditures on active measures, are designed to create and maintain jobs. These include programs of relief work, self-employment support, and recruitment and job subsidies for youth, refugees and immigrants, the long-term unemployed, and the disabled. **Supply-oriented programs,** accounting for about one-third of active measure expenditures, include training programs and relocation grants to prepare the labor force for available and emerging areas of employment. Between 1990 and 1992, when the nation plunged into a deep recession, enrollment in training programs more than doubled, rising to about 92,000, or about 2 percent of the labor force. **Matching programs,** accounting for about 10 percent of active expenditures, are designed to enhance the short-term flexibility and efficiency of the labor market. These include job information and placement services.[25] During the 1980s and early 1990s, the Swedish governments assigned rising priorities to supply-oriented and matching programs, reducing the dominance of demanded-oriented programs.

Management of Swedish labor market policy is the responsibility of the national Labor Market Board (LMB), the 24 county labor boards, and the public employment service (PES). The PES maintains about 360 local employment offices, and until 1993 it had a monopoly on job placements. In the late 1980s, the average PES officer had to serve only 14 unemployed persons—a very low number in international perspective. Thus, each client received intensive assistance. In 1994, with unemployment rising, the average

[23]Olsen, "Re-Modeling Sweden," 5.

[24]*OECD Economic Surveys:* Sweden 1993–1994, 39.

[25]Gösta Rehn, "Swedish Active Labor Market Policy: Retrospect and Prospect," *Industrial Relations* 24 (Winter 1985): 62; updated with information from Pär Trehörning, *Measures to Combat Unemployment in Sweden: Labor Market Policy in the Mid-1990s* (Stockholm: The Swedish Institute, 1993), 58–77.

■ **FIGURE 13.1**

UNEMPLOYMENT IN SWEDEN
AND OECD, 1985–1994 (PERCENT)

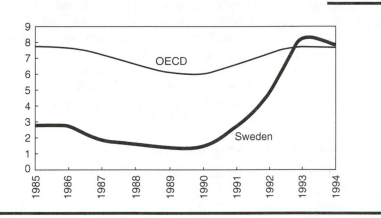

caseload increased to more than 50 clients. Although still a small number internationally, this was a serious deterioration in the Swedish context.[26]

Traditionally, the national and county labor market boards all included representatives from government and from business and labor organizations. In 1992, however, the national LMB was reorganized, allowing the labor and employer organizations to play only an advisory role. Board members now are purportedly chosen to represent the broader public interest.

Because a wide range of governmental programs are administered by the labor boards, they can respond to a problem such as a plant closing in a variety of ways. They can increase public-service employment, attract new firms or support existing ones with subsidies, increase the issue of building permits, expand occupational training courses, and/or pay for job searches and moving expenses for workers who must leave the target area.

What contribution did active labor market programs make to Sweden's economic performance? Unfortunately, formal studies of this question have been inconclusive. Efforts to measure the effectiveness of training programs, for example, have produced mixed results.[27] Extensive public-sector employment and private-sector subsidies may have reduced Swedish productivity and economic efficiency, but defenders of the system argue that relief work is economically and psychologically preferable to unemployment. In fact, the Swedish system faintly resembles some of the work-for-welfare schemes that have been adopted by conservative governments in other industrial countries (Figure 13.1).

Again, a major purpose of the active labor market policy is to avoid the passive payment of unemployment insurance benefits. Traditionally, this strategy seemed to work; unemployment rates remained low before the

---

[26]*OECD Economic Surveys:* Sweden 1995, 67–68.

[27]Ibid, 68–69; and Richard B. Freeman, "The Large Welfare State as a System," *American Economic Review* 85 (May 1995): 18.

1990s, and expenditures on active programs were usually about three times larger than expenditures on unemployment compensation. This was true despite the fact that Sweden had perhaps the most generous system of unemployment insurance benefits in the world, and it does today.

In 1991, the unemployment insurance system replaced up to 90 percent of a jobless person's previous pay. This **replacement rate** was up sharply from 58 percent in 1971, and was much higher than the 56 percent average for other OECD countries in 1991. In an effort to strengthen work incentives, the Moderate government reduced the replacement rate to 80 percent in 1993 and to 75 percent in 1995, but the SDP government, under pressure from the LO, restored the rate to 90 percent in 1996.[28]

CODETERMINATION AND EMPLOYEE OWNERSHIP

Like their counterparts in Germany, Swedish workers are able to participate in management through their involvement in works councils (which play a consulting role on hiring and firing policy, employee safety, and other manpower issues) and through their representation on company boards of directors. Under legislation passed in the mid-1970s, each company with 25 or more employees must allow the local union to appoint two board members. The employee representatives are not allowed to participate on the board when it considers industrial relations and collective bargaining issues.

Although the system of codetermination has been controversial, it was eclipsed for many years by the movement to transfer a large share of corporate ownership to laborers through the formation of **wage earner funds**.[29] These were first proposed by Rudolph Meidner, the chief LO economist, in a report presented in 1975, and the issue dominated the 1982 and 1985 elections.

The funds were established by an act of parliament in 1982 and became operational in 1984. They were financed through a tax on corporate profits and a supplementary payroll tax. Whereas the original Meidner plan would have created one large fund under the control of the LO, the actual legislation avoided concentration of economic power by establishing five regionally based funds. Each was controlled by a government-appointed board of worker representatives.

To some observers, the funds represented a Swedish road to socialism, transferring a share of wealth and ownership to the workers. Proponents at the LO argued that the funds would make the public more tolerant of large corporate profits and more moderate in their wage demands. Indeed, the funds were established in exchange for a pledge from the LO to accept very small wage increases for its members in 1984.

On the other hand, public opinion polls indicated that a majority of Swedes were opposed to the wage earner funds. They feared that the funds

---

[28]*OECD Economic Surveys: Sweden 1995*, 60–61; and *Wired from Sweden*, May 12, 1996, 4 <http://www.si.se/wired.html>.

[29]See Kristina Ahlen, "Sweden Introduces Employee Ownership," *The Political Quarterly* 56 (April–June 1985): 186–193; and Jonas Pontusson and Sarosh Kuruvilla, "Swedish Wage-Earner Funds: An Experiment in Economic Democracy," *Industrial and Labor Relations Review* 45 (July 1992): 779–791.

would increase the power of the already-powerful union bureaucrats. Thus, the funds were discontinued when the Moderate government entered office in 1991. Most of their capital was transferred into regional holding companies that fund research and new businesses.

THE FINANCIAL SYSTEM

The Swedish financial system is similar in most respects to the financial systems of other continental European nations that we have considered. It is directed by the Sveriges Riksbank, the oldest central bank in the world, which has been governmentally owned and operated since its establishment in 1668. The nation's largest commercial bank, Nordbanken, was partially privatized in 1995, and all Sweden's other commercial banks are owned privately.[30] The system also includes a small stock exchange and networks of savings banks, cooperative agricultural credit societies, mortgage institutions, and finance companies.

Accounting for over half of all long-term funds, the largest lender in the Swedish credit market is the National Pension Insurance Fund. Established in 1960 to partially fund the then new supplementary earnings-related pension program, the system is divided into nine sub-funds to prevent any one from dominating the capital markets. These are governed by boards that differ in various ways, but generally include government and employee representatives. Thus, the government has been able to implement some of its investment priorities through the credit market. In particular, the pension funds have been used to support the housing industry.[31]

THE GOVERNMENTAL SECTOR

As we have noted, the influence of the government is seen everywhere in Sweden. Generally speaking, the Swedes have led the rest of the world in stabilization policy, redistribution of income, health insurance, and environmental and consumer protection. On the other hand, direct control of production through nationalized industries usually has been limited.

FISCAL AND MONETARY POLICY

In 1930, even before the Great Depression reached Sweden, a group of Social Democrats made a proposal to the Parliament to use expansionary fiscal and monetary policies to reduce the rate of unemployment. When the Social Democrats entered office in 1932, these recommendations became governmental policy. The result? The annual unemployment rate, which hit a Depression peak of 15 percent in Great Britain and 22 percent in the United States, never exceeded 7 percent in Sweden.

---

[30]In 1992, during the onset of recession, Nordbanken was rescued by the government in the face of huge losses. Its turnaround was "swift and dramatic." See Rupert Bruce, "A Scandinavian Success Story," *Institutional Investor,* January 1996, 84.

[31]Leif Haanes-Olsen, "Investment of Social Security Reserves in Three Countries: Canada, Japan, Sweden," *Social Security Bulletin* 53 (February 1990): 2.

Fiscal activism remained an important element of the Swedish model in the postwar era. Beginning in 1955, the traditional instruments of monetary and fiscal policy were supplemented with the use of the **investment reserve funds system.**[32] The investment reserve was designed to stabilize investment expenditure by awarding tax advantages to companies that saved during boom periods and invested during downturns. The system was flexible and responsive because it was controlled by the Labor Market Board, and could be used without a new act of Parliament.

The reserve system worked roughly as follows. A Swedish company could escape taxation on up to 40 percent of its profits in any year by setting them aside in a noninterest-bearing investment reserve account with the central Riksbank. Money placed in the account could be used for capital investments, but the timing, nature, and location of the investments were approved by the Labor Market Board. Through its control over the funds, the Labor Market Board was able to influence the timing of about one-eighth of all private investment. A careful econometric investigation by John B. Taylor indicated that the system was quite successful in stabilizing Swedish investment during the 1950s and 1960s.[33]

According to critics of the investment reserve system, it added to the complexity of the tax system, and it distorted the economy because it favored capital-intensive industries with historically high rates of profit. Furthermore, it encouraged companies to use their funds internally, rather than making them available to the broader capital market. This reduced the availablity of venture capital needed to finance smaller businesses, which are underrepresented in the Swedish business system.

Thus, the investment reserve system was abolished in 1991 in connection with a comprehensive reform and simplification of corporate taxes. The basic tax rate on corporate profits was reduced in stages from 52 percent in 1989 to 28 percent in 1992. Today, among industrial countries, only Finland has a lower rate of taxation on corporate profits.[34]

Along with corporate taxes, the top rate of taxation on personal income was also reduced in stages from 80 percent in 1985 to 51 percent in 1991 (20 percent for the central government and 31 percent for the counties). These tax reductions were offset, however, by an increase in the rate of the value-added taxation from 23.5 percent to 25 percent in 1990, and by extending its base in 1991 to include passenger transport, entertainment, telecommunications, construction, and a wide range of personal services.

Taking this all together, central government taxes on income and profits fell from 6 percent of GDP in 1980 to 2 percent of GDP in 1993, while central government taxes on goods and services increased from 10 percent of GDP to 13 percent of GDP. Also between 1980 and 1993, social security contributions

---

[32]The investment reserve funds were actually established in 1938, but they were not used for countercyclical purposes until 1955.

[33]John B. Taylor, "The Swedish Investment Reserve Funds System as a Stabilization Policy Rule," *Brookings Papers on Economic Activity,* No. 1 (1982): 97.

[34]John Burton, "Imbalances to Be Corrected: The Tax Reform of the Century," *Financial Times,* July 3, 1990, supplement, 4; and Invest in Sweden Agency <http://www.isa.se/taxation.htm>.

were raised from 12 percent of GDP to 15 percent of GDP.[35] Total government revenue—central, county, and local—increased from 56 percent of GDP in 1980 to a peak of nearly 64 percent of GDP in 1989, and then declined to 58 percent of GDP in 1994.[36]

While revenues declined in relation to GDP between 1989 and 1993, relief and training programs associated with the recession caused expenditures to surge from 58 percent of GDP to a staggering 71 percent of GDP.[37] This is a level of government spending that has seldom (if ever) been matched by any country during peacetime. The budget balance, which recorded surpluses between 1987 and 1990, descended to a deficit in 1993 exceeding 13 percent of GDP. Since that time, an export-oriented economic recovery and a series of governmental austerity programs have been working together to reduce the deficit. When the SDP leaders returned to power in 1994, they launched an ambitious 118-billion-kronor ($17.5 billion) savings plan, and 8 billion kronor ($1 billion) of additional savings was announced in April 1996. About two-thirds of these savings were to come from spending cuts, and one-third from new taxes.

In its handling of monetary policy, the Swedish central bank has traditionally utilized a broader arsenal of controls than its counterparts in the United States, Great Britain, or Germany. In addition to its use of traditional tools, such as open-market operations, reserve requirements, and discounting, the Riksbank has also exercised direct control over bank lending. In the mid-1980s, for example, banks were instructed to increase their lending in Swedish kronor by no more than 4 percent for purposes other than housing.[38]

In recent years, and particularly after the decision in 1994 to join the European Union, monetary policy has been focused more and more narrowly on control of inflation and external stabilization of the kronor.[39] Thus, Swedish inflation was below the OECD average in the 1980s and early 1990s (Table 13.1). In 1995, in line with the requirements for participation in European monetary union, the governors of the Riksbank asked Parliament to change its charter, providing it with greater independence from political authority.[40]

SOCIAL WELFARE AND INCOME REDISTRIBUTION

Sweden devotes about one-third of its GDP to public social protection expenditures—a larger proportion than any other industrial country (Table 13.3). The Swedish welfare system includes cash maternity benefits;

---

[35]World Bank, *World Development Report 1995* (Oxford: Oxford University Press, 1995), 183.

[36]*OECD Economic Outlook,* June 1997, A32.

[37]Ibid., A28.

[38]*OECD Economic Surveys: Sweden 1984/1985,* 71

[39]For a brief period in 1992, in a move to crush speculation against the kronor, the Riksbank raised its lending rate to a staggering 500 percent. See *Financial Times,* September 17, 1992, 2.

[40]"Sweden's Riksbank Seeks More Constitutional Freedom," Reuter News Service, October 19, 1995.

■ TABLE 13.3

PUBLIC EXPENDITURES ON SOCIAL PROTECTION, 1959–1994

Percentage of GDP

	1959-60	1980	1990	1994
Austria	10.0	23.4	24.5	30.2
Belgium	10.1	25.4	26.9	27.1
Canada	8.1	—	18.8	n.a.
Denmark	9.6	26.0	26.9	30.8
Finland	7.1	21.4	25.4	34.8
France	9.0	23.9	27.7	30.5
Germany	11.0	25.4	26.9	30.8
Ireland	7.7	20.6	19.4	21.1
Italy	8.4	19.8	23.6	25.3
Luxembourg	n.a.	26.0	22.5	24.9
Netherlands	8.8	27.2	32.2	32.3
Norway	7.5	21.4	28.7	n.a.
Portugal	n.a.	13.6	15.3	n.a.
Spain	n.a.	16.8	20.7	23.6
Sweden	10.0	32.4	33.1	n.a.
United Kingdom	8.8	21.3	22.7	28.1
United States	4.8	14.1	14.6	n.a.

SOURCES: For 1959–1960: Margaret S. Gordon, *Social Security Policies in Industrial Countries* (Cambridge: Cambridge University Press, 1988), 348–350. For 1980 and 1990: OECD, *Employment Outlook*, July 1994, 151. For 1990 and 1994: *Eurostat Yearbook 1996*, 243.

family allowances for each child under 16 years of age, regardless of family income; free childcare; and free public education through graduate school. According to an analysis by OECD, Sweden not only has a comprehensive system of benefits, but also ranks persistently among the top countries in every category of social welfare spending.[41]

The nation's system of comprehensive health insurance, which is administered by the 23 county governments, covers medical and dental treatment, hospitalization and surgery, and pharmaceutical costs. The government also provides vacation grants for housewives, free marital counseling, generous retirement and disability pensions, and a network of paid Samaritans to dispense home help to the elderly.

Particularly generous are the parental insurance benefits, which provide income compensation for up to 450 days, divided between the parents however they wish until a child reaches eight years of age. During the first

[41]*OECD Economic Surveys: Sweden 1993/1994*, 81.

360 days, the benefit provides approximately 90 percent of the parent's normal income, and during the last 90 days a fixed amount is paid to all parents.

On the positive side of the ledger, the welfare state, together with the legacies of the system of wage solidarity, contributes to the fact that Sweden has the most even distribution of after-tax income in the Western world, and, by most measures, the lowest incidence of poverty.[42] Moreover, Swedish social welfare spending has had a demonstrable impact on the health and education of the population. No nation, other than Japan, has a significantly longer life expectancy or a lower level of infant mortality than Sweden.

On the other hand, a number of studies have shown that the Swedish level of equality could have been accomplished with a much smaller system of transfer payments and taxes. Many of the programs are provided to all members of the population, without an income requirement. One of the most powerful results of these universal programs, according to Sherwin Rosen, is the high level of labor participation among women, who have accounted for nearly all of the growth in public-sector employment:

In Sweden, a large fraction of women work in the public sector to take care of the children of other women who work in the public sector to care for the parents of the women who look after their children.[43]

As we have noted, the welfare state requires a heavy burden of taxation and other revenue, accounting for about 60 percent of Swedish national income—roughly double the American or Japanese proportions. The high level of taxation has clearly damaged work incentives. The average Swedish workweek is one of the shortest in the world, and its rate of absenteeism is among the highest. On an average day, one in every four workers is away from work on sick leave, child-care leave, study leave, or for one of many other reasons.[44] Of course, this may only reflect the value placed on leisure by an increasingly affluent society. In the early 1980s, Swedish salaried workers were asked, "If you had to choose between a salary raise and a longer vacation, which would you choose?" Fifty-eight percent answered that they would prefer a longer vacation—on top of the five weeks they already received.[45]

Despite its cost in taxation and productivity, political support of the welfare state is strong in Sweden, partly because about half the population receives some part of its income from the public system. Swedish political leaders are trying to trim and reform the system, but ultimately they are trying to find its sustainable core.

---

[42]Ibid., 84; Timothy M. Smeeding et al., "Poverty, Inequality, and Family Living Standards Impacts Across Seven Nations: The Effect of Noncash Subsidies for Health, Education, and Housing," *Review of Income and Wealth* 39 (September 1993): 249–252.

[43]Sherwin Rosen, quoted in Martin Wolf, "The Limits of Socialism," *Financial Times,* April 18, 1995, 25.

[44]"A Change of Course: Something Rotten in the Welfare State," *The Economist,* March 3, 1990, 10.

[45]Hans Zetterberg and Greta Frankel, "Working Less and Enjoying It More in Sweden," *Public Opinion,* August–September, 1981, 43.

SWEDEN IN THE EUROPEAN UNION

The Swedish decision to join the EU, which became effective at the beginning of 1995, was the culmination of a struggle between two priorities. The first priority, which dominated policy during the years before 1994, was the maintenance of an independent foreign and domestic policy. Membership in the EU, participation in EU institutions, and direct exposure to EU competition would jeopardize Sweden's ability to maintain a unique welfare state, an active labor market policy, a clean natural environment, a flexible exchange rate for the kronor, and a policy of military neutrality. The other priority, which dominates policy today, is Sweden's necessity as a small country to remain competitive on the world market, and to have full access to its largest trade and investment partners in Europe.

European issues draw some of the clearest lines between Swedish politicians. Members of the Left party and traditionalists in the SDP are generally opposed to EU membership, and they certainly oppose projects such as European monetary union. At the other end of the spectrum, members of the Moderate party support full participation in Europe. They generally believe that Sweden should adapt to the EU, rather than pressing for the EU to adapt to Swedish practices. Members of the Center party and so-called renewers in the SDP attempt to establish a middle ground. Sweden must participate in the EU, they say, and it should attempt to participate in monetary union, but the EU should not force Sweden to abandon the "core" of the welfare state; Sweden should serve as a "conscience" for Europe, and should encourage other countries to protect their poor, their workers, their natural environments, and the poor of other nations.

SUMMARY

Sweden is a small, geographically isolated country. Its isolation has lightened its military burden and promoted a cultural homogeneity that is conducive to cooperation and egalitarianism. The reform-socialist Social Democratic Party has ruled with few interruptions since 1932, but it has never pressed for nationalization of industry. Many Swedish workers are employed in large companies, and, because Sweden is a small country, many of its industries are highly concentrated. Still, firms face foreign competition and a strong system of consumer cooperatives.

Sweden has a tradition of peaceful labor-management relations, despite the fact that over 80 percent of the labor force is unionized. This is explained in part by the orderly system of conflict resolution established in the Basic Agreement of 1938 and in part by the centralized system of collective bargaining created in the 1950s. However, centralized collective bargaining has deteriorated in recent years as labor unions have split on the issue of wage solidarity.

Until the 1990s, unemployment remained at very low levels, supported by an active labor market policy of governmental support for job creation, information, training, and relocation, and by an active fiscal policy. For many years, the latter included a special investment reserve program that allowed the government to stimulate and stabilize the level of investment expenditure.

The lifelong social welfare system is one of the most comprehensive in the world. Thus, Sweden has the most even distribution of after-tax income in the Western world and one of the healthiest and best-educated populations. High taxes seem to weaken work incentives, but popular support for welfare-state policies is very strong.

The decision to enter the EU, beginning in 1995, represented a shift of Swedish priorities from economic and political independence to economic interdependence. The EU is still a matter, though, of political controversy.

Discussion and Review Questions

1. Describe the Swedish industrial structure. What is the government's policy concerning nationalization? Is industry relatively concentrated? Why? How is monopoly power contained?

2. Explain the operation of centralized collective bargaining. What caused labor and management to adopt the system? How has it been weakened in recent years?

3. What is the purpose of an active labor market policy? What does it include? Does it have any drawbacks?

4. How was the investment reserve fund used to stabilize the economy? How did it differ from the conventional tools of fiscal policy?

5. How has the high level of welfare-state taxation affected the operation of the Swedish labor market?

6. How do Swedish political parties differ on the subject of European participation?

Suggested Readings

Bosworth, Barry P., and Alice M. Rivlin, eds. *The Swedish Economy.* Washington, D.C.: The Brookings Institution, 1987. *Based on a conference held in 1986, this book includes eight chapters by American authors with comments by Swedes. The emphasis is on macroeconomic policy, but attention is also given to the operation of the labor market, the systems of public expenditure and finance, and the political foundations of economic policy.*

Lachman, Desmond, Adam Bennett, John H. Green, Robert Hagemann, and Ramana Ramaswamy. *Challenges to the Swedish Welfare State.* Occasional Paper No. 130. Washington, D.C.: International Monetary Fund, 1995. *The authors are mildly critical of the Swedish model in their analyses of recent monetary, fiscal, labor, foreign exchange, and social policies.*

Lundberg, Erik. "The Rise and Fall of the Swedish Model." *Journal of Economic Literature* 23 (March 1985): 1–36. *A good general survey. Argues that the*

Social Democrats were radicalized under Olaf Palme while out of office during 1976–1982, and their subsequent policies (such as the employee investment funds) departed from those in the "golden decades" of the 1950s and 1960s.

Milner, Henry. *Sweden: Social Democracy in Practice.* Oxford: Oxford University Press, 1989. *Written by a political scientist, this is a sympathetic analysis of the social, cultural, and economic building blocks of Swedish social democracy. Against those who predict an "end of the Swedish model," Milner predicts its renewal.*

Trehörning, Pär. *Measures to Combat Unemployment in Sweden: Labor Market Policy in the Mid-1990s.* Stockholm: The Swedish Institute, 1993. *A concise and nontechnical discussion of Swedish labor markets, with a full description of training programs, placement and relocation services, and other weapons in an arsenal of active labor market policy.*

INTERNET RESOURCES

Aftonbladet (News in Swedish)
http://www.aftonbladet.se/

Aktiespararna (Business News in Swedish)
http://www.aktiespararna.se/

Center Party
http://www.centerpartiet.se/

Dagens Industri (Business News in Swedish)
http://www.di.se/

Embassy of Sweden (Washington, D.C.)
http://www.sweden.nw.dc.us/sweden/

Finance Ministry—Expert Group on Public Finance
http://www.infopak.ministry.se/eso.htm

Information Rosenbad—Swedish Government
http://www.sb.gov.se/

Institute of Economic Research
University of Lund
http://www.ec.lu.se/ekforsk/

Invest in Sweden Agency
http://www.isa.se/

LO (Landsorganisationen i Sverige)
Swedish Labor Confederation
http://www.lo.se/

Moderate Party
http://www.moderat.se/Mod2.htm

National Board for Industrial and Technical Development
http://www.nutek.se/home_page_eng.html

On Sweden
gopher://gopher.si.se:70/11/english/onsweden

Radio Sweden News
http://www.sr.se/rs/english/news.htm

SAF (Svenska Arbetsgivareforeningen)
Swedish Employers' Confederation
http://www.spray.se/safproto/saf/

SAP (Sveriges Socialdemokratiska Arbetarepartiet)
Swedish Social Democratic Party
http://www.sap.se/

Statistics Sweden
http://www.scb.se/indexeng.htm

Svenska Dagenbladet (News in Swedish)
http://www.svd.se/svd/

Sweden Online
http://www.swedentrade.com/

Sweden: Welfare-State Sclerosis
http://www.cato.org/main/pa-160.html

Swedish Corporations
http://www.netg.se/Oppen/Foretagsinfo/UKindex.html

Swedish Data Archive
http://www.ssd.gu.se/enghome.html

Swedish Economic History
http://www.scb.se/snabb/keyeng2.htm

Swedish Economic Indicators
http://www.westnet.se/sweden/industry/dev/

Swedish Economy
http://www.informatik.umu.se:80/sweden_info/SI/economy.html

Swedish Information Service
http://www.webcom.com/sis/

Swedish News and Media
http://www.it-kompetens.se/swedish/media.html

CENTRAL EURASIA

Regions of Central Eurasia

14

RUSSIA, EAST-CENTRAL EUROPE, AND CENTRAL ASIA: OVERVIEW AND ECONOMIC HISTORY

Nature has given us [Slavic nobles] a prime advantage. *Our people are not ambitious.* They do not yearn for power and therefore readily submit themselves to anyone who knows their nature, who can thus easily force them to do hard work or engage in war. Most other nations are different. We are content with simple food and drink and do not make any special effort to prepare it.[1]

—IURII KRIZHANICH, *POLITIKA*, 1666

The men of the Communist Party, the leaders of the KGB and the military and the millions of provincial functionaries who had grown up on a falsified history, could not bear the truth. Not because they didn't believe it. They knew the facts of the past better than anybody else. But the truth challenged their existence, their comfort and privileges. Their right to a decent office, a cut of meat, a month of vacation in the Crimea—it all depended on a colossal social deception, on the forced ignorance of 280 million people.

—DAVID REMNICK, *LENIN'S TOMB*, 1993

ime and time again, historic events in Russia, east-central Europe, and central Asia have transformed the economic, political, and military fortunes of the world. The inhabitants of this region endured the invasions of European and Asiatic empires, provided battlefields for two world wars and a

---

[1]English Translation from John M. Letiche and Basil Dmytryshyn, *Russian Statecraft: The Politika of Iurii Krizhanich* (Oxford: Basil Blackwell, 1985), 161.

lengthy cold war, and participated in the rise and fall of communism. Today, several countries in the region are seeking membership in the European Union and NATO, and all are seeking new paths to economic development and external security. In this chapter and the three that follow, we shall survey the economic and institutional history of this pivotal region, and examine the transition strategies being implemented today.

For simplicity of expression, we use the term **central Eurasia** to refer to an area encompassing 27 contemporary nations—15 that previously were republics of the Soviet Union and 12 in east-central and southern Europe that fell under Soviet influence after World War II.[2] This is a region of enormous diversity, but a shared legacy of Soviet influence caused all these countries (or their predecessors) to have some experience with nationalized industry, collectivized agriculture, and central economic planning. Before 1991, most of them were allied economically through the Council for Mutual Economic Assistance (CMEA) and militarily through the Warsaw Pact.[3] Today, they are embarking on many different paths from the totalitarian past to the uncertain future.

OVERVIEW OF CENTRAL EURASIA

Although the nations of central Eurasia share many historical legacies and developmental challenges, the region is also marked by enormous diversities of geography, economy, and culture. The highest rates of urbanization, for example, are found in the northern regions—Russia and the Baltic states— where agricultural opportunities are limited; the lowest rates of urbanization are found in the central Asian area, south of Kazakhstan, and in the Balkan region, south of Slovenia (Table 14.1).

The undisputed giant of the realm is the Russian Federation, accounting for 36 percent of the region's population, 40 percent of its production of goods and services, and 73 percent of its surface area. Russia is geographically the largest nation on earth, spanning 11 time zones and an area 70 percent larger than Canada, China, or the United States. It has perhaps one-fourth of the world's reserves of natural gas, about 12 percent of its oil, and major reserves of many other natural resources.[4]

Outside Russia, the largest nations in the region are Ukraine and Poland (in population and national income) and Kazakhstan (ranked ninth in the

---

[2]Please note that our operational definition of the term *Central Eurasia* is only a matter of convenience. Different agencies and authors use the term in different ways, and no special accuracy is pretended here. Also note the difference between Central Eurasia—the entire region under consideration—and central Asia—the subregion consisting of five Asiatic nations of the former Soviet Union.

[3]Former Yugoslavia had only associate membership in the CMEA and was never a member of the Warsaw Pact. Albania ceased to particpate in both organizations when it broke relations with the Soviet bloc in 1961.

[4]These oil and gas figures are based on the ultimate reserve concept. See C. D. Masters, D. H. Root, and E. D. Attanasi, "Resource Constraints in Petroleum Production Potential," *Science* 253 (July 12, 1991): 146–152.

■ TABLE 14.1

CENTRAL EURASIA IN 1995: BASIC INDICATORS

	Popu-lation (millions)	Area (thou-sands of sq. km.)	Total GDP (billion dollars at purchas-ing power parity)	GDP per Capita (dollars at purchas-ing power parity)	Infant Mor-tality Rate*	Urban popu-lation (% of total)
Total Region	**415.7**	**23,445**	**1,653.4**	**3,980**	**19**	**65**
Former Soviet Union	**293.0**	**22,277**	**1,024.9**	**3,500**	**21**	**67**
Central Slavic Area	*210.1*	*17,887*	*831.2*	*3,960*	*18*	*72*
Belarus	10.3	208	43.5	4,220	13	71
Russia	148.2	17,075	663.9	4,480	18	73
Ukraine	51.6	604	123.8	2,400	17	70
Caucasus/Black Sea Area	*21.0*	*221*	*33.5*	*1,600*	*21*	*58*
Armenia	3.8	30	8.6	2,260	16	69
Azerbaijan	7.5	87	11.0	1,470	25	56
Georgia	5.4	70	7.9	1,460	18	58
Moldova	4.3	34	6.0	1,400	22	52
Baltic Area	*7.7*	*175*	*29.9*	*3,880*	*17*	*72*
Estonia	1.5	45	6.3	4,200	14	73
Latvia	2.5	65	8.4	3,360	16	73
Lithuania	3.7	65	15.2	4,110	20	72
Central Asian Area	*54.2*	*3,994*	*130.3*	*2,400*	*32*	*46*
Kazakhstan	16.6	2,717	50.0	3,010	27	60
Kyrgyz Republic	4.5	199	8.1	1,800	30	39
Tajikistan	5.8	143	5.2	900	41	32
Turkmenistan	4.5	488	13.0	2,890	46	45
Uzbekistan	22.8	447	54.0	2,370	30	42
East-Central European Region	**64.5**	**534**	**393.9**	**6,110**	**12**	**65**
Former Czechoslovakia	*15.7*	*128*	*120.1*	*7,650*	*9*	*63*
Czech Republic	10.3	79	100.6	9,770	8	65
Slovak Republic	5.4	49	19.5	3,610	11	59
Hungary	10.2	93	65.4	6,410	11	65
Poland	38.6	313	208.4	5,400	14	65
Balkan Region	**58.2**	**634**	**234.6**	**4,030**	**21**	**56**
Albania	3.3	29	9.1	2,760	30	37
Bulgaria	8.4	111	37.6	4,480	15	71
Romania	22.7	238	99.0	4,360	23	55
Former Yugoslavia	*23.8*	*256*	*88.9*	*3,740*	*20*	*54*
Bosnia/Herzegovina	4.4	51	6.6	1,500	30	

Continued

■ TABLE 14.1

(CONTINUED)

	Population (millions)	Area (thousands of sq. km.)	Total GDP (billion dollars at purchasing power parity)	GDP per Capita (dollars at purchasing power parity	Infant Mortality Rate*	Urban population (% of total)
Croatia	4.8	57	17.5	3,650	16	64
Macedonia	2.1	26	7.4	3,520	23	60
Serbia/Montenegro	10.5	102	37.8	3,600	20	
Slovenia	2.0	20	19.6	9,800	7	64

*Deaths during first year of life per 1,000 live births.
SOURCES: World Bank, *World Development Report 1997*, supplemented by sources listed in Tables 14.2 and 14.3 and by the author's calculations.

world in land area). The smallest countries are Estonia and Macedonia (in population and national income), Slovenia (in population and land area), and Albania (in national income).

With relatively high per capita GDPs and low infant mortality rates, the highest standards of living in the region are found in Slovenia, the Czech and Slovak republics, Estonia, Belarus, and Hungary. Four of these countries (Slovenia, the Czech and Slovak republics, and Hungary) were members of the relatively prosperous Austro-Hungarian empire during the nineteenth century. The Estonians have linguistic and cultural ties to Finland and Sweden, the advantage of a thriving port in Tallinn, and more capacity to produce electrical power for each of its residents than Germany, Japan, or the United Kingdom.[5]

The lowest standards of living in Central Eurasia are found in the southern regions—in central Asia (particularly in Tajikistan), the Balkan area (particularly in Albania), and the Caucasus and Black Sea areas (particularly in Armenia and Azerbaijan, nations torn by violent territorial disputes). Many of these countries are rich in natural resources, but most were latecomers to economic development, having spent much of their history under the domination of Mongol and Turkish sultans.

A longer view of demographic trends is provided in Table 14.2. During the years between 1910 and 1920, the turmoil leading to World War I, the Russian revolution, and the Russian civil war caused most of the region to lose population. According to official statistics, regional population growth resumed between 1920 and 1940, but official Soviet statistics apparently were

---

[5]World Bank, *World Development Report 1995*, 224–225.

■ **TABLE 14.2**

POPULATION OF CENTRAL EURASIA, 1910–1995 (MILLIONS)

	c. 1910	c. 1920	c. 1940	1960	1980	1995
Central Eurasia	—	224.5	296.5	308.2	382.4	415.7
Former Soviet Union	159.2	142.9	194.0	208.9	264.8	293.0
Central Slavic Area	132.0	118.3	160.4	167.5	198.6	210.1
Belarus	6.9	4.3	9.0	8.1	9.6	10.3
Russia	89.9	87.8	110.1	117.5	138.8	148.2
Ukraine	35.2	26.2	41.3	41.9	50.2	51.6
Caucasus/Black Sea Area	8.0	7.1	10.7	12.4	18.3	21.0
Armenia	1.0	0.8	1.3	1.8	3.1	3.8
Azerbaijan	2.3	1.9	3.3	3.7	6.1	7.5
Georgia	2.6	2.4	3.6	4.0	5.1	5.4
Moldova	2.1	2.0	2.5	2.9	4.0	4.3
Baltic Area	6.3	4.9	5.9	6.0	7.4	7.7
Estonia	1.0	1.1	1.1	1.2	1.5	1.5
Latvia	2.5	1.8	1.9	2.1	2.5	2.5
Lithuania	2.8	2.0	2.9	2.7	3.4	3.7
Central Asian Area	12.8	12.6	17.0	23.0	40.5	54.2
Kazakhstan	5.6	5.4	6.1	9.3	14.8	16.6
Kyrgyz Republic	0.9	0.9	1.5	2.1	3.6	4.5
Tajikistan	1.0	1.0	1.5	2.0	3.8	5.8
Turkmenistan	1.0	0.9	1.3	1.5	2.8	4.5
Uzbekistan	4.3	4.4	6.6	8.1	15.5	22.8
East-Central European Region	47.3	48.4	59.4	53.3	61.6	64.5
Former Czechoslovakia	13.6	13.6	15.5	13.7	15.3	15.7
Czech Republic	10.1	10.6	12.2	9.5	10.3	10.3
Slovak Republic	3.5	3.0	3.3	4.2	5.0	5.4
Hungary	7.6	8.0	9.1	10.0	10.7	10.2
Poland	26.1	26.8	34.8	29.6	35.6	38.6
Balkan Region	—	33.2	43.1	46.0	56.0	58.2
Albania	—	0.8	1.1	1.5	2.7	3.3
Bulgaria	4.3	4.8	6.3	7.9	8.8	8.4
Romania	12.0	15.6	20.0	18.4	22.2	22.7
Former Yugoslavia	13.0	12.0	15.7	18.4	22.3	23.8
Bosnia/Herzegovina	1.9	—	2.3	3.4	4.1	4.4
Croatia	—	—	3.9	3.9	4.4	4.8
Macedonia	—	—	1.1	1.5	2.0	2.1
Serbia/Montenegro	—	—	6.9	8.1	9.9	10.5
Slovenia	—	—	1.5	1.5	1.9	2.0

NOTE: When possible, these data have been adjusted to conform with current boundaries. The population figures for the Soviet Union in 1940 may be seriously overstated. See Nickolai Shmelev and Vladimir Popov, *The Turning Point: Revitalizing the Soviet Economy* (New York: Doubleday, 1989), 56–58.

SOURCES: B. R. Mitchell, ed., *European Historical Statistics, 1750–1975* (New York: Facts on File, 1980), 29–34, 67–83; M. Hauner, "Human Resources," in *The Economic History of Eastern Europe 1919–1975*, ed. M. C. Kaser (Oxford: Clarendon Press, 1985), 75; Goskomstat, *Narodnoe khoziaistvo SSSR: statisticheskii ezhegodnik* (Moscow: Finansy i statistika, various years); World Bank, "Eastern Europe and Central Asia Overview," <http://www.worldbank.org/html/extdr/eca.html>; and author's estimates.

distorted during this period to conceal the number of deaths associated with collectivization of agriculture and other programs of Stalinist terror.[6] Outside of central Asia, losses during World War II caused populations throughout the region to decline or grow slowly between 1940 and 1960. Population growth resumed between 1960 and 1980, but decelerated between 1980 and 1993. Again, the most rapid rates of population growth were in central Asia. The population of the entire Central Eurasia region did not double between 1920 and 1993, but the population of central Asia quadrupled.

Approximate trends in GDP growth are outlined in Table 14.3. Russia has long had the dominant economy in the region, but stronger growth in other countries caused the Russian share of regional GDP to decline from about 45 percent in 1940 to 40 percent in 1995.[7] The most impressive rates of economic growth apparently were achieved in Kazakhstan, Moldova, Estonia, and Lithuania between 1940 and 1960, and in Armenia, Albania, and Yugoslavia between 1960 and 1980. Most of the region experienced a serious downturn in measured national income between 1980 and 1995 (and particularly between 1990 and 1995), associated with the decline of central planning, with difficult programs of economic transformation, and with hostilities in former Yugoslavia, the Caucasus, and central Asia.

Similar trends are reflected in the per capita GDP figures in Table 14.4. We see that some countries have advanced more rapidly than others, but we also detect an underlying continuity in the Central Eurasian income distribution. It appears that Slovenia, Estonia, Latvia, and the Czech and Slovak republics have long enjoyed relative prosperity, and the central Asian, Caucasian, and other Balkan states have long endured relative poverty. Hungary presents an interesting case because it apparently had a per capita GDP below the regional average in 1940 (and below our estimate for the Soviet Union in 1920), but it rose above the regional average during the years after 1960. Georgia recorded one of the region's best growth performances between 1940 and 1980, but a horrible civil war caused the economy to collapse between 1990 and 1995.

BEGINNINGS

The history of central Eurasia cannot be summarized adequately in a few pages. The subject is complicated by the enormous size and diversity of the region, by the countless alterations of political boundaries, cultural arrange-

---

[6]See Steven Rosefielde, "Excess Mortality in the Soviet Union: A Reconsideration of the Demographic Consequences of Forced Industrialization 1929–1949," *Soviet Studies* 35 (July 1983): 385–409; Barbara A. Anderson and Brian D. Silver, "Demographic Analysis and Population Catastrophes in the USSR," *Slavic Review* 44 (1985): 528; Mark Tolts, "How Many of Us Were There Then?" *Ogonyok* 51 (December 1989), translated in *Current Digest of the Soviet Press* 40 (February 17, 1988): 12; and Nikolai Shmelev and Vladimir Popov, *The Turning Point: Revitalizing the Soviet Economy* (New York: Doubleday, 1989), 56–58.

[7]These figures would be slightly different if we had adopted the estimates of G. I. Khanin rather than those of Abram Bergson and the Central Intelligence Agency. See Mark Harrison, "Soviet Economic Growth Since 1928: The Alternative Statistics of G. I. Khanin," *Europe-Asia Studies* 45 (1993): 141–167.

GROSS DOMESTIC PRODUCT OF CENTRAL EURASIA, 1920–1995
(BILLION 1995 U.S. DOLLARS AT PURCHASING POWER PARITY)

	1920	1940	1960	1980	1990	1995
Central Eurasia	—	461	922.9	2,219.4	2,706.0	1,653.4
Former Soviet Union	191.3	364.0	681.2	1,522.5	1,996.6	1,024.9
Central Slavic Area	—	*316.6*	*553.1*	*1,229.2*	*1,617.9*	*831.2*
Belarus	—	10.4	18.0	47.3	74.9	43.5
Russia	—	248.8	443.8	996.2	1,277.1	663.9
Ukraine	—	57.4	91.3	185.7	265.2	123.8
Caucasus/Black Sea Area	—	*13.2*	*30.0*	*79.7*	*89.8*	*33.5*
Armenia	—	1.9	4.8	14.3	20.5	8.6
Azerbaijan	—	5.0	8.9	25.8	26.8	11.0
Georgia	—	4.7	10.7	26.8	26.5	7.9
Moldova	—	1.6	5.6	12.8	15.9	6.0
Baltic Area	—	*8.7*	*20.4*	*45.9*	*63.4*	*29.9*
Estonia	—	1.3	3.8	10.1	8.9	6.3
Latvia	—	3.8	5.7	12.6	16.5	8.4
Lithuania	—	3.7	11.0	23.2	38.0	15.2
Central Asian Area	—	*25.6*	*77.6*	*167.8*	*225.6*	*130.3*
Kazakhstan	—	9.3	43.0	89.5	109.5	50.0
Kyrgyz Republic	—	2.9	4.8	9.7	15.9	8.1
Tajikistan	—	1.7	4.2	9.3	12.9	5.2
Turkmenistan	—	3.5	7.0	14.0	21.5	13.0
Uzbekistan	—	8.2	18.6	45.4	65.7	54.0
East-Central European Region	8.1	61.7	126.6	391.1	402.7	393.9
Former Czechoslovakia	*17.4*	*37.9*	*81.9*	*137.2*	*140.6*	*120.1*
Czech Republic	—	—	—	118.8	117.8	100.6
Slovak Republic	—	—	—	18.5	22.9	19.5
Hungary	8.1	14.1	35.4	64.7	73.9	65.4
Poland	—	47.5	91.2	189.2	188.2	208.4
Balkan Region	2.9	35.3	115.2	305.8	306.7	234.6
Albania	—	1.5	3.1	10.7	10.5	9.1
Bulgaria	2.9	5.9	15.6	34.2	45.3	37.6
Romania	—	27.9	53.0	118.5	112.3	99.0
Former Yugoslavia	*11.3*	*18.9*	*43.5*	*142.4*	*138.6*	*88.9*
Bosnia/Herzegovina	—	—	8.7	29.1	19.4	6.6
Croatia	—	—	8.2	24.6	24.9	17.5
Macedonia	—	—	3.2	14.6	12.4	7.4
Serbia/Montenegro	—	—	17.6	53.7	61.5	37.8
Slovenia	—	—	5.7	20.4	20.4	19.6

NOTE: Estimates in this and the following table are highly approximate, derived from a variety of sources and estimation procedures, and should be interpreted with caution.

SOURCES: Where available, estimates for 1995 are based on figures for population and per-capita GDP in international dollars in World Bank, *World Development Report 1997*, 214–215. Others are based on estimates in the United Nations Development Program, *Human Development Report 1997*, 146–147. These are linked to earlier years with data from Mitchell, ed., *European Historical Statistics, 1750–1975*, 817–836; E. Lethbridge, "National Income and Product," in *The Economic History of Eastern Europe 1919–1975*, 532, 538; Herbert Block, "Soviet Economic Power Growth," in *Soviet Economy in a New Perspective*, U.S. Congress, Joint Economic Committee, 1976, 246; World Bank, *World Tables, 1995*; Goskomstat, *Narodnoe khoziaistvo SSSR: statisticheskii ezhegodnik*; (various years); International Monitary Fund, *World Economic Outlook*, May 1997, 141; and author's estimates.

ments, and demographic structures that have followed major wars and the expansion and decline of empires, and by the grotesque efforts of political leaders to distort the historical record. Still, a brief outline of economic and cultural history will help us to make sense of contemporary conditions and events in the region.

Settled populations inhabited some areas of central Eurasia during deep antiquity. Paleolithic settlements (dating beyond 20,000 B.C.) apparently existed in the Caucasus area, and relatively large tribes were organized in Armenia by about 1,000 B.C. Settlements were organized in the areas that are now Tajikistan and Estonia by about 3,000 B.C. The modern Albanian language is the only surviving remnant of the Thraco-Illyrian group, which formed the primitive speech of early inhabitants of the Balkan peninsula. An area stretching from eastern Hungary to the southeastern steppes of Russia was populated by the ancient Scythian people by the eighth century B.C. Evidence of early Slavic tribes has been traced back to about 2,000 B.C., when they appeared in the eastern Carpathian region between the Vistula and Dnieper rivers, and these consolidated into a distinguishable ethnic group by about the seventh century B.C. They pressed slowly westward into the Czech lands, eastward into Russia, and eventually southward into the Balkans, establishing themselves as a dominant population in about the seventh century A.D.

Macedonia played a most important role in antiquity. Together with sections of modern Bulgaria and the Caucasus area (modern Armenia, Azerbaijan, and Georgia), ancient Macedon was a border region of the Persian empire in the sixth century B.C. A Greek victory in 480 B.C. forced Persia to withdraw from the Aegean area, and Macedon became an independent region of ancient Greece. Beginning in 359 B.C., Philip of Macedon conquered and united the Greek realm, and, beginning in 334 B.C., Philip's son, Alexander the Great, conquered most of the Persian empire and added new territories in modern Albania, India, Kyrgyzia, and Pakistan—the largest empire the world had yet known. As a former student of Aristotle, Alexander spread Greek culture throughout his empire.

After Alexander's death, the Romans conquered his empire west of modern Iran, and ultimately controlled all of Europe south of the Danube and Rhine rivers. Thus, the Roman empire included the Balkan and Caucasus areas of central Eurasia and the western half of Hungary. North of the Danube, modern Romania (known at the time as Dacia) was one of the last territories to be conquered by the Romans in 105 A.D., and it was one of the first to be abandoned in 207 when the empire was besieged by northern tribes. Still, Romania's modern name, its Romance language, and other elements of its culture are important legacies of its relatively brief connection to Rome.

In 285 A.D., Diocletian attempted to strengthen the Roman empire against external invasion and internal strife by dividing it into a **Western empire,** including modern Croatia, Slovenia, and western Hungary, and an **Eastern empire,** including the remaining southern Balkan area and modern Armenia

■ TABLE 14.4

GDP PER CAPITA OF CENTRAL EURASIA, 1920–1995
(1995 U.S. DOLLARS AT PURCHASING POWER PARITY)

	c. 1920	c. 1940	1960	1980	1990	1995
Central Eurasia	—	**1,550**	**2,990**	**5,800**	**6,570**	**3,980**
Former Soviet Union	**1,200**	**1,880**	**3,260**	**5,750**	**6,920**	**3,500**
Central Slavic Area	—	*1,970*	*3,300*	*6,190*	*7,700*	*3,960*
Belarus	—	1,160	2,220	4,930	7,350	4,220
Russia	—	2,260	3,780	7,180	8,620	4,480
Ukraine	—	1,390	2,180	3,700	5,120	2,400
Caucasus/Black Sea Area	—	*1,230*	*2,420*	*4,350*	*4,420*	*1,600*
Armenia	—	1,460	2,640	4,600	5,700	2,260
Azerbaijan	—	1,500	2,410	4,230	3,780	1,470
Georgia	—	1,300	2,680	5,260	4,820	1,460
Moldova	—	640	1,940	3,210	3,880	1,400
Baltic Area	—	*1,470*	*3,400*	*6,200*	*7,920*	*3,880*
Estonia	—	1,150	3,150	6,730	5,530	4,200
Latvia	—	1,990	2,700	5,040	6,110	3,360
Lithuania	—	1,260	4,060	6,810	10,280	4,110
Central Asian Area	—	*1,510*	*3,370*	*4,140*	*4,490*	*2,400*
Kazakhstan	—	1,520	4,620	6,050	6,520	3,010
Kyrgyz Republic	—	1,940	2,310	2,690	3,880	1,800
Tajikistan	—	1,130	2,110	2,450	2,490	900
Turkmenistan	—	2,690	4,650	4,990	5,970	2,890
Uzbekistan	—	1,250	2,290	2,930	3,210	2,370
East-Central European Region	—	**1,040**	**2,370**	**6,350**	**6,280**	**6,110**
Former Czechoslovakia	*1,280*	*2,790*	*5,280*	*8,970*	*8,960*	*7,650*
Czech Republic	—	—	—	11,530	11,320	9,770
Slovak Republic	—	—	—	3,690	4,310	3,610
Hungary	1,010	1,550	3,540	6,040	7,110	6,410
Poland	—	1,370	3,080	5,310	4,950	5,400
Balkan Region	—	—	**2,500**	**5,460**	**5,220**	**4,030**
Albania	—	1,390	2,040	3,960	3,190	2,760
Bulgaria	610	930	1,980	3,890	5,200	4,480
Romania	—	1,390	2,880	5,340	4,840	4,360
Former Yugoslavia	*870*	*1,580*	*2,360*	*6,390*	*5,870*	*3,740*
Bosnia/Herzegovina	—	—	2,570	7,100	4,310	1,500
Croatia	—	—	2,100	5,590	5,180	3,650
Macedonia	—	—	2,160	7,280	6,190	3,520
Serbia/Montenegro	—	—	2,170	5,420	5,970	3,600
Slovenia	—	—	3,810	10,750	10,210	9,800

NOTE AND SOURCES: See notes to Tables 14.2 and 14.3.

and Georgia. The Eastern empire, with its longer record of civilization, was relatively strong and prosperous at this time, but the West was not able to withstand the invasions of northern tribes.[8]

During the first half of the fourth century A.D., Constantine temporarily reunited the Eastern and Western empires, built a new capital at Byzantium (later to be known as Constantinople and Istanbul), and caused the entire empire to embrace Christianity. After Rome was captured in 476 A.D. by German invaders, the Eastern empire survived for another millennium, and became known as the **Byzantine empire.** From its capital in Constantinople, the Eastern empire maintained a thriving commerce, and preserved classical civilization while the West passed through its so-called Dark Ages.

Equally important for the cultural history of Europe, a Christian religious tradition developed in Constantinople that grew more and more disconnected from the Church in Rome. The Byzantine emperors did not recognize the pope as leader of the Christian church, and did not allow their own priests to gain political power. The Eastern church adopted Greek rather than Latin for its liturgy, allowed its priests to marry, and maintained a tolerant stance toward Islam and other non-Christian religions. These and many other differences culminated in a formal schism between the Roman Catholic and the Eastern Orthodox churches in 1054, adding to the cultural distance between eastern and western Europe.

BULGARIA AND KIEVAN RUSSIA (NINTH–TWELFTH CENTURIES A.D.)

Bulgaria became the first Slav state in the sixth century A.D. when the Bulgar people intermarried with Slavs with whom they were allied against the Byzantine empire. In 865, a Bulgarian prince accepted Orthodox baptism, setting a precedent, according to J. M. Roberts, for the Christianizing of all the Slav peoples "from the top downwards, by the conversion of their rulers."[9] Unwittingly, the prince may have set a precedent for many other programs of top-down reform that would be undertaken in the Slavic world during subsequent centuries.

During the ninth and tenth centuries, an alliance of Russian city-states developed with its capital in Kiev, at the center of a network of trade routes. Kiev was linked directly to Constantinople in the south and the fur trade in the north by the Dnieper River and the Black Sea. Less directly, it was connected by river and overland transport to central Europe in the west and the Baltic region in the northwest.

The Kievan Russians became a cosmopolitan people, with commercial and cultural ties to most of the known world. In 980, when Prince Vladimir

---

[8]Indeed, Diocletian kept the East for himself, and appointed a co-emperor, Maximian, to manage the Western empire.

[9]J.M. Roberts, *The Penguin History of the World* (London: Penguin Books, 1976), 351.

decided to adopt Christianity as a state religion, he could have followed the example of his Slavic neighbors in Poland, who had already been converted to Roman Catholicism by the Germans. Instead, like the Bulgarians, he was attracted by the beauty and wealth of the Orthodox churches in Constantinople, and by the apparent potential for economic and political relations with the Byzantine empire.

J. M. Roberts is far from alone in his belief that Vladimir made the "single decision which, more than any other, determined Russia's future."[10] Together with Bulgaria and the other Byzantine nations, Russia became culturally isolated from the West. This was symbolized by the fact that the Orthodox Slavs—Russians, Belorussians, Bulgarians, Macedonians, Serbs, and Ukrainians—adopted the Cyrillic alphabet (a mixture of Greek, Latin, and Glagolitic characters), while the Roman Catholic Slavs—Croats, Czechs, Poles, Slovaks, and Slovenes—adopted the Latin alphabet.

THE MONGOL AND TURKISH CONQUESTS (THIRTEENTH–SEVENTEENTH CENTURIES)

Beginning in the thirteenth century, a series of invasions from the east created deeper divisions within Central Eurasia. Between 1221 and 1223, after their conquest of Persia, Mongols (or Tatars, as they also are known) led by Genghis Khan conquered and occupied a portion of the Caucasus area and all of central Asia. Genghis died in 1227, but his grandson, Batu, returned to central Eurasia in 1236, where he looted and destroyed a vast area stretching through Russia, Poland, Moravia (the eastern province of the modern Czech republic), and Hungary. Kiev, Moscow, Cracow, and other major cities were destroyed by fire.

After their initial conquest, the Mongols withdrew quickly from east-central Europe, but economic development was interrupted in that region for several decades by loss of life and property. In western Russia, Mongol occupation continued another century, and in eastern Russia and central Asia, the khanates of the Golden Horde and the White Horde ruled for two centuries. According to the ancient chronicles, two-thirds of the Russian population perished during the Mongol holocaust.

In eastern Russia, the Golden Horde established its capital at Sarai, near modern Volzhsky on the lower Volga. From this stronghold, they organized collection of tribute and conscription of labor. Many of the best Russian craftsmen were taken from their homeland to serve the Mongol rulers, forcing others to return to agriculture. To enforce payment of tribute, the Mongols exercised control over international trade and payments. Thus, Russian ties to international technology and culture were severed, and Russian economic development fell far behind that of the West.

---

[10]Ibid., 355.

To distance themselves from Mongol terror, many Russians moved northward to the areas around Moscow and Novgorod. The Russian princes in these areas continued to collect and pay tribute, so the Mongols awarded them with a measure of autonomy. Gradually, the Moscow princes were able to rebuild their economic and military power, and in 1326 the metropolitan of the Russian Orthodox Church decided to move his seat from the city of Vladimir to the greater security of Moscow. The presence of the metropolitan, in turn, helped to establish Moscow as a new capital of Russia, a suitable successor for fallen Kiev.

In 1453, one year after Russia gained independence from the Mongols, central Eurasia was shaken by another assault from the east. After a long siege, the Turks conquered Constantinople, the capital of the Byzantine empire, changed its name to Istanbul, and proclaimed it to be the capital of their Ottoman empire. The church of St. Sophia, the center of Eastern Orthodox Christianity, was immediately transformed into an Islamic mosque.

In Russia, the fall of Constantinople meant that Moscow was now the only major center of Eastern Orthodoxy—the so-called Third Rome. Also, despite Russia's newfound independence from the Mongols, its opportunities to expand trade with Europe through the Black Sea were disrupted by Istanbul's strategic position on the Bosporus Strait. Thus, Russia was encouraged to continue its traditions of cultural isolation and slow, inward economic development.

In southeastern Europe, the rise of the Ottoman empire was even more important. The Bulgars had already been subdued in 1371, and Serbia became a vassal principality in 1389. In 1463, the Turks took Bosnia and Herzegovina, and, 20 years later, Albania. In 1526, Hungary (including a portion of modern Croatia) was defeated by the Turks, and the young Hungarian king was killed. These conquests were followed by an exceptionally long occupation. Hungary, the first nation to be liberated by the Habsburgs in 1699, was under Turkish control for about 170 years. Serbia, Romania, and Bosnia gained their independence by 1878, Bulgaria in 1908, and Albania in 1913. Thus, a number of countries were occupied by the Turks for 500 years or more.

The Ottoman influence on the Balkan nations was similar in some respects to the Mongol influence on Russia. The Ottomans required payment of tribute and strict regulation of commerce. Many of the Balkan people were converted to the Islamic faith, and the region was economically and culturally isolated from developments in the West.

The areas that are now the Czech and Slovak republics, Poland, and Slovenia were able to avoid Ottoman domination altogether. Indeed, it was a Polish king, Jan Sobieski, who rescued Vienna when it was besieged by the Turks in 1683. We noted that Hungary and Croatia were devastated by the Turks, but were liberated long before the other Balkan states. Thus, all these countries maintained ties to the West, supported by their shared Roman Catholicism, and most of them (Poland being the exception) were members of the Holy Roman and Habsburg empires. Today, they all have per capita incomes above the Central Eurasian average.

PETER THE GREAT AND RUSSIAN EXPANSION (EIGHTEENTH–NINETEENTH CENTURIES)

Long experience with Mongol rule (later reinforced by the efforts of Napoleon and Hitler) caused the Russians to develop a fear and suspicion of foreigners that lingers in their national psyche. When the Russians regained independence in 1452, the capital was located in Moscow, a remote outpost from Western Europe. Foreign travel and commerce were limited; the few outsiders permitted to live in the country were quarantined from the native population. To support a strong military, a strict set of feudal institutions was established under control of the tsar. "In the sway he holds over his people," one sixteenth-century ambassador declared, the tsar "surpasses all of the monarchs of the whole world."[11]

At the beginning of the eighteenth century, on the eve of the Industrial Revolution in England, Russian despotism was no match for Western technology. Peter the Great became convinced of this fact during his grand tour of Europe in 1697–1698. Drawing charges from pious Muscovites that he was the Antichrist, Tsar Peter initiated a crash program to introduce Western science, technology, art, and architecture in Russia. He hired foreign technicians, established an Academy of Sciences, built new state industries, and forbade his nobles to marry before they had some knowledge of mathematics. He forsook Moscow and moved his capital closer to the Western world, on the Gulf of Finland. At untold cost of resources and human lives he built St. Petersburg on swampland and patterned it after Venice and Versailles.

Peter was careful to avoid the adoption of Western political and economic philosophies while importing foreign technology. His Westernization program paradoxically led to stronger autocratic repression and a wider gulf between the aristocracy, who adopted Western ways, and the peasants, who did not.

Peter's military adventures, his program of industrialization, and the building of St. Petersburg required that taxes be levied on everything imaginable: the wearing of beards, the keeping of bees, and the grinding of knives and axes to name a few.[12] Tax revenues increased fivefold during Peter's reign, requiring repressive measures to maintain domestic order and to support his system of forced labor.

Peter and his immediate successors accomplished most of his goals. Between the beginning of his reign and the end of the eighteenth century, new territory was added to the Russian empire in the Baltic area, the Crimea, the northern Caucasus, the Ukraine, part of Central Asia, and Belorussia. Thus, Russia gained access to the Baltic and Black Sea trade routes, the farmlands of the Ukraine, and the iron and coal deposits of Krivoi Rog and the Donets Basin that would support the development of a steel industry in the next

---

[11]The ambassador of the Holy Roman Empire, quoted in Michael Kort, *The Soviet Colossus: A History of the USSR* (New York: Charles Scribner's Sons, 1985), 13.

[12]Peter I. Lyashchenko, *History of the National Economy of Russia* (New York: Macmillan, 1949), 269.

CENTRAL EURASIA IN 1815

Central Eurasia in 1815

century. The number of factories increased from less than 200 in 1725 to about 2,500 at the end of the century.

EMANCIPATION AND INDUSTRIALIZATION (1853–1900)

The maintenance of autocratic and feudal institutions placed limits on Russian economic development. The immobility of the feudal labor force thwarted the growth of agricultural productivity. A repressive society may be able to buy, borrow, and steal technologies from abroad, but it provides a poor environment for the development of new ideas at home. Despite several significant achievements, Russia lagged behind the West in technological progress.

The persistent backwardness of Russian society was dramatized by the Crimean War (1853–1856), when a disastrous defeat was handed to the army by a small but modern force of Europeans. Five years later, Alexander II signed the Emancipation Decree that nominally abolished serfdom in Russia. The decree was long and complex, and had positive and negative elements.

On the positive side, some 47 million serfs, making up about three-quarters of the population, were freed from the arbitrary rule of their masters. Unlike the emancipated Poles and the victims of the European enclosure movement, the Russian serfs were not left landless. About half of the nation's agricultural land was assigned to them.

Unfortunately, the better land was kept by the gentry and the freed serfs were required to pay for their land through a system of so-called redemption payments. The land was not owned individually by the peasants, but as members of village communal organizations (the *mir* or *obshchina*). The commune was responsible for collection of taxes and redemption payments and for the fair apportionment of land to its members. The commune divided its land into small strips. Each family was assigned several strips to tend (sometimes as many as 40), some with higher fertility and some with lower. From time to time, the strips were rotated among the families.

The communal system of strip agriculture may have been equitable, but it was grossly inefficient.[13] The workers lost time traveling from one strip to another and the rotation of plots between families provided little incentive for improving the land. For these and other reasons, the level of productivity in Russian agriculture remained very low after emancipation, and chronic food shortages continued.

Despite low productivity, the peasants were forced to market a large part of their output to pay taxes, redemption payments, and other monetary obligations. Thus, Russia became the world's largest grain exporter during the latter half of the nineteenth century. Grain exports made it possible to import more foreign equipment, and a wave of railroad construction began. Encompassing less than 700 miles of track before the emancipation, the Russian railroad network grew to more than 21,000 miles in 1894.

The railroads made it possible to link the coal of the Donets Basin with the iron ore of Krivoi Rog, and production of iron and steel tripled during the 1890s. Petroleum production also tripled during the decade and production of cotton cloth doubled.

Unfortunately, the industrialization program caused little improvement in the living standards of the common people. The benefits of economic growth were dissipated by rapid population growth and imperial taxation. Between the 1860s and the early 1900s, when infant mortality rates fell

---

[13]Karl Marx suggested in 1882 that the Russian experience with "primeval common ownership" might make it possible to "pass directly to the higher form of communist common ownership." See the preface to the Russian edition of the *Communist Manifesto*, in *The Marx-Engels Reader*, 2d ed., ed. Robert Tucker (New York: W. W. Norton, 1978), 472.

■ TABLE 14.5

INFANT MORTALITY RATES IN EUROPE, 1867–1911 (ANNUAL DEATHS OF INFANTS UNDER ONE YEAR OLD PER THOUSAND LIVE BIRTHS)

	1867–1869	1909–1911
Austria	248	202
Belgium	133	147
Denmark	135	102
England	155	115
Finland	252	114
France	180	128
Germany	304	175
Italy	225	151
Netherlands	204	115
Norway	120	67
Russia	272	252
Sweden	151	73

SOURCE: Mitchell, ed., *European Historical Statistics, 1750–1975*, 137–143.

dramatically in most of Europe, the Russian rate barely declined (Table 14.5) and real wages barely increased.

In a vain attempt to control labor unrest, the tsarist government prohibited the formation of trade unions. This prohibition only contributed to the growth of underground revolutionary organizations. One of these organizations, Liberation of Labor, was founded by George Plekhanov in 1883. Plekhanov's group established close ties with socialist organizations in Western Europe, and laid the foundation for the Russian Social Democratic movement.

THE RUSSIAN REVOLUTIONS AND WORLD WAR I (1900–1918)

The Russian Social Democrats held their first congresses in 1903. Their program called for the overthrow of the tsarist monarchy and the eventual adoption of socialism. The faction that came to be known as the Mensheviks believed that Russia must pass through a bourgeois democratic period before it would be ready for socialism and that the party should be a broad-based mass organization. As we noted in the previous chapter, Lenin's followers, the Bolsheviks, believed that Russia was already ripe for socialism and that party membership should be restricted to an elite group of dedicated revolutionaries. While the Mensheviks won the vote on membership policy, the Bolsheviks gained control of the party's central committee and its newspaper, *Iskra* (The Spark).

The revolutionary movement gained momentum in January 1905 when the palace guard opened fire on thousands of workers assembled at the Winter Palace in St. Petersburg to protest the hardships caused by the war with Japan. Bloody Sunday, as it was called, precipitated a wave of demonstrations and strikes, culminating in a general strike in October. Although few socialist goals were attained, the tsar was forced to grant several concessions, including the formation of a parliament (the Duma). The ensuing Stolypin reforms of 1906 to 1910 released the agricultural peasants from the communes and canceled their debts.

Meanwhile, in the Balkans, a struggle for Slavic independence from the Austro-Hungarian empire led to the outbreak of World War I. In 1909, the Austrians had offended the Russians and Serbs by annexing Bosnia, a Slavic region, as it departed from the Ottoman empire. In 1914, a Serbian nationalist assassinated the Austrian archduke during his visit to the Bosnian capital, Sarajevo. The Austrians, supported by the Germans, responded with a declaration of war, intent to crush the Serbian menace to their monarchy. The Serbs were supported, however, by Russia, France, Britain, Belgium, Montenegro, and, later, Romania. In the end, rather than preserving their monarchy, the Austrians lost it entirely. The Serbs established themselves as the leaders of a strong movement for south Slavic unity.

These new realities were formalized in the **Treaty of Versailles,** signed in 1919. The former Habsburg holdings in Bosnia, Croatia, and Slovenia were united under effective Serbian control with Montenegro and Macedonia, forming a new kingdom that was later named Yugoslavia. Bohemia, Moravia, Slovakia, and part of Ruthenia were merged into a new state of Czechoslovakia. An independent state of Poland was established, but, with few natural borders, its territory became a matter of endless disagreement that eventually contributed to the outbreak of another world war.

In Russia, the war exacted a horrible price. More than 14 million soldiers were enlisted in the war effort, and about 2 million were killed in combat. In 1916, nearly three-fourths of industrial workers were engaged in military production. These commitments of labor and capital caused civilian production to plummet. The annual grain harvest, for example, declined by about 30 percent between 1914 and 1917. These problems were compounded by an inefficient and corrupt system of food distribution.

Food riots broke out in St. Petersburg in February 1917 and the Tsar was forced to abdicate the throne. The Duma established a moderate provisional government, which was eventually headed by Alexander Kerensky of the Labor Party. The provisional government acted very slowly at a time when major reforms were needed and it gradually lost popular support. After several months of planning and a brief exchange of fire, the Bolsheviks (who split from the Mensheviks to form their own party in 1912) took control of the Winter Palace in November 1917.

WAR COMMUNISM (1918–1921)

After seizing power in Russia, the new Bolshevik leaders faced several immediate problems. First, they had to deliver on their promise to create a socialist society. To this end, on the very day of the overthrow they issued a decree that allowed the confiscation of all private and church land and livestock without compensation. Local committees were appointed to distribute the use of the land (but not its ownership) among the peasants in each area.

Second, the Bolshevik victory was won only in St. Petersburg; the consolidation of their rule in the rest of the empire required a long civil war against forces loyal to the tsarist regime. Their efforts to establish domestic control and reform were vastly complicated by Russian cooperation with the Allies in World War I.

After a heated debate, Lenin and his associates decided to cut their losses by negotiating a separate peace with the Germans. In exchange, they were required to recognize German control over several territories in Georgia, the Ukraine, Poland, and the Baltic states that were not yet under Bolshevik rule. Thus, in the 1918 Treaty of Brest-Litovsk, the Bolsheviks signed away their rights to the trade routes, croplands, and iron and coal fields that were the backbone of the economy.

The truce with Germany precipitated an invasion of Allied soldiers, whose mission was to draw Russia back into the war, to recover munitions stored there, and to protect investments that had been nationalized by the Bolsheviks. The new leaders had traded German hostility for Allied intervention in 1918–1919 and were engaged in a civil war and a war with Poland until 1920.

The institutional response to these events was the formation of a military style of economic organization known as **War Communism.** The inefficiency of small-scale agriculture and the loss of Ukraine contributed to severe food shortages; police and party activists were sent into the countryside to forcibly collect the agricultural "surpluses" of the peasants. These and other consumer goods were rationed to workers and their families by governmental agencies. Little use was made of money, and private trade was outlawed. The leaders attempted to justify these measures in ideological terms, claiming that they represented a giant step toward the moneyless economy of full communism. In retrospect, they seem to have been little more than a pragmatic response to a desperate situation.

In industry, some 37,000 enterprises were nationalized, including all those that employed more than ten workers and those with more than five workers where mechanical power was used. These were administered by a complex and confused bureaucracy of central and regional commissariats and councils, led by the Supreme Council of National Economy (*Vesenkha*). The ability of the government to coordinate the work of the nationalized industries was rendered all but impossible by the lack of centralized information. A committee of investigation set up in 1920 found that many of the central authorities not only "do not know what goods and in what amounts are kept in the warehouses under their control, but are actually ignorant even of the number of warehouses."[14]

A strict system of military discipline was exercised over much of the labor force. Labor armies were formed to rebuild the roads and railways (some 7,200 road and rail bridges had been destroyed by the hostilities) and to speed the recovery of coal mining, forestry, and oil extraction. The movement of workers was restricted and deserters were given severe penalties.

How did the system of War Communism perform? Agricultural and industrial production both plummeted during its operation. The uncompensated requisitioning of agricultural surpluses certainly reduced the farmers' work incentives and encouraged them to conceal their surpluses from the authorities. However, it is difficult to determine how much of the reduction in output was caused by poor work incentives and chaotic management practices and how much was caused by the disruption and devastation of war. According to Maurice Dobb, the Soviet authorities were forced by extreme circumstances to adopt their requisitioning and rationing system: "Without it there is small doubt that starvation in the towns in the winter of 1919–1920 would have been very much more extensive, and the army might well have collapsed."[15]

THE NEW ECONOMIC POLICY (1921–1928)

By the end of 1920, the Bolsheviks had won the civil war, consolidated their power, and regained most of the territory surrendered in the Brest-Litovsk Treaty. A series of workers' and soldiers' revolts made it painfully obvious that: (1) the government was not able to administer the entire economy, (2) forced requisitioning provoked anger from the peasants rather than productivity and, (3) the civilian labor force was no longer willing to work under military conditions.

The War Communism controls were no longer necessary or sustainable and in 1921 Lenin replaced them with his New Economic Policy (NEP). The NEP system was, in many ways, an experiment in market socialism. Lenin described it as a temporary step backward to capitalism, designed to get the economy back on its feet, so that it would become possible to take "two steps forward" toward full communism.

First, and perhaps most important, a progressive agricultural tax replaced the system of forced requisitioning, and private trade was legalized. The farmers were able to keep or sell a larger part of any increase in their production, and their incentive to work was restored. Governmental rationing of consumer goods was quickly replaced by private retail trade.

---

[14]Quoted in Maurice Dobb, *Soviet Economic Development Since* 1917 (New York: International Publishers, 1948), 112.

[15]Ibid., 103.

Second, the enterprises with 20 persons or fewer that had been national-ized under War Communism were leased to independent entrepreneurs. Many of the larger enterprises were allowed to operate as autonomous trusts and expected to operate at a profit. The only enterprises kept under direct governmental control were those in the commanding heights of industry—fuel, metallurgy, war industries, transportation, banking, and foreign trade. By controlling these industries, Lenin believed, it would be possible to set the course for the rest of the economy.

Third, the restrictions on labor mobility under War Communism were abolished and income equality gave way to market-determined wages. Labor legislation in 1922 entitled workers to an 8-hour day, a 2-week paid holiday, social insurance benefits, and collective bargaining rights. The re-turn of the profit motive was accompanied by the return of unemployment, which climbed to 1.6 million in 1929.[16]

The performance of the NEP system, like the performance of War Communism, was obscured by exceptional conditions. A drought in 1920–1921 led to a famine in 1921–1922 that caused some 5,000,000 deaths—twice the number of Russian combat casualties in World War I. Even more deaths would have occurred without $70 million of aid provided by the United States and smaller amounts given by other countries. After 1921, however, the NEP system supported a rapid recovery. The prewar levels of agricultural and industrial production were regained in 1925 and 1927, respectively.

The famine of 1921–1922 caused agricultural prices to rise at the beginning of the NEP period; they gradually declined as production recovered in 1922–1923. Industrial prices, on the other hand, were driven upward by mo-nopolistic practices and by the slower recovery of industrial production. If drawn on a chart, the falling agricultural prices and rising industrial prices resembled a pair of scissors, giving rise to the so-called Scissors Crisis of 1923–1924. The Soviet leaders feared, irrationally it seems, that falling agri-cultural prices would eventually cause the peasants to reduce their market-ing of food in the cities. They feared that in order to maintain their production incentives, it would be necessary to allow the farmers to accu-mulate more wealth. This policy seemed inconsistent with socialist ideals; thus, the entire NEP program came under attack.

THE INDUSTRIALIZATION DEBATE

The Scissors Crisis and Lenin's death in 1924 stimulated a heated debate over the proper strategy for Soviet industrialization. Impressed with the rapid re-covery experienced after 1921, Bukharin and his "right-deviation" faction ar-gued for continuation of the market-oriented policies of NEP. They admitted that the Soviet Union would remain an agrarian society for several years if

---

[16] Alec Nove, *An Economic History of the USSR* (London: Penguin, 1969), 115.

market forces were allowed to operate: the country's comparative-cost advantage was currently in agriculture. They defended policies favoring agriculture, however, on both political and economic grounds.

First, the right believed that the legitimacy of the Soviet government was based on the so-called *smychka,* or alliance, between agricultural and industrial workers. Any serious effort to distort market forces to the advantage of industry would alienate the farmers. The *smychka* would be broken and the political basis of Soviet rule would disappear.

In economic terms, the right believed that investment expenditures directed toward modernization of the primitive agricultural sector would reap large returns and these would eventually generate the savings needed for industrial investment. Agricultural development in the short run would most effectively support industrial development in the long run, they argued.

In reply to the *smychka* argument, Trotsky and other members of the "left-deviation" wing of the Bolshevik Party warned that if NEP were continued, and if private agriculture and trade were allowed to grow and prosper, the capitalist system would return. They particularly disliked the slogan that Bukharin launched in 1925 to encourage the farmers: "Get rich." Furthermore, they warned that the Soviet Union, the only socialist country in the world, was surrounded by enemies and that a rapid expansion of heavy industry was necessary to support the military.

In economic terms, the left argued that a big push toward industrialization could be accomplished by exploitation—as they called it—of the private sector. Preobrazhensky, their leading theorist, estimated that between one-third and one-half of all profits in trade and industry in 1922 were accumulated by private traders and capitalists. These resources could be captured by the socialist sector, he suggested, by reviving the state trade monopoly that existed under War Communism, by levying high taxes on the peasants, and by controlling agricultural prices at low levels. If the peasants reacted by reducing their shipments of food to the cities, he suggested that they be forcibly assembled on collective farms where their actions could be controlled and where mass-production techniques could be used.

The industrialization debate was closely connected with two other important debates in the 1920s. The first concerned revolutionary strategy. Would the protection of socialism in the Soviet Union require a worldwide socialist revolution or would it be possible to build socialism in one country? Trotsky and the left adopted the former position, arguing that rapid development of heavy industry and military production was necessary to support the worldwide socialist revolution. Bukharin and the right believed that socialism must be strengthened in Russia before it could be carried to the outside world. They warned that coercive measures against the peasants would provoke a hostile reaction from Western countries (as evidenced by the aid received from the United States during the famine).

Industrialization strategy was also an important theme in the economic planning debate. On one side were the **geneticists,** who believed that any realistic long-term plan must be based on a careful analysis of present and past conditions and experiences—on the "genetic" heritage of the economy. The geneticists adopted the conservative (right) view that any shift from agricultural to industrial production should be gradual. On the other side were the **teleologists,** whose name comes from the Greek word for *end.* They believed that the purpose of economic planning was to accomplish a sharp break from tradition and market forces and that emphasis should be placed on goals rather than beginnings. The support of the workers for the socialist system should open a whole new realm of possibilities, they believed; thus their plans need not be constrained by conventional "genetic" criteria.

THE PLANNING ERA BEGINS (1929–1945)

Stalin initially aligned himself with the right, but problems with grain procurement in 1927 turned him against the peasants and provoked the return of forced requisitioning. Bukharin began to speak of Stalin as a new Genghis Khan (recalling the two centuries of Mongol domination) and of military-feudal exploitation of the peasantry. Stalin responded by declaring, early in 1929, that Bukharin was living in the past.

With the First Five-Year Plan, inaugurated in 1928, Stalin adopted a strategy that was unabashedly leftist and teleological. The plan was predicated on wildly optimistic assumptions and called for rapid rates of growth in all sectors of the economy (Table 14.6). The highest rates of growth were planned for producer goods, the next highest were those for industrial consumer goods, and the lowest priority was given to agriculture.

Statistics on the fulfillment of the plan suggest an even more leftist orientation. A massive effort was devoted to expansion of machinery production, and this portion of the plan was more than fulfilled. All the other sectors of

■ **TABLE 14.6**

THE FIRST SOVIET FIVE-YEAR PLAN, 1928–1933
(TOTAL PERCENTAGE INCREASES)

	Target Growth	Actual Growth (Soviet Estimate)	Actual Growth (Western Estimates)
Industrial Production	136	113	49
Intermediate Goods	181	95	98
Machinery	157	359	359
Consumer Goods	84	63	1
Agriculture	55	−19	−16

SOURCES: First column—Alec Nove, *An Economic History of the USSR* (London: Penguin, 1969), 145–146; second column—Roger Clark, ed., *Soviet Economic Facts 1917–1970* (New York: John Wiley and Sons, 1972), 8–10, 68, and author's estimates; and third column—G. Warren Nutter, *Growth of Industrial Production in the Soviet Union* (Princeton, N.J.: Princeton University Press, 1962), 525–526; and Holland Hunter and Janusz M. Szyrmer, *Faulty Foundations: Soviet Economic Policies 1928–1940* (Princeton, N.J.: Princeton University Press, 1992), 34, 105.

THE LONG WAR AGAINST THE KULAKS

In 1956, in his so-called secret speech, Soviet premier Nikita Khrushchev acknowledged the atrocities committed by his predecessor, Joseph Stalin, and in November 1987, Mikhail Gorbachev told a television audience that the "guilt of Stalin and those close to him before the Party and the people for the mass repressions and lawlessness that were permitted are immense and unforgivable."

While they heaped shame on Stalin, Khrushchev and Gorbachev protected the name of Vladimir Lenin, the father of the Soviet state. In fact, Gorbachev claimed that his purpose in criticizing Stalin was to advance "the final and irreversible assertion of Lenin's ideal of socialism." To hear the historical truth about Lenin from their national leaders, the Russian people had to wait until the months following August 1991, when a failed coup led to the collapse of the Communist party and the opening of secret archives.

For example, Stalin's violent collectivization of agriculture, which caused massive losses of life and liberty during the 1930s, was grounded in Lenin's war against the *kulaks* (rich farmers) during the Russian civil war. On August 11, 1918, the following order was sent to communist leaders in Penza, a town not far from Simbirsk, where Lenin was born:

> Comrades! The kulak revolt in the five districts must be suppressed without mercy. The interest of the entire revolution demands this, because we have now before us our "final and decisive battle" with the kulaks. We need to set an example.
>
> 1. You must hang (and I mean hang so that the *people can see them*) at *least 100* known kulaks, rich men, bloodsuckers.
> 2. Publish their names.
> 3. Take away all of their grain.
> 4. Identify hostages in accordance with yesterday's telegram.
>
> This needs to be accomplished in such a way that people for hundreds of miles will see, tremble, know and scream out: they are choking and strangling those bloodsucking kulaks. Telegraph us acknowledging receipt and execution.
> Yours, Lenin
> P.S. Use your toughest people for this.

In his recent biography of Lenin, Dmitri Volkogonov, a former general of the Soviet army, offered this memorandum as evidence that Lenin employed "inhuman terrorist methods" to support his revolution. Compared to the "bestialities of the civil war," says Volkogonov, "the tragedies of tsarist Russia pale into insignificance."

Continued

CONTINUED

Although the war with the kulaks began 80 years ago, its final battles are still being fought. In June 1996, President Yeltsin found it necessary to issue a decree, "On the Peasant Rebellions of 1918–1922," to restore "historical justice and the legitimate rights of Russian citizens who have been subject to repression for participating in the peasant rebellions." According to the decree, "the right to exoneration" also extends to "children who have been subject to reprisals for the participation of their parents in these rebellions."

sources: "Collectivization and Industrialization," Soviet Archives Exhibit, U.S. Library of Congress, <http://www.ncsa.uiuc.edu:80/SDG/Experimental/soviet.exhibit/collect.html>; David Remnick, *Lenin's Tomb* (New York: Vintage Books, 1993), 50; Dmitri Volkogonov, *Lenin: A New Biography* (New York: The Free Press, 1994), 69–71; and RIA Novosti News Service, June 19, 1996.

the economy fell short of their goals. According to Western estimates, production of industrial consumer goods increased by only 1 percent in 5 years. Official Soviet data revealed that agricultural production declined sharply.

What caused the drop in agricultural production? First, the plan devoted the lion's share of investment resources to industry, and pay incentives attracted millions of workers from agriculture into industry. Second, in his effort to maintain food deliveries to the cities, Stalin again borrowed from Preobrazhensky and, in 1929, launched a massive drive to collectivize agriculture. The land reform, he reasoned, had reduced the number of large, efficient farms and the size of the agricultural surplus marketed in the cities: "The way out lies, firstly, in the transition from the small, backward and scattered peasant farms to amalgamated, large-scale socialized farms, equipped with machinery, armed with scientific knowledge and capable of producing a maximum of grain for the market."[17]

Collectivization was violently resisted by the peasants, who wanted to keep their land, their livestock, and their independence. Rather than surrender them to the government, the peasants slaughtered millions of head of livestock and destroyed large numbers of buildings. The battle over collectivization, the consequent disruption of food production, and Stalin's use of forced labor in the Gulag caused at least 5 million deaths in the 1930s and perhaps as many as 20 million (see "The Long War Against the Kulaks")

At enormous cost, the First Five-Year Plan and the collectivization of agriculture initiated a radical shift toward industrialization of the Soviet economy. Industrial production increased from 28 percent to 45 percent of net national product between 1928 and 1937, building the military-industrial base that repelled Hitler's invasion during World War II and contributed to the country's superpower status after the war. On the other hand, the low priority placed on agricultural production eventually turned the world's largest exporter of grain into the world's largest importer.

---

[17]From Stalin's 1928 address, "On the Grain Front," in *A Documentary History of Communism,* ed. Robert V. Daniels (New York: Random House, 1960), 303.

AFTER WORLD WAR II: SOCIALIST INTEGRATION AND DISINTEGRATION

Before World War II, the Soviet leaders believed (with some justification) that their country was surrounded by capitalist enemies. For this reason, and because it was difficult to forecast and plan foreign trade, the Soviets followed a policy of autarky—they tried to minimize their dependence on foreign trade. After the war, the Soviets occupied most of east-central Europe and were able to install Communist regimes throughout the region. To one degree or another, all the members of the new Soviet bloc adopted Soviet-style systems of autocratic government, collectivized agriculture, and detailed central planning. Stalin proclaimed the establishment of a new socialist trading area:

> The disintegration of the single, all-embracing world market must be regarded as the most important economic sequel of the Second World War. . . . The economic consequence of the existence of two opposite camps was that . . . we now have two parallel world markets also confronting one another.[18]

To consolidate his control of eastern Europe, Stalin required the "fraternal" countries to break most of their ties with the West. He vetoed the plans of Poland and Czechoslovakia to apply for Marshall Plan aid and countered by establishing a socialist **Council for Mutual Economic Assistance (CMEA).**[19] For several years the CMEA remained little more than a press release. It provided little assistance to Eastern Europe; the Soviet Union required its wartime enemies—East Germany, Romania, and Hungary—to pay exorbitant reparations. The East Germans, for example, were required to deliver commodities worth about $4 billion; they were also required to dismantle factories and equipment worth about $12 billion and move them to the Soviet Union. Before the war, the east-central European nations purchased only 17 percent of their imports from one another and from the Soviet Union. By 1953, the figure was 72 percent.[20] From the beginning, there were rumblings in the Soviet camp, and once again the noise was coming from Yugoslavia.

TITO'S YUGOSLAVIA

World War II had a devastating impact on Yugoslavia. Nearly 300,000 farms were destroyed, and the systems of transportation and communication were rendered inoperable. Eleven percent of the population lost their lives in the

---

[18]Joseph Stalin, *Economic Problems of Socialism in the USSR* (New York: International Publishers, 1952), 26.

[19]The CMEA was also known as Comecon. Its members eventually included the Soviet Union, Bulgaria, Czechoslovakia, the German Democratic Republic, Hungary, Poland, Romania, Mongolia, Cuba, and Vietnam. Yugoslavia, North Korea, Angola, Laos, and Ethiopia had observer status. Albania dropped out in 1962.

[20]Franklyn Holzman, *International Trade Under Communism* (New York: Basic Books, 1976), 70.

war, and 3 million people were left homeless.[21] Nevertheless, the Yugoslavs were proud of the fact that they expelled the Nazis without foreign assistance.

The war also produced a national hero, Marshall Tito, who had been captured by the tsarist Russians in 1915 and, as a result, lived in Russia during the revolution. When he returned to Yugoslavia in 1920, Tito became a founding member of the Yugoslav Communist Party (YCP). He was appointed general secretary of the YCP in 1937, and in 1941 he left Belgrade to lead the Partisans in their fight for national liberation. Tito was seriously wounded in combat in 1943, contributing to his reputation as a war hero. He established a new socialist government after the war and ruled until his death in 1980.

Immediately after the war, Tito and his associates attempted to transplant the Soviet political and economic systems into Yugoslavia. He initiated a program of agricultural collectivization, but was unwilling to use excessive force against peasants who had supported his struggle against the Nazis. Against orders from Moscow, Tito wanted to accept Western economic aid to speed recovery from the war and to establish an independent federation of Balkan nations.

Joseph Stalin was unhappy with Tito's relative independence, and he initiated a war of words. In 1948, a meeting of the Comintern (the Soviet-bloc political grouping) expelled Yugoslavia from the organization, and, in 1949, the Soviet Union and its allies attempted to topple the Tito government by imposing a trade embargo. The Yugoslavs attempted to regain Soviet favor by continuing their practice of central planning and by accelerating the collectivization of agriculture until the end of 1949. In 1950, though, Tito accepted aid from the West, and replaced Soviet-style central planning with a new system of labor self-management.

AFTER STALIN (1953–1960)

Central Eurasia was shaken by Stalin's death in 1953 and by Khrushchev's denunciation of Stalin's terror at the 1956 Party Congress. The Albanian leaders criticized Khrushchev for his blasphemy, and dropped out of the Soviet bloc, but Poles and Hungarians were encouraged, and started designing programs of democratic and market reform. When Hungary attempted to resign from the Warsaw Pact in 1956, the effort was crushed by Soviet troops and tanks, but János Kádár, the Hungarian leader installed by the Soviets in 1956, was eventually able to resume progress toward market reform.

The CMEA became a more active organization after the Hungarian uprising. Twelve standing commissions were established in 1956 to exchange technical information. A fledgling attempt was made to coordinate the national five-year plans for 1956–1960. A detailed set of rules was formulated in 1958 for the negotiation of CMEA foreign-trade prices, and plans were ap-

---

[21]Martin Schrenk, Cyrus Ardalan, and Nadal A. El Tatawy, *Yugoslavia: Self-Management Socialism and the Challenge of Development* (Baltimore: The Johns Hopkins University Press, 1979), 12.

proved in that same year to build the 3,000-mile Druzhba (Friendship) Pipeline, that would carry most of the Soviet exports of oil to East Germany, Czechoslovakia, Hungary, and Poland. A set of CMEA articles was finally published in 1960 to codify the structure and governance of the organization.

As the Soviet strategy of economic development, with its emphasis on heavy industrial production, was adopted in all the socialist countries, wasteful duplication of production facilities became a notorious problem. All the countries built huge iron and steel complexes and increased production of machinery, chemicals, and other products of heavy industry. A 1962 policy statement, the Basic Principles of the International Socialist Division of Labor, called for improvements in efficiency through greater specialization and integration of production.

To implement the Basic Principles, Khrushchev called for an amendment to the articles that would give the CMEA new powers of compulsory plan coordination for large investment projects. Romania, the most backward country in the organization (after Albania left in 1962), was afraid that a supranational planning body would force it to specialize in primary production and abandon its modern industries; thus it threatened to withdraw from the CMEA if the amendment was adopted. Khrushchev capitulated and the principle of voluntarism prevailed.

EARLY REFORMS (1960–1970)

By the late 1950s, many economists and some politicians in east-central Europe were convinced that the Soviet economic system, designed for a large, self-sufficient country, was not appropriate for their small, trade-dependent countries. Several countries, led by Hungary and Poland, introduced limited programs of economic reform. By the early 1960s, Soviet economic performance had begun to deteriorate, and Soviet economists, influenced by their European neighbors, gained more freedom to discuss programs of reform. In the mid-1960s, the Soviet government led by prime minister Kosygin implemented a very limited program of reforms, introducing profitability as a measure of enterprise performance.

During this season of reform, Czechoslovakia pressed the Soviet leaders too far, calling for creation of democratic institutions and independent trade unions. In 1968, the so-called Prague Spring was crushed by Warsaw Pact troops. Also in 1968, however, Hungary was able to successfully launch a bold (by standards of that time) new program of market-oriented reforms, known as the New Economic Mechanism.

PRELUDE TO THE FALL (1970–1985)

The decade of the 1970s opened with a bang in Poland. When the Gomulka regime introduced major increases in food prices a few days before the 1970 Christmas holidays, strikes and demonstrations spread from the Baltic town of Gdansk to other cities. Repression of the workers' movement caused about 300 deaths, mostly of civilians, and Gomulka was forced to resign.

A new era of normalization of East-West relations (or detente, as it was known at the time) was symbolized by the visit of U.S. President Richard Nixon to Moscow in 1972. Normalization gave the region easier access to Western credit, and most of the countries took advantage of this opportunity. The new prime minister of Poland, Edward Gierek, adopted an import-oriented growth strategy, causing Polish indebtedness to swell from about 1 billion dollars in 1971 to more than 20 billion dollars at the end of the decade. The challenge of debt repayment forced the Gierek regime to abandon its growth strategy, and an attempt to increase food prices again in 1976 caused another series of demonstrations, strikes, riots, and repression.

In 1978, when the Roman Catholic church selected a new pope from Poland, the indirect effect was to strengthen the workers' movement in Poland, which was supported by the Church. Two years later, Solidarity was organized—the first independent trade union in the Communist bloc. After a series of strikes and political upheavals in 1980 and 1981, the Communist leadership imposed martial law, but the seeds of an anti-Communist revolution already had been sown.

THE END AND THE NEW BEGINNING (1985–PRESENT)

Mikhail Gorbachev came to power in the Soviet Union in 1985, and introduced a new measure of flexibility into the Communist system that eventually led to its destruction. His policy of *glasnost* (openness) led, step-by-step, to democratic political reforms, and his policy of *perestroika* (restructuring) eventually led to market-oriented economic reforms. His repudiation of the so-called Brezhnev Doctrine, which had committed the Soviet Union to preserve communism in other countries, allowed the nations of east-central Europe (and ultimately those of the Soviet Union) to determine their own destinies. Mass demonstrations in October and November 1989 led to the destruction of the Berlin Wall and the resignation, removal, or, in the Romanian case, execution of Communist leaders throughout the region. In August 1991, responding to an abortive coup attempt against Gorbachev's government, Russian President Boris Yeltsin suspended the activities of the Communist Party and Gorbachev agreed to dissolve the Soviet Union.

Since 1991, the countries of Central Eurasia have adopted a wide variety of programs to transform their political and economic systems. As we shall find in Chapter 17, they have adopted different approaches to privatization, price reform, labor relations, industrial policy, social policy, international financial relations, and many other aspects of economic policy. Some of these differences are explained by the simple fact that economic reform is a trial-and-error process—we may not be able to confidently identify the optimal transition process for *any* individual country. As we have seen in this chapter, however, differences among national systems and policies may also be justified by different historical experiences, economic conditions, and social traditions. "Why fight what's known to be decisive?" asked Pushkin. "Custom is the despot of mankind."[22]

SUMMARY

Despite their shared experience of Communist totalitarianism and central planning, states of Central Eurasia are marked by enormous diversities of geography, economy, and culture. The lowest standards of living are found in the central Asian, Balkan, Caucasus, and Black Sea areas. The highest are found in Slovenia, the Czech and Slovak republics, Estonia, Belarus, and Hungary. These patterns have persisted over time.

Some important ethnic groups have existed in Central Eurasia since deep antiquity, but the Slavs are relatively new on the scene. The divisions of Europe caused by the split of the Roman empire, the schism in the Christian church, and the influence of Mongol and Turkish conquests have left an important imprint on the economic and social development of the region. In Russia, the Mongol invasion led to 200 years of foreign oppression and established autocratic and xenophobic traditions. An inward pattern of Russian development was encouraged by the fall of Constantinople.

During the eighteenth century, Peter the Great initiated a period of closer contact with the West, imperial expansion, and industrial growth, while continuing the autocratic tradition. Although serfdom was finally abolished in 1861, several provisions of the emancipation decree restricted labor mobility and rural living standards. A railroad boom began in the 1870s and industrial production grew rapidly during the 1890s, but few of the benefits trickled down to the lower classes.

The end of the Ottoman era in east-central Europe caused a major realignment of the region, and contributed to the outbreak of World War I. In Russia, the privation of World War I led to riots that drove the tsar from the throne in February 1917, clearing the way for the Bolshevik revolution.

During the period of War Communism (1917–1921), the new Soviet government nationalized industry, confiscated agricultural surpluses, and used a military style of organization. This was followed by an experiment in market socialism known as the New Economic Policy (1921–1928). After an extended period of debate, the planning era began in 1928 with the publication of the ambitious First Five-Year Plan. Under this plan, heavy industry was given a higher priority than agriculture.

After World War II, new institutions were established to support the reorientation of eastern European trade to the Soviet Union, but relations between the Communist countries were always strained. This was demonstrated in the struggle between Stalin and Tito, and in uprisings in Hungary, Czechoslovakia, and Poland. During the 1960s, careful steps were taken to

---

[22]Alexander Pushkin, *Eugene Onegin* (1823), ch. 1, st. 25.

reform the central planning system, and East-West normalization during the 1970s raised new expectations for economic growth and reform.

The development of a workers' movement in Poland, supported by the Catholic church, played an important role in the transformation of communism. In the Soviet Union, Mikhail Gorbachev set forces in motion that eventually led to the collapse of communism. Today, countries in the region are following a number of different transition strategies.

DISCUSSION AND REVIEW QUESTIONS

1. What do the Central Eurasian nations have in common? How do they differ?

2. How did the division of the Roman empire and the fall of Constantinople affect the subsequent history of Central Eurasia?

3. Discuss the role of Peter the Great in Russian economic and political history. Why do you suppose that Maximillian Voloshin, a Russian poet, called Peter "the first Bolshevik"?

4. Discuss the Russian Emancipation Decree of 1861, and explain its connection to the railroad boom of the 1870s.

5. Contrast the systems of War Communism and New Economic Policy. What purpose was each of these systems designed to serve?

6. What role did Central Eurasia play in the outbreak of World War I, and what were the economic consequences of the war?

7. What were the positions taken during the industrialization debate of the 1920s? How were these positions supported?

8. Was the Soviet economic system well suited for the economic development needs of nations in east-central Europe? Discuss the factors that led to the demise of Soviet-style central planning.

SUGGESTED READINGS

Aldcroft, Derek H., and Steven Morewood. *Economic Change in Eastern Europe Since 1918.* Aldershot, U.K.: Edward Elgar Publishing, 1994. *This is one of the best and most readable contemporary histories of Eastern Europe, particularly for the period since the 1970s.*

Allworth, Edward, ed. *Central Asia: A Century of Russian Rule.* New York: Columbia University Press, 1967. *Some of the contemporary material is outdated, but this is still a lively introduction to the region, discussing everything from agriculture, industry, and demography to music, art, and literature.*

Berend, Iván T., and Görgy Ránki. *Economic Development in East-Central Europe in the 19th and 20th Centuries.* New York: Columbia University Press, 1974. *The first half of this book provides one of the best and most concise accounts of developments in the region before the twentieth century.*

Dobb, Maurice. *Soviet Economic Development Since 1917*. New York: International Publishers, 1948. *A vivid account of the confusion and terror of War Communism, the experimentation of the NEP period, and the early days of central planning.*

Erlich, Alexander. The *Soviet Industrialization Debate, 1924–1928*. Cambridge, Mass.: Harvard University Press, 1967. *A fascinating chronicle of the arguments, the changing positions and alliances, and the aftermath of one of the most important debates in world history.*

Gregory, Paul R., and Robert C. Stuart. *Soviet Economic Structure and Performance*. 4th ed. New York: Harper and Row, 1990. *A popular textbook on the Soviet economy, with an extended discussion of its history.*

Kaser, M. C., and E. A. Radice, eds. *The Economic History of Eastern Europe 1919–1975*. Oxford: Clarendon Press, 1985. *This monumental and authoritative collection of five volumes provides encyclopedic, if somewhat unwieldy, coverage of economic issues in Eastern Europe during the years listed.*

Kort, Michael. *The Soviet Colossus: A History of the USSR*. New York: Charles Scribner's Sons, 1985. *Well written and accessible to a general audience.*

Manz, Beatrice F., ed. *Central Asia in Historical Perspective*. Boulder, Colo.: Westview Press, 1994. *In ten chapters written by an interdisciplinary team of historians, economists, anthropologists, and political scientists, this book succinctly ties the early history of the region together with the Russian, Soviet, and contemporary periods.*

Nove, Alec. *An Economic History of the U.S.S.R.* London: Penguin, 1969. *An advanced treatment of Soviet economic history.*

INTERNET RESOURCES

Albanian History and Culture
http://www.ug.cs.sunysb.edu/~bardhie/Albanian/

Balkan Pages
http://www.peacenet.org/balkans/

Brief History of Albania
http://www.middlebury.edu/~como/Historia/hist.shtml

Chechnya Chronology
http://www.cnn.com/Interactive/Faces/Chronologies/CHEWCRE.html

Chronology of Russian History
http://www.bucknell.edu/departments/russian/chrono.html

Czech History and Geography
http://www.bsf.cz/project/histgeo.htm

Dazhdbog's Grandchildren
http://sunsite.oit.unc.edu/sergei/Grandsons.html

Early Polish History
http://www.msstate.edu/Archives/History/hungary/austria/chap23.html

East-Central European History Resources
http://www.idbsu.edu:80/history/nmiller/

Eastern Europe and Central Asia Overview
http://www.worldbank.org/html/extdr/eca.html

Essays on Georgian History
http://alexia.lis.uiuc.edu/~stvilia/hist.html

Estonian History
http://www.estemb.org/pages/ajalugu.htm

Eurasia Research Center
http://ourworld.compuserve.com/homepages/eurasiarc/

History of Bosnia-Herzegovina
http://www.cco.caltech.edu/~bosnia/history/history.html

History of Czech Industry
http://www.bsf.cz/project/economy/industry/history/industry.htm

Hungarian History
http://www.fsz.bme.hu/hungary/history.html

History of Ukraine
http://www.un.kiev.ua/Ukraine/About_Ukraine-History.html

Illustrated History of Russia
http://www.cs.toronto.edu/~mes/russia/history.html

Macedonia in History
http://vislab-www.nps.navy.mil/~fapapoul/macedonia/macedon.html

Muslim Life in the Nineteenth-Century Russian Empire
http://www.uoknor.edu/cybermuslim/russia/rus_home.html

Romanian History
http://www.vicnet.net.au/~romclub/florin/history.htm

Romanov Page
http://www.angelfire.com/pages2/romanov/index.html

Russian History Page
http://darkwing.uoregon.edu/~jeseaman/index.html

Russian Revolution
http://history.hanover.edu/modern/russrevo.htm

Slavic Review
http://ccat.sas.upenn.edu/slavrev/slavrev.html

Soviet Archives Exhibit
(U.S. Library of Congress)
http://www.ncsa.uiuc.edu/SDG/Experimental/soviet.exhibit/
soviet.archive.html

Tito's Home Page
http://www.fri.uni-lj.si/~tito/tito-eng.html

Treasures of the Czars
http://www.times.st-pete.fl.us/Treasures/Default.html

Central Slavic and Baltic Areas of Central Eurasia

15

THE POLITICAL ECONOMY OF SOVIET-STYLE CENTRAL PLANNING

Social ownership does away with anarchy of production and spontaneity, and production is developed in the interests of the people as a whole. This being so, the national economy can develop only on planned lines. Through their own state, workers under socialism make a prior calculation of all the needs of society and of its productive resources, and direct production in the interests of the people. In conformity with set aims, society also establishes the necessary proportionality which it then constantly and consciously maintains.

—P. NIKITIN
FUNDAMENTALS OF POLITICAL ECONOMY, 1966

How has our economy developed over the years? An uninformed person might say it developed according to plan, but he would of course be wrong. A specialist would say that it had not developed according to plan, but he would be unlikely to have any better explanation than this purely negative one. . . . Today we can only assert that the entire process of real economic growth in the short and long term is not under the Center's control—it remains a dark secret. We don't decide where we should go, we don't even know which way we are going. There isn't a knowledgeable Gosplan worker or a wise and experienced economist who could say what will happen to shortages tomorrow or how production capacity will change.

—NIKOLAI SHMELEV AND VLADIMIR POPOV
THE TURNING POINT, 1989

few years after its demise, the Soviet-style system of central planning lingers in our memory as if it were a strange custom of an ancient or mythological civilization. Despite recent victories of moderate socialist parties in central and eastern Europe, it seems unlikely that any country in the region will ever return to a system of detailed planning, command, and control.

Why, then, should we bother to study this antiquated system? Why not skip past all this, and begin our survey of market transition strategies in central Eurasia? Several reasons can be suggested. First, the Soviet-style system of central planning has enduring historical significance. This was the system that exacted a heavy and violent toll on Soviet agriculture, that supported mobilization for World War II (perhaps affecting the outcome of the war), and that launched the USSR into superpower status after the war. When it operated in countries stretching from Cuba and Czechoslovakia to China and Vietnam, the Stalinist system dominated the lives of nearly one-third of the earth's inhabitants.

The Soviet-style system has even greater historic significance as our best-documented example of a broader class of command economies. Little is known of the dynastic and dictatorial regimes in ancient Egypt, Mesopotamia, and Middle America; more is known about Nazi Germany, but its history was relatively brief. Despite a long Soviet campaign of secrecy, false reporting, and propaganda, a great deal of information is available on the structure and performance of the Stalinist system, and on its evolution, rise, and fall. However, as we are reminded by Nikolai Shmelev and Vladimir Popov (in the preceding title quotation), there is much that we still do not understand about the dynamics of the system.

Most important for our purposes, some knowledge of the Stalinist system is necessary before one can understand and appreciate current programs of market transition in central Eurasia, China, and elsewhere in the post-Stalinist world. According to Richard Ericson of Columbia University, the system "is as much an organism as a mechanism, tending to counteract forces impinging from outside and to equilibrate the natural forces and tendencies that arise within it."[1] Like the Soviet geneticists of the 1920s who argued that an economic development strategy must take account of the nation's economic heritage, we may reasonably insist that a market transition strategy must also take account of national resources, cultural traditions, financial conditions, the legacies of central planning, and previous programs of economic reform.

In this chapter, we shall explore the system of central planning with heavy emphasis on its application in the former Soviet Union. We do this because the Soviet Union had the longest experience with the Stalinist system, was the largest country in the region, and was able to transfer the system to other

---

[1]Richard E. Ericson, "The Classical Soviet-Type Economy: Nature of the System and Implications for Reform," *Journal of Economic Perspectives* 5 (Fall 1991): 11.

countries with few initial modifications. If we understand how the system operated in the Soviet Union, we will understand how it initially operated in most other countries.

OWNERSHIP

In the Soviet model of socialism, the state, rather than collectives, cooperatives, corporations, or, of course, private individuals, owned most of the nation's productive resources. The Soviet constitution gave the state an exclusive right to own land, forests, and mineral and water resources, and the state also owned the nation's factories, public utilities, news organizations, facilities for transportation, communication, health, education, and culture, and most agricultural equipment and urban housing. As recently as 1990, the Soviet state sector still employed 77 percent of the labor force, accounted for 83 percent of production, and owned 89 percent of the capital stock.[2] Until 1988, when Soviet legislation allowed formation of independent producer cooperatives, the so-called cooperative sector consisted almost entirely of collective farms, which had little independence from the state.

According to the Soviet constitution, individuals were allowed to own "articles of everyday use, personal consumption and convenience, the implements and other objects of a small-holding, a house, and earned savings." In practice, most urban dwellers lived in state-owned apartments, often provided by their employers, for which they paid nominal rent. Many rural families owned private houses, but they could not own the land on which their houses were built. Private production was legally restricted to small-scale agriculture, construction of private housing, arts and crafts, and some personal and professional services.[3]

POLITICAL AND ECONOMIC INSTITUTIONS

Politics and economics are linked in all societies, but this was particularly true in the Soviet-style system, based on state ownership and control of productive resources. Soviet constitutional law did not recognize a principle of separation of powers, but, pedagogically, it will be useful to divide the Soviet-style political system into three large and interconnected branches: the Communist party apparatus, the legislature, and the administrative apparatus (Figure 15.1). In the Soviet Union, these three branches were organized at the national level and in each of the 15 republics. The Soviet-style system had a judiciary, of course, but it was formally subordinate to the legislative branch; it had little formal or informal political power. The Soviet Supreme Court, for example, did not claim authority to review acts of the Party, the legislature, or the administration.

---

[2]Goskomstat SSSR, *Narodnoe khoziaistvo SSSR v 1990 g.: statisticheskii ezhegodnik* (Moscow: Finansy i statistika, 1991), 51.

[3]The most important exception to this rule was found in Poland, where peasants refused to forfeit their land, and the government refused to force them onto collective farms. About three-quarters of Polish agricultural land remained under private control.

THE SOVIET-STYLE COMMUNIST PARTY
AND GOVERNMENT

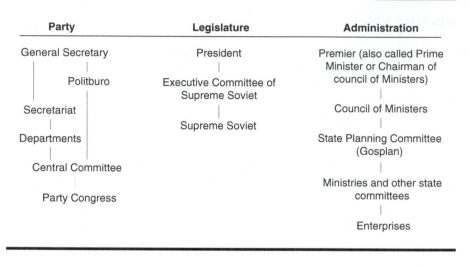

Party	Legislature	Administration
General Secretary	President	Premier (also called Prime Minister or Chairman of council of Ministers)
Politburo	Executive Committee of Supreme Soviet	
Secretariat		Council of Ministers
	Supreme Soviet	
Departments		State Planning Committee (Gosplan)
Central Committee		
Party Congress		Ministries and other state committees
		Enterprises

THE COMMUNIST PARTY

Article 6 of the Soviet constitution proclaimed that the Communist party was "the leading and guiding force of the Soviet society and the nucleus of its political system, of all state organizations and public organizations." The general secretary of the Communist party was the most powerful person in a Soviet-style society. This was the office held by such people as Stalin, Khrushchev, Brezhnev, and Gorbachev in the Soviet Union, by Gomulka, Gierek, and Jaruzelski in Poland, by Dubcek and Husák in Czechoslovakia, and by Kádár in Hungary, Zhivkov in Bulgaria, and Ceausescu in Romania.[4]

The Politburo was the board of directors of the Party and the senior board of directors of the entire political system. In the Soviet Union, it usually had about 12 voting members, including the general secretary, several of the other Party secretaries (who collectively composed the Secretariat), the leaders of major regional Party organizations, and representatives from other branches of government. The Soviet Politburo held weekly meetings and exercised control over all aspects of foreign and domestic policy. With approval of the Central Committee, it controlled appointments to important positions on **Nomenklatura No. 1,** a list that included heads of republic and regional Party organizations, heads of government ministries, military officials, and ambassadors to important countries.[5]

---

[4]That the party leader had such an exalted position may seem strange to American readers, who probably do not know the names of their Democratic or Republican party chairmen.

[5]This procedure was established in 1925. See Dmitri Volkogonov, *Lenin: A New Biography* (New York: The Free Press, 1994), 309–310.

The Secretariat also had about 12 members, all of whom were full-time Party leaders overseeing the work of Central Committee departments. The departments were the agencies through which the Party exercised control over other branches of government. For example, the Agriculture and Food Industry Department monitored the work of the Ministry of Agriculture. The departments exercised authority by controlling appointments to **Nomenklatura No. 2,** a list of some 200,000 key positions held by factory managers, foreign trade officials, directors of research institutes, and many other influential people.

The Central Committee of the Party had about 300 members who were, with few exceptions, the most powerful members of the national and regional Party and governmental agencies. The full committee usually had only two or three brief meetings each year, hardly providing enough time to deal with complex issues. Nonetheless, the Central Committee was a very important organization. It elected the Politburo and Secretariat and controlled the Party's press organizations and journals. It provided a forum for communication and debate among national leaders, and sometimes challenged the authority of the General Secretary and the Politburo. In the Soviet Union, Central Committee debates preceded the 1964 ouster of Khrushchev as General Secretary and the 1968 invasion of Czechoslovakia. In 1987, Boris Yeltsin provoked a crisis in the Party when he delivered a speech to the Central Committee that criticized the slow pace of Gorbachev's reforms.

The Party Congress, theoretically the supreme body of the Party, usually convened every fifth year. Each congress was an enormous media event. Thousands of delegates gathered to unanimously approve the new economic plan and to unanimously "elect" a new Central Committee. The congress provided a forum for national leaders to deliver their most important policy speeches, and for local officials to solicit support for investment projects.

THE LEGISLATURE

Until 1989, when Gorbachev introduced a major parliamentary reform in the Soviet Union, the Supreme Soviet was an ineffectual "rubber stamp" legislature. Its 1,500 elected delegates, who generally held other full-time jobs outside government, gathered one or two times each year to approve laws and administrative appointments prepared in the Party departments and government ministries. Debates were rare in the Supreme Soviet, and votes were almost always unanimous.

A more influential body was the Presidium of the Supreme Soviet. It had about 40 members, most of whom were full-time governmental officials, and held meetings every other month. Between meetings of the full Supreme Soviet, the Presidium had all the constitutional powers of the legislature.

The chairman of the Presidium, or president, was the Soviet head of state. The president performed the traditional duties of signing legislation, receiving the credentials of diplomats, and the like. The position was heavily ceremonial, like the vice presidency of the United States, but the president sometimes had other sources of power. Brezhnev and Gorbachev, for example, both served concurrently as general secretary of the Party and president.

THE ADMINISTRATIVE BRANCH

The premier, or prime minister, headed the administrative branch of the Soviet-style political system. As a Politburo member, the premier was involved in all aspects of national policy, but had direct responsibility for management of the economy. In the Soviet Union, the premier usually delivered a major speech at each Party Congress to introduce a new five-year plan, and he was usually responsible for major programs of economic reform.

Led by the premier, the Council of Ministers was the supreme administrative body in the Soviet-style system. Its membership included the heads of government ministries, state committees, the state bank, and, in the case of the Soviet Union, the chairmen of the councils of ministers of the 15 republics. Based on its authority to issue decrees, the Council supplanted many of the legislative functions of the Supreme Soviet. A Soviet economic reform that began in 1979, for example, was based on a decree (*postanovlenie*) jointly issued by the Central Committee and the Council of Ministers, with no involvement of the nominal legislature.

The most influential administrative agency under the Council of Ministers was the State Planning Committee, or Gosplan. Although many other agencies participated in the planning effort, it was Gosplan's responsibility to coordinate the process, to forge the proposals of other agencies into an integrated document, and to resolve problems that inevitably arose during execution of the plans.

Aside from Gosplan, several other agencies performed tasks that cut across all sectors of the economy. The State Price Committee was responsible for setting and controlling all wholesale and retail prices in the country. The State Committee for Material and Technical Supply, or Gossnab, played an important role in the planning of production and distribution; it ran a nationwide network of industrial supply warehouses and stores. The Ministry of Finance and the State Bank handled monetary and financial policy and administered enormous systems of taxes and subsidies through the state budget. The Ministry of Foreign Trade prepared export and import plans and conducted almost all the nation's international transactions through its worldwide network of trade organizations and representatives.

Actual production of goods and services was administered by 50-odd industrial ministries. These included, for example, a Ministry of Agriculture, a Ministry of Ferrous Metallurgy, and a Ministry of the Automobile Industry, each responsible for the work of farms and factories under its jurisdiction. The ministries prepared economic plans for their subordinate enterprises, administered systems of material incentives, and handled the hiring and firing of enterprise directors.

At the bottom of the administrative hierarchy were the farms, factories, and other enterprises that actually produced goods and services. Each enterprise had a director appointed by the ministry with the advice and consent of the Party. It also had a Party committee and a trade union committee, each with its own leadership.

Formally, each enterprise had little autonomy in the Soviet system. The ministry and the other central agencies told it what and how much to produce, how many workers to hire, what raw materials to use and where to buy them, what prices to charge for its products, and what to do with any profits that were earned. The incomes of enterprise employees were based on their faithful performance of instructions handed down by superior authorities. Informally, the enterprise maintained a modicum of autonomy because the central authorities did not have the desire, the ability, or the information necessary to regulate all its actions.

At all levels, advancement of careers in the Soviet-style system was a bureaucratic and political process, with heavy reliance on personal relationships and exchanges of favors. In the somewhat jaded view of Anatoly Sobchak, the former mayor of St. Petersburg, connections were usually more important than qualifications:

> *Americans like to use the expression, a "self-made man." The sum of our system of protectionism, nepotism, and graft has been the disappearance of any equivalent expression from the Russian language. Faced with a successful individual, all we can think to ask is: "Who backed him? Whose protégé is he?" The legacy of the communist system is a looking-glass world in which the original and talented are persecuted and mediocrity rises to the top.[6]*

CENTRAL PLANNING

All the organizations and institutions outlined in the preceding section were involved in the formulation and implementation of economic plans. General economic priorities were set by the Party leadership. Under the leadership of the Council of Ministers, operational economic plans were prepared by the State Planning Committee and the other administrative agencies. The plan was given the force of law by the legislature and was implemented by the ministries and enterprises.

Economic plans were prepared for interlocking time periods. Annual plans provided the greatest detail, with specific instructions for individual enterprises. Five-year plans set goals for the growth of national income and for broad commodity groups, but included few targets for individual enterprises. Even less detail was included in long-term plans, covering periods of 10 years or more, and these were usually little more than exercises in wishful thinking.[7] In the discussion that follows, we will primarily consider the formulation and implementation of annual plans.

PLANNING OF PRODUCTION AND DISTRIBUTION

The annual plan was divided into several sections. One covered the production and distribution of goods and services, another controlled the allocation of capital investments, and others were prepared to regulate the financial

---

[6]Anatoly Sobchak, *For a New Russia* (New York: The Free Press, 1992), 182.

[7]In 1961, for example, Khrushchev issued a long-term plan to bring Soviet society to the threshold of full communism—that is, material abundance—by 1980 (see *Pravda*, October 18, 1961). In the end, even according to inflated official statistics, Soviet national income fell nearly 40 percent short of Khrushchev's target.

and foreign trade systems. In principle, all these plans were coordinated, but the hub of the system was the production plan. All the other plans were designed to support the production process and to keep the economy in financial balance.

Formulation of an annual production plan would begin at the top of the political hierarchy, where the general secretary and other members of the Politburo would formulate general priorities for the economy. Khrushchev, for example, set a high priority on the development of the chemicals industry, Brezhnev paid special attention to agriculture (particularly after the American grain embargo of 1980), and Gorbachev emphasized the production of industrial consumer goods.

Based on these general priorities and prospects, the economists at the State Planning Committee would prepare a set of **control figures**—a first draft of the plan for broad categories of commodities, designed to guide the planning activities of the ministries and enterprises. Based on these guidelines, the ministries would prepare a more detailed set of plan targets and pass them down to the individual enterprises. The ministries would often inflate the initial targets, expecting their enterprises to bargain for lower, less demanding goals.

Based on the targets assigned by their ministries and on their own assessments of production possibilities and their customers' needs, the enterprises would prepare an even more detailed set of plans. These would include specific final products and requests for raw materials and other inputs. Again, these plans were prepared in the context of a bargaining process. Knowing that plan fulfillment would directly affect their incomes and careers, enterprise directors would do almost anything to obtain achievable plan targets.

After an initial round of enterprise bargaining, the ministries would send their detailed production plans and input requirements back to the State Planning Committee. At this point, the focus of the planning process would shift to the question of **consistency**—planned uses of each product must coincide reasonably well with planned sources of that product. For some 2,000 to 4,000 products that were considered most important, the planned allocations were prepared by economists at Gosplan. About 400 of these, including key raw materials and high-capacity computers, were "funded" allocations that required direct approval by the Council of Ministers. The State Committee for Material and Technical Supply (Gossnab) handled plan allocations for about 15,000 items that were used throughout the economy, but were considered less important. The ministries prepared plans for some 40,000 to 50,000 items that were used within their individual industries.[8]

In each case, the internal consistency of the plan was established through the so-called system of **material balances.** A material balance table (see Table 15.1) was a statement of planned sources and uses of a product, each measured in physical terms. If this were, for example, a material balance for

[8]N. F. Fedorenko, "Planning and Management: What Should They Be Like?" *Problems of Economics* 28 (December 1985): 45.

■ **TABLE 15.1**

Sources	Uses
Production	Productive uses
Imports	Exports
Beginning Stocks	Ending stocks
	Personal consumption
Total	Total

oil, the most important source was domestic production, and data for planned oil production and stocks were provided to the State Planning Committee by the Ministry of the Petroleum Industry. Information on planned imports and exports of oil was furnished by the Ministry of Foreign Trade, based on trade agreements with other countries. Other industrial ministries would provide estimates of their planned requirements for oil, and the Ministry of Trade would estimate the level of consumer demand.

Based on these sources of information and many others, the State Planning Committee compiled its material balance tables. Ideally, the proposed sources of each product would match requested uses. Unfortunately, though, the first drafts of the tables usually yielded product deficits; the ministries and enterprises had strong incentives to pad their requests for resources and to bargain for low output targets. In a market system, these shortages would be resolved by price increases, but in the traditional Soviet system, with controlled prices and no significant profit motive, shortages could be removed only by adjusting the planned allocations.

Therefore, one of the most difficult and important tasks undertaken by central planners was adjustment of material balance tables to achieve consistency—if only on paper. Suppose, for a moment, that we were central planners and it was our job to remove an impending shortage of oil. First, on the sources side, we could tell the petroleum ministry that it would have to produce more oil. This, however, could cause a number of problems. In order to produce more oil, the industry would probably need more drilling and pumping equipment. Thus, we would need to make a new entry on the uses side of the material balance tables for oilfield equipment. In our effort to remove one shortage, we would often create others. Alternatively, we could tell the petroleum ministry that it would need to produce more oil, but without additional equipment. Would this be an unreasonable assignment? Perhaps, but it could prove feasible if the petroleum ministry had been understating its production capabilities to obtain easy plan targets. From our planning office in Moscow, Prague, or Bucharest, we could only guess.

A similar problem would arise if we tried to reduce the productive uses of oil. Sending less oil to the chemicals industry, for example, would reduce the planned shortage of oil, but it could also create a shortage of chemicals. Alternatively, we could tell the chemicals industry to maintain its production with a smaller allocation of oil. Again, we could be asking the impossible, or we could be requiring a higher level of productivity, or we could be encouraging the production of low-quality goods.

We could also rely on our control of foreign trade to reduce an expected shortage of oil; we could increase our imports of oil or reduce exports. Either of these actions, however, could cause a deficit in our international balance of payments, requiring additional exports of some other product. We could delay the payments problem by increasing our international debt, but this approach could cause more serious problems in the future.[9]

Finally, we could resolve the oil shortage by reducing planned deliveries of oil and petroleum products to our consumers. Austerity programs of this kind were used many times in Soviet-style societies, but they had their limits. In the extreme, solving our planning problems at the expense of domestic consumers could cause political unrest. Short of this, insufficient provision of consumer goods would reduce the effectiveness of our material incentive system, which could lead again to shortages of other products.

Enough has been said to illustrate the main point: Any stratagem to reduce a planned shortage could cause a range of other problems, including shortages of other products, trade imbalances, low-quality production, consumer austerity, and political instability. In modern countries with millions of people and products, with complex and dynamic patterns of interdependence among sectors of the economy, and with limited and imperfect information available to central planners, it was impossible to compile a fully consistent plan.

If its assignments were not fully *consistent*, the plan was even less likely to prescribe an *optimal* allocation of resources, maximizing the satisfaction of the Party, the planners, or the public. Computers and mathematical methods, such as input-output economics, could provide some help to the planners, but they had serious limitations (see the Appendix to this chapter). In practice, the output targets for many products were simply derived from the **achieved level**—that is, the target for next year would be equal to this year's production plus an arbitrary percentage markup.

After the sources and uses of each important commodity were drawn into balance on paper, the State Planning Committee issued a final list of plan targets and raw material allotments to the ministries. These were disaggregated into targets and allotments for the individual enterprises. The final plan was approved by the Supreme Soviet; noncompliance was an infraction of the law. In the Soviet case, annual plan targets and product orders were usually

---

[9]In Poland, for example, a program of debt-financed economic growth during the early 1970s led to austerity programs during the late 1970s, which contributed to the rise of an independent trade union movement during the early 1980s and the demise of communism during the early 1990s.

sent to the enterprises in April, so enterprises had to work through the first quarter of the year "practically in the blind."[10]

IMPLEMENTATION OF THE OUTPUT PLAN

For a number of reasons, production plans were seldom implemented precisely as they were written. First, as we just noted, it was virtually impossible for planners to devise a program that was fully consistent and feasible. Second, plan implementation was often interrupted by the uneven rhythm of Soviet production. Just as college students tend to procrastinate until the end of the school term to write term papers and study for tests, Soviet-style enterprises tended to wait until the last few days of the quarter and the year, when plan fulfillment reports were due, to meet their production quotas. This process, known as **storming,** explained why about 70 percent of all construction jobs were usually completed in the last quarter of the year, and why industrial enterprises found it difficult to obtain raw materials at the right time to meet their plan targets.[11]

For these and other reasons, the plan was subject to constant revision and evasion. Throughout the year, troubled enterprises appealed to their ministries, and ministries appealed to Gosplan, for lower output targets and larger allocations of raw materials. Failing that, the enterprises sent out procurement agents (*tolkachy*), who operated on the fringe of legality to locate supplies of raw materials and to arrange unplanned transactions.[12]

The enterprises also dealt with supply problems through vertical integration, or self-supply. That is, they attempted to produce the necessary raw materials and subassemblies themselves, rather than depending on plan allocations and deliveries from other enterprises. According to Soviet planning officials, only 4 percent of standard metalworking products were produced in specialized plants, compared to 70 percent in the United States.[13] This practice reduced the efficiency of the Soviet-style economy by encouraging small-scale production and discouraging specialization. It also reduced the controlling power of the central planners; each enterprise tried to maintain its private hoard of raw materials.

Some of the problems in the plan were solved through black-market activities. The so-called second economy provided everything from industrial raw materials to ballpoint pens and taxi rides. Although these activities reduced the authority of the central planners and gave rise to graft and corruption, they also remedied some of the more glaring deficiencies of the planning system.

---

[10]Ibid., 47.

[11]A Soviet estimate, cited in Peter Rutland, *The Myth of the Plan* (La Salle, Ill.: Open Court, 1985), 128.

[12]For a discussion of the process of continuous plan revision and of the welfare effects of this process, see Raymond P. Powell, "Plan Execution and the Workability of Soviet Planning," *Journal of Comparative Economics* 1 (March 1977): 51–76.

[13]Vladimir Kontorovich and Vladimir Shlapentokh, "Soviet Industry Grows Its Own Potatoes," *The Wall Street Journal*, January 11, 1985, 14.

INVESTMENT PLANNING

In a capitalist country, investment resources will flow to a particular sector of the economy if the rate of return in that sector, adjusted for risk, is higher than the market rate of interest. Put simply, money will be available to build widget factories if the widget industry is sufficiently profitable. Market demand influences profitability; profitability influences the pattern of investment; and the pattern of investment influences the pattern of production.

In the Soviet-style system, the chain of causation was different. Political priorities (which were influenced by consumer demand) determined the structure of output; the structure of output determines the required structure of the capital stock; and profitability influenced the operation of the financial system. Profitable enterprises were taxed heavily and unprofitable enterprises were subsidized to serve official priorities.

The political process that allocated capital resources in the Soviet economy was similar to that used in the U.S. military. The U.S. Army, Navy, and Air Force compete for their shares of the new weapons systems, and states and municipalities compete for the location of military bases. In many cases, new installations are located in the home states of key members of Congress, regardless of their economic or military justification. Similarly, Soviet-style industrial ministers, enterprise managers, and local officials contended for investment resources; their relative success was determined by their position in the government, by their bargaining power, and by other political and economic considerations.

After the general level of investment in a particular industry was determined by official priorities and political processes, economic criteria were used to make more specific investment decisions. Suppose, for example, that the chemicals ministry was told to increase its production of sulfuric acid by a certain amount and was allotted investment resources for that purpose. Further suppose that sulfuric acid could be produced by either of two processes, one of which is more capital intensive, the other more labor intensive. Which process should be used and what kind of factory should be built?

According to the official Soviet procedure, the ministry was supposed to build the factory that minimized the cost of producing the planned quantity of sulfuric acid. The full cost of producing sulfuric acid in a particular kind of factory would include wage and raw materials expenses and a charge for use of the proposed capital resources. The percentage charge on capital in the calculations performed a function similar to a rate of interest in a capitalist economy. A high capital charge would encourage the use of capital-saving, labor-intensive techniques; a low charge would have the opposite effect. Unlike a market rate of interest, however, the capital charge was set by central planners, was differentiated according to industry, and was only used to choose between production methods.[14]

---

[14]See David Dyker, *The Process of Investment in the Soviet Union* (Cambridge: Cambridge University Press, 1983); and Janice Giffen, "The Allocation of Investment in the Soviet Union: Criteria for the Efficiency of Investment," *Soviet Studies* 33 (October 1981): 593–609.

AGRICULTURAL ORGANIZATION AND PLANNING

Despite the Stalinist development strategy that designated a higher priority to industrial growth than to agriculture or the service sector, agriculture has continued to play an important role in most of the central Eurasian countries. In the late 1980s, the share of agriculture in the total labor force was only about 6 percent in the European Union, but it was about 12 percent in former Czechoslovakia; around 20 percent in Bulgaria, Hungary, and the former Soviet Union; 28 percent in Poland and Romania; 33 percent in former Yugoslavia; and more than 50 percent in Albania.[15]

Three basic kinds of agricultural institutions existed in the Soviet-style system. First, the collective farm, or *kolkhoz,* was supposedly a cooperative organization, jointly owned and managed by its members, who shared in its profits. In reality, the ownership rights of *kolkhoz* members were extremely limited. The chairman of the farm, if formally elected by the members, was usually the single nominee approved by the Party. A primary motive of the Soviet collectivization drive of the 1930s, which created the *kolkhozy,* was to extend state control over independent farmers.

The state farm, or *sovkhoz,* was owned and operated directly by the state; it had an organization similar to that of an industrial enterprise. Designed to take advantage of economies of scale, the state farms were enormous. In the Soviet Union, the average *sovkhoz* had a harvested area of 12,000 acres, compared to about 2,500 acres of total area on the average U.S. corporate farm. The chairman of the *sovkhoz* was appointed by the government, and its employees were paid through the same kind of wage and bonus system that was used in factories. The state farms were treated preferentially because, according to Stalinist dogma, they were the highest form of socialist agriculture.

The *kolkhozy* and *sovkhozy* were required to sell a portion of their output to the state at relatively low prices. Known as "compulsory deliveries" or "state procurements," these quotas took a large proportion of total output during the Stalin years, and the procurement prices were far below costs of production. The *sovkhozy* were given subsidies to support the wages of their workers, but the *kolkhozy* were impoverished during those years. After Stalin's death in 1953, and particularly after about 1958, the procurement prices were raised to cover production costs. After meeting their plan quotas, the *kolkhozy* were allowed to sell any additional output to the state at higher incentive prices, or they could sell their additional goods directly to consumers at collective farm markets. About 8,000 of these market areas operated in the Soviet Union, with prices set uncharacteristically by supply and demand.

The third form of agricultural organization in central Eurasia was the private sector. In Poland and in some other countries of central and eastern Europe where collectivization of agriculture was abandoned at an early stage, peasants were allowed to own their own farms. Still, they had to deliver

[15]Sovet Ekonomicheskoi Vzaimopomoshchi, *Statisticheskii ezhegodnik stran-chlenov Sovieta Ekonomicheskoi Vzaimopomoshchi* (Moscow: Finansy i Statistika, 1988), 409–413.

products to the state at fixed prices; strict limits were imposed on the size of their holdings, on their ability to hire laborers, and on their ability to transfer land to others.

In the Soviet Union, the legal private sector in agriculture was confined to the so-called private plots. These were small holdings (about 1.5 acres per worker) allotted to families that worked on the *kolkhozy* and *sovkhozy*, and smaller plots (usually .5 acre or less) that were cultivated by residents of the towns and cities. The land was formally owned by the state, but production on the plots was not subject to compulsory deliveries; it could be consumed by the family or sold at the collective farm markets. Because he considered them to be a remnant of the capitalist system, Stalin intended to phase the plots out of existence. They were treated more favorably by later Soviet leaders, and, beginning in 1982, the plots gained legal access to equipment, fertilizers, pesticides, and other resources. In 1987, Gorbachev announced his intention to lease 800,000 unoccupied village houses with small plots of land to city dwellers who agreed to farm them part-time.

Although they used only about 3 percent of the land, private plots accounted for about 29 percent of agricultural output in the Soviet Union. With some justification, Western observers often cited this kind of information to prove the superiority of private agriculture over socialist agriculture. Other factors, however, should also be considered. The private plots were primarily used to produce high-priced, labor-intensive goods, such as fruit, garden vegetables, spices, and meat, while the socialist sector provided the population with low-priced land and capital-intensive products, such as grain. Also, private livestock were allowed to graze on socialist land, and the generous rewards for private activity often caused farmers to neglect their responsibilities on the *kolkhozy* and *sovkhozy*.

FOREIGN TRADE ORGANIZATION AND PLANNING

In a market economy, international trade is an extension of domestic trade. Import decisions are ultimately made by individual consumers, based on their comparisons of prices and other characteristics of domestic and foreign goods. Export decisions are made by individual businesses, based on the profits they can earn on the domestic and foreign markets. Within each country, the profit motive encourages each producer to specialize according to comparative advantage—to produce at a relatively low opportunity cost.

In the traditional Soviet-style economy, where production targets and price controls replaced the market mechanism, foreign-trade decisions were controlled and coordinated by the central authorities. Individual consumers and producers were not trusted to buy and sell products overseas that would fit the requirements of the plan, and they could not be trusted, under the influence of inflexible prices and exchange rates, to maintain an acceptable balance of international payments.

In order to administer foreign trade in a centrally planned economy, a specialized Ministry of Foreign Trade (MFT) was established under the leadership of the State Planning Committee. The MFT, in turn, operated several

Foreign Trade Organizations (FTOs), which handled the actual negotiation and conclusion of export and import transactions. In the Soviet Union, about 65 FTOs had monopolies on the export and/or import of particular categories of goods.

The profits and losses of the FTOs were largely determined by differences between international market prices and controlled domestic prices. Consider, for example, the case of Soviet coal exports in 1972. *Soyuzpromeksport,* the relevant FTO, purchased coal from industrial enterprises at the controlled domestic price of 23 rubles per ton. It sold the coal abroad at the international price of $14 per ton, which translated into a price of 13 rubles per ton at the official exchange rate of $1.11 per ruble. Accordingly, because the foreign-trade ruble export price was lower than the domestic ruble purchase price, *Soyuzpromeksport* suffered a financial loss of about 10 rubles per ton on its 10 million tons of net exports of coal in 1972. The FTO engaged in these unprofitable exports because it was told to do so by the central planners. Subsidies from the governmental budget were required to spare *Soyuzpromeksport* and many other FTOs from bankruptcy. Profitable FTOs were taxed to help finance these subsidies.

Because of the intervention of the Ministry of Foreign Trade and its FTOs, industrial ministries and their enterprises had little direct contact with foreign customers and suppliers. They transacted their business with the FTOs at roughly the same prices that prevailed in any other domestic transaction. Privileges of foreign contact and travel were reserved for the Party faithful who worked for the FTOs, and the domestic economy supposedly was protected from foreign inflationary pressures.

The export and import plans were prepared in conjunction with the other sections of the annual and five-year plans. Based on control figures provided by the State Planning Committee, combined with their knowledge of existing trade agreements, international market conditions, and the specific resources and requirements of the domestic economy, each FTO prepared a detailed plan for the export and/or import of its commodity group. The FTO plans were adjusted by other officials at the Ministry of Foreign Trade to assure an acceptable balance of payments, and were assembled into a comprehensive (but preliminary) foreign-trade plan. The latter was sent to the State Planning Committee, which made additional adjustments during the compilation and revision of its material balance tables. Finally, the entire plan was resubmitted to the political leaders for their approval.[16]

Of the many problems associated with the traditional Soviet-style system of foreign-trade administration, the most fundamental was this: Most of the important variables in a foreign-trade plan—international prices, exchange rates, and international production and demand—could not be controlled by the central planners of any single nation. Therefore, it was virtually impossible to construct a reliable foreign-trade plan for even one year; a five-year trade plan was only a rough forecast.

---

[16]For a detailed account of this procedure, see H. Stephen Gardner, *Soviet Foreign Trade: The Decision Process* (Boston: Kluwer-Nijhoff, 1983).

The socialist countries attempted to make trade more predictable by coordinating their plans and by signing long-term trade agreements among themselves and with the governments of capitalist countries. These agreements, however, were often made to be broken. In 1975, when international oil prices were soaring, the Soviet Union abandoned its commitment to sell oil to its socialist neighbors at fixed prices. According to the Soviet–American long-term grain agreement for 1983–1988, the Soviet Union was obligated to purchase at least 4 million tons of wheat each year from the United States. Instead, the Soviets bought about 3 million tons in 1984–1985 and less than 200,000 tons in 1985–1986.

Even when the actions of foreigners were predictable, central planners found it impossible to take full advantage of the gains from international trade. Without a system of market prices, they had no dependable way to identify the particular products that their country should export and import. A planned economy, with inflexible, irrational, and tightly controlled prices and exchange rates, had little objective basis on which to compare domestic and foreign costs of production.[17]

Another problem was presented by the system of material incentives in the Soviet-style planned economies. Because their factories were oriented toward fulfillment of quantitative output targets, these countries generally produced low-quality manufactured goods and provided little service after the sale. Thus, they found it difficult to sell their goods on competitive world markets. This problem was exacerbated by the fact that domestic manufacturers had little knowledge of the international market because foreign contacts were usually handled by the Ministry of Foreign Trade. For these and other reasons, the relatively small, trade-dependent countries of central and eastern Europe quickly learned that the Soviet-style system, developed in a large, self-sufficient country, was not appropriate for their needs.

FINANCE, INCENTIVES, AND PRICES

As we have seen, the Soviet-style system of central planning was based on physical output targets, rather than on monetary values. This was true because, in many respects, central planning was a large engineering puzzle. For example, the planners had to order the production of x tons of coal and y tons of iron in order to direct the production of z tons of steel, making it possible to demand the production of a, b, and c tons of the final products that used steel as an input. Ideally, all these engineering relationships would be handled in physical quantities, and enterprises would be rewarded for fulfilling their plan assignments in physical terms.

---

[17] A small number of optimistic Soviet economists believed that mathematical programming methods could be used to identify an optimal structure of foreign trade. However, if these methods had been used to make trade decisions in a continuous, dynamic, and flexible way for a detailed list of products, the data and computational requirements would have been unthinkable. Little progress was made toward the construction of large-scale programming models. See Gardner, *Soviet Foreign Trade*, Chapter 6.

Planning based on monetary values was treated with suspicion in the traditional Soviet-style economy because it implied the presence of market-oriented or profit-oriented decisions, which implied the possibility of economic development based on Ricardian comparative advantage.[18] As we noted in the previous chapter, market-oriented economic development was unacceptable to Stalin because he thought it would cause the Soviet Union to remain a backward, agricultural country, unable to defend itself from the "capitalist encirclement."

Thus, for many years it was dangerous for a Soviet economist to say that the "law of value" had any relevance in a centrally planned economy. In the last years of his life, in the early 1950s, Stalin was still arguing that value-based financial criteria must not be used to make strategic decisions about the development of the economy:

> If this were true, it would be incomprehensible why a number of our heavy industry plants which are still unprofitable, and where the labor of the worker does not yield the "proper returns," are not closed down, and why new light industry plants, which would certainly be profitable and where the labor of the workers might yield "big returns," are not opened.[19]

For these and other reasons, financial institutions and financial planning played a subordinate role in the Stalinist system, but they could not be eliminated altogether. Workers were still compensated with money, which they used to buy goods and services, so their material incentive system included a financial dimension. Enterprises were required to maintain financial accounts, and, because all major transactions were handled by the branch offices of a single State Bank, the bank was able to monitor and enforce the fulfillment of output and investment plans. In the Soviet Union, this surveillance was known as **control by the ruble.** Many enterprises produced a wide assortment of goods, so their overall plan fulfillment could not be measured in physical terms; it had to be measured in terms of monetary value.

FINANCIAL PLANNING

To support the physical output plan, the State Planning Committee, the Ministry of Finance, and the State Bank prepared a set of financial plans to ensure the balance of the household, business, governmental, and international sectors. Centralized control of the financial system was necessary because interest rates, exchange rates, and other prices were not allowed to perform a spontaneous equilibrating role in the planned economy.

In the *household sector*, financial balance meant that the population's disposable income, minus expected saving, should be roughly equal to the supply of consumer goods and services. If a surplus of income over consumer

---

[18]Recall the discussion of David Ricardo's theory in Chapter 3, which said that a country should specialize in lines of production that it can offer at relatively low cost.

[19]Joseph Stalin, *Economic Problems of Socialism in the USSR* (New York: International Publishers, 1952), 21.

goods production was expected—too many rubles chasing too few goods—the central planners could increase retail prices, tax rates, or consumer goods production, or they could reduce wage rates or social security benefits. Unfortunately, these remedies were either difficult (increased production) or politically sensitive (price increases or wage decreases). Traditionally, the planners avoided the unpopular practice of raising retail prices, contributing to financial imbalances and shortages of consumer goods.

In the *business sector*, financial balance required that the state-owned enterprises receive sufficient incomes to cover their payroll and other costs of production. These enterprises were not fully responsible for their profits or losses because their output levels and prices were set by higher authorities. Accordingly, money-losing enterprises were kept afloat through subsidies from the government; successful enterprises were required to surrender most of their profits to the government.

Financial balance in the *international sector* was reflected in the balance of payments. Planned earnings from exports, arms sales, and tourism, together with international borrowing, had to finance the planned level of imports. Actually, several different balances of payments had to be planned and regulated in the Soviet-style system because trade was conducted with Western countries in convertible currencies and with other socialist countries in complex barter arrangements. Control of the international balance was difficult, particularly in trade with capitalist countries, because international prices, exchange rates, and production levels could not be controlled unilaterally by central planners.

Finally, the financial balance of the *governmental sector* was planned through the state budget. Business profits were the largest source of governmental revenue. Aside from military outlays, subsidies and other payments to businesses were the largest categories of expenditure. Thus, the budget provided a huge system of transfer payments from profitable to money-losing enterprises, mitigating the financial imbalances caused by systems of price control and central planning.

THE INCENTIVE SYSTEM

In Chapter 1, we spoke of three kinds of incentives: coercive, material, and moral. In the Soviet-style system, all three were used extensively at one time or another. Prison labor and other forms of coercion were used routinely during the Stalin era, and a corps of political and religious dissidents and criminals was still being used to build pipelines, military facilities, and other projects in the 1980s.[20]

Maintenance of moral incentives was the special mission of the Communist party apparatus and the labor unions. Laggards were criticized, socialist

---

[20]Walter Mossberg, "Soviets Are Using Forced Labor to Build Pipelines, Other Projects, U.S. Study Says," *The Wall Street Journal*, February 14, 1983, 7.

competitions for productivity improvement were organized, and the victory over fascism in World War II was memorialized, providing a constant reminder of the need for personal sacrifice and military-industrial readiness. Party Congresses were orchestrated to build enthusiasm for the five-year plans and to encourage virtuous socialist behavior.

Nevertheless, despite the continued use of coercion and moral incentives, the relative importance of *material incentives* grew through the years. Coercion became a crude instrument when most workers were free to move between jobs, and skills and creativity grew more important than raw labor power. Moral sentiments grew more difficult to arouse as the 1917 revolution and World War II faded farther into the past. Material incentives eventually were used to encourage plan fulfillment, hard work, technological development, higher rates of childbirth, relocation of workers to Siberia, combat service of soldiers, and a wide range of other priorities.[21]

In most cases, a Soviet worker received two important forms of income. Her basic wage or salary was based on her branch of industry, vocation, skills, location, and other factors, and accounted for about 70 percent of her income. The other 30 percent was received in the form of salary bonuses, dependent on fulfillment of plan targets.

Under the traditional Soviet system, the average wage that an enterprise could pay was set by higher authorities in the ministries, the State Planning Committee, and the Ministry of Finance. Some enterprises were allowed to pay much higher wages than others. For example, during Stalin's industrialization drive, workers were attracted from the farms to the cities by wages in industry that were far above those in agriculture. In 1960, the average rural wage remained about 40 percent lower than the average industrial wage. In the early 1960s, when the Soviet Union became a net importer of food, agriculture gained a higher priority. In the 1980s, the wage levels of farmers were much closer to those of factory workers.

Enterprises were also able to pay higher wages in some geographic areas than in others. Like Americans who work for high wages in Alaska, Soviets could increase their pay by up to 50 percent in Siberia, 70 percent in some regions of the far north, and 100 percent in the islands of the Arctic ocean.[22]

Within each enterprise, managers and trade union representatives assigned workers to occupations and skill levels according to standards that were set by the State Committee for Labor and Social Questions. Workers with higher skill ratings could receive higher wages according to a fixed

[21]On the use of material and moral incentives to encourage higher birthrates, see Murray Feshbach and Stephen Rapawy, "Soviet Population and Manpower Trends and Policies," in U.S. Congress, Joint Economic Committee, *Soviet Economy in a New Perspective* (Washington, D.C.: USGPO, 1976), 122. On material incentives to encourage combat service, see Ludmilla Thorne, "Inside Afghanistan: War of Innocents," *The Wall Street Journal*, September 21, 1983, 28.

[22]Janet G. Chapman, "Recent Trends in the Soviet Industrial Wage Structure," in *Industrial Labor in the USSR*, ed. Arcadius Kahan and Blair Ruble (New York: Pergamon Press, 1979), 160.

schedule. For example, in 1975, workers in the machinery industry were paid the following multiples of the base wage for their factory:

Skill Level	Wage
1	1.00
2	1.09
3	1.20
4	1.33
5	1.50
6	1.71

During the Stalin era, large differentials were included in wage schedules to encourage workers to upgrade their skills. During the years that followed, these differentials were reduced—minimum wage rates were increased more than the higher rates. By 1986, the pay of a bus driver was equal to that of a university professor.[23]

Reduced to its basics, the industrial bonus system was quite simple. If the physical plan targets (in tons, square meters, or other units) for the most important products were met, bonuses were added to the base salaries of the employees of the enterprise. Underfulfillment of the plan, even by a small margin, could mean that no bonus was paid at all; overfulfillment resulted in small increases in the bonus. According to a decree introduced in 1986, the bonuses of enterprise directors could amount to as much as 75 percent of their base pay.

An incentive system that rewarded plan fulfillment was a natural and necessary element of a centrally planned economy, but it presented several problems. First, it encouraged enterprise managers to bargain for easier plan targets. To that end, they were likely to provide distorted information to the central planners concerning their production capacities and input needs. Enterprises were not likely to overfulfill their plan targets by a very large margin—even if they were able to do so—because a high level of production one year was likely to result in a difficult plan target the next year.

Second, the emphasis on plan fulfillment contributed to production inefficiency. Industrial managers had strong incentives to hoard labor, equipment, and raw materials to insure that their enterprises would be able to handle their plan targets. Many enterprises engaged in inefficient small-scale production of raw materials and components, rather than risk plan fulfillment on supplies provided by other enterprises.

Third, even when enterprises were able to abide by the letter of the plan, they often found it necessary or convenient to ignore the spirit. The quality of output was routinely sacrificed to fulfill quantitative plan targets. For example, Soviet automobile factories were reluctant to produce spare parts and accessories because they were rewarded more heavily for their most important products, finished cars.

---

[23]N. Rimashevskaya, "Income Distribution and Justice," *Current Digest of the Soviet Press*, 10, 1986, 6.

Shoe factories often simplified their operations by producing all their shoes in a few sizes. Thus, many Soviet shops were full of shoes, but customers spoke of shortages. A classic Soviet cartoon showed one enormous nail hanging in a large workshop. "The plan to produce 100 tons of nails is fulfilled," beamed the manager.

Finally, the planning and incentive systems discouraged technological innovation. An enterprise that developed a new, more advanced product received little reward for its work. Time and effort spent on innovation made it difficult for the enterprise to meet its basic plan targets. A new product often required raw materials that were difficult to acquire in the supply system. If an enterprise adopted a new technique that increased its production capacity, the plan targets assigned to the enterprise were increased accordingly, and the innovators were left where they started.[24]

THE PRICE SYSTEM

The role of prices in a centrally planned economy was quite different from that in a market economy. In the market system, prices react spontaneously and continuously to the forces of supply and demand; production is guided by prices and profitability. Soviet prices, in contrast, were set and controlled by the State Price Committee; production was guided by the annual plan. Setting millions of prices for a modern economy was an enormous task, so prices were not changed very often. Significant revisions of wholesale prices were undertaken in 1948, 1952, 1955, 1967, 1973, and 1982; they were changed very little during the intervening years.

Although prices did not play the same allocative role that they play in a market economy, they were still important for several reasons. They influenced the managerial incentive system because plan targets were stated in monetary units for enterprises with multiple products. Prices were among the levers used to regulate the financial balance of the economy. The incomes and outlays of consumers, enterprises, and the governmental budget were all influenced by prices; an imbalance in any of these sectors could cause shortages or surpluses of goods.

The rules and principles used to set wholesale prices, which Soviet enterprises received for their products, and retail prices, which consumers paid, were quite different. In general, the **wholesale price** of a product was equal to the average unit cost of producing that item in the entire industry, plus a small profit markup related to the capital intensity of the product. During the 1980s, Soviet enterprises were allowed to keep about 40 percent of their profits to finance material incentive funds, internal investments, and the like.[25]

Basing wholesale prices on average industry costs was probably the simplest method available to the State Price Committee, but it caused many problems. Enterprises with higher costs than the industry average ran losses,

---

[24]For a full discussion of these issues, see Joseph S. Berliner, *The Innovation Decision in Soviet Industry* (Cambridge, Mass.: MIT Press, 1976).

[25]Tsentral'noe Statisticheskoe upravlenie SSSR, *Narodnoe khoziaistvo SSSR v 1984 g.* (Moscow: Finansy i Statistika, 1985), 563.

requiring subsidies from the state budget. A large part of the state budget was used to redistribute income from profitable enterprises to unprofitable ones. In contrast, the price of a product in a competitive market economy will normally rise to a level sufficient to cover marginal costs for all firms needed to meet market demand.

Although cost-oriented, demand-insensitive prices may have given enterprises an incentive to hold down their costs of production, they provided little incentive for enterprises to respond to consumer demand. Average-cost prices were poor guides for central planners to use for investment and foreign trade decisions. By their nature, these were usually marginal decisions: Will the cost of additional energy production outweigh the additional benefits? Will an increase in export production cost more or less than the domestic cost of import substitution? Such questions could have been addressed more effectively with prices based on marginal, rather than average, costs and benefits.

Several principles influenced the determination of **retail prices** in the Soviet-style system. Here again, most prices were not controlled by markets, but by the State Price Committee, and were changed very infrequently. The maintenance of stable retail prices traditionally was claimed as one of the major strengths of the system. To maintain some semblance of order and equilibrium in the consumer goods sector, the retail price of each product was initially set at a level that roughly equated the quantity demanded with the quantity supplied (as controlled by the central planners). On the other hand, an effort was made to redistribute purchasing power from the rich to the poor by holding down the relative prices of food, shelter, and other necessities and by padding the prices of luxuries.

Because price stability, supply-demand equilibrium, and distributive equity were competing objectives, none of them could be fully achieved. The failure of retail prices to maintain an equilibrium between supply and demand gave rise to shortages, long lines, and black-market activities. These in turn encouraged corruption, dilution of work incentives, and other social problems. According to a survey of immigrants from the Soviet Union, Soviet women spent about 20 percent of their leisure time standing in lines.[26] Shortages and lines may also indicate the presence of pent up inflationary pressure.

In the Soviet Union, the fact that wholesale and retail prices were formed by very different principles caused a serious budgetary problem. In most cases, the retail prices were higher than the wholesale prices, and the difference between the two—the so-called turnover tax—was pocketed by the state. In the agricultural sector, however, the situation was quite different. Soviet agriculture was notoriously inefficient, requiring high cost-based wholesale prices, but the retail prices of food items were held down for ideological and political reasons. Consequently, retail prices of most agricultural goods were actually lower than the wholesale prices, requiring the payment

---

[26]Cullen Murphy, "Watching the Russians," *The Atlantic* (February 1983): 50.

of governmental subsidies. During the 1980s, the subsidy for meat and milk products alone amounted to 40 billion rubles annually, or about 10 percent of all budgetary expenditures.[27]

THE SECOND ECONOMY

Intertwined with the planned sector of the Soviet-style economy was a second economy of unplanned production and exchange. Much of this unplanned activity was legal; the system of small-scale private-plot agriculture, for example, allowed farmers to set their own production and price levels. Within strict limits, private activities of physicians, teachers, beauticians, photographers, and hunters were permitted in the Soviet Union, and the Law on Individual Enterprise, which took effect in May 1987, legalized the private provision of repair and taxi services and a broader range of handicrafts.

On the other hand, even after passage of the Law on Individual Enterprise, the Soviet Union continued to disallow: (1) employment of workers outside the immediate family; (2) production of a list of prohibited items, such as fur hats, precious jewelry, weapons, and copying equipment; (3) operation of amusement rides or games; (4) teaching subjects or courses that were not offered in public schools and colleges; and (5) organization of entertainment activities. The law did not allow a worker to quit her regular job to engage in full-time individual enterprise, nor did it give the worker access to raw materials or supplies in the wholesale trade network. These legal limits on private activity, coupled with widespread shortages, caused the illegal portion of the second economy to flourish.

The Soviet newspapers reported prosecution of cases in which entire factories produced goods for the plan during the day and for the black market at night. Some of the entrepreneurs who ran these operations amassed large fortunes.[28] To run illegally at night, a factory had to obtain raw materials. These could be stolen from state enterprises or purchased from other black-market outlets. A distribution network for final products had to be established, often requiring payment of bribes to local police, party, trade union, and government officials. The ability of governmental officials to collect bribes, in turn, placed an economic value on their positions.

A 1982 law imposed fines ranging from the equivalent of $420 (more than the average monthly wage) to $1,400 for economic crimes such as profiteering and stiffened the prison sentences for theft of public property. Judges

---

[27]Interview with V. Yesipov in *Leningradskaia Pravda*, September 22, 1984, 2; translated in Joint Publications Research Service, *USSR Report: Economic Affairs*, January 3, 1985, 2. Also, see Vladimir Treml, "Subsidies in Soviet Agriculture: Record and Prospects," in U.S. Congress, Joint Economic Committee, *Soviet Economy in the 1980s: Problems and Prospects*, Part 2 (Washington, D.C.: USGPO, 1982), 171–185.

[28]For an account of the underground business world during the Soviet era, written by a former Moscow attorney, see Konstantin Simis, *USSR: The Corrupt Society* (New York: Simon and Schuster, 1982), Chapter 6.

were instructed to assign more convicts to forced labor brigades instead of sending them to prison. Gorbachev spoke in 1986 of the need to "intensify the struggle against unearned income," stating "we should conduct an uncompromising fight against all parasitic elements, that is, against those who try to live off the money of others and of society."[29]

In retrospect, it is difficult to evaluate the influence of the second economy on the Soviet-style system. It provided a mixture of benefits and costs. On the positive side of the ledger, private activity filled many of the voids missed by central planning. Private-plot farmers and moonlighting workers contributed to the quantity, quality, and variety of goods and services that were available to the population. Industrial expediters provided an invaluable service to factories needing raw materials to meet their plan targets. These activities obviously created employment and incomes for the participants. According to estimates by Soviet economists, the second economy represented between 10 percent and 20 percent of GNP during the late 1980s and provided 36 percent to 40 percent of consumer products.[30] Emigrant interviews indicate that these activities already accounted for more than a third of the urban population's income during the late 1970s.[31]

The second economy also supported the survival of entrepreneurial talent in a social system that generally discouraged individual initiative. During the early 1990s, after the fall of central planning, this pool of talent grew more important. Businesspeople who had been working "in the shadow" for decades were able to see the light of day.

On the negative side, the second economy diverted the efforts of workers from their official jobs, and encouraged them to steal raw materials and other resources from state industries. Agricultural workers spent an inordinate amount of time on their tiny private plots. Industrial managers complained that workers were not interested in their full-time jobs because they could make more money working on the side. According to Western estimates based on emigrant surveys, Soviet employees spent about 12 percent of their paid work time in state factories on private or personal activities.[32]

In a more general way, broad acceptance of illegal activities in the second economy caused long-term damage to the legal culture of many of the central Eurasian countries. Mafia activities expanded in the region after 1990, but they originated during the central planning era when private activities required protection from state interference. The network of crime became organized over a large geographic area, and was able to survive the breakup of the Soviet Union. During the Communist era, mafia activities already included

---

[29]*Pravda,* March 17, 1986, 3.

[30]G. Yavlinsky et al., *500 Days: Transition to the Market* (New York: St. Martin's Press, 1991), 126–128; and Goskomstat SSSR, *Narodnoe khoziaistvo SSSR v 1990 g.* (Moscow: Finansy i Statistika, 1991), 9 and 50.

[31]Gregory Grossman, "Roots of Gorbachev's Problems: Private Income and Outlay in the Late 1970s," in U.S. Congress, Joint Economic Committee, *Gorbachev's Economic Plans,* Part 1 (Washington, D.C.: USGPO, 1987), 213–230.

[32]Vladimir G. Treml, "A Study of Labor Inputs into the Second Economy of the USSR," *Berkeley-Duke Occasional Papers on the Second Economy of the USSR,* Paper no. 33 (January 1992), 38–39.

everything from sale of public property, bootleg liquor, and narcotics to organized prostitution and gambling.

Finally, the second economy apparently had a significant impact on the distribution of household income. According to information gathered from Soviet emigrants, the poorest decile obtained about 6 percent of their income from private sources while the richest decile obtained almost 39 percent of their income privately. The Gini index of income inequality was 0.27 if private incomes were excluded and 0.30 if they were included—a rise of 10 percent. The distribution of second economy income was considerably more unequal in central Asia and the Caucasus than in northern areas of the Soviet Union.[33]

PERFORMANCE OF THE CENTRAL PLANNING SYSTEM

To fairly evaluate the Soviet-style system of central planning and administrative control, we must consider several dimensions of performance, including those that were emphasized by its strongest advocates and severest critics. Once again, our discussion will emphasize the performance of central planning in the Soviet Union; many, but certainly not all, of these observations are also true of the economic performance of centrally planned economies in central and eastern Europe.

PLAN FULFILLMENT AND ECONOMIC GROWTH

The creators of the central planning system said that it would allow countries to accelerate their economic growth and development, orient that development toward the most important needs of society; and avoid the "chaotic" business cycles, unemployment, and inflation associated with capitalism and market-oriented development.

It would take us far afield here to determine whether economic planning generally helped countries to accelerate their rates of economic development. In the Russian/Soviet case, estimates of long-term national income growth during the pre-Soviet era (1885–1913) range from 2.5 percent to 3.4 percent per annum.[34] During the central planning era (1928–1985), the Soviet authorities claimed an annual growth rate of 8.8 percent, but Western estimates suggest a rate of 4.3 percent, and an alternative Russian estimate suggests a rate of 3.3 percent.[35] Did Russian economic growth accelerate over a long period of time? If it did, was the acceleration caused by central planning? The evidence is not clear.

[33]Gur Ofer, "The Distribution Effects of Private Incomes," *Radio Liberty Research,* June 19, 1987, 4–7; and Michael V. Alexeev and Clifford G. Gaddy, "Trends in Wage and Income Distribution Under Gorbachev," *Berkeley-Duke Occasional Papers on the Second Economy of the USSR,* Paper no. 25 (February 1991), 19–21.

[34]Paul R. Gregory, *Russian National Income, 1885–1913* (Cambridge: Cambridge University Press, 1982), 71.

[35]Richard E. Ericson, "The Soviet Statistical Debate: Khanin vs. TsSu," in H. S. Rowen and C. Wolf, Jr., eds., *The Impoverished Superpower* (San Francisco: ICS Press, 1990), Table 2.1 and 2.4.

Another approach to this question is suggested by the work of Abram Bergson, who has carefully explored the statistical relationships between national products and inputs of land, labor, and capital in the Soviet Union, Hungary, Poland, Yugoslavia, and seven capitalist countries. According to Bergson's estimates for 1975, the four socialist countries utilized their resources between 25 percent and 34 percent less efficiently than their capitalist competitors. Interestingly, the productivity shortfall was not statistically significant for Yugoslavia, the socialist country that had the longest history of market reform.[36] These are measures of static (point in time) productivity rather than productivity growth, but they seem to imply that any growth advantage of central planning must arise from extensive utilization of inputs (drawing women into the labor force, cultivating more agricultural land, expanding the capital stock by restricting consumer goods production, and so on), rather than from efficient utilization of existing resources.

Still another way to evaluate the growth performance of the Soviet-style economy is to survey its ability to meet specific plan targets. Instead of comparing its growth to historical experience or to international competitors, we ask whether planned societies have been able to meet their self-imposed goals.

Information on the record of Soviet fulfillment of its medium-term (usually five-year) plans is presented in Table 15.2. If we look at national income statistics for the entire period between 1929 and 1990, the Soviet statistical authorities claimed that they achieved an average rate of growth of 7.5 percent, which was very near the 7.7 percent average planned rate of growth. They claimed overfulfillment of the first, fourth, fifth, sixth, and eighth plans, and conceded underfulfillment of the others (including all the plans for the period between 1971 and 1990). Soviet official statistics indicate that the highest growth rates and best records of plan fulfillment were in the producer goods industries. They indicate that long-term growth in the agricultural sector was less than half the planned average.

Western estimates, which attempt to remove double counting of production and hidden inflation, tell a different story. They indicate that none of the Soviet medium-term national income plans were fulfilled; the average growth rate between 1929 and 1990 was little more than half the planned average. Shortfalls in plan fulfillment were spread throughout the economy, but, again, they were largest in the agricultural sector.

On many occasions, the initial goals of medium-term plans were substantially revised during the formulation of annual plans. When problems developed during the execution of annual plans, the affected enterprises would plead with central authorities for more resources, or they would try to obtain raw materials extralegally: through private barter arrangements or other second economy transactions. In 1981, at the 26th Soviet Party Congress, General Secretary Brezhnev lamented the excessive revision of plans:

The plan is law because only its observance assures the harmonious functioning of the national economy. Let us speak frankly: This axiomatic truth has begun to be forgotten. The

---

[36]Abram Bergson, "Comparative Productivity: The USSR, Eastern Europe, and the West," *American Economic Review* 77 (June 1987): 342–357.

■ TABLE 15.2

SOVIET MEDIUM-TERM PLANS AND PLAN FULFILLMENT, 1928–1990 (AVERAGE ANNUAL PERCENTAGE GROWTH RATES)

Plan Number and Period	National Income			Industrial Producer Goods Production		
	Planned Growth	Official Outcome	Western Estimate	Planned Growth	Official Outcome	Western Estimate
1. 1929–32	15.2	16.2	3.6	24.9	28.6	21.6
2. 1933–37	17.1	16.2	8.4	14.5	19.0	13.7
3. 1938–40	12.5	10.0	3.2	15.7	8.9	4.8
4. 1941–50	3.3	5.1	2.4	4.9	7.4	4.6
5. 1951–55	9.9	11.3	7.6	11.8	13.8	7.9
6. 1956–58	9.9	10.2	7.9	11.2	11.2	6.6
7. 1959–65	7.3	6.8	5.3	9.3	10.1	8.5
8. 1966–70	6.9	7.1	5.6	8.5	8.6	4.7
9. 1971–75	6.7	5.1	3.7	7.9	7.9	6.1
10. 1976-80	4.7	3.9	2.6	6.5	4.7	1.0
11. 1981-85	3.4	3.1	1.6	4.9	3.7	2.3
12. 1986-90	4.1	1.7	1.5	4.4	1.9	0.4
Average 1929–1990	7.7	7.5	4.2	9.5	10.0	6.6

Plan Number and Period	Industrial Consumer Goods Production			Agricultural Production		
	Planned Growth	Official Outcome	Western Estimate	Planned Growth	Official Outcome	Western Estimate
1. 1929–32	15.2	11.7	−1.5	9.2	−3.6	−4.6
2. 1933–37	18.5	14.8	9.9	14.9	9.0	8.9
3. 1938–40	11.5	10.0	1.6	8.7	15.3	−1.0
4. 1941–50	2.3	2.1	0.2	2.4	−0.1	−0.5
5. 1951–55	9.9	12.0	11.9	8.4	4.1	2.2
6. 1956–58	9.9	8.5	7.7	11.2	8.8	7.1
7. 1959–65	7.3	6.9	5.3	7.9	1.9	1.9
8. 1966–70	7.6	8.3	7.7	4.6	4.3	3.4
9. 1971–75	8.2	6.5	5.1	4.0	0.6	−2.3
10. 1976–80	7.0	3.9	4.0	3.0	1.5	0.2
11. 1981–85	5.1	3.9	1.6	2.5	2.1	1.2
12. 1986–90	4.9	4.3	2.1	2.7	0.9	0.2
Average 1929–1990	8.1	7.1	4.4	6.1	2.9	1.2

NOTES: The first, third, and sixth plans were originally prepared to conclude in 1933, 1942, and 1960, respectively, but were terminated early for various reasons (the third plan, for example,

(*Continued*)

practice of downward plan revision has become widespread. Such a practice disorganizes the economy, demoralizes personnel, and accustoms them to irresponsibility. . . . There may be rare occasions, and we do have them, when plan amendment is necessary. But they have to be precisely rare occasions, exceptions.[37]

Despite Brezhnev's wishes, the plans continued to require frequent and large revisions, causing many analysts in the West and in the East to question whether it was accurate to describe the Soviet-style economies as "centrally planned."[38] Without getting bogged down in semantics, it seems clear that the Soviet-style economies were not planned in a highly accurate or inflexible way. Particularly in agriculture, the plans bore little resemblance to reality. On the other hand, the plans did send strong forward-looking signals to subordinates about the priorities of central authorities. Furthermore, the nation's system of managerial pay and bonuses was based on plan fulfillment. Even unplanned activities were frequently directed toward fulfillment of plan assignments.

Therefore, it seems inadequate, as some have suggested, to describe these merely as "command" or "administered" economies.[39] During the years before 1970, the plan targets reflected traditional Stalinist growth priorities:

NOTES CONTINUED: was interrupted by World War II). Planned growth rates reported here are average annual rates for the original period of the plan. Official and Western measures of outcomes are calculated for the effective duration of the plans (the years listed in the first column). The fourth plan operated during 1946–1960, but its growth targets were based on 1940 as their base year, so the growth targets and outcomes listed here are averages for entire period, 1941–1950.

SOURCES: Plan figures for 1929–1958 and Western measures of growth for 1929–1950 are taken from Naum Jasny, *Essays on the Soviet Economy* (New York: Praeger, 1962), 266. Plan figures for 1950–1990 were gathered from Alec Nove, *An Economic History of the U.S.S.R.* (London: Penguin Books, 1989), 333, 346–347; Gregory Grossman, "An Economy at Middle Age," *Problems of Communism* 25 (March–April 1976): 22; Ed A. Hewett, *Reforming the Soviet Economy: Equality versus Efficiency* (Washington, D.C.: The Brookings Institution), 52; and Soviet press reports. Official fulfillment data are from Goskomstat, *Narodnoe khoziaistvo SSSR: statisticheskii ezhegodnik* (Moscow: Finansy i Statistika, various years). Western estimates for 1950–1990 were calculated by the author, based on CIA estimates of net material product (derived from its GNP estimates), and on components of its indexes of industrial and agricultural production. See CIA, *USSR: Measures of Economic Growth and Development, 1950–1980*, U.S. Congress, Joint Economic Committee (Washington, D.C.: USGPO, 1982), passim; CIA, *Measures of Soviet Gross National Product in 1982 Prices*, U.S. Congress, Joint Economic Committee (Washington, D.C.: USGPO, 1990), passim; and articles by James Noren, Laurie Kurtzweg, Douglas Diamond, and Gregory Kisunko in *The Former Soviet Union in Transition*, vol. 1, U.S. Congress, Joint Economic Committee (Washington, D.C.: USGPO, 1993), passim.

[37]L. I. Brezhnev, "Report of the Central Committee of the CPSU to the 26th Congress of the CPSU," in *Documents and Resolutions of the 26th Congress of the CPSU* (Moscow: Novosti, 1981), 64.

[38]See the opening quotation for this chapter, taken from Nikolai Shmelev and Vladimir Popov, *The Turning Point* (New York: Doubleday, 1989), 100–101. Also, see Vitali A. Naishul, "Communism: Death or Transformation?" <http://www.fe.msk.ru/libertarium/library/nayshul/edeathtran.html>; John Howard Wilhelm, "The Soviet Union Has an Administered, Not a Planned, Economy," *Soviet Studies* 37 (January 1985): 118–130; and Rutland, *The Myth of the Plan*, passim.

[39]The phrase "command economy" was coined to describe the system in Nazi Germany. See Gregory Grossman, "Command Economy," in John Eatwell, Murray Milgate, and Peter Newman, eds., *Problems of the Planned Economy* (New York: W. W. Norton & Company, 1990), 58–62.

producer goods, followed by industrial consumer goods, followed by agriculture (Table 15.2). These priorities and plans were consistent with actual performance. Between 1971 and 1990, the central priorities apparently changed: Planned and actual growth rates for industrial consumer goods were both higher, on average, than the rates for producer goods.

The data in Table 15.2 also indicate a long-term deterioration of Soviet growth rates—both planned and actual. The deceleration of economic growth was particularly steady after the mid-1950s, eventually playing a most important role in the collapse of Soviet-style socialism.

What caused the **growth slowdown?** Inputs of labor and capital grew at fairly steady rates through the 1950s and 1960s, so the slowdown of the 1960s was caused entirely by a deceleration of factor productivity. In the 1970s, long-term demographic patterns caused the growth rate of the labor force to decelerate, and attempts to improve the standard of living caused the capital stock to grow more slowly. Thus, the slowdown of output growth during the 1970s and 1980s can be blamed in fairly equal measures on slower input growth and slower (indeed, negative) productivity growth.[40]

The slow or negative growth rates of factor productivity, which explained most of the reduction in economic growth after 1950, apparently had several causes. First, the capital stock grew much more rapidly than the labor force, so diminishing returns to capital slowed the growth of output. This has several econometric studies.[41]

Second, the growth of factor productivity was undoubtedly fettered by the depletion of accessible natural resources. As deposits of oil, coal, iron ore, and other materials dwindled in the European portion of the Soviet Union, it was necessary to develop resources in Siberia and the Far East. This, in turn, required construction of new factories, roads, bridges, and living quarters, often under unfavorable conditions. Thus, each unit of output required a relatively large volume of capital investment.

Third, slower growth of technological progress apparently contributed to slower growth of factor productivity. A slowdown in technological improvement was indicated by a number of factors: slower introduction of new machinery into the economy, slower growth in the number of technological innovations, and slower growth or decline in the importation of Western equipment.[42]

Closely related to the slower growth of technological progress was the aging of the nation's capital stock and its detrimental effect on productivity growth. According to international statistical comparisons, the Soviets retired their old machinery and equipment less than half as quickly as the

[40]See Stanley Fischer, "Russia and the Soviet Union Then and Now," Working Paper No. 4077, National Bureau of Economic Research (May 1992): 9–18.

[41]See, for example, Robert Whitsell, "The Influence of Central Planning on the Economic Slowdown in the Soviet Union and Eastern Europe: A Comparative Production Function Analysis," *Economica* 52 (May 1985): 235–244, and the sources cited therein.

[42]Vladimir Kontorovich, "Technological Progress and Productivity Growth Slowdown in the Soviet Economy, 1951–1982," presented to the American Economic Association, Dallas, December 28–30, 1984, 54.

United States and other Western countries.[43] The decrepit capital stock was technologically backward and required more repair. At times, 40 percent of the nation's machine tools were used to repair old equipment, rather than to build new models.[44]

Finally, we may surmise that an increasing strain on the central planning system contributed to the slowdown. As the economy grew larger and more technologically advanced, as the size of the governmental bureaucracy expanded, and as the Soviet-style economies increased their involvement in international trade, the task of central planning grew ever more complex.

INDUSTRIAL PERFORMANCE

In the Soviet Union, the central planning system was designed in the late 1920s to place a high priority on development of industry, particularly on the metallurgical and producer goods industries. At the time, this was done in the name of modernization and national defense (protecting socialism from the "capitalist encirclement"). From the perspective of Stalin and his peers, these early efforts were quite successful. Steel production, which had grown about 6 percent annually between 1900 and 1913, sped to a rate of more than 12 percent between 1928 and 1940. In 1928, the Soviet Union was the world's eighth largest producer of electrical power; by 1946, the USSR was the largest electrical power producer in Europe, and second in the world only to the United States.[45]

Soviet industrialization and militarization helped to defeat the fascist powers in World War II. After the war, Soviet science and industry recorded a succession of stunning technical achievements, including: the detonation of a hydrogen bomb in 1953; the launch of Sputnik, the first satellite, in 1957; the commissioning of what was then the world's largest hydroelectric station in 1958; and the first manned space flight by Yuri Gagarin in 1961. These and other Soviet successes seem to illustrate a single truth: Soviet scientists, engineers, and industry workers were able to perform amazing technical feats when they worked on isolated, high-priority projects that could summon the nation's best talent, scarce resources, and, when necessary, foreign technology. The strength of the central planning system was its ability to focus resources on projects that were most important to the Party leadership.

To support rapid development of high-priority industrial and military sectors, people living in Soviet-style societies were denied personal liberties and had to endure shortages of agricultural products, consumer goods, services, and housing. In 1980, production of services accounted for only 37 percent of GDP in Russia and Estonia, and about 30 percent of GDP in Belarus,

---

[43]Stanley H. Cohn, "Sources of Low Productivity in Soviet Capital Investment," in U.S. Congress, Joint Economic Committee, *Soviet Economy in the 1980s* (Washington, D.C.: USGPO, 1982), 181.

[44]Herbert Levine, "Possible Causes of the Deterioration of Soviet Productivity Growth in the Period 1976–80," *Soviet Economy in the 1980s*, 159.

[45]B. R. Mitchell, *European Historical Statistics, 1750–1975*, 2d ed. (New York: Facts on File, 1980), 420–422, 500–503.

Bulgaria, former Czechoslovakia, and Lithuania. In comparison, services claimed 43 percent of GDP in an upper-middle-income country and 59 percent in an average high-income country.[46] The average resident of Russia had about 16 square meters of housing in the late 1980s, compared with 29 square meters in Japan, 44 in Germany, 49 in France, and 71 in the United States.[47]

As we noted earlier, the Soviet-style incentive system, based on plan fulfillment measured in physical quantities, provided little motivation for firms to strive for high-quality production, to hold down their costs of production, to use the best available technologies, or to provide spare parts and repair services for their products. In 1983, Soviet General Secretary Andropov disclosed that 500,000 televisions, 250,000 cameras, and 160,000 refrigerators were sitting unsold in warehouses, despite shortages, because their quality was so poor.[48] Soviet five-year plans routinely included goals to increase the share of machinery and equipment in export sales, but these goals were never fulfilled.[49]

The Soviet-style system also tended to create a highly monopolized industrial sector. In the mid-1980s, firms with 1,000 or more employees accounted for 51 percent of total employment in Poland and 73 percent in the Soviet Union, compared to 25 percent in the United States.[50] About 80 percent of the products of the Soviet machinery industry were manufactured by monopolies.[51] To reduce the complexity of their efforts, central planners preferred to communicate with a few enterprises in each industry.

The Soviet preference for huge enterprises, known as **gigantism,** apparently had several motivations. First, Soviet political leaders believed that big projects would draw international attention to the achievements of socialism. Second, they seemed to have a mistaken belief that large factories were almost always more technically efficient than smaller ones. Third, it was simpler to coordinate the construction of a smaller number of big factories. And fourth, it was simpler to formulate economic plans and monitor their execution for a smaller number of enterprises. This was particularly true in countries of central Eurasia, countries that had poor systems of long-distance communication.

AGRICULTURE

Perhaps the most costly and notorious failure of the Soviet-style system was the destruction of the agricultural sector. Before the revolution, from 1909 to 1913, Russia was the world's largest exporter of grain, accounting for

---

[46]World Bank, *World Development Report 1996* (Oxford: Oxford University Press, 1996), 210–211.

[47]The Russian figure is taken from U.S. Central Intelligence Agency, *Handbook of International Economic Statistics 1992*, CPAS 92–10005 (September 1992), 60. Figures for other countries are from Keizai Koho Center, *Japan 1994: An International Comparison* (December 1993), 85.

[48]Ed A. Hewett, *Reforming the Soviet Economy: Equality versus Efficiency* (Washington, D.C., 1988), 81.

[49]See Paul Ericson, "Soviet Efforts to Increase Exports of Manufactured Products to the West," in *Soviet Economy in a New Perspective*, 709–726.

[50]Fischer, "Russia and the Soviet Union Then and Now," 32.

[51]Yavlinsky et al., *500 Days: Transition to the Market*, 66.

30 percent of the world total. The agricultural sector suffered during the Stalinist era of collectivization and industrialization, and did not respond well to the higher priority given to it by Khrushchev and Brezhnev. In the 1960s, the Soviet Union became a chronic importer of grain, and during the 1980s it became the world's largest grain importer, accounting for about 15 percent of the world total.

Between the 1960s and 1980s, the Soviet Union consistently used at least 50 percent more land and eight times as many workers in agriculture as the United States, but Soviet output was usually about 20 percent below the American level. Agricultural performance was not quite as dismal in some of the countries of central and eastern Europe, but there was little cause for celebration. Between 1980 and 1990, when agricultural production grew at a 2.5 percent annual rate in an average upper-middle-income country, the growth rates were −2.1 percent in Bulgaria, 0.6 percent in Hungary, 0.7 percent in Poland, and 0.6 percent in Slovakia.[52]

What explained the poor performance of agriculture in centrally planned economies? A large part of the problem could be explained by the low priority afforded to agriculture, particularly during the Stalin era. The land mass of the Soviet Union was more than twice as large as that of the United States, but during the 1970s the Soviet road system was only one-fourth as large. More than one-quarter of the farms in the Russian Republic had no roads to connect them with the outside world, and most rural roads were not paved. Storage facilities were too few and too distant from one another. The result was that about 20 percent of the grain, fruit, and vegetables produced, and as much as 50 percent of the potato crop, rotted in the fields or was lost on the way to the grain elevator.[53]

Part of the agricultural weakness of the Soviet Union could be explained, of course, by the climate. Most of its sown area was comparable to the prairie provinces of Canada and to the northwestern United States; little could compare to the climate of the American corn belt. The annual distribution of precipitation was also unfavorable in the Soviet Union. Still, according to a prominent Russian agricultural economist, these factors should not be overemphasized:

The main reasons for the instability of agriculture are not natural and climatic factors in themselves, but rather the technological and organizational-economic conditions of farming that have not been sufficiently flexible to make it possible to adapt continuously and efficiently to existing natural and climatic conditions.[54]

In other words, central planning was simply too bureaucratic and inflexible to work well in the agricultural sector. Ideally, all the important decisions in a centrally planned economy were made at the beginning of the year (or five-year period) and were carried out during the remainder of the year.

[52]World Bank, World Development Report 1996, 208–209.

[53]Marshall Goldman, *USSR in Crisis: The Failure of an Economic System* (New York: W. W. Norton, 1983), 80–81.

[54]V. Tikhonov, "The Soviet Food Program," *Problems of Economics* 26 (June 1983): 12.

Agricultural decisions, however, must be adjusted continuously to deal with the climate, insects, incidence of plant disease, consumer demand, and other factors. In most cases, timely and informed judgments can be made only by the farmer on the scene, not by a central planner in the capital city.

EMPLOYMENT AND LABOR MOBILITY

One of the most important advantages of the Soviet-style system was its ability to maintain a very low level of unemployment. During the 1930s, when the future of the capitalist world was open to question, John Maynard Keynes acknowledged that "the authoritarian state systems of today seem to solve the problem of unemployment," but he quickly added that their solution required an excessive "expense of efficiency and freedom."[55] When Soviet leaders were criticized for abuses of human rights, they usually called attention to their protection of the right to work, and to abuses of this right in the West. In 1987, while he acknowledged the need for "radical" restructuring (*perestroika*), Soviet General Secretary Gorbachev still rejected the opinion "that we ought to give up planned economy and sanction unemployment," because "we aim to strengthen socialism, not replace it with a different system."[56]

Unemployment was not entirely absent in the Soviet-style economies. Workers moving from one job to another generated a small rate of frictional unemployment. Most of this movement was voluntary. Rapid population growth in Soviet central Asia caused a significant amount of rural unemployment, particularly among women.[57] Still, these were the exceptions; full employment was the rule. In the Soviet-style system, the government did not operate an unemployment compensation program because, officially, this problem simply did not exist.

Employers in Soviet-style economies typically wished to hire more workers than they could find. Political leaders and central planners placed a high priority on rapid economic growth, and much of this growth was accomplished with extensive use of labor. Public subsidies kept unprofitable enterprises from failing. Protected by these subsidies, and determined to meet output targets, industrial managers had little incentive to economize on the use of labor. A reserve of extra workers could be very useful when the time was drawing near to file a plan fulfillment report. Furthermore, it was difficult to dismiss an employee under Soviet law.

Thus, conventional unemployment was rare in the Soviet-style system, but "unemployment on the job" or underemployment was pervasive.[58] In the Soviet Union, estimates of the general level of overstaffing ranged from 5 percent

---

[55]John Maynard Keynes, *The General Theory of Employment, Interest, and Money* (New York: Harcourt, Brace, and World, 1964), 381.

[56]Mikhail Gorbachev, *Perestroika: New Thinking for Our Country and the World* (New York: Harer and Row, 1987), 86.

[57]See "Central Asia Faces Unemployment Problem," *Current Digest of the Soviet Press*, May 6, 1987, 4.

[58]Janos Kornai, *The Economics of Shortage* (Amsterdam: North Holland, 1980), 255–256.

to 25 percent.[59] This problem apparently worsened during the early 1990s, when production in factories throughout central Eurasia began to decline, but jobs remained protected. When factories in the region were privatized, some of them were able to release half their workers without cutting production.

During the Stalin era, Soviet restrictions on labor mobility were quite severe. The rate of labor turnover was very high in the early 1930s and draconian methods were devised to solve the problem. Job changers were penalized with inferior housing and the loss of social insurance; an internal passport system was established to monitor the movement of the population. Millions of peasants who resisted collectivization, political prisoners, prisoners of war, resettled minorities, and others were sent to labor camps.

Beginning in the mid-1950s, workers in Soviet-style societies had greater freedom to enter the occupations of their choice and to move between jobs. Many of the labor camps were closed after 1956, and many other restrictions on mobility were abolished at that time. Still, Party approval was necessary for thousands of high-level jobs on the *nomenklatura* lists. Church members, whose names were registered by the state, were not allowed to work as school teachers. Jews, Chechnyans, Gypsies, and people of many other ethnic groups experienced discrimination in hiring.

INCOME DISTRIBUTION AND POVERTY

Another purported advantage of Soviet-style socialism was its potential to reduce the unfair income inequalities and poverty that existed under capitalism. In 1965, a Soviet propaganda publication conceded that a "small number" of capitalist countries were producing large volumes of consumer goods, but reported that "these goods remain inaccessible to the overwhelming majority of the population in the capitalist world" because of the "uneven (and, to our mind, unjust) distribution of incomes among the populations of these countries." In contrast, the authors claimed that "all the riches of the country belong to the whole population" in the Soviet Union, so "the basis of inequality has been eliminated."[60]

In reality, none of the central Eurasian countries attempted to completely "eliminate" inequality. Income differentials were explicitly used to reward plan fulfillment, to compensate workers for achieving high levels of skill, and to attract workers into high-priority professions, industries, and regions. Special benefits were distributed to the Party elite, the *nomenklatura*, who were able to shop in special stores, ride in chauffeured limousines, enroll their children in the best schools, and vacation at private resorts.

In fairness, a great deal was done to reduce certain categories of inequality. Food prices and housing rents were heavily subsidized; public transportation, child care, education, and medical services were provided at little

---

[59]Shmelev and Popov, *The Turning Point*, 181.

[60]"Why Are Living Standards in the Soviet Union Lower Than in Capitalist Countries?" reprinted from *Soviet Life*, June 1966, 21, in Harry G. Shaffer, ed., *The Soviet Economy: A Collection of Western and Soviet Views*, 2d ed. (New York: Appleton-Century-Croft, 1969), 311.

or no immediate cost to patrons. Officially approved wage differentials were usually moderate, and individuals were not permitted to amass "unearned" fortunes from rents, interest, profits, or stock dividends.

In the end, it is difficult to measure and compare the levels of income inequality or poverty in socialist and capitalist countries. Comparisons are made complicated by differences in national statistical systems, income categories, relative prices, product shortages, in-kind incomes, and taxes.

With these limitations in mind, Christian Morrisson made a brave attempt to compare distributions of total income (including the value of Party privileges) in central Eurasia, western Europe, and the United States during the mid-1970s. Morrisson found that Czechoslovakia was in a class by itself, with perhaps the most equal distribution of income in the world. Bulgaria, Romania, and Hungary had relatively egalitarian distributions of income similar to those in Denmark, Sweden, and the United Kingdom. Poland, Yugoslavia, and the Soviet Union had less egalitarian distributions, not unlike those of Canada, the United States, and West Germany.[61]

Some of Morrisson's findings are supported by data from the mid-1980s, surveyed by Atkinson and Micklewright and by economists at the World Bank.[62] By all accounts, former Czechoslovakia and Hungary had the most egalitarian income distributions in the region at that time. The former Soviet Union had a more unequal income distribution than its neighbors in central and eastern Europe; its level of inequality was comparable to the average level of inequality of the OECD countries.

In summary, it seems that the Soviet-style system promoted income equality, but did not live up to its propaganda. Income inequality declined substantially in the Soviet Union between 1956 and 1968, and it was relatively low compared to developing countries in Latin America and Africa, but it apparently was never lower than the OECD average.[63] Czechoslovakia had a very low level of inequality, but this was already true as early as 1956; Czech and Slovak income equality may have preceded the introduction of the Soviet-style system.[64]

FINANCIAL STABILITY

During the 1950s and 1960s, before the first experiments with market-oriented reform in eastern Europe and before the explosion of international oil prices, the nations of central Eurasia all maintained a high level of financial stability—that is, they maintained control of their governmental budget balances, prevented excessive growth of their money supplies, and had low

---

[61]Christian Morrisson, "Income Distribution in East European and Western Countries," *Journal of Comparative Economics* 8 (June 1984): 121–138.

[62]Anthony B. Atkinson and John Micklewright, *Economic Transformation in Eastern Europe and the Distribution of Income* (Cambridge, UK: Cambridge University Press, 1992), passim; and World Bank, *World Development Report 1996*, 66–72.

[63]On the decline in Soviet income inequality, see Atkinson and Micklewright, *Economic Transformation in Eastern Europe*, 88.

[64]Ibid., 86.

rates of consumer price inflation. During the 1960s, Bulgaria and Czechoslovakia had the highest inflation rates in the region; both countries had an average rate of 3.2 percent per year. The Soviet inflation rate during the 1960s was only 1 percent per year.[65]

During the 1970s and 1980s, financial balances deteriorated in several countries, but the problem was most obvious in Yugoslavia, Poland, and Hungary—the countries that introduced the most extensive programs of market-oriented reform. Therefore, it seems that the traditional, unreformed Soviet-style system, when managed properly, was able to sustain a high level of financial stability.

If this financial system was stable, though, it had its weaknesses. Prices, for example, were centrally controlled and administered. They bore little relation to market conditions, and could not resolve product shortages or surpluses. Investment and foreign trade decisions were highly politicized; in the absence of market prices, interest rates, and exchange rates, they could not support a high level of economic efficiency.

FOREIGN ECONOMIC RELATIONS

The system of central planning was developed during the 1920s and 1930s in the Soviet Union when it was a relatively isolated country with few reliable trading partners. Thus, at that time, foreign trade was included in plans only when it was necessary to obtain products that simply could not be produced domestically. The Soviet-style system did not attempt to take full advantage of gains from international trade. The financial system prevented planners from basing their export and import decisions on principles of comparative advantage.

We have noted that the system of central planning also provided poor incentives to produce high-quality goods that could compete on international markets. Furthermore, enterprises were not allowed to interact directly with their foreign customers and suppliers; they were required to handle all transactions through agencies of the Ministry of Foreign Trade. This bureaucratic process allowed the central authorities to maintain firm control of foreign trade, but it placed additional limits on export performance, and interfered with efficient and timely import decisions. In the end, economic reforms were embraced most quickly during the 1960s by countries that had the greatest need to improve their foreign trade performance.

NATURAL ENVIRONMENT

In principle, the centrally planned economies should have been able to maintain excellent records of environmental protection. With central control of investment decisions and selection of technologies—a "scientific" approach to economic development—they should have been able to avoid many of the ecological problems encountered by capitalist societies.

---

[65]These are estimates of the U.S. Central Intelligence Agency, which exceed national estimates. See their *Handbook of Economic Statistics 1986,* 53.

THE DEATH OF THE ARAL SEA

The entire central Asian region is shaped like a large basin, surrounded by uplands and mountain ranges, with the Aral Sea in its center. The sea is fed by the two largest rivers in the region, the Amu Darya and the Syr Darya.

During the nineteenth century, when supplies of imported cotton were interrupted by the American Civil War, the Russian imperial authorities decided to expand cotton farming by irrigating desert lands in central Asia. In the Farghana region, the area sown in cotton increased from 14 percent of the land farmed in 1885 to 44 percent in 1915.

Heavy reliance on cotton production, rather than food crops, caused serious difficulties for the central Asian population during World War I, the Russian revolution, and the Russian civil war, and serious damage was inflicted on the irrigation system. After their victory, however, the Soviet authorities announced that it was necessary to free themselves entirely from foreign imports of cotton. They decided to greatly expand production in central Asia, requiring a huge increase in the amount of irrigated land under cultivation. Between 1929 and 1932 alone, irrigation facilities were installed on about 500,000 acres of new land.

Over a long period of time, these economic development policies have exacted a disastrous toll on the central Asian people and on their environment. The flow of water into the Aral Sea from the Amu Darya and Syr Darya declined from 55 cubic kilometers per year during the 1950s to zero in the 1980s. Over that same period, the volume of the Aral Sea declined by about two-thirds; it continues to decline today. The remaining water has grown increasingly saline, killing the local fishing industry, which provided 40,000 tons of fish in its best years, and endangering the water supplies of almost 50 million people. As the surface of the sea recedes, it exposes vast areas of salty flatland; salt and dust from these areas blow across the plains onto croplands and pastures, causing additional damage.

Heavy emphasis on irrigated cotton farming has created a pattern of economic development in central Asia that is difficult to change today. "If nothing is done," Shmelev and Popov reported several years ago, "in two decades we'll have to redraw the maps and geography textbooks—the Aral Sea will have dried up."

SOURCES: Ian Murray Matley, "Agricultural Development," in Edward Allworth, ed., *Central Asia: A Century of Russian Rule* (New York: Columbia University Press, 1967), 274–308; World Bank, *World Development Report 1992* (Oxford: Oxford University Press, 1992), 38; and Nikolai Shmelev and Vladimir Popov, *The Turning Point* (New York: Doubleday, 1989), 108.

We have noted, however, that a centrally planned system is driven by the priorities of the leadership. In the countries of central Eurasia, a high priority was placed on rapid industrial development; preservation of the natural environment was low on the political agenda. Industrial ministries and enterprises were rewarded for fulfilling output targets, not for economy or sensitivity in their use of labor, capital, or natural resources.

The Soviet-style system was predicated on the idea that the highest form of socialist ownership was state, rather than cooperative, ownership. A system of state ownership is most susceptible, however, to the so-called **tragedy of the commons**—if property belongs to everybody, it belongs to nobody. Aristotle's words are worth repeating: "That which is common to the greatest number has the least care bestowed upon it."[66] Under a system of state socialism, no individual or small group of people is willing or able to maintain the value and quality of public property.

For these and other reasons, it is now widely understood that the environmental performance of the Soviet-style system was disastrous. International attention was attracted to the problem in 1986 by the Chernobyl catastrophe, but scattered throughout central Eurasia one can find unsafe nuclear power plants, polluted and abandoned military and industrial sites, and water-diversion projects that have caused large-scale desertification and erosion (see "The Death of the Aral Sea").[67]

SUMMARY

Soviet-style socialism was based on state ownership of productive resources. The political system was led by the general secretary and the Communist Party hierarchy. The prime minister, the Council of Ministers, and the State Planning Committee coordinated the work of the ministries, which directed the industrial enterprises. The roles of the parliament (Supreme Soviet) and the president were mostly ceremonial.

The economic plans were formulated for several time periods, with the annual plans being the most specific and operational. The production plans were formulated through a process of disaggregation and bargaining and were adjusted for rough consistency through the method of material balances. During its implementation, departures from the production plan were coordinated by administrative guidance, by the practice of self-supply within enterprises, and by black-market transactions between enterprises. An investment plan was designed to provide the capital stock needed for the production plan.

Agriculture was organized around collective farms (*kolkhozy*) that were owned and managed cooperatively, state farms (*sovkhozy*) that were run like factories, and small private plots. Procurement prices for the state and

---

[66]Aristotle, *Politics* 2.3.1261b34.

[67]Marshall Goldman, *The Spoils of Progress* (Cambridge, Mass.: MIT, 1972); Murray Feshbach and Alfred Friendly, Jr., *Ecocide in the USSR: Health and Nature Under Siege* (New York: Basic Books, 1992); and Murray Feshbach, *Ecological Disaster: Cleaning Up the Hidden Legacy of the Soviet Regime* (New York: Twentieth Century Fund Press, 1995), passim.

collective farms were set by the state; the private plots could sell all their output at market prices. Retail prices of food were heavily subsidized.

In the traditional Soviet-style system, foreign trade transactions were all handled by agencies of the Ministry of Foreign Trade, which was firmly controlled by the State Planning Committee. Imports were used to fill gaps in the material balance tables, and exports were sold to pay for the imports. Little account was taken of comparative advantage.

Financial criteria played a limited role in economic decisions, but financial plans were designed to balance the incomes and expenditures of the household, business, and governmental sectors, and to equilibrate the international balance of payments.

The material incentive system was based on wage and bonus payments. Workers received a basic wage that was differentiated by industry, vocation, skills, location, and other factors. Bonuses were based on plan fulfillment. The heavy emphasis on fulfillment of physical output targets encouraged producers to provide distorted information to central planners, and discouraged high-quality production.

Wholesale and retail prices were heavily controlled. The former were designed to cover average costs of production, and the latter to roughly equate the demand and planned supply of each product, with lower prices set for necessities.

A second economy of unplanned production and exchange included legal activity on private plots and in handicrafts and illegal production for the black market. The second economy provided incomes and supplies of scarce goods and services, and contributed in some ways to the performance of the planned sectors, but it also contributed to a culture of illegality and apparently caused greater income inequality.

The contribution, if any, of economic planning to rapid economic development is uncertain. According to Western estimates, the national income goals of Soviet medium-term plans were never fulfilled. However, economic planning apparently did allow the central authorities to concentrate economic development on high-priority sectors. Thus, the heavy industrial sectors were developed rapidly, but at a high cost of agricultural and consumer goods production and product quality. The central planning system also created a highly monopolized industrial sector.

The poor performance of Soviet agriculture can be explained by climatic and geographic factors, the low investment priority that was placed on food production for many years, and the fact that agricultural production was difficult to plan and manage centrally.

The low rates of unemployment in Soviet-style systems were explained by the high priority accorded to economic growth, the managerial incentive system that stresses output targets, the prevention of bankruptcies through a large system of public subsidies, and a legal system that provided employment protection to workers. A certain amount of frictional and rural unemployment existed. Severe limits were imposed during the Stalin era, but beginning in the mid-1950s, Soviet workers were generally free to enter the occupation of their choice and move between jobs.

Soviet-style socialism never attempted to fulfill exaggerated promises to eliminate inequality, but it provided low-cost food, housing, medical care, and other necessities to the general population. Some of the central Eurasian countries achieved much higher levels of equality than others.

Before market-oriented reforms were introduced, the centrally planned economies maintained high levels of financial stability, evidenced by low rates of consumer price inflation. Central planning was a poor instrument, however, to exploit international comparative advantage. Because of the high priority it placed on economic growth and its distant system of property rights, Soviet-style socialism also caused catastrophic damage to the natural environment.

DISCUSSION AND REVIEW QUESTIONS

1. What functions were performed by the Communist Party in the Soviet system of government?

2. Suppose that the material balance table for paper goods indicated a deficit. What options were available to clear the deficit? What were the possible problems associated with each option?

3. How did investment decision making differ in capitalist and centrally planned socialist countries?

4. How were wholesale prices set? Why do you think this method was adopted? What problems did it cause?

5. Describe the Soviet record of fulfillment of medium-term plans. Was it appropriate to refer to the Soviet Union as a centrally planned economy?

6. What were several factors that explained the low level of productivity in Soviet agriculture?

7. How did the unplanned second economy support the performance of the planned economy? How did it interfere?

8. How were foreign trade decisions made in planned economies? What purpose did this arrangement serve, and what problems were caused by it?

9. What were some of the causes of environmental disasters in the centrally planned economies? Was this a necessary outgrowth of socialism?

SUGGESTED READINGS

Abouchar, Alan, ed. *The Socialist Price Mechanism.* Durham, N.C.: Duke University Press, 1977. *Much, but not all, of this is rather advanced material.*

Alexeev, Michael V., Gregory Grossman, and Vladimir G. Treml, eds. *Berkeley-Duke Occasional Papers on the Second Economy in the USSR.* Bala

Cynnwyd, Penn.: The WEFA Group, 1985–1993. *One of the richest sources of information on the unplanned portion of the Soviet economy; 38 papers were published in the series, including studies of income, wealth, agriculture, alcohol production, poverty, housing, drug sales, prostitution, and religious and funeral services.*

Berliner, Joseph S. *The Innovation Decision in Soviet Industry.* Cambridge, Mass.: MIT Press, 1976. *Provides an extended discussion of prices and incentives in a planned economy and their impact on technological progress.*

Eatwell, John, Murray Milgate, and Peter Newman, eds. *Problems of the Planned Economy.* New York: W. W. Norton & Company, 1990. *Thirty-seven brief articles, extracted from* The New Palgrave: A Dictionary of Economics. *Most of these are excellent, and most are written from a historical perspective. These include, for example, articles on "Command Economy" and "Material Balances" by Gregory Grossman, on "Central Planning" by Tadeuz Kowalik, and on "Planned Economy" by Alec Nove.*

Ericson, Richard E. "The Classical Soviet-Type Economy: Nature of the System and Implications for Reform." *Journal of Economic Perspectives* 5 (Fall 1991): 11–27. *Argues that the component institutions of the classical Soviet system were organically connected and mutually supporting, so partial reforms were likely to fail.*

Goldman, Marshall. *USSR in Crisis: The Failure of an Economic System.* New York: W. W. Norton, 1983. *Written in a lively style by the associate director of the Russian Research Center at Harvard University, the opening chapter on "The Stalinist Model" and the third chapter on agriculture provide statistical and anecdotal evidence on the failures of the traditional Soviet system.*

Gregory, Paul R., and Robert C. Stuart. *Soviet Economic Structure and Performance.* 4th ed. New York: Harper and Row, 1990. *A popular textbook on the Soviet economy with an extended discussion of economic planning.*

Hewett, Ed A. *Reforming the Soviet Economy: Equality versus Efficiency.* Washington, D.C.: The Brookings Institution, 1988. *The purpose of this volume is to explore economic reform, but the first four chapters provide one of the best dissections of the formal and de facto Soviet systems available in print.*

Hough, Jerry F., and Merle Fainsod. *How the Soviet Union Is Governed.* Cambridge, Mass.: Harvard University Press, 1979. *A comprehensive and authoritative treatment of Soviet political institutions.*

Kahan, Arcadius, and Blair Ruble, eds. *Industrial Labor in the USSR.* New York: Pergamon Press, 1979. *Sixteen articles on the demography, organization, standard of living, and political positions of Soviet workers.*

Nove, Alec. *The Soviet Economic System.* London: George Allen and Unwin, 1977. *Nove's analysis is somewhat advanced and should be preceded by simpler texts.*

Rutland, Peter. *The Myth of the Plan.* La Salle, Ill.: Open Court, 1985. *A critique of the planning system, harkening back to the von Mises–Lange debate.*

Simis, Konstantin. *USSR: The Corrupt Society.* New York: Simon and Schuster, 1982. *An inside view of Soviet political corruption and its roots in the system of central planning.*

Voslensky, Michael. *Nomenklatura.* Garden City, N.Y.: Doubleday, 1984. *An explanation of the personnel system operated by the Party, and a biting account of the class structure it has created.*

INTERNET RESOURCES

Cockshot, W. Paul. "Laibman and the Phases of Planning"
http://www.cs.strath.ac.uk/Contrib/wpc/reports/mfs2/node2.html

Communist Party of the Soviet Union
http://www.ida.liu.se/%7Evaden/communism/

Constitution of the USSR, 1977
gopher://wiretap.spies.com:70/00/Gov/World/ussr77.con

Feshbach, Murray. *Introduction to Ecological Disaster: Cleaning Up the Hidden Legacy of the Soviet Regime*
http://epn.org/tcf/xxfesh03.html

Hoover Institution Library
http://www-sul.stanford.edu/depts/hoover/pubs.html

Levine, Herbert. "Why Soviet Central Planning Failed"
http://mcneil.sas.upenn.edu/east/spring95/levin.html

Linear Programming FAQ
http://www.skypoint.com/subscribers/ashbury/linear-programming-faq.html

Martens, Ludo, "Another View of Stalin"
http://koza.eri.harvard.edu/~knut/Stalin/book.html

Medley, Joseph, ed. "Soviet Agriculture: A Critique of Myths"
http://macweb.acs.usm.maine.edu/economics/Soviet.html

Melberg, Hans, "The Soviet System and Model Building"
http://home.sol.no/hansom/papers/940301.htm

Naishul, Vitali A. "Communism: Death or Transformation?"
http://www.fe.msk.ru/libertarium/library/nayshul/edeathtran.html

Spalding, Elizabeth E. Review of *The Soviet Tragedy*, by Martin Malia
http://www.heritage.org/heritage/library/categories/forpol/inaugbk.html

Stalin, Joseph. "On Problems of Organizational Leadership"
http://www.brainlink.com/~Anesi/stalin.htm

Ukraine: The Environment Bites Back
http://www.un.kiev.ua/UNonLine/hdr_press/unprhdr0.html

Waal-Palms, Pyotr J. "Command vs. Market Capital Allocation"
http://www.aa.net/~russia/texts/pd119.html

APPENDIX: INPUT-OUTPUT ECONOMICS

In our discussion of the material balance method, we saw that formulating a consistent plan was a difficult, if not impossible, task. Adjustment of the production or use of one product logically required adjustments in the production and use of many other products. These technical relationships could be complex and circular: Steel is used to produce trucks and trucks are used to produce steel.

Faced by these difficulties, the central planners were aided by a technique that earned its inventor, Wassily Leontief, the 1973 Nobel Prize in economics. Input-output analysis makes it possible, in principle, for a planner to formulate a set of mutually consistent gross output targets for each industry. A condensed input-output table for Soviet transactions in 1972 is presented in Table 15A.1. For the sake of pedagogical simplicity, all the productive sectors of the economy are combined here into three large groups—industry, agriculture, and services. The table could have been divided, however, into hundreds of sectors.

Each row on the table shows how the gross output of a particular sector was distributed through the economy in 1972. For example, about half the output of the industrial sector was used within industry itself for productive purposes. Part of the output of the steel industry, for example, was used by the automobile industry. Relatively small shares of industrial output were used by the agricultural and service sectors; less than half was used by consumers and other final demanders.

Looking down any of the first three columns of the table, we see the inputs that were delivered to a particular industry. For example, in order to produce its 522 billion rubles of gross output, the Soviet industrial sector used 266 billion rubles of its own output, 62 billion rubles of agricultural goods, and 50 billion rubles of services.

■ TABLE 15A.1

SOVIET UNION: SIMPLIFIED INPUT-OUTPUT TABLE, 1972
(BILLIONS OF RUBLES IN PURCHASERS' PRICES)

To/From	Industry, Construction	Agriculture	Services, Other	Total Intermediate	Final Demand	Gross Output
Industry, Construction	266	18	10	294	228	522
Agriculture	62	24	0	86	29	115
Services, Other	50	6	1	57	3	60

SOURCE: U.S. Bureau of the Census, Foreign Demographic Analysis Division, *Input-Output Structure of the Soviet Economy: 1972.* Foreign Economic Report No. 18 (Washington, D.C.: USGPO, 1983), p. 102.

Dividing the inputs in the first three columns by the gross outputs of the sectors that use them, we obtain a matrix of direct input coefficients, denoted by the letter A:

$$A = \begin{bmatrix} 266/522 & 18/115 & 10/60 \\ 62/522 & 24/115 & 0/60 \\ 50/522 & 6/115 & 1/60 \end{bmatrix} = \begin{bmatrix} .51 & .16 & .17 \\ .12 & .21 & 0 \\ .10 & .05 & .02 \end{bmatrix}$$

Matrix A is sometimes called a technology matrix because it contains useful information about the technical interrelationships among different sectors of the economy. If it is multiplied by any vector of gross outputs, x, it will provide us with a vector of intermediate inputs that are needed to produce these gross outputs: Ax = intermediate demand. If, for example, we multiply matrix A by the actual gross outputs that were produced in 1972 (given in Table 15A.1), we obtain the vector of intermediate demands for 1972 (also given in the table):

$$\begin{bmatrix} .51 & .16 & .17 \\ .12 & .21 & 0 \\ .10 & .05 & .02 \end{bmatrix} \begin{bmatrix} 522 \\ 115 \\ 60 \end{bmatrix} = \begin{bmatrix} 294 \\ 86 \\ 57 \end{bmatrix}$$

If we use f to denote final demand, then:

$$x = Ax + f, \tag{1}$$

or gross output is equal to intermediate output plus final output. If we collect terms and solve Equation 1 for gross output, we obtain:

$$x = (I - A)^{-1}f, \tag{2}$$

where I is the identity matrix—a square matrix of the same order as A, but with ones along its principal diagonal (from upper left to lower right) and zeros elsewhere.

Equation 2 provides one of the principal conclusions of input-output analysis. If a political decision is made to provide a particular collection of goods (f) to consumers and other final demanders, we can multiply that vector by the matrix $(I-A)^{-1}$ to obtain the vector of gross outputs that will satisfy that final demand. In our example:

$$(I - A)^{-1} = \begin{bmatrix} 2.2370 & 0.4776 & 0.3880 \\ 0.3998 & 1.3380 & 0.0589 \\ 0.2456 & 0.1170 & 1.063 \end{bmatrix}$$

Hence, if we decided to supply final demanders with 100 billion rubles of industrial goods, agricultural goods, and services, we would need to set gross output targets of 310, 174, and 143 billion rubles, respectively.

APPLICATION AND LIMITATIONS OF INPUT-OUTPUT

In the 1960s, when electronic computers, input-output methods, and other mathematical techniques were in their infancy, it was widely believed that they would make it possible for the Soviet Union to compile fully consistent, and even optimal, economic plans. Subsequent events caused many Soviet economists to lose this hope.

It certainly was true that computers provided invaluable aid to central planners. Input-output (I-O) and other methods made it possible for the planners to explore alternative growth strategies for the economy and to compile highly aggregated versions of their plans. For several reasons, however, the application of mathematical techniques never lived up to original expectations.

First, the I-O method ran into ideological and political opposition. It was not firmly grounded in the Marxist-Leninist theory of value, and its use was resisted by the ministries and other organizations that feared they would lose bargaining power under a computerized system of planning. Thus, according to an analyst at the Research Institute of Gosplan:

> *The true reasons for insufficient use of input-output tables are to be found in the slow pace with which the organization and methodology of planning are being restructured. Planning practice has not yet completely overcome the outmoded approach that looks on the formation of a plan as a process of "meshing" the drafts submitted by the various agencies.*[1]

Second, the I-O tables were not compiled with sufficient frequency or detail to accurately guide the planning effort. Compiling a large table is an expensive and complicated enterprise, much like taking a census. Soviet tables were constructed only for 1959, 1966, 1972, 1977, and 1982. By the time a table became available for use, many of its technical relationships were already out of date. At most, they were disaggregated into hundreds of sectors; yet the State Planning Committee alone compiled material balances for thousands of products. Even if it were possible to compile much larger I-O tables, Soviet computers were not able to perform the matrix inversions necessary for their effective use.

Third, if it were possible to compile and manipulate large, up-to-date input-output tables, the results of these calculations would still have limited application. An I-O table can reveal how many inputs were actually *used* during some previous year to produce a given level of output, but not how many inputs were actually *needed*. Thus, the use of I-O tables could cause the inefficiencies of the past to be perpetuated in plans for the future.

In addition, a number of other technical problems interfered with input-output planning. The output plans usually were compiled in physical terms, but I-O tables usually were aggregated in rubles. I-O analysis is based on an unusual assumption about the nature of the production function. Inputs, it is assumed, must be combined in fixed proportions to produce their output.

Finally, we should emphasize that I-O analysis may assist in the formulation of an internally consistent plan, but it does not generate an optimal plan—one that serves the objectives of consumers or political leaders at the lowest possible cost. For this purpose, we would have to go beyond I-O

---

[1] F. Klotsvog, "The Utilization of Input-Output Tables in Planning Practice," *Current Digest of the Soviet Press*, May 7, 1980, 16.

analysis to linear programming methods; the theoretical, statistical, and computational problems would become even larger.

For these and other reasons, I-O analysis was most useful during the early stages of the planning process—during the preparation of highly aggregated control figures. At that stage, I-O made it possible to prepare several broad options for the plan, one of which was chosen by the political leadership. When the plan was disaggregated into thousands of product groups, no suitable substitute was ever found for the traditional system of material balance tables. "Computopia," as Peter Wiles called it, remained a distant dream.

East-Central Europe and the Balkan Region

16

CENTRAL EURASIA:
SOCIALIST ECONOMIC REFORMS

Blind is the one who but half sees the chasm, and half recoils because he lost his way, half mutineer and half suppresser of the rebellion he has spawned.

—YEVGENIY YEVTUSHENKO, "HALF MEASURES," 1990

Not a single reform in Russia has ever been completed. . . . If we look at the reforms of various ages, everywhere radical reform has been attempted, there is a rollback, a sharp backlash. This is particularly true of the twentieth century. In Russia, not two land reforms, three revolutions, Lenin's new economic policy, Stalin's industrialization, Khrushchev's thaw, or Kosygin's quiet reforms changed anything fundamental in Russia.

—BORIS YELTSIN, *THE STRUGGLE FOR RUSSIA*, 1994

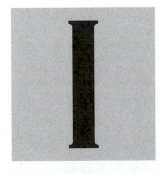

n the previous chapter, we found that Soviet leaders were able to accomplish many of their chief objectives with a system of central planning and authoritarian control. They mounted a rapid program of industrialization that made the Soviet Union a major military power, able to support an Allied victory in World War II. For many years, the Soviet Union was able to challenge the United States in arms production and space exploration, maintain positive economic growth with little inflation or unemployment, control a vast multinational empire, and play a central role in the world communist movement.

After World War II, the extension of Soviet influence through central Eurasia exposed conflicts and inefficiencies in the Stalinist system that led, step-by-step, to its reappraisal, reform, and destruction. Soon after the war, a confrontation between Joseph Stalin and Marshall Tito caused Yugoslavia to go its own way, shifting to a system of workers' self-management and market socialism. Yugoslavia opened the first fracture in a seemingly monolithic communist bloc, setting a precedent for alternative systems of socialism.

In 1955, two years after Stalin's death, Nikita Khrushchev led a Soviet delegation to Belgrade to mend relations with Tito. The communiqué of their meeting provided a strong endorsement for socialist experimentation: "Differences in practical forms of socialism are exclusively the affair of individual countries."[1] Early in 1956, in his so-called Secret Speech to the Twentieth Party Congress, Khrushchev renounced Stalin's system of terror; several months later, however, he sent troops into Hungary to crush a democratic uprising. In 1957, Khrushchev initiated a major decentralization of the Soviet administrative system, giving new hope to reformers in Czechoslovakia, Hungary, and Poland. They formulated major programs of market-oriented reform during the late 1950s, and were able to implement lesser programs during the early 1960s.

In 1965, the deterioration of Soviet economic performance and the infiltration of ideas from East-Central Europe led Soviet Premier Alexei Kosygin to adopt a modest program of economic reform. Kosygin's program gained international attention, but gained little support from General Secretary Brezhnev, and faltered in the face of strong opposition from the ministerial bureaucracy. Still, the Soviet experiments encouraged leaders in East-Central Europe to advance their reforms to the next level. In 1968, a market-oriented New Economic Mechanism was adopted in Hungary, and a more ambitious program of economic and democratic reforms was attempted in Czechoslovakia. This time, the Hungarian reforms were allowed to stand, but Czechoslovakia was invaded by Soviet tanks. Two months after the destruction of the so-called Prague Spring, a commentary in *Pravda* enunciated the **Brezhnev Doctrine,** setting ideological limits on national sovereignty:

> . . . [T]he peoples of the socialist countries and the communist parties have and must have freedom to determine their country's path of development. However, any decision of theirs must damage neither socialism in their own country nor the fundamental interest of the other socialist countries. . . . [E]very communist party is responsible not only to its own people but also to all the socialist countries and to the entire communist movement.[2]

During the first half of the 1970s, East-West *dé tente* and the growing availability of petrodollar credits provided opportunities for closer economic relations with the capitalist world. Poland adopted a particularly aggressive and unsuccessful economic development strategy based on debt financing of machinery imports from the West. In 1972, following the lead of Yugoslavia, Hungary tested the limits of cooperation between capitalism and socialism when it invited Western partners to share in the ownership of joint enterprises on Hungarian soil. In 1975, at the Helsinki Conference on European

---

[1] Edward Crankshaw, *Khrushchev: A Career* (New York: The Viking Press, 1966), 210.

[2] Quoted in Derek H. Aldcroft and Steven Morewood, *Economic Change in Eastern Europe Since 1918* (Aldershot: Edward Elgar, 1995), 150.

Security, the Soviet Union and other Warsaw Pact countries formally relinquished the Brezhnev Doctrine:

> *The participating States will respect each other's sovereign equality and individuality . . . including in particular the right of every State to juridical equality, to territorial integrity and to freedom and political independence. They will also respect each other's right freely to choose and develop its political, social, economic and cultural systems as well as its right to determine its laws and regulations.*[3]

The constituencies for democratic and market-oriented reform were strengthened during the 1970s by the spirit of Helsinki and by expanded contact with the West. At the time, however, little practical progress could be made; the Eastern economies were destabilized by rising international oil prices and debt burdens. During the mid-1970s, Hungary and Yugoslavia were forced to restore central controls on prices and foreign exchange transactions. At the end of 1981, Polish authorities responded to a debt crisis, a collapsing economy, and a confrontation with the Solidarity trade union by imposing martial law.

Hungary returned to the reform path in 1980 with a major revision of its price system, and expanded the scope of cooperative and private enterprise in 1982. In the Soviet Union, Mikhail Gorbachev gained power in 1985, and introduced his policies of economic *perestroika* and political *glasnost*. Initially, Gorbachev's economic proposals were quite reserved, but they grew progressively more ambitious. Equally important, Gorbachev made it clear that the Brezhnev Doctrine was truly dead; the nations of East-Central Europe were free to pursue radical reforms, even if they threatened the survival of communism.

In this chapter, we survey programs of economic reform introduced in central Eurasia between World War II and the revolutions that began in 1989. Unlike the transition strategies discussed in the next chapter, the reforms in this chapter were all predicated on preservation of socialist ownership and continued dominance of the Communist party. They were important, however, for several reasons. They restored a semblance of market-oriented behavior in some countries, and encouraged the development of skills that would be needed in more ambitious programs of market transition. They demonstrated that market systems are ineffective when excessive controls are imposed on property ownership, market entry, and price adjustments, and when profits are diluted by excessive taxes and subsidies. They created a constituency for additional reform, and provided experimental data on institutional arrangements such as worker self-management that would later be useful to designers of privatization programs.

Here, we focus on socialist reforms in three countries: former Yugoslavia, Hungary, and the former Soviet Union. Yugoslavia had a unique, experimental economic system that represented the first major revision of Stalinism. Before 1989, Hungary had the most ambitious program of economic

---

[3]Helsinki Conference on Security and Cooperation in Europe, Final Act, 1975, <http://www.hri. org/docs/Helsinki75.html>.

reform in the Warsaw Pact. The Soviet Union was, of course, the dominant power in central Eurasia, and here it represents several countries that searched for conservative solutions to the problems of central planning.

YUGOSLAVIA: WORKER-MANAGED MARKET SOCIALISM

In its idealized form, the Yugoslav system of worker-self management and market socialism had the following features:

- Each enterprise or workers' collective was owned by society at large, and was governed by its workers through a system of direct or representative democracy, with equal representation for workers in all categories of rank, skill, and income.

- Enterprises interacted with one another, with domestic consumers, and with foreign firms through a market system with relatively uncontrolled prices and exchange rates. As a secondary system of coordination, the authorities prepared indicative plans, based on voluntary or contractual compliance of workers' collectives.

- The workers in each enterprise were paid a portion of residual income—enterprise sales revenue, net of production costs, taxes, capital charges paid to the government, and enterprise investments. In effect, the workers shared a portion of enterprise profits (although this word was seldom used), giving them a motivation to serve the demands of consumers and to minimize nonlabor costs of production.

- Aside from its obligation to protect the system of self-management, the government played an economic role quite similar to that of a capitalist government. Its objectives were usually implemented through traditional instruments of fiscal, monetary, commercial, labor, environmental, and regional policy.

These, once again, were important elements of the *idealized* economic system in Yugoslavia. They were implemented partially and imperfectly over a period of several decades. At any point after World War II, the actual Yugoslav system also included elements of the Soviet system and several layers of legal and illegal private activity.

BACKWARDNESS AND CENTRAL PLANNING

Most of the Yugoslav republics were dominated for centuries by the Ottoman Turks, trapped in relative backwardness. After World War I, the republics were joined together by foreign powers, not by a natural and voluntary union. Serbia became the dominant republic, accounting for nearly one-half of the population and one-third of national income; Croatia followed, contributing one-fifth of the population and one-fourth of national income (refer to Table 14.1).

Before World War II, Yugoslavia was primarily an agricultural country; property ownership was semifeudal and early-capitalist. Land reforms were undertaken during the 1920s and 1930s, but enormous inequalities persisted. On the eve of World War II, two-thirds of the farms were still smaller than 12 acres.

After the war, Yugoslavia achieved a modicum of national unity under its authoritarian leader, Marshall Tito. It joined the Soviet camp, and adopted a system of state ownership and central planning. In 1945, a new land reform redistributed all holdings larger than 87 acres, and in 1946 a cautious collectivization of agriculture commenced. The First Five-Year Plan, adopted in 1947, was highly ambitious, with a Soviet-style emphasis on industrialization.

THE 1950s: WORKER'S SELF-MANAGEMENT AND THE VISIBLE HAND

When the Soviet Union, Hungary, and other socialist countries adopted reforms, their purpose was usually simple: to improve economic performance. In Yugoslavia, the first stage of economic reform grew out of a political confrontation with the Soviet Union. The Yugoslavs had been faithful to the Soviet-style system for several years, but turned against it when Stalin employed a series of overbearing tactics, including a trade embargo, in his attempt to overthrow Tito's regime. The Yugoslav leaders declared that Stalinism had become an exploitive system of state capitalism or, at best, an immature system of socialism. It bore little resemblance to the Marxian ideal of a "free association of producers."[4]

In 1950, the Basic Law on the Management of State Industries by Work Collectives gave each enterprise the right to handle its own affairs through an elected workers' council (analogous to the stockholders of a capitalist firm), an elected management board (analogous to the board of directors), and an appointed manager.[5]

In the following years, the Yugoslavs continued to distance themselves from the Soviet model. A 1951 law replaced the system of detailed central planning with a system that Egon Neuberger called the **Visible Hand.** Enterprises were allowed to set their own production targets; planners in Belgrade continued to control investment, foreign trade, the distribution of profits, and the basic structure of the economy. In 1952, compulsory deliveries of agricultural commodities were abolished and price controls were lifted from a wide range of goods. In 1953, the program of forced collectivization of agriculture was discontinued altogether. In 1954, local

---

[4] This political and ideological interpretation of Yugoslav behavior is based on evidence presented in David A. Dyker, *Yugoslavia: Socialism, Development and Debt* (London: Routledge, 1990), Chapter 2.

[5] An English translation of the Basic Law is available in *Self-Governing Socialism*, Vol. 1, ed. Branko Horvat, Mihailo Markovic, and Rudi Supek (White Plains, N.Y.: International Arts and Sciences Press, 1975), Chapter 35.

authorities were allowed to establish **communal banks,** breaking the monopoly previously held by the National Bank and its branches. The number of bureaucrats in central agencies was cut by almost 80 percent between 1948 and 1956.[6]

THE 1960s: WORKER-MANAGED MARKET SOCIALISM

During the 1960s, while most socialist countries were introducing cautious programs of reform, the Yugoslav authorities continued to take bold steps. By the end of the decade, they had dismantled the Visible Hand controls and introduced a broader system of market socialism.

In 1961, the National Bank ceased to perform commercial banking functions; these were transferred to the communal banks and to specialized banks for agriculture, investment, and foreign trade. At the same time, the communal banks were removed from the direct control of local politicians. The workers' councils of local enterprises were given two-thirds of the seats on the management boards.

In 1965, the Yugoslav authorities introduced a particularly broad package of reforms, similar in some respects to the "shock therapy" programs that would be undertaken 25 years later in Poland and Czechoslovakia. Their major actions included the following:

- Price controls were lifted on many products; by 1968, nearly 60 percent of producer prices and 70 percent of retail prices were unregulated. For products still subject to control, subsidies were reduced, and prices were adjusted to world market levels.

- Social investment funds, previously allocated on a political basis by the federal government, were transferred to banks, which were encouraged to lend on a profit-and-loss basis.

- The domestic market was exposed to more foreign competition, and a cumbersome system of multiple exchange rates was replaced with a single rate for the dinar (the Yugoslav currency).

- Enterprises gained greater authority and freedom to distribute profits between capital investment and employee income.

- Central planning of basic proportions gave way to an even less detailed and more voluntary system of indicative planning.

In 1967, the communal banks were reorganized into independent **basic banks,** controlled by their founders, which could include governmental or business organizations. The founders participated in management and profits according to their investment shares. A group of basic banks could create an **associated bank** to organize check-clearing and foreign-exchange activities in their region, and to arrange financing for major projects. A large, diversified industrial enterprise could organize its own **internal bank** to pool the financial resources of its units.

---

[6]Laza Djodjic, "Thirty-Five Years of Socialist Self-Management in Yugoslavia," *Socialist Thought and Practice* 25 (November 1985): 36–37.

The reforms of the 1960s increased the flexibility and allocative efficiency of the Yugoslav economy, but also increased its vulnerability to international price movements and inflationary pressures. Small enterprises were shaken by foreign competition and by smaller subsidies, forcing them to merge with larger and stronger producers. Unable to compete in the new capital market, the underdeveloped regions received a smaller share of total investment.

THE 1970S: RADICAL DECENTRALIZATION

During the 1970s, Yugoslavia had to cope with a growing list of economic, social, and political problems. Like many other countries, it had to absorb macroeconomic shocks from rising oil prices and unstable international markets. Economic instability contributed to political tensions among the republics.[7] Marshall Tito was growing old, and the country needed a system to choose his successor. Business enterprises were growing larger, so individual workers found it difficult to play a meaningful role in management.

The Yugoslav leaders addressed these problems by pressing the concepts of self-management, federalism, and decentralization to new extremes. To resolve the leadership succession problem and to relieve tension between the republics, a new constitution adopted in 1974 included an unusual system of political institutions. The regions were given equal representation in the collective leadership of the national League of Communists. After Tito's death, the job of party president would rotate each year to a representative of a different region. The state would be headed by a collective presidency, which would include one member from each of the eight regions, plus the Party president. Each year, according to a set order of rotation, a representative from a different region would become the national president.

At the enterprise level, actions were taken under the constitution and the 1976 Law on Associated Labor to strengthen self-management. In the large enterprises, each department or other unit that could construct its own set of financial accounts was organized into an independent **Basic Organization of Associated Labor (BOAL).**[8] The larger enterprise, now called a **Work Organization of Associated Labor (WOAL),** was still a legal entity, headed by a workers' council and a general manager, but it directed the work of the BOALs by their mutual consent.

Each BOAL had its own assets, its own workers' council, and its own representation on the workers' council of the larger enterprise. Each was free to hire and fire its own workers, to set its own prices and production levels, to negotiate contractual agreements with other BOALs, to withdraw from the WOAL in accordance with its contractual obligations, and to join another

---

[7]On regional disputes during the 1970s, see Steven Burg, *Conflict and Cohesion in Socialist Yugoslavia* (Princeton, N. J.: Princeton University Press, 1983), Chapter 3.

[8]For example, 20 BOALs were established in Beogradska Konfeksia, a clothing company with 5,600 workers. These ranged in size from an 80-member association of maintenance engineers to a 700-member association of retail workers. See Christopher Prout, *Market Socialism in Yugoslavia* (London: Oxford University Press, 1985), 65–67.

WOAL or operate independently. This was a system of enterprise decentralization without parallel in the industrial world.

THE 1980S: AFTER TITO

In May 1980, Marshall Tito died at the age of 87, leaving Yugoslavia without a strong authoritarian leader or a familiar symbol of national unity.[9] The presidency was placed on a one-year rotation, so it was impossible for any new leader to implement a long-term program of stabilization or unification. Macroeconomic policy spun out of control. The consumer price inflation rate escalated steadily from 30 percent in 1980 to more than 100 percent in 1987, and then exploded to 10,000 percent at the end of 1989. The unemployment rate, which had been about 7 percent during the second half of the 1970s, rose from 10 percent in 1980 to 15 percent in 1990.[10]

In 1990, in an effort to quell growing social tension, the Communist party surrendered its exclusive "leading role," paving the way for non-Communist parties to prevail in free elections held in Croatia and Slovenia. In May 1991, the leadership of Serbia provoked a constitutional crisis by blocking the scheduled rotation of a Croat into the federal presidency.[11] One month later, Croatia and Slovenia declared independence from Yugoslavia, followed by Macedonia, Bosnia, and Herzegovina. Serbia and Montenegro organized a new, diminished Yugoslavia, and the new countries continued their political, economic, and military struggles.

EVALUATION OF THE YUGOSLAV SYSTEM

Because it was unique, the Yugoslav system has attracted the attention of economists around the world who have analyzed its theoretical and operational strengths and weaknesses. A full review of their arguments and findings would carry us far afield, but we can summarize several key issues.

SELF-MANAGEMENT. Long ago, John Stuart Mill argued that leadership by a single capitalist has "great advantages over every description of collective management," but cooperation has "one thing to oppose to those advantages—the common interest of all the workers in the work."[12] Self-management is meant to carry the democratic principle into the workplace—to make workers the masters of their fate. According to its proponents, participatory management can reduce worker alienation, strengthen work incentives, and, consequently, increase labor productivity.

Four major criticisms have been leveled against the Yugoslav system of self-management. First, its assailants claim the system was *inconsistent*—that

---

[9]Was Tito a great unifier or a petty dictator? For an interesting analysis, see Aleksa Djilas, "Tito's Last Secret," *Foreign Affairs* 74 (July–August 1995): 116–122.

[10]Tomasz Telma, "Economic Situation in Yugoslavia in 1990," *Planecon Report*, March 20, 1991, 1.

[11]See Celestine Bohlen, "New Crisis Grips Yugoslavia Over Rotation of Leadership," *The New York Times*, May 16, 1991, A1.

[12]John Stuart Mill, *Principles of Political Economy*, Book 4 (London: Penguin Books, 1985 [1848]), 139.

Yugoslavia employed the authoritarian powers of a one-party state to install a system of economic democracy and free markets. The Communist party maintained its monopoly on power and its "leading role" in society, supposedly to safeguard a system of economic pluralism. In fact, the political leaders never fully relinquished control over appointments of enterprise directors and other key officials. According to János Kornai, "the principle of 'direct' democracy has been championed primarily by those who wanted it as a substitute for genuine political democracy."[13]

It is undoubtedly true that Yugoslav political economy was inconsistent and contradictory, but Kornai's criticism also seems slightly inconsistent. Did economic freedom and democracy serve as a substitute for political liberalism in Yugoslavia? Kornai, together with Milton Friedman, Friedrich von Hayek, and other classical liberals have usually argued that economic and political freedoms are complementary, if not inseparable. If central planning leads a nation down Hayek's road to serfdom, what is the destination of a system of democratic cooperation? One could argue that worker-management supported a political culture in Yugoslavia that provided freedoms unknown in other communist countries. Beginning in 1963, for example, Yugoslav citizens were free to travel and work in the West with little interference. Few limits were placed on religious and artistic expression.

According to a second criticism, the Yugoslav system was *not genuine*—most workers never played an active role in management. Control of the enterprise was dominated by the general manager, whose appointment was often controlled by local politicians. The workers were usually forced to accept the judgments of enterprise accountants, economists, and other experts. In public opinion surveys, most workers agreed with such statements as, "I don't have a feeling of being a self-manager in the work organization."[14]

Its defenders are willing to concede that the Yugoslav system never fully embodied the ideals of economic democracy, but they ask whether the democratic ideal has ever been fulfilled in any complex society. Voters in Western nations may not feel they have personal control over the actions of political organizations and leaders, but they remain dedicated to democracy.

According to a third criticism, worker self-management was a slow and *cumbersome* system for making and implementing business decisions. This was particularly true in Yugoslavia after the enterprises were divided into independent BOALs. Within the Rakovica Motor Works, for example, about 18,000 labor hours were devoted each year to negotiating agreements between the BOALs.[15] The actions of a single department could cause managerial gridlock and work stoppages in a large enterprise.

---

[13]János Kornai, *The Road to a Free Economy* (New York: W. W. Norton and Company, 1990), 100.

[14]Vlado Arzensek, "Problems of Yugoslav Self-Management," in *International Yearbook of Organizational Democracy*, Vol. 1, ed. Colin Crouch and Frank Heller (Chichester: John Wiley, 1983), 307; and Harold Lydall, *Yugoslavia in Crisis* (Oxford: Clarendon Press, 1989), 107.

[15]Barry Newman, "Change of Heart: Yugoslavia's Workers Find Self-Management Doesn't Make Paradise," *The Wall Street Journal*, March 25, 1987, 1, 18.

Today, defenders of the former Yugoslav system would generally agree that the BOALs created an excessive level of decentralization and confusion, although they arose from a well-intended effort to strengthen self-management. Before the BOALs were created, advocates contend that Yugoslav labor management was no more cumbersome than the leadership of a capitalist firm with a board of directors.

According to the fourth and broadest criticism, the Yugoslav system of ownership and management caused enterprises to make the *wrong decisions*—wrong because they generated low levels of allocative efficiency and stability and high rates of inflation and unemployment. We shall explore these arguments in the following paragraphs. Once again, however, the defenders of self-management contend that any economic inefficiency must be balanced against the intrinsic value of economic democracy, and that problems in the performance of the Yugoslav economy were caused primarily by policy blunders and by a hostile socioeconomic environment.

SUPPLY RESPONSE AND PRODUCTIVITY. Theoretical analysis suggests the supply behavior of a labor-managed firm may be very different from that of a capitalist firm. Under certain assumptions, the labor-managed firm will respond to a price increase by reducing its employment of labor and production of goods. This, in turn, may cause markets to be unstable (unable to sustain equilibrium), and may prevent the economy from achieving high levels of allocative efficiency and productivity. These results are sensitive, however, to changes in theoretical assumptions and model structures. Under a different set of assumptions, the behavior of a labor-managed firm may be virtually identical to that of an analogous capitalist firm (see chapter Appendix, "The Theory of the Labor-Managed Firm").

Although the Yugoslav system has inspired a wealth of theoretical analysis, few of the underlying assumptions, models, or conclusions have been tested empirically. Until recently, Western scholars did not have access to microeconomic data from Yugoslavia; their statistical inferences were based on information from producer cooperatives in Western Europe, Israel, and the United States. For example, in the American plywood manufacturing industry, Katrina and Matthew Berman found a negative relationship between price and product supply in the cooperative sector, but only at a low level of statistical significance. More confidently, they found that supply elasticities were lower among cooperatives than among capitalist firms.[16]

Several microeconomic studies have found that Western cooperative firms are able to operate as productively as their capitalist competitors. In Western Europe, cooperatives using profit-sharing schemes have achieved particularly high levels of productivity. In Italian cooperatives, workers have been found to work longer hours with lower rates of absenteeism than their

---

[16]Katrina V. Berman and Matthew D. Berman, "An Empirical Test of the Theory of the Labor-Managed Firm," *Journal of Comparative Economics* 13 (June 1989): 281–300.

capitalist counterparts.[17] Based on macroeconomic data, Abram Bergson found that Yugoslavia employed its resources more productively than other socialist countries, but less productively than industrial capitalist countries.[18]

In the late 1980s, when former Yugoslavia was near its end, a team of economists finally gained access to a rich set of panel data for Yugoslav firms.[19] Their findings were similar in some respects to those of the Berman study; prices were found to be negatively related to employment and product supplies, but at a low level of statistical significance. More confidently, the authors were able to conclude that the price-employment behavior of a Yugoslav firm was "stodgy or rigid rather than perverse."[20]

MARKET ENTRY AND ENTREPRENEURSHIP. For a market economy to work efficiently in a dynamic environment, new firms and production facilities must be able to enter markets where demand is increasing, where monopolies are developing, and where opportunities exist for new products and technologies. In Yugoslavia, new production facilities were usually established by existing enterprises that wished to expand or diversify, or by governmental units pursuing national or local priorities.[21]

The Yugoslav system provided little opportunity or incentive for an individual entrepreneur to undertake risk, and to invest time, effort, and resources in a new enterprise. After the enterprise was created, it would quickly fall under the control of workers and government officials, and profits would be divided within the collective. Thus, a creative individual had little motivation to introduce a new product or to take advantage of other market opportunities. This may have been one of the most serious shortcomings of the Yugoslav economic system.

SAVING AND INVESTMENT. In principle, the after-tax profits of a Yugoslav enterprise were controlled by its active work force. Within limits imposed by the government, the worker-managers could divide the profits among themselves as current income, or they could invest a portion of the profit back into the enterprise, hoping for larger incomes in the future. Ordinarily,

---

[17]J. Defourney, S. Estrin, and D. C. Jones, "The Effects of Workers' Participation on Enterprise Performance," *International Journal of Industrial Organization* 3 (1985): 197–217; Saul Estrin, Derek C. Jones, and Jan Svejnar, "The Productivity Effects of Worker Participation," *Journal of Comparative Economics* 11 (March 1987): 40–61; and Saul Estrin, "Some Reflections on Self-Management, Social Choice, and Reform in Eastern Europe," *Journal of Comparative Economics* 15 (June 1991): 349–361.

[18]Abram Bergson, "Comparative Productivity: The USSR, Eastern Europe, and the West," *The American Economic Review* 77 (June 1987): 352–353.

[19]Specifically, they gained access to a stratified random sample of 147 Yugoslav firms (5 percent of the population) during the years between 1975 and 1979. See Janez Prasnikar, Jan Svejnar, Dubravko Mihaljek, and Vesna Prasnikar, "Behavior of Participatory Firms in Yugoslavia: Lessons for Transforming Economies," *Review of Economics and Statistics* 76 (November 1994): 728–741.

[20]Ibid., 733.

[21]See S. A. Sacks, *Entry of New Competitors in Yugoslav Market Socialism* (Berkeley, Calif.: Institute of International Studies, University of California, 1973), passim.

however, reinvestment of profits was opposed by two groups of workers: (1) those who simply preferred to have the income immediately; and (2) those who expected to retire or change jobs, or who feared the loss of their jobs, preventing them from sharing in the income of the enterprise in the future.

Unlike capitalist stockholders, who can share in the income of an enterprise without working in it, and who can recover the value of reinvested profits by selling their stock, Yugoslav workers did not have portable ownership rights. When they departed from the enterprise for any reason, they lost any claim on its residual income.[22] Thus, under most circumstances, a group of Yugoslav-style worker-managers would have a weaker motivation to reinvest profits than would a capitalist owner.

Although they were reluctant to finance investments from retained earnings, Yugoslav worker-managers were perfectly willing to invest if they could obtain credit financing. Indeed, under certain conditions, the workers would favor investments, even if their expected rate of return was lower than the interest rate. They could benefit from the investments in the short run, and, if they did not remain at the enterprise, they could pass the burden of repayment to future generations of workers.

The enterprises gained easier access to external credit during the 1960s, when economic reforms placed the banks under the control of enterprises, and during the 1970s, when the domestic market for promissory notes expanded. To support their lending, the banks received large injections of credit from the central bank, contributing to the inflationary growth of the money supply. Excessive reliance on debt rather than equity caused the enterprises to be financially weak, and caused them to undertake inefficient investments.[23]

INFLATION. Throughout its postwar existence, the Yugoslav authorities maintained poor control of monetary growth and price inflation. With each decade, Yugoslavia's average inflation rate accelerated, and was always higher than the OECD average; it was almost always the highest rate in socialist central Eurasia (Table 16.1). In 1990, the last full year before Yugoslavia was dismembered, the annual consumer price inflation rate was 583 percent.[24]

The inflationary bias of the Yugoslav economy was apparently rooted in financial weaknesses of the labor-managed firms, and in the unwillingness of central authorities to impose financial discipline—or, to use János Kornai's terminology, the absence of a **hard budget constraint.** It was difficult for Yugoslav enterprises to maintain internal financial discipline because: (1) the

---

[22]More exactly, they could receive repayment of principle and interest (at regulated rates) for loans they personally made to the enterprise, but they could not receive a continuing return on reinvested profits.

[23]See Eirik Furubotn and Svetozar Pejovich, *The Economics of Property Rights* (Cambridge: Ballinger, 1974), passim; Svetozar Pejovich, "Why Has the Labor-Managed Firm Failed?" *Cato Journal* 12 (Fall 1992): 461–473; and Michael Keren and David Levhari, "Some Capital Market Failures in the Socialist Labor-Managed Economy," *Journal of Comparative Economics* 16 (December 1992): 655–669.

[24]Paul Marer, et al., *Historically Planned Economies: A Guide to the Data* (Washington, D.C.: The World Bank, 1992), 221.

■ TABLE 16.1

ECONOMIC GROWTH AND INFLATION IN
CENTRAL EURASIA, 1951-1990

	1951–1960	1961–1970	1971–1980	1981–1990
Average annual growth of real GNP/GDP (%)				
Soviet Union	5.7	4.9	2.4	1.2
Bulgaria	6.9	5.8	2.8	1.5
Czechoslovakia	4.8	2.9	2.8	0.9
Hungary	4.5	3.4	2.6	0.1
Poland	4.5	4.2	3.6	−0.4
Romania	6.0	5.2	5.3	−1.8
Yugoslavia	6.2	6.3	5.0	0.1
OECD Average	4.2	5.1	3.2	2.8
Average annual consumer price inflation (%)				
Soviet Union	n.a.	0.9	1.8	4.1
Bulgaria	n.a.	3.3	4.9	5.5
Czechoslovakia	n.a.	3.1	2.4	2.4
Hungary	4.8	2.0	5.2	10.7
Poland	6.3	2.5	7.2	70.3
Romania	n.a.	n.a.	3.3	5.1
Yugoslavia	5.2	11.6	18.7	144.7
OECD Average	3.3	3.9	9.1	8.1

NOTE: In most cases, the data for Central Eurasian countries are based on alternative estimates of the U.S. Central Intelligence Agency.

SOURCES: B. R. Mitchell, *European Historical Statistics, 1750–1975* (New York: Facts on File, 1980); *OECD Economic Outlook,* December 1986 and December 1995; World Bank, *World Tables,* 1980 and 1995; Irving Kravis, Alan Heston, and Robert Summers, *World Product and Income* (Baltimore: Johns Hopkins University Press, 1982), 343; Angus Maddison, *Phases of Capitalist Development* (Oxford: Oxford University Press, 1982), appendices A, C, and E; U.S. Central Intelligence Agency, *Handbook of Economic Statistics,* annual; World Bank, *Historically Planned Economies: A Guide to the Data,* 1992 and 1993; and European Bank for Reconstruction and Development, *Transition Report, 1995.*

workers were in a position to vote for their own pay raises; and (2) the worker-managers were motivated to rely heavily on debt to finance their investments. It was difficult for the authorities to impose a hard budget constraint on the enterprises because: (1) in the absence of a true capital market, it was difficult to design a meaningful system of bankruptcy and liquidation of assets; (2) efforts by the National Bank to slow the growth of the money supply and to tighten the availability of credit to the basic banks and enterprises were circumvented by expanded circulation of trade credits and other promissory notes among enterprises; and (3) when the National Bank was successful in its efforts to control the money supply, it caused unemployment to rise and real incomes to fall, contributing to political instability in the poorest regions of the country.[25]

After Yugoslavia established a pattern of financial mismanagement and inflation, and after its market was opened to foreign competition and exchange rate movements during the 1960s, the inflation problem was frequently exacerbated by instabilities in the foreign exchange market. Yugoslavia was caught in a vicious circle of rising product prices, balance of payments deficits, devaluation or depreciation of the dinar, and rising import costs, leading again to rising product prices. This pattern became most pronounced during the years after 1979, when Yugoslavia posted a record trade deficit of about $6.4 billion.

UNEMPLOYMENT. It was ironic and troubling that Yugoslavia, a labor-managed socialist economy, was plagued by more unemployment than most capitalist countries. From an average rate below 2 percent between 1952 and 1964, the unemployment rate climbed to an average above 11 percent between 1984 and 1988.[26] In any given year, another 3 percent to 6 percent of the Yugoslav labor force was working outside the country, most often in Germany.[27]

Why so much unemployment? First, the labor force grew rapidly—by about 100,000 per year—and a similar number moved out of agriculture every year. Many of the new entrants lived in backward areas of the country with few job opportunities. Linguistic and cultural barriers prevented workers from moving between republics, yielding a high rate of structural unemployment. Thus, between 1976 and 1987, the average unemployment rate was less than 2 percent in Slovenia, but over 20 percent in Macedonia and nearly 30 percent in Kosovo.[28]

Another possible cause of structural unemployment was the reluctance of some worker-managed enterprises to take on new workers. Successful enterprises may have been unwilling to absorb unemployed workers because they did not wish to share income and managerial control with a larger number of employees.

ECONOMIC GROWTH. Although it posted poor records of price and employment stability, Yugoslavia maintained very respectable rates of economic growth during the 1950s, 1960s, and 1970s. During each of those decades, Yugoslav GDP growth was higher than the OECD average, and was challenged

---

[25]See Shirley Gedeon, "Monetary Disequilibrium and Bank Reform Proposals in Yugoslavia: Paternalism and the Economy," *Soviet Studies* 39 (April 1987): 281–291; and Brune Schönfelder, "Reflections on Inflationary Dynamics in Yugoslavia," *Comparative Economic Studies* 32 (Winter 1990): 85–106.

[26]James H. Gapinski, *The Economic Structure and Failure of Yugoslavia* (Westport, Conn.: Praeger, 1993), 8.

[27]Sample surveys indicated, however, that high income abroad, not a lack of employment opportunities in Yugoslavia, was the major force motivating emigration. Prout, *Market Socialism in Yugoslavia*, 134–135.

[28]Evan Kraft, "Evaluating Regional Policy in Yugoslavia, 1966-1990," *Comparative Economic Studies* 34 (Fall–Winter 1992): 13.

in socialist Central Eurasia only by Bulgaria and Romania (Table 16.1). According to the World Bank, Yugoslav GNP per capita grew at an annual rate of 3.2 percent between 1965 and 1989—well above the 2.6 percent average rate for upper-middle-income developing countries.[29]

According to the growth accounting methodology developed by Edward Denison, the determinants of Yugoslav economic growth were similar in several respects to those of the Soviet Union. In both countries, rapid growth of the capital stock accounted for a very large proportion of total economic growth—43 percent in Yugoslavia and 54 percent in the USSR. These are the largest capital contributions observed in the industrial world. In both countries, about one-fifth of total growth was explained by growth of the size and quality of the labor force, and about one-fourth of the total was explained by growth of total factor productivity—more output from each unit of inputs. In most of the industrial Western countries, the contribution of productivity growth was about twice as large.[30]

INCOME INEQUALITY AND POVERTY. During its four decades of socialism, Yugoslavia never developed a remarkably even distribution of income. In his study of six European socialist countries and seven industrial capitalist countries in the mid-1970s, Christian Morrisson found that the United States was the only country with greater income inequality than Yugoslavia.[31] Between the 1970s and the mid-1980s, the Yugoslav distribution was apparently fairly stable, and continued to be less egalitarian than those in Hungary, Poland, Germany, or Sweden.[32]

With a low level of national income and an uneven income distribution, Yugoslavia had a relatively high poverty rate. The proportion of the population living below a subsistence income of about $900 per person increased from 17 percent in 1978 to 25 percent in 1987. Among 25 countries studied by the World Bank, only Poland experienced a larger increase in its poverty rate during these years.[33]

The causes of income inequality and poverty in Yugoslavia were numerous and complex. Regional inequalities accounted for a large part of the problem. When economic performance deteriorated during the 1970s and 1980s, the low-income regions were hit hardest. Thus, in 1947, income per capita was already three times larger in Slovenia than in Kosovo; by 1965, it was five times larger, and, by 1989, nearly eight times larger. In the late 1980s,

[29]The World Bank, *World Development Report* 1991, 205.

[30]Robert J. Jerome, Jr., "Estimates of Sources of Growth in Bulgaria, Greece, and Yugoslavia, 1950–1980," *Comparative Economic Studies* 27 (Fall 1985): 31–82.

[31]Christian Morrisson, "Income Distribution in East European and Western Countries," *Journal of Comparative Economics* 8 (June 1984): 131–132. Yugoslavia ranked more favorably among developing countries. See Wouter van Ginneken and Jong-goo Park, *Generating Internationally Comparable Income Distribution Estimates* (Geneva: International Labour Office, 1984), 5.

[32]See World Bank, *World Development Report* 1990 (Oxford: Oxford University Press, 1990), 236–237.

[33]See World Bank, *World Development Report* 1990, 43, 48; and Aleksandra Posarac, "Poverty in Yugoslavia 1978-1987," World Bank Background Paper No. 23, November 1989.

the gap between Slovenia and Kosovo was three or four times larger than the regional income gap in any country of the European Union.[34]

A smaller portion of Yugoslav income inequality was caused directly by the self-management system. In a capitalist market economy, incomes tend to equalize for workers who have comparable occupations, skills, and experience. In Yugoslavia, the labor market worked very differently. Because residual incomes were distributed within successful enterprises, and because entry of new competitors was restricted in labor and product markets, large income differentials emerged among workers in each occupation who worked in different enterprises. This form of inequality was apparently greatest during the late 1960s, when Estrin found the ratio of the highest to lowest incomes for a given skill type across sectors normally exceeded 2:1, with the largest differentials among blue collar workers.[35] This form of inequality evidently grew less important during the 1970s when incomes fell under stronger political control.[36]

In the end, it appears that regional inequalities, rooted in early developmental experiences in the Ottoman and Hapsburg empires, accounted for much of Yugoslav income inequality. Any suggestion that self-management was inconsistent with moderate income equality seems to be contradicted by the fact that Slovenia, considered apart from its low-income neighbors, had one of the most egalitarian distributions of income in the world.[37]

CONSUMER SOVEREIGNTY. Because Yugoslavia had a market economy, and because the enterprises had a strong profit motive, the pattern and assortment of production was largely governed by consumer demand. Thus, Yugoslav consumers had a clear advantage over their counterparts in centrally planned economies where production was governed by the preferences of planners and politicians. Yugoslav consumer goods and services were often superior in their style, variety, and quality to those in many of the more developed countries of Eastern Europe, and they could be obtained without standing in long lines.[38]

---

[34]Branko Horvat, *The Yugoslav Economic System* (Armonk, N.Y.: M. E. Sharpe, 1976), 62; and Daniel Gros and Alfred Steinherr, *Winds of Change: Economic Transition in Central and Eastern Europe* (London: Longman, 1995), 336–337.

[35]Saul Estrin, "Income Dispersion in a Self-Managed Economy," *Economica* 38 (1981): 181–194; and Saul Estrin, Robert E. Moore, and Jan Svejnar, "Market Imperfections, Labor Management, and Earnings Differentials in a Developing Country: Theory and Evidence from Yugoslavia," *Quarterly Journal of Economics* 103 (August 1988): 465–478.

[36]Janez Prasnikar and Jan Svejnar, "Workers' Participation in Management vs. Social Ownership and Government Policies: Lessons for Transforming Socialist Economies," *Comparative Economic Studies* 33 (Winter 1991): 35–36; and Milan Vodopivec, "Appropriability of Returns in the Yugoslav Firm," *Eastern Economic Journal* 20 (Summer 1994): 337–348.

[37]In 1987–1988, Slovenia's Gini ratio was an extremely low 0.24. See World Bank, *World Development Report 1996*, 69, 196–197.

[38]According to Leonid Abalkin, a prominent Russian economist, Soviet visitors in Yugoslavia were usually astounded by the selection of food available in the stores: "Meat consumption per capita is lower in Yugoslavia than in the Soviet Union, but there is a sense of abundance. If I want, I can always come and buy it, as much as I want, without a line." Quoted in Bill Keller, "Soviet Planning Big Labor Shift Out of Industry," *New York Times,* July 4, 1987, 2.

Yugoslav performance in consumer goods production was closely related to its activities in the tourism industry. With its enviable location near Italy and Greece on the Adriatic Sea, and with its relatively open borders, Yugoslavia was in a better position to attract tourists than most other socialist countries in central Eurasia. Earnings from tourism grew most rapidly between 1965 and 1976, from $81 million to about $800 million, and then climbed to a peak of $1.3 billion in 1982 before they were disrupted by currency devaluations and political instability.[39]

With thousands of tourists present in the country and endless opportunities to earn foreign currency, Yugoslav enterprises were more aware of competitive trends in Western style and production quality than their counterparts in other socialist countries. In his memoirs, Nikita Khrushchev said he once asked Marshall Tito how he handled the problem, so common in socialist countries, of "fashion-conscious young men and women chasing after tourists, trying to buy all sorts of trinkets off them, especially around the hotels." "We don't really have that problem here," Tito replied. "When some item becomes fashionable among our young people, we buy the necessary equipment for a factory and start manufacturing the item ourselves."[40]

THE NATURAL ENVIRONMENT. The system of self-management provided an interesting, if only partial, solution to the problem of environmental pollution. In capitalist and centrally planned economies, decisions to pollute the air and water in a particular location are made by stockholders and planners who often live elsewhere. A decision to pollute Lake Michigan may be made in New York, and Lake Baikal was sacrificed by officials in Moscow. Under local control, a Yugoslav workers' council could, in principle, take a better account of the needs and desires of the community.

If it operated democratically, a workers' council would attempt to balance the community's desire for income growth against its needs for environmental health and sustainable development. For example, if the additional income that could be generated by allowing a lake to be polluted was smaller than the perceived value of the lake for health and recreation, pollution would not be approved.[41] In this sense, a system of self-management could provide an approximation to Milton Friedman's goal of a free-to-choose society; it could protect the environment with a minimum of governmental interference. Unfortunately, little information seems to be available on the actual record of environmental decision making in Yugoslavia.[42]

---

[39]Martin Schrenk, Cyrus Ardalan, and Nadal EI Tatawy, *Yugoslavia: Self-Management Socialism and the Challenge of Development* (Baltimore: Johns Hopkins University Press, 1979), 213; and Dyker, *Yugoslavia: Socialism, Development and Debt,* 129, 135–136.

[40]*Khrushchev Remembers* (New York: Bantam Books, 1971), 427.

[41]This, of course, would not remedy a situation in which pollutants are dumped into a river in one location with most of the ill effects experienced in other locations downstream.

[42]Perhaps it is indicative that Slovenia derives a large proportion of its GDP from manufacturing, but maintains a relatively low percapita level of CO_2 emissions. See World Bank, *World Development Report 1996,* 203, 211.

INSTITUTIONAL COMPETITION. All things considered, we can say again that Yugoslavia was a country with a tortured history. Again and again, the Balkan republics were dominated by foreign powers, shaken by war, and pitted against one another in national and religious rivalries. For about 40 years, under authoritarian rule, a larger Yugoslavia wore a thin veneer of national unity, but was never able to develop a fully integrated market.[43]

In the midst of all this, an experimental system of worker-management and market socialism was introduced without a clear blueprint. It worked well enough to support high rates of economic growth for three decades, and to offer limited systems of industrial democracy and consumer sovereignty; the self-management system did not prevent Slovenia from achieving a very high standard of living for its citizens.

In the opinions of many authors, including János Kornai and Svetozar Pejovich, Yugoslavia's disastrous records of inflation, unemployment, international payments imbalance, and income inequality have demonstrated conclusively that labor-management provided a failed and irreparable foundation for an economic system.[44] On the other hand, a recent study by Gros and Steinherr concluded that "the Yugoslav experience is not an indictment of a self-managed economy."[45] Many of its problems were caused by broad environmental factors, and others by policy failures, particularly under the rotating presidency. Basic economic reforms, such as the creation of a market for tradeable enterprise memberships, could have resolved many of Yugoslavia's problems.

Even if we can defend the viability and efficiency of the worker-management system, however, it is much more difficult to argue that this system should ever have been established by fiat. Today, international competition has made it difficult for a national government to impose any uniform, inflexible, or arbitrary system of ownership and management on its business community. If labor-managed cooperatives can compete in some industries with traditional capitalist firms, they will survive and prosper. In a dynamic economy, we expect to find a complex mixture of capitalist proprietorships, corporations, franchise relationships, foreign holdings, and producer and consumer cooperatives.

What does the future hold for systems of participatory management? Can they compete in the international marketplace for institutional arrangements? This is a subject of continuing disagreement. Some authors argue that the institutions of industrial democracy have failed to emerge spontaneously, so they obviously are inefficient and noncompetitive.[46] According to others, participatory management provides benefits to society that are external to

---

[43]See Melica Zarkovic Bookman, "The Economic Basis of Regional Autarchy in Yugoslavia," *Soviet Studies* 42 (January 1990): 93–109.

[44]Kornai, *Road to a Free Economy*, 97–100; and Pejovich, "Why Has the Labor-Managed Firm Failed," 461–473.

[45]Gros and Steinherr, *Winds of Change*, 346.

[46]Again, see Pejovich, "Why Has the Labor-Managed Firm Failed," 461.

the firm, so it should be encouraged, even if it does not pass the market test.[47] A third group remains committed to the proposition that industrial democracy will be the wave of the future, and is progressing quietly today. Embryonic systems of participation may be found in the West in cooperative sectors and employee stock-ownership programs; in the East, workers have gained a share of ownership and control in many of the recent privatization programs. Like John Stuart Mill, some economists still believe that we will evolve into societies of workers "collectively owning the capital with which they carry out their operations, and working under managers elected and removable by themselves."[48]

HUNGARY:
ADMINISTRATIVE MARKET SOCIALISM

Relatively small in population and poor in mineral resources, Hungary was the most trade-dependent country in the Soviet bloc. With fertile plains and a mild climate, its comparative advantage lay in agricultural production. The Stalinist system, with its preference for heavy industry and its rigid system of central planning, was unable to respond to the unpredictable needs of agriculture and foreign trade; it was a most inappropriate system for Hungary.

The First Five-Year Plan (1950–1954), which conformed to the Stalinist model, worked well enough for two years, but agricultural production declined sharply in 1952 and became increasingly unstable. The harvests of wheat, rye, barley, and oats all declined between the beginning and end of the five-year plan.

In 1956, after Khrushchev denounced the crimes of Stalin, a peaceful demonstration in Budapest against the Communist regime drew a brutal response from security forces and Soviet tanks. A new government was installed, headed by Imre Nagy, and was authorized to initiate a series of moderate reforms. Instead, Nagy's government supported freedom of the press, disbanded the security police, repudiated Hungary's association with the Warsaw Pact, and appealed to the United Nations to pressure Soviet troops out of Hungary. Yugoslav-style workers' councils spontaneously appeared in many of the factories. In November, while the world's attention was distracted by U.S. presidential politics and the Suez crisis, Soviet tanks and troops crushed the rebellion. About 2,900 Hungarians were killed (Nagy and about 200 others were executed) and 200,000 fled the country.

János Kádár, the new Soviet-installed leader, skillfully balanced Soviet demands for orthodoxy with Hungarian demands for independence. In 1957, he was required by the Soviets to resume the collectivization of agriculture.

[47]Gregory K. Dow, "Democracy versus Appropriability: Can Labor-Managed Firms Flourish in a Capitalist World?" in *Markets and Democracy: Participation, Accountability, and Efficiency,* ed. Samuel Bowles, Herbert Gintis, and Bo Gustafsson (Cambridge: Cambridge University Press, 1993), 176–195.

[48]Mill, *Principles of Political Economy,* Book 4, 133.

To satisfy domestic demands, he spread the program over four years and employed incentives rather than coercion to increase membership in co-operatives.[49] In the end, state farms obtained only 10 percent of the land; about 35 percent was controlled by cooperatives and the remainder was owned and cultivated by individual families.[50]

Between 1965 and 1967, Hungary introduced a series of important agricultural reforms. Obligatory plan targets were abandoned and the farms were allowed to formulate their own plans for most products. State purchase prices were raised to strengthen agricultural profits; the farms were allowed to use their profits to finance decentralized investments. Individual farmers were provided credit and equipment for their private plots. These reforms were apparently quite successful. Wheat production, for example, increased by more than 50 percent between 1964 and 1968.

In industry, Kádár dissolved the Yugoslav-style workers' councils, but introduced a modest program of reforms in the late 1950s. He reduced the number of compulsory plan targets, amended the material incentive system to reward profitability and technological improvements, and introduced an interest charge to encourage efficient use of fixed assets. These measures, however, had little effect. After a period of rapid growth in the late 1950s, Hungarian industry began to stagnate in the early 1960s. In 1964, the Central Committee called for a full-scale discussion of the management of the economy. Based on early successes in agriculture, a 1966 decree called for major reforms of the entire economic system.

THE NEW ECONOMIC MECHANISM

Introduced in 1968, the **New Economic Mechanism (NEM)** was the boldest program of reform adopted in any country of the Warsaw Pact before the 1990s. Specifically, the NEM included the following elements of market socialism:

- Detailed central planning of output and delivery was replaced with a regulated market mechanism and a system of macroeconomic indicative planning.

- In place of bonuses for plan fulfillment, the profit motive became the centerpiece of the material incentive system.

- Aside from raw materials and consumer staples, price controls were lifted from a wide range of products, and many other prices were allowed to fluctuate within limits.

- The state monopoly of foreign trade was weakened; several enterprises were allowed to trade without the intervention of the foreign trade ministry. To guide the decisions of these enterprises, the existing

---

[49]See Michael Marrese, "Agricultural Performance and Policy in Hungary," *Journal of Comparative Economics* 7 (September 1983).

[50]Péter Mihályi, "Hungary: A Unique Approach to Privatization," in *Hungary: An Economy in Transition*, ed. István P. Székely and David M. G. Newbery (Cambridge: Cambridge University Press, 1993), 92

system of multiple exchange rates was replaced with a single, more realistic rate.

Although these were major changes in the Eastern European context, Hungarian reformers did not threaten the existing power structure. They preserved the leading role of the Communist party and accepted Hungary's role in the Warsaw Pact. Hungary built a system of market socialism, but, unlike Yugoslavia, it did not adopt workers' self-management. The party-ministry hierarchy, not workers' councils, wielded authority to hire and fire enterprise managers. Furthermore, the government maintained direct control over half of all investment expenditures.

To assure domestic support, the reformers protected the population from many of the unpleasant consequences of the market system. Most important, they subsidized money-losing enterprises to prevent unemployment. Without the discipline of a hard budget constraint, inefficient producers were able to continue operations, and were forced to make few market adjustments.

The NEM proceeded smoothly for several years. Real national income, which had grown about 5.5 percent annually between 1965 and 1967, accelerated to a rate of 6 percent between 1968 and 1971. The growth rate of total factor productivity doubled between 1967 and 1972.[51] At the same time, Hungary began to encounter several of the problems that plagued market socialism in Yugoslavia. In both countries, the reformers inherited a monopolistic market structure from central planners who preferred to control a small number of large firms. Critics of the NEM questioned the efficiency of market socialism in the presence of monopolies, warning that it would generate income inequality. Indeed, Hungarian wages apparently grew more unequal between 1966 and 1974.[52]

For these and other reasons, support for the NEM began to crumble during the early 1970s. Central controls were reintroduced in 1973, and grew stronger when the country was shaken by rising international oil prices. In a vain attempt to prevent inflation, the government increased its price subsidies. In 1974, 70 percent of the increase in import prices was neutralized by payments from the state budget. Shielded from price movements, Hungarians had little incentive to reduce their demand for imports. The export-import balance moved from a small surplus in 1973 to a deficit of more than $1 billion in 1975.

In 1976, when the nation's reserves of foreign exchange began to dwindle, the government introduced an expanded system of import quotas and quantitative restrictions. Nevertheless, the external situation continued to deteriorate. The Hungarian debt to the West increased from $3 billion in 1975 to $9 billion in 1980. In Eastern Europe, only Poland and Romania had lower credit ratings, and both of these countries were forced into insolvency in 1981.

---

[51]A study by Marton Trados of the Hungarian Institute for Market Research, cited in Bela Balassa, "The Hungarian Economic Reform, 1968–1981," World Bank Staff Working Paper No. 506 (February 1982), 11.

[52]Henryk Flakierski, *Economic Reform and Income Distribution: A Case Study of Hungary and Poland* (Armonk, N.Y.: M. E. Sharpe, 1986), Chapter 2.

THE 1980S: THE NEW IMPROVED MECHANISM[53]

In 1977, faced with the failure of central controls and restricted in their access to international borrowing, Hungarian leaders returned to the principles of the New Economic Mechanism. Furthermore, the Solidarity movement in Poland prompted demands for more effective employee participation in management.

PRICES. Measures first were taken to rationalize the subsidy-ridden price system. Consumer price inflation, which had been held artificially low during the 1970s, was allowed to rise above the rates of the OECD countries during the 1980s (Table 16.1). Beginning in 1980, under the **competitive price system,** about 70 percent of industrial prices were adjusted to approximate world market levels and another 20 percent were allowed to fluctuate with domestic supply and demand. In principle, the authorities attempted to maintain prices at levels that would prevail if all markets were competitive.

INDUSTRIAL ORGANIZATION AND COMPETITION. Monopolistic behavior of large enterprises was a serious obstacle to relaxation of price controls, and directors of large enterprises were among the strongest opponents of reform. Thus, in 1979 a special commission was created to oversee the dissolution of large enterprises and trusts. By 1983 about 300 new enterprises had been broken off of the old giants—a significant number considering that Hungary had only 702 state enterprises in 1979.

Beginning in 1982, the law also allowed the establishment of several new kinds of small, competitive organizations. In the socialist sector, these included small enterprises and cooperatives created by ministries and local councils, independent subsidiaries of state enterprises, and independent joint ventures created by two or more enterprises and/or cooperatives.

Bridging the gap between the public and private sectors, **enterprise contract work associations (ECWAs)** were partnerships of individuals who contracted with enterprises to provide overtime labor. The ECWAs were able to use the facilities and equipment of state enterprises, so they required few capital investments. The wages paid by the enterprise to ECMA members were exempt from traditional wage controls, and were usually much higher than traditional wages. Thus, the creation of ECWAs represented a major decentralization of the Hungarian labor market. Their number increased rapidly from about 3,500 in 1982 to a peak of 21,500 in 1986, and then declined slowly.[54]

---

[53]The following discussion is based on Paul Marer, "Economic Reform in Hungary: From Central Planning to Regulated Market," in U.S. Congress Joint Economic Committee, *East European Economies: Slow Growth in the 1980s,* Vol. 3 (Washington, D.C.: USGPO, 1986), 247–271; and Paul Marer, Economic Transformation in Central and Eastern Europe," in *Making Markets: Economic Transformation in Eastern Europe and the Post-Soviet States,* ed. Shafiqul Ilam and Michael Mandelbaum (New York: Council on Foreign Relations Press, 1993), 55–66.

[54]Catherine Sokil-Milnikiewicz, "Struggles over a Growing Private Sector: The Case of Hungary," in *Capitalist Goals, Socialist Past,* ed. Perry L. Patterson (Boulder, Colo.: Westview Press, 1993), 75.

Organizationally similar to the ECWAs, but more private, were the **independent contract work associations (ICWAs).** Unlike the ECWAs, the ICWAs were not affiliated with a single enterprise. They owned their own equipment, found their own work, and took entrepreneurial risks. In many cases, they were successors of underground operations. The number of ICWAs increased quickly and steadily from about 2,300 in 1982 to nearly 12,000 in 1988. In one celebrated case, members of a mountain-climbing club formed an ICWA to wash the windows of high-rise buildings.

ENTERPRISE AUTONOMY AND DEMOCRACY. To reduce the scope of bureaucratic meddling in enterprise affairs, three major industrial ministries were merged in 1980 into a single Ministry of Industry, with about half the former personnel. Decentralization of foreign trade also continued; more enterprises were allowed to deal directly on foreign markets without the intervention of the Ministry of Foreign Trade.

In 1984, the Law on Enterprise Democracy assigned all state companies to one of three categories. About one-fifth of industrial enterprises, including public utilities, defense industries, and other natural monopolies, were kept under traditional administrative control. Their directors were still appointed by the Ministry, but advisory boards were created to represent the interests of workers, consumers, and social organizations.

Medium-size and large competitive enterprises, comprising the majority of Hungarian establishments, were placed under the control of enterprise councils. With up to 50 members, the councils had equal numbers of labor representatives (elected by secret ballot for 5-year terms) and managers (some elected and some appointed by the director). The director, who handled day-to-day operations, was appointed by the board, based on a competitive application process, with consent of the ministry. Despite the role of the enterprise council in decisions relating to economic plans, investment, merger, and appointment of directors, this was still a modified "one-person" system of management.

Companies with fewer than 500 employees, accounting for about 25 percent of all state enterprises, were allowed to establish Yugoslav-style systems of labor self-management. A general assembly of all enterprise employees had authority to make strategic decisions and to elect a director without obtaining state approval.

FINANCE AND MONETARY POLICY. Reforms resumed in the financial sector in 1983, when a small market for bonds issued by enterprises, cooperatives, financial institutions, and local governments was established. Secondary trade commenced in 1984. For the next few years, bond sales grew very rapidly because: (1) the market was well organized, and they were highly liquid; (2) they generally carried government guarantees, so they were very safe; (3) yields set by the Ministry of Finance were sometimes 4 points higher than deposit rates or the inflation rate; and (4) yields on bonds were not subject to income tax. In 1987, the value of bonds in circulation reached nearly 20 billion forints. Beginning in 1988, sales declined sharply because state guarantees were terminated and other financial instruments, including certificates of deposit, became available.[55]

In 1986, Hungarian authorities decided that the country's centralized banking system, which performed surveillance and control functions in the old system of central planning, was not appropriate for a market economy. In 1987 the National Bank of Hungary was transformed into a Western-style central bank; its commercial and investment banking operations were moved into five new commercial banks and nine venture capital operations. The large commercial banks were still owned entirely by the state, but they had to compete for customers, and were expected to operate at a profit. In 1988, when the government stopped providing bond guarantees, the banks were allowed to provide underwriting services. In 1989, the banks were allowed, for the first time, to provide personal banking services to individuals.[56]

The National Bank was now responsible for the formulation and implementation of monetary policy, but approval still rested with the government. Thus, Hungary gained a Western-style central bank, but not an independent one. Between 1987 and 1989, the bank had to provide three-quarters of its financial assets to finance state budget deficits, imposing an enormous strain on the entire financial system.[57]

BANKRUPTCY. Despite their efforts to encourage competition and enterprise autonomy, in 1985 the Hungarian authorities provided 157 billion forints of budgetary subsidies to unprofitable enterprises—roughly one-quarter of the national income.[58] The government decided it could no longer provide such a large proportion of the nation's resources to inefficient enterprises. Thus, a new bankruptcy code was implemented in 1986. For political reasons, however, few state enterprises were threatened by the law. During the first few years of its operation, enterprise reorganizations and plant closures affected only 0.3 percent of the labor force.[59]

While the government took a cautious approach to bankruptcies, it also established systems of job placement and financial support for displaced workers. Insolvent businesses were allowed to keep operating for as many as 9 months while their workers looked for jobs. A system of unemployment compensation, deemed unnecessary under the Soviet-style system, replaced 75 percent of income during the first 3 months and 60 percent during the next 3 months.[60]

[55]István Abel and István Székely, "Changing Structure of Household Portfolios in Emerging Market Economies: The Case of Hungary, 1970–1989," in *Hungary: An Economy in Transition,* ed. Székely and Newbery, 175–176.

[56]Ian Jeffries, *Socialist Economies and the Transition to the Market: A Guide* (London: Routledge, 1993), 283.

[57]Éva Várhegyi, "The Modernization of the Hungarian Banking Sector," in *Hungary: An Economy in Transition,* ed. Székely and Newbery, 149–151.

[58]Gyorgy Ney, "Official Interviewed on Workforce, Work Environment," in Joint Publications Research Service, *Eastern Europe Report,* October 28, 1986, 17.

[59]Jeffries, *Socialist Economies and the Transition to the Market,* 282.

[60]Gyorgy Ney, "Official Interviewed on Workforce," 18–19.

TAXATION. One of the final reforms during the socialist era was a major overhaul of the tax system. To draw Hungary in line with standards in Western Europe, and to strengthen the entrepreneurial motive, the profit tax was revised in 1989, and its basic rate was reduced from 50 percent to 40 percent in 1990. To prevent a reduction of revenue, a stiff value-added tax (with rates as high as 25 percent) and a revised personal income tax (with rates ranging from 15 percent to 50 percent) were introduced a year earlier, in 1988.[61]

EVALUATION OF THE HUNGARIAN SYSTEM

Throughout the socialist era, Hungarian politicians and economists received high marks for their willingness to experiment, and for their efforts to press the limits of reform in the Soviet bloc. Supporters of the reforms were able to claim that Hungary had the highest rate of industrial labor productivity growth in Eastern Europe during the early 1980s.[62] Reforms were particularly successful in agriculture, where Hungary consistently maintained the highest level of per capita agricultural production in Eastern Europe.[63]

During the 1980s, Hungary expanded its export sales more rapidly than other countries in its income category and remained solvent through the debt crisis of the early 1980s against tremendous odds; Poland and Romania were not as successful.[64] Despite concerns that market-oriented reforms would cause a high level of inequality, Hungary ended the 1980s with a more even distribution of income than any country in central Eurasia except Czechoslovakia.[65]

On the negative side of the ledger, Hungary had a lower rate of income growth during the 1980s than the Soviet Union, Bulgaria, or Czechoslovakia, and its inflation rate was twice as high (Table 16.1). Many workers had to work overtime in contract work associations (ECWAs and ICWAs) simply to maintain their standards of living. The country was able to avoid insolvency, but it had the highest level of foreign debt, on a per capita basis, in central Eurasia. In a recent international survey, the Gallup organization found that

---

[61]Organization for Economic Cooperation and Development, *OECD Economic Surveys: Hungary* (Paris: OECD, 1991), 62–63; and Jeno Koltay, "Tax Reform in Hungary," in *Hungary: An Economy in Transition*, ed. Székely and Newbery, 249–270.

[62]United Nations Economic Commission for Europe, *Economic Survey of Europe in 1984–85*, Part 2 (Geneva: 1986), 4.71.

[63]Gregor Lazarcik, "Comparative Growth of Agricultural Output, Inputs, and Productivity in Eastern Europe, 1965-82," in *East European Economies: Slow Growth in the 1980s*, Vol. 1, 419–420. Also, see Michael Marrese, "Hungarian Agriculture: Lessons for the Soviet Union," *Comparative Economic Studies* 32 (Summer 1990): 155–169.

[64]*World Development Report 1990*, 204–205.

[65]*World Development Report 1996*, 68–69. Apparently, Ukraine and Belarus had even distributions of income, but they were not independent countries during the 1980s. See Anthony B. Atkinson and John Micklewright, *Economic Transformation in Eastern Europe and the Distribution of Income* (Cambridge: Cambridge University Press, 1992), 136–137.

only 21 percent of Hungarians professed to be "totally satisfied" with their lives—a much smaller proportion than in any of 17 other countries.[66]

More fundamentally, economists in the East and West have questioned whether the Hungarian reforms were genuine, deep, and significant. The state retained ownership and ultimate control of the most important enterprises and banks, and continued to regulate the foreign exchange and capital markets. Ministry personnel continued to meddle in business affairs, and enterprises were frequently spared from the chopping blocks of bankruptcy and hard budget constraints. Price and enterprise subsidies were reduced during the 1980s, but they still consumed 16 percent of GDP in 1989.[67]

According to Marton Tardos, the scope of governmental control remained sufficiently large during the mid-1980s to say that Hungary had a system of modified central planning rather than a market socialist economy.[68] János Kornai argued that market socialism was itself an insufficient basis for genuine reform:

> It is futile to expect that the state unit will behave as if it were privately owned and will spontaneously act as if it were a market-oriented agent. It is time to let go of this vain hope once and for all. Never, no more. There is no reason to be astonished at the fact that state ownership permanently recreates bureaucracy, since the state-owned firm is but an organic part of the bureaucratic hierarchy.[69]

THE SOVIET UNION: TREADMILL OF CONSERVATIVE REFORMS

Here, because of their own importance, and because they resembled programs adopted by conservative governments in other countries, we briefly consider the socialist reforms introduced in the Soviet Union between 1957 and 1991. For political and ideological reasons, Soviet reformers were more hesitant than their Yugoslav and Hungarian counterparts to embrace the profit motive and price flexibility, or to abandon the state monopoly of foreign trade. Instead, they usually did little more than tinker with the existing system, attempting to improve organizational structures, incentive formulas, investment priorities, and systems of price control. With small variations, programs of reform were replayed over and over again by successive governments. Thus, Gertrude Schroeder characterized socialist reforms as an

---

[66]The other country at the bottom of the satisfaction list was Mexico, with a rating of 36 percent. The survey did not include other central Eurasian countries, but it did include low-income countries, such as China, India, and the Dominican Republic. David W. Moore and Frank Newport, "People Throughout the World Largely Satisfied with Their Lives," *The Gallup Poll Monthly,* June 1995, 4. Also available at <http://www.gallup.com/international/6–95.html>.

[67]Koltay, "Tax Reform in Hungary," 265.

[68]Marton Tardos, "How to Create Efficient Markets in Socialism," Kennan Institute for Advanced Russian Studies, Woodrow Wilson International Center for Scholars, Washington, D.C., October 1984, 17.

[69]Kornai, *The Road to a Free Economy,* 58.

endless treadmill, creating an appearance of activity, but producing little forward motion.[70]

KHRUSHCHEV: REGIONAL DECENTRALIZATION[71]

The first major administrative reform of the Stalinist system began in 1957, when Nikita Khrushchev shifted control of major enterprises from the branch ministries in Moscow to a new network of approximately 100 regional economic councils (*sovnarkhozy*). Many of the ministries were disbanded, and the central planners in Moscow were able to control distribution of only the most critical national commodities and centralized commodities whose production was dispersed.

Khrushchev's reform was designed to break the excessive political power of the ministries in Moscow and to allow each region to organize a rational division of labor. Under the centralized system, raw materials and supplies were sometimes shipped from one region to another across the vast Soviet Union when local supplies were available. The planners in Moscow, unable to stay abreast of changes in local production conditions, sometimes issued plan assignments that were infeasible.

The *sovnarkhoz* system may have alleviated these problems of excessive centralization, but it created equally costly problems of local protectionism, as the Soviet Union split into a near-feudal system of local, self-sufficient economies. Beginning in 1959, the growth rates of national income and labor productivity dropped sharply, and the *sovnarkhoz* reform was judged a failure. For this and his other "hare-brained schemes," Khrushchev was ousted in 1964, and was succeeded by a collective leadership headed by General Secretary Leonid Brezhnev and Premier Alexei Kosygin. The ministries and state committees in Moscow were modified and rebuilt; the *sovnarkhozy* were dissolved.

THE LIBERMAN/KOSYGIN REFORMS

During the years after Stalin's death, standards of censorship were relaxed, allowing the publication of novels by Solzhenitsyn, poems by Yevtushenko, and a series of surprising articles in *Pravda* by Evsei Liberman, an economist from Kharkov University in Ukraine. Liberman shifted the debate away from broad organizational matters to a more technical discussion of incentive systems, planning methods, and, most surprising at that time, the role of profits in a socialist economy.

---

[70]See Gertrude E. Schroeder, "The Soviet Economy on a Treadmill of Reforms," in U.S. Congress, Joint Economic Committee, *Soviet Economy in a Time of Change*, Vol. 1 (Washington, D.C.: USGPO, 1979), 312–340; and Gertrude E. Schroeder, "Soviet Economic 'Reform' Decrees: More Steps on the Treadmill," in U.S. Congress, Joint Economic Committee, *Soviet Economy in the 1980s: Problems and Prospects*, Part 1 (Washington, D.C.: USGPO, 1982), 65–88.

[71]This section is based on Ed A. Hewett, *Reforming the Soviet Economy: Equality versus Efficiency* (Washington, D.C.: The Brookings Institution, 1988), 223–227.

According to Liberman, the existing incentive system rewarded enterprises for fulfilling plan assignments, but provided little incentive for them to seek more challenging targets. Indeed, to the contrary, enterprise managers were motivated to bargain for low, achievable targets. Afterwards, they had little reason to overfulfill their assignments, because: (1) a large bonus was paid for fulfillment of the plan, but the reward for above-plan production was small; and (2) according to the so-called **ratchet principle,** a high level of production in year 1 usually led to an unwelcome boost in plan assignments in year 2. Liberman also observed that the existing incentive system, based on fulfillment of physical *output* targets, provided little motivation for an enterprise to economize on its use of *inputs,* and it provided little reward for the *quality* of production.

Responding to these shortcomings of the existing system, and incorporating many of Liberman's proposals, Prime Minister Kosygin introduced a series of enterprise reforms in 1965 and price reforms in 1966–1967 that included the following:

■ To encourage product quality and sensitivity to consumer demand, sales volume rather than gross output would be the basic determinant of bonuses.

■ Bonus income and other employee benefits would be paid from enterprise funds, financed from a portion of enterprise profits according to a stable set of formulas. Thus, the enterprises would be motivated to hold down costs, and the formulas, or "normatives," would be designed to counteract the ratchet principle.

■ To encourage enterprises to economize on their use of capital, they would be required to pay a 6 percent annual charge to the state for their fixed and circulating assets.

■ Rather than setting as many as 40 groups of targets for each enterprise, the ministries would be allowed to set only eight: physical output of principal products, sales volume, total profit and rate of profit on capital, total wage fund, state budget contributions, centrally funded capital investments, technological tasks, and allocations of important raw materials and supplies.

■ New industrial prices would be set according to a new set of formulas, permitting enterprises to accumulate incentive funds and to pay capital charges.

On paper, these reforms appeared to represent a modest, but significant, improvement of the economic system. Modest, because they retained the one-party political system, retained the obligatory system of economic planning, did not change the basic systems of ownership or control, did not allow any free movement of prices, and did not attack the state monopoly of foreign trade.

The reforms appeared significant, however, because they introduced elements of a profit motive, attempted to counteract the ratchet principle, and attempted to set limits on bureaucratic interference in the work of the enterprises. Unfortunately, these improvements proved to be illusory. With an inflexible system of prices, production could not be guided by profits, so detailed central planning was still necessary. Unwilling to sacrifice their authority, power, and privileges, the ministries simply refused to implement many elements of Kosygin's program. In particular, they often refused to pay bonuses to enterprises that failed to fulfill a longer list of plan assignments, and they continuously revised those assignments to resolve day-to-day shortages. With limited support from General Secretary Brezhnev, the reforms failed. They apparently gave a temporary boost to light industry, but growth rates in the remainder of the economy were little affected.[72]

Despite their failures during the 1960s, Soviet leaders continued to tinker with the system, addressing the declining growth rate of the economy with one partial reform after another. Special bonuses were established to reward all manner of virtuous behavior, including high-quality production, technological innovation, and export sales. In all cases, these supplementary programs were rendered insignificant by larger bonuses for fulfillment of basic plan targets and by deficiencies of the central planning system that could not be remedied by the incentive system.

Beginning in 1971, Soviet leaders introduced a complex new system of **counterplanning** to encourage enterprises to adopt more ambitious plans. Under this system, the enterprise first negotiated a set of obligatory plan targets with its ministry; no bonuses would be paid if these basic targets were not fulfilled. The enterprise was then encouraged to propose a more challenging counterplan, which, if fulfilled, would be rewarded with additional bonuses. As long as the directive plan was fulfilled, failure to meet the counterplan would not cause a complete loss of bonuses.

The counterplanning system was, again, unsuccessful. Because obligatory plan targets had to be fulfilled before any bonuses were paid, enterprises continued in their attempts to obtain unchallenging assignments. If an enterprise adopted and fulfilled an ambitious counterplan in one year, the ratchet principle caused it to obtain a more difficult obligatory plan in the following year, leading to a possible loss of bonuses. Thus, most enterprises were unwilling to propose counterplans; only 7 percent of all enterprises adopted them in 1981.[73]

In 1976, following the lead of Yugoslavia and Hungary, the Soviet Politburo attempted to introduce a significant foreign trade and investment reform, allowing foreign partners to invest in joint ventures on Soviet soil. The Ministry of Foreign Trade (MFT) was able to defeat these efforts, though, and

---

[72]According to CIA estimates, annual growth of light industrial production doubled from 2.7 percent during 1961–1965 to 6.4 percent during 1966–1970, and then fell again to 2.5 percent during the 1970s. If light industry and government administration are removed from the totals, the remainder of Soviet GNP grew at equal annual rates—5.2 percent—during 1961–1965 and 1966–1970. See Central Intelligence Agency, *Measures of Soviet Gross National Product in 1982 Prices*, a study for the U.S. Congress, Joint Economic Committee (Washington, D.C.: USGPO, 1990), Appendix A-1.

[73]Philip Hanson, "Success Indicators Revisited: The July 1979 Soviet Decree on Planning and Management," *Soviet Studies* 35 (January 1983): 8.

a much more limited foreign trade reform was introduced in 1978.[74] The export-import organizations under the MFT were reorganized with new boards of directors, including representatives from the industrial ministries. It was hoped that a closer working relationship between the producers and the MFT would improve Soviet export performance, reducing its reliance on exports of oil and other raw materials. Again, however, the results were discouraging. The share of machinery and equipment in Soviet exports fell from 22 percent in 1970 to 14 percent in 1985.

In 1979, in another vain attempt to fine-tune the economy by revising the official list of plan fulfillment indicators, the authorities replaced gross sales with **net normative value added (NNVA).** The NNVA of an enterprise was roughly equal to the gross value of its output minus its purchases of intermediate inputs. By evaluating enterprise performance according to value added, the authorities hoped to discourage enterprises from using expensive raw materials and assemblies to inflate the value of their output.

In principle, NNVA was a better measure of enterprise productivity than gross sales. In practice, it required a much more complex accounting system, and required more information from the State Price Committee. At any rate, this reform, like so many others during the Brezhnev-Kosygin years, was never fully implemented.

THE ANDROPOV EXPERIMENTS

In 1982, Leonid Brezhnev was succeeded as General Secretary by Yuri Andropov, director of the KGB since 1967. During the 1950s, when Andropov was Soviet ambassador to Hungary, he arranged for Soviet troops to stop the 1956 uprising. Afterwards, though, he supported Hungarian economic reforms, and apparently developed an appreciation for the Hungarian system.

Predictably, the former KGB chief believed that many of the Soviet Union's problems could be solved by enforcing stricter codes of order and discipline. He quickly moved to fire corrupt government ministers, local officials, and policemen. Bars and retail stores were raided during the day; factory managers were reprimanded if their employees were found drinking or shopping during work hours. These steps apparently had a measurable influence on Soviet industrial production during the mid-1980s.[75]

More generally, Andropov, at age 78, gave new energy to the subject of economic reform. Complaining that previous reforms had been managed on an "irrational trial-and-error" basis, Andropov commissioned a series of studies on the long-run needs of the Soviet economy. Noteworthy among these was the **Novosibirsk Report,** a study by Tatiana Zaslavskaya, an economic sociologist at a progressive research institute in western Siberia. A paternalistic and highly centralized social system may have made sense in the 1930s, said Zaslavskaya, when the population was compliant and uneducated, but it was not appropriate in the Soviet Union or in the world of the 1980s. The system could not be reformed, however, with simple adjustments

---

[74]For a detailed account of these and other controversies over foreign trade reform, see H. Stephen Gardner, *Soviet Foreign Trade: The Decision Process* (Boston: Kluwer-Nijhoff, 1983).

[75]Marshall Goldman, *Gorbachev's Challenge* (New York: W.W. Norton, 1987), 69–70.

of the incentive system: "At the root of the problem lies a deeper cause." The reforms of the 1960s and 1970s were defeated by interference and resistance from the ministries and other state bureaucracies in Moscow. For meaningful reforms to be successful, the power of the regulatory bureaucracies must be broken; the enterprises must gain broader scope for independent action.[76]

Based on this sort of analysis, Andropov and his protégé, Mikhail Gorbachev, launched a major economic experiment in January 1984. On paper, the experiment was not a radical departure from the reform programs of the 1960s and 1970s—in five industrial ministries, some 700 enterprises were instructed to link their incentive payments to three indicators—product sales, product quality, and profits—according to a stable set of formulas. The experiment was different, though, because special measures were taken to limit the breadth and depth of ministry interference in the enterprises. In the end, these measures were not able to counteract the old patterns of behavior; enterprises continued to present evidence of bureaucratic interference. Still, the performance of the enterprises in the experiment was judged sufficiently successful to extend the program to another 1,600 enterprises in 1985.[77]

THE GORBACHEV ERA: STAGES OF PERESTROIKA

Andropov's death in 1984 was followed by the brief caretaker regime of Konstantin Chernenko, and then, in 1985, by the energetic leadership of Mikhail Gorbachev. During his 7 years in office, Gorbachev introduced an evolutionary series of reforms; when moderate actions were unsuccessful, he moved, step-by-step, to bolder measures. In the process, he gradually lost the support of conservatives, who resisted any significant change, and radical reformers, who believed that gradualism would cause the Soviet Union to miss its best opportunities for economic recovery and growth.[78] To the end, he remained loyal to principles of socialist ownership, and was unwilling or unable to launch a revolutionary transition to a market economy.

In many respects, the first two years of Gorbachev's rule (1985 and 1986) were an extension of the Andropov era. Gorbachev believed that a *perestroika* (restructuring) of Soviet society based on hard work, discipline, and moderate programs of economic reform would be sufficient to accelerate economic growth and technological achievement. Gorbachev apparently believed that reforms similar to those proposed by Liberman and Kosygin would be sufficient for the Soviet Union if they were supported by a young, energetic General Secretary, willing to battle the forces of corruption, laziness, and bureaucratism.[79]

---

[76]Zaslavskaya's study was highly classified and circulated in 70 numbered copies, but became more influential when it leaked to the Western Press. See Dusko Doder, "End to Central Control Advocated; Soviet Study Urges Economic Changes," *The Washington Post*, August 3, 1983, Al; and Tatiana Zaslavskaia, "The Novosibirsk Report," *Survey* 28 (Spring 1984): 91–95.

[77]Hewett, *Reforming the Soviet Economy*, 260–273.

[78]On the views of this second group, see Marshall Goldman, *Lost Opportunity: Why Economic Reforms in Russia Have Not Worked* (New York: W. W. Norton, 1994), passim.

[79]Indeed, Gorbachev confirmed that many of his proposed reforms were derived directly from the Kosygin program. See *Nineteenth All-Union Conference of the CPSU: Documents and Materials* (Moscow: Novosti, 1988), 96.

During his next three years (1987, 1988, and 1989), Gorbachev became convinced of the need for a "radical" or "revolutionary" *perestroika*. He supported much stronger measures to insure enterprise independence, including the development of certain forms of private enterprise, and he supported a truly revolutionary democratization of the political system.

During his final two years (1990 and 1991), while Soviet society was torn between forces of democracy and reactionary nationalism, Gorbachev declared that he was dedicated to the principles of regulated market socialism. He stated his case extensively to the 28th Party Congress in 1990:

> *The advantages of a market economy have been proven on a world scale and the question now is only whether a high level of social security—which is characteristic of our socialist system, the system of the working people—can be assured under market conditions. The answer is this: it is not only possible but it is precisely a regulated market economy that will make it possible to increase social wealth and consequently to raise everyone's living standards.*[80]

Unfortunately, Gorbachev was never willing or able to introduce a market economy in the Soviet Union. His ministers and advisors developed at least a dozen plans, including the familiar 500-Days Plan, but Gorbachev could not resolve their differences, and he was never convinced that any of the plans included sufficient social guarantees.[81] "If we continue to act in this way," he admitted, "we will bankrupt the country."[82] Seventeen months later, the Soviet Union officially ceased to exist.

POLITICAL ENVIRONMENT. During his first two years in office, Gorbachev consolidated his political power by arranging the retirement of several rivals, and he relaxed some of the oppressive policies of previous regimes. He allowed the human rights leaders Andrei Sakharov and Yelena Bonner to return to Moscow from internal exile; he released hundreds of other political prisoners; and, in keeping with his policy of *glasnost* ("openness"), he encouraged the news media to criticize bureaucratic practices in the government and in the Communist party.[83] On the other hand, he suggested few structural reforms in the Soviet political system.

In 1987, Leonid Abalkin, director of the Soviet Institute of Economics and one of Gorbachev's top advisors, convened a conference of Soviet economists to explore the lessons of earlier programs of economic reform. A major conclusion of the conference, published openly in the Soviet press, was that fundamental economic reform could not succeed without parallel political

---

[80]*Twenty-Eighth Congress of the Communist Party of the Soviet Union: Documents and Materials* (Moscow: Novosti, 1988), 60.

[81]For a list of these plans, see Goldman, *Lost Opportunity: Why Economic Reforms in Russia Have Not Worked,* 76. For a most interesting example (which, by the way, apparently never mentions the word *socialism*), see G. Yavlinsky, et al., *500 Days: Transition to the Market* (New York: St. Martin's Press, 1991).

[82]*Twenty-Eighth Congress of the Communist Party of the Soviet Union: Documents and Materials,* 60.

[83]For an excellent chronology of events during the Gorbachev years, see Ed A. Hewett and Victor H. Winston, eds., *Milestones in Glasnost and Perestroyka: Politics and People* (Washington, D.C.: The Brookings Institute, 1991), 499–536.

democratization.[84] One year later, at a major Communist party conference, Gorbachev proposed a major reform of the political system. The party would retain its political monopoly, but the president and members of a reorganized parliament would be selected in multicandidate elections for limited terms of office. The new parliament was elected in 1989 with a diverse membership; its proceedings were televised, providing an unprecedented forum for discussion and debate of national issues.

In 1990, Gorbachev grew frustrated with the Communist party; he supported the development of a multiparty system, and Article 6 of the Soviet Constitution, which assigned a "leading role" in society to the party, was abolished. In 1991, a new set of state structures was created, including a Federation Council, a National Security Council, and a Cabinet of Ministers. Gorbachev attempted to transfer power from the party to the presidency and to these other state structures. His efforts were interrupted by the coup attempt in August 1991, and by the subsequent dissolution of the Soviet Union.

DISCIPLINE.   Among Gorbachev's first actions in office was to launch a campaign against alcoholism and drunkenness on the job. He cut vodka production, closed two-thirds of the liquor stores, forbade restaurants to serve drinks before two P.M., and increased the fine for drinking at work to 50 rubles (about one-fourth of the average monthly wage). About three years after its introduction, public resistance and declining state revenues from alcohol sales forced Gorbachev to abandon his antialcohol campaign.

To strengthen discipline *within* enterprises, Gorbachev borrowed several ideas from the military. Most enterprises in industry and agriculture were organized into work teams known as brigades (10 to 30 workers) and links (5 to 10 workers). Each team concluded a collective contract with the enterprise, and bonuses were paid in a lump sum to the team based on their fulfillment of the contract. This system attempted to combine moral incentives (peer pressure) with material incentives.[85]

A new system of product quality inspection, also based on military procedure, was introduced in 1987. The State Committee on Standards was empowered to post teams of inspectors in some 1,500 enterprises that produced vital products. The inspectors had broad powers to block the shipment of substandard goods and to advise enterprise managers on improvements in product quality.[86] The system was quickly abandoned, though, because tough quality standards were unrealistic in the Soviet system and were inconsistent with ambitious goals for economic growth.[87]

---

[84]See discussion of the conference in Anders Aslund, *Gorbachev's Struggle for Economic Reform* (Ithaca, N.Y.: Cornell University Press, 1989), 180–181.

[85]For more on this and other military precedents to the Gorbachev reforms, see George G. Weickhardt, "The Soviet Military-Industrial Complex and Economic Reform," *Soviet Economy* 2 (July–September 1986): 193–220.

[86]See Gertrude Schroeder, "Gorbachev: 'Radically' Implementing Brezhnev's Reforms," *Soviet Economy* 2 (October–December 1986): 294–295.

[87]James Noren, "The Soviet Economic Crisis: Another Perspective," *Soviet Economy* 6 (January–March 1990): 25.

Enforcement of discipline was also among Gorbachev's motives in his program of *glasnost*. He publicly reprimanded officials who continued to work "in the old way" and encouraged the news media to expose derelictions of duty: "Those who have grown used to doing slipshod work, to practicing deception, indeed feel really awkward in the glare of publicity, when everything done . . . is in full public view."[88]

ENTERPRISE AUTONOMY AND CENTRAL PLANNING. Throughout his leadership, Gorbachev opposed the petty interference of central planners and ministry officials in the everyday work of enterprises, and he encouraged broader and deeper participation in the reforms launched by Andropov. In 1985, he organized a major administrative reform to curtail the dictatorial powers of industrial ministries; he created seven **superministries** by merging closely related ministries and agencies, allowing reductions of their supervisory staff. For example, the State Agroindustrial Committee was formed in 1985 by merging five ministries and one state committee, allowing the release of nearly half the ministries' employees.[89]

Legislation adopted in 1987 called for the scope of enterprise autonomy to increase dramatically. Central planners would now be primarily responsible for long-term planning and investment policy. The enterprises would be required to cover their own expenses, but they would be able to prepare their own annual plans and control their own payrolls. In place of obligatory plan assignments, encompassing all production, the enterprises would only be required to fill **state orders** for strategic products. The workers in each enterprise would be able to elect their manager.

According to Gorbachev, however, the ministries conspired with the State Planning Committee and other organs of the Council of Ministers to undermine this reform: "What is most intolerable is that enterprises are being compelled by the means of state orders to manufacture goods that are not in demand, compelled for the simple reason that they want to attain the notorious gross output targets."[90] Frustrations of this kind eventually caused Gorbachev to abandon his faith in central planning, to search for an acceptable market alternative.

NEW FORMS OF ENTERPRISE. As Gorbachev's approach to economic reform became more radical, he gradually expanded the scope of private and cooperative activities. A law on private economic activity, passed in 1986 and implemented in 1987, permitted individuals to engage in a range of paid services and handicrafts that were previously forbidden. A private firm, or, more officially, an **individual enterprise,** could employ family members, but could not employ other hired labor.

---

[88]Mikhail Gorbachev, *Political Report of the CPSU Central Committee to the 27th Party Congress* (Moscow: Novosti Press Agency, 1986), 76.

[89]Philip Hanson, "Superministries: The State of Play," *Radio Liberty Research,* April 21, 1986, 6. Also, see Hewett, *Reforming the Soviet Economy,* 335–340.

[90]*Nineteenth All-Union Conference of the CPSU: Documents and Materials,* 17.

More significantly, regulations issued in 1986 and 1987 allowed groups of workers to form **producer cooperatives.** The defining characteristic of a Soviet cooperative was that all the owners had to work (physically, as a worker, or mentally, as a manager) in the firm. A cooperative could be owned by a single person, who could be its manager, and it could hire workers. Thus, the door was opened to the creation of a large, quasi-capitalist sector in the Soviet Union. By the end of 1990, some 245,000 cooperatives had been created, employing more than 6 million people.[91]

Initially, development of the individual and cooperative sectors was restricted by their limited access to buildings, equipment, and other facilities owned by the state. This problem was resolved in 1989, when legislation allowed the creation of **leased enterprises.** In this arrangement, which had been common during the New Economic Policy of the 1920s, state-owned facilities were leased and managed by private individuals, cooperatives, or joint ventures with foreign partners. According to the negotiated terms of the lease, the tenant paid rent to the proprietor—a ministry or local authority—and, after payment of taxes, was able to keep any residual income. One year after their legalization, some 6,200 leased enterprises were operating in the Soviet Union with 3.6 million employees.[92]

INCENTIVES. An important component of Gorbachev's reform was his effort to adjust material incentives, unleashing what he called the "human factor." The only limit on an individual's income, he argued, should be whether it is earned. The basic wage scales were adjusted to raise the pay of highly skilled workers, including engineers, scientists, and teachers. The 1987 Law on State Enterprise gave broad new powers to the enterprises to control wages and salaries. As one would expect, actions and attitudes such as these led to a more uneven distribution of income.[93]

PRICES. In 1987, Gorbachev called for a radical reform of prices, and declared it must be completed by 1990. Unlike earlier price reforms, this one was supposed to encompass the whole range of wholesale, retail, and procurement prices. The prices of strategic products, such as oil, would be controlled, but other wholesale prices would be allowed to fluctuate. Retail prices would be increased to remove subsidies from the system, but savings arising in the state budget would be distributed to the population in additional income to compensate them for the price increases. Unfortunately, this compensation formula caused endless disagreement between Gorbachev and his advisors, many of whom believed it would be inflationary. Retail prices were finally raised in April 1991, by an average of 60 percent; prices of

---

[91]Alexander S. Bim, Derek C. Jones, and Thomas E. Weisskopf, "Hybrid Forms of Enterprise Organization in the Former USSR and the Russian Federation," *Comparative Economic Studies* 35 (Spring 1993): 7.

[92]Ibid., 11.

[93]See Michael V. Alexeev and Clifford G. Gaddy, "Trends in Wage and Income Distribution under Gorbachev," *Berkeley-Duke Occasional Papers on the Second Economy of the USSR,* Paper no. 25 (February 1991), passim.

foodstuffs were raised 240 percent. The government attempted to compensate the public for 85 percent of their loss of purchasing power.

FOREIGN TRADE AND JOINT VENTURES. Beginning in 1987, a flurry of new activity began in the field of foreign economic relations. Initially, 21 industrial ministries and 70 manufacturing enterprises were allowed to handle foreign-trade transactions without intervention of the Ministry of Foreign Trade or its superministry successor, the State Foreign Economic Commission. Several of the existing export-import firms were placed under direct control of industrial ministries. New export incentives were established, including a system whereby the exporting enterprises would have greater control over the foreign currency they earned. Regulations issued in 1987 allowed the creation of joint ventures between Soviet enterprises and foreign firms on Soviet soil. Nearly 3,000 of these were established by the end of 1990, but the interest of foreign partners was restricted by the inconvertibility of the ruble and by an uncertain system of property rights. Initial steps were taken to make the ruble an internationally convertible currency, but this could not be accomplished in the presence of pervasive price controls.

PERFORMANCE. By almost any conventional economic measure, the Soviet economy performed badly during the Gorbachev era. National income, which grew at an annual rate of about 1.8 percent between 1976 and 1985, slowed to a rate of 0.9 percent between 1986 and 1990. Between those same periods, the consumer price inflation rate accelerated from 2.2 percent annually to 5.9 percent annually. The international current account balance, which registered surpluses during all the years between 1982 and 1988, descended into deep deficits in 1989 and 1990. Accordingly, the convertible currency debt increased from $29 billion in 1985 to about $54 billion in 1989.[94]

Most of the accomplishments of the Gorbachev era cannot be measured in dollars or rubles. History and truth were rediscovered. Political prisoners and captured territories were released. Elections were organized, and new leaders were discovered. Travel restrictions were abolished. Political and economic relations were restored with the outside world. First steps were taken toward an uncertain future.

EVALUATION OF SOCIALIST REFORMS

Looking back across the record of socialist economic reform in Yugoslavia, Hungary, and the Soviet Union, we notice a few common elements. In all cases, the reformers attempted to preserve a system of socialist ownership, increase the scope of enterprise autonomy, and encourage some form of market-oriented behavior. Blending these institutional elements, the reformers hoped to establish a "golden mean," avoiding the inefficiency of Stalinism and the inequity of unfettered capitalism.

---

[94]Marer, et al., *Historically Planned Economies: A Guide to the Data*, 204–211.

Unfortunately, none of these reforms was successful over an extended period. They were plagued, in part, by external, cultural, and environmental problems. Yugoslavia was torn by internal divisions and shaken by the international economy. Hungary was also vulnerable to international oil prices and constrained by membership in the Warsaw Pact. The Gorbachev team in the Soviet Union had to contend with a nuclear disaster in Chernobyl, an earthquake in Armenia, and falling prices during the late 1980s for its exports of oil.

On the other hand, it appears that many of the economic difficulties in Yugoslavia, Hungary, and the Soviet Union were caused by the reforms, themselves. The specifics are different, of course, from one country to another, but they seem to support an argument made many years ago by Frederic Pryor. Based on the experiences of the 1960s, he concluded that mixed plan-market economies are likely to combine the worst elements of capitalism and socialism rather than the best.[95] Instead of seeking a "golden mean" between capitalism and socialism, countries may be better advised to choose one of the "grand alternatives." Countries with relatively pure systems of central planning, such as Czechoslovakia and East Germany, and countries with relatively pure market systems, such as the East Asian nations, usually outperformed the reformist countries.

In many cases, mixtures of market and central control have created institutional irrationalities and contradictions. For example, in the Soviet case, Gorbachev's reforms allowed enterprises to compete against one another for workers, offering higher wages, but generally did not allow them to adjust the prices of their final products. With rising wage costs and fixed sales revenues, the enterprises were forced to seek loans or subsidies from the government, or they could seek loans from one another. Thus, the Soviet financial system carried the burden of enormous subsidies and inter-enterprise credits.

In one reformist country after another, we also find that governments have poor records of granting independence or enforcing responsibility. Even when concerted efforts have been made by national leaders over long periods of time, it has been difficult in the reforming countries to prevent government agencies from interfering in the everyday decisions of enterprises. Why do they interfere? Sometimes to serve a national priority. Sometimes to prevent bankruptcy and unemployment. Sometimes to enrich a member of the government. Sometimes to undermine the reforms, to maintain a position of authority.

For these and other reasons, the nations of central Eurasia have abandoned their piecemeal efforts to reform the Stalinist system. Today, they are engaged in broader strategies of market transition and privatization. Still, as we shall find in the next chapter, the market transition offers its own collection of contradictions and irrationalities.

---

[95]Frederic L. Pryor, *Property and Industrial Organization in Communist and Capitalist Nations* (Bloomington, Ind.: Indiana University Press, 1973), 276–277.

SUMMARY

Yugoslavia launched the first major reform of the Stalinist system in the early 1950s when it created a system of workers' self-management and replaced detailed central planning with planning of basic proportions. Price controls were gradually released and forced collectivization of agriculture was abandoned. In 1965, Yugoslav leaders introduced new reforms that broadened the spectrum of market activity, gave the banks a role in investment decisions, and replaced the system of basic proportions planning with a looser system of indicative planning. In the 1970s, self-management was decentralized to the enterprise department level, and a new system of contractual planning was adopted. Cooperation between the independent departments (BOALs) became slow and bureaucratic.

According to its proponents, the Yugoslav system carried the democratic principle into the workplace; it outperformed other middle-income countries in terms of economic growth and income equality, and provided a natural system of protection for the natural environment. The Yugoslav borders were open; those who disliked the system were free to leave. Yugoslavia had a number of other economic and social problems, but, according to proponents, these were not created by the economic system.

According to critics, the Yugoslav system was not consistently democratic or genuinely based on self-management. Instead, it was a cumbersome system of management that frequently caused enterprises to make wrong, inefficient decisions. Enterprises were inclined to finance investments from debt rather than from internal savings, and they may have responded inappropriately to price changes. Critics believe that the economic system was also responsible for the country's persistently high rates of unemployment and inflation, and for inequalities in the Yugoslav income distribution.

Stalinist central planning proved to be an inappropriate economic system for small, trade-dependent Hungary. Opposition to political repression and forced collectivization eventually led to a 1956 revolt that was crushed by Soviet forces. János Kádár, installed as the new national leader, resumed collectivization, but simultaneously introduced agricultural reforms. Based on successes in agriculture, he carried moderate reform to industry, and in 1968 the country moved toward market socialism with the New Economic Mechanism (NEM).

The NEM replaced detailed central planning with indicative planning and a limited market mechanism. It based the incentive system on profits, lifted some price controls, and allowed some enterprises to engage directly in foreign trade. These measures boosted productivity growth, but also caused greater income inequality; when the international oil crisis of 1973 threatened to accelerate inflation, the NEM floundered. Centralized price control was strengthened in the 1970s, causing repressed inflation and contributing to balance of payments problems. To deal with these problems, the principles of the NEM were reaffirmed beginning in 1980. Price controls were eased, monopolistic firms were broken into smaller units, other small firms were established, the state bureaucracy was trimmed, the banking system was reformed, bankruptcy laws were adopted, and a Western-style tax code was adopted.

Under market socialism, the Hungarian economy recorded rapid rates of productivity and export growth, a relatively even distribution of income, and a high level of agricultural production per capita, while maintaining international solvency. On the other hand, income growth was relatively slow, and the debt burden was very large on a per capita basis. More fundamentally, the market socialist system never extended full independence to Hungarian companies; bureaucratic interference and subsidized production persisted.

In the Soviet Union, Khrushchev introduced a major administrative reform in 1957, shifting authority to the regions. This system was eventually judged a failure, and was displaced by the Liberman-Kosygin reforms of 1965, which adjusted the incentive system to emphasize sales and profits rather than gross output. The Liberman-Kosygin reforms were never fully implemented, and Soviet economic growth continued to stagnate. A system of counterplanning was introduced in 1971 to encourage ambitious planning, but the enterprises were not interested. The authorities continued to tinker with the incentive system during the 1970s, and a limited foreign trade reform was introduced in 1978, but these efforts had little effect.

Yuri Andropov became General Secretary in 1982, and attempted to instill a stronger system of discipline in the Soviet Union; he commissioned new research on the problems of the Soviet economy, and initiated an incentive reform experiment in five ministries. These experiments and discipline programs were continued and expanded by Mikhail Gorbachev when he became General Secretary in 1985. With regard to discipline programs, Gorbachev conducted a campaign against alcohol, organized production in brigades, initiated a new system of quality inspection, and exposed laggard workers to public ridicule. Gorbachev also allowed greater enterprise autonomy in managing material incentives, and he approved a new system of retail and wholesale prices. As the economy continued to stagnate, Gorbachev was driven to attempt more radical measures. He introduced a major reorganization of the administrative, political, and foreign trade systems; transferred progressively more authority to individual enterprises; encouraged the formation of family firms, cooperatives, and leased enterprises; supported work incentives that broadened the income distribution; and, finally, approved a major increase of consumer prices, compensated with higher incomes. The Gorbachev economic programs, like other programs of socialist reform, were insufficient to save the Soviet economy, but his political reforms proved to be revolutionary for all of central Eurasia.

DISCUSSION AND REVIEW QUESTIONS

1. How did the policies of Stalin, Khrushchev, Brezhnev, and Gorbachev differ on the subject of national autonomy in Central and Eastern Europe?

2. What would be the condition of the former Yugoslav republics today if Tito had adopted a capitalist system in 1951 instead of a worker-managed system?

3. What was a BOAL? When and why were they created? What were their rights and responsibilities?

4. What were some of the causes of Yugoslav unemployment? Is there any reason to believe that labor management contributed to the problem?

5. Why were Yugoslav enterprises unwilling to invest out of their retained earnings? Did this reluctance have any macroeconomic significance?

6. Would a system of labor management alleviate some problems of environmental pollution? Would any problems of this kind be more difficult to control under a system of labor management?

7. How did the Hungarian New Economic Mechanism resemble the Yugoslav system of market socialism? How did it differ?

8. What caused the decline of the New Economic Mechanism in the 1970s? What caused its recovery in the 1980s?

9. Based on evidence from Yugoslavia and Hungary, is it clear that market socialism is inconsistent with an even distribution of income?

10. What problems were addressed by the Soviet reforms of the 1960s? How successful were these reforms?

11. This chapter adopts the position that Gorbachev presented his reforms in a series of progressively radical stages. What were these stages, and how did they develop? Can a case be made (as some have suggested) that Gorbachev planned this entire strategy in 1985?

12. Is it possible to design an institutional arrangement that will impose a hard budget constraint on enterprises in a state socialist system?

SUGGESTED READINGS

Adam, Jan. *Planning and Market in Soviet and East European Thought, 1960s–1992.* New York: St. Martin's Press, 1993. *The author draws on primary source materials in four languages to discuss the development of reform doctrine in the Soviet Union, Czechoslovakia, Hungary, and Poland between the 1960s and 1990s.*

Dyker, David A. *Yugoslavia: Socialism, Development, and Debt.* London: Routledge, 1990. *A lively chronological account of Yugoslav economic affairs from the birth of the state in 1918 until the eve of its dissolution.*

Hewett, Ed A. *Reforming the Soviet Economy: Equality versus Efficiency.* Washington, D.C.: The Brookings Institution, 1988. *An authoritative analysis of Soviet reforms from the time of Khrushchev to the middle of the Gorbachev era.*

Horvat, Branko. *The Yugoslav Economic System.* Armonk, N.Y.: M. E. Sharpe, 1976. *An insider's account of the operation and performance of Yugoslav institutions and the academic debates that formed them.*

Prout, Christopher. *Market Socialism in Yugoslavia*. London: Oxford University Press, 1985. *A brief survey of the system with separate chapters on the markets for goods, labor, and capital.*

Schrenk, Martin, Cyrus Ardalan, and Nadal El Tatawy. *Yugoslavia: Self-Management Socialism and the Challenge of Development*. Baltimore: The Johns Hopkins University Press, 1979. *A wide-ranging World Bank report, this is one of the most comprehensive assessments of the Yugoslav system.*

U.S. Congress, Joint Economic Committee, *East European Economies: Slow Growth in the 1980s*. 3 vols. Washington, D.C.: USGPO, 1985–1986. *A compendium of articles on a wide range of Eastern European themes, covering the period through the early 1980s.*

Vanek, Jaroslav. *The Theory of Labor-Managed Market Economies*. Ithaca, N.Y.: Cornell University Press, 1970. *A good general introduction to the body of theoretical literature addressed in the chapter Appendix.*

INTERNET RESOURCES

Cockshott, W. Paul and Allin Cottrell. "Socialism: Towards a Post-Soviet Model"
http://www.cs.strath.ac.uk/University/wpcbook.html

Hammel, E. A. "The Yugoslav Labyrinth"
http://boserup.qal.berkeley.edu/~gene/labyrinth.eeurrev.html

Helsinki Conference on Security and Cooperation in Europe, Final Act, 1975
http://www.hri.org/docs/Helsinki75.html

McCain, Roger A. "Libertarian Socialism and Cooperative Enterprise"
http://william-king.www.drexel.edu/top/political.html

Naishul, Vitali. "Liberalism, Customary Rights, and Economic Reforms"
http://www.fe.msk.ru/libertarium/library/nayshul/ecright.html

Naishul, Vitali. "The Final and Highest Stage of Socialism"
http://feast.fe.msk.ru/libertarium/library/nayshul/brezhnev.html

Yugoslav Economy: Memorandum of the Serbian Academy of Sciences, 1993
http://suc.suc.org/~kosta/tar/memorandum/memorandum.html#crisis

APPENDIX:
THE THEORY OF THE LABOR-MANAGED FIRM

A large body of theoretical analysis, including hundreds of articles in the English language alone, was inspired by the introduction of workers' self-management in Yugoslavia after 1951. A brief look at this literature reveals something about the peculiarities of the worker-managed firm and, equally interesting, about the role of assumptions in economic theory.

The seminal work in this field was Ben Ward's 1958 study of an idealized firm in Illyria (the ancient name for the region that later became Yugoslavia).[1] Unlike the capitalist firm, which theoretically attempts to maximize total profits, Ward assumed that the worker-managed firm would attempt to maximize profits per worker. Whereas the capitalist firm can hire additional employees at a market-fixed wage, the new employee in a worker-managed firm will receive a share of the company's profits.

Assume, for simplicity's sake, that a firm employs L workers as its only variable input, and pays a fixed rent of R dinars per month to the government for the use of its factory. Also assume that the firm produces Q units of output according to the same kind of production function that is employed in the standard textbook theory of the capitalist firm, and sells its output in a competitive market at a price of P dinars per unit. Income per worker (Y/L) is equal to total revenue (PQ) minus total cost (R), divided by employment (L):

$$Y/L = (PQ - R)/L = P(Q/L) - R/L$$

As rearranged, this equation states that income per worker is equal to the value of the average product of labor minus rental cost per worker. According to the standard production function, which states that the average product of labor (Q/L) first rises and then falls as more workers are hired, the value of the average product of labor will also rise and then fall. A graph of Q/L and P(Q/L) is presented in Figure 16A.1 for two different values of P. Notice that an increase in P shifts the P(Q/L) curve upward and changes its shape as its sides become steeper.

In Figure 16A.2, the graph of P(Q/L) is joined by a graph of R/L, the other half of the income formula. In the short run, with the amount of capital fixed, R/L slopes downward to the right as the fixed rental cost is spread over a larger number of workers (technically, it is represented by a rectangular hyperbola). Income per worker is represented by the vertical distance between the P(Q/L) and R/L curves.

How many workers should the firm hire to maximize income per worker? According to the graph, the firm can maximize sales revenue per worker—P(Q/L)—by hiring 30 employees. If additional workers are hired, it will reduce P(Q/L) but, up to a certain point, it will yield an even larger reduction in cost per worker—R/L. To maximize income per worker, hiring should continue until the last worker reduces P(Q/L) and R/L by the same amount. Graphically, this will occur at the level of employment where lines drawn tangent to the two curves (AA and BB) have identical slopes. Thus, the firm depicted in Figure 16A.2 will hire 40 workers.

Now, how will the firm react if the price of its product increases? In Figure 16A.1, an increase in P will cause the P(Q/L) curve to shift upward and become steeper. In terms of Figure 16A.2, the slope of AA will become steeper than the slope of BB if 40 workers are employed. A reduction in employment

---

[1]Benjamin Ward, "The Firm in Illyria: Market Syndicalism," *American Economic Review* 48 (September 1958): 566–589.

■ FIGURE 16A.1

THE AVERAGE PRODUCT OF LABOR AND THE VALUE OF THE AVERAGE PRODUCT OF LABOR

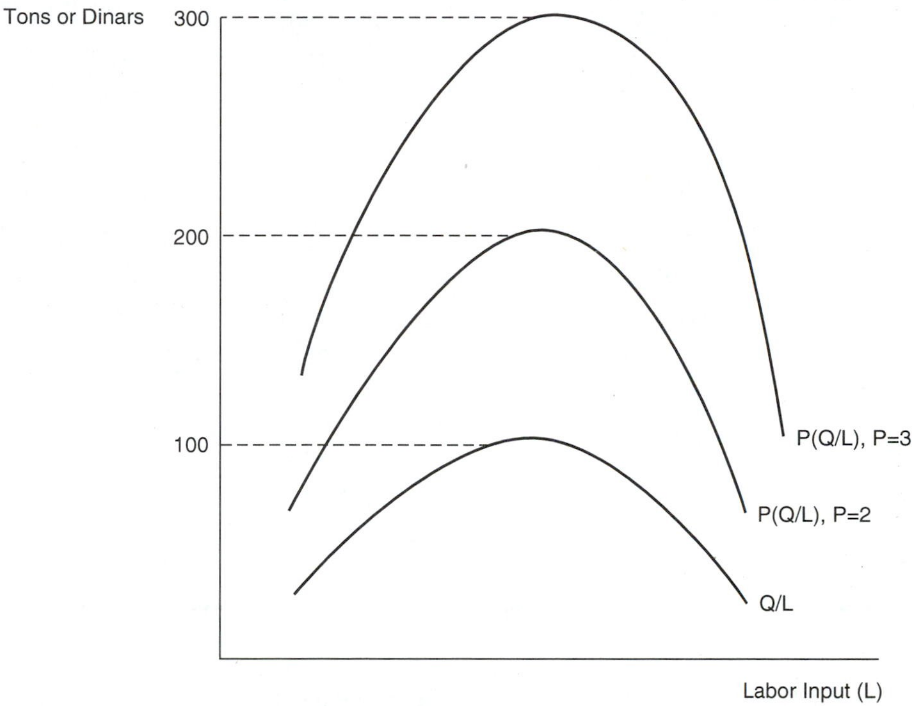

will be necessary to flatten AA and to steepen BB until their slopes are equal again and Y/L is at a new maximum. If the increase in P causes a reduction in employment, however, it will also cause a reduction in the output of the firm. Thus, the firm has a negatively sloped supply curve for its product.

The result just obtained is significant in several respects. First, if nothing else, it tells us that a seemingly small change in assumptions can cause a major change in the outcome of an economic theory. In this version of his theory, Ward retained all the technology and market-structure assumptions of the theory of perfect competition, but replaced maximization of profits with maximization of profits-per-worker. This single alteration reversed the basic conclusion of the theory—the upward-sloping capitalist supply curve became a downward-sloping Illyrian supply curve.

More important, the theory suggests that markets in a Yugoslav-style economy could be unstable. If a product is in short supply, causing its price to rise, this could cause a decline in production that would make the shortage even more severe. If the majority of markets were to work in this way, worker management would surely be an unworkable system.

The theoretical stability of the labor-managed market economy can be salvaged in any of several ways. First, even if a supply curve is negatively

■ **FIGURE 16A.2**

MAXIMIZATION OF INCOME PER WORKER

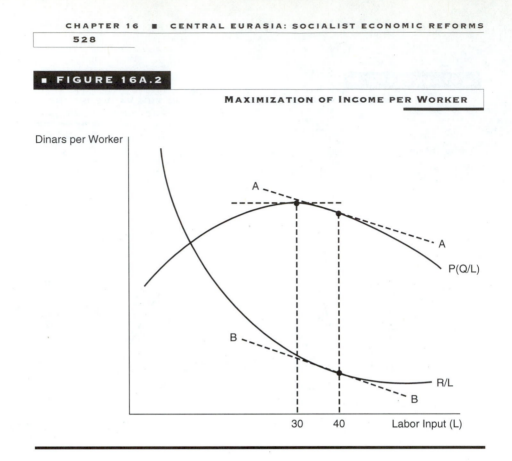

sloped, the corresponding market will be stable if the supply curve is steeper than the demand curve. In this circumstance, a price above the equilibrium level will generate a surplus of the product, causing the price to fall back toward equilibrium.[2]

Second, the labor-managed firm may have a positively sloped supply curve if labor is not its only variable input or if it produces more than one final product. Like a capitalist firm, the Illyrian firm will employ each nonlabor input up to the point where the value of its marginal product equals its price. Depending on the relative height and steepness of the marginal productivity curves of labor and other inputs, the supply curve may be positively or negatively sloped. In general, we can only say that the supply curve of the labor-managed firm will be less elastic than that of a comparable capitalist firm.[3]

Third, the current output of the labor-managed firm should depend not only on current prices, but also on future price expectations. If an increase

[2]Technically, this assumes a Walrasian price-adjustment mechanism rather than a Marshallian quantity-adjustment mechanism. For Marshallian stability, the demand curves must be steeper than the negatively sloped supply curves.

[3]Jaroslav Vanek, *The Theory of Labor-Managed Market Economies* (Ithaca, N.Y.: Cornell University Press, 1970), Chapter 3.

in a price today causes us to expect that price to fall again in the future, then the supply elasticity of the firm will be greater than is usually supposed. On the other hand, if price expectations are elastic—a price rise causes us to expect more price rises—the possibility of a negative supply response is enhanced.[4]

Fourth, even if individual Illyrian firms have negatively sloped supply curves, the market long-run supply curve for a product may be positively sloped if new enterprises are able to enter the market. According to results from a dynamic model developed by Christophre Georges, if unemployed workers are free to open their own firms, the allocation of labor in a labor-managed economy may be identical to that in a competitive capital-managed economy.[5] Murat Sertel has derived similar results from a model that assumes the existence of a market for memberships in worker co-operatives.[6]

Finally, several authors have disputed the validity of the entire body of Illyrian literature based on maximization of income per worker. According to Branko Horvat, "It is a great merit of Ward's original article, which so bluntly stated the absurd neoclassical consequences, that it has forced us to undertake the reexamination of the theoretical foundations."[7] Horvat argues that the behavior of a Yugoslav firm could be described more accurately by the solution of a multiyear dynamic program, in which income per worker is maximized subject to a set of six constraints. These include upper and lower boundaries on wages and a requirement that a certain fraction of the firm's investments must be financed out of the firm's own funds. Horvat was not able to derive conclusions from his program, however, "since our knowledge about the behavior of worker-managers is still very imperfect."[8]

Likewise, Nava Kahana and Shmuel Nitzan have explored partial equilibrium models that assume income-per-worker maximization subject to an employment constraint and employment maximization subject to an income-per-worker constraint. Under these circumstances, an increase in product price does not cause a reduction in employment, and, if labor is a normal input, it does not cause a reduction in the quantity of production and supply.[9]

---

[4]David C. Wong, "A Two-Period Model of the Competitive Socialist Labor-Managed Firm," *Journal of Comparative Economics* 10 (September 1986): 313–324.

[5]Christophre Georges, "A Dynamic Macroeconomic Model of the Labor-Managed Economy," *Journal of Comparative Economics* 18 (February 1994): 46–63.

[6]Murat R. Sertel, "A Rehabilitation of the Labor-Managed Firm," in *Workers and Incentives,* ed. Murat R. Sertel (Amsterdam: North-Holland, 1982), 11–26; and Murat R. Sertel, "Workers' Enterprises in Imperfect Competition," *Journal of Comparative Economics* 15 (December 1991): 698–710.

[7]Branko Horvat, "Farewell to the Illyrian Firm," *Economic Analysis and Workers' Management* 20 (1986): 29.

[8]Branko Horvat, "The Theory of the Worker-Managed Firm Revisited," *Journal of Comparative Economics* 10 (March 1986): 20–25.

[9]Nava Kahana and Shmuel Nitzan, "More on Alternative Objectives of Labor-Managed Firms," *Journal of Comparative Economics* 13 (December 1989): 527-538.

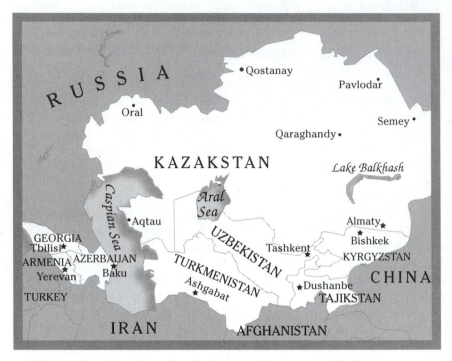

Central Asia and the Caucasus Area

CENTRAL EURASIA: MAKING MARKETS

[H]owever much one may wish a speedy return to a free economy, this cannot mean the removal at one stroke of most of the wartime restrictions. Nothing would discredit the system of free enterprise more than the acute, though probably short-lived, dislocation and instability such an attempt would produce. . . . [A] carefully thought-out policy of gradual relaxation of controls . . . may have to extend over several years.

—FRIEDRICH A. HAYEK, *THE ROAD TO SERFDOM*, 1944

It is cruel to cut off a dog's tail slowly.

—POLISH PROVERB

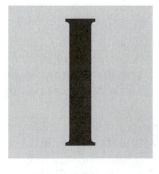n the previous chapter, we surveyed the programs of economic reform undertaken in the Soviet Union and Eastern Europe between the 1950s and the 1980s. We found that some of these programs were quite significant; they caused extensive modifications of Stalinist systems of central planning and control. Still, all these reforms were predicated on the preservation of socialist ownership and Communist rule. In the end, they failed to address the problems of economic stagnation, technological backwardness, inferior production quality, or international indebtedness.

During the years between 1989 and 1991, for reasons that may never be fully understood, the Berlin Wall was breached, the international communist system collapsed, the Soviet Union disintegrated, and the nations of Central Eurasia embarked on new programs of democratization, market transition, and globalization. During subsequent years, the strategies and performances of the individual countries have differed widely. In this chapter, we shall survey these differences and explore the elements of the transition programs. Why did communism finally collapse? Why have some countries moved more rapidly than others? What are the relative merits of a "big bang" or a gradual transition strategy? What are the present prospects for continued progress? These are a few of the questions we shall explore.

THE FALL OF COMMUNISM

We have already discussed several of the systemic weaknesses and historical developments that contributed to the decline and fall of the Stalinist system. Among the important items, we could include the following:

■ The long-term deterioration of Soviet economic growth, beginning in the 1960s, caused in part by the rising complexity of central planning, by a rapid decline in the productivity of capital investments, and by a heavy burden of military expenditures.[1]

■ Normalization of East-West political and economic relations in the 1970s, causing political and intellectual leaders to gradually shift their interests, ideologies, and attitudes.

■ The rapid rise of international energy prices during the 1970s, which destabilized the economies of oil importing countries in Eastern Europe, and the sharp reduction of those prices during the early 1980s, which destabilized the Soviet export sector.

■ The rise of an independent labor movement in Poland during the 1970s and early 1980s, encouraged in 1978 by the selection of a new Polish pope.

■ Soviet involvement, beginning in 1979, in a costly war in Afghanistan, opening the country to drug traffic and a variety of other social problems.

■ The death of Marshall Tito in 1980, leading to new instability in Yugoslavia.

■ During the early 1980s, the realization that Western industrial countries were extending their technological lead, and that Taiwan, Singapore, and the other new industrial countries of East Asia were pulling ahead of the socialist world.[2]

■ The leadership of Mikhail Gorbachev, beginning in 1985, who progressively extended new liberties to the news media, the public, a reorganized parliament, the Soviet republics, and resistance movements in other socialist countries. According to Marie Lavigne, Gorbachev "triggered the collapse" when he allowed the legitimacy of the Soviet Communist party to be questioned, and when he "renounced support of that legitimacy in the 'brother' countries."[3]

---

[1]See William Easterly and Stanley Fischer, "Living on Borrowed Time: Lessons of the Soviet Economy's Collapse," *Transition* 5 (April 1994): 1–3.

[2]According to the U.S. Central Intelligence Agency, in the mid–1980s the Soviet Union lagged at least 8 years behind the United States in microprocessor, mainframe, and minicomputer technology, and at least 10 years in supercomputer technology. These lags, according to CIA analysis, were still growing. See testimony and exhibits in *Allocation of Resources in the Soviet Union and China—1986*, Hearings before the Subcommittee on National Security Economics, Joint Economic Committee, U.S. Congress (Washington, D.C.: USGPO, 1988), 17–18 and 86–88.

[3]Marie Lavigne, *The Economics of Transition: From Socialist Economy to Market Economy* (New York: St. Martin's Press, 1995), 94.

- A series of natural and human disasters, including the Chernobyl nuclear explosion in 1986 and the Armenian earthquake in 1988, which interfered with Gorbachev's plans for acceleration of economic growth.
- Boris Yeltsin's public attack, beginning in 1987, on the systems of privilege, corruption, and resistance to change in the Communist party.
- The failure of a coup attempt against Gorbachev's government in 1991, causing the Communist party to lose its last shred of legitimacy, and triggering dissolution of the Soviet Union.

Once again, these are only a few of the factors that led to the collapse of the Stalinist system. A more complete account would include a wider range of political, economic, and social phenomena and would acknowledge the acts of Andrei Sakharov, Vaclav Havel, and thousands of other critics, dissidents, and revolutionaries. Still, enough has been said to illustrate two important points. First, the fall of communism cannot be reduced to a simple formulation; it resulted from a complex interaction of historical trends and events. Second, few of the problems that *contributed* to the fall of communism were quickly *resolved* by its failure. The transformation of Central Eurasia was initiated against a backdrop of economic collapse, financial imbalance, political disintegration, labor unrest, ethnic hostility, environmental emergency, and international indebtedness. When the new governments were unable to respond quickly to all these crises, individual people and families were forced to devise their own survival strategies. By necessity, market-oriented behavior began to spread throughout the region.

THE STARTING LINE

On the eve of economic transition, the nations of Central Eurasia faced many common challenges, but some countries were more favorably equipped to begin the process. As we found in Chapter 14, many national differences were rooted in centuries of historical experience. Generally, the largest incomes, the highest educational levels, and the strongest legal and civil traditions were found in the Czech Republic, Slovakia, Hungary, and Slovenia— countries that spent their formative years in the Austro-Hungarian empire.[4] The nations of Central Asia, the southern Balkans, and the Caucasus traditionally had the lowest income levels and the highest rates of civil unrest.

Several indicators of initial conditions are presented in Table 17.1. On the eve of economic transformation, the highest levels of private sector development were found in Poland, Yugoslavia, Hungary, and Bulgaria. During the socialist era, all these countries maintained substantial private sectors in agriculture. Yugoslavia and Hungary had extensive experience with market socialism.

---

[4]Czechoslovakia was divided into two countries—the Czech Republic and Slovakia—on January 1, 1993.

■ TABLE 17.1

INITIAL CONDITIONS: CENTRAL EURASIA
IN THE LATE 1980s

	1989 GNP per Capita ($ at PPP)	1989 Private Sector Share of GDP (percent)	1986–89 Industrial Firms with 1,000+ Workers (% of industrial employment)	1988 Military Spending (percent of GDP)	1989 Unemployment Rate (percent)
Albania	1,250	5	n.a.	5	0
Bulgaria	5,710	15	49	13	0
Czechoslovakia	7,880	11	94	7	0
Hungary	6,110	15	65	6	0.3
Poland	4,570	29	51	9	0.1
Romania	3,450	13	87	7	0
Soviet Union	5,000	6	73	12	0
Yugoslavia	5,460	18	27	3	14
United States	22,040	99	26	6.3	5.3

	1989 Budget Balance (percent of GDP)	1989 Growth of Broad Money Supply (percent)	1989 Consumer Price Inflation (percent)	1989 Black Market Exchange Rate Premium (percent)	1989 External Debt (percent of GDP)
Albania	−9	15	0	n.a.	n.a.
Bulgaria	−1	13	6	325	21
Czechoslovakia	−2	5	1	171	6
Hungary	−1	15	17	56	32
Poland	−8	515	251	261	25
Romania	8	5	1	779	1
Soviet Union	−10	16	7	1,195	2
Yugoslavia	1	2,347	1,240	0	34
United States	−1.7	6	5	0	n.a.

SOURCES: *Statisticheskii ezhgodnik stran-chlenov soveta ekonomicheskoi vzaimopomoshchi 1988* (Moscow: Finansy i Statistika, 1988); International Monetary Fund, *World Economic Outlook,* May 1996, 78; International Monetary Fund, *The Economy of the USSR: Summary and Recommendations* (Washington, D.C., 1990); U.S. Arms Control and Disarmament Agency, *World Military Expenditures and Arms Transfers 1989* (Washington, D.C.: USGPO, 1990); Paul Marer, et al. *Historically Planned Economies: A Guide to the Data* (Washington, D.C.: World Bank, 1992 and 1993); *Transition* (World Bank newsletter), July–August 1996, 9; and national statistical yearbooks.

With the possible exception of Yugoslavia, all countries in the region had industrial sectors that were dominated by a small number of very large firms. This was particularly true in Czechoslovakia, where enterprises with more than 1,000 workers accounted for nearly all industrial employment.[5] When the market transition commenced and price controls were lifted, large firms could attempt to exploit their monopoly power and charge exorbitant prices. To prevent or ameliorate this problem, most of the transitional nations adopted programs to regulate or dismember existing monopolies, to encourage creation of new competitive enterprises, and to allow more import competition.

The highest levels of military spending, expressed as a percentage of GDP, were found in Bulgaria, the Soviet Union, and Poland. Large defense cuts during recent years have forced these nations to undertake massive programs of military conversion, involving costly adjustments of their industrial, scientific, labor, educational, and financial sectors. Far more difficult have been the new military burdens in Bosnia, Serbia, Croatia, Georgia, Armenia, Tajikistan, and other nations that have encountered border disputes, separatist movements, and civil war. Albania, Hungary, Romania, Slovakia, and the Czech Republic started their transitions with relatively small military burdens, and have been able to proceed with relative tranquility.

Almost all countries in the region began their transitions with extremely low unemployment rates. Unfortunately, this was primarily a reflection of the cost insensitivity and overstaffing that characterized enterprises in the Soviet-style systems. Effective transition programs would force enterprises to control costs and adjust their production to meet market demand, both of which would certainly cause rising unemployment. The exception, again, was Yugoslavia, which had a long record of market-oriented behavior, and was beset with a host of problems in its labor market.

Several indicators of financial stability are included in Table 17.1. In 1989, the largest governmental budget deficits, relative to GDP, were recorded in the Soviet Union, Albania, Poland, and Romania. Poland and Yugoslavia had the highest rates of money supply growth and inflation. In all countries other than Hungary, the rate of monetary growth was substantially higher than the recorded rate of inflation, generally indicating the presence of price controls, hidden or repressed inflation, and a growing **monetary overhang** that would cause a burst of inflation when price controls were lifted.

In the external sector, Yugoslavia, Hungary, Poland, and Bulgaria started their market transitions with heavy debt burdens; Romania, the Soviet Union, and Czechoslovakia had relatively light burdens. Distortion in the foreign exchange market is usually measured by the *black market exchange rate premium*, the percentage by which the black market exchange rate exceeds the official exchange rate. By this measure, the currencies of the Soviet Union and Romania were most seriously overvalued in 1989; market distortions

---

[5]These observations, based on data for the 1980s, are remarkably similar to previous findings for the 1960s. See Frederic L. Pryor, *Property and Industrial Organization in Communist and Capitalist Nations* (Bloomington, Ind.: Indiana University Press, 1973), 187–195.

were smallest in Yugoslavia and Hungary, countries that had systems of market socialism.[6]

TRANSITION TASKS AND STRATEGIES

Although Yugoslavia and Hungary introduced important programs of market socialism during the 1960s, the first substantial program of market transition and privatization was the so-called Balcerowicz Plan, named for the finance minister who administered "shock therapy" to the Polish economy in 1990. Since that time, transition programs in the Central Eurasian countries have usually included the following tasks:

■ *Macroeconomic stabilization:* Reduce budget deficits and excessive monetary growth.

■ *Price liberalization:* Release price controls and regulations.

■ *Privatization:* Organize the sale, distribution, or restitution of ownership of large and small enterprises, land, and residential housing.

■ *Military conversion:* Reorganize and restructure factories, educational facilities, and other institutions to meet the needs of the civilian sector.

■ *Antimonopoly reform:* Dismember or regulate large public and private firms.

■ *Labor market reform:* Liberalize controls of hiring and firing, and create new information services and other institutions to increase labor market flexibility and prevent excessive unemployment.

■ *Banking reform:* Reorganize the monolithic state banking system into a two-level system of central and commercial banks and savings institutions.

■ *Financial market reform:* Create markets and regulatory structures for stocks, bonds, mutual funds, privatization vouchers, and other securities.

■ *Tax reform:* Reorganize tax systems to strengthen profit and saving motives, reduce distortions of relative prices, and strengthen collections from individuals and from a larger universe of business firms.

■ *Legal reform:* Develop safeguards to strengthen the independence of the courts and to define and enforce a new system of property rights and commercial codes.

■ *Social welfare reform:* Develop new institutions to help needy people no longer protected by systems of guaranteed unemployment, controlled prices, and equalitarian wages.

---

[6]An illegal market for foreign exchange existed in each of the Soviet-style economies because: (1) legal entry on the supply side of the market was limited by the state bank, which had an exclusive right to sell foreign currency; (2) limits on the demand side of the market were established by foreign trade planning and import licensing systems; and (3) the state bank established official rates at which foreign currency could be bought and sold legally, usually overvaluing the local currency.

- *Foreign exchange market reform*: Develop wider international convertibility of the national currency.

- *Foreign trade reform:* Dissolve state monopolies of foreign trade, liberalize trade regulation and licensing, and participate in market-oriented world trade organizations.

- *Foreign investment reform:* Liberalize and protect foreign ownership of real property and securities.

To start working on these and other specific tasks, the Central Eurasian leaders have had to address some broader issues. First, each has chosen a **strategic concept** of transition. They have decided, for example, how forcefully the government should attempt to manage the transition process, and whether their highest immediate priorities are to maintain political stability, attract international private investment, obtain support from the International Monetary Fund and other international agencies, prepare for future membership in the European Union, or develop a framework of economic and political independence.

Stemming from their strategic concepts, the leaders of the various countries have made key decisions about the **pace** of transition. Shall price controls be released in a single program of **shock therapy,** or shall they be removed in phases? Shall subsidies to unprofitable enterprises be discontinued quickly, or shall they be reduced slowly to avoid a steep rise of unemployment? Shall ownership of large enterprises be redistributed to the population with a rapid program of voucher privatization, or shall privatization be designed and implemented on a case-by-case basis?

Because market processes and institutions are interdependent, many of the tasks of transition should, in principle, be performed simultaneously. For example, foreign trade reform and price liberalization should be bundled together because: (1) expansion of foreign trade will limit the power of local monopolies, reducing the inflationary impact of price liberalization, and (2) liberalized prices will provide better guidance for rational foreign trade decisions.

Even in countries that undertake shock therapy, however, it is impossible to prepare, legislate, and implement all the elements of transition in a single stroke; the leaders of each country must assign priorities and design a strategic **sequence** of transition. A typical strategy for a country in East-Central Europe is presented in Figure 17.1. In this example, programs of macroeconomic stabilization and unemployment compensation are introduced quickly to prevent or ameliorate some of the most explosive problems of the transition—hyperinflation and mass poverty. Soon thereafter, programs of price liberalization, small-scale privatization, monopoly regulation, tax reform, and foreign market reform may be introduced. Longer periods of preparation and implementation are usually required for large-scale privatization and broad programs of military conversion, legal reform, and development of financial securities markets.

In each country, the concept, pace, sequence, and results of economic transition are influenced by national political culture, by initial economic

■ **FIGURE 17.1**

TYPICAL SEQUENCE OF ECONOMIC TRANSITION

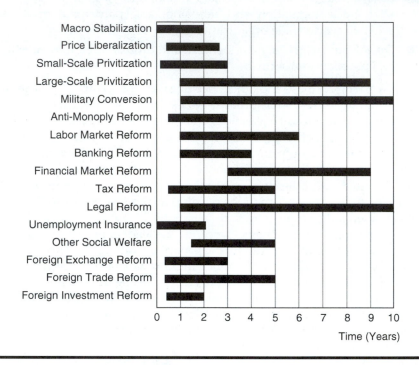

SOURCES: Adapted from Alan Gelb, "Socialist Transformations: An Overview of Eastern Europe and Some Comparators," in *Rebuilding Capitalism: Alternative Roads after Socialism and Dirigisme,* ed. Andres Solimano, Osvaldo Sunkel, and Mario I. Blejer (Ann Arbor: University of Michigan Press, 1994), 113; Marie Lavigne, *The Economics of Transition* (New York: St. Martin's Press, 1995), 122–125; and author's estimates.

conditions, and by the prospects for foreign investment and other international assistance. Transition programs seem to be more aggressive in countries that have historical experience with political democracy, that have a new generation of political leaders with little allegiance to the old Soviet-style system, that entered the transition period with low levels of financial imbalance and ethnic rivalry, and that have geographic locations, resources, and other accommodations attractive to foreign investors. The Czech Republic, for example, fits this mold extremely well, but some countries, such as the Kyrgyz Republic, have made impressive progress with fewer initial advantages (Table 17.2).[7]

---

[7]The Kyrgyz Republic does not have a long democratic tradition, but its president, Askar Akayev, is a former physics professor, preisdent of the Kyrgyz Academy of Sciences, and protege of Soviet leader Mikhail Gorbachev, rather than a member of the old Communist elite. Akayev won the presidency in 1990, and garnered 72 percent of the votes in his 1995 reelection bid against five opponents. His stated goal is to make the Kyrgyz Republic the "Switzerland of Central Asia." The country has experienced little ethnic rivalry, and its substantial gold and oil reserves have attracted foreign investors.

On the surface, it appears that countries with aggressive transition programs have experienced smaller and briefer downturns of national income than countries that have moved cautiously (Table 17.3). The nations of East-Central Europe, for example, have been among the most aggressive reformers, and they have been among the first to recover from the so-called transformational recession. However, according to statistical analysis by Laza Kekic of the Economist Intelligence Unit, it is far from certain that rapid transition programs *prevented* sharp downturns of production. Most of the variations in cross-country performance, he says, can be explained by initial conditions and capital inflows.[8] Countries with desirable initial conditions tend to undertake aggressive transition programs and they tend to perform well under almost any circumstances.

MONEY, PUBLIC FINANCE, AND PRICES

With few exceptions, the early stages of transition in Central Eurasia were associated with very high rates of price inflation (Table 17.4). According to World Bank analysts, these inflationary episodes can be divided into three stages.[9] In the first stage, when price controls were released, decades of repressed inflation and excessive monetary balances were quickly transformed into bursts of open inflation. This process began in Poland, where consumer prices lunged forward by nearly 600 percent in 1990. It spread through the states of the former Soviet Union beginning in 1992. The Czech and Slovak republics, which had traditions of fiscal discipline, and Hungary, which had little repressed inflation under its market socialist system, were the only countries in the region that avoided huge bursts of inflation.

After an initial surge of inflation, most countries entered a second stage of adjustment, spanning two or three years, when inflation rates declined to levels that were still very high, sustained by the traditional formula: too much money chasing too few goods. Rapid monetary growth and declining production were caused, in turn, by several circumstances:

■ Extension of large central bank credits to finance governmental budget deficits caused by large subsidies to state enterprises, small contributions to the budget from those same enterprises, and poor enforcement of tax collections from the new private sector.

■ Extension of highly subsidized central bank credits directly to unprofitable state enterprises. In some cases, the credits provided in these direct industry subsidies were three times larger than credits extended to finance governmental deficits.

■ Disruption caused by reorientation of production from planners' priorities to consumers' market demand.[10]

---

[8]See Laza Kekic, "Quotation of the Month," *Transition* (World Bank newsletter) 7 (July–August 1996): 9–10.

[9]World Bank, *World Development Report 1996* (Oxford: Oxford University Press, 1996), 35–41.

[10]See János Kornai, "Transformational Recession: The Main Causes," *Journal of Comparative Economics* 19 (August 1994): 39–46.

CENTRAL EURASIA IN 1995: STATUS OF TRANSITION

	1994 Population (millions)	1994-GDP per Capita (dollars at PPP)	1995 QII Unemploy-ment Rate (percent)	1995 Consumer Inflation Rate (percent)	Private Sector Share of GDP (percent)		1995 Transition Index*
					1989	1995	
Total Region	**415.7**	**3,980**	**6.6**	**205**	**11**	**50**	**24**
Former Soviet Union	**293.1**	**3,500**	**2.2**	**251**	**6**	**47**	**22**
Central Slavic Area	*210.6*	*3,960*	*2.2*	*262*	*5*	*50*	*22*
Belarus	10.4	4,220	2.4	709	5	15	19
Russia	148.3	4,480	2.8	190	5	55	23
Ukraine	51.9	2,400	0.6	376	5	35	20
Caucasus/Black Sea Area	*20.9*	*1,600*	*2.7*	*223*	*9*	*32*	*18*
Armenia	3.7	2,260	6.6	177	8	45	19
Azerbaijan	7.5	1,470	1.0	412	5	25	14
Georgia	5.4	1,460	3.4	163	18	30	18
Moldova	4.3	1,400	1.4	30	5	30	23
Baltic Area	*7.7*	*3,880*	*5.3*	*31*	*10*	*59*	*26*
Estonia	1.5	4,200	1.8	29	10	65	29
Latvia	2.5	3,360	6.3	25	10	60	24
Lithuania	3.7	4,110	6.1	40	10	55	25
Central Asian Area	*53.9*	*2,400*	*1.1*	*293*	*9*	*27*	*19*
Kazakstan	16.8	3,010	1.5	176	15	25	19
Kyrgyz Republic	4.5	1,800	1.9	53	5	40	25

Tajikistan	5.8	900	1.8	610	5	15	14
Turkmenistan	4.4	2,890	2.0	1,005	5	15	10
Uzbekistan	22.4	2,370	0.3	305	5	30	21
East-Central European Region	**64.4**	**6,110**	**12.4**	**22**	**21**	**63**	**31**
Former Czechoslovakia	*15.6*	*7,650*	*6.6*	*9*	*11*	*67*	*30*
Czech Republic	10.3	9,770	2.9	9	11	70	31
Slovak Republic	5.3	3,610	13.8	10	10	60	29
Hungary	10.3	6,410	10.6	28	15	60	31
Poland	38.5	5,400	15.2	28	29	60	30
Balkan Region	**58.2**	**4,030**	**22.2**	**48**	**15**	**42**	**24**
Albania	3.2	2,760	13.0	8	5	60	21
Bulgaria	8.4	4,480	11.1	62	15	45	23
Romania	22.7	4,360	9.9	32	13	40	22
Former Yugoslavia	*23.9*	*3,740*	*39.0*	*55*	*18*	*41*	*26*
Bosnia/Herzegovina	4.4	1,500	50.0	10	—	—	—
Croatia	4.8	3,650	17.6	2	15	45	25
Macedonia	2.1	3,520	37.2	16	10	40	22
Serbia/Montenegro	10.6	3,600	50.0	120	13	35	—
Slovenia	2.0	9,800	14.0	13	37	45	28

*Sum of scores in nine areas of transition, including large-scale and small-scale privatization, price liberalization, and reforms of competition policy, foreign trade, banking, securities markets, and legal institutions. In each area, the EBRD assigns a score between one (little progress) and four (standards similar to advanced market economies). Thus, the highest possible score is 36. Regional averages of inflation, private sector shares, and transition indexes are weighted by GDP; average unemployment rates are weighted by population.

SOURCES: European Bank for Reconstruction and Development, *Transition Report 1995*; OECD Center for Cooperation with Economies in Transition, *Short-Term Indicators for Transition Economies*, No. 4, 1996; World Bank, *World Development Report 1997*; International Monetary Fund, *World Economic Outlook*, May 1997; press releases of national statistical offices; and author's estimates.

■ TABLE 17.3

CENTRAL EURASIA:INDEXES OF
REAL GDP, 1989–1996

	1989	1990	1991	1992	1993	1994	1995	1996
Total Region	**100.0**	**96.2**	**85.7**	**73.2**	**66.5**	**60.0**	**58.5**	**58.2**
Former Soviet Union	**100.0**	**97.0**	**86.2**	**70.9**	**62.3**	**53.2**	**50.2**	**48.8**
Central Slavic Area	*100.0*	*96.9*	*85.5*	*70.6*	*61.9*	*52.8*	*49.6*	*47.7*
Belarus	100.0	98.0	97.0	87.5	79.2	63.4	56.9	58.1
Russia	100.0	97.0	84.6	68.3	60.1	52.5	50.4	49.0
Ukraine	100.0	96.4	85.2	73.5	63.1	51.1	45.0	40.5
Caucasus/Black Sea Area	*100.0*	*81.9*	*53.8*	*44.1*	*35.9*	*35.5*	*34.7*	*35.3*
Armenia	100.0	94.5	86.2	41.1	35.0	37.0	39.6	42.2
Azerbaijan	100.0	88.3	87.7	67.9	52.2	40.7	36.2	36.7
Georgia	100.0	84.9	67.8	37.4	27.9	24.7	25.3	27.9
Moldova	100.0	98.6	80.1	57.5	54.7	38.3	37.2	34.2
Baltic Area	*100.0*	*95.7*	*88.6*	*59.2*	*48.8*	*49.0*	*49.9*	*54.1*
Estonia	100.0	91.9	82.7	71.0	65.5	63.4	65.4	67.5
Latvia	100.0	102.7	92.0	59.9	51.0	52.1	52.3	53.6
Lithuania	100.0	93.1	80.9	49.1	35.8	36.1	37.2	38.5
Central Asian Area	*100.0*	*98.8*	*92.5*	*80.6*	*73.5*	*62.5*	*59.7*	*60.3*
Kazakstan	100.0	99.0	87.4	76.0	66.2	49.6	45.2	45.6
Kyrgyz Republic	100.0	104.8	100.4	83.9	70.1	52.6	23.3	56.3
Tajikistan	100.0	100.2	91.7	63.3	52.4	46.1	40.3	37.5
Turkmenistan	100.0	101.8	97.0	91.9	82.7	67.1	61.6	59.8
Uzbekistan	100.0	99.3	98.8	87.8	85.7	82.3	81.6	882.9
East-Central European Region	**100.0**	**92.8**	**82.3**	**83.1**	**83.5**	**86.9**	**91.6**	**95.9**
Former Czechoslovakia	*100.0*	*98.4*	*84.3*	*78.7*	*77.2*	*79.7*	*84.0*	*88.2*
Czech Republic	100.0	98.8	84.7	79.2	78.5	80.5	84.4	87.9
Slovak Republic	100.0	97.5	83.3	77.5	74.3	77.9	83.2	89.0
Hungary	100.0	96.5	85.0	82.4	81.8	84.1	85.4	86.2
Poland	100.0	88.4	82.2	84.4	87.5	91.9	97.9	103.3
Balkan Region	**100.0**	**92.7**	**80.6**	**70.7**	**68.5**	**70.7**	**73.9**	**75.3**
Albania	100.0	90.0	65.1	58.8	65.2	71.3	77.7	84.0
Bulgaria	100.0	90.9	80.2	74.4	72.6	73.6	75.5	68.7
Romania	100.0	94.4	82.2	74.0	75.0	77.7	83.2	86.6
Former Yugoslavia	*100.0*	*92.5*	*80.2*	*67.6*	*62.8*	*65.0*	*67.0*	*69.8*
Bosnia/Herzegovina	100.0							
Croatia	100.0	91.5	72.3	65.3	62.9	63.4	64.4	67.6

Continued

	1989	1990	1991	1992	1993	1994	1995	1996
Macedonia	100.0	89.8	78.9	68.4	58.7	54.5	53.7	54.3
Serbia/Montenegro	100.0	91.6	81.3	60.0	51.0	54.2	56.3	59.1
Slovenia	100.0	91.9	84.5	79.9	80.9	84.9	88.2	91.3

NOTE: Regional averages are weighted by the distribution of GDP in dollars at purchasing power parity in 1994.

SOURCES: U.N. Economic Commission for Europe, *Economic Bulletin for Europe* 47, 1995; International Monetary Fund, *World Economic Outlook*, May 1997; press accounts, and author's estimates and calculations.

■ Disruption of demand and supply caused by disintegration of political, monetary, and trade relations among the new Central Eurasian states.

To reverse these processes, most of the national governments introduced measures during the early 1990s to reduce subsidies and other expenditures, to strengthen tax collections, and to avoid inflationary financing of budget deficits. Of 26 countries in the region, only 7 failed to significantly reduce their budget deficits, relative to GDP, between 1992 and 1995.[11] In Russia, for example, the deficit was reduced from 19 percent of GDP in 1992 to 5 percent in 1995, and then to 4 percent during the first 7 months of 1996.[12] A key feature of the 1996 Russian budget was a commitment to finance nearly two-thirds of the deficit (roughly equivalent to $10 billion) by selling treasury securities to the general public, rather than by requiring the central bank to issue new money.[13]

In several countries, the fight against inflation included a strict **incomes policy,** designed to prevent a cost-push spiral of rising wages and prices. This was considered necessary during the early stages of transition, before significant privatization of industry, because managers of state enterprises had little incentive to resist excessive wage increases, and many sectors of the economy were already unprofitable. In Poland and Hungary, taxes were imposed on excessive wage increases. In the Czech and Slovak republics, real wage reductions were fixed by agreements among government officials, employers, and union leaders.[14] Studies have demonstrated that methods such

---

[11]These seven were Azerbaijan, Belarus, Hungary, Latvia, Lithuania, Slovenia, and Turkmenistan. See International Monetary Fund, *World Economic Outlook,* May 1996, 78; and *Vprosy ekonomiki,* 1996, No. 2, 71.

[12]*OMRI Daily Digest,* September 10 1996.

[13]Russian Economic Monitor," *PlanEcon Report,* May 20, 1996, 23.

[14] Lavigne, *The Economics of Transition,* 114.

CENTRAL EURASIA: CONSUMER PRICE INFLATION, 1991-1996

	1991	1992	1993	1994	1995	1996
Total Region	**101**	**802**	**1,002**	**940**	**205**	**53**
Former Soviet Union	**96**	**1,225**	**1,540**	**1,459**	**251**	**61**
Central Slavic Area	*92*	*1,311*	*1,525*	*492*	*262*	*55*
Belarus	84	969	1,188	2,220	709	52
Russia	93	1,353	896	302	190	48
Ukraine	91	1,210	4,735	891	376	80
Caucasus/Black Sea Area	*110*	*963*	*2,136*	*5,560*	*223*	*27*
Armenia	100	825	3,732	5,273	177	19
Azerbaijan	106	913	1,130	1,664	412	20
Georgia	79	887	3,125	15,606	163	40
Moldova	162	1,276	789	330	30	24
Baltic Area	*191*	*1,012*	*239*	*55*	*33*	*23*
Estonia	211	1,069	89	48	29	23
Latvia	124	951	109	35	25	19
Lithuania	225	1,021	410	72	40	25
Central Asian Area	*93*	*758*	*1,817*	*7,394*	*293*	*130*
Kazakstan	79	887	3,125	17,272	176	39
Kyrgyz Republic	85	855	1,209	278	53	30
Tajikistan	112	1,157	2,195	350	610	443
Turkmenistan	103	493	3,102	1,748	1,005	992
Uzbekistan	105	645	534	1,568	305	54
East-Central European Region	**61**	**30**	**29**	**23**	**22**	**17**
Former Czechoslovakia	*59*	*11*	*22*	*11*	*9*	*8*
Czech Republic	59	11	21	10	9	9
Slovak Republic	59	11	23	13	10	6
Hungary	34	23	23	19	28	24
Poland	70	43	35	32	28	20
Balkan Region*	**200**	**176**	**196**	**119**	**48**	**57**
Albania	36	225	85	23	8	163
Bulgaria	334	82	73	96	62	123
Romania	161	210	256	137	32	39
Former Yugoslavia	*170*	*8,999*	*2.6×10[a]*	*131*	*55*	*4610*
Bosnia/Herzegovina	—	—	—	—	—	—
Croatia	250	938	1516	98	2	4
Macedonia	230	1,925	335	123	16	3
Serbia/Montenegro	117	19,810	6×10[a]	200	120	100
Slovenia	118	201	32	20	13	10

*Excluding former Yugoslavia. Regional averages are weighted by GDP.

SOURCES: See sources for Table 17.3.

as these cannot substitute for fiscal and monetary restraint, but they can play a useful supporting role.

In their programs of financial stabilization, a number of countries, including Croatia, the Czech and Slovak republics, Estonia, Hungary, and Poland, introduced **fixed exchange rates** between their currencies and the dollar, mark, European Currency Unit, or some other strong anchor. These policies frequently contributed to rapid reductions of inflation rates by imposing additional discipline on central banks and by making their policies more credible and predictable. On the other hand, a fixed exchange rate could also cause a massive overvaluation or undervaluation of a nation's currency during a time of financial instability, with undesired consequences for the international balance of payments. Hence, some countries have found it beneficial to allow more exchange rate flexibility after the initial program of stabilization.[15]

According to World Bank researchers, reduction of inflation to moderate levels (around 40 percent per year) is unambiguously beneficial to economic growth. Most of the Central Eurasian countries, though, have progressed to a third stage of inflation reduction whose benefits are less certain. On the positive side of the ledger, a country that undertakes additional stabilization may inspire confidence in its currency, relieve the fears of its citizens, and strengthen its applications for support from and membership in the European Union, International Monetary Fund, World Bank, and other international organizations.[16] On the negative side, additional reductions of inflation may reduce the flexibility of relative prices.[17] This may hinder the performance of transitional economies that are experiencing major adjustments in the structure of production, requiring large adjustments of relative prices, and where price reform is still incomplete.

PRIVATIZATION

A defining characteristic of the socialist economic system is social ownership of the means of production. Hence, if price liberalization signaled the end of traditional central planning, extensive privatization signaled the end of traditional socialism. Like other components of the transition project, programs of privatization have differed markedly between countries in their underlying objectives, structure, sequence, pace, and depth.

---

[15]World Bank, *World Development Report 1996*, 39; and Thomas D. Willett and Fahim Al-Marhubi, "Currency Policies for Inflation Control in the Former Centrally Planned Economies," *The World Economy* 17 (November 1994): 795–815.

[16]In a poll administered throughout Russia in 1996, 73 percent of respondents listed inflation on their top-ten list of worries, ahead of crime (63 percent), unemployment (51 percent), or any other cause of fear. See the findings of Richard Rose of the University of Strathclyde reported in Leon Aron, "Will Communism Rise Again?" *The American Enterprise*, July–August 1996, 55–57.

[17]Because nominal prices (prices measured in money) tend to be inflexible downward, a moderate rate of inflation seems to improve relative price (the price of one product relative to the prices of other products) flexibility. See Paula De Masi and Vincent Coen, "Relative Price Convergence in Russia," *IMF Staff Papers* 43 (March 1996): 97–121.

OBJECTIVES OF PRIVATIZATION

Perhaps the most fundamental objective of privatization is to raise **efficiency** by strengthening the independence and responsibility of enterprise managers. Relieved of direct governmental controls and deprived of automatic subsidies, enterprises are allowed and required to operate efficiently, to respond to consumer demand, and to withstand excessive wage increases.[18] This objective can, of course, be undermined if the government continues to impose excessive regulations and provide large subsidies to the new private sector. Market discipline and consumer sovereignty may also be undermined if the new enterprises have excessive monopoly power.

A second objective of many privatization programs is to improve the access of each enterprise to needed **skills** and **capital**. Removed from political control, enterprises may select and reward officials for their skills and performance, rather than their personal connections or partisan loyalties. If foreign investors and managers are permitted to participate in privatization, they may be able to provide new technologies, methods of management, capital investments, and connections to new markets.

A third objective of privatization is **budgetary**—to reduce public expenditures for subsidies and economic administration, and to collect public revenues from property sales. As we shall note below, the amount of revenue collected is highly dependent on the specific method of privatization. In principle, however, it is risky and improper for governments to make a habit of financing their annual operations with revenues from self-limiting asset sales.

Fourth, privatization programs are usually affected by considerations of **social justice**. If a factory is to be held privately, who should own it? Should it be returned to family members of the pre-Communist owners, or should it be sold to the highest bidder? Perhaps a share of ownership should be given to each worker employed in the factory, or perhaps the shares of ownership should be distributed to a larger segment of the population.

Finally, other things equal, a privatization method is preferable if it can be implemented with **simplicity** and **speed**. A typical Central Eurasian country must privatize thousands of enterprises with scarce administrative and legal talent; this is a big and costly project that can delay implementation of other transition programs.

As one would expect, these objectives can interact and conflict with one another. The privatization method that seems most socially just, for example, may not generate a lot of revenue for the treasury, and it may not be simple to implement. A method that provides revenue to the government may provide little investment capital to needy enterprises.

METHODS OF PRIVATIZATION

Because their political, economic, legal, and financial conditions are not the same, and because they have a variety of objectives and priorities, each of the Central Eurasian nations has employed a different mixture of methods to

---

[18]For a general and elegant analysis of this issue, see Maxim Boycko, Andrei Shleifer, and Robert W. Vishny, "A Theory of Privatization," *The Economic Journal* 106 (March 1996): 309–319.

privatize existing enterprises and to encourage the creation of new firms in the private sector.

A practical and legal distinction is usually drawn between **small privatization,** involving the transfer of small shops, restaurants, trucks, and other service companies, and **large privatization,** involving the transfer of enterprises too valuable to be purchased by a family or small group of individuals. Generally, the small privatizations were accomplished much more quickly and easily than the large. Small-company assets were relatively easy to value, capital requirements were relatively small, political considerations (unemployment, subsidies, environmental problems) were limited, and the transactions could sometimes be handled by local governments. In Russia, small firms usually were sold to their managers or employees; in Central and Eastern Europe, more of the firms were sold in public auctions.

A distinction is also made between **managed privatization,** which is initiated, audited, and regulated by a state property agency, and **spontaneous privatization,** which is initiated and undertaken by the managers and employees of a state enterprise. In some Central Eurasian countries, the governments established legal procedures for spontaneous privatization. In Hungary, for example, a privatization statute was adopted in 1988, two years before the formation of the State Property Agency. Under the law, managers of a state enterprise could take initiative to appraise company assets, identify an outside investor who would assume at least 20 percent of ownership, conduct the sale, and remit 80 percent of the proceeds to the government for reduction of public debt. Under these rules, about 15,000 limited liability corporations were created in Hungary between 1988 and 1990, including many with foreign participation.[19]

Despite their legality, spontaneous privatizations were unpopular in Hungary because they were controlled by enterprise managers—members of the old Communist elite—with little regulation.[20] A firmer regulatory structure was created in March 1990, when the Hungarian State Property Agency was established, but enterprise managers continued to initiate and organize most of the privatizations. In Poland and Czechoslovakia, the anti-Communist governments that gained power in 1989 adopted stricter policies against the old elite. Spontaneous privatizations were forbidden, and institutions were created during 1990 and 1991 to organize and regulate the transfer of ownership.[21]

---

[19]Organization for Economic Cooperation and Development, *OECD Economic Surveys: Hungary 1991* (Paris, 1991), 109–114.

[20]Péter Mihályi argues that spontaneous privatization was necessary, even if it benefited the old managerial elite, because: (1) independent specialists with technical and commercial competence were scarce, and (2) studies have shown that claims of exploitation and individual enrichment were "grossly overstated." See his "Hungary: A Unique Approach to Privatization—Past, Present, and Future," in *Hungary: An Economy in Transition,* ed. István P. Székely and David M. G. Newbery, (Cambridge: Cambridge University Press, 1993), 103–104.

[21]See Kálmán Mizsei, "Privatization in Eastern Europe: A Comparative Study of Poland and Hungary," *Soviet Studies* 44 (1992): 283–296; and Dennis Rondinelli, "Developing Private Enterprise in the Czech and Slovak Federal Republic," *Columbia Journal of World Business* (Fall 1991): 26–36.

In other Central Eurasian countries, the early stages of privatization were more chaotic. Political systems were disintegrating, and spontaneous privatization proceeded with little or no legal framework. Russian president Boris Yeltsin described the situation in late 1991:

> For impermissibly long, we have discussed whether private property is necessary. In the meantime, the party-state elite has actively been engaged in their personal privatization. The scale, the enterprise, and the hypocrisy are staggering. The privatization of Russia has gone on [for a long time], but wildly, spontaneously, and often on a criminal basis. Today, it is necessary to grasp the initiative, and we are intent on doing so.[22]

Soon after these words were spoken, state property agencies were established in most of the Central Eurasian countries, and strategies were devised for programs of managed privatization. These programs have taken many forms.

Initially, officials in several countries, including the Czech and Slovak republics, Bulgaria, Romania, Slovenia, and the Baltic states, attempted to handle a portion of privatization by **restitution**. That is, they attempted to return property to pre-Communist owners. Unlike spontaneous privatization, which seemed to reward the old Communist *nomenklatura,* restitution represented an attempt to reverse the errors of the Communist era. On practical grounds, however, a spontaneous program could be undertaken much more quickly and simply than a program of restitution.

In a program of restitution, how should former owners be located and identified, and what evidence of previous ownership should be required? Should property be restored only if it was taken by a Communist regime? What if it was taken by the Nazis? If the former owner is not living, how should the estate be divided? If new buildings have been constructed on land that was formerly barren, does their ownership transfer to the estate without compensation? If ownership of an apartment building is transferred by restitution, what legal rights should be accorded to existing tenants? Should institutions, including churches, be able to regain large holdings of land and other property?

In countries that have grappled with restitution, these difficult issues have contributed to social tension, have burdened the judicial systems, and have caused interruptions and delays in privatization programs. In the three Baltic states, which have a combined population of 8 million people, about 1 million have filed claims for urban and rural land. In former Czechoslovakia, about 100,000 properties were returned to their previous owners during 1992. In Romania, restitution led to the creation of about 2.4 million private farms. In Estonia, about 10 percent of nonagricultural privatizations have been handled by direct restitution.[23] Some countries, including Hungary and Croatia,

---

[22]Boris Yeltsin, quoted in Andres Aslund, *How Russia Became a Market Economy* (Washington, D.C.: The Brookings Institution, 1995). 228.

[23]World Bank, *World Development Report 1996,* 53 and 59.

have chosen to avoid the complexities of in-kind restitution by compensating former property owners with cash, vouchers, or other financial instruments.[24]

Perhaps the boldest programs of property transfer in Central Eurasia have been the **equal-access voucher privatizations,** which have made it possible for a country to privatize hundreds of large enterprises in a short period of time and to distribute their ownership to a large proportion of the national population. This was the predominant method of large privatization in former Czechoslovakia and Lithuania, but it has also been used in Russia, Kazakstan, Poland, Romania, and a growing list of other countries (see "Voucher Privatizations in the Czech Republic," pp. 550).

Voucher programs are usually popular with voters, who receive their "fair" share of ownership of the nation's wealth, and they can prevent some of the backroom bargaining and influence peddling that damages the legitimacy of other methods. They can also contribute to the growth of national securities markets and other financial institutions. According to their critics, however, these are giant "giveaway programs" that contribute nothing to the managerial efficiency of the affected enterprises, nothing to the nation's stock of investable capital, and nothing to the governmental budget.

Another politically popular program of privatization is a **management-employee takeover,** effected by a state giveaway or a preferential sale. "Inside" privatizations of this kind are supported by some on grounds of social justice—the enterprise becomes the property of the people who "built" it, and they have the potential advantage or disadvantage (depending on your point of view) of strengthening the role of employees in management and control.[25] Otherwise, like a broader voucher program, they promise little contribution of managerial efficiency, investment resources, or budget revenue. Croatia, Georgia, Poland, Romania, Russia, and Slovenia have relied heavily on management-employee buyouts in the large privatization programs.

If the objective of the privatization program is to attract revenue, capital, and managerial talent, the quickest and simplest procedure is to hold an open **auction** for each enterprise. The auction may involve the actual sale of the enterprise, or it may set the rental rate for a long-term lease.[26] Depending on political and national security considerations, the auction may or may not include foreign investors.

In Hungary, the Czech Republic, and many other countries, small privatization programs were handled predominantly by auction. The method is often impractical for a large privatization because a pool of qualified and independent bidders cannot be assembled. Furthermore, an open auction

---

[24]In October 1996, for example, the Croatian House of Representatives enacted a bill to compensate 25,000 of its citizens for property seized by the Yugoslav state between 1945 and 1991. See Foreign Broadcast Information Service, *Eastern Europe: Daily Report,* October 11, 1996.

[25]For a discussion of these issues, see Stephen C. Smith, "On the Law and Economics of Employee Ownership in Privatization in Developing and Transition Economies," *Annals of Public and Cooperative Economics* 65 (1994): 437–468.

[26]In the small privatization program of former Czechoslovakia, for example, about 21,000 auctions were held in 1991, but property was actually sold in only one-quarter of these cases. See Marko Simonetti, "A Comparative Review of Privatization Strategies in Four Former Socialist Countries," *Europe-Asia Studies* 45 (1993): 79–102.

VOUCHER PRIVATIZATIONS IN THE CZECH REPUBLIC

"Privatize as quickly as possible." This was the slogan and the central principle of economic reform demanded by Vaclav Klaus, who became the finance minister of Czechoslovakia in 1990 and prime minister in 1992. On July 1, 1996, Klaus declared victory and closed the Privatization Ministry, which had substantially completed its work.

Much credit for the rapid completion of Czech privatization is due to an innovative voucher distribution system, first proposed by Jan Svejnar, a Czech-American economist, developed by Dusan Triska, a long-time Klaus associate, and implemented by Tomas Jezek, the first Privatization Minister. According to its authors, the voucher program was inspired by Milton Friedman's proposals during the 1960s for a school voucher system in the United States, and by privatization programs undertaken in Canada and Chile.

Czech privatization also was accelerated by Klaus's decision to privatize enterprises without first restructuring them. In many other countries, government agencies prepared firms for sale by closing unprofitable units and reorganizing management. Klaus decided that issues such as these could best be resolved by the new owners.

The first wave of voucher privatization was implemented in 1992, when Czechoslovakia was still a single country. Any citizen over 18 could purchase and register a book of ten 100-point vouchers for 1,035 crown—roughly one week's average wage. A list of firms whose shares could be purchased for vouchers was made available to the public. A total of 1,491 corporations were included in the first wave, of which 988 were in the Czech Republic. The most popular investments, with prices sometimes rising as high as 800 points per share, were in hotels, breweries, banks, and glass factories. The prices of the least popular firms were as low as 90 shares for 100 points.

The second wave of privatization took place in the Czech Republic between October 1993 and December 1994. The offer comprised property in 861 corporations, including 184 companies that were offering shares left from the first wave. Only 30 percent of the property included in the second wave was handled by coupon privatization; the remainder was privatized by individual tender.

Individuals could participate directly in competitive bidding if they wished, but about 70 percent of the Czechs entrusted the management of their vouchers to one of 400 new investment companies. The nine largest funds, which gained control of nearly half the vouchers, were founded by and associated with the largest banks in the country. According to critics of the Czech system, the firms have not been fully privatized or restructured because they are controlled by the investment companies, which are controlled by the banks, which are still effectively controlled by the state. According to its supporters, the Czech system

Continued

CONTINUED

has supported rapid privatization, rapid growth of the stock market, broad participation of the public in ownership, and financial stability. Its imitation throughout Central Eurasia is the sincerest form of flattery.

SOURCES: Jan Svejnar, "A Framework for the Economic Transformation of Czechoslovakia," *PlanEcon Report*, December 29, 1989, 7–9; Barry D. Wood, "Privatization in the Czech Republic and Slovakia," *International Economic Insights*, March/April 1993, 47–48; Cheryl W. Gray, "In Search of Owners: Privatization and Corporate Governance in Transition Economies," *The World Bank Research Observer* 11 (August 1996): 179–197; "Privatization in Former Socialist Countries: The Revolution Continues," *Moscow News*, September 19, 1996, 1; Jaroslav Veis, "Czech Republic Grows by Giving Away," *WorldPaper*, September 1996, 1.

may be inappropriate if it is unclear that a company should be owned and managed by the highest bidder. What should be done if the highest bidder is a direct competitor, and the sale would create a monopoly? Should special limitations, concessions, or incentives be applied to foreign investors, employees of the affected enterprise, war veterans, or any other group?

When an enterprise is too large to sell in an open auction, a large share of ownership may be sold to one or more **strategic investors** participating in a closed-bid tender offer. This, we noted in Chapter 11, was the method employed on a massive scale by the agency Treuhandanstalt in Germany, but it also has been the predominant method of large privatization in Hungary and Estonia. The state property agency that selects a winning tender offer can take a wide range of criteria into account, including sale price, market structure, quality of managerial personnel, investment resources, intended maintenance of employment, and so on. On the other hand, the lack of transparency in this process can cause real or imagined graft and corruption with grave political consequences.[27]

Finally, most of Russia's large privatization in 1995 was handled through a complex and controversial **loans for shares program**. This program grew out of the Yeltsin administration's desire to raise revenue for the budget and to reduce the power of the "red barons" (Soviet-era directors still running large enterprises) by selling federal share holdings in the energy, mineral, and aircraft industries. The Communist-dominated parliament would not approve the sales. Thus, instead of formally selling the shares, the administration offered them to Russian banks as collateral on loans. Control over each block of shares was transferred to the bank that offered the largest loan in a closed tender auction.[28] After an agreed period of time, if the government failed to repay the loans (which was probable), the bank would be able

[27]In 1996, for example, a series of scandals in Hungary led to suspension of the privatization program, dismissal of the Industry and Trade Minister, and destablization of the entire government. See Kyle Pope, "Hungary's Privatization Czar Is Unloaded," *The Wall Street Journal*, October 21, 1996, A19.

[28]For example, in the first two auctions, Euroresursy won 15 percent of the shares of Nafta Moskva by offering a $35 million loan, and Oneksimbank gained 38 percent of Norilsk Nickel with a $170 million loan. See ITAR-TASS, November 17, 1995.

to sell its collateral shares; if the proceeds of the sale exceeded the debt, the surplus would be divided between the bank and the government.

Loans-for-shares auctions provided about 3.6 trillion rubles ($8 billion) of credit to the Russian government at the end of 1995, but several of the transactions remain under litigation.[29] Thus, if we recall the objectives of privatization, this method can generate large sums of revenue, but it rates poorly on grounds of simplicity and transparency. It may contribute to managerial efficiency by breaking the excessive power of the red barons, but it transfers much of that power to another group that has little legitimacy with the general public—the directors of large banks.

RESULTS OF PRIVATIZATION

We have noted wide variations between the objects and methods of privatization in the nations of Central Eurasia. According to data presented in Table 17.2, there are also wide variations in the outcomes of privatization programs. For the region as a whole, the private sector share of GDP increased from 11 percent in 1989 to 50 percent in 1995. The most aggressive programs were undertaken in East-Central Europe, the Baltic states, Russia, and Albania. Least aggressive were Belarus, Tajikistan, and Turkmenistan.

What has been the deeper significance of these privatization programs? It is too early to answer this question definitively, but a few points are clear. First, on a macroeconomic level, the privatization programs have provided temporary revenues for governments during critical stages of transition, and have distanced governments from money-losing enterprises, allowing them to reduce budgetary subsidies. In Bulgaria, the Czech Republic, Hungary, and Poland, the share of subsidies in GDP declined from an average of 16 percent in 1989 to 3 percent in 1994.[30]

On a microeconomic level, it is not yet clear that privatization programs have made major contributions to the efficiency of enterprise operations in Central Eurasia. Evidence of efficiency gains is strongest for small retail trade and service enterprises that have simple systems of ownership and governance.[31] However, even in small enterprises, efficiency gains tend to be small when a new private company is left in the hands of an old Soviet-era manager. A recent study of managerial practices in 452 small shops in seven Russian cities found that "restructuring requires new people who have new skills more suitable to a market economy." About 30 percent of the shops in the study were, in fact, transferred to new owners and managers. When privatization only served to strengthen the property rights of existing managers, this was not found "particularly effective in bringing about significant change."[32]

---

[29]See "Russia Reports Greater Revenue from Privatization in 1995," British Broadcasting Corporation, February 8, 1996.

[30]International Monetary Fund, *World Economic Outlook*, May 1996, 81.

[31]Daniel Gros and Alfred Steinherr, *Winds of Change: Economic Transition in Central and Eastern Europe* (New York: Longman, 1995), 285–287.

[32]Nicholas Barberis, Maxim Boycko, Andrei Shleifer, and Natalia Tsukanova, "How Does Privatization Work? Evidence from the Russian Shops," *Journal of Political Economy* 104 (August 1996): 788.

The impact of large privatizations on microeconomic efficiency is even more ambiguous. When ownership of an enterprise is given or sold to "insiders" (workers and managers), the change in performance usually is very small. When ownership is transferred to the general population through a voucher program, old enterprise directors are frequently able to exercise effective control and make few changes.

The results of privatization are sometimes dramatic, however, when foreign investors are willing and able to participate. In 1991, for example, a Polish lighting company was purchased by a Dutch businessman. The new owner invested heavily in training and new equipment. After three years, the company reportedly was able to maintain employment at about 3,000 persons, raise its salaries by about 10 percent each year, reduce its prices by about 25 percent, double its sales, reduce environmental emissions, and move from losses to profits.[33]

BANKING AND FINANCE

In Chapter 15, we noted that monetary and financial criteria played a very limited role in Soviet-style central planning. When possible, output targets were formulated in physical, rather than monetary, units. Enterprises were rewarded for fulfilling output targets, not for earning profits. Capital investments were selected by central planners and engineers to support production priorities, not by producers and their bankers to seek high rates of financial return. Products were chosen for import or export based on domestic shortages and surpluses, not on domestic and international costs of production.

For these reasons, and because there was little need for a capital market when most enterprises were owned by the state, financial institutions were few in number and limited in strength during the central planning era. A monolithic state banking system existed to facilitate and monitor planned transactions between enterprises, but it had little independent authority to extend credit to enterprises, played no significant role in investment decision making, offered few services to the general public, and had no provision for competition between independent banks.

In Chapter 16, we noted that modifications of the Soviet-style financial system were undertaken in some Central Eurasian countries during the era of socialist reform. In Yugoslavia, the National Bank lost its monopoly status when communal banks were formed in 1954; a **two-level banking system** was created in 1961, confining the National Bank to central banking operations and entrusting commercial operations to communal and specialized banks. Similar reforms began in Hungary in 1986 and in Poland and the Soviet Union in 1987. Still, these administrative reforms had little effect on the banks' behavior.

During their early stages of market transition, Central Eurasian countries struggled with a long list of financial challenges. Independent currencies were introduced in nations emerging from the former Soviet Union, former

---

[33]World Bank, *World Development Report 1996*, 63–64.

Czechoslovakia, and former Yugoslavia. Countries throughout the region attempted to stabilize their currencies and make them internationally convertible. In most countries, central bankers gained legal authority to conduct their monetary policies free of domestic political interference, and evidence suggests that the central banks had substantial autonomy in some countries. In 1994, for example, the Bulgarian central bank was able to force the government to finance more of its deficit by borrowing from the public, rather than by expanding the money supply.[34]

To alleviate shortages of market-oriented banking services, authorities in several countries placed few restrictions on creation of new commercial banks. Also, with help from international agencies, professional organizations, and universities, hundreds of programs have been organized to teach banking skills unknown in planned economies: risk evaluation, property appraisal, project selection, cash management, credit and debit card transactions, savings instruments, and so on. In the Czech Republic, employment in banking increased from 8,000 in 1991 to 55,000 at the end of 1994.[35] In Russia, the number of commercial banks increased from 5 in 1989 to 1,500 in 1992 and 2,500 in 1995.[36] Within strict limits, most countries also have allowed foreign banks to establish representative offices and to provide selected services, particularly to their national clients.

In most countries, rapid growth of the banking sector has provided a wider array of needed services, but it has also contributed to the weakness and instability of the financial system. Throughout the region, a large proportion of the banks are undercapitalized and poorly managed. Operating in unstable economies with poorly diversified portfolios, many of the banks are carrying large volumes of nonperforming loans. In Russia, one third of the banks reported losses in 1995.

To reduce the number of weak banks, many Central Eurasian countries are now tightening their regulatory structures. Authorities are setting higher auditing and reporting standards, are examining applications for new bank charters more carefully, are requiring banks to tighten their lending standards, and, in some cases, are encouraging bank mergers to raise efficiency and to dilute losses. In some countries, including Armenia, Hungary, and Kyrgyzstan, domestic banks may also seek funds from foreign investors.

When all else fails, the authorities frequently have resorted to debt forgiveness, recapitalization, and other methods to "bail out" troubled banks. Used sparingly in concert with other regulatory measures, a recapitalization may contribute to stabilization of the financial system. Otherwise, it may permit continuation of irresponsible behavior. In Hungary, some banks have been recapitalized as many as five times.

The financial systems of the Central Eurasian countries continue to be dominated by the major banks, but a variety of other financial institutions

---

[34]European Bank for Reconstruction and Development, *Transition Report 1995* (London, 1995), 37. Also, see "Central Banking Reforms in Baltic and CIS Countries," *IMF Survey*, July 29, 1996, 249–250.

[35]European Bank for Reconstruction and Development, *Transition Report 1995*, 4.

[36]World Bank, *World Development Report 1996*, 100.

are developing in the region. Securities markets were established in Slovenia in 1989, in Hungary in 1990, in Poland in 1991, and in most other countries since 1992. Typically, these exchanges are very small by Western standards; they handle trading in treasury securities and over-the-counter transactions in small collections of stocks and bonds. The major exception to this rule is the Prague exchange, where shares are traded in more than 1,750 Czech companies. The market value of traded shares, taken as a percentage of GDP, is actually larger in the Czech Republic than in France.[37]

In most countries, investment companies have been established at the retail level, offering shares in diversified mutual investments. The investment companies have provided a convenient hedge against inflation for members of the general population and, particularly in countries that have undertaken voucher privatization programs, have provided for diversification of investment. Unfortunately, the reputations of these companies, and the image of the entire transition program, have been tainted by several high-profile instances of fraud (see "Sergei Mavrodi: The Perils of Russian Capitalism," p. 556).

In several countries, the financial systems also have been distorted by so-called **nonpayments crises**. When enterprises are unable to meet their financial obligations, they simply withhold payments for long periods of time. In mid-1996, for example, Russian enterprises owed about 200 trillion rubles ($38 billion) to their industrial suppliers, 86 trillion rubles ($16 billion) to the government budget, 62 trillion rubles ($12 billion) to pensions and other nonbudgetary funds, 33 trillion rubles ($7 billion) to their employees, and 18 trillion rubles ($3 billion) to commercial banks.[38] Tax arrears range from 1.1 percent of GDP in Turkmenistan to 7.5 percent of GDP in Hungary.

The nonpayments problem is a natural outcome of a system in which enterprises are unable to pay their bills, bankruptcy procedures are poorly developed, and workers and suppliers are willing to support production in the hope of future payment. It causes problems for workers who sometimes must live for months without regular payment of wages, and for governments attempting to reduce their budget deficits. It exerts pressure on the central bank to support economic growth by bailing out debtors with an inflationary expansion of the money supply.[39]

Nonpayments can also interfere with plans for privatization and attraction of foreign investment. In 1996, when the Russian government was ready to offer shares of its largest company, Gazprom, on the international market, the deal was temporarily threatened because regional governments were able to freeze the bank accounts of some Gazprom subsidiaries. The chairman of the natural gas monopoly, Rem Vyakhirev, acknowledged that the company owed 15 trillion rubles ($2.8 billion) in federal and local taxes, but he told the Parliament the company could not pay because it was awaiting

---

[37]Ibid., 108.

[38]Data from *Ekonomika i zhizn,* No. 36, 1996, reported in Open Media Research Institute, *Daily Digest,* September 10, 1996.

[39]For a full discussion of related issues, see Lavigne, *The Economics of Transition,* 179–183; International Monetary Fund, *World Economic Outlook,* May 1996, 88–89; and M. Afanas'ev, P. Kuznetsov, and P. Isaeva, "The Payments Crisis in Russia: What Is Really Going On?" *Problems of Economic Transition* 39 (May 1996): 5–25.

SERGEI MAVRODI: THE PERILS OF RUSSIAN CAPITALISM

Most of the people in Central Eurasia have accepted the demise of central planning, but they also have learned that the transition to a market economy is perilous. Particularly dangerous are the early stages of transition, when the economy is unstable, prices are racing upward, market behavior is unfamiliar, reliable information is difficult to find, and new laws, regulations, and institutions are needed to protect the population from force, fraud, or other unfair business practices.

Aside from the broader network of mafia activities, perhaps the most notorious symbol of unfettered capitalism in Central Eurasia is Sergei Mavrodi, a Russian businessman and con artist. In 1988, Mavrodi founded a cooperative that specialized in computer imports, but it subsequently was transformed into the AO-MMM investment company. Early in 1994, AO-MMM started an aggressive campaign to sell investment shares to the general public, promising enormous rates of return. Night after night, slick advertisements ran on television (reportedly costing $100 million), featuring a fictional working-class character, Lyonya Golubkov, whose AO-MMM investments allowed him to buy a fur coat for his wife, a flat in Paris, and a vacation on the beaches of California. In other television spots, AO-MMM claimed the endorsement of major entertainment personalities.

After decades of Communist propaganda, many Russians believed that anything shown on television had official approval. They knew that a class of "new Russians" was getting rich quick, that high inflation and low interest rates were eroding their savings in bank accounts, and that the banks themselves were on shaky ground. They heard that Mavrodi's initial investors were collecting hundred-fold returns after only six months. Thus, perhaps as many as 10 million people were lured by AO-MMM, many of them investing all their life savings.

Unfortunately, Mr. Mavrodi was familiar with the methods developed in 1920 by Charles Ponzi, a con artist in Boston who collected the modern equivalent of $150 million from 40,000 of his fellow Italian immigrants. Mavrodi, like Ponzi before him, used much of the money he received from new investors, not to purchase stocks or other properties, but to pay large dividends to earlier investors. The dividends, in turn, attracted additional investors, and the deception continued to grow.

The Russian government was aware of Mavrodi's scheme, but had no law against it. President Yeltsin undermined confidence in AO-MMM, however, when he warned the public that its television advertisements were misleading. A few weeks later, in July 1994, the bubble burst; the price of an AO-MMM share dropped almost overnight from 115,000 rubles to 1,000 rubles. The fortunes of the remaining AO-MMM investors were destroyed.

CONTINUED

Unable to prosecute Mavrodi for his Ponzi scheme, the government arrested him for failing to report 24.5 billion rubles (about $12 million) of company revenue to the tax authorities. Mavrodi blamed the problems of AO-MMM on government and central bank officials who were trying to prevent common people from sharing in the riches of capitalism, and he vowed to keep the company operating. Hoping to recover their fortunes, his investors continued to support him. Two weeks after the AO-MMM crash, with Mavrodi still in jail, the offices were re-opened, and more than 10,000 people gathered to buy additional AO-MMM shares at a price of 1,515 rubles.

In November 1994, with continued support from his long-suffering investors, Mavrodi gained release from jail and immunity from prosecution by winning a seat in the Russian parliament. He never attended meetings of the Duma, and in October 1995 his fellow deputies finally ejected him from the parliament on a technicality. Stripped of immunity, he still was not charged with a crime.

In 1996, Mavrodi attempted to run for the Russian presidency, but the Central Electoral Commission rejected nearly half his qualifying petitions, denying him a place on the ballot. He also launched still another investment fund. The Securities and Exchange Commission prevented Mavrodi from operating in the United States, but the man who bilked millions of people of their savings was still doing business in Russia.

SOURCES: Helen Womack, "Rouble Trouble," *The Independent,* August 21, 1994, 7; "Thousands Seek to Buy Shares as MMM Offices Reopen," ITAR-TASS, August 22, 1994; Michael Kaser, "Privatization in the CIS," in *Challenges for Russian Economic Reform,* ed. Alan Smith (Washington, D.C.: Brookings Institution, 1995), 189–190; Dmitry Borodenkov, "Mavrodi Expands MMM Political Party," *Moscow News,* August 4, 1995, 1; David Segal, "Money for Nothing; Mr. Ponzi Showed Us the Real American Dream," *The Washington Post,* June 2, 1996, 1C; and Elizabeth Sullivan, "Reforms Sour for Disenchanted," *The Plain Dealer,* June 9, 1996, 1A.

even larger payments from consumers: "The situation is now such that the overwhelming majority of Russian consumers don't pay for the gas that we produce."[40]

UNFINISHED BUSINESS AND THE WAY FORWARD

Here, we have discussed only a few of the most pressing issues that have dominated the early stages of market transition. Dozens of other issues are still in early stages of resolution.

---

[40]Betsy McKay, "Russia's Gazprom Battles Tax Liens, Rattling Foreigners as Share Sale Nears," *The Wall Street Journal,* October 3, 1996, A11.

In most countries, for example, little has been done to build new **social safety nets** appropriate for the needs of workers and pensioners in market economies. During the era of central planning, individuals could usually rely on stable jobs, prices, and pensions to provide reasonable income security. By destroying these guarantees, the market transition has led to rising income inequality and poverty throughout the region.[41] Tatiana Zaslavskaya, a well-known Russian sociologist, recently observed, "The well-being of the majority of the groups of the population has sharply fallen, while the system of social protection does not actually exist at all."[42]

Typically, proposals for social welfare reform have included establishment of minimum retirement benefits, unification of treatment across occupations, increases in the retirement age, steps to reduce access to benefits by younger working pensioners, and measures to strengthen collection of payroll taxes. In most countries, however, deep-seated disagreements among market reformers, Communist and Social Democratic parties, and high-income constituencies have prevented enactment of meaningful reforms targeted at basic needs.[43]

Rebuilding of foreign trade and investment relations is another major area of unfinished business. Normal trade ties with the West were disrupted during the Communist era, and trade among Central Eurasian countries was disrupted by the disintegration of the Communist world. Trade within the region fell by roughly 60 percent between 1990 and 1993, and trade within the former Soviet Union fell even more steeply.[44] With new access to Western markets and financial institutions, consumers and businesses in Central Eurasia increased their imports of Western goods, but their export performance lagged far behind. Foreign investors were invited to enter Central Eurasia, but the response has been sluggish: In 1995, Russia attracted only $2 billion of foreign direct investment, while China absorbed $38 billion.[45]

To rebuild trade and investment within Central Eurasia, leaders of neighboring states will need to overcome age-old rivalries, ethnic antagonisms, and territorial disputes. They may be able to achieve rapid gains by identifying and reactivating any trading relations that existed during the Communist era that are now considered profitable. For example, when a customs union was recently created between Russia, Kazakstan, Kyrgyzstan, and Belarus, trade between Russia and Kazakstan quickly increased by some 80 percent.[46]

Several countries in the region still need to dismantle extensive systems of import restrictions and export controls, and create more reliable systems of

---

[41]According to World Bank estimates, expenditure-based poverty rates in 1993 ranged from 1 percent of the Czech population to 35 percent of the Russian and 57 percent of the Kyrgyz populations. See World Bank, *World Development Report 1996*, 69.

[42]Tatiana Zaslavskaya, "Social Adaptation Difficult but Possible," *Power in Russia*, September 9, 1996.

[43]See "Transition Economies Need to Reform Social Safety Nets," *IMF Survey*, August 12, 1996, 261 and 269–270.

[44]Lavigne, *The Economics of Transition*, 192–194.

[45]Estimates of the United Nations Conference on Trade and Development, reported in Open Media Research Institute, *Daily Digest*, September 26, 1996.

[46]Open Media Research Institute, *Daily Digest*, October 3, 1996. Also, see Gabor Bakos, "After COMECON: A Free Trade Area in Central Europe?" *Europe-Asia Studies* 45 (1993): 1025–1044.

financial accounts. In 1996 and 1997, Russia conducted its fourth round of negotiations to join the World Trade Organization or its predecessor, the General Agreement on Tariffs and Trade. Its earlier applications were denied because Russia maintained excessive nontariff trade barriers, its energy prices were seriously distorted from world market levels, and questions remained concerning the capabilities of Russian regulatory and statistical authorities.[47] In Kazakstan, a government official recently blamed a "corrupted system of trade" for the fact that payments for over $500 million of oil sales were simply never received.[48]

The reintegration of Central Eurasia into the world economy will also be affected by decisions made in the West. Under what circumstances will Western investors be willing to make a stronger commitment to the region? In light of tight governmental budgets in most of the Western nations, how much economic assistance will be extended to the region, and for how long? Under what circumstances, and with what privileges, will countries in the region be allowed to join the European Union, World Trade Organization, NATO, OECD, and other international organizations? How will Western nations deal with such countries as Serbia that are emerging from economic sanctions, and how will they react to other regional conflicts and instances of political chauvinism? And finally, will the Western nations practice what they preach, and keep their own markets open when the nations of Central Eurasia become formidable economic competitors?

SUMMARY

The transformation of Central Eurasia began against a backdrop of economic collapse, financial imbalance, political disintegration, labor unrest, ethnic hostility, environmental emergency, and international indebtedness. Generally, the Central European countries had the most favorable starting conditions and the nations of Central Asia, the southern Balkans, and the Caucasus faced the most difficult challenges.

Since 1990, when the Balcerowicz Plan introduced a program of "shock therapy" in Poland, transition programs usually have included elements of macroeconomic stabilization, price liberalization, privatization, military conversion, and reform of antimonopoly practices, labor markets, banking, financial markets, taxes, legal systems, social welfare, foreign exchange markets, foreign trade, and foreign investments. An effective reform program is usually based on a strategic concept, which determines its direction, pace, and sequence. These, in turn, are influenced by national political culture, by initial economic conditions, and by prospects for foreign investment and other international assistance.

The early stages of transition were associated with high rates of inflation. In each country, a burst of open inflation was usually followed by a struggle, lasting a few years, against rapid demand-pull inflation. Eventually, the benefits of additional stabilization become less certain.

---

[47]Open Media Research Institute, *Daily Digest,* October 16, 1996.
[48]Open Media Research Institute, *Daily Digest,* October 30, 1996.

Programs of privatization may be undertaken to raise efficiency, to acquire needed skills and capital, to provide revenues and reduce subsidies in the budget, to serve the needs of social justice, and to accomplish these tasks as simply and quickly as possible. Distinctions are drawn between privatizations that are large or small; between those that are managed or spontaneous; and between those that are handled by restitution, voucher distribution, management-employee turnover, auction, sale to strategic investors, or exchange of loans for shares. Each method has its advantages or disadvantages in a particular circumstance, and may provide a different set of results.

Financial institutions were few in number and limited in strength during the central planning era. Market transition programs have required the development of two-level banking systems, introduction of new currencies, encouragement of new financial institutions, and creation of new regulatory structures to stabilize the growing financial systems. Financial transition programs have been complicated and distorted by instances of large-scale fraud and by widespread nonpayments crises.

Market transition programs have been associated with rising inequality and poverty, but Central Eurasian countries have made little progress in their reform of social safety nets. They have made more progress toward rebuilding their systems of foreign trade and investment, but much remains to be done.

DISCUSSION AND REVIEW QUESTIONS

1. How have historical legacies and other initial conditions affected the design and implementation of transition programs in Central Eurasia?

2. What arguments can be made for a "shock therapy" approach to economic transition? What arguments can be made for gradualism?

3. What have been the major causes of inflation in Central Eurasia, and what instruments have been used to fight it?

4. What is spontaneous privatization? How has it differed between countries? What are its advantages and disadvantages, if any, as a method of privatization?

5. If a country places a high value on microeconomic efficiency, what method of privatization is most beneficial?

6. In the early stages of economic transition, what restrictions should be placed on the formation of new banks and other financial institutions?

7. During early stages of economic transition, should countries in the former Soviet Union give a higher priority to expansion of East-West trade, or should they focus on rebuilding and reformulating trade within their region?

SUGGESTED READINGS

Aslund, Anders. *How Russia Became a Market Economy*. Washington, D.C.: Brookings Institution, 1995. *Written by a leading advisor to the Russian and Ukrainian governments, this book provides a behind-the-scenes view of the early stages of Russian transition and a broad analysis of the continuing issues.*

Clague, Christopher, and Gordon C. Rausser, eds. *The Emergence of Market Economies in Eastern Europe*. Cambridge, Mass.: Blackwell, 1992. *Nineteen studies by a distinguished team of international scholars covering institutional, macroeconomic, antitrust, and privatization issues.*

Gros, Daniel, and Alfred Steinherr. *Winds of Change: Economic Transition in Central and Eastern Europe*. New York: Longman, 1995. *This is a remarkable volume, drawing on historical information, theoretical analysis, and editorial cartoons to provide a comprehensive account of transition issues.*

Herr, Hansjörg, Slke Tober, and Andreas Westphall, eds. *Macroeconomic Problems of Transformation*. Aldershott: Edward Elgar, 1994. *A collection of sixteen studies by twenty European and American scholars. Macroeconomic and structural issues are discussed on an applied level that should be accessible to advanced undergraduate students.*

Islam, Shafiqul, and Michael Mandelbaum, eds. *Making Markets: Economic Transformation in Eastern Europe and the Post-Soviet States*. New York: Council on Foreign Relations Press, 1993. *Studies by four recognized scholars—Richard Portes, Paul Marer, Robert Campbell, and Jeffrey Sachs—provide background information in transition processes on issues related to Western aid.*

Kornai, János. *The Road to a Free Economy*. New York: W. W. Norton, 1990. *Written by a renowned Hungarian scholar, this book provided an early and spirited argument against half measures in economic transition strategies.*

Lavigne, Marie. *The Economics of Transition: From Socialist Economy to Market Economy*. New York: St. Martin's Press, 1995. *Written by an established authority in the field, this is a comprehensive, yet compact and balanced, presentation of issues ranging from the breakdown of communism to privatization, stabilization, and Western aid.*

Solimano, Andrés, Osvaldo Sunkel, and Mario I. Blejer, eds. *Rebuilding Capitalism: Alternative Roads after Socialism and Dirigisme*. Ann Arbor: University of Michigan Press, 1994. *In twelve concise studies, the problems of market transition in Central Eurasia are compared to developmental challenges in Latin America.*

World Bank. *World Development Report 1996*. Oxford: Oxford University Press, 1996. *This edition of the annual report is dedicated to the theme, "From Plan to Market." It summarizes the results of nineteen background studies, and provides a wealth of data supporting the so-called Washington Consensus on the economics of development and market transition.*

RELATED PERIODICALS

Comparative Economic Studies, Association for Comparative Economic Studies

Economic Bulletin for Europe, U.N. Economic Commission for Europe

Economics of Transition, Oxford University Press for the European Bank for Reconstruction and Development

Europe-Asia Studies (continuation of *Soviet Studies*), Carfax, Inc. for University of Glasgow

Journal of Comparative Economics, Academic Press

Post-Soviet Affairs, V. H. Winston & Son, Inc.

Problems of Economic Transition (continuation of *Problems of Economics*), M. E. Sharpe, Inc.

Transition, Open Media Research Institute

Transition, World Bank Transition Economies Division

Transition Brief, OECD Center for Cooperation with Economies in Transition

Transition Report, European Bank for Reconstruction and Development

INTERNET RESOURCES

Business Information Service for the Newly Independent States (BISNIS), U.S. Department of Commerce
http://www.itaiep.doc.gov/bisnis/bisnis.html

Center for Civil Society International
http://solar.rtd.utk.edu/~ccsi/ccsihome.html

OECD Center for Cooperation with Economies in Transition (CCET)
http://www.oecd.org/ccet/

Center for Economic Reform and Transition (CERT)
Heriot-Watt University
http://www.hw.ac.uk/ecoWWW/cert/certhp.htm

Central European Online (CEO) Navigator
http://www.ceo.cz/

Civic Education Project (CEP)
http://cep.nonprofit.net/

Competition Policy and Economic Transformation
http://www.economics.tcd.ie/jfinglet/cec/book.htm

Economies and Societies in Transition (EAST) Newsletter
University of Pennsylvania
http://www.ssc.upenn.edu/east/

Economic Reform Today
Center for International Private Enterprise
http://www.cipe.org/ert.html

European Bank for Reconstruction and Development
http://www.ebrd.com/intro/index.htm

Friends and Partners
http://solar.rtd.utk.edu/friends/home.html

Institute for the Economy in Transition
Directed by Dr. Yegor Gaidar, Moscow, Russia
http://www.online.ru/sp/iet/

Institutional Reform and the Informal Sector (IRIS)
University of Maryland
http://www.inform.umd.edu:8080/IRIS/

Klaus, Vaclav. "Transition to Free Markets"
http://www.scimitar.com/revolution/by_topic/commerce/economic/
czech.html

Polish Ministry of Privatization
http://www.urm.gov.pl/mpw/indexnif.html

Russia Today
http://www.russiatoday.com/

Russian and East European Network Information Center (REENIC)
University of Texas at Austin
http://reenic.utexas.edu/reenic.html

Russian Economy Resource Center
http://mail.eskimo.com/~bwest/rerc.html

St. Petersburg Times
http://www.spb.su/times/index.html

Soft Road to Hungarian Economy
http://www.bekkoame.or.jp/~hyoko/

Stocks and Funds in the Czech Republic
http://194.212.110.9/en/

Transition, The World Bank
http://www.worldbank.org/html/prddr/trans/trans.htm

Wiener Institut für Internationale
Wirtschaftsvergleiche (WIIW)
The Vienna Institute for Comparative Economic Studies
http://www.wsr.ac.at/wiiw-html/

Wolfe, James W. "Privatization in the Former Soviet Union"
http://www.ibs.ee/economics/privatization.html

Zijlstra, Kees. "Czech Republic: A Case Model," NATO, 1995
http://www.friends-partners.org/oldfriends/economics/czech.rep.case.
study.html

ASIA AND AFRICA

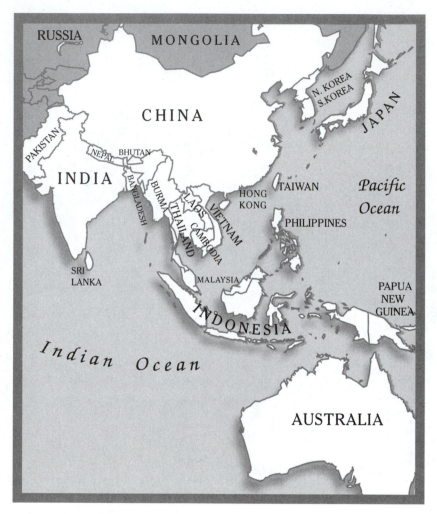

South and East Asia

18

ASIA AND THE PACIFIC AREA: AN OVERVIEW

From the very dawn of human history, philosophies, religions, culture, and the arts have flourished in Asia. Until the Middle Ages, science and technology flowed from Asia to Europe. It was only for the last four hundred years that Asia has been eclipsed by Europe. What is happening now in Asia could mark a reversal of this eclipse.

—SURENDRA J. PATEL, *ASIA-PACIFIC DEVELOPMENT JOURNAL*, JUNE 1994

. . . The Asian system is powerful precisely because it has become a broad regional system, reaching across national borders and taking on different characteristics in each place it is applied. . . . Its economic power is based on a political model at odds with the ideals Westerners have propounded since the time of Locke and Rousseau. No one outside Asia will be forced to adopt or imitate the system, but outsiders should be sure they understand how the new system works.

—JAMES FALLOWS, *LOOKING AT THE SUN*, 1994

In this chapter and the two that follow, we turn our attention to the southern and eastern nations of Asia and to their neighbors in the Pacific. For present purposes, we exclude the Asian region of Russia, the central Asian nations of the former Soviet Union, and the Asian nations of the Middle East. Nevertheless, the region under consideration accounts for more than half the world's population, more than one-fourth its production of goods and services, and nearly one-fourth its surface area. Here we find some of the world's richest economies (Japan, Hong Kong, Australia, and New Zealand), some of its poorest (Myanmar, Vietnam, Nepal, and Bhutan), and its champions of economic growth (Thailand, China, South Korea, and Taiwan). See Table 18.1.

TABLE 18.1

ASIA AND PACIFIC AREA: BASIC INDICATORS FOR 1995

	Population (millions)	Area (thousands of sq. km.)	Total GDP (billion dollars at purchasing-power parity)	GDP per Capita (dollars at purchasing-power parity)	1985–1995 Annual Growth of GDP per Capita (percent)	Infant Mortality (per 1,000 live births)	Urban Population (% of total)
Total Region	**3,144.4**	**31,576**	**10,295**	**3,270**	**5.3**	**49**	**32**
South Asia	**1,219.4**	**6,891**	**1,816**	**1,490**	**2.9**	**71**	**27**
Bangladesh	119.8	1,330	140	1,170	2.1	79	18
Bhutan	0.7	1,270	876	1,260	4.9	124	6
India	929.4	3,288	1,301	1,400	3.2	68	27
Nepal	21.5	141	25	1,180	2.4	91	13
Pakistan	129.9	796	290	2,230	1.2	90	34
Sri Lanka	18.1	66	59	3,250	2.6	16	22
East Asia	**1,422.3**	**11,762**	**6,263**	**4,400**	**7.6**	**30**	**36**
China	1,200.2	9,561	2,424	2,020	8.3	34	29
Hong Kong	6.2	1	142	22,950	4.8	5	95
Japan	125.2	378	2,768	22,110	2.9	4	78
Korea, North	22.0	120	72	3,250	−2.8	24	60
Korea, South	44.9	99	514	11,450	7.7	10	80
Mongolia	2.5	1,566	5	1,950	−3.8	55	60
Taiwan	21.3	37	338	15,870	6.8	6	84

Continued

	Population (millions)	Area (thousands of sq. km.)	Total GDP (billion dollars at purchasing-power parity)	GDP per Capita (dollars at purchasing-power parity)	1985–1994 Annual Growth of GDP per Capita (percent)	Infant Mortality (per 1,000 live births)	Urban Population (% of total)
Southeast Asia	**214.8**	**2,271**	**873**	**4,060**	**5.0**	**49**	**26**
Cambodia	10.0	181	11	1,120	2.7	108	19
Laos	4.9	237	13	2,570	2.7	90	21
Malaysia	20.1	330	181	8,440	5.7	12	53
Myanmar	45.1	677	49	1,090	−0.8	80	26
Singapore	3.0	1	68	22,770	6.2	4	100
Thailand	58.2	513	439	7,540	8.4	35	20
Vietnam	73.5	332	112	1,520	6.0	41	21
Pacific Area	**287.9**	**10,652**	**1,342**	**4,660**	**4.5**	**48**	**42**
Australia	18.1	7,713	343	18,940	1.4	6	85
Indonesia	193.3	1,905	735	3,800	6.0	51	34
New Zealand	3.6	271	59	16,360	0.8	7	86
Papua New Guinea	4.3	463	10	2,420	2.3	64	16
Philippines	68.6	300	196	2,850	1.5	51	53

NOTE: Regional averages in the last three columns are weighted by population.

SOURCES: World Bank, *World Development Report 1997*; World Bank, *Historically Planned Economies 1993*; United Nations Development Program, Human Development Report 1997; United Nations Economic and Social Commission for Asia and the Pacific, *Statistical Yearbook for Asia and the Pacific 1996*; United Nations Conference on Trade and Development, *Handbook of International Trade and Development Statistics 1994*; "How Poor Is China?" *The Economist*, October 12, 1996, 35; and author's estimates.

THE ENVIRONMENT

Because of its vast territory, enormous population, and timeless history, the economies of the Asia-Pacific region operate in a diversified and complex environment. Geologically, the region includes everything from the snow-covered Himalayan peaks, crowned by Mount Everest, to the arid plains of Australia. Some countries in the region have large endowments of arable land (India and Thailand), others are amply endowed with mineral and other natural resources (Australia, Indonesia, Myanmar, and Vietnam), others have advantages of location, particularly for shipping (Hong Kong, Japan, and Singapore), and others seem to be naturally poor (Bangladesh and Nepal).

Demographically, the region includes three of the world's four most populous nations (China, India, and Indonesia), its three most crowded nations (Hong Kong, Singapore, and Bangladesh), and many of its largest cities (Tokyo, Calcutta, Bombay, Shanghai, and Jakarta). On the other hand, the region includes many island nations with populations of fewer than 1 million people (Fiji, Kiribati, Tonga, Tuvalu, and Vanuatu).

RELIGION AND CULTURE

Cultural traditions in most of the Asia-Pacific region are tied to Eastern religions and philosophies. Unlike the monotheistic and particularistic religions of the West and the Middle East, the Eastern religions are characterized by polytheism and syncretism. Ordinarily, in an Asian city or village, the local system of belief is based on indigenous animisms and atavisms, blended with imported religions and philosophies.

Rooted in a collection of texts composed in India between 1500 B.C. and 600 B.C., **Hinduism** is the oldest major religion native to the Asia-Pacific region. According to Hindu belief, every individual soul (*atman*) is part of a larger universal soul (*Brahman*). Because most humans pursue material riches, personal pleasure, and other dead-end goals, their lives are full of suffering and pain. The objective of Hindu life is to achieve and accumulate a record of spiritual understanding and action, or *karma*, that allows the individual to escape the bondage of worldly existence (*moksha*) and unite fully with Brahman. Because this process requires more than a single lifetime, Hindus believe that the soul is transferred into another body after each death. Depending on one's karma in the previous life, the soul may be reincarnated as a lower animal, a higher animal, a human of lower caste, a human of higher caste, or, best of all, a human of the priestly Brahman caste.

Buddhism arose, in some respects, as a protestant movement within Hinduism. Its prophet, Siddhartha Gautama, was born about 563 B.C. as a member of the wealthy warrior caste. Gautama renounced his privileges to search for the cause of human suffering, but found no satisfactory answer in the ancient Hindu texts. After six years of wandering, he discovered the "Four Noble Truths" during a period of meditation, and from that time forward he was known as the Buddha, or "Enlightened One."

Superficially, the doctrines of Buddhism were similar to those of traditional Hinduism, but they were quite different in detail. According to the Four Noble Truths: (1) life is full of pain and suffering (*dukka*); (2) the causes of suffering are inappropriate desire (*tanha*) and ignorance (*avija*); (3) to escape suffering, one must overcome desire and move to a higher state of consciousness (*nirvana*); and (4) to pursue nirvana, one must follow the disciplines of the Eightfold Path, seeking balance between extremes of self-indulgence and total abstinence. Following Hindu tradition, the Buddha accepted the doctrines of karma and reincarnation, but believed that any person, regardless of caste, could achieve nirvana *on earth* by following the Eightfold Path. Accordingly, he rejected the caste system and the view that priests were spiritually superior.

During several centuries that followed the Buddha's death, his disciples divided and subdivided into large and small sects, spread their teachings throughout Asia, and adapted their ideas in each locality to the existing philosophies and religions. The relatively conservative *Theravada* sect, which resisted any departure from ancient Buddhist scripture or ritual, spread from India into Southeast Asia. Today, Theravada Buddhism is the dominant religion in Cambodia, Laos, Singapore, Sri Lanka, Thailand, and Vietnam.

Between the second centuries B.C. and A.D., a collection of new scriptures appeared, purporting to provide the Buddha's most advanced and complete teaching. These were rejected by the Theravada, but accepted by those who called themselves the *Mahayana,* or followers of the "Greater Vehicle." Relatively expansive and flexible in belief, the Mahayana gradually subdivided into numerous traditions. These ranged from the Pure Land school, whose simple doctrine of faith appealed to poor farmers, to the Hua-yen, which developed a sophisticated epistemology, and the Zen, which emphasized meditation and the possibility of sudden enlightenment. These Mahayana Buddhist traditions have been most influential in the cultures of China, Korea, and Japan.

A third broad sect of Buddhism, known as *Vajrayana* (the "Diamond Vehicle"), became prominent in India in the seventh century A.D. This was an esoteric system requiring strict guidance under an accomplished master, and involving elaborate ritual usage of *mudras* (sacred gestures), *mantras* (sacred sounds), and *mandalas* (maps of the spiritual cosmos). Vajrayana influenced the development of Buddhism in Mongolia and Tibet.

In many Asian countries, the Buddhist tradition, native to India, was adopted in combination with one or both of the major Chinese philosophies. Taoism and Confucianism both emerged in China during the sixth century B.C., during an era of political instability and social disintegration. Accordingly, both of these philosophies directed attention to ethical issues associated with social structure and governance.

Based on the writings of Lao-tzu (c. 604–c. 531 B.C.), **Taoism** was similar in some respects to Hinduism and Buddhism; it found that "there is no calamity greater than lavish desires," and "no guilt greater than discontentment." Thus, it encouraged a simple and introspective style of life, seeking the mystical ecstasy associated with knowledge of ultimate reality (the *Tao*).

However, breaking new ground, Lao-tzu advised government leaders to seek social harmony with a policy of "strength through weakness," extending the scope of individual freedom and spontaneity. "The more laws and order are made prominent," he predicted, "the more thieves and robbers there will be." Thus, Taoism anticipated the relatively libertarian stance of Thomas Jefferson: "That government is best which governs least."

First as a philosophy and later as a religion, Taoism played a notable role in the development of Chinese, Korean, Japanese, and Vietnamese culture, but its laissez-faire social policy was unacceptable to Asian leaders. **Confucianism** was grounded more realistically in the hierarchical nature of Chinese society; it became the dominant philosophical system, in large part, because the Han emperors (206 B.C.–220 A.D.) adopted it as the basis of their civil service examinations. From China, Confucianism spread with Taoism to Korea, Japan, and Vietnam.

Unlike Lao-tzu and the Indian sages who recommended solitary lives of introspection, Confucius (551–479 B.C.) promoted a practical system of social ethics, based on the mutual obligations of servants and masters. He encouraged people in leadership positions (political rulers, parents, husbands, and older brothers) to exercise their authority wisely and charitably, always seeking the welfare of their inferiors. In response, subordinates should serve their leaders cheerfully, obediently, and honorably, upholding the welfare of the larger social unit. Familial and social obligations were held above individual rights.

In addition to the native traditions, the Asian countries also have been influenced by religions and philosophies introduced by missionaries and colonialists. Islam is the dominant religion in Bangladesh, Indonesia, Malaysia, and Pakistan. Christianity is dominant in Australia, New Zealand, Papua New Guinea, and the Philippines.

In the opinions of many writers and analysts, religious and ethical traditions have significantly influenced the relative levels of economic development in the Asia-Pacific region. Allegedly, the poor economic performance of India and Nepal can be explained, in part, by certain aspects of Hinduism. The caste system restricts occupational mobility, educational opportunity, housing choice, and access to community wells and other social facilities.[1] The work ethic allegedly is weakened by caste-oriented limitations of opportunity and by an otherworldly fatalism that derives from doctrines of persistent human misery, karma, and reincarnation. In some localities, Hindu beliefs have interfered with family planning activities.[2]

By lifting the burden of the caste system, Buddhism allegedly improved the economic fortunes of Southeast Asia. However, according to a widely held view, Singapore, Vietnam, and the East Asian countries are particularly

---

[1]See, for example, Stefan Wagstyl, "Poverty in a Class of Its Own," *Financial Times,* September 30, 1993, supplement, XII; and Dennis D. Miller, "A New System for India," *Christian Science Monitor,* July 28, 1992, 18.

[2]Large families are encouraged, for example, by the importance many Hindus attach to having their funeral pyre lit by a son. See K. K. Sharma, "India Fights to Control Population Growth," *Financial Times,* April 7, 1989, 4.

fortunate because their cultures combine the strengths of Buddhism and Confucianism. Thus, the first Asian miracles lifted the economies of Japan, Hong Kong, Singapore, South Korea, and Taiwan; economic growth has been explosive in China and Vietnam during their recent era of market reform.

Confucianism allegedly promotes economic development because it encourages social stability, hard work, and a reverential attitude toward education. Within each business enterprise, it encourages cooperation, teamwork, and loyalty. Furthermore, Confucianism may partially explain the East Asian penchant for long-range decision making and frugality. "If a man takes no thought about what is distant," said Confucius, "he will find sorrow near at hand."[3]

These cultural interpretations of Asian economic performance are enormously popular,[4] but not universally accepted. It is not altogether clear, for example, that poor, uneducated Hindus are less motivated and more "otherworldly" than poor, uneducated members of other world religions.[5] If ancient Confucianism provides strong support for economic progress, why is the East Asian growth miracle such a recent historical phenomenon? In 1820, after more than a millennium of Hindu and Confucian development, and until the 1980s, when China introduced its market-oriented reforms, average incomes evidently were higher in Hindu India than in Confucian China (Table 18.2).

■ TABLE 18.2

ASIA AND LATIN AMERICA: REAL GDP PER CAPITA, 1820–1995 (1995 U.S. DOLLARS AT PURCHASING-POWER PARITY)

	China	India	Brazil	Mexico
1820	180	450	460	1,250
1870	180	450	480	1,230
1913	220	590	810	1,600
1950	190	560	1,480	3,150
1980	610	870	5,320	7,200
1995	2,020	1,400	5,400	6,400

SOURCES: Base income levels for 1995 are from World Bank, *World Development Report 1997*; and, in the case of China, from an estimate based on the benchmark described in "How Poor is China?" *The Economist*, October 12, 1996, 35. Growth indexes are from Angus Maddison, "A Comparison of Levels of GDP Per Capita in Developed and Developing Countries, 1700–1980," *Journal of Economic History* 43 (March 1983): 30; International Monetary Fund, *International Financial Statistics Yearbook 1996*; and International Monetary Fund, *World Economic Outlook*, May 1997.

---

[3]*Confucian Analects*, 15:11.

[4]See, for example, W. J. O'Malley, "Culture and Industrialization," in *Achieving Industrialization in Asia*, ed. H. Hughes (Cambridge: Cambridge University Press, 1988), 332 and 341; Anis Chowdhury and Iyanatul Islam, *The Newly Industrializing Economies of East Asia* (New York: Routledge, 1993), 14; Keun Lee, *New East Asian Economic Development: Interacting Capitalism and Socialism* (Armonk, N.Y.: M. E. Sharpe, 1993), 14–18; James Fallows, *Looking at the Sun* (New York: Vintage, 1995), 283; and Dinesh D'Souza, "Confucius Meets Max Weber," *Forbes*, November 4, 1996, 86.

[5]For evidence and arguments that Hinduism may contribute *positively* to economic development, see Jogindar S. Uppal, *Economic Development in South Asia* (New York: St. Martin's, 1977), 136–140.

LEGACIES OF COLONIALISM

If the economic influence of religion and philosophy in the Asia-Pacific region is diverse and complex, the same is true of the colonial heritage. In fact, the two subjects are interrelated because colonial powers introduced several religious traditions and political philosophies into the region.

COLONIALISM IN SOUTH ASIA

The colonial conquest of Asia began in the northwestern regions of India, near the mountain passes that link Asia with Europe and the Near East. About 1500 B.C., Aryan invaders descended through the Khyber Pass and absorbed or destroyed the aboriginal Indus Valley civilization. The Aryans developed a hierarchical Hindu civilization, and eventually assembled India's first large empires, the Magadha (between 500 B.C. and 321 B.C.) and the Maurya (between 321 B.C. and 183 B.C.).

In 326 B.C., after conquering Persia, Alexander the Great found his way through the Khyber Pass and marched into the Indus Valley. When his army withdrew, Greek outposts remained in the area, facilitating trade and cultural exchange between India, Persia, and Greece. Like other invaders, Alexander's remnant, the Bactrian Greek civilization, eventually was absorbed into Indian culture.

In the eighth century A.D., Moslem invaders entered India again through the northwest portal, and began to carve out principalities. A vast network of trade was established between the Asian and Islamic worlds. The conquest of India continued for hundreds of years until, during the sixteenth century, the Moslem-led Moghul empire unified most of the subcontinent. Today, the Islamic populations of Pakistan and Bangladesh and the Taj Mahal in India stand as reminders of the Moslem influence on South Asian culture.

During the twelfth and thirteenth centuries, when the Crusades supported development of the Italian shipping industry, merchants from Venice and Genoa established contacts with Middle Eastern traders who, in turn, had access to Asian products. Europeans quickly developed an insatiable demand for pepper from India, cinnamon from Ceylon, nutmeg from the East Indies, and tea and silks from China.

Probably written in 1298, **Marco Polo's** book, *Description of the World,* publicized the fantastic riches of the Orient to a broad European audience. Polo, a Venetian merchant, claimed that he traveled throughout central China for seventeen years as a servant of Kublai Khan, the Mongol emperor. On his return trip to Europe, Polo claimed that he visited coastal areas of Southeast Asia, the East Indies, and India. Today, some scholars believe that Polo's descriptions were based on Persian and Arabic reports rather than on first-had experience.[6] Nevertheless, his book was trans-

---

[6]Frances Wood, *Did Marco Polo Go to China?* (Boulder, Colo.: Westview Press, 1996); and John Critchley, *Marco Polo's Book* (Aldershot: Variorum, 1992).

lated into more than a dozen languages and dialects, and was read throughout Europe.

Intrigued by Polo's account, European adventurers started searching for an oceanic trade route to Asia. Most resolute were Spanish and Portuguese sailors who hoped to outflank the Arabs and Italians who controlled the overland and Mediterranean passages. With Spanish support, Christopher Columbus sailed westward, and thought he had won the oceanic race to Asia in 1492 when he arrived in the Caribbean islands. Six years later, Vasco da Gama of Portugal found his way around the southern tip of Africa to the southwestern coast of India. Building on that success, Portugal established a near monopoly of the spice trade between Asia and Europe for nearly a century.

In 1600, England established its East India Company to challenge the Portuguese monopoly; similar companies were established by Holland in 1602 and by France in 1664. The Dutch company, having a superior fleet of ships and using ruthless military tactics, quickly established dominance in the region, and cornered the lucrative spice trade in the East Indies (now known as Indonesia).

England focused its attention on the Indian subcontinent, and by 1612 it had replaced Portugal as the dominant Western power in that area. Initially, England established simple trading relationships with the local Indian merchants and accepted the sovereignty of the Moghul elite. Over a period of two centuries, however, England subdued the Moghul leadership and established its own trade monopoly. The East India Company became a military and bureaucratic arm of the British government and supplemented its trading profits with tax revenues.

In 1857, the East India Company was shaken when a mutiny among its Indian soldiers ignited a broader peasant rebellion. British troops put down the rebellion, and, in 1858, the British Parliament established direct rule over India. Control was shifted from the East Asia Company to a viceroy, a member of the British cabinet, who managed a colonial government that eventually had about 1,000 British officials.

The colonial governors introduced British laws and institutions, and created a new elite of Indian civil servants and professionals with British educations. They discouraged development of local industries and encouraged production of raw materials for British factories. In agriculture, they encouraged cultivation of cotton, which was useful in the British textile industry, but reduced the local supply of food. To extend colonial development and control, the British governors organized construction of a huge network of canals, roads, and railways.

In 1920, Mahatma Ghandi captured control of the Indian National Congress and used it as a platform to launch the fight for independence from British colonial rule. By the end of the Second World War, Britain was ready to surrender its empire. A timetable was set for Indian independence in 1947. Unfortunately, when British influence diminished, differences emerged among the native sects and ethnicities. Wary of Hindu domination in India, the Moslems sought a state of their own. India was therefore partitioned, and the new nation of Pakistan gained little of its industrial wealth.[7]

British colonialism provided significant economic and social benefits to India, particularly by strengthening the transportation and higher educational systems, causing some historians to argue that the benefits of colonialism exceeded the costs.[8] However, the bulk of historical analysis and statistical evidence seems to lean heavily in the opposite direction.[9] Colonial priorities, rather than local needs, dictated the structure of Indian production. Millions of lives were lost in years of famine because colonial cotton farming displaced food production. Colonial taxes and remittances deprived India of a large share of its saving and investment resources.

The statistical record is incomplete, but it seems to provide little support for colonialism. In 1820, around the time that England established its hegemony, incomes in India were not much lower than those in Brazil. Brazil gained independence from Portugal in 1822, but India remained under British control until 1947. Free to control its own destiny, Brazil was far more successful between 1820 and 1950 than British India (Table 18.2).

COLONIALISM IN SOUTHEAST ASIA AND THE PACIFIC

A large part of Southeast Asia is also known by the name Indochina, because the cultural traditions of the region descended from mixtures of Indian, Chinese, and local customs. To this day, Chinese immigrants are the majority population in Singapore and constitute important segments of the professional populations in most other Southeast Asian nations.

European influence in the area began early in the sixteenth century when Portugal established a commercial outpost on the Malay peninsula. Spain arrived in 1571, when it conquered the Philippines and placed them under a Spanish governor-general. The Philippines became the hub of trade between Asia and Spanish territories in the New World.

Next came the Dutch, who became the dominant power in the Southeast Asia–Pacific area during the seventeenth and eighteenth centuries. The focus of their colonizing effort was in Indonesia, which became known as the Dutch East Indies. To obtain large quantities of rice, rubber, coffee, spices, and other commodities for export, the Dutch transformed the Indonesian

---

[7]After another period of ethnic agitation and fighting, the state of Eastern Pakistan gained independence in 1971 to form still another poor nation with few resources, Bangladesh.

[8]For example, see Morris David Morris et al., *Indian Economy in the Nineteenth Century: A Symposium* (Delhi: Delhi School of Economics, 1969).

[9]See Neil Charlesworth, *British Rule and the Indian Economy, 1800–1914* (London: Macmillan, 1982); A. Krishna Dutt, "The Origins of Uneven Development: The Indian Subcontinent," *American Economic Review* 82 (May 1992): 146–150; K. N. Chaudhiri, "Foreign Trade and the Balance of Payments (1757–1947)," in *The Cambridge Economic History of India*, vol. 2, ed. Dharma Kumar (Cambridge: Cambridge University Press, 1983), 804–877; Uppal, *Economic Development in South Asia*, 153–159; and Lance E. Davis and Robert A. Huttenback, *Mammon and the Pursuit of Empire* (Cambridge University Press, 1986), 191.

agricultural sector, which had been based on small-scale subsistence farming, into a system of large plantations.

Late in the eighteenth century, empowered by its industrial revolution, England broke the Dutch imperial monopoly in the Southeast Asia–Pacific area. The British claimed possession of Australia in 1770, established their first prison settlements there in 1788, began their conquests of Burma (now Myanmar), Malaysia, and Singapore during the 1820s, and began an organized program to settle colonists in New Zealand in the 1840s. France entered Vietnam in 1786, seized control of territories in southern Vietnam during the 1860s, and controlled nearly all Indochina by the end of the nineteenth century.

Lured to the East by the opening of China and Japan, the United States obtained a naval base in Samoa in 1878 that remains an American possession. In 1898, American ships paved the way to a U.S. victory in the Spanish-American War by destroying a Spanish fleet in Manila Bay. In the peace settlement that followed, the United States gained control of Spanish colonial holdings in the Philippines and Guam.

Thailand (then known as Siam) was the only nation in Southeast Asia to successfully avoid the domination of European or American colonialists during the nineteenth century. Exploiting their country's position as a neutral buffer between British Burma and French Indochina, the Siamese leaders signed commercial treaties of friendship with all sides—England, France, and the United States—in 1855 and 1856, and formed a cabinet of foreign advisors. In a series of top-down reforms, the king dismantled feudal institutions, abolished slavery, and encouraged importation of Western technology.

Britain granted independence to Australia in 1901 and New Zealand in 1907, but Japan seized control of most of the region from Western colonialists during World War II. The Western powers reclaimed their colonies after the war, but a movement for political independence quickly spread through the region. By the end of 1949, Malaysia and Singapore were the only sizable countries in the region remaining under Western control; Britain granted their independence eight years later.[10]

The impact and imprint of the colonial era was different in each Southeast Asia–Pacific country. The sparsely populated countries that attracted large numbers of permanent European settlers (Australia and New Zealand) became successful extensions of Western culture. Thailand escaped colonialism, and enjoyed a gradual development of democratic and market institutions. After centuries of imperial rule, most of the other countries had little experience with self-government and had plantation-based agricultural systems that exposed the native people to world market fluctuations. Thus,

---

[10]For several years thereafter, Western countries controlled some smaller nations in the region. Thus, Fiji and Tonga became independent from the United Kingdom in 1970, followed by the Solomon Islands in 1978, Vanuatu in 1980, and Brunei in 1984.

much of the region remained politically and economically unstable, vulnerable to communist insurgency and Western intervention.

COLONIALISM IN EAST ASIA

The economic histories of Japan and China, the two major powers of East Asia, will be surveyed in the next two chapters. For present purposes, it seems that Western colonialism had an important impact on the history of East Asia, but less important than in South and Southeast Asia.

Aside from Portuguese control of Macau (1557–1999) and British control of Hong Kong (1841–1997), the Western powers never took direct possession of the East Asian nations. The countries maintained independent governments and, for the most part, controlled their own financial and production - structures. The most important colonial powers in the area were not England, Spain, Portugal, Holland, or America, but Japan and China, themselves.

The most outrageous episodes of Western intrusion in East Asia were the Opium Wars, which erupted in 1839 when the Chinese government attempted to prevent importation of narcotics. Chinese purchases of opium from British India were important to England because they financed British imports of Chinese tea. In China, however, the imports contributed to a troubling incidence of addiction. After a crushing military defeat, China signed the Treaty of Nanking, requiring: (1) transfer of Hong Kong to British control; (2) creation of five treaty ports where the British would have residence and trade rights; (3) limitation of import and export duties to modest rates; and (4) permission of British nationals to be tried in British courts. Soon, China was forced to sign similar treaties with Russia, Japan, France, and Germany, carving the Chinese and Korean coastal areas and river valleys into so-called **spheres of influence.** The United States took a different approach, insisting on equal access to trade and investment in China for all countries. This **Open Door Policy** gave East Asia some protection from the wholesale colonialism that destroyed the sovereignty of nations in other parts of Asia. Still, the influences of foreign commerce, culture, and religion were distasteful to Chinese nationalists. In 1900, partisans in the Boxer Rebellion attempted to expel foreign influence from China, but, in the end, they were repaid with the stationing of foreign troops on Chinese soil.

For many years, Japan allowed only China and Holland to operate trading depots on its soil, restricting each to a single port. After the spectacle of the Opium Wars, the Japanese were even more determined to avoid foreign penetration. In 1854, however, under threat from Commodore Perry's fleet, Japan accepted a commercial treaty with the United States that opened two additional ports. In short order, similar treaties were signed with the European powers, opening additional ports and extending extraterritorial rights to foreigners. Again, though, the Japanese government maintained its essential independence, and international contact led to a series of reforms that ended Japanese feudalism and launched its industrialization.

ASIAN COOPERATION AND SOCIALISM

Throughout Asia, extended families traditionally have been responsible for care of children, the elderly, and the disabled, and, in some cases, for ownership of property. Beyond the family, at the levels of village, province, and nation, institutions of community service and ownership have differed widely across Asian space and time.

In the Hindu cultures of South Asia, the caste system has obstructed development of social interaction and cooperation. Even today, when members of lower castes have broad constitutional rights and a major political voice, they continue to suffer from harsh discrimination and violence, particularly in rural villages.[11] Believing that individual poverty is the outcome of bad karma in a previous life, wealthy Hindus have provided little support for programs of public or private charity.[12]

With lower barriers of caste, the Theravada Buddhist and Islamic countries of Southeast Asia would seem to have greater capacities for social cooperation. However, most have found it difficult to cope with ethnic, racial, and tribal divisions. Cambodia is the only country in the region with a relatively homogeneous population. Thus, with a population of only 3 million, Singapore has four official languages. With 5 million people, Laos has six major ethnic and tribal groups. According to Sharon Siddique, recent patterns of economic growth in the region are explained, in large part, by noneconomic factors; prosperity has been the reward for countries (including his native Singapore) that embrace heterogeneity, ensure minority representation, and thereby promote political stability, ethnic harmony, and religious tolerance.[13]

The East Asian societies that combine Confucianism with Mahayana Buddhism seem to encourage the highest levels of social cooperation. By promoting educational opportunity, by emphasizing the importance of the group over the individual, and by encouraging leaders to serve the interests of their inferiors, the Confucian philosophy seems to encourage the development of cooperative institutions and relative equality of income. Thus, the East Asian countries have overturned the conventional view that income inequality is a necessary by-product of economic growth.

---

[11]On the new political power of lower castes, see M. R. Narayan Swamy, "Hindu 'Untouchable' Set to become Indian President," Agence France Presse, June 17, 1997. On the continuing caste divisions, see Barbara Crossette, "Caste May be India's Moral Achilles' Heel," *The New York Times*, October 20, 1996, section 4, 3; and Ajay Singh, "Curse of the Castes," *Asiaweek*, October 18, 1996, 34.

[12]Uppal, *Economic Development in South Asia*, 144–146.

[13]Sharon Siddique, "Economics Aside, Other Lessons from Southeast Asia," *Business Times* (Singapore), February 27, 1993, 3. Ironically, the region's worst episode of genocide in modern times occurred in culturally homogeneous Cambodia. Between 1975 and 1979, the Khmer Rouge regime exterminated or starved between 1 million and 2 million people–perhaps 40 percent of the entire population, including large proportions of its middle-class and intellectual communities—who were declared to be enemies of the regime.

In China, the home of Confucianism, a strain of communitarianism has existed for hundreds of years. The idea of communal utilization of land was discussed in the ancient Chinese work, *The Rites of Zhou,* and was practiced during the brief Xin dynasty (8–23 A.D.). During the Taiping Revolution (1850–1864), a huge army of peasants briefly gained control of southern China in their campaign against unfair land holdings, excessive taxes, and foreign imperialism. The Taiping rulers attempted to abolish private ownership of land and other property, proposing an elaborate and equalitarian system of land tenure.[14] In 1897, influenced by British Fabian Socialists, Sun Yat-sen included socialism, together with nationalism and democracy, among the Three Fundamental Principles that would lead his Nationalist Party in its revolution against Manchu rule.[15] A Chinese republic was established in 1911 by Sun and his Nationalists, but the government was unable to forge national unity or to withstand Western and Japanese interference.

Marxian socialism gained popularity in some Chinese intellectual circles after the Russian Bolshevik revolution. In 1918, Li Dazhao, the librarian at Beijing University, established a socialist New Tide Society that attracted a younger generation of university students, including his assistant, Mao Zedong. In 1921, Mao and eleven other delegates met secretly in Shanghai to create the Chinese Communist Party. In 1949, after long years of internal and external conflict, the Nationalist party established a government in Taiwan, and the Communist party, led by Mao, established the People's Republic of China on the mainland.

During the early years of their leadership, the Chinese Communists accepted advice and assistance from the Soviet Union, and built a Soviet-style system of central planning. However, beginning in 1958, during the so-called Great Leap Forward, China adopted a more radically equalitarian form of socialism. Ideological purity became more important than practical experience, and material incentives were replaced with moral exhortation.

In India, socialist programs were supported by Mahatma Gandhi (1869–1948) and Jawaharlal Nehru (1889–1964). Both men were exposed to Fabian Socialism when they studied law in England, and both participated in the fight for independence from British colonialism. Unlike the revolutionary and authoritarian systems of socialism in Russia and China, Gandhi and Nehru favored nonviolence and democracy.

Gandhi condemned the caste system and the unequal distribution of agricultural land. He supported nationalization and state control of public utilities and other industries that must operate on a large scale. Otherwise, he believed that India should rebuild a traditional society of self-contained rural villages, each governed by democratic principles. These should support development of agricultural production and small-scale handicraft industries.

---

[14]Immanuel C. Y. Hsü, *The Rise of Modern China,* 5th ed. (New York: Oxford University Press, 1995), 233.

[15]Ibid., 459.

Poverty should be eliminated, but society should avoid the spiritually and ecologically destructive quest for greater riches.

Nehru accepted Gandhi's ethical approach to life, but, as India's first independent prime minister, he also was strongly influenced by the policies of the British Labor party. Thus, Nehru's model of socialism was more urban, more industrial, and more oriented toward social modernization. The "commanding heights" of industry, including public utilities, steel, heavy machinery, and chemicals were nationalized, and were developed according to a series of five-year plans. Smaller industries and service firms remained under private ownership, but they were heavily regulated. Land reforms were designed to equalize holdings and to break the power of absentee landlords, but generally they were unsuccessful.[16]

Most of the smaller Asian countries had little experience with socialism before the end of World War II. During their postwar struggles for independence from Japanese and European colonial rule, many of the countries developed socialist revolutionary movements. When they gained independence, socialism provided a rationale for state control of assets seized from colonialists.

Under Indian and British influence, most of the South Asian countries adopted systems of democratic socialism. Initially, China and the Soviet Union worked together to support Communist movements in Cambodia, Laos, Myanmar, Vietnam, and North Korea. Beginning in the 1960s, after the Sino-Soviet split, the two major Communist powers had to compete for influence in Asia. Since 1976, when the death of Mao Zedong initiated a chain of events that led to a more pragmatic policy in China, market reforms have spread to most of the socialist countries of Asia (North Korea being the notable exception at the time of this writing).

The socialist influence was weakest in countries that escaped colonial control (Japan and Thailand), in countries that were permanently settled by colonists (Australia and New Zealand), in Hong Kong, controlled by the British until 1997, and in South Korea, aided by the United States and Japan in its confrontation with a Communist neighbor. In several of these countries, democratic socialist and labor parties have played significant roles in government, promoting nationalization of key industries and redistribution of income. With a few notable exceptions, though, investments in nationalized companies have attracted a declining share of Asian investment since the 1980s (see Table 18.3).

In Thailand, where socialists have not played a significant role in the parliament, and where Communists are not allowed to function legally, an interesting system of grassroots socialism has developed in a sect of the Buddhist community. Followers of Ajarn Buddhadasa (1906–1993), who established the Suan Mokkhabalarama sanctuary in southern Thailand, practice a system of **Dhammic socialism,** meaning a "preference for society over

---

[16]Allan G. Gruchy, *Comparative Economic Systems,* 2d ed. (Boston: Houghton Mifflin, 1977), 633–635; and Uppal, *Economic Development in South Asia,* 176–181.

■ **TABLE 18.3**

SHARES OF STATE-OWNED ENTERPRISES IN GROSS DOMESTIC INVESTMENT, 1978–1991

	1978–1985	1986–1991
South Asia		
Bangladesh	11	30
India	43	39
Nepal	35	53
Pakistan	36	29
Sri Lanka	31	26
East Asia		
Japan	10	6
Korea, South	26	15
Taiwan	30	18
Southeast Asia		
Malaysia	17	16
Myanmar	54	31
Thailand	16	14
Pacific Area		
Australia	18	15
Indonesia	15	10
Papua New Guinea	8	7
Philippines	17	7

SOURCE: World Bank, *Bureaucrats in Business* (Oxford: Oxford University Press, 1995), Table A.3.

the individual" derived from the "Law of Nature." Ideally, this is a socialism based on spiritual enlightenment and recognition of human interdependence, not a materialist system predicated on class conflict.[17] Similar in some respects to Christian socialist communities or Israeli *kibbutzim*, Dhammic societies are communitarian and voluntary, emphasizing rural development.[18]

---

[17]See Bhikkhu Buddhadasa, *Dhammic Socialism* (Bangkok: Inter-Religious Commission for Development, 1986); Santikaro Bhikkhu, "Why Dhammic Socialism?" at <http://www.suanmokkh.org/dhamsoc1.htm>; Justin Hall, "Buddhadasa's Dhammic Socialism: An Internet Vision" at <http://www.links.net//vita/swat/course/dasanet.html>; and Daren Johnson, "Ravages of Economic Development," *The Daily Yomiuri,* July 28, 1991, 7.

[18]On Christian communitarianism, see Martin Buber, *Paths in Utopia* (New York: Macmillan, 1950). On Israeli kibbutzim, see Haim Barkai, "The Kibbutz as a Social Institution," *Dissent* (Spring 1972): 354–370; and Christopher Warhurst, "High Society in a Workers' Society: Work, Community and Kibbutz," *Sociology* 30 (February 1996): 1–19.

THE ASIAN GROWTH MIRACLES

Since World War II, several countries in East and Southeast Asia have posted "miraculous" rates of economic growth. First among these was Japan, where per capita GDP grew at an annual rate of about 10 percent during the 1960s. When Japan's economy decelerated during the 1970s, the epicenter of economic growth moved to the first generation of Newly Industrializing Economies (NIEs)—Hong Kong, Singapore, South Korea, and Taiwan.[19] Between 1965 and 1985, these economies grew three times faster than their neighbors in South Asia and seven times faster than the poor nations of Sub-Saharan Africa (see Table 18.4). During the 1980s, explosive growth began in China and in a second generation of NIEs in Southeast Asia. With annual growth rates in the neighborhood of 6.5 percent, the NIEs have doubled their per capita incomes with each passing decade. At the same time, they have reduced income inequality, increased literacy rates, and extended life expectancy.

Many would agree with Michael Prowse that "the biggest challenge for economists today is understanding the extraordinary success of East Asia."[20] The policy community needs to understand the Asian miracle to maintain its vitality, to forecast its future, and to assess its relevance for other developing and transitional economies. After decades of research, social scientists have accumulated an enormous volume of statistical and qualitative evidence on this subject, but their conclusions have generated equal measures of scholarly light and emotional heat. In the following pages, we shall briefly consider the influences of culture, government, trade policy, saving, investment, productivity growth, and income distribution on East Asian economic growth. Finally, we shall conclude the chapter with a more extensive review of regional cooperation and integration in the Asia-Pacific region, considering, again, its contribution to the regional economic growth.

CULTURE

Cultural traditions in Japan, China, and the first generation of NIEs were strongly influenced by Confucianism, with its emphases on cooperative and honorable behavior, education, hard work, discipline, and frugality. Thus, as we noted previously, many believe that the mixture of Confucianism and Mahayana Buddhism in East Asia provided a supportive environment for economic growth and development. At the same time, and for several reasons, other people consider this line of analysis to be offensive and unconvincing. First, it seems to argue that one cultural tradition is superior to another. Second, it implies that the lessons of East Asia cannot be applied in other regions. Third, the cultural hypothesis seems to be contradicted by the second generation of growth miracles in Indonesia and

---

[19]In the past, these were known as Newly Industrializing Countries (NICs), but international agencies now use the word *economy*, rather than *country*, because Hong Kong and Taiwan are considered to be provinces of China.

[20]Michael Prowse, "Miracles Beyond the Free Market," *The Financial Times*, April 26, 1993, 15.

■ TABLE 18.4

INCOME AND GROWTH OF ASIAN INDUSTRIAL
ECONOMIES, 1965–1996

	GDP per Capita (dollars at purchasing-power parity)	Annual Growth of GDP per Capita (percent)		
	1994	1965–1985	1985–1994	1995–1996
Major Economies				
Japan	21,140	4.7	3.2	1.3
China	1,800	4.8	7.8	8.9
India	1,280	1.7	2.9	5.4
Newly Industrializing Economies				
First Generation:	16,950	6.7	6.5	5.4
Hong Kong	20,950	6.1	5.3	4.1
Korea, South	10,330	6.6	7.8	7.0
Singapore	21,900	7.6	6.1	5.8
Taiwan	14,630	6.6	6.8	4.8
Second Generation:	6,340	4.4	6.7	6.4
Indonesia	3,600	4.8	6.0	6.3
Malaysia	8,440	4.4	5.6	6.4
Thailand	6,970	4.0	8.6	6.6
Emerging Generation:	2,080	2.1	3.4	3.7
Bangladesh	1,330	0.4	2.0	3.2
Pakistan	2,130	2.6	1.3	2.2
Philippines	2,740	2.3	1.7	2.9
Sri Lanka	3,160	2.9	2.9	3.2
Vietnam	1,050	n.a.	6.0	7.2
For Comparison				
South Asia	1,650	1.9	2.7	4.8
Sub-Saharan Africa	1,420	1.0	−1.2	1.5
Latin America	5,970	2.5	0.6	0.5
High-Income Countries	18,520	2.4	1.9	1.7

NOTE: Averages for tier groups are simple and unweighted. Averages for comparison regional groups are weighted. For some countries, estimates of per capita income growth during 1995–1996 are based on the assumption that population growth continued at rates prevailing in 1990–1994.

SOURCES: Sources for Table 18.1; and International Monetary Fund, *World Economic Outlook,* May 1997.

Malaysia, where the majority populations are Muslim, and, fourth, it fails to explain the unexceptional performance of Confucian economies in earlier periods of history.

GOVERNMENT

The governmental role in East Asian economic growth is nearly as controversial as the role of culture. Indeed, in recent years, East Asia has been a major ideological battlefield in the timeless struggle between philosophies of laissez-faire and state intervention.

According to neoclassical economists, including advocates of the so-called Washington Consensus, East Asian growth has been supported by the "market friendly" policies of national governments.[21] By avoiding regulation of prices, interest rates, rents, and other payments, and by maintaining small budget deficits, stable monetary policies, low levels of foreign debt, and low barriers to internal and external trade, the governments have provided stable and flexible environments for market-oriented development. These market conditions have encouraged high rates of domestic saving and large inflows of foreign capital, supporting high rates of investment. According to this view, the East Asian governments are strong and sometimes authoritarian, but, fortunately, they usually have focused on appropriate governmental services; they have protected the public from violence and injustice, have provided educational services for the young, and have invested in infrastructure for transportation, communications, and other public utilities.

According to an opposing interpretation, the East Asian economies are led by **developmental states** that have supported economic growth not by following markets, but by leading them. Particularly in the cases of Japan, South Korea, and Taiwan, national planning agencies formulated active industrial policies, picked key industries for preferential development, and supported them with selective credit policies, production and export subsidies, import substitution schemes, and an arsenal of other market-bending weapons. Recent research suggests that private investors in these countries would have been unwilling to shift their activities from traditional to modern sectors without strong encouragement and coordination by their governments.[22]

The active industrial policies of the East Asian governments are documented extensively in anecdotal evidence. In South Korea, for example, Hyundai Heavy Industries was created in the 1970s with state-subsidized credit and eventually became the world's largest shipbuilding company. Also in the 1970s, Korean leaders were denied support from the World Bank to build an integrated steel mill because Korea did not seem to have a comparative advantage in steel production. After the government built the

---

[21]Recall our discussion of the Washington Consensus in Chapter 5.

[22]Dani Rodrik, "Getting Interventions Right: How South Korea and Taiwan Grew Rich," *Economic Policy* 20 (April 1995): 55–107.

POSCO mill with its own resources, the World Bank eventually acknowledged that it was "arguably the world's most efficient producer of steel."[23] According to James Fallows, Koreans only wish that their government had taken this aggressive stance earlier:

> When Koreans ask themselves why their country took so long to get going industrially, they usually say the problem was too weak a government—too weak to rig the economy to get extra savings out of the public, too weak to "get prices wrong" and artificially encourage investment. They do not complain that the government was too strong.[24]

In 1993, the World Bank published a controversial report, *The East Asian Miracle: Economic Growth and Public Policy*, based on a major research project financed by the Japanese government.[25] In a subtle shift of the Washington Consensus, the World Bank team acknowledged that strong and intelligent bureaucratic institutions in the Northeast Asian countries—Japan, South Korea, and Taiwan—contributed to the growth miracles in those countries. However, to the apparent dismay of its Japanese sponsors, the report found no broader evidence that industrial targeting policies had raised productivity growth in East Asia. Furthermore, according to the report, interventionist policies that worked in Northeast Asia during the 1960s and 1970s were dependent on unique historical and institutional features in that region, and they would provoke retaliatory trade sanctions today. In the end, therefore, the report suggested that developing countries should learn from the experience of Singapore, Hong Kong, and the second generation of NEIs in Southeast Asia, where governments have been strong and stable, but markets have remained free and relatively unregulated.[26]

TRADE POLICY

According to the neoclassical view, much of East Asian success can be attributed to liberal trade regimes and strong performances on export markets. The import tariffs of NIEs are much lower than those of South Asian countries (Table 18.5), and their trade volumes are much larger. The first generation NIEs account for only 10 percent of the total GDP of the Asia-Pacific region, but they supply about 27 percent of total exports from Asia-Pacific to the world. The second generation NIEs account for 9 percent of regional GDP and 13 percent of regional exports (Table 18.1 and Table 18.6).

Certainly, most of the East and Southeast Asian economies have benefited from strong export performance, and the smallest economies in the region—Hong Kong and Singapore—could hardly exist without the foreign

---

[23]Ibid., 91. For additional evidence, see A. H. Amsden, *Asia's Next Giant: South Korea and Late Industrialization* (New York: Oxford University Press, 1989), 269–290.

[24]Fallows, *Looking at the Sun*, 214.

[25]World Bank, *The East Asian Miracle: Economic Growth and Public Policy* (Oxford: Oxford University Press, 1993). On the political environment in which the report was prepared, see Prowse, "Miracles Beyond the Free Market," 15; and Edith Terry, "An East Asian Paradigm?" *Atlantic Economic Journal* 24 (September 1996): 183–185.

[26]World Bank, *The East Asian Miracle*, 81–90.

■ TABLE 18.5

SIMPLE AVERAGE TARIFF RATES FOR
SELECTED ASIAN COUNTRIES, 1992

	Percent
South Asia	
Bangladesh	75
India	66
Pakistan	71
Sri Lanka	44
East and Southeast Asia	
Indonesia	20
Malaysia	10
Philippines	24
Singapore	6
South Korea	10
Thailand	31

SOURCE: World Bank, *Industrial Competition and Performance in Asia* (Washington, D.C., 1995), 27.

sector. In the larger countries, though, we should neither underestimate nor overestimate the importance of commerce. With few natural resources, Japan is dependent on international trade, but, in 1994, its export share of GDP was smaller than in any of 24 other high-income economies of the world.[27] In South Korea and Taiwan, recent research suggests that export performance was a symptom or a secondary cause of economic development; the primary engine of growth, according to this interpretation, was domestic investment.[28]

SAVING AND INVESTMENT

In the 1950s, national saving rates were relatively low in the first generation NIEs, ranging from 3 percent of GDP in South Korea to 10 percent in Taiwan. Inflows of foreign capital supported gross investment rates that were significantly higher—10 percent in Korea and 16 percent in Taiwan. In all the first generation NIEs, investment grew rapidly during the 1960s and 1970s, and domestic saving grew even more rapidly. By the 1970s, Taiwan had saving and investment rates above 30 percent of GDP; similar levels were achieved

---

[27]World Bank, *World Development Report 1996* (Oxford: Oxford University Press, 1996), 213.
[28]Rodrik, "Getting Interventions Right," 55–107.

■ TABLE 18.6

DESTINATIONS OF EXPORTS FROM ASIA AND THE PACIFIC AREA, 1995 (BILLIONS OF U.S. DOLLARS)

Exports to:	World	United States	European Union	Japan	Other Industrial	China	Other Asian Developing	Other Developing
Exports from:								
Asia and Pacific	**1,459.0**	**322.5**	**228.3**	**141.0**	**67.7**	**76.4**	**510.0**	**112.3**
South Asia	**51.7**	**10.2**	**16.4**	**3.9**	**2.0**	**0.6**	**10.3**	**8.4**
Bangladesh	4.0	1.3	1.7	0.1	0.1	—	0.4	0.3
India	35.1	6.1	10.4	2.9	1.3	0.4	7.7	6.2
Nepal	0.4	0.1	0.2	—	—	—	—	—
Pakistan	8.5	1.3	2.7	0.6	0.4	0.2	1.8	1.54
Sri Lanka	3.8	1.3	1.4	0.2	0.1	—	0.3	0.4
East Asia	**1,019.8**	**241.5**	**153.6**	**70.4**	**45.8**	**62.7**	**364.7**	**80.7**
China	231.9	48.5	30.9	35.9	8.6	—	94.7	13.3
Hong Kong	63.0	10.7	15.5	2.7	2.7	8.6	14.5	8.2
Japan	479.2	127.2	75.8	—	24.2	29.0	184.9	37.8
Korea, South	118.8	24.9	14.6	17.3	5.1	10.3	32.9	13.8
Taiwan	126.6	30.2	16.7	14.3	5.2	14.8	37.6	7.7

Exports to:	World	United States	European Union	Japan	Other Industrial	China	Other Asian Developing	Other Developing
Exports from:								
Southeast Asia	**238.9**	**49.0**	**35.8**	**29.4**	**8.8**	**7.6**	**93.8**	**14.3**
Cambodia	0.4	—	0.1	—	—	—	0.3	—
Laos	0.4	—	0.1	—	—	—	0.2	—
Malaysia	85.6	18.0	11.5	10.5	2.9	2.1	36.4	4.2
Myanmar	1.1	0.1	0.1	0.1	—	0.2	0.6	—
Singapore	89.2	18.9	13.4	6.8	3.3	3.4	37.8	5.4
Thailand	56.5	11.9	9.1	10.1	2.2	1.6	17.1	4.4
Vietnam	5.7	0.2	1.5	1.7	0.3	0.3	1.3	0.3
Pacific Area	**148.6**	**21.8**	**22.6**	**37.4**	**11.2**	**5.5**	**41.2**	**8.9**
Australia	55.0	3.6	6.6	14.5	4.2	2.6	20.3	3.3
Indonesia	47.4	8.0	8.0	14.2	1.8	2.1	10.6	2.7
New Zealand	14.7	1.6	2.4	2.5	3.1	0.3	3.5	1.1
Papua New Guinea	2.8	0.1	0.5	0.7	1.0	—	0.6	—
Philippines	19.9	7.4	3.0	3.5	0.7	0.3	4.5	0.5
Other Pacific	8.7	1.3	2.0	1.9	0.4	0.2	1.7	1.2

NOTE: Entries may not sum to stated totals because of rounding.

SOURCE: Compiled from International Monetary Fund, *Direction of Trade Statistics Yearbook 1996* (Washington, D.C., 1996).

in Korea, Hong Kong, and Singapore during the 1980s and in the second generation NIEs during the early 1990s.[29]

We noted earlier the possibility that these investment booms were the major force, on the demand side, behind explosive growth in Taiwan and Korea, and perhaps in several other NIEs. More certainly, these investments were critical on the supply side, providing the capital and social infrastructure needed for higher levels of production and improved standards of living.

According to the neoclassical view, rapid growth of saving and investment in the NIEs began spontaneously when they gained independence from colonialism and introduced market-friendly policies. According to the cultural view, East Asian frugality was encouraged by the Confucian heritage and by a survivor mentality in the region, developed during periods of warfare and forced migration. According to the developmental state view, governments in the region encouraged saving by creating postal saving systems, by restricting consumer credit, and by providing few retirement benefits; they encouraged investment by creating state enterprises and by coordinating activities in the private sector.[30]

PRODUCTIVITY GROWTH

In almost any country, the level and growth of national production can be explained, in large part, by the availability and quality of productive resources (labor, capital, and natural resources) and by how fully they are employed. If a country's output is higher or lower than the level predicted by a simple analysis of its resources, we may conclude that it exhibits a high or low level of **total factor productivity (TFP).** Growth arising from higher TFP, in turn, may indicate improvements in labor motivation or industrial organization, gains from domestic and international trade, and a host of other factors.

If a large portion of East Asia's growth could be attributed to TFP, the performance of the region would seem more genuinely "miraculous" because output growth would be considerably more than the sum of productive inputs. High historical TFP growth also may imply that significant East Asian growth will continue in the future, when high levels of saving and international investment may be difficult to sustain. Furthermore, it may imply that market-oriented policies can generate significant growth in other developing countries, even if they have limited capacities to save and invest.

Unfortunately, the statistical evidence on East Asian TFP growth is quite unclear. Depending on the country and time period analyzed, the measurement of outputs and inputs, and the formulae used to relate outputs to

---

[29]United Nations Conference on Trade and Development, *Trade and Development Report, 1996* (Geneva, 1996), 109–110.

[30]Joseph E. Stiglitz and Marilou Uy, "Financial Markets, Public Policy, and the East Asian Miracle," *The World Bank Research Observer* 11 (August 1996): 250–256.

inputs, one can obtain a wide range of estimates. For example, measures of Singaporean annual TFP growth range from −0.01 percent to 3.1 percent.[31]

In 1993, when it published *The East Asian Miracle,* the World Bank emphasized higher estimates of TFP growth, as it had done many times in the past.[32] One year later, Paul Krugman of Stanford University drew attention to the lower TFP estimates; he claimed that East Asian growth was comparable to the ill-fated, input-driven growth of the former Soviet Union, and he concluded that the East Asian miracle was a mirage. "If there is a secret to Asian growth," he said, "it is simply deferred gratification, the willingness to sacrifice current satisfaction for future gain."[33]

Krugman's analysis provoked outrage. The international business press declared that his evidence and conclusions were "tendentious," "entirely misconceived," and "ripped up at the roots."[34] Krugman gave undue emphasis, they said, to the poor TFP growth of tiny Singapore during the 1970s. Based on more recent data, a new study by the Union Bank of Switzerland claims that all the Asian NIEs, except Indonesia, have achieved TFP growth rates significantly above the world average: "Our results restore the 'miracle' to Asian growth, at least until better measures of capital and labor become available."[35]

INCOME DISTRIBUTION

For hundreds of years, many economists believed that income inequality was both cause and consequence of economic growth. Inequality caused growth, according to the so-called "trickle-down theory," by encouraging a high rate of saving, supporting a high level of investment in the instruments of production.[36] Inequality was a consequence of the early stages of growth, according to the Kuznets hypothesis, because the benefits of growth were seldom shared evenly across social classes or geographic areas.[37]

The experience of East Asia poses a serious challenge to the conventional wisdom on inequality and growth. According to Gini ratios for the

---

[31]World Bank, *World Development Report 1987* (Oxford: Oxford University Press, 1987), 93; and International Monetary Fund, *World Economic Outlook,* May 1997, 82–83.

[32]World Bank, *World Development Report 1987,* 92; World Bank, *World Development Report 1991,* 42–51; and World Bank, *The East Asian Miracle,* 46–69.

[33]Paul Krugman, "The Myth of Asia's Miracle," *Foreign Affairs* 73 (November–December 1994): 78. Krugman's conclusions are based on studies by Jong-Il Kim and Lawrence Lau, "The Sources of Economic Growth of the East Asian Newly Industrialized Countries," *Journal of the Japanese and International Economies* 8 (September 1994): 235–271; and Alwyn Young, "The Tyranny of Numbers: Confronting the Statistical Realities of the East Asian Growth Experience," NBER Working Paper No. 4680 (March 1994).

[34]"The Spectre of Soviet Disease? Wrong Again, Krugman," *Asiamoney,* May 1997, 18–19; "Is It Over?" *The Economist,* March 1, 1997, 23.

[35]Sarah Davison, "Continued High Growth Seen in Asia," Reuter Asia-Pacific Business Report, November 17, 1996.

[36]During the 1930s, John Maynard Keynes argued against the broad sweep of this argument, claiming that saving may encourage or discourage growth, depending on the state of the business cycle. A better understanding of this relationship, he said, would remove "one of the chief social justifications of great inequality of wealth." See his book, *The General Theory of Employment, Interest, and Money* (New York: Harcourt, Brace, and World, 1964), 373.

[37]Refer to the discussion of Kuznets's Law in Chapter 5.

decades of the 1960s, 1970s, and 1980s, inequality was consistently lower in high-growth Asia than in low-growth Africa or Latin America, and inequality *declined* steadily in Singapore, Malaysia, and Hong Kong. Inequality increased marginally in South Korea, Taiwan, and Indonesia during the 1970s, but remained far below the average for developing countries.[38]

Clearly, then, inequality was not a notable cause or consequence of rapid East Asian growth. Indeed, a growing body of literature suggests that Asian growth was encouraged by the same policies that reduced inequality, and growth was encouraged by equality itself. Growth and equality both seem to be supported by programs of public health and education, land reform, trade liberalization, and support for small business.[39] Income equality contributes directly to economic growth by strengthening political stability, by reducing the probability of political stalemate that prevents progress in divided societies, and by reducing demands for protectionism.[40]

REGIONAL ECONOMIC INTEGRATION

According to Ippei Yamazawa of Hitotsubashi University in Japan, an important engine of economic growth among East Asian economies is their "growing interdependence."[41] This assertion will come as a surprise to many, because economic cooperation among Asian countries is a relatively recent phenomenon.

After World War II, the environment for regional economic cooperation was extremely unfavorable in Asia. Independence and fragmentation were the orders of the day. In South Asia, to mitigate religious and ethnic rivalries, national borders were drawn between India, Pakistan, and Bangladesh. In East Asia, the Communist leadership of China attempted to cooperate with the Soviet Union, but eventually drifted into a deep isolationism. Japan, a defeated and desperate country, lost its colonial holdings in Taiwan and Korea, and the latter was divided, north and south. In Southeast Asia, former French Indochina was divided and subdivided, spawning civil and national wars, ethnic hostilities, and foreign intervention.

Against this historical background, and because of Asia's alleged penchant for protectionism, many Westerners believed that Asians would be slow to develop effective systems of economic cooperation. In his well-known work on regional trade blocks, Lester Thurow suggested that economic integration would languish in East Asia because Japan, the major power in the region, was unwilling to open its markets for labor and im-

---

[38]Jose Edgardo Campos and Hilton R. Root, *The Key to the Asian Miracle: Making Shared Growth Credible* (Washington, D.C.: Brookings Institution, 1996), 9.

[39]Ibid., Chapter 3.

[40]World Bank, *World Development Report 1991,* 137–139; and Rodrik, "Getting Interventions Right," 92.

[41]Ippei Yamazawa, "On Pacific Economic Integration," *The Economic Journal* 102 (November 1992): 1523.

ported manufactures; other Asian countries were wary of Japanese neocolonialism:

> Japan's history and culture may make it impossible for it to create a quasi trading block on the Pacific Rim to rival that of Europe or the Americas. Korea and the Chinese-based economies (mainland China, Taiwan, Hong Kong, and Singapore) may prefer to have special arrangements with their best market—the United States—rather than their chief rival—Japan.[42]

Despite these and other doubts, countries in the East-Pacific region have made surprising progress toward regional integration in recent years. Trade between Asian countries accounted for 37 percent of Asian world trade in 1980, 41 percent in 1990, and 46 percent in 1995.[43] Asian developing countries now provide the most important export market for products from South Asia, East Asia, Southeast Asia, and the Pacific Area (Table 18.6). By their willingness to set aside age-old animosities to pursue commercial relations, the Asian nations "may offer a model for the rest of the world."[44]

Asian economic integration seems to be supported by three groups of institutional arrangements: multilateral organizations, growth triangles, and multinational business networks. Let us consider each of these in turn.

MULTILATERAL ORGANIZATIONS

Efforts to pursue multilateral integration in Asia have a relatively short history. Organizations now known as the United Nations Economic and Social Council for Asia and the Pacific (ESCAP) and the Pacific Islands Commission were created after World War II to promote general economic development in the region, but, as we noted, the time was not ripe for significant cooperation.

The Asian Development Bank and the **Association of Southeast Asian Nations (ASEAN)** were established in 1967, during the Vietnam War, as bulwarks against the spread of communism (Table 18.7). In 1977, after American troops withdrew from Vietnam, ASEAN shifted more of its attention to economic issues, and established a system of Preferential Trading Arrangements (PTAs). The PTAs called for lower tariffs on intra-ASEAN trade, but initial progress was minimal.[45]

In 1992, member countries agreed to establish an **ASEAN Free Trade Area (AFTA)** that would gradually reduce internal tariffs on most manufactured products to no more than 5 percent by the year 2008. Again, initial progress was slow, but tariff reductions were accelerated in 1993 to attract foreign investors who were looking to China; "normal track" tariff reductions would now be completed by 2003, and fast-track reductions would

---

[42]Lester Thurow, *Head to Head: The Coming Economic Battle Among Japan, Europe, and America* (New York: William and Morrow Co., 1992), 251.

[43]United Nations Statistical Office, *Monthly Bulletin of Statistics*, June 1993, 256–261, and June 1996, 258–263. For present purposes, Asia consists of Japan and the category "developing countries—other Asia."

[44]Wasahide Shibusawa, quoted in James C. Abegglen, *Sea Change: Pacific Asia as the New World Industrial Center* (New York: Free Press, 1994), 246–247.

[45]Arvind Panagariya, "East Asia and the New Regionalism in World Trade," *World Economy* 17 (November 1994): 817–839.

MEMBERSHIP OF ASIA-PACIFIC COUNTRIES IN ECONOMIC ORGANIZATIONS, 1997

	ADB	APEC	ASEAN	ESCAP	PIC	SAARC	WTO
South Asia							
Bangladesh	M			M		M	M
Bhutan	M			M		M	
India	M			M		M	M
Nepal	M			M		M	C
Pakistan	M			M		M	M
Sri Lanka	M			M		M	M
East Asia							
China	M	M		M			C
Hong Kong	M	M		A			M
Japan	M	M		M			M
Korea, North				M			
Korea, South	M	M		M			M
Mongolia	M			M			M
Taiwan	M	M					C
Southeast Asia							
Cambodia	M		C	M			C
Laos	M		C	M			O
Malaysia	M	M	M	M			M
Myanmar	M		C	M			M
Singapore	M	M	M	M			M
Thailand	M	M	M	M			M
Vietnam	M	C	M	M			C
Pacific Area							
Australia	M	M		M	M		M
Brunei Darussalam		M	M	M			M
Indonesia	M	M	M	M			M
New Zealand	M	M		M	M		M
Papua New Guinea	M	M	O	M	M		M
Philippines	M	M	M	M			M

ADB–Asian Development Bank
APEC–Asia Pacific Economic Cooperation
ASEAN–Association of Southeast Asian Nations
ESCAP–Economic and Social Commission for Asia and the Pacific
PIC–Pacific Islands Commission (formerly South Pacific Commission)
SAARC–South Asian Association for Regional Cooperation
WTO–World Trade Organization

A–Associate Member
C–Candidate for Membership
M–Member
O–Observer

SOURCES: Compiled from U.S. Central Intelligence Agency, *The World Factbook 1996, appendix;* organizational web sites and news reports.

be completed by 1998. At the same time, the scope of tariff reduction was expanded to include agricultural and other primary commodities. According to Australian estimates, full implementation of AFTA may increase intra-ASEAN trade by 10 percent, total ASEAN exports by 2 percent, and regional GDP by 2 percent.[46]

Initiatives for multilateral integration in South Asia were even later to begin, and have moved more slowly than those in Southeast Asia. **The South Asian Association for Regional Cooperation (SAARC)** was established in 1985 with a long list of lofty goals, but its annual meetings during the 1980s were dominated by security concerns—ethnic disputes in border areas, the nuclear arms race between India and Pakistan, and the Tamil separatist movement in Sri Lanka. Nearly half the early SAARC projects were abandoned because member countries failed to attend organizational meetings. The intra-SAARC share of total SAARC trade was only 5 percent in 1980, and it actually *declined* to 3 percent in 1990 (Table 18.8). In 1990, a New Delhi newspaper declared that "of the many regional groupings that have emerged in the world, SAARC certainly takes its place among the least effective."[47]

During the 1990s, SAARC began to show signs of life. In 1992, it established a SAARC Chamber of Commerce and Industry, based in Karachi, to coordinate the work of the national chambers. In 1993, following the long lead of ASEAN, a SAARC Preferential Trading Arrangement (SAPTA) was established; again, however, it was implemented slowly. In 1997, SAARC members displayed new resolve to settle political differences, and they agreed to establish a free trade area by 2001. Indian industrialists estimated that intra-SAARC investment could grow from insignificant levels to $15 billion by the turn of the century.[48]

■ TABLE 18.8

	INTERNAL TRADE OF REGIONAL TRADING GROUPS, 1970–1993		
	1970	**1980**	**1990**	**1993**
APEC	57.1	57.5	69.0	67.2
ASEAN	21.1	16.9	18.7	20.0
European Union (12)	53.2	55.7	60.6	56.0
SAARC	4.6	5.0	3.0	3.5

SOURCE: United Nations Conference on Trade and Development, *Handbook of International Trade and Development Statistics* 1994 (New York, 1995), 35.

---

[46]Department of Foreign Affairs and Trade, Australia, East Asia Analytical Unit, "ASEAN Free Trade Area: Trading Bloc or Building Block?" April 1994 <http://www.dfat.gov.au/dept/eaau/asean_free_trade.html>.

[47]Dilip Mukherjee of the *Economic Times,* quoted in Rajiv Tiwari, "South Asia: Clipped Wings Prevent Cooperative Take-off," Inter Press News Service, November 23, 1990.

[48]Amal Jayasinghe, "South Asians Set Free Trade Deadline," *Financial Times,* May 15, 1997, 6; and "India Study Assesses Scope for SAARC Cooperation," *Business Line* (FT Asia Intelligence), April 21, 1997, 9.

In 1989, the **Asia Pacific Economic Cooperation (APEC)** was created on principles of "open regionalism" to provide a forum for resolution of trade disputes between the United States and countries in the Asia-Pacific region.[49] The organization attracted little attention initially, but its importance increased dramatically in 1991. At that time, the United States was concluding a free trade agreement with Canada, the European Community was preparing for its single market program, and the Uruguay Round of GATT negotiations was proceeding slowly. To strengthen the Asian position in what seemed to be an emerging system of regional trade blocs, Malaysian Prime Minister Mahathir Mohamad proposed that the capitalist East Asian countries—Hong Kong, Japan, South Korea, and Taiwan—which were not members of a regional association, should be invited to join an expanded ASEAN, which would be called the East Asian Economic Group (EAEG).[50]

The United States quickly voiced its strong opposition to the EAEG proposal, and Japan decided not to support creation of the organization, fearing it would provoke a new round of protectionism in the United States and Europe. Instead, the two countries decided to raise the profile of APEC, giving it more financial and political support. Under these circumstances, China, Hong Kong, and Taiwan decided to join APEC at its 1991 meeting, and discussions commenced on creation of a permanent secretariat.[51]

APEC held its first summit meeting in 1993, and one year later the national leaders agreed to create the world's largest free trade area. The industrial countries would remove trade and investment barriers by 2010, and developing countries would do the same by 2020. The group adopted an implementation plan in 1995, and several developing countries—Chile, Hong Kong, Philippines, Singapore, and Taiwan—pledged in 1996 and 1997 to accelerate their schedules of trade liberalization.[52]

According to a computable general equilibrium analysis performed for the World Bank, all the APEC members will gain in GDP if the region completes a trade liberalization program, but the excluded European Union will lose slightly from trade diversion. The gains will be larger for the poorer countries, for whom potential gains from trade are most significant. Gains are largest if the free trade area is as large as possible. Exclusion of any region (the United States, China, or ASEAN) is harmful to that region, and reduces the estimated gains of all other members.[53]

---

[49]On open regionalism, recall our discussion of regional trading organizations in Chapter 5.

[50]This was only one of several attempts by Mahathir to distance Asia from the West. See Fallows, *Looking at the Sun*, 307–314.

[51]Gwen Robinson, "Asia Forum Cutting Political Teeth; APEC Meeting Lays Groundwork for Broader Scope of Cooperation," *The Nikkei Weekly*, November 23, 1991, 24.

[52]Vikram Khanna, "The Glacial Progress of APEC," *Business Times*, April 7, 1997, 4; and Juliana E. Dancel, "Developing Nations Ready Full Liberalization by 2010," *Business Daily*, May 22, 1997.

[53]Jeffrey D. Lewis, Sherwin Robinson, and Zhi Wang, "Beyond the Uruguay Round: The Implications of an Asian Free Trade Area," World Bank Policy Research Working Paper, No. 1467, February 1995, <http://www.worldbank.org/html/dec/Publications/Workpapers/intlecon.html>.

GROWTH TRIANGLES

In the 1970s, after Japan relaxed some of its external controls, several Asian countries attempted to attract Japanese investments by establishing Export Processing Zones, special business parks with few taxes or tariffs. In some cases, it was discovered that these zones could operate more efficiently, exploiting complementary resources, if they crossed over national borders. Thus, the first of the so-called **growth triangles** were created. Representing a lower level of multilateralism than the free trade organizations, growth triangles involve intergovernmental agreements or informal arrangements between smaller groups of countries.

In 1989, the participating governments recognized a growth triangle linking Singapore, the southern part of the Johore state of Malaysia, and the island of Batam in Indonesia. Known as the Southern Triangle, this zone allows Singaporean businesses to take advantage of lower labor costs in Indonesia and Malaysia. At various levels of legal formality and informality, other triangles include the Chinese Economic Area, linking Southern China, Hong Kong, and Taiwan; the Baht Zone, covering border areas of Southeast Asia; and the Yellow Sea Zone, involving areas of Northeast China, North Korea, South Korea, and Japan.[54]

Unlike trading blocs, which usually focus on development of internal markets, growth triangles are more outward looking. At the present stage of Asian development, when markets in North America and Europe continue to be critically important, this may be an appropriate system of cooperation. Also, because a growth triangle initially may cover only a limited geographic area and product mix, it can be established at relatively low cost in a short period of time with little policy coordination.[55]

MULTINATIONAL BUSINESS NETWORKS

The most important networks supporting Asian economic integration are handled by the private sector, with little or no involvement of governments or international organizations. Of these, the most important are organized by Japanese multinational corporations and by networks of Overseas Chinese.

During the 1980s, when it was amassing trade surpluses, Japan became a major overseas investor. Nearly half of Japan's external capital was invested in the United States, but in 1994 Japan had a stock of about $76 billion dedicated to direct investments in Asia.[56] In Southeast Asia, Japan was the most important foreign investor during the early 1990s, accounting for about 26 percent of all foreign direct investment.[57] Official development assistance from Japan was even more important in Asia than direct private investment;

---

[54]P. J. Lloyd, "Intraregional Trade in the Asia and Pacific Region," *Asian Development Review* 12 (1994): 127–129.

[55]United Nations, *Economic and Social Survey of Asia and the Pacific in 1994*, 52.

[56]United Nations Conference on Trade and Development, *Trade and Development Report, 1996*, 82.

[57]Ibid., 85.

most Asian countries received more than half their foreign aid from Japan.[58] Nearly one-third of that aid was paid from the Japanese government to Japanese companies working in the recipient countries.[59]

Japanese investment and aid in Asia supports an international pattern of industrial development known as the **flying geese formation.** Developed during the 1930s by Kanemae Akamatsu to describe changes in the industrial structure of a single country over time, this model now is used to analyze the evolving industrial structure of a cooperative group of countries. According to the usual formulation, Japan is the lead goose in Asian technology and industry, followed sequentially in a V-shaped formation by the first generation NIEs, the second generation NIEs, China and Vietnam, and the other emerging NIEs of Southeast and South Asia. As Japan progresses technologically, it pulls the entire formation forward, creating new industries, shedding old ones that have become uncompetitive in Japan, and investing in other Asian countries to sustain a dynamic pattern of regional comparative advantage.[60]

The Japanese government, represented in this case by the Ministry of International Trade and Industry, plays a supporting role in the flying geese formation by coordinating the industrial policies of compliant East Asian economies and by providing foreign aid to complement private investments.[61] The leading role in this network is played, however, by Japanese multinational corporations and business groups (*keiretsu*), and by their counterparts in the NIEs, frequently organizing their activities in the subregional growth triangles. Toyota, for example, manufactures transmissions in the Philippines, diesel engines in Indonesia, steering parts in Malaysia, and gas engines in Thailand. In Singapore, it operates a trading center to oversee shipments of vehicle parts throughout Southeast Asia.[62]

The factor intensity ratios in Table 18.9 provide an interesting view of the underlying patterns of comparative advantage supported, in part, by the flying geese formation. In 1993, Japan exported relatively few products produced with unskilled labor, and relatively large numbers of products produced with physical capital, human capital, and, most of all, advanced technology. None of the other East Asian countries was a major exporter of products embodying physical and human capital. Malaysia and Singapore were significant exporters of technology-intensive goods; the other countries, and particularly China, were dependent on exports produced with unskilled labor.

---

[58]Abegglen, *Sea Change,* 66 and 260.

[59]Lloyd, "Intraregional Trade in the Asia and Pacific Region," 129.

[60]Kanemae Akamatsu, "A Theory of Unbalanced Growth in the World Economy," *Weltwirtschaftliches Archiv* 86 (1961): 196–217; Terry, "An East Asian Paradigm?" 185–190; and United Nations Conference on Trade and Development, *Trade and Development Report, 1996,* 75–105.

[61]See Bernard Wysocki, Jr., "In Asia the Japanese Hope to 'Coordinate' What Nations Produce," *The Wall Street Journal,* August 20, 1990, A1.

[62]Artemio F. Cusi III, "Japanese Ties to Keep Machinery, Transport Equipment Imports Up," *Businessworld* (Manila), June 10, 1997, 15.

■ **TABLE 18.9**

**RELATIVE FACTOR INTENSITIES OF
ASIAN EXPORTS, 1993**

	Unskilled Labor	Physical Capital	Human Capital	Technology
Japan	**0.39**	**1.29**	**1.44**	**1.60**
Newly Industrializing Economies				
First Generation	2.03	0.57	0.65	1.62
Hong Kong	3.50	0.29	0.63	1.21
Korea, South	1.95	0.72	0.97	1.38
Singapore	0.53	0.63	0.31	2.35
Taiwan	2.15	0.64	0.68	1.53
Second Generation	1.53	0.29	0.34	1.04
Indonesia	1.88	0.15	0.24	0.21
Malaysia	0.70	0.36	0.34	1.84
Thailand	2.02	0.35	0.43	1.06
China	**3.58**	**0.43**	**0.47**	**0.56**

NOTE: Country X has an index greater than 1.0 for factor Y if the share of Y-intensive goods in country X exports is larger than the share of Y-intensive goods in total world exports.

SOURCE: United Nations Conference on Trade and Development, *Trade and Development Report, 1995* (New York, 1995), 150.

At an even lower level of multilateralism, beyond the coordinating authority of any international organization, government ministry, or multinational business enterprise, a major role in Asian economic integration is played by a loose network of about 50 million Chinese expatriates living throughout East and Southeast Asia.[63] Although the **Overseas Chinese** account for fewer than 10 percent of the population of Southeast Asia, they include about 86 percent of its billionaires. Their businesses generate an annual income of about $450 billion—a figure exceeded by the national incomes of only ten countries in the world.

Chinese settlements have existed in several regions of Asia since the fifteenth century, but the most important waves of migration from China occurred during the nineteenth and twentieth centuries, spawned by episodes of famine and political upheaval. Away from home and excluded from political or social influence, the Chinese focused on organizing trade, building businesses, and buying property. By 1990, ethnic Chinese residents

[63]The discussion that follows is based on an excellent report by the East Asia Analytical Unit of the Australian Department of Foreign Affairs and Trade, *Overseas Chinese Business Networks in Asia* (August 1995) <http://www.dfat.gov.au/dept/eaau/ocbn.html>; on a review of the Australian report and related literature by Syed Tariq Anwar in *Journal of International Business Studies* 27 (December 1996): 811; and on Abegglen, *Sea Change,* 117–120 and 200–203; and F. J. Khergamvala, "The Bamboo Empire as Asia's Growth Engine," *The Hindu,* June 11, 1997, 11.

controlled 81 percent of the listed companies in Thailand, 73 percent in Indonesia, 60 percent of the economy in Vietnam, and 60 percent in the Philippines, but they accounted for no more than 10 percent of the population in any of these countries.

Chinese business empires are different in several respects from Japanese business groups. Most obviously, the Japanese groups have their headquarters in a single country—Japan; the Chinese groups are a diaspora, based in countries throughout Asia. The Chinese groups are more likely to be family owned, centrally controlled by a single founder or his children. They usually expand through acquisition rather than enlargement of existing companies. The resulting Chinese groups may be enormous, but their individual firms typically are small and medium-sized.

None of this would have significance for Asian economic integration if the Chinese entrepreneurs confined their activities to individual countries. However, the Overseas Chinese network is decisively international in scope. The holdings of a single family may extend to several countries, like the Indonesia-based Salim Group, with hundreds of companies operating across Asia. Most of the business groups have representation on capital markets in Hong Kong and Singapore, providing access to regional and international credit.

In many cases, Chinese business networks are based on ethnic clans, tied together by a dialect of spoken Chinese. For example, a large segment of Southeast Asia's food trade is handled by a clan of Teochiu speakers. Some of these ethnic clans have established formal international associations.

The Overseas Chinese also participate in a large share of international investment in Asia, perhaps now exceeding the share of Japanese investors. In particular, the Chinese-dominated economies of Hong Kong, Taiwan, and Singapore are significant net exporters of capital to China, Thailand, Indonesia, the Philippines, Vietnam, Cambodia, and Myanmar.

The regional and global importance of the Overseas Chinese community increased immeasurably during the 1980s, when the Chinese mainland opened its doors to trade and investment. The expatriates were vitally interested in the success of China's reforms, and they had obvious advantages over others who attempted to enter the new Chinese market. Although a state of war technically continued to exist between China and Taiwan, their business leaders were able to conclude major agreements and conduct enormous volumes of trade and investment through Hong Kong and other third parties. Both nations accepted the idea that ships from one could sail directly to the ports of the other if the ship flew the flag of another country.

The results? Between 1990 and 1995, overseas investors pumped about $240 billion through Hong Kong and Taiwan into China, accounting for 65 percent of China's total contracted investments.[64] Much of the investment

---

[64]These figures probably overstate the volume of net foreign investment into China by as much as 25 percent because part of China's internal investment is funneled through foreign accounts to obtain preferential tax treatment. See United Nations Conference on Trade and Development, *Trade and Development Report, 1996.*

is going into the regions of ancestral origin of clan members, based on personal connections and cultural preferences. By maintaining an entrepreneurial tradition that was nearly lost in China during the era of radical communism, and by reconnecting the world's most populous country to the modern global economy, the Overseas Chinese are leaving an important mark on world history.

SUMMARY

The Asia-Pacific economies operate in a complex geographic and cultural environment. The culture of each region is influenced by a syncretic blending of religious and philosophical systems. Some people believe that the Confucian societies have an economic advantage over the Hindu societies, but the evidence is unclear.

The colonial experience also has a lasting influence throughout the region, adding another layer of cultural and economic diversity. The fortunes of nations were affected by the national origins of their colonial masters, by the depth and duration of colonial control, by building of transport facilities and other infrastructure, and by the introduction of plantation agriculture and other extractive institutions.

The cultural and colonial heritage also influenced the receptivity of each Asian nation to socialism after World War II. Generally, the countries that had the most destructive colonial experiences adopted the most radical systems of communism. Japan and Thailand maintained independence from colonialism, and never adopted socialism. The South Asian countries were influenced by English Fabian socialism.

The so-called East Asian growth miracles have supported rapid economic development in Japan and in two generations of newly industrializing economies. The high growth rates variously and controversially have been attributed to the influence of Confucian culture, to market-friendly or developmental state systems of public policy, to export-oriented trade policies, to cultural dispositions or governmental policies that supported high rates of saving and investment, and to egalitarian policies that promoted growth and prevented income inequality. Questions concerning the nature, sustainability, and transferability of Asian economic growth are raised by the continuing debate on total factor productivity growth.

International trade and investment have grown rapidly within Asia in recent years, despite cultural and historical divisions that caused many to question the possibility of Asian economic integration. In recent years, Asian cooperation has been supported by the development of multilateral organizations and free-trade agreements, subregional growth triangles, Japanese investment, aid, and industrial coordination, following the so-called flying geese formation, and the relatively unregulated network of trade and investment links created throughout Southeast Asia and China by a wealthy group of Overseas Chinese entrepreneurs.

DISCUSSION AND REVIEW QUESTIONS

1. Is it possible to objectively analyze the economic influences of Asian religions and philosophies? If so, how should this be done?

2. What did India gain, and what did it lose, during its experience with British colonialism? Which were greater, the benefits or the costs?

3. How did the colonial experiences of East Asia and Southeast Asia differ? What if any, are the legacies of those differences?

4. "When the Eastern countries adopted socialism, they replaced one Western social and philosophical system with another Western system." Comment.

5. Of the "emerging generation" of NIEs listed in Table 18.4, which ones are most likely to succeed? How closely will their "miracles" resemble those of the first two generations of NIEs?

6. Is it possible for a developmental state to pursue a market-friendly set of policies in support of economic growth?

7. How did the East Asian countries support high rates of growth and income equality, simultaneously?

8. Should the East Asian countries create an exclusive trading bloc to improve their collective bargaining power in the world economy?

9. Compare Joseph Schumpeter's analysis of the rise and fall of capitalist firms, discussed in Chapter 3, with Akamatsu's flying geese model. Do you notice any common elements?

SUGGESTED READINGS

Abegglen, James C. *Sea Change: Pacific Asia as the New World Industrial Center.* New York: Free Press, 1994. *Abegglen, an established authority on Japanese industrial organization and management, carries his analysis to the remainder of the Asia-Pacific region, and concludes that "there is nothing temporary or fragile about the enormous economic changes taking place across East Asia."*

Bhagwati, Jagdish. *India in Transition: Freeing the Economy.* Oxford: Clarendon Press, 1993. *Written by an eminent specialist at Columbia University, this book provides a market-oriented prescription for Indian economic development.*

Campos, Jose Edgardo, and Hilton R. Root. *The Key to the Asian Miracle: Making Shared Growth Credible.* Washington, D.C.: Brookings Institution, 1996. *Debunking the view that economic growth must initially entail rising income inequality, this book persuasively argues that East Asian leaders have been able to maintain a consensus for rapid economic growth by ensuring that its benefits are shared by a large segment of the population.*

Fallows, James. *Looking at the Sun.* New York: Vintage, 1995. *Written clearly, candidly, and insightfully by a prominent American journalist who lived in Asia for four years, this book heralds the creation of an integrated East Asian economic system, but one based on different principles than the Western economic communities.*

Lee, Keun. *New East Asian Economic Development: Interacting Capitalism and Socialism.* Armonk, N.Y.: M. E. Sharpe, 1993. *The author, a young professor at the National University in Seoul, South Korea, explains the interaction between interventionist "hard" states and dynamic market systems in East Asia, and contrasts their reform programs with those in the former Soviet Union, China, and, most interestingly, North Korea.*

Lele, Jayant, and Kwasi Ofori-Yeboah, eds. *Unravelling the Asian Miracle: Explorations in Development Strategies, Geopolitics, and Regionalism.* Brookfield, Vt.: Dartmouth Publishing, 1996. *Drawn from papers presented at a conference in 1993, this volume includes 12 chapters written by 13 scholars from Asia and North America. These include, for example, a brief survey article on East Asian growth theories and strategies and a study of the governmental role in industrial restructuring in Thailand.*

So, Alvin Y., and Stephen W. K. Chiu. *East Asia and the World Economy.* Thousand Oaks, Calif.: Sage, 1995. *Written by two professors in Hong Kong, this book employs the conceptual framework and terminology of Immanuael Wallerstein's world-systems analysis to interpret the broad sweep of East Asian history since the early days of the nineteenth century.*

World Bank. *The East Asian Miracle: Economic Growth and Public Policy.* Oxford: Oxford University Press, 1993. *Provides a subtle revision of the so-called Washington Consensus on market-oriented development in its East Asian context, and provides a wealth of statistical information on the region.*

ANNUAL REPORTS

Asia Pacific Economic Cooperation Secretariat, *Economic Cooperation in the Asia-Pacific Region,* annual.

Asian Development Bank, *Asian Development Outlook,* annual.

United Nations Conference on Trade and Development, *Trade and Development Report,* annual.

United Nations Economic and Social Commission for Asia and the Pacific, *Economic and Social Survey of Asia and the Pacific,* annual.

INTERNET RESOURCES

APEC Secretariat
http://apecsun.apecsec.org.sg/

ASEAN Infosite
http://faraday.clas.virginia.edu/~cep2t/asean.html

ASEAN Institute
http://www.w-internet.com/verein/asean/engl.htm

ASEANWEB
http://www.asean.or.id/

Asia Business News
http://www.abn-online.com/abn/

Asia Channel
http://www.asia-ch.org/

Asia, Inc. Online
http://www.asia-inc.com/

Asia in the World Economy
http://tpc.harvard.edu/pbrc/asiaworld/

Asian Business Watch
http://www.webcom.com/darrel/

Asian Development Bank
http://www.asiandevbank.org/

Asian Human Rights Commission
http://www.hk.super.net/~ahrchk/

Asian Studies Virtual Library
http://coombs.anu.edu.au/WWWVL-AsianStudies.html

AsiaOne
http://www.asia1.com.sg/

Asia Online
http://www.asiadragons.com/

Asia Pacific Economic Review
http://www.moshix2.net/APER/

Asia Times
http://www.asiatimes.com/

Asia Ville
http://www.asiaville.com/

Asiaweek
http://www.pathfinder.com/@@AXkirsAYFAAAQJEz/Asiaweek/

AskAsia
http://www.askasia.org/

@Asia
http://www.jaring.my:80/at-asia/

Australian Government
http://www.nla.gov.au/oz/gov/federal.html

Best of Asia and the Pacific
http://www.sintercom.org/makan/award/ap.html

BusinessAsia News
http://www.businessasia.com/

Business Line of India
http://www.indiaserver.com/news/bline/bline.html

Business Recorder
(Pakistan Financial Daily)
http://www.brecorder.com/

CNN: Asia-Pacific
http://www.cnn.com/WORLD/asiapcf/index.html

Council on East Asian Libraries
http://darkwing.uoregon.edu/~felsing/ceal/welcome.html

Department of Foreign Affairs and Trade, Australia
http://www.dfat.gov.au/

Discover India
http://www.indiagov.org/

East Asia Virtual Library
http://coombs.anu.edu.au/WWWVLAsian/VLEast.html

Economics on East Asia
http://tenjin.glocom.ac.jp/eco/economics.html

Fairbank Center for East Asian Research
http://www.fas.harvard.edu/~fairbank/index.html

Far Eastern Economic Review
http://www.feer.com/

Hong Kong Information Center
http://www.info.gov.hk/

Hong Kong: Lives in Transition
http://www.pbs.org/pov/hongkong/

Hong Kong Standard
http://www.hkstandard.com/online/news/001/hksnews.htm

Hong Kong Trade Development Council
http://www.tdc.org.hk/

IndiaReview
http://www.indiareview.com/

Indonesia Central Bureau of Statistics
http://www.bps.go.id/

Indonesian Home Page
http://www.uni-stuttgart.de/indonesia/

Indus News
http://www.indusnews.com/

International Confederation of Free Trade Unions' Asian and Pacific Regional Organization
http://singnet.com.sg/~icftu/welcome.html

Korean History
http://socrates.berkeley.edu/~seoul/

Land of Genghis Khan (National Geographic)
http://www.nationalgeographic.com/modules/genghis/index.html

Lavergne, Stephen, "North Asian Integration"
http://www.dfait-maeci.gc.ca/english/foreignp/dfait/policy~1/1995/part1—03.htm

Malaysia Home Page
http://www.newhomes.com.my/

National Bureau of Asian Research
http://www.nbr.org/

News India-Times
http://www.newsindia-times.com/

Pacific Rim Review
http://pacificrim.bx.com/

Philippines National Statistical Board
http://users.info.com.ph/~nscbrscs/

Singapore Business Times
http://biztimes.asia1.com/

South Asian Association of Regional Cooperation (SAARC) Chamber of Commerce and Industry
http://www.sccinet.com/

South Asian Review
http://www.georgetown.edu/users/khemkak/

Thai Financial Network
http://home.theidea.com/tfn/

This Is Australia
http://springboard.telstra.com.au/australia/index.htm

Times of India
http://www.timesofindia.com/

Top News from Asia
http://www.asianmall.com/top10news/

U.N. Economic and Social Commission for Asia and the Pacific (ESCAP)
http://www.un.org/Depts/escap/

U.S. Department of Commerce
International Trade Administration
Asia-Pacific Section
http://infoserv2.ita.doc.gov/apweb.nsf

Vietconnection
http://www.vietconnection.com/

Vietnam Information
http://www.batin.com.vn/

Weekly Financial Review
Overseas Union Bank of Singapore
http://www.oub.com.sg/wkreview.htm

Weekly Report on the Asia Pacific
http://www.apec.org/wrap.html

Japan

19

JAPAN: REBUILDING AFTER THE BUBBLE

For all the brilliance and energy of Japan's postwar economic miracle, interlocking business and bureaucracy has led to a domination of entrenched interests that make a mockery of the free enterprise that business and government spokesmen publicly support.

—FRANK B. GIBNEY, *JAPAN QUARTERLY*,
JULY–SEPTEMBER 1996

I am not at all convinced that an American-style economy is the only way for Japan to succeed. And I don't think we are seeing much convergence in the two systems. . . . The fact of the matter is that convergence is running in the other direction: Asian countries are moving toward the Japanese-style economic structure, with strong state involvement rather than the myth of laissez faire that is commonly accepted in the United States.

—ROBERT M. ORR, JR., *TOKYO BUSINESS TODAY*,
FEBRUARY 1996

n an age of East Asian economic miracles, one country set the pace for the entire region. With few natural resources to support it, Japan climbed from the ashes of World War II to build the second largest industrial economy in the world. During the 1960s, 1970s, and 1980s, its growth rates were sometimes double the OECD average; its unemployment rates were consistently lower than half the norm (Table 19.1). Today, Japan can claim the longest average life expectancy, the lowest rate of infant mortality, the smallest per capita prison population, and one of the most even distributions of income in the industrial world.[1]

---

[1]World Bank, *World Development Report 1997* (New York: Oxford University Press, 1997), 215, 223, and 225; and United Nations Development Program, *Human Development Report 1995* (New York: Oxford University Press, 1995), 198.

■ **TABLE 19.1**

RELATIVE PERFORMANCE OF
THE JAPANESE ECONOMY, 1951–1996

	1951–1960	1961–1970	1971–1980	1981–1990	1991–1996
Average annual growth of real GDP (%)					
Japan	6.3	10.9	4.7	4.0	1.8
OECD Average	4.2	5.1	3.2	2.8	2.0
Average annual consumer price inflation (%)					
Japan	4.0	5.6	9.1	2.1	1.2
OECD Average	3.3	3.9	9.1	8.1	4.9
Unemployment rate (%)					
Japan	2.0	1.2	1.8	2.5	3.0
OECD Average	3.6*	2.8*	4.5	7.3	7.5

*Based on data for Canada, France, Germany, Italy, Japan, Sweden, the United Kingdom, and the United States.

SOURCES: *OECD Economic Outlook*, December 1986 and June 1997; World Bank, *World Tables*, 1980 and 1995; Irving Kravis, Alan Heston, and Robert Summers, *World Product and Income* (Baltimore: Johns Hopkins University Press, 1982), 343; and Angus Maddison, *Phases of Capitalist Development* (Oxford: Oxford University Press, 1982), appendices A, C, and E.

Because of its many achievements, the Japanese economic system has long been touted as a model for other countries. Herman Kahn announced in 1970 that Japan was an emerging "superstate."[2] Nine years later, Ezra Vogel spoke of Japan as "number one," and claimed that it had become "a more effective democracy than America."[3] More recently, the title of a book by William Dietrich suggested that the United States is living *In the Shadow of the Rising Sun.* "The Japanese are way out in front of the pack and are gaining ground daily," said Dietrich; "It is the considered opinion of this work that we must become more like Japan."[4]

According to its admirers, what aspects of the Japanese system should be copied by other countries? Martin Weitzman advocates the Japanese system of labor compensation—the so-called share economy. This, he claims, could help all nations to eradicate unemployment.[5] According to Chalmers

[2]Herman Kahn, *The Emerging Japanese Superstate* (Harmondsworth: Penguin Books, 1970).

[3]Ezra Vogel, *Japan As Number One* (Cambridge, Mass.: Harvard University Press, 1979), 97.

[4]William Dietrich, *In the Shadow of the Rising Sun* (University Park, Penn.: The Pennsylvania State University Press, 1991), 268–269.

[5]Martin L. Weitzman, *The Share Economy: Conquering Stagflation* (Cambridge: Harvard University Press, 1984).

Johnson, the key to Japanese success is its cooperative system of government-industry relations, known as "Japan, Inc."[6] Others suggest that we should emulate Japan's "humanistic enterprise system," based on lifetime employment, egalitarianism, teamwork, and cooperation between labor and management.[7]

The Japanese economic and social system also has its critics. Jon Woronoff, a journalist, has written books since the 1970s with such titles as *Japan as—anything but—Number One*.[8] What benefit does a country derive from its industrial power, Woronoff asks, if its women and ethnic minorities suffer from discrimination, its men work endless hours for meager standards of living, its children live in constant fear of "examination hell," and its elderly resort to suicide at one of the world's highest rates? James Fallows, a prominent journalist who worked in Tokyo during the 1980s, raises similar questions:

> *We had heard for years that Japan was rich. Yet normal life, as we lived and observed it in a Tokyo suburb, would be considered needlessly grinding and difficult by most American and European standards. Homes were usually unheated. Modern plumbing was rare. In the country that produced more automobiles than any other nation, most of our neighbors had no cars. . . . I had been taught that the ultimate purpose of economic growth was to make individuals rich; in Japan, individuals remained poor so that the industries could grow strong.*[9]

Woronoff and Fallows are not alone in their views; scores of Japanese scholars are equally critical of their nation's economic and social system.[10] Indeed, since the early 1990s, the tide of domestic criticism has grown ever stronger, fueled by a series of financial crises, political scandals, and troubling demographic and international trends. These include:

■ The rise and fall of the "bubble economy," characterized by wide gyrations of stock and real estate prices

■ The collapse of Japan's housing-loan companies (*jusen*), causing heavy losses and requiring government bailouts for large banks that owned them

[6]Chalmers Johnson, *MITI and the Japanese Miracle* (Stanford: Stanford University Press, 1982).

[7]William Ouchi, *Theory Z: How American Business Can Meet the Japanese Challenge* (Reading, Mass.: Addison-Wesley, 1981); Robert Ozaki, *Human Capitalism: The Japanese Enterprise System as a World Model* (Harmondsworth: Penguin Books, 1991); and Hiroyuki Itami, "The 'Human Capitalism' of the Japanese Firm as an Integrated System," in *Business Enterprise in Japan: Views of Leading Japanese Economists*, ed. Kenichi Imai and Ryutaro Komiya (Cambridge, Mass.: The MIT Press, 1994), 73–88.

[8]Jon Woronoff, *Japan: The Coming Economic Crisis* (Tokyo: Yohan, 1979); Jan Woronoff, *Japan as—anything but—Number One* (Armonk, N.Y.: M. E. Sharpe, 1990); and Jan Woronoff, *The Japanese Economic Crisis* (New York: St. Martin's Press, 1993).

[9]James Fallows, *Looking at the Sun: The Rise of the New East Asian Economic and Political System* (New York: Vintage Books, 1995), 8. Even more pointedly, see Fallows's article, "The Hard Life," *The Atlantic*, March 1989, 16–26.

[10]For example, see Tadashi Fukutake, *Japanese Society Today* (Tokyo: University of Tokyo Press, 1981); Takahashi Nobuaki, "Superpower Japan, the Closet Pauper," *Japan Echo* 16, no. 2 (1989): 47–51; and Mikio Sumiya, "Japan: Model Society for the Future?" *Annals of the American Academy of Political and Social Sciences* 513 (January 1991): 139–150.

■ Political, financial, and sexual scandals in the dominant Liberal Democratic Party that contributed to political instability, causing Japan to appoint six prime ministers between 1990 and 1996[11]

■ Instances of negligence and corruption in government agencies that regulated financial institutions, in police units that mishandled a terrorist attack on a Tokyo subway in 1994 and an earthquake in 1995, and in government health agencies that concealed information on HIV-tainted blood that was distributed during the 1980s

■ Impatience of women for greater equality in Japanese society

■ Heavy demands on the health and social security systems caused by the shifting age structure of the Japanese population

■ Rising competition on international markets caused by the strong Japanese currency, by the economic development of other East Asian nations, and by the formation of regional trading blocs in Europe and the Americas

According to the Japanese Economic Planning Agency, existing institutions are no longer able to accommodate these "tidal shifts" in history. An effective response, according to the planners, "will require radical reforms of Japan's social and economic structure, and changes in the way we as individuals think."[12]

Radical reform? Should Japan abandon the system that supported its postwar economic miracle? What institutional arrangements should be changed, and what should be retained? Will environmental changes, such as demographic trends, provide support for systemic reform, or will traditional culture stand in the way? Should some aspects of the Japanese system be copied by other countries? We have much to explore in this chapter.

THE ENVIRONMENT

Japan has little land, but many people. Scattered over four major islands, its territory is smaller than California, but it has nearly half the population of the United States. Furthermore, most of its terrain is mountainous; less than 20 percent is arable. Thus, Japan must import about half its food and nearly all its energy, iron ore, copper, tin, aluminum, nickel, and uranium.

TAMING THE WORK ETHIC

Through the centuries, the Japanese people learned to compensate for their scarcity of natural resources: "We must work very hard" became their refrain, "because we are a poor island nation." The Japanese work ethic grew

---

[11] For a full list of Japanese prime ministers, see <http://www.lg.ehu.es/~ziaoarr/japan.htm>.

[12] Economic Planning Agency and Economic Council, "Social and Economic Plan for Structural Reforms," November 29, 1995 <http://www.epa.go.jp/e-e/keikaku/sumwin.html>.

ever more necessary after the carnage and destruction of World War II, and played a vital role in the postwar "miracle." The hero of the new era was the "corporate warrior."

Today, when their battle for survival has been won, and when the Japanese have joined the ranks of the affluent democracies, they have decided it is time to moderate their work ethic. The average adult male, they believe, spends too many hours working overtime, attending unpaid quality control sessions and other group meetings, socializing with work associates and clients, and riding long distances on crowded commuter trains. He has little time for leisure activities, and he provides little help, relief, or companionship to his wife and children.

More than half of eighth graders claim that they never speak with their fathers on weekdays.[13] In 1995, the average Japanese worker was authorized to take 17 days of paid vacation, but elected to take only 9.[14] Among workers above age 50, about 60 percent say their job is their main reason for living.[15] Since the late 1980s, telephone hotlines have been operating in major cities to aid families victimized by *karoshi,* or "death from overwork." By the end of 1995, nearly 2,000 cases had been reported.[16]

Slowly but surely, the culture of workaholism seems to be softening. In 1996, a record 59 percent of adults reported their intention to find more time for leisure and relaxation rather than work and income; this was up from 37 percent in 1972, the first year this survey question was asked.[17] Accordingly, the government hopes to (1) reduce the length of the standard workweek, (2) encourage workers to use more of their authorized vacation time, (3) reduce commute times by making more housing available near places of work, and (4) provide more opportunities for leisure, continuing education, and civic involvement to enrich the lives of workers and pensioners.[18]

The Labor Ministry reduced the legal workweek from 48 hours to 44 hours in 1991, and set 1997 as the deadline for all companies to adopt a 40-hour workweek. Late in 1996, when about 33 percent of the small and midsized companies reported that they could not meet the deadline, the government threatened to fine offending companies or incarcerate their managers.[19]

---

[13] Nicholas Kristof, "Japan: For Better or for Worse," *The New York Times,* February 11, 1996, 1.

[14] The average number of paid holidays was 19 in the United States, 24 in the United Kingdom, and 29 in Germany. See Economic Planning Agency, *Annual Report on the National Life for Fiscal 1993* (Tokyo, 1994), 38; and data relating to leisure activities at <http://www.jinjapan.org/ stat/ index.html>.

[15] Economic Planning Agency, *Annual Report on the National Life for Fiscal 1993,* 37.

[16] National Defense Counsel [sic] for Victims of Karoshi, *Karoshi: When the "Corporate Warrior" Dies* (Tokyo: Mado-Sha, 1990), 6; and Chuah Bee Hwa, "Karoshi and the Winds of Change," *New Straits Times,* June 20, 1996, 4.

[17] "More Japanese See Mental Health, Comfy Life as Vital," Japan Economic Newswire, November 23, 1996.

[18] Economic Planning Agency and Economic Council, "Social and Economic Plan for Structural Reforms," 3–4.

[19] "40-Hour Mandate Strains Small Firms," *The Nikkei Weekly,* October 28, 1996, 4.

The Culture of Conformity

As an island nation, Japan spent many of its formative years in relative seclusion. Particularly during the seventeenth and eighteenth centuries A.D., while military dictators of the Tokugawa family enforced a strict system of isolationism, the Japanese people developed a remarkable uniformity of race, language, and culture. The homogeneous culture, in turn, encouraged the development of a social philosophy, known as **groupism,** that elevates the importance of the group over the individual.[20] Today, Japan seems to derive a mixture of benefits and burdens from its uniform culture and its group orientation.

First, Japanese groupism seems to encourage a tight system of familial and social obligations. The Japanese divorce rate is less than half the American level, and, although the strength of extended family relationships is declining, two-thirds of the elderly still live in multigenerational households.[21]

Frequently, the familial relations in Japanese society are extended into the business world. The Japanese worker, for example, may become a member of a company "family" through a bond of lifetime employment. Furthermore, a company may engage in familial relationships with other companies by participating in a *zaibatsu* or *keiretsu* conglomerate. On an even broader level, the "Japan, Inc." thesis suggests that the entire economy is knit together under the leadership of a paternalistic government.

All these family ties play a vital role in the traditional structures of Japanese society. The individual worker derives security, stability, and protection from relationships with his extended family and company family; each company relies on the support of its loyal employees and on stable relations with its *keiretsu* partners. The system of familial relations encourages resolution of conflicts through conciliation and compromise rather than conflict and litigation. Thus, all of Japan requires the services of fewer lawyers than the city of Philadelphia.[22]

The cost of security and conciliation, however, is a low level of social, occupational, and managerial flexibility. A Japanese elder son may be compelled to continue in his father's business; a worker under the lifetime employment system may be tied to an unsatisfying job; a company in a *keiretsu* organization may be forced to trade with other companies in the group, forsaking other opportunities.

One of the most troubling aspects of Japanese groupism is its potential to encourage excessive conformity, which may discourage individual initiative and creativity. "The nail that sticks out," says a Japanese proverb, "will be pounded down." The educational system emphasizes rote memorization

---

[20] On the significance of groupism and its relationship to individualism, see Ozaki, *Human Capitalism*, 88–92.

[21] Akiko Hashimoto, "Family Relations in Later Life: A Cross-Cultural Perspective," *Generations*, December 22, 1993, 22; "Whither the Extended Family?" *Asiaweek*, December 15, 1995, 86.

[22] According to data compiled by the Institute for Legal Studies at the University of Wisconsin (reported in *World Monitor*, November 1992, 8–9), for every million members of the population there were 2,753 lawyers in the United States, 1,511 in Germany, 919 in the United Kingdom, and 872 in Japan.

and respect for authority rather than critical thinking, and offers little opportunity or reward for originality. Values of humility and respect for age and authority are reinforced by the Confucian, Buddhist, and Shinto traditions.

Thus, the Japanese system produces students who excel on standardized exams, particularly in mathematics and the natural sciences, but few scientists who can push forward the frontiers of knowledge. According to Susumu Tonegawa, a Japanese national who won the 1987 Nobel Prize in medicine, "talented scientists have no choice but to get out of Japan."[23] Tonegawa performed his prize-winning research in Switzerland and the United States, and claims that subordination to the Japanese scientific establishment would have made his work impossible.

On the other hand, if Japan has performed poorly as a nation of inventors, it is unsurpassed as a nation of assimilators. Repeatedly, Japanese engineers have mastered technologies from other countries, incorporated them into marketable products, and developed sequential improvements in quality standards and production processes. As Rosenberg and Steinmuller have noted, these modest, incremental innovations do not win Nobel Prizes, but they are often the "essence of success in the competitive process."[24]

Historically, Japan's ability to assimilate foreign technology was strengthened by the Confucian culture. Superstitions and taboos may have inhibited the advance of technology in many countries, but Japanese Confucianism was characterized by intellectualism and rationalism. Thus, Morishima claims it was "entirely" owing to Confucianism that Western science was transplanted quickly and painlessly in Japan.[25]

Finally, at its worst, Japanese homogeneity seems to encourage patterns of intolerance, racism, and xenophobia. For example, more than 600,000 ethnic Koreans who were born and raised in Japan have not been offered citizenship, so they are ineligible for many civil service jobs. Many of these are grandchildren of laborers who came to the country against their will during the 1920s.[26] Notably, at the end of the Vietnam War, less than 5,000 Indochinese refugees were willing or able to settle in Japan, while more than 600,000 traveled around the world to settle in the United States.[27] Also notable is the fact that Japanese companies operating in the United States have a relatively poor record of racial diversity in hiring and promotion.[28]

---

[23] Stephen Yoder, "Japan's Scientists Find Pure Research Suffers Under Rigid Life Style," *The Wall Street Journal*, October 31, 1988, A1.

[24] Nathan Rosenberg and W. Edward Steinmuller, "Why Are Americans Such Poor Imitators?" *American Economic Review* 78 (May 1988), 230.

[25] Michio Morishima, *Why Has Japan 'Succeeded'?* (Cambridge: Cambridge University Press, 1982), 61.

[26] See Christopher B. Johnstone, "'Virtual' Citizens: Japan's Foreign Residents and the Quest for Expanded Political Rights," *Japan Economic Institute Report* 27A (July 19, 1996), 3–12.

[27] These are figures for the years between 1971 and 1984. See George Fields, "Racism Is Accepted Practice in Japan," *The Wall Street Journal*, November 10, 1986, 19; and U.S. Department of Commerce, Bureau of the Census, *Statistical Abstract of the United States 1986*, 86.

[28] See hiring data presented in Rochelle Sharpe, "Japanese Bank in U.S. Built for One Minority, Is Pressed to Aid Others," *The Wall Street Journal*, December 30, 1996, A1.

A Brief History

From the seventh century A.D., when the monarchy was established, until 1603, when a unified military dictatorship was founded by the Tokugawa family, the Japanese lived in a chronic state of civil war. The Tokugawa regime provided 250 years of peace, law, and order, but imposed a feudal economic order and a policy of total isolation from the outside world. The Japanese people developed culturally and achieved a relatively high rate of literacy, but fell far behind the West in science and technology.

The Japanese became aware of their backward state in 1853, when Commodore Perry arrived with his fearsome fleet of steam-powered ships and delivered a letter from U.S. President Franklin Pierce demanding the opening of trade relations. The ensuing domestic debate led to a civil war in 1867; the military dictatorship was overthrown and the monarchy was restored under the young emperor Meiji.

The Meiji Reforms and Modern Economic Growth

The new Meiji regime opened the door to foreign trade, abolished many feudal institutions, and attempted to close the technology gap. It established the legal equality of all social classes and gave everyone the legal (if not social) freedom to choose their trade or occupation. Feudal guilds were eliminated, agricultural land was distributed to peasants, and monetary taxes were replaced with payments in kind. Internal travel restrictions were abolished, and the transportation system was improved. Primary education (with a Western curriculum) was made compulsory, and foreigners were employed as educators, advisors, and corporate officers. The government established a number of large state-run businesses and supported private industry through extension of loans and subsidies. Government enterprises accounted for about 40 percent of total investment during the Meiji period.[29]

The Meiji reforms drew Japan into the modern world and launched a period of rapid economic growth. The nation's emerging industrial and military power led to territorial gains in wars with China (1894–1895) and Russia (1904–1905) and in the First World War (1914–1918). An overvalued exchange rate caused Japanese economic growth to moderate during the 1920s, despite an economic boom in the United States. On the other hand, the Japanese economy grew at a 6 percent annual rate between 1931 and 1938, despite a continuing depression in the West, because the government devalued the currency and pursued an expansionary program of military expenditures.[30]

This triumphal era of economic growth ended with the devastation of World War II. The war destroyed about one-fourth of the nation's buildings and structures, one-third of its industrial machinery, and more than 80 percent of its ships. Japan was stripped of its colonies and investments in Manchuria, Korea, and Formosa; reparations payments required the dismantling of some industrial capacity. Unlike Germany, Japan was not surrounded

---

[29] Angus Maddison, *Economic Growth in Japan and the USSR* (New York: W. W. Norton, 1969), 23.

[30] Takatoshi Ito, *The Japanese Economy* (Cambridge, Mass.: The MIT Press, 1993), 13–17.

by countries experiencing rapid recoveries. In 1948, a member of the American Occupation team held out little hope for the Japanese economy:

> *In the light of an analysis of its resources, the Japan of the next three decades appears likely to have one of two aspects if its population continues to grow to 100 million or more. (1) It may have a standard of living equivalent to that of 1930–4 if foreign financial assistance is continued indefinitely. (2) It may be "self-supporting," but with . . . a standard of living approaching the bare subsistence level.*[31]

THE ECONOMIC GROWTH MIRACLE

Indeed, postwar economic recovery initially proceeded slowly. Japan did not regain its prewar level of GNP until 1954.[32] However, the outbreak of the Korean War in 1950 caused the demand for Japanese exports to grow rapidly. It also induced the United States to recognize the importance of Japan as an outpost against communism in the Far East. Hence, American policy toward Japan shifted from punishment to encouragement. For these and other reasons, a period of "miraculous" growth began around 1953 and continued with few interruptions until the oil shocks of 1973 and 1979.

Economic growth can be caused either by increasing the availability and employment of labor or capital inputs, or by improving factor productivity— growth in output per unit of factor inputs. During the 1960s, Japan did all three, simultaneously maintaining a higher growth rate for labor hours, for the capital stock, and for factor productivity than any other major capitalist or socialist country. How was this accomplished?

According to careful measurements by Edward Denison and William Chung, the largest contribution was made by growth of the capital stock.[33] This high rate of capital accumulation was driven by a high rate of saving, which was, in turn, the result of several factors. These included the modesty of the social security system, the importance of bonus income, a tax exemption on savings accounts held in post office, a low overall tax burden, and a tendency of consumer spending to lag behind the growth of income. Furthermore, the sharing of risk within *zaibatsu* and *keiretsu* company families may have increased the willingness of the business community to engage in long-term capital investments. Based on this heritage, Japan continues to have a very high rate of saving today (Table 19.2).

Denison and Chung found that the second largest cause of Japanese growth was the contribution of knowledge and technology to factor productivity. A major element here was the process of adopting technologies that were developed earlier in other countries. The intellectualism of the Confucian heritage may have assisted the catching-up process, and the lifetime employment system may have encouraged employees to accept new technologies and employers to provide more training. In addition, the industrial

---

[31] E. A. Ackerman, quoted in Andrea Boltho, Japan: An Economic Survey, 1953–1973 (Oxford: Oxford University Press, 1975), 192.

[32] Maddison, *Economic Growth in Japan and the USSR*, 46.

[33] Edward F. Denison and William K. Chung, *How Japan's Economy Grew So Fast* (Washington, D.C.: The Brookings Institution, 1976), 49.

■ **TABLE 19.2**

GROSS SAVING AS A PERCENTAGE OF
GDP, 1977–1995

	1977	1980	1985	1990	1995
Total OECD	22.7	22.5	21.3	21.0	—
Japan	32.0	31.1	31.7	33.6	30.8
OECD North America	19.7	20.2	18.1	15.9	16.2
Canada	20.9	22.9	19.6	16.4	17.1
Mexico	19.7	22.2	22.5	19.2	19.5
United States	19.6	19.8	17.6	15.6	15.9
OECD Europe	22.3	21.6	20.5	21.3	19.5
France	24.4	23.6	18.9	21.5	19.7
Germany	21.7	21.7	22.0	24.9	21.4
Italy	26.0	24.7	21.6	19.6	19.7
Netherlands	22.8	20.5	24.3	26.0	24.6
Sweden	17.8	17.8	17.5	17.7	16.6
United Kingdom	18.5	17.7	17.6	14.3	13.9

SOURCE: *OECD Economic Outlook* 61 (June 1997): Annex Table 27.

policy of the government may have stimulated the development of new products and technologies.

Growth in the quantity and educational quality of labor was the third largest source of output expansion. In addition to fortuitous demographic trends and a strong work ethic, the low rate of unemployment also contributed to the quantitative growth of the labor input. Low unemployment, in turn, may have resulted in part from the lifetime employment system and from the flexibility of the bonus income system. The Confucian culture and the understanding that labor was Japan's only natural resource may have encouraged rapid improvement in educational levels.

Economies of scale, the fourth contributor to growth, were made possible by expansion of markets; improvement of the allocation of resources, the fifth contributor, was caused by movement of workers from agriculture and other low-productivity sectors into industry. The proportion of the labor force engaged in primary goods production dropped from 33 percent in 1960 to 19 percent in 1970.

THE BUBBLE ECONOMY

During the early 1980s, Japanese growth was discouraged by a recession in the United States, which was employing a tight monetary policy to fight inflation. When the U.S. economy recovered in 1983 and 1984, its imports from Japan soared. Both economies experienced strong economic growth, but they developed a troublesome trade imbalance.

In 1985, in the so-called **Plaza Accord**,[34] Japan agreed to accept a substantial appreciation of the yen, allowing it to double against the dollar by 1988. Fearing that the strong yen would cause slow export growth, the Japanese government mounted an expansionary monetary policy to stimulate domestic demand. The narrow money supply grew 10 percent in 1986, and the official discount rate was cut to a postwar low of 2.5 percent.

The government's easy-money policy caused little inflation of consumer prices, but it triggered one of the most remarkable episodes of financial speculation in world history—the so-called **bubble economy.** The value of commercial property in central Tokyo, already the most expensive real estate in the world, climbed tenfold between 1985 and 1989. The Ministry of Finance allowed Japanese companies to take out bank loans, backed by their inflated real estate wealth, to purchase securities. Thus, despite a temporary decline caused by the international Black Monday crash in 1987, the average price of a share on the Nikkei stock exchange tripled between 1985 and 1989. With new confidence in their economy, and encouraged by the increasing values of their real estate and securities, Japanese consumers and purchasers of capital equipment went on a buying spree. Between 1987 and 1990, while the North American and European economies grew at an average rate of about 3 percent, Japan posted a 5 percent real growth rate.

During the first few years of the bubble, it was possible to argue that the high asset prices were sustainable, based on expectations of future earnings and other traditional market criteria.[35] When prices continued to climb rapidly in 1988 and 1989, though, the speculative nature of the boom grew increasingly evident. Japanese industrial stocks, for example, were sold in 1989 for an average of 54 times their annual earnings, compared with a multiple of 15 for similar U.S. firms.[36] According to whimsical calculations by the Ministry of Construction, in 1989 the aggregate real estate value of Japan was theoretically four times larger than the value of the United States—a country 25 times larger.[37]

The bubble grew more fragile when its sustainability was called into question. Then, in May 1989, the Bank of Japan shifted to a more restrictive monetary stance, and raised its official discount rate for the first time in more than two years.[38] The expansion paused, and then the bubble burst. Between 1989 and 1996, real estate and stock prices both fell by about 50 percent. Falling

---

[34]On September 22, 1985, finance ministers and treasury officials from the Group of Five (G5) countries—France, Germany, Japan, the United Kingdom, and the United States—met at the Plaza Hotel in New York City to devise a coordinated plan to push down the value of the dollar and contain the United States payments deficit, which then stood at $124 billion.

[35]Ito, *The Japanese Economy,* 407–436.

[36]Kenneth French and James Poterba, "Were Japanese Stock Prices Too High?" *Journal of Financial Economics* 29 (October 1991): 337–364.

[37]David L. Asher, "What Became of the Japanese 'Miracle'?" *Orbis* 40 (Spring 1996): 216.

[38]Monetary policy was the main factor that burst the bubble, according to Ryuichiro Tachi, *The Contemporary Japanese Economy: An Overview* (Tokyo: University of Tokyo Press, 1993), 200, and is also emphasized by Naoki Tanaka, "The Japanese Economy After the 'Bubble,'" *Japanese Economic Studies* 23 (May–June 1995): 6.

asset prices left a trail of bad debts and bankruptcies of borrowing and lend-ing institutions.

The end of the bubble also caused a reversal of consumer and investor ex-pectations, dragging Japan's average economic growth rate to less than 1 percent per year between 1992 and 1995. During those same years, the aver-age growth rate of other OECD countries was about 2 percent, and the rate for newly industrializing countries in East Asia was about 7 percent. Fur-thermore, in 1995, Japan's unemployment rate climbed above 3 percent for the first time in the postwar era. These are among the realities that inspired new proposals for deep structural reform.

Late in 1995, the Japanese economy began to improve, and the recovery gained momentum during 1996. This is good news, of course, but it raises a new question: Will demands for institutional reform persist if the economic crisis is past?

INDUSTRIAL ORGANIZATION

In an average Japanese industry, about 27 percent of output is produced by the largest firm, 54 percent is produced by the three largest firms, and 83 per-cent is produced by the ten largest firms. This suggests a level of industrial concentration somewhat higher than that in the United States, roughly com-parable to the rates in Germany and the United Kingdom, and somewhat lower than the levels in France and Sweden.[39]

Conventional measurements such as these, however, do not reflect the hi-erarchical nature of Japanese business, wherein many small firms are mem-bers of industrial families dominated by large firms. The large companies that produce cars and consumer electronics, such as Toshiba, Mitsubishi, Toyota, and Sony, are familiar to us all. Their influence extends far beyond the Japanese domestic market. The names of the small firms are less familiar, but they employ the majority of Japanese workers. Most of these firms, large and small, are woven together in complex webs of subsidiary relationships, interlocking directorates, and subcontracting arrangements.

ZAIBATSU AND KEIRETSU

In 1965, only two Japanese companies could be counted among the world's 100 largest industrial corporations. By 1970, eight Japanese companies were on the list, and by 1990 there were sixteen. In 1995, among the world's 100 largest corporations (industrial, financial, and otherwise), 37 were Japanese. The three largest companies in the world, measured by sales, were the Mit-subishi, Mitsui, and Itochu trading companies, and largest by asset valuation was Sumitomo Bank. The 25 largest Japanese corporations (measured by sales) are listed in Table 19.3. Of these, nine are trading companies, six are manufacturers of electronic and electrical equipment, five are insurance or banking firms, three are automotive companies, and two are public utilities.

---

[39] OECD Survey of Japan in 1991/1992 (Paris, 1992), 82–83.

■ **TABLE 19.3**

JAPAN'S LARGEST CORPORATIONS, 1995

	Rank in World (by sales)	Sales (U.S. $ millions)	Employees
Mitsubishi (Trading)	1	184,365	36,000
Mitsui (Trading)	2	181,519	80,000
Itochu (Trading)	3	169,165	7,182
Sumitomo (Trading)	5	167,531	6,193
Marubeni (Trading)	6	161,057	6,702
Toyota Motor	8	111,052	146,855
Nissho Iwai (Trading)	11	97,886	17,005
Hitachi	13	84,167	331,852
Nippon Life Insurance	14	83,207	89,690
Nippon Telegraph & Telephone	15	81,937	231,400
Matsushita Electric Industrial	19	70,398	265,538
Tomen (Trading)	21	67,756	2,943
Nissan Motor	23	62,569	139,856
Dai-Ichi Mutual Life	26	58,052	70,038
Toshiba	32	53,047	186,000
Tokyo Electric Power	33	52,362	43,448
Nichimen (Trading)	35	50,842	2,443
Sumitomo Life Insurance	36	50,711	70,000
Kanematsu (Trading)	37	49,839	11,759
Sony	40	47,582	151,000
NEC	45	45,557	152,719
Honda Motor	46	44,056	96,800
Fujitsu	54	38,976	165,056
Industrial Bank of Japan	56	38,229	5,362
Meiji Mutual Life	57	38,047	46,936

SOURCE: "The Global 500," *Fortune*, August 5, 1996.

A few of Japan's large companies, including those in the Mitsui and Sumitomo groups, date back to the feudal Tokugawa years. The big jump in industrial concentration began in the 1880s, however, when a fiscal crisis forced the government to sell some of its nationalized companies to the public. Because few people could afford them, the privatized companies fell into the hands of a few wealthy families and eventually grew into conglomerates that were known as the *zaibatsu* (the "financial clique").[40]

By the turn of the century, the four major *zaibatsu* groups—Mitsui, Mitsubishi, Sumitomo, and Yasuda—developed their own characteristic form of

---

[40] Edwin O. Reischauer, *Japan: The Story of a Nation*, 3d ed. (New York: Alfred A. Knopf, 1981), 130–131.

organization. Each was organized around a family-owned holding company that controlled shares in a diversified and interdependent group of industrial corporations, banks, trading companies, and other businesses. The larger firms controlled shares in smaller subsidiaries and suppliers, creating a pyramid arrangement under the holding company. The *zaibatsu* bank provided financing for all the firms in the group, the trading company handled the intelligence and marketing function for the entire group, and other firms performed other specialized functions for the *zaibatsu* family.

Aided by their close connections with the government, by their country's lack of antitrust legislation, and by their role in world trade, colonialism, and mobilization for war, the *zaibatsu* organizations grew in economic and political influence. In 1928, the four largest *zaibatsu* owned about 15 percent of the paid-in capital of Japanese incorporated business; by the end of World War II, their share grew to about 25 percent, including about one-half of banking and insurance, shipping, and machinery production.[41]

After the war, American occupation forces attempted to create a more competitive and decentralized industrial structure in Japan. Through a series of laws, some drafted by the Antitrust Division of the U.S. Justice Department, the *zaibatsu* were broken up, their holding companies were dissolved, and thousands of their officers and stockholders were purged for their wartime activities. Banks were forbidden to hold more than 5 percent of the stock of a nonbank subsidiary, mergers were placed under strict limits, and a number of unfair business practices were prohibited.

When the Allied occupation ended in 1952, the Japanese government relaxed enforcement of the antitrust laws. Restoration of big business was considered necessary for Japan to exert its economic power on world markets. Less pejorative words were found to replace the term *zaibatsu,* namely *kigyo shodan* (meaning "industrial group") and **keiretsu** (or "lineage").[42] These new groups took several different forms, but they generally involved cross holdings of stock, interlocking directorates, presidents' clubs, and other cooperative arrangements. Today, nearly all the large and mid-sized Japanese enterprises are connected to one or more of the *keiretsu* organizations.

Three of the *keiretsu*—Mitsui, Mitsubishi, and Sumitomo—were formed by regrouping former *zaibatsu* networks. These and three others—Fuyo (or Fuji), Sanwa, and Dai-Ichi Kangyo—are sometimes called the **financial keiretsu** because they include not only manufacturing firms but also banks, insurance companies, and trading companies. In 1993, each of these six groups had at least 20 member companies and 125,000 employees. Together, they accounted for 16 percent of Japan's total sales and 38 percent of its market capitalization.[43]

---

[41] Ito, *The Japanese Economy,* 179; and Hidemasa Morikawa, *Zaibatsu: The Rise and Fall of Family Enterprise Groups in Japan* (Tokyo: University of Tokyo Press, 1992), xix.

[42] Chalmers Johnson, "*Keiretsu:* An Outsider's View," *Economic Insights* (September–October 1990), 16.

[43] William Dawkins, "Loosening of the Corporate Web," *The Financial Times,* November 30, 1994, 13.

The big holding companies that led the *zaibatsu* before World War II were dissolved, but many of their functions were assumed by the leading banks and trading companies in the financial *keiretsu*. The economic power of the leading banks was enhanced by the absence of a strong securities market after World War II; businesses had to depend on bank loans to finance their investments. Bank officers serve on the boards of member companies and organize joint investments.

The huge general trading companies (or *sogo shosha*) have no counterpart in other countries. They procure raw materials for their clients, distribute products at home and abroad, control key ports and shipping facilities, and gather intelligence. In 1993, the nine largest trading companies handled about 10 percent of Japan's wholesale trade, 34 percent of its exports, and 56 percent of its imports.[44] They also provide an important link in the nation's financial system by extending short-term trade credits to customers, many of whom do not have ready access to bank loans.[45]

Another kind of enterprise group, the so-called **production** *keiretsu*, is composed of a large industrial concern and its subsidiaries and subcontractors. The largest of these groups, such as Hitachi and Bridgestone, may have as many as 600 subsidiaries and affiliates. The distinguishing feature of a production *keiretsu* is a tight, stable relationship between the large firm and its subcontractors, usually reinforced by cross shareholdings. This stands in contrast to American and European practice, where ties between large companies and their suppliers are typically weak and uncertain.

The large firm in a production *keiretsu* is able to reap several advantages. By purchasing its raw materials, parts, and assemblies through the so-called just-in-time (*kanban*) system, the dominant firm is able to shift the cost of holding inventories to subcontractors (see "Toyota: Less Is More"). During recessions, the large firm is able to maintain the employment of its permanent laborers by reducing the amount of subcontracted work. Because the wages of workers in small firms are relatively low, large firms can reduce their labor costs by subcontracting. According to their critics, however, the benefits gained by lifetime employees and owners of the large firms do not justify the losses imposed on other companies and on the general public by industrial collusion and restrictive business practices.[46]

Still another variety of enterprise group, the **distribution** *keiretsu*, is an exclusive organization that moves products from manufacturers to consumers. Operating like networks of company-controlled auto dealerships in the United States, these are found in the automotive, cosmetic, electrical, and electronic sectors in Japan. For example, Matsushita Electric sells its Panasonic and National products through its private chain of 24,000 stores. Foreign critics claim that these arrangements are designed to exclude

---

[44] Keizai Koho Center, *Japan 1995: An International Comparison* (Tokyo: 1994), 43 and 45.

[45] Jon Choy, "Japan's Sogo Shosha: Old Dogs and New Tricks," *Japan Economic Institute Report* 30A (August 9, 1996), 3.

[46] For example, see Goto Akira, "The Myth of *Keiretsu* Efficiency," *Japan Views Quarterly* 1 (Summer 1992): 19–23.

TOYOTA: LESS IS MORE

In 1994, Toyota Motor generated more than one-half the sales of General Motors with only one-sixth as many employees. How was this possible? Toyota operates at a high level of efficiency and relies on outside suppliers for most of its parts and components. By holding down its size, the company is able to remain flexible and dynamic. According to a company slogan, "A large man has difficulty exercising his wits."

Standing at the head of a large production *keiretsu*, Toyota owns stock in many of the 230 regular suppliers that provide about 75 percent of the tools and materials it needs to build a car. Most of these companies have been serving Toyota for decades. About 140 of their factories are located in Toyota City, the company complex near Nagoya. In contrast, General Motors produces most of its own components, relying on outside suppliers for only about 30 percent, and has a more distant relationship with its 2,000 subcontractors.

By working closely with suppliers, Toyota is able to exercise strict control over product quality and delivery schedules, adjust production rapidly in response to consumer demand, and maintain very small inventories of parts and finished vehicles. This is the essence of the so-called *kanban*, or "just-in-time inventory system," which originated at Toyota in the 1950s. Under this system, parts are not ordered and production schedules are not finalized until specific orders are received from dealers.

The just-in-time system allows Toyota to produce cars on a made-to-order basis, take advantage of high-technology and mass-production methods, and minimize inventory costs. This has proved to be a very profitable combination. By 1990, Toyota had accumulated enough cash to buy both Ford and Chrysler at current stock prices, with nearly $5 billion to spare. *Fortune* magazine concludes that Toyota is simply "the best carmaker in the world."

According to a 5-year, $5-million study at MIT, some aspects of the less-is-more philosophy have been adopted by auto manufacturers in other countries. The best American-owned automobile plants in North America are now more productive than the average Japanese auto plant, and are nearly equal in quality. American tradition and antitrust law will make it difficult, though, to emulate the Japanese system of supplier relationships, cross ownership, and labor discipline.

SOURCES: James P. Womack, Daniel T. Jones, and Daniel Roos, "How Lean Production Can Change the World," *The New York Times Magazine* (September 23, 1990), 20–38; Alex Taylor III, "Why Toyota Keeps Getting Better and Better and Better," *Fortune*, November 19, 1990, 66–79; Masaru Yoshitomi, "Keiretsu: A Legitimate, Viable Capitalist Approach," *The International Economy* (May–June 1991), 68–75; and "The Global 500," *Fortune*, April 7, 1995, F1.

competition. Japanese producers, they say, are able to earn monopoly profits on their domestic sales, and use these to offset temporary losses when they invade foreign markets.

Contrary to the claims of their critics, Japanese companies apparently do not join *keiretsu* groups to earn monopoly profits; indeed, member companies have been found to earn lower profits and grow at lower rates than independent companies.[47] Instead, members seem to be seeking the security and stability of a family relationship. Each company offers a steady market for the products of other members, and the *keiretsu* bank provides financial support for the whole group. Crossholdings of shares, seldom transacted, protect members from stock fluctuations and hostile takeovers. If a shift of consumer demand causes one company to have excess labor, it may be able to transfer workers to an affiliate. The keiretsu system may restrict competition and permit some inefficiencies, but it seems to be a natural expression of Japan's protective culture.

How will the *keiretsu* organizations be affected by current and planned programs of structural and financial deregulation? They will be strengthened, it appears, by cancellation of the postwar ban on holding companies. These were outlawed in the 1947 Antimonopoly Law to break the economic and political power of the *zaibatsu* groups, but now the government has decided that holding companies can contribute to the flexibility and diversity of the financial system.[48] On the other hand, the failure of the "bubble" economy and the unfolding programs of deregulation are introducing new competitive pressures in Japan. To obtain higher yields, institutional investors have been forced to liquidate some of their *keiretsu*-based crossholdings of stock; to earn higher profits, some Japanese manufacturers have abandoned their former sources of supply.[49]

THE ZAIKAI

Traditionally, large corporations have wielded an unusual measure of influence over the government through their participation in four big business federations, whose leaders are known collectively as the *zaikai*. The most important of these federations, with 970 corporate members, is the Keidanren (Federation of Economic Organizations). Established in 1946, Keidanren has about 60 departments and 30 committees that formulate policy on everything from taxation and transportation to computer research and cooperation with Latin America.

Prominent members of the *zaikai* hold regular meetings with government leaders and serve as chairmen of advisory boards and panels. These include,

---

[47] See the studies by Caves, Uekusa, and Nakatani reviewed in Ito, *The Japanese Economy*, 194–195.

[48] Formation of a holding company will make it possible, for example, to break the telecommunications giant Nippon Telegraph and Telephone Corp (NTT) into three companies. See Fumiko Fujisaki, "Japan Set to End Ban on Holding Companies," Reuter European Business Report, December 10, 1996.

[49] See Robert Steiner and Jathon Sapsford, "Japanese Stock Plunge Signals Painful Fallout of Deregulation Trend," *The Wall Street Journal*, January 10, 1997, A1.

for example, the Economic Council (attached to the Economic Planning Agency) and the Industrial Structure Council (which advises the Ministry of International Trade and Industry).

Recommendations from the business community are backed by contributions to the dominant Liberal Democratic Party (LDP). Until 1993, Keidanren served as an intermediary, funneling about 13 billion yen ($120 million) each year to the LDP, but now contributions are handled by the individual corporations.[50] Corporate influence is further strengthened by the practice of *amakudari* ("descent from heaven"), whereby senior bureaucrats are allowed to retire into well-paid jobs in the private sector in exchange for political favors. During the early 1990s, more than 30 former officials of the Ministry of Finance held senior positions in private securities firms.[51]

Until recently, the captains of Japanese industry exercised extraordinary control over governmental policy. In the 1980s, for example, it was found that "no legislation strongly opposed by the zaikai is introduced by the government or passed by the Diet [parliament]."[52] Another study alleged that "the country's economic policy is not really determined by the Prime Minister or the bureaucrats," but by "three old men in their seventies and eighties who are in charge of the leading businessmen's associations."[53]

In recent years, however, the *zaikai* have encountered important challenges. The needs of the traditional industrial sector, the high-technology sector, and the service sector have grown more distinct, making it difficult to forge a consensus on many policy issues.[54] A series of political and economic scandals have eroded public confidence in the established system, have weakened the LDP, and have led to recent administrative reforms. According to Tetsuji Okazaki of the University of Tokyo, "The political-economic system that supported Keidanren's influential role for the past 50 years is gone. . . . The organization won't disappear, but it will not return to its former glory."[55]

SMALL BUSINESSES

The visibility of the large companies and conglomerates should not obscure the fact that 99 percent of all Japanese companies, accounting for more than 75 percent of the labor force, have fewer than 100 employees. Small firms

---

[50] In 1993, Keidanren suggested that it might discourage individual corporate donations, but it recently decided that these are acceptable if they are "based on a set of rules." Unfortunately, such rules do not seem to exist. "Keidanren Not to Scrap Political Donations," Japan Economic Newswire, October 31, 1996; and Linda Sieg, "Japan Business Lobby Turns 50, Has Mid-Life Crisis," Reuters Business Wire, August 16, 1996.

[51] "Hidden Japan," *Business Week*, August 26, 1991, 38.

[52] S. Prakash Sethi, Nobuaki Namiki, and Carl Swanson, *The False Promise of the Japanese Miracle* (Boston: Pitman, 1984), 21.

[53] Jon Woronoff, *The Japan Syndrome* (New Brunswick, N.J.: Transaction Books, 1986), 125.

[54] Edmund Klamann, "Keidanren: A Vision Dim with Age?" *The Japan Economic Journal*, December 8, 1990, 17.

[55] Sieg, "Japan Business Lobby Turns 50," 1.

account for a larger share of employment in Japan than in any other major industrial country.

In manufacturing, almost two-thirds of the small firms are subcontractors for *keiretsu* groups. In several sectors—including machinery, motor vehicles, clothing, and construction—subcontracted work represents as much as 90 percent of a company's output. Subcontractors provide everything from manufactured components to marketing and janitorial services.

Typically, subcontractors have little bargaining power in their relations with leading production *keiretsu* firms. According to Woronoff, small firms are given "the most painful, tedious, and unproductive jobs while the more pleasant, mechanized, and profitable ones are kept in-house."[56] To make matters worse, small firms usually find it difficult to obtain the bank financing they need during lean years; they are far more vulnerable to business cycles than are large firms.

Retail stores are particularly small in Japan. The average store has only 4 employees, compared with 5 in Germany, 9 in the United Kingdom, and 13 in the United States.[57] Because economies of scale are substantial in this sector, most analysts believe that the Japanese distribution system is grossly inefficient. According to estimates based on purchasing power parity exchange rates, labor productivity in the Japanese distribution sector is 25 percent below the OECD average; only Portugal and Finland have lower levels of productivity.[58]

Japanese retail stores have remained small for several reasons. During the early 1990s, the rate of automobile ownership was 40 percent lower in Japan than in the United States, and the amount of housing space per person was, respectively, 50 percent smaller. When the Japanese went shopping, more than 70 percent of the time they walked or rode a bicycle. Hence, considerations of transportation and storage space encouraged them to purchase small quantities in neighborhood stores. The small retailers, in turn, were able to purchase food products on a competitive basis through a national system of wholesale auction markets.[59] Furthermore, during the bubble economy, high real estate prices made it all but impossible to build large stores in the major cities.

Bureaucratic obstacles also slowed the pace of change in the Japanese distribution system. The Large-Scale Retail Store Law of 1974 authorized the government to regulate the establishment of new stores with more than 1,500 square meters of floor space. In 1979, the law became more intrusive; the regulations were extended to all stores larger than 500 square meters, and approvals for new construction required the consent of neighboring

[56] Woronoff, *The Japan Syndrome*, 79.

[57] "Japan, Still a Nation of Small Neighborhood Stores," *Japan Pictorial* 17, no. 4 (1994), 33.

[58] Organization for Economic Cooperation and Development, *OECD Economic Surveys 1994–1995: Japan* (Paris: 1995), 84.

[59] David Flath, "Why Are There So Many Retail Stores in Japan?" *Japan and the World Economy* 2 (1990): 365–386.

mom-and-pop stores. Applications to open new large stores fell substantially during the 1980s.

Responding to pressure from the United States and from local entrepreneurs, the Japanese government liberalized the Large-Scale Retail Store Law in 1990, 1992, and 1994. For outlets larger than 1,000 square meters, the law still requires review by the government and by local shopkeepers, but prescribes a tighter schedule for approvals. The new regulations also allow stores to remain open more days each year and for longer hours each day.[60] Retailers have responded enthusiastically by opening new superstores and discount outlets. Additional reforms are under discussion.[61]

THE LABOR MARKET AND LABOR RELATIONS

Aside from its people, Japan has few natural resources. Labor management and motivation, therefore, are critical components of the economic system. Japan's achievements in this area are well known. Labor productivity has grown rapidly, unemployment has remained consistently low, strike activity has been moderate, and labor unions have accepted new manufacturing technologies with a minimum of resistance. These are the achievements of a unique system of labor-market institutions.

COLLECTIVE BARGAINING

Organized labor has a brief history in Japan. Before World War II, experiments with unionism met with little success. After the war, in line with efforts to weaken the *zaibatsu* organizations, the Allied authorities introduced reforms that guaranteed basic rights to organized labor and encouraged the formation of unions. Membership soared to almost 7 million by 1948, accounting for more than 50 percent of the industrial labor force.[62] The unions, with socialist ties, lost some legislative ground during the Cold War and suffered another blow in 1955 with the election of the conservative Liberal Democratic Party (which has dominated Japanese politics since that time). After the oil price shocks of the 1970s, the unions found it more difficult to organize local units in new enterprises. These forces, together with the rise of the nonunionized service economy, reduced union membership to about 24 percent of the labor force in the mid-1990s—somewhat higher than the U.S. level.

About 90 percent of Japanese union members are aligned with comprehensive enterprise-based organizations. The unions are comprehensive in that their membership includes all the permanent employees of the enterprise, including white-collar personnel with ranks lower than section chief. Relations within the Japanese companies are not always harmonious, but

---

[60] For details, see Organization for Economic Cooperation and Development, *OECD Economic Surveys 1994–1995: Japan*, 93–103.

[61] "MITI to Review Large Store Law in Reform Plan," Jiji Press Service, December 3, 1996.

[62] Solomon Levine, "Japan," in *International Handbook of Industrial Relations*, ed. Albert Blum (Westport, Conn.: Greenwood Press, 1981), 323–330.

every effort is made to keep all disagreements within the family. Indeed, according to theoretical work by David Weinstein, cooperative interactions between an oligopolistic firm and its enterprise union may provide mutual benefits for workers and stockholders—the employees *and* the firm may be better off with the union than without it.[63]

Most of the enterprise unions are affiliated with industrial, regional, and national federations, but these have little authority to conduct collective bargaining, call strikes, or initiate grievance procedures. Until the late 1980s, four national federations served as political lobbying units for organized labor, provided forums for information and discussion, and coordinated the so-called Spring Labor Offensive. In 1987, most of the private-sector unions merged into a single federation, known as the *Rengo* (literally, "coalition"), and in 1989 the Rengo was expanded to include public-sector employees. Together, Rengo-affiliated unions account for about two-thirds of organized labor, but internal disagreements over such issues as deregulation and privatization have diluted the group's political influence.[64]

The **Spring Labor Offensive** (*Shunto*) is the most coordinated activity of the Japanese labor unions. Initiated in 1955, it begins each December or January when the Rengo announces targets for basic wage increases. These are usually countered by a recommendation from Nikkeiren, the Federation of Employers' Associations. In early April, when the corporations are hiring new graduates for permanent employment, the unions stage brief 1- or 2-day strikes and demonstrations to assert their solidarity. Next, negotiations are conducted at the industry level and settlements are reached at the company level. In the end, actual wage increases typically are only 60 percent to 70 percent of the unions' initial demands.

Like the Swedish system of centralized collective bargaining, Shunto provides a forum for coordinated negotiations between national labor and employer confederations, setting benchmarks for subsequent local negotiations. The Japanese labor confederations are neither willing nor able to discipline the independent enterprise unions. According to its supporters, who advocate its adoption in other countries, the Shunto procedure allows the Japanese labor market to work smoothly, generating reasonable wage increases and limited strike activity.[65] According to its critics, Shunto is "losing its relevance" because it requires an excessive commitment of time to obtain relatively predictable results. Led by the influential Federation of Iron and Steel Workers' Unions, several of the labor organizations are planning to shift from an annual to a biennial system of wage negotiations.[66]

---

[63] David E. Weinstein, "United We Stand: Firms and Enterprise Unions in Japan," *Journal of the Japanese and International Economies* 8 (March 1994): 53–71.

[64] Ehud Harari, "Japanese Labor Organization and Public Policy," *Social Science Japan* 6 (February 1996): 1–4, available at <http://www.iss.u-tokyo.ac.jp/center/SSJ/SSJ6/Harari.html>.

[65] Robert Evans, "Lessons from Japan's Incomes Policy," *Challenge* 27 (January–February 1985): 33–39.

[66] Tsuyoshi Tsuru, "It's Time to Change the Shunto System," *The Nikkei Weekly*, March 11, 1996, 7; and "Steelworkers' Unions Considering Biennial Wage Offensive," *Japan Weekly Monitor*, September 16, 1996, 1.

LIFETIME EMPLOYMENT

Perhaps the most distinctive feature of the Japanese labor market is the permanent commitment system of employment. Under this arrangement, the large corporations and selected employees are honor-bound to maintain their employment relationship until retirement. The corporations promise that they will not dismiss their permanent employees, except under the most extreme circumstances (for example, embezzlement). The employees pledge that they will not abandon their employer for a more attractive job. The system is another reflection of the family aspect of Japanese business.

Lifetime employment agreements have existed since the beginning of the twentieth century, but they were uncommon during the feudal era. After the Russo-Japanese War, during an era of labor unrest and rapid technological progress, some of the major enterprises adopted programs of "familyism," characterized by vocational training programs and regular pay raises, to maintain staffs of skilled labor. After World War II, during another era of rapid growth and labor unrest, the lifetime employment system was introduced more explicitly into a larger number of enterprises.[67]

Lifetime employment never applied to the majority of workers. It always excluded women, who traditionally quit their jobs when they married, and returned to paid employment in their late thirties or forties when their children were grown. Today, the labor participation rate for young Japanese women (between 25 and 34 years of age) is about 60 percent; this is significantly higher than the Japanese rate in previous decades, but lower than current rates of 75 percent in the United States and 80 percent in France and Sweden.[68] In large Japanese corporations, an average female employee has less than half as many years of service as an average male, and her income is less than half as large.[69]

The permanent commitment system is not practiced in smaller enterprises, which employ the majority of Japanese workers, and it does not even apply to all the males in large corporations. About 33 percent of the labor force was covered by an employment guarantee in 1972, but that proportion fell below 25 percent during the late 1980s and early 1990s.[70] Thus, the system does not provide a universal guarantee of employment, but it covers enough people to influence the operation of the economic system.

On the positive side of the ledger, lifetime employment provides security to workers included in the system and strengthens their loyalty to the

---

[67] Johannes Schregle, "Dismissal Protection in Japan," *International Labour Review* 132 (1993): 511–512.

[68] Based on data published by the International Labour Office in *Yearbook of Labour Statistics*, 1994 and 1995.

[69] Organization for Economic Cooperation and Development, *OECD Economic Surveys 1986/1987: Japan* (Paris: 1986), Table 25B; and Keizai Koho Center, *Japan 1995: An International Comparison*, 67.

[70] Motohiro Morishima, "Japanese Employees' Attitudes Toward Changes in Traditional Employment Practices," *Industrial Relations* 31 (Fall 1992): 434; and Atsushi Yamakoshi, "Restructuring, Reengineering and Japan's Management System," *Japan Economic Institute Report* 25A (July 15, 1996): 8.

company family. Thus, it partially explains the low level of labor unrest and the willingness of employees to participate after working hours without pay in quality control circles and other programs to improve the efficiency and quality of production.

The permanent commitment system may also help explain Japan's quick assimilation of modern production technologies. With little fear of technological unemployment, employees under the system seldom resist the introduction of robots and other innovations that make their jobs easier. Employers are willing to spend time and money to train their employees for new technologies, knowing that their company—not a competitor—will reap the benefits.[71]

Lifetime employment also has its problems. From the employer's perspective, many workers who are redundant, incompetent, or unmotivated must be retained. Some of these are assigned such tasks as messengers and doorkeepers; sidelined middle managers are sometimes assigned to the *madogiwa-zoku*, "the window-seat tribe." As the name implies, they are expected to do little more than look out the windows, while the valued employees work in the inner offices (which often have no windows).[72]

From the workers' perspective, lifetime employment, together with the seniority wage system, makes it difficult to leave a job for a better one with another employer. In a survey conducted by the prime minister's office, only 59 percent of young Japanese workers said that they were satisfied with their jobs, compared to 83 percent of young American workers.[73] The proportion of male workers between the ages of 20 and 45 who change jobs in any given year is about four times larger in the United States than in Japan.[74] The fate of the lifetime employee is in the hands of his employer.

The lifetime employees are considered an elite class of workers. According to Woronoff, "This means that the others are much worse off," because they serve as a buffer. "Since they are the buffer and regular employees are not fired, the ordinary worker is exposed to even greater chances of losing a job than otherwise."[75]

Despite their traditional place of honor in Japanese society, older employees are another buffer group in the job market. The mandatory retirement age in most companies is 55, although Japanese life expectancy (79 years) is the world's longest. When employment cuts are needed, companies often resort to the "golden handshake" or "the tap on the shoulder"—payment of bonuses to employees, aged 45 or older, who agree to early voluntary retirement. After losing their prestigious permanent position, these older workers

[71] In 1993, Japan had a stock of 368,000 industrial robots, compared with 50,000 in the United States and 44,000 in Germany. Keizai Koho Center, *Japan 1995: An International Comparison* (Tokyo: 1994), 27.

[72] Sethi, Namiki, and Swanson, *The False Promise*, 232, 235.

[73] Toyohiro Kono, "An Excerpt from Strategy and Structure of Japanese Enterprises," *Japanese Economic Studies* 13 (Fall–Winter 1984–85): 194.

[74] Isao Ohashi, "A Comparison of the Labor Market in Japan and the United States," *Japanese Economic Studies* 11 (Summer 1983): 63.

[75] Woronoff, *The Japan Syndrome*, 66.

are often forced to find new jobs at lower pay. While cause and effect is impossible to establish, it should be noted that the elderly Japanese have one of the highest suicide rates in the industrial world.[76]

In recent years, Japanese employers and employees have reduced their commitment to the lifetime employment system. After the collapse of the bubble economy, a protracted economic slump has made it difficult for companies to offer new employment guarantees, and some companies have been forced to cancel their existing commitments.[77] Influenced by Western culture, a growing number of young workers are known as "job hoppers"—people who are willing to move between employers for better pay. In the past, respectable Japanese companies were unwilling to hire these people. Today, at such companies as Sony and Toshiba, about 40 percent of the managerial personnel started their careers under different employers.[78]

SENIORITY PAY AND BONUSES

The Japanese wage system is characterized by two interesting practices. First, in many private and public organizations, wage levels are determined largely by the length of service of the employee, rather than by skill, performance, or position. Although the seniority system does not completely exclude other considerations (and some Japanese corporations claim to base wages on merit alone), the statistical evidence indicates that seniority has a greater impact on wages in Japan than in the United States.[79] The seniority system reinforces the loyalty of employees to the lifetime employment system because it is costly to lose seniority with a job change.

On the other hand, seniority pay has reduced the loyalty of employers to the lifetime system, and has encouraged companies to force their older, higher-paid workers into early retirement. A 1993 survey by the Japan Productivity Center found that 94 percent of companies were planning to modify or dismantle their seniority systems. In 1970, college-educated manufacturing workers with 25 years of service earned about 2.6 times as much as workers with fours years of service. By 1992, the differential had declined to about 2.0, and it was expected to continue downward.[80]

---

[76]Of 13 nations reporting suicide rates in the early 1990s, elderly Japanese, aged 75 and over, had the highest rate among women and the fifth highest rate among men. See U.S. Department of Commerce, Bureau of the Census, *Statistical Abstract of the United States 1994* (Washington, D.C.: USGPO, 1994), 859.

[77]"Japan Reneging on Lifetime Guarantee," *The Dallas Morning News,* January 11, 1993, 4D; and William Dawkins, "Japan's Silent Knife," *The Financial Times,* November 17, 1995, 10.

[78]Takeshi Ozaki, "Job Hopping Encouraged by Some Firms," *Nikkei Weekly,* June 6, 1992, 25.

[79]Ohashi, "A Comparison," 60.

[80]Michael Williams, "Japan Labor System: A Two-Edged Sword," *The Wall Street Journal,* November 4, 1994, A18. On the other hand, in a recent survey of large Japanese corporations, only 25 percent of their representatives believed that seniority was declining in importance for promotion decisions. About 52 percent believed that its importance was unchanged, and 23 percent said that its importance was increasing. See Norio Kambayashi, "Changes in Organizational Structure and New Developments in Personnel Management," *Japanese Economic Studies* 23 (September–October 1995): 86.

The other unique aspect of the compensation system is the extensive use of bonuses. In contrast to the practice in other Western countries, where salary bonuses usually are paid only to top management, Japanese companies pay semiannual bonuses to all regular employees—from janitors to presidents. For managerial personnel, the size of the bonus varies according to individual performance; all other employees usually receive the same percentage of their regular salary. On average, production workers in manufacturing receive about 20 percent of their compensation in bonuses, compared with less than 1 percent in the United States and the United Kingdom.[81]

The system of bonuses is important in many ways. First, like profit-sharing schemes in other countries, it may contribute to the employees' interest in the performance of their company and to their motivation to work. Second, if the bonuses are regarded as transitory income by the workers, Friedman's permanent income hypothesis suggests that a relatively large portion of bonus income will be saved. Thus, the bonuses may help explain the Japanese population's high savings rate, which finances the high rate of investment and economic growth.

IS JAPAN A SHARE ECONOMY?

One interesting result of the bonus system is suggested by Martin Weitzman of MIT. According to Weitzman, Japan is a living laboratory for an economic system that he calls a *share economy*, in which workers are paid a fixed share of the revenue of their company instead of a fixed wage.[82] In a pure share economy, Weitzman claims that profit-maximizing employers would expand employment and output until "every qualified person in the economy seeking work has a job."[83] Briefly put, this is based on the fact that revenue-sharing employers would maximize their profits by maximizing revenues, which would usually call for a larger level of production than profit maximization with a fixed wage. Thus, Weitzman argues that the bonus system may help explain the very low level of unemployment in Japan, and he advocates the adoption of a similar system in other countries.

Weitzman's assertion that the wage system is *the* cause of unemployment in capitalist economies, and his argument that unemployment can be eradicated by the adoption of a share economy, have both met stiff disagreement.[84]

[81] U.S. Department of Labor, Bureau of Labor Statistics, *Handbook of Labor Statistics* (Washington, D.C.: USGPO, 1985), 439–440. In 1986, Japanese manufacturers with more than 500 employees paid 30 percent of total compensation in bonuses; firms with 30 to 99 employees paid 18 percent in bonuses. See Organization for Economic Cooperation and Development, *Employment Outlook*, July 1995, 149.

[82] Weitzman, *The Share Economy*, 73.

[83] Ibid., 6. For a technical proof of this proposition, see Martin L. Weitzman, "The Simple Macroeconomics of Profit Sharing," *The American Economic Review* 75 (December 1985): 937–953.

[84] See Kurt Rothschild, "Is There a Weitzman Miracle?" and Paul Davidson, "The Simple Macroeconomics of a Nonergodic Monetary Economy versus a Share Economy: Is Weitzman's Macroeconomics Too Simple?" both in *Journal of Post Keynesian Economics* 9 (Winter 1986–1987): 198–225; and papers by William Nordhaus and James Tobin in *The Share Economy: A Symposium*, ed. William Nordhaus and Andrew John, *Journal of Comparative Economics* 10 (December 1986): 414–473.

Critics say that a theory of unemployment based on wage rigidity cannot explain, for example, how the world economy slipped into the Great Depression and takes little account of the influence of expectations and uncertainty.

There was a time when a share economy—better known as sharecropping—dominated the world agricultural system. It gradually disappeared as the need to economize on labor and to introduce new agricultural technologies increased. If we were to return to a pure share economy today, Paul Davidson argues, perhaps unemployment would decrease, but "we would see an auto industry where workers hand-carried car frames down the assembly line."[85]

Even if a pure share economy would perform according to Weitzman's analysis, the Japanese bonus system may not explain the low rate of unemployment in that country. The bulk of Japanese income still is paid in wages rather than bonuses, and this is particularly true in the smaller firms that employ a large proportion of the labor force. The bonus rate usually is settled in the annual Shunto wage negotiations, and is sometimes advertised to recruit new employees. Thus, bonuses may be little more than another form of wage payment. According to econometric estimates, fluctuations of bonus payments are correlated more closely with wages than with profits.[86] Weitzman's critics propose that traditionally low rates of Japanese unemployment have been explained by several factors outside his theory:

- ■ The rapid rate of output growth caused by the high savings rate, assimilation of foreign technology, and other factors;

- ■ The stabilizing influences of lifetime employment and retention of jobs on aggregate demand;

- ■ The willingness of workers and employers to respond to business fluctuations with adjustments of overtime work, rather than with fluctuations of employment; and

- ■ The observed tendency of unemployed Japanese workers (particularly women) to leave the labor force during times of recession, so that they are counted only as discouraged workers. In 1993, for example, the recession caused the number of female "housekeepers" outside the labor force to jump by 420,000.[87]

---

[85]Davidson, "The Simple Macroeconomics," 220.

[86]Merton J. Peck, "Is Japan Really a Share Economy?" in *The Share Economy: A Symposium*, 428–431; and Organization for Economic Cooperation and Development, *Employment Outlook*, July 1995, 149–151.

[87]Koichi Hamada and Yoshio Kurosaka, "Trends in Unemployment, Wages, and Productivity: The Case of Japan," *Economica* 53 (Supplement 1986): S285–S286; Stuart Weiner, "Why Is Japan's Unemployment Rate So Low and So Stable?" *Federal Reserve Bank of Kansas City Economic Review* (April 1987), 3–18; and Williams, "Japan Labor System: A Two-Edged Sword," A18.

THE FINANCIAL SECTOR

By encouraging the public to save vigorously, and by directing public savings into productive investments, Japanese financial institutions played a vital role in the growth miracle of the 1960s. Today, six of the world's ten largest banks are based in Japan.[88] Recently, however, instabilities in Japanese financial markets have become a major cause of concern, not only within the country, but throughout the world. Shaken by the collapse of the bubble economy and tested by programs of financial deregulation, financial institutions have been forced to make painful adjustments.

Striding atop the Japanese system, the **Ministry of Finance (MOF)** has exceptionally broad regulatory and administrative authority. It bears general responsibility for the conduct of fiscal policy, and has considerable influence over monetary policy, implemented by the Bank of Japan. Described as a "titan among Japanese government agencies," the MOF wields powers that are dispersed in the United States among the Department of the Treasury, the Internal Revenue Service, the Federal Reserve, the Securities Exchange Commission, the Federal Deposit Insurance Corporation, and the Office of the Comptroller.[89] Because of its high ranking in the Japanese economic and social hierarchy, the MOF can attract the brightest graduates of the top universities, and retire its senior officials into leading positions in government and industry.

The MOF exercises informal powers that extend far beyond its legal mandate. In a constant stream of memoranda and closed-door meetings, ministry officials provide **administrative guidance** to financial institutions, influencing their day-to-day decisions. For example, during recent economic crises, when insolvent financial institutions have been unable to meet all their obligations, the MOF has been able to determine which creditors would receive payments. Usually, these instructions are issued privately, off the public record, sometimes at variance with policies set by the prime minister and the Diet. Hence, Japanese reformers are seeking support to break the excessive power of the MOF by dividing it into four independent agencies: a budget agency, a treasury agency, a financial commission, and a securities and exchange commission.[90]

Established in 1882, the **Bank of Japan** is the nation's central bank. Its supreme decision-making body is a seven-member Policy Board, chaired by the Governor of the bank, and including one representative from each of the following: the Ministry of Finance, the Economic Planning Agency, the city banks, the regional banks, commerce and industry, and agriculture.[91]

---

[88] These are Industrial Bank of Japan, Sanwa, Mitsubishi, Fuji, Dai-ichi Kangyo, and Long-Term Credit Bank. See "The Global 500," *Fortune*, August 5, 1996, F-17.

[89] Eamonn Fingleton, "Japan's Invisible Leviathon," *Foreign Affairs* 74 (March/April 1995): 72.

[90] Saito Seiichiro, "Rebuilding a Bankrupt Financial Regulatory System," *Japan Echo* 23 (Summer 1996): 15–20; and Miyao Takahiro, "A Proposal for Dismantling the Ministry of Finance," *Japan Echo* 23 (Spring 1996): 25–27.

[91] Yoshio Suzuki, *The Japanese Financial System* (Oxford: Clarendon Press, 1992), 313.

Formally, the Bank of Japan has independent control of monetary policy. Informally, though, the Bank falls under the guidance of the MOF, and some of its actions (such as any change in bank reserve requirements) require explicit approval of the MOF.

Because Japanese markets for government securities have developed slowly, the Bank of Japan has used discount lending, rather than open market operations, as its primary tool of monetary policy. Indeed, in a system where companies are highly dependent on bank financing, and banks are highly dependent on central bank funding (because their loans typically exceed their private deposits), the Bank of Japan is able to exercise extraordinary control over the economy through its discount policy.

Traditionally, the Bank of Japan has used its discounting authority not only to control the overall growth of the money supply, but also to direct funds to sectors targeted by the nation's industrial policy. This has been handled through moral suasion, or **window guidance,** and through direct controls. Generally, the system of window guidance grew more strict during years of tight monetary policy, and was relaxed during years of monetary ease. Today, in an environment of financial deregulation, these extraordinary controls are expected to decline gradually, and the Bank of Japan is expected to gain more independence.[92]

Below the MOF and the Bank of Japan, the financial system is highly stratified and differentiated. **Commercial banks,** for example, are divided into two categories: city banks and regional banks. These are allowed to handle short-term commercial and personal deposits and loans, but severe limits have restricted their ability to handle long-term deposits and loans (they gained permission to issue certificates of deposit in 1979), and, until the Banking Law was liberalized in 1993, they were not allowed to engage in trust-related activities (such as pension fund management) or securities transactions.

Because their securities market is relatively small and underdeveloped, Japanese companies obtain a large proportion of their financing from short-term commercial bank loans rather than from sales of long-term bonds or equity ownership. In this respect, the Japanese financial system differs markedly from the American system (Table 19.4). Heavy reliance on short-term debt exposes Japanese companies to the risk of insolvency. Traditionally, this risk has been reduced by the mutual support of *zaibatsu* and *keiretsu* members and by the cushion of rapid economic growth, but it has been an increasing cause of concern since the slowdown of the 1970s and the financial crises of the 1990s.

The ten **city banks** are among the most powerful financial institutions in the nation, accounting for 29 percent of all private-sector lending. Beyond Japan, they include 6 of the world's 20 largest banks.[93] Each has its head-

---

[92] Ibid., 326; and Douglas Ostrom, "Bank of Japan Reform Appears a Step Closer," *Japan Economic Institute Report* 44B (November 22, 1996): 4.

[93] The six largest city banks are Sanwa, Mitsubishi/Bank of Tokyo, Fuji, Dai-Ichi Kangyo, Sumitomo, and Sakura. The four smaller city banks are Asahi, Daiwa, Tokai, and Hokkaido Takushoku. See "The Global 500," *Fortune,* August 5, 1996, F-17. For information on the distribution of private lending, see *OECD Economic Surveys 1994–1995: Japan,* 44.

■ **TABLE 19.4**

COMPOSITION OF LIABILITIES OF NON-FINANCIAL
ENTERPRISES, 1994 (PERCENTAGES)

	Japan	United States	Canada	France	Germany	Italy	Sweden
Equity	20.1	48.4	52.5	38.8	39.7	23.5	33.8
Short-Term Debt	46.9	24.9	24.7	37.7	44.7	52.3	39.5
Bank Loans	18.2	7.0	—	4.3	—	10.2	4.9
Trade Credits	15.4	9.9	—	26.2	—	28.8	7.9
Long-Term Debt	33.0	26.7	18.3	23.5	15.2	24.3	26.7
Bonds	4.4	16.9	6.6	5.7	—	2.8	—
Total Liabilities	100.0	100.0	100.0	100.0	100.0	100.0	100.0

SOURCE: Organization for Economic Cooperation and Development, *Non-Financial Enterprises Financial Statements 1995* (Paris: 1995).

quarters in a major city, and each maintains a nationwide network of hundreds of branches. The city banks have attempted to diversify their activities in recent years, but their traditional depositors and debtors are large and upper-middle-sized corporations. Several of the banks serve as hubs of financial *keiretsu* organizations, and all serve as **main banks** for companies that require regular financing and guidance.[94]

Below the city banks in the financial pyramid are the **regional banks,** each of which has a branch network confined to a single city or prefecture. In 1995, 129 regional bank networks were operating (half of which were converted from mutual banks to regional banks in 1989), accounting for about 24 percent of all private lending. The traditional depositors and debtors of the regional banks are small and lower-middle-sized companies.

Also in the private sector, to handle banking activities that traditionally were forbidden in the commercial banks, Japan has three long-term credit banks (which underwrite securities and finance fixed capital investments), 23 trust banks, one specialized foreign exchange bank, a variety of consumer and agricultural cooperative societies, and 282 investment companies. Until they were liquidated at enormous cost to the taxpayers in 1996, the private financial system also included seven housing loan companies (*jusen*) that fell victim to the collapse of the real estate market in the 1990s. Thus, the Japanese financial system is far more differentiated than the German unified banking system, and perhaps even more segmented than the American system.

In the public sector, a network of governmental financial institutions provides funding directly to nonfinancial corporations. These include the Japan Development Bank, which makes long-term loans for investment and

[94]For an extended account of the significance of company relations with their main banks, see *The Japanese Main Bank System,* ed. Masahiko Aoki and Hugh Patrick (Oxford: Clarendon Press, 1994).

research in target industries; the Export-Import Bank, which provides long-term financing for export promotion; the Small Business Finance Corporation; and the Housing Loan Corporation. All these investment activities are financed through the Fiscal Investment and Loans Program (FILP), which is prepared by the Ministry of Finance in parallel with the general-account budget. Governmental financial institutions account for a much larger proportion of lending in Japan than in the United States.[95] Thus, the government has been able to use lending as an important lever to implement its industrial policy.

The largest single source of FILP funds for the governmental financial institutions, and the largest financial institution in the world, is the Japanese **postal savings system,** which has operated since 1875.[96] Accounting for about 25 percent of national savings since the 1950s, postal savings accounts have been attractive to Japanese families for several reasons. First, they are convenient: An individual can open a savings account at any of 24,600 post offices around the country, can arrange automatic deposit of incomes and automatic payment of public utilities, and can take advantage of cash card and automatic teller services.[97] Second, before a withholding tax was imposed in 1988, most of the interest earned on postal accounts was exempt from taxation. Third, since the confidence of the public in private financial institutions has been shaken by the rise and fall of the bubble economy, money has been flooding into postal accounts. The share of postal accounts in the total stock of personal saving increased from 18 percent in 1990 to 22 percent in 1995.[98] To end their dominance, the Japanese Federation of Bankers' Associations is calling for a partial privatization of the postal savings facilities and accounts.[99]

More generally, Prime Minister Hashimoto called in 1996 for a "Big Bang" package of financial reforms, based on the British program by the same name that was launched in 1986. The reforms are designed to strengthen the efficiency of Japanese financial institutions and markets by removing barriers to competition. Major provisions of a first wave of reforms would include:

■ Allowing banks, brokerage houses, and insurance firms to establish subsidiaries that would compete in all their respective markets.

■ Allowing financial institutions to issue innovative financial instruments that presently are illegal, such as stock index funds.

[95] Eisuke Sakakibara and Robert Feldman, "The Japanese Financial System in Comparative Perspective," *Journal of Comparative Economics* 7 (March 1983): 10.

[96] Kent Calder, "Introducing the World's Largest Financial Institution," *The International Economy,* May/June 1993, 53–55.

[97] Suzuki, *Japanese Financial System,* 288–290; and "Privatization of 'Kampo' Postal Insurance Possible," Japan Economic Newswire, November 10, 1996.

[98] Jon Choy, "Financial Market Reform in Japan: Postbubble Economy Shocks Continue," *Japan Economic Institute Report* 9A (March 8, 1996), 5.

[99] "Bankers Federation Recommends Partial Privatization of Post Funds," Tokyo Financial Wire, December 3, 1996.

■ Allowing greater freedom to set flexible brokerage commissions and other fees for financial services.

■ Removing regulations on the mix of assets required in private pension programs, and considering privatization of the public pension program.

■ Allowing a larger number of intermediaries to participate in the foreign exchange market.

■ Removing the postwar ban on financial holding companies, and allowing them to manage the reorganization of inefficient companies.[100]

Hashimoto's plan, coupled with news of weak economic growth, caused an initial destabilization of Japanese financial markets. The Nikkei stock average fell by more than 16 percent during the first five weeks after the prime minister's announcement. Still, the need for deregulation and structural adjustment is widely understood. In early 1997, a report by the influential Association of Corporate Executives affirmed that "Japan needs to implement economic structural reform as quickly as possible."[101]

THE GOVERNMENT

Conventional indicators seem to suggest that the government plays a relatively small role in the Japanese economy. Government expenditures, for example, amounted to 36 percent of GDP in 1995; the average OECD figure was 41 percent.[102] The Japanese government also collects a smaller percentage of national income in taxes, employs a smaller percentage of the population, and controls a smaller fraction of total investment through nationalized industries than does the average OECD country.[103] Nevertheless, many believe that Japanese government agencies, through their regulatory, advisory, and financial activities, have been able to direct the development of the economy. According to this point of view, powerful government agencies stand at the head of a public-private partnership known as **Japan, Inc.:**

> *The Japanese government corresponds to corporate headquarters, responsible for planning and coordination, formulation of long-term policies and major investment decisions. The large corporations of Japan are akin to corporate divisions, with a good deal of operating autonomy within the overall policy framework laid down by corporate headquarters, free to compete with each other within broad limits, and charged with direct operating responsibility.*[104]

---

[100] Jon Choy, "Hashimoto Lights Fuse for 'Big Bang' in Japan's Financial Sector," *Japan Economic Institute Report* 44B (November 22, 1996), 1–3.

[101] Steiner and Sapsford, "Japanese Stock Plunge Signals Painful Fallout," A5.

[102] Notably, the U.S. figure was only 33 percent. *OECD Economic Outlook*, June 1996, A31.

[103] On this last point, for example, the nationalized share of investment between 1978 and 1991 was 8 percent in Japan, which was lower than 15 percent in France, 12 percent in Germany, and 11 percent in the United Kingdom, but higher than 4 percent in the United States. See World Bank, *Bureaucrats in Business* (Oxford: Oxford University Press, 1995), 276–281.

[104] James C. Abegglen, *Business Strategies for Japan* (Tokyo: Sophia University, 1970), 71.

The Japan, Inc. model is only a caricature of the Japanese system. It exaggerates the economic power of the government, but takes little notice of the political power of the business community. Furthermore, it implies that the government speaks with a single voice. In reality, the "corporate headquarters" role is divided between at least three governmental agencies—the Economic Planning Agency (EPA), the Ministry of International Trade and Industry (MITI), and the Ministry of Finance—often in disagreement with one another. The EPA typically advocates stable growth and efficient resource allocation; MITI presses for rapid growth and technological innovation; the Ministry of Finance is responsible for maintaining stable prices and a balanced budget.

Despite its limitations, Japan, Inc. may have been a reasonably accurate model during the high-growth 1960s, when the government was able to intervene in the economy with few constraints. The model seems to be losing relevance, however, in the post-bubble economy, when the government faces serious financial limits, and when central control is giving way to global competition, international accountability, and domestic deregulation.

ECONOMIC PLANNING

The EPA, connected to the prime minister's office, was created to operate in a manner quite similar to that of the General Planning Commissariat in France. It works closely with the Economic Council—a group of 30 advisors from business, organized labor, academia, and other government agencies—to operate a broad system of indicative planning. The tasks of the EPA are to provide information, to improve communication between segments of society, and to draw their individual proposals into a comprehensive and consistent plan. Adherence to the plan is voluntary, and the EPA, which has little legal, administrative, or financial authority, must rely on the private sector and other government agencies for implementation.

As with French planning, the success or failure of Japanese planning is difficult to assess. Between 1956 and 1995, 13 long-term plans were adopted (Table 19.5). Most of these were designed to run 5 years or longer, but their average life was only 3 years; plans were scrapped as they lost touch with reality. During the era of miraculous growth, encompassing the first five plans, and during the early bubble era, encompassing the tenth and eleventh plans, actual economic growth exceeded planned growth. Otherwise, planned growth rates during the 1970s and 1990s have proved overly optimistic.

Despite their frequent revisions and inaccuracies, many observers believe that the Japanese plans have served a useful purpose. According to their supporters, the plans have set a general course for the economy, and have encouraged private investment by proclaiming governmental support for rapid economic growth. This leadership and encouragement may have been especially important during the 1950s and early 1960s, when economic expectations were dampened by Japan's wartime losses, and it may have helped Japan to overcome market inflexibilities caused by the lifetime employment system and by other long-term agreements. Furthermore, in recent

■ **TABLE 19.5**

JAPANESE ECONOMIC PLANS, 1956–2000

		Annual Growth of GDP	
Name of Plan	Period	Target	Actual
Five-Year Plan for Economic Independence	1956–1960	5.0	8.8
New Long-Term Economic Plan	1958–1962	5.8	9.7
National Income Doubling Plan	1961–1970	7.8	10.0
Mid-Term Economic Plan	1964–1968	8.1	10.1
Economic and Social Development Plan	1967–1971	8.2	9.8
New Economic and Social Development Plan	1970–1975	10.6	5.1
Economic and Social Basic Plan	1973–1977	9.4	3.5
1976–1980 Economic Plan	1976–1980	6.0	4.5
New Seven-Year Economic and Social Plan	1979–1985	5.7	3.9
Prospects and Guidelines for the 1980s	1983–1990	4.0	4.5
Economic Management in a Global Context	1988–1992	3.8	5.4
Sharing a Better Quality of Life Around the Globe	1992–1996	3.5	1.2
Plan for Structural Reforms: Towards a Vital Economy and Secure Life	1995–2000	3.0	n.a.

SOURCES: Takatoshi Ito, *The Japanese Economy* (Cambridge: The MIT Press, 1992), 66–67; *The Nikkei Weekly*, January 25, 1992, 4; and Japanese Economic Planning Agency <www.epa.go.jp>.

years, Japanese plans have become important tools of economic diplomacy; they are used to explain the nation's policy stance and long-term goals to other nations.[105]

INDUSTRIAL POLICY

Even among those who doubt that the EPA's plans have significantly influenced Japanese economic performance, many ascribe an important role to the industrial policy coordinated by MITI. In collaboration with the Industrial Structure Council, MITI designates certain industries for priority development, based on their growth potential and their contribution to the growth of other sectors. These included the steel, automotive, shipbuilding, and petrochemical industries in the 1950s; consumer electronics in the 1960s; computer chips in the 1970s; and energy, computer, and other knowledge-intensive industries in the 1980s and 1990s.

Governmental support of target industries takes many forms. First, the Bank of Japan practices a selective policy of bank credit control—window guidance—and the Japan Development Bank and other public institutions

---

[105]William V. Rapp, "Japan: Its Industrial Policies and Corporate Behavior," *The Columbia Journal of World Business* (Spring 1977): 42; Isamu Miyazaki, *The Japanese Economy: What Makes It Tick?* (Tokyo: Simul Press, 1990), 100–105; and Kazuo Sato, "Indicative Planning in Japan," *Journal of Comparative Economics* 14 (December 1990): 625–647.

account for more than one-quarter of all lending from the financial sector. Thus, MITI is able to channel governmental funds into targeted areas of investment, research, and export financing.

Second, with cooperation from the Ministry of Finance, MITI is able to provide special tax concessions, such as accelerated depreciation, to target industries. Third, it has sponsored the formation of rationalization and recession cartels to promote efficient production and to support prices. Fourth, it has protected certain industries from import competition through various tariff and nontariff barriers and, until the 1960s, through a system of foreign exchange controls.

How much has industrial policy contributed to the Japanese miracle? Again, opinions are sharply divided. Proponents of the system find it difficult to believe that the postwar industrialization would have succeeded without governmental assistance:

Conscious management of the industrial structure has been a driving force behind the Japanese advance, but the process could be accomplished only with the enthusiastic backing of the state. The Japanese government is willing and able to create the institutions and policies that accelerate the specific growth industries while cushioning the decline of the less-promising ones.[106]

Critics believe that Japan has prospered despite its industrial policy, not because of it. They note that some of Japan's most successful companies, including Sony and Honda, were on MITI's list of losers; likewise, the bicycle and motorcycle industries blossomed without governmental aid. Despite enormous sums of financial support, MITI was unable to create winners in the aluminum, petrochemical, and nuclear-powered steel industries.[107]

Critics also insist that MITI is not as powerful as it seems. They point out that tax concessions are not terribly important in a country that has a light tax burden for everyone. Only a small proportion of industrial investment is financed directly with governmental loans; most of the government's investment funds are used for housing, railways, and highways. "The great global economic lesson of the last generation," says Karl Zinsmeister, "is that earnest centralized management—even in as mild a form as existed in postwar Japan—always will bring less prosperity than open market competition."[108]

Advocates of industrial policy concede that MITI-sponsored lending is small in relation to the entire economy, but they claim it is important in priority sectors. Furthermore, it could be argued that MITI supports its target industries in the same way that the Federal Deposit Insurance Corporation (FDIC) supports the banking system in the United States. The FDIC is able to maintain public confidence in insured bank accounts that are much larger than its reserve fund because the FDIC represents the commitment of the

---

[106] Dietrich, *In the Shadow of the Rising Sun*, 63.

[107] Carla Rapoport, "Great Japanese Mistakes," *Fortune*, February 13, 1989, 108–111.

[108] Karl Zinmeister, "MITI Mouse: Japan's Industrial Policy Doesn't Work," *Policy Review* 64 (Spring 1993): 35.

U.S. government to support the banking industry. Likewise, loans from the Japan Development Bank have been shown to support a larger volume of private lending and investment.[109] In the 1970s, when the Japanese government committed $350 million to a research program for large integrated circuits, companies in the project responded by spending 20 times more.[110]

In recent years, the Japanese authorities have fallen under mounting pressure to reform their system of industrial regulation. The first complaints came from abroad, where the United States claimed that Japan was employing unfair trading practices in support of its industrial policy. In response, the Japanese government dismantled many import barriers, cut subsidies, and amended tax laws.

During the 1990s, foreign pressure has continued to grow, but Japanese industrial policy also has been subject to rising *domestic* criticism. Shaken by a series of public scandals and financial crises, the Japanese people have lost much of their faith in the honesty and effectiveness of MITI, the Ministry of Finance, and other powerful public agencies.[111] Under duress, both foreign and domestic, all these agencies are now participating in programs of deregulation. Public officials have conceded that their methods must change, but, according to one of its vice-ministers, MITI will continue to serve as a "stage manager" for the economy:

> *MITI used to play a slightly different role in the early stages of the recovery of the Japanese economy after the war. If you look a bit more closely at MITI's history, it is not a long history, but just about 50 years or so . . . It seems to me that MITI is entering into a totally new era to play a different role to facilitate the business environment. It means that the private firms should be dancing on the stage, but the stage has to be prepared rightly and adequately by the Government . . .[112]*

FISCAL AND MONETARY POLICY

Presently, monetary and fiscal policy operate under the general oversight of the Ministry of Finance. Budgetary decisions must be approved by the cabinet and the Diet (parliament), and monetary policy is executed by the Bank of Japan, but recommendations of the ministry usually are adopted with little opposition. This is quite different from the situation in the United States, where the Treasury Department is faced by a powerful Congress and an independent Federal Reserve.

Traditionally, the monetary policy of the Ministry of Finance and the Bank of Japan has been accommodative. Over short periods of time, the Bank of Japan has regulated monetary growth to maintain stable short-term interest

---

[109] Joseph E. Stiglitz and Marilou Uy, "Financial Markets, Public Policy, and the East Asian Miracle," *The World Bank Research Observer* 11 (August 1996): 265–266.

[110] Douglas Ramsey, et al., "Japan's High-Tech Challenge," *Newsweek*, August 9, 1982, 51.

[111] See Leonard Silk and Tom Kono, "Sayonara, Japan Inc." *Foreign Policy* 93 (Winter 1993–94): 115–131.

[112] Hisashi Hosokawa, vice-minister of MITI for International Affairs, remarks at a press conference on August 29, 1996; <http://www.jef.or.jp/news/press0906.html#8>.

rates. Over long periods of time, monetary policy has been regulated to sustain full employment.[113] Accordingly, during the 1950s and 1960s, Japan's inflation rate was higher than the OECD average. During the 1970s and early 1980s, when Japan was avoiding an appreciation of the yen, the Japanese inflation rate was roughly equal to the average OECD rate. Since the Plaza Accord of 1985, when Japan agreed to accept an appreciation of the yen, the Japanese inflation rate has been among the lowest in the industrial world (Table 19.1).

During the period of rapid growth, fiscal policy played a relatively unimportant role in economic stabilization. The Fiscal Law of 1947 permitted the government to issue bonds only to raise money for public works projects; it did not permit the issue of securities to finance current expenditures. Without access to debt financing, the government was forced to maintain a balanced budget. This was relatively easy to accomplish during the "miracle" years; military spending was low, and economic growth generated sufficient tax revenues.

The fiscal balance was upset by the oil price shock of 1974, slowing the growth of incomes and tax revenues. Special legislation in 1975 allowed the government to finance current expenditures from bond sales, and the deficit began to climb. As a proportion of GNP, the central government deficit grew from 1.6 percent in 1974 to 3.6 percent in 1975, and then to a peak of 6.1 percent in 1979. In 1983, the government adopted a medium-term fiscal plan aimed at deficit reduction, leading to an across-the-board spending freeze.

In 1987 and 1988, a major reform of the tax system was undertaken to improve the balance between income, consumption, and property taxes, taking into account the aging of the population and the internationalization of the economy. The top rate of income taxation was reduced from 70 percent to 50 percent, and the number of brackets was reduced from 15 to 5. A tax exemption for interest earned on small savings was abolished, and individual indirect taxes were replaced by a 3 percent consumption tax (raised to 5 percent in 1997). The standard rate of corporate income taxation was reduced from 42 percent to 37.5 percent.

By 1990, the central government managed to reduce its budget shortfall to less than 1 percent of GNP. Unfortunately, at that point in time, the financial bubble burst, and the subsequent recession caused the deficit to reappear. In 1994, the Diet provided assistance to farmers affected by the Uruguay Round trade agreement, provided relief to victims of the Kobe earthquake, and enacted an across-the-board income tax cut. Hence, the central government deficit climbed above 4 percent of GDP in 1995 and 1996. Japanese leaders are hoping that an economic recovery soon will resolve the deficit problem.

---

[113] This is demonstrated empirically by Hiroshi Yoshikawa, *Macroeconomics and the Japanese Economy* (Oxford: Oxford University Press, 1995), 342–371.

REDISTRIBUTION OF INCOME

Our ability to compare the Japanese income distribution to those of other nations is impaired because Japan has not participated in initial rounds of the
Luxembourg Income Study.[114] According to figures published by the Economic Planning Agency, Japan had a more even distribution of income during the 1970s and 1980s than the United States, the United Kingdom, or
Germany.[115] These reports seem to be consistent with information published
by OECD, the World Bank, and other international agencies.[116] On the other
hand, they seem inconsistent with the estimates of independent Japanese
scholars, who find a significantly higher level of inequality in Japan.[117]

The period of rapid economic growth was accompanied by a very high investment rate, causing a rapid increase in the share of property income (profits, interest, and rent) in national income. Because property income tends to
be distributed less evenly than wages, Japan apparently experienced a significant deterioration of income equality during the late 1950s and 1960s, and
it may have extended into the 1980s.[118]

Progressive income taxation has reduced Japanese income inequality, but
its influence apparently has been relatively small. This is true because Japanese rates of taxation are generally low, because capital gains on the sale of securities and real estate are taxed separately from normal income after
allowing for special deductions, and because wealthy individuals are able to
escape high rates of taxation by responding to governmental incentive programs, known as "tax measures." Thus, in 1991, when the top rate of income
taxation was formally 50 percent, the effective rate for high-income taxpayers was only 22 percent.[119]

On the other side of the budget, Japan traditionally has had a conservative
system of social expenditures. During the high-growth years, the population
was relatively young, and families were expected to care for their poor and
elderly. Many companies provided their employees with low-cost housing,
subsidized meals, health care, and other welfare-like benefits. Free of heavy

---

[114] For a description of the Luxembourg Income Study, which provides the most reliable international comparisons of income distribution and poverty, see Chapter 2 of this book.

[115] Specifically, in 1985, the Gini coefficients were 0.27 in Japan, 0.36 in the United States, 0.37 in
the United Kingdom, and 0.49 in West Germany. See Douglas Ostrom, "Economic Equality in
Japan," *Japan Economic Institute Report* 4A (February 1, 1991), 5.

[116] Boltho, *Japan: An Economic Survey 1953–1973*, Chapter 8; Malcolm Sawyer, "Income Distribu-
tion in OECD Countries," *OECD Economic Outlook Occasional Studies* (July 1976): 16–17;
United Nations Development Program, *Human Development Report* 1995, 197; and World
Bank, *World Development Report 1996*, 197.

[117] According to Tadao Izhizaki, the after-tax Gini coefficient in 1968 was about 0.40. See his article, "Is Japan's Income Distribution Equal? An International Comparison," *Japanese Economic
Studies* 14 (Winter 1985–1986): 31–55; and Hiromitsu Ishi, *The Japanese Tax System*, 2d ed. (Oxford: Clarendon Press, 1993), 170–171.

[118] Royal Commission on the Distribution of Income and Wealth, "The International Comparison
of Income Distributions," in *Wealth, Income, and Inequality*, 2d ed., ed. A. B. Atkinson (Oxford:
Oxford University Press, 1980), 95; Ishi, *The Japanese Tax System*, 173–174; and Ostrom, "Economic Equality in Japan," 4.

[119] Ishi, *The Japanese Tax System*, 107.

responsibilities in the defense and social welfare categories, the government was able to spend much of its money on projects contributing to economic growth.

A modest (by American and European standards) expansion of the social security system was introduced in 1973. Free medical care for the aged was introduced, and the ratio of old-age benefits was raised from 20 percent of the average salary to 43 percent. These measures apparently had a significant influence on income equality during the 1980s; as in the United States, Japanese transfer payments had a more progressive redistributional effect than the tax system.[120]

In 1991, Japan still had a more modest social security system than its industrial peers; benefits represented 15 percent of national income in Japan, 18 percent in the United States, 25 percent in the United Kingdom, 30 percent in Germany, 35 percent in France, and 49 percent in Sweden.[121] Still, despite its modesty, Japan's public pension scheme is not prepared to absorb the rapid growth of the elderly population expected in the coming years. Thus, the Japanese pension scheme must resolve a large projected deficit during the years between 1995 and 2050.[122]

In 1970, the Japanese population was relatively young—only 7 percent were aged 65 or over. By the mid-1990s, that proportion had grown to 15, and by 2050, it should be about 28 percent—the largest elderly share in the industrial world. The consequences of an aging population for Japanese social welfare, saving, investment, and economic growth are simply enormous.

SUMMARY

With few natural resources and devastated by World War II, Japanese workers performed the ultimate economic miracle of the postwar era, but now they are learning how to relax. Their homogeneous population is organized into a cooperative network of interlocking families of individuals, companies, and conglomerates. However, cultural homogeneity and groupism may also impede technological creativity and encourage xenophobia and racism.

Modern economic growth was launched in 1868, when the Meiji restoration abolished feudal controls and opened the nation to foreign trade and technology. After the devastation of World War II, rapid economic growth resumed in the 1950s and 1960s, caused first by the growth of the capital stock and then by the contributions of knowledge and technology, the growth of the size and quality of the labor force, economies of scale, and the shift of laborers from primary production to industry.

---

[120]Tachi, *The Contemporary Japanese Economy*, 127.

[121]According to estimates of the prime minister's office, found at the following site: <http://www.stat.go.jp/161162.htm>.

[122]Among seven other OECD countries, only Germany and France face equally large deficits, relative to their national incomes. See International Monetary Fund, *World Economic Outlook*, May 1996, 56.

The Japanese economy was shaken by the oil shocks of the 1970s, the bubble economy of the late 1980s, and the collapse of the bubble during the early 1990s. Now it is passing through a difficult process of administrative reform and deregulation.

The business community is organized in a dual market structure—very large businesses and very small businesses with few in the middle. Many of the big companies are members of *zaibatsu* and *keiretsu* conglomerates, which provide protected markets and financing for their members and exert considerable influence over governmental policies. The small companies are centered in distribution and subcontracting; they serve to reduce labor and inventory costs and to absorb the effects of business cycles for the larger firms.

The labor market, which is credited with much of Japan's success, is organized around a relatively docile network of company unions that participate in a semicentralized system of collective bargaining known as the Spring Labor Offensive. The lifetime employment system, which applies to about one-quarter of the work force, strengthens the family spirit of enterprises and may encourage technological innovation, but it reduces labor mobility and may impose a burden on employees who are not covered by the system. Support for lifetime employment seems to be waning among both employers and employees. Pay is strongly influenced by seniority and a relatively large proportion is paid in bonuses. The latter may help to explain the high saving rate and the low unemployment rate in Japan.

Led by the Ministry of Finance and centered around the large city banks, the Japanese financial system played a pivotal role in the growth miracle and in the rise and fall of the bubble economy. During the early years, the Ministry and the Bank of Japan were able to regulate a large segment of the economy by guiding the lending activities of banks. Individual families were encouraged to save by the convenience and tax advantages of the postal savings system. Today, Japan is passing through a "Big Bang" program of financial reforms, designed to strengthen the efficiency and competitiveness of the system.

The government plays a limited role in the economy in direct taxation, expenditure, and nationalization. It plays an important role, however, in regulation, lending, and the formulation of indicative plans and industrial policies. Global integration and domestic scandals have generated pressure for reform of the regulatory systems. Monetary policy generally has been accommodative, geared to stabilize interest rates and maintain full employment. Before the 1970s, the government was required to maintain a balanced budget. Since that time, deficits have been more variable. Macroeconomic policy has attempted to balance the need for stimulus to reduce unemployment and excessive trade surpluses and the need to control the public debt.

The era of rapid growth apparently contributed to income inequality, but, despite some uncertainty on the matter, Japan appears to have a relatively even distribution of income today. Progressive income taxation apparently caused a small reduction of inequality, and the social expenditures seemingly caused a larger reduction. It will be difficult, however, for Japan to maintain its existing system of social benefits into the twenty-first century as the elderly proportion of the Japanese population grows much larger.

DISCUSSION AND REVIEW QUESTIONS

1. To what extent are the Japanese economic system and the "growth miracle" of the 1960s rooted in the national culture?

2. What were the most important factors that contributed to the rapid growth of the Japanese economy in the 1960s?

3. What was the "bubble economy"? What caused its rise and fall?

4. What is the difference between the *zaibatsu* and *keiretsu* forms of industrial organization? What is the value of membership in one of these conglomerates?

5. How do the big companies allegedly benefit from the existence of small subcontractors in Japan?

6. How is the Shunto system in Japan similar to the centralized system of collective bargaining in Sweden? How do they differ?

7. What are the advantages and disadvantages of the lifetime employment system? What is happening to this institution today? Would you be willing to enter such a commitment with an employer?

8. What is a share economy? To what extent does Japan fit this theoretical model? Would you be willing to take a job under a share contract?

9. "Economic planning and industrial policy made a valuable contribution during the high-growth era, but they are outmoded today." Evaluate this statement.

SUGGESTED READINGS

Denison, Edward F., and William K. Chung. *How Japan's Economy Grew So Fast.* Washington, D.C.: The Brookings Institution, 1976. *A comprehensive statistical picture of growth in the 1960s and comparisons with other countries.*

Ito, Takatoshi. *The Japanese Economy.* Cambridge, Mass.: The MIT Press, 1992. *Based on lectures he delivered at Harvard and the University of Minnesota, Professor Ito provides a most comprehensive assessment of the Japanese system, including discussions of the product, labor, and financial markets, the distribution system, international trade and finance, economic growth, and asset prices.*

Johnson, Chalmers. *MITI and the Japanese Miracle.* Stanford: Stanford University Press, 1982. *An enthusiastic assessment of industrial policy.*

Morishima, Michio. *Why Has Japan 'Succeeded'?* Cambridge: Cambridge University Press, 1982. *Deals primarily with cultural factors in Japanese development.*

Suzuki, Yoshio, ed. *The Japanese Financial System.* Oxford: Clarendon Press, 1992. *First published in 1986, this is a revised edition of a Japanese publication, prepared by the staff of the Institute for Monetary and Economic Studies of the Bank of Japan. As such, it provides an authoritative description of the institutional structure of the financial system.*

Tachi, Ryuichiro. *The Contemporary Japanese Economy: An Overview.* Tokyo: University of Tokyo Press, 1993. *A good, compact assessment of the Japanese system, emphasizing the factors affecting the growth and fluctuation of the economy. Includes a discussion of the formation and collapse of the Japanese "bubble" during the 1980s and early 1990s.*

Weitzman, Martin L. *The Share Economy: Conquering Stagflation.* Cambridge: Harvard University Press, 1984. *Attributes Japanese success to its system of bonus pay and provides a theoretical argument for this position.*

Woronoff, Jon. *The Japan Economic Crisis.* New York: St. Martin's Press, 1993. *Written by a correspondent for* Asian Business, *this book presents an extremely critical assessment of the economic and social system in Japan.*

Yoshikawa, Hiroshi. *Macroeconomics and the Japanese Economy.* Oxford: Oxford University Press, 1995. *This is a sophisticated account, but should be accessible to advanced undergraduates who have a basic understanding of econometrics. The author argues for the usefulness of Keynesian tools of analysis by applying them to the Japanese economy.*

INTERNET RESOURCES

American Visit to Japan, 1923
http://www.dorsai.org/~whitfb/chas.html

Asahi News
http://www.asahi.com/english/english.html

Constitution of Japan
http://www.ntt.jp/japan/constitution/english-Constitution.html

Constitution of Japan, 1946
gopher://wiretap.spies.com:70/00/Gov/World/japan.con

Dai-Ichi Kangyo Bank
http://www.infoweb.or.jp/dkb/welcome-e.html

Daiwa Research Institute
http://www.dir.co.jp/Reception/welcome.html

Economic Notes
(Japan Development Bank)
http://www.jdb.go.jp/english/info/econote/index.html

Economic Planning Agency
http://www.epa.go.jp/

Gateway Japan
http://www.gwjapan.org/html/gjhome.html

History of Japan
http://www.io.com/~nishio/japan/history.html

International Economics (Ministry of Foreign Affairs)
http://infomofa.nttls.co.jp/infomofa/economy/index.html

Japan Development Bank
http://www.jdb.go.jp/index_e.html

Japan Economic Foundation
http://www.jef.or.jp/index.html

Japan Economic Update (Dai-Ichi Kangyo Bank)
http://www.infoweb.or.jp/dkb/infoecon/index-e.html

Japan External Trade Organization (JETRO)
http://www.jetro.go.jp/

Japan Federation of Economic Organizations (Keidanren)
http://www.keidanren.or.jp/index.html

Japan Free Press
http://www.twics.com/~infoplan/interest.html

Japan in Figures
http://www.stat.go.jp/1611.htm

Japan Information Network (JIN)
(Japan Center for Intercultural Communications)
http://www.jinjapan.org/

Japan News Weekly
http://www.aabion.co.jp/

Japan Online
http://www.japanonline.com/

Japan Press Network
http://www.jpn.co.jp/

Japan Research Institute
http://www.jri.co.jp/

Japan That Can Say No
gopher://hoshi.cic.sfu.ca/1m/dlam/business/japan

Japanese Economic Forecasts
(Nikko Research)
http://www.nikko.co.jp/NRC/doc/res_rep/keizai/index.html

Japanese Economic Statistics (from JIN)
http://www.jinjapan.org/stat/index.html

Kyodo News
http://www.kyodo.co.jp/

Liberal Democratic Party of Japan
http://www.sphere.ad.jp/ldp/english/e-index.html

Ministry of Foreign Affairs, Japan
http://www2.nttca.com:8010/infomofa/

Ministry of International Trade and Industry
http://www.miti.go.jp/index-e.html

Mitsubishi Research Institute
http://www.mri.co.jp/index_e.html

National Institute for Research Advancement
http://nira.nira.go.jp/

Nikkei Net
http://www.nikkei.co.jp/enews/

Nomura Research Institute
http://www.nri.co.jp/nri/index-e.html

Prices in Japan
http://www.root.or.jp/Dipper'sJapan/Prices/Prices.html

Prime Minister of Japan
http://www.kantei.go.jp/index-e.html

Sakura Research Institute
http://www.sakura.co.jp/sir/index-e.htm

Social Democratic Party of Japan
http://www.omnics.co.jp/politics/SDPJ/SDPJ-E.html

Social Science Japan
(Institute of Social Science, University of Tokyo)
http://www.iss.u-tokyo.ac.jp/center/SSJ/SSJ.html

Takao, Yoshikazu, and Nobuya Nemoto. "Long-Term Outlook: Japan's Economy in an Era of Structural Change," 1995.
http://www.nri.co.jp/nri/publications/nriqF/95summer/gaiyo.html

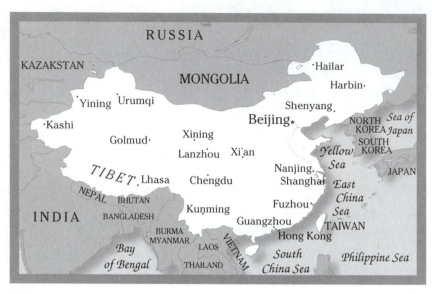

China

20

China: The Continuing Revolution

China's economic boom seems to have been a chemical
reaction of sorts. The first ingredient was the Confucian
heritage that emphasized education and savings. Then
came the Maoist revolution that unified the country, broke
the entrenched interests, divided up the land, and supplied
financial and human capital. Third were the quasi-
capitalist policies of Deng Xiaoping. None of these factors
was enough by itself; in combination they have been
explosive.

—Nicholas D. Kristof and Sheryl Wudunn,
China Wakes, 1994

hina is a land of ceaseless continuity and revolutionary change. For a large fraction of the rural
population, life has changed little in the last millennium; the struggle for subsistence has continued without interruption. However, for hundreds
of millions of Chinese, the past 50 years have
required adaptation to a series of political, economic, and cultural revolutions, punctuated by
cycles of order and chaos, liberalization and repression, plan and market, social protection and
individual responsibility.

During the mid-1990s, after a decade of gradual market reform, China
recorded the world's most rapid rate of economic growth—nearly 10 percent
per year.[1] Based on comparisons of economic performance, many observers
concluded that the policy of gradualism in China had proved more effective
than "shock therapy" in Russia and Central Europe. Indeed, based on its
enormous population, its expanding consumer market, and its strategic position in Asia, a rising chorus of voices claimed that China would be the economic superpower of the twenty-first century.[2]

---

[1]International Monetary Fund, *World Economic Outlook*, October 1996, 26.

[2]See, for example, "China: The Titan Stirs," *The Economist*, November 28, 1992, supplement, 1–18;
"China: The Emerging Economic Powerhouse of the 21st Century," *Business Week*, May 17, 1993,
54–69; and Murray Weidenbaum, "The World's Next Economic Superpower," *Journal of Commerce*, November 27, 1996, 7A.

More recently, others have questioned the sustainability of China's rapid economic growth, and the tide of opinion has shifted. Many observers have rejected the "hype" of earlier years, and a few have even predicted the imminent collapse of the Chinese system.[3] According to its critics, the Chinese economy already has pocketed most of its easy gains; continued improvement will require deeper and more genuine political and institutional reforms that threaten the stability of the existing social system.

What can we realistically expect for the Chinese future? Will it be characterized by growth and stability or stagnation and disorder? Will economic and political reform continue to follow a gradual path, or will the revolutionary pulse of Chinese history reassert itself? Will China continue to integrate itself into the world economy, or will a new generation of leaders, like many of their predecessors, find it difficult to live with an "open door"?

HISTORY AND ENVIRONMENT

With about 1.2 billion people, China constitutes more than one-fifth of the world's population. In surface area, only Russia and Canada are larger. Unfortunately, only 10 percent of China's land is suitable for cultivation. Thus, with more than 70 percent of the Chinese labor force engaged in agriculture, the average farm worker controls less than one acre of land. In contrast, the average Indian farmer works on about two acres, and the average American farmer handles about 100 acres.

The Chinese empire was the only giant of the ancient world to survive into the twentieth century. Despite several episodes of barbarian conquest and internal strife, China remained intact long after the Egyptian, Persian, Greek, and Roman empires were dismembered. Let us briefly consider the economic significance of China's longevity.[4]

Sometime between 3000 B.C. and 2000 B.C., Chinese civilization began to take form in the lower Yellow River basin, several hundred miles from the Pacific coast. According to one interpretation of its history, China's physical setting caused it to quickly develop strong institutions of authority; coordinated measures were needed to control flooding and irrigation.[5] At the beginning of recorded history, during the Shang dynasty (1766–1122 B.C.), this authority structure already included a primitive network of feudal states.

During the Zhou dynasty (1122–256 B.C.), Chinese civilization extended over a large region north of the Yangtze Valley. As this territory grew larger, the feudal states gained greater autonomy, and warfare became ever more common. In this setting, several decades before Socrates established his

---

[3]Jack A. Gladstone, "The Coming Chinese Collapse," *Foreign Policy* 99 (Summer 1995): 35–53; "China Miracle Hype," *The International Economy*, November/December 1996, 27–31; Liz Sly, "The Bloom Is Off China's Boom," *Chicago Tribune*, February 4, 1997, 1; and John Maggs, "The Myth of the China Market," *The New Republic*, March 10, 1997, 15–18.

[4]For an interesting analysis of the endurance of the Chinese empire, see Mark Elvin, *The Pattern of the Chinese Past* (Stanford, Calif.: Stanford University Press, 1973).

[5]Karl Wittfogel, "Imperial China—A 'Complex' Hydraulic (Oriental) Society," in *The Pattern of Chinese History*, ed. John Meskill (Lexington, Mass.: D. C. Heath and Co., 1965), 85–95.

school of philosophy in the streets of Athens, **Confucius** (551–479 B.C.) traveled the roads of China, seeking to convert warring rulers to his way of thinking. The educated son of an aristocratic family in present-day Shandong, Confucius called for a return to the "good old days" of peace, honor, and stability that prevailed during the early years of the Zhou dynasty. His philosophy glorified the family as a model for all human relations, elevated familial and social obligations over individual rights, and held governmental rulers responsible for the welfare of their subjects. Although Taoism, Buddhism, and other doctrines gained acceptance, Confucianism became firmly established as the philosophical basis of Chinese civilization.

China was transformed from a loose confederation of feudal states into a unified empire during the **Qin dynasty** (221–206 B.C.). Hereditary aristocracies were abolished, and their territories were merged into a system of prefectures ruled by appointed bureaucrats. To protect his people from the influence of northern barbarians, the first Qin emperor joined local fortifications into a Great Wall, and, behind its protection, a wave of cultural unification spread to the south and west.

The **Han emperors** (206 B.C.–A.D. 220) were faithfully Confucian in their selection and training of administrative personnel. Appointments were based on merit, measured by performance on written examinations, rather than on heredity or patronage. An imperial university, established in the second century B.C., trained prospective bureaucrats in the classics of Confucianism.

To promote economic growth, the early Han emperors reduced taxes sharply and adopted a policy of laissez-faire. Later, they standardized weights and measures and established a unified currency. Today, the Hanren (Han people) constitute about 94 percent of the Chinese population.

Imperial China made remarkable strides in the development of science and technology. The Chinese knew how to cast iron about 1,500 years before the Europeans, and they used it to replace wood and bronze in the manufacture of weapons and tools. Gunpowder was invented in China no later than the sixth century A.D., about 500 years before it was discovered by a British alchemist. Woodblock printing emerged during the ninth century and movable type was invented during the eleventh century, about 400 years before Gutenberg's discovery. By the thirteenth century, a machine was introduced that could simultaneously spin 32 spindles of hemp thread, and Chinese mathematicians discovered theorems in algebra and trigonometry that were unknown in Europe for another 300 years. In sum, medieval China was "the most numerate as well as the most literate country in the world," and by the thirteenth century it also had "probably the most sophisticated agriculture in the world."[6]

On the eve of the fourteenth century, China seemed to be poised on the threshold of an industrial revolution similar to the one that commenced in England 400 years later. Instead, for reasons yet unclear, Chinese cultural and technological development lost its vitality. Several competing explanations have been suggested for this reversal. According to the most familiar

---

[6]Elvin, *The Pattern of the Chinese Past*, 129, 181.

hypothesis, China was a victim of her own success—she was drawn into a **high-level equilibrium trap.** Improvements in agricultural and medical technology, limited urbanization, and a cultural preference for early marriages and large families caused excessive population growth and a rising labor-to-land ratio. The large population exacted a heavy strain on the raw material base, reduced the market value of labor, and reduced the demand for labor-saving technology. By the eighteenth century, the continuing burden of excess population on Chinese economic development was evident to Adam Smith:

> China has long been one of the richest, that is, one of the most fertile, best cultivated, most industrious, and most populous countries in the world. It seems, however, to have been long stationary. . . . The poverty of the lower ranks of people in China far surpasses that of the most beggarly nations in Europe. In the neighborhood of Canton many hundred, it is commonly said, many thousand families . . . live constantly in little fishing boats upon the rivers and canals. The subsistence which they find there is so scanty that they are eager to fish up the nastiest garbage thrown overboard from any European ship.[7]

According to its critics, the high-level equilibrium trap hypothesis is unconvincing because the Chinese labor-to-land ratio did not rise to excessive levels until the sixteenth century, long after the economy lost its vitality. Indeed, during its early history, China's large and relatively homogeneous population of artisans and farmers (always significantly larger than the entire population of continental Europe) probably accounted for its large number and wide dispersion of technological discoveries. Unfortunately, though, according to recent research by Justin Yifu Lin, Chinese discoveries continued to arise from happenstance, individual needs, and the law of large numbers. Unlike Europe, China failed to develop a scientific method based on theoretical innovation and systematic experimentation. The best and brightest of Chinese society were drawn into the civil service, where the systems of admission, evaluation, and promotion provided little opportunity or incentive for scientific research.[8]

Undoubtedly, Chinese economic development also was disrupted by the long era of Mongol domination (1234–1368), when the population was subjected to harsh taxation and slave-like servitude. However, the Mongol influence was not entirely negative. The Grand Canal, which was repaired and completed during this period, strengthened transportation between the north and the south, and the economy temporarily was opened to foreign trade and technology. Marco Polo visited China, for example, between 1275 and 1292. When the Chinese expelled the Mongols, the **Ming emperors** (1368–1644) supported a revival of Confucian teaching, restored the civil service system, and attempted to erase all evidence of foreign rule.

In the early 1600s, invaders from Manchuria overwhelmed the Ming dynasty, and established a new capital in Beijing. **The Qing (or Manchu)**

---

[7]Adam Smith, *An Inquiry into the Nature and Causes of the Wealth of Nations* (New York: P. F. Collier and Son, 1909), 75–76. For a full discussion by the author of the high-level equilibrium trap hypothesis, see Elvin, *The Pattern of the Chinese Past*, 298–316.

[8]Justin Yifu Lin, "The Needham Puzzle: Why the Industrial Revolution Did Not Originate in China," *Economic Development and Cultural Change* 43 (January 1995): 269–292.

dynasty (1644–1912), was an alien force, but it adopted many Chinese customs and won the support of the Confucian official class. The early Qing emperors built a powerful and prosperous empire. Like Communist leaders who would rule China in later years, the Qing emperors placed a high priority on political stability. In rural areas, they organized households into self-policing groups that required each member of a village to inform on others. An environment of fear and suspicion prevented villagers from entering into seditious plots, reducing the danger of rural uprisings.[9]

Toward the end of the Qing dynasty, China's economic and social development was burdened by a horrible incidence of drug addiction. The Chinese had used opium medicinally for centuries, but its abuse became so widespread that the emperor forbade its production and sale in 1729. When this had little effect, importation of the drug was prohibited in 1800.

China's import ban was particularly troubling to the British, who profited from colonial opium trade between India and China. In 1839, when the Chinese government destroyed a large quantity of imported opium in Canton, the British responded with overwhelming military force. In the end, China suffered an ignominious defeat in the so-called **Opium Wars** (1839–1842), and was forced to open five additional treaty ports. Domestic cultivation of opium poppies expanded along with imports; by 1923 they accounted for about two-thirds of the winter planting in Yunnan province. This aggravated the food shortage, and, in some cities, 90 percent of the men and 60 percent of the women were said to be addicts.[10]

Burdened by population pressure, technological backwardness, foreign colonialism, political corruption, and social decay, the Chinese economy continued to stagnate during the nineteenth century. The dynastic system finally collapsed in 1911, and a republic was established by Sun Yat-sen. The republic was weak, however, and the government in Beijing eventually fell under the control of warlords.

In 1917, Sun Yat-sen established a rival government in Canton under the control of his Nationalist (Kuomintang) Party. Sun was opposed by many provincial officials, but he was supported by the working population. His "three fundamental principles" were nationalism, democracy, and socialism, and he secured wage increases for the Canton workers.

In 1923, Sun turned to the Soviet Union for help in his campaign against the northern government. Moscow sent aid and advisors and persuaded Sun to cooperate with the Chinese Communist Party, which had been organized in Shanghai two years earlier. Sun died in 1925 and Chiang Kai-shek, the new leader of the Kuomintang, joined hands with the Communists in a northern military expedition to unify the country. In 1927, with victory and national unification in sight, Chiang launched a bloody purge against his Communist allies.

---

[9]Immanuel C. Y. Hsü, *The Rise of Modern China*, 5th ed. (New York: Oxford University Press, 1995), 58.

[10]L. Carrington Goodrich, *A Short History of the Chinese People*, 3d ed. (New York: Harper and Brothers, 1959), 223.

The Communists who survived the purge established headquarters in southern Jiangxi province with Mao Zedong as their leader. Kuomintang forces attacked in 1934 and forced the Communists to retreat northward. During their famous Long March, covering a distance of some 6,000 miles, the Communists fought through the southern and western provinces of China for more than a year. They eventually established their headquarters in Yenan, a desolate and remote outpost in northern Shaanxi province, where Mao rebuilt the party and military around himself.

In 1937, Japan occupied a large part of northern China and the Nationalist government fled to Chongqing in the south. Thus, the Communist government in Yenan became the command center for a growing number of anti-Japanese bases in the north. By 1945 the party claimed over 1.2 million members and governed areas with a population of 95.5 million.[11] During the Yenan period, Chairman Mao also completed some of his most important theoretical writings, emphasizing the principles of self-reliance and mass political participation, and establishing his preference for moral over material incentives.

After World War II, when the Communists and Nationalists no longer faced a common enemy, the civil war resumed. Drawing on their strength in rural regions, the Communists drove the Nationalists onto the island of Taiwan in 1949, and established the People's Republic of China on the mainland.

IMPORTING THE SOVIET MODEL, 1949–1957

Shortly before the People's Republic was established, Mao Zedong declared his allegiance to the Soviet model of economic and social development:

We must overcome difficulties, we must learn what we do not know. . . . The Communist Party of the Soviet Union is our best teacher and we must learn from it.[12]

In 1950, the Soviet and Chinese leaders signed a 20-year Treaty of Friendship, Alliance, and Mutual Assistance. During the following years, territories captured by Japan were returned to China, enormous factories were built, thousands of Soviet economists and technicians were sent to work in China, and tens of thousands of Chinese specialists were trained in the Soviet Union.

In agriculture, the Communists initiated a massive program of land reform. Between 1950 and 1952, about 45 percent of all farmland was confiscated from the former landlords and distributed to the poorer peasants. A system of local tribunals was established "to try and punish . . . the hated despotic elements who have committed heinous crimes, whom the masses of the people demand to be brought to justice, and all persons who resist or

[11]James R. Townsend and Brantly Womack, *Politics in China,* 3d ed. (Boston: Little, Brown, 1986), 74.

[12]"On the People's Democratic Dictatorship," in *Mao Tse-tung and Lin Piao: Post Revolutionary Writings,* ed. K. Fan (Garden City, N.Y.: Anchor Books, 1972), 19.

violate the provisions of the Land Reform Law."[13] At least 2 million landlords died in the process, many in summary executions after brief public trials. The elite hierarchy of the traditional society was destroyed.

In 1953, immediately after the first stage of land reform was completed, the government initiated a program to collectivize agriculture into rural co-operatives and Soviet-style collective farms. Unlike the Soviet collectivization campaign, this program was undertaken in China with little disruption or destruction of property. In 1957, when the program was completed, about 800,000 cooperative farms had been created.[14]

In industry, the Communists initially assumed ownership of about two-thirds of the nation's capital stock, taken from the outgoing Nationalist government and from foreign "imperialists" who fled the country. Following the example of the Soviet New Economic Policy of the 1920s, the Chinese attempted to nationalize only the commanding heights of industry, including metallurgy, energy, chemicals, engineering, electrical machinery, and railroads. The remaining enterprises were left in private hands, with the understanding that they would gradually be socialized. Thus, the program of nationalization avoided the excesses of Soviet War Communism, and began with little domestic opposition.

During these early years, the Communists also enacted an extensive program of social reforms. Their campaign to improve public health included stiff penalties for sale or consumption of opium. A new marriage law strengthened the legal status of women and protected them from "tyrannical husbands." Educational reforms were initiated, but a shortage of teachers prevented introduction of compulsory schooling.

By 1952 the Chinese economy had regained its pre-revolutionary peak level of production, and the First Five-Year Plan (1953–1957) was prepared with the help of Soviet economists to speed industrialization. Reflecting the traditional Soviet emphasis on heavy industry, the plan called for 20 percent annual growth of industrial output and 5 percent annual growth of agricultural production. With Soviet financial and technical assistance, China surpassed its plan assignments and roughly doubled its income per capita between 1949 and 1957.

THE GREAT LEAP FORWARD, 1958–1960

Agricultural production grew steadily during the First Five-Year Plan, but rapid growth of the industrial labor force led to urban food shortages in 1956 and 1957. By early 1958, Chairman Mao openly questioned whether the Soviet development model was appropriate for China. Was it wise for a poor, overpopulated country with a primitive communications system to rely on nationwide central planning and to assign heavy industry a higher priority

---

[13]*The Land Reform Law of the People's Republic of China* (Peking: Foreign Languages Press, 1976), 13.
[14]Hsü, *The Rise of Modern China*, 653.

than agriculture? Dogmatic adherence to the Soviet model fell out of favor:

> In the period following the liberation of the whole country (from 1950 to 1957), dogmatism made its appearance both in economic and in cultural and educational work. . . . In economic work dogmatism primarily manifested itself in heavy industry, planning, banking, and statistics, especially in heavy industry and planning. Since we didn't understand these things and had absolutely no experience, all we could do in our ignorance was to import foreign methods. . . . In short, the Soviet Union was tops.[15]

To declare his independence from the Soviet model, Mao introduced a leftist program with a misleading name: the Great Leap Forward (GLF). The GLF represented Mao's first major attempt to develop a higher form of socialism, based on revolutionary fervor, strict equalitarianism, and moral incentives rather than Soviet-style bureaucratic organization and material rewards. By unleashing the full potential of the working class, the government claimed that it would be possible for Chinese industrial production to surpass the British level within 15 years.

The GLF was supposed to replace the Soviet pattern of unbalanced growth with a Chinese policy of "walking on two legs"—industry and agriculture would develop simultaneously. In principle, this was probably a good idea, but the goals of the GLF were unrealistic, and the program ignored basic laws of economic scarcity. Mao apparently believed that proletarian zeal would make it possible for industry and agriculture to "leap forward" together.[16]

THE PEOPLE'S COMMUNES

The most important systemic outcome of the GLF was the reorganization of the rural sector into **people's communes.** Each of these was formed by merging several rural cooperatives or collective farms under a single administration with many of the powers of a local government. Thus, in addition to the farms, each commune typically operated its own tax office, schools, hospitals, power stations, irrigation systems, and recreational facilities. This integrated form of organization was retained with modifications until 1979, when the political and economic functions were again divided between townships, Party organizations, cooperatives, and households.

Each commune included about 3,000 to 5,000 households, divided into 100 to 200 **production teams,** and these, in turn, were divided into 10 to 20 **production brigades.** The production team was the basic unit of agricultural organization. Its leaders decided which specific crops to grow and issued work assignments to households. The brigade leaders coordinated the teams in such activities as equipment repair and construction, and assisted the teams in obtaining fertilizer, insecticides, electricity, and other resources.

---

[15]Chairman Mao quoted in Alexander Eckstein, *China's Economic Revolution* (Cambridge: Cambridge University Press, 1977), 55.

[16]On the denial of the doctrine of opportunity cost during the GLF, see Chih-Yu Shih, "The Decline of a Moral Regime: China's Great Leap Forward in Retrospect," *Comparative Political Studies* 27 (July 1994): 279–280.

In line with the radicalism of the GLF, the communes were formed very quickly, causing disruption of economic management and local governmental services. Furthermore, the administrators of the communes initially gave greater attention to ideology than to incentives. A large portion of income was distributed "to each according to his needs," and households were deprived of their private plots. Some communes drove the doctrine of social ownership to the extreme and collectivized all personal property down to cooking pots.

SMALL-SCALE INDUSTRY

Industrial policy during the GLF emphasized the development of small-scale, labor-intensive facilities in the interior of the country, far from traditional industrial centers on the Pacific coast. This strategy was designed to provide industrial inputs to agriculture, absorb underemployed and unemployed labor, and modernize the more isolated parts of the country. Small plants were established by local governments to produce agricultural tools, fertilizers, pesticides, iron, steel, and many other goods. By the fall of 1958, some 600,000 of the so-called backyard blast furnaces were operating all over the country.

The GLF successfully spread industrial production through a large part of the country. The share of pig-iron production contributed by the northeastern region dropped from 48 percent to 18 percent between 1957 and 1960; the share of the central region increased from 6 percent to 21 percent.[17] With the exception of Tibet, all the provinces and regions were steel producers by 1959.

On the negative side, many of the small factories were extremely inefficient. Many were unable to obtain raw materials, and were operated only a few hours a day by unskilled agricultural workers during spare time. Moreover, the quality of their output often was very poor; about 27 percent of the steel produced in 1958 was found unfit for industrial use. When industrial production fell in 1961, it became clear that investments in larger enterprises would yield larger returns, and many of the smaller plants were closed.

THE LEGACY OF THE GREAT LEAP

The Great Leap Forward contributed to a famine that was, "undoubtedly, the worst catastrophe in human history."[18] The chaotic formation of the communes, the liquidation of private agricultural plots and rural markets, destruction of material incentives, and disruption of the social security system exacerbated the effects of poor weather conditions. Between 1958 and 1961, grain production fell by 24 percent, excess deaths numbered between 15 million and 30 million, and about 33 million births were lost or postponed.[19]

---

[17]Willy Kraus, *Economic Development and Social Change in the People's Republic of China* (New York: Springer-Verlag, 1982), 146.

[18]Justin Yifu Lin, "Collectivization and China's Agricultural Crisis in 1959–1961," *Journal of Political Economy* 98 (December 1990): 1229.

[19]Etisham Ahmad and Gang Zou, "Deprivation and Prosperity in Chinese History," World Bank Background Paper (September 1989), 48–49.

The collapse of agricultural production and experimentation with inefficient production techniques combined to reduce industrial production by roughly 40 percent in 1961. The GLF also disrupted education, technological progress, foreign trade, and control of population growth. On the other hand, the formation of the communes made it possible to mobilize millions of workers each year to dig irrigation ditches and build dikes and dams for flood control.

The GLF also had enormous importance in the international political realm. It contributed to an ideological dispute between Beijing and Moscow that effectively ended their diplomatic relations in 1960. Soviet advisors were called home, technological and financial aid was withdrawn, and border conflicts erupted. The international Communist movement that appeared monolithic at the end of World War II became deeply divided.

READJUSTMENT AND RECOVERY, 1961–1965

As the Great Leap Forward faltered, Chairman Mao was openly criticized in the Chinese press, and he confessed that "I am absolutely no good at construction, and I do not understand industrial planning."[20] In 1959, Mao was able to retain chairmanship of the Central Committee of the Party, but he was forced to relinquish his titles as President and General Secretary, respectively, to two of the leading moderates—Liu Shaoqi and Deng Xiaoping.

During the early 1960s, under pragmatic leadership, the agricultural communes were reduced in size, work incentives were strengthened, and the private plots were restored. Inefficient small-scale factories were closed and investment was directed toward the production of agricultural equipment. The system of central planning was strengthened to resolve raw material shortages, and trade was increased with Japan and the West. The focus of the educational system was shifted from ideology to technical subjects. Birth control and family planning were encouraged under the slogan: "Two children are just right, three are too many, and four is an error."

In economic terms, these moderate policies were quite successful. Agricultural and industrial incomes grew rapidly during the mid-1960s (Figure 20.1). Other problems began to appear, however, on a political and social plane. In the upper reaches of power, the bureaucracy expanded its size, power, and privilege. In the countryside, the free markets and private plots created a class of relatively wealthy farmers who threatened the authority of the Communist Party. Because of the shortage of qualified teachers, the educational system seemed to promote elitism.

Beginning in 1962, Mao staged a political comeback with his socialist education campaign, designed to broaden the base of the educational system and to increase its ideological content. Mao consolidated his power by the beginning of 1965 and began to criticize those in power who were "taking the capitalist road."

---

[20]Hsü, *The Rise of Modern China*, 693.

CHINA: ANNUAL GROWTH OF INCOME IN INDUSTRY AND
AGRICULTURE, 1953–1995 (PERCENT)

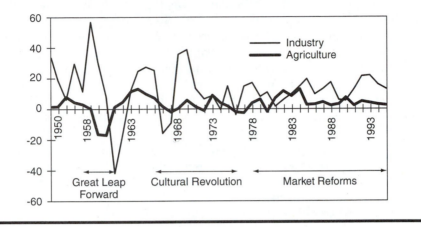

THE CULTURAL REVOLUTION, 1966–1976

The Great Proletarian Cultural Revolution was primarily a political and an ideological movement, but it had important economic consequences. Its underlying purpose was to return China to the path of utopian communism. With this in mind, Mao and his followers had at least three objectives: (1) to overturn the existing power structure and to reverse the Soviet-style trend toward bureaucratism and state capitalism, (2) to cleanse "New China" of all traditional Chinese and Western cultural expressions that could encourage the resurgence of feudalism or capitalism, and (3) to raise the socialist consciousness of the masses.

In his effort to break the bureaucratic power structure, Mao carried his appeal to the masses. In place of the Communist Youth League and other orderly political organizations, Mao formed the Red Guard—a vast, loosely organized, revolutionary army of disaffected young people. With some of its members only 12 and 13 years old, the Red Guard conducted a series of tribunals and purges to cleanse the country of "capitalist roaders." All counterrevolutionaries and rightists were subject to condemnation, from shopkeepers and teachers to journalists and governmental leaders at local and national levels. Confessions of guilt were often obtained by torture.

All in all, the government now says that as many as 2.9 million people were persecuted during the Cultural Revolution and its aftermath, causing about 34,000 deaths.[21] Conspicuous among the victims was Liu Shaoqi, the moderate leader who was president of the People's Republic, deputy Party

---

[21]In comparison, about 34,000 Americans died in the Korean War, and 47,000 Americans died in Vietnam.

chairman, and chairman of the National Defense Council. Liu was expelled from the Party and stripped of all his governmental duties. He eventually died while under house arrest.

In 1967, Chinese politics degenerated into utter chaos. The relatively pluralistic Central Committee of the Party was replaced by a Central Cultural Revolution Group, dominated by radicals. Red Guard groups roamed the countryside performing their rectification campaign and feuding with rival groups. Workers were encouraged to oppose revisionist leaders of factories, communes, and local governments. Industrial production fell sharply for the first time since the latter days of the Great Leap Forward.

To restore a semblance of order, Mao finally instructed the People's Liberation Army to intervene. Once in control, the army placed Revolutionary Committees in charge of the factories and the local governments. Each committee included representatives from the army, the Red Guard, and the repentant veteran managers—the "three-way alliance." After the purge of the political leadership and the formation of the Revolutionary Committees, the old power structure was thoroughly undermined.

The cultural component of the Cultural Revolution was pursued with similar zeal. Campaigns were waged against Confucianism, Western fashion, art, and music, and traditional Chinese literature and performing arts. All this had a devastating effect on foreign economic and political relations. Foreign ambassadors and crews on foreign ships were attacked, provoking outrage in both the East and the West. After growing by about 60 percent between 1962 and 1966, the dollar value of Chinese foreign trade fell by about 11 percent between 1966 and 1968.

The campaign against bourgeois culture was closely connected with the third component of the Revolution—the effort to create a new proletarian society with its own philosophy, technology, music, and style of dress. Maoist philosophy was presented as a replacement for Confucianism, and all were expected to study it. Intellectuals and bureaucrats were required to work in the fields to get in touch with the masses. The masses, in turn, were admonished to learn from Tachai—a production brigade in the mountains that increased its agricultural yields against serious obstacles. "The Tachai spirit meant working for the revolution and not for 'filthy lucre,' seven-day workweeks and twelve-hour working days, remuneration according to political reliability, doing without private plots and side occupations, . . . and especially self-reliance and delivery of large amounts of grain to the state."[22]

Despite all this, the leaders of the Cultural Revolution did not order any basic institutional changes in the countryside, apart from the formation of the Revolutionary Committees. No national effort was made to abolish private-plot agriculture or to move the focus of rural organization from the production teams to the communes, although these actions were taken by some of the more zealous Revolutionary Committees. Accordingly, the agricultural disaster that attended the Great Leap Forward was not repeated during the Cultural Revolution.

---

[22]Kraus, *Economic Development and Social Change in the People's Republic of China*, 193.

During the Cultural Revolution, Mao called on the army to oust Liu Shaoqi and the other "right deviationist" forces in the Party, and, in the end, Mao extended extraordinary powers to the army to restore order. Thus, the military elite gained unprecedented political powers, and, in 1969, Defense Minister Lin Biao was designated to be Mao's eventual successor. Soon thereafter, the relationship between Mao and Lin deteriorated. Threatened by the strong role of the military, Mao attempted to shift power to his civilian prime minister, Zhou Enlai. Lin feared he would lose his status as Mao's successor, and he objected to Mao's plan to normalize relations with the West. In 1971, Lin attempted to seize power in a coup d'etat, but was betrayed by one of his conspirators. Lin tried to escape from the country with his wife (a Politburo member), his son, and six others, but they died in a mysterious plane crash in Outer Mongolia.[23]

Within a month of Lin's death, Zhou Enlai held talks with Henry Kissinger that led to President Nixon's historic visit to Beijing. Zhou strengthened his power base by rehabilitating moderates who were purged during the 1960s. Chief among these was Deng Xiaoping, who, as general secretary of the Central Committee, had been denounced as the number-two person taking the capitalist road (Liu Shaoqi was number one). Zhou made Deng his vice-premier in 1973 and vice-chairman of the Party and chief of staff of the army in 1975.

Under the leadership of Zhou and Deng, many of the policies of the Cultural Revolution were reversed. Material incentives, foreign contacts, and the bureaucratic machinery of the government were strengthened. Knowledge of foreign languages was again encouraged, and English-language courses were introduced in some primary schools. Greater attention was given to economic planning, which had fallen into disarray during the 1960s. National income reversed its decline and grew continuously between 1969 and 1975. In his speech to the 1975 National People's Congress, Zhou laid groundwork for what was later called Four Modernizations campaign, setting goals for development of agriculture, industry, defense, and technology.

TRANSITION OF POWER: 1976–1978

In 1976, China was shaken by the death of Zhou Enlai in January, an earthquake in July that killed 240,000 people, the death of Marshal Zhu De in July, major floods on the Yellow River in August, and the death of Mao Zedong in September. An intense battle for succession erupted between Deng Xiaoping, Zhou's hand-picked successor, and Jiang Qing, who was Mao's widow, a leader of the Cultural Revolution, and a member of the radical **Gang of Four**. The power struggle, together with mass demonstrations, riots, and natural disasters interrupted economic growth in 1976 and caused Deng Xiaoping to

---

[23]For a recent account of this strange and momentous event, see Hsü, *The Rise of Modern China*, 710–714. For documentation and analysis, see Michael Y. M. Kau, ed., *The Lin Piao Affair: Power Politics and Military Coup* (White Plains, N.Y.: International Arts and Sciences Press, 1975). For a fascinating semi-fictionalized interpretation, see John Ehrlichman's novel, *The China Card* (New York: Simon and Schuster, 1986).

fall from power once again. The Party was left in the hands of a compromise candidate—a relative newcomer named Hua Guofeng. Late in 1976, one month after Mao's death, Hua had the Gang of Four arrested in an attempt to consolidate his power.

As a compromise leader, Hua vainly attempted to please both ends of the political spectrum. For the moderates and rightists, he arrested the Gang of Four and strengthened the system of material incentives. In 1977 he ordered the first general wage increase in 20 years and restored the payment of bonuses for plan fulfillment. Most important, he grudgingly allowed Deng Xiaoping to be rehabilitated for the second time in two years.

Despite his relative moderation, Hua leaned to the left on several issues. He supported the so-called "two whatevers" faction—those who adopted the slogan: "We must resolutely support whatever decision Chairman Mao made and follow whatever directives Chairman Mao issued." In agriculture, Hua continued to promote the Maoist Tachai production brigade as an ideal organizational model. In industry, Hua supported a seven-year plan to build 120 large-scale projects—most of them in heavy industry, energy, and transport. Announced early in 1978, this was the most ambitious industrialization scheme since the disastrous Great Leap Forward, 20 years earlier.

China reached an important crossroads in December 1978 at a Party Central Committee meeting. Hua's industrialization plan, which had been approved only months earlier, was found to be imbalanced, unrealistic, and harmful to consumers. In contrast, the communiqué of the meeting declared that during Deng Xiaoping's previous period of leadership, "there were great achievements in all fields of work, with which the whole party, the whole army and the people throughout the country were satisfied."[24] Several of Deng's supporters were added to the Politburo and the Central Committee, giving him effective control of the Party and the government. Furthermore, the following decisions were taken:

- The focus of the party's work would shift from political agitation and class struggle to socialist modernization and improvement of living standards.

- To remedy the effects of long-term ruination and neglect, economic modernization would begin in the agricultural sector, supported by a substantial increase in agricultural prices paid by the government.

- Work incentives would be strengthened in the communes, based on the Marxian prescription for early stages of socialism: "To each according to his work."

- Local authorities and industrial and agricultural enterprises would gain greater autonomy under the guidance of unified state planning.

- The Party would continue to play a leading role in society, but clear lines would be drawn between the responsibilities of Party, government, and enterprise leaders.

---

[24]"Communique of the Third Plenary Session of the Eleventh Central Committee of the Communist Party of China," Xinhua Overseas News Service, December 24, 1978.

SOCIALISM WITH CHINESE CHARACTERISTICS (1979-PRESENT)

Early in 1979, Deng initiated an enormous agricultural reform—the household responsibility system—that led to dissolution of the people's communes. He also made a historic state visit to the United States to continue progress toward normalization of relations.

In 1980, Jiang Qing and her Gang of Four were convicted of crimes causing more than 34,000 deaths during the Cultural Revolution. In the same year, six influential leftists were found guilty of conspiring with Lin Biao in his 1971 plot against Mao Zedong. During these trials, Hua Guofeng was implicated as an accomplice in the activities of the Gang of Four. Late in 1980, Hua offered his resignation as Party chairman, and Deng, with few competitors remaining, became the undisputed "'core' of the Party's second generation of central collective leadership."[25]

With Deng Xiaoping firmly in power, China entered a remarkable phase of economic transformation. A new philosophy of pragmatism displaced the leftist ideologies of Mao Zedong and the Gang of Four. Reforms proceeded most rapidly in agriculture, population policy, and foreign trade, and were accompanied by more modest efforts in industry and finance. Reform in the political sphere was slow and unsteady, and was concentrated at local levels.

After a few years of smooth sailing, the reform agenda was tested severely during the second half of the 1980s. A wave of consumer price inflation began in 1985, causing a temporary tightening of economic controls. In 1986, the course of political reform was disrupted when Party conservatives initiated a new "anti-bourgeois liberalization" campaign. Against this background, students demonstrated in December 1986 for broader democratic freedoms. Conservatives immediately retaliated by forcing the resignation of Hu Yaobang, the reform-oriented General Secretary, and by creating a new agency for censorship of the press.

Late in 1987, the Thirteenth Party Congress reaffirmed China's commitments to ideological pragmatism, economic reform, and the Open Door, but it continued to oppose national political reform at the national level. In April 1989, when Hu Yaobang died, university students honored his memory with a memorial service in Tienanmen Square. The subsequent events are well known. The memorial service attracted thousands of demonstrators; they remained in the square for six dramatic weeks, and their numbers swelled to more than 1 million. Again, conservatives forced the resignation of a relatively liberal General Secretary, Zhao Ziyang, for tolerating the demonstrations. Under orders from Deng Xiaoping and Premier Li Peng, military troops entered the square on June 4 and killed hundreds or, perhaps, thousands of demonstrators.

Following the June massacre, conservative leaders were able to disrupt progress toward economic liberalization; in November, a Party plenary

---

[25]"Eternal Glory to Our Beloved Comrade Deng Xiaoping," *Beijing Review*, March 10–16, 1997, 1.

session called for recentralization of authority and imposition of controls on prices and foreign investment. However, two years later, Deng Xiaoping led another campaign for acceleration of economic reforms, culminating in the declaration of the 1992 Party Congress that China would build a "socialist market economy." At the same time, Deng reshuffled the Party leadership and transferred power to a new generation of leaders who were committed to his policies of economic reform and political stability. After his death in 1997, Deng's successors declared their continuing allegiance to his pragmatic ideology and policies.

THE IDEOLOGY OF PRAGMATISM

Chinese leaders have a lasting enthusiasm for philosophy and ideology. In the premodern era, public servants were required to study the sayings of Confucius; after 1945, they studied the wisdom of Chairman Mao, recorded in his little red book. Traditionally, Chinese political decisions have been publicized in slogans and exhortations. In recent years, Deng Xiaoping and his successors have not abandoned ideology, but have supplanted Mao's teachings on revolution and class struggle with an ideology of pragmatism and modernization.

In 1962, when China was suffering from a horrible famine associated with the Great Leap Forward, Deng Xiaoping called for market-oriented reforms, and supported his position with a proverb from his native Sichuan province: "Yellow cat, black cat, as long as it catches mice, it is a good cat."[26] During later years, Deng was criticized and punished for this ends-justify-the-means approach to ideology, but his proverb gained wide familiarity, helping Deng to establish his reputation as a pragmatic leader.

In 1978, when China was recovering from the Cultural Revolution, Deng restated and disseminated his philosophy in two compact slogans: "Practice is the sole criterion of truth" and "Seek truth from facts." These statements may seem unexceptional today, but they stood in stark contrast to the prevailing whatever-Mao-said dogma.

Indeed, many of Deng's followers took his words more seriously than he intended. They sought truth from the facts of world history, and some of them detected a global trend toward political liberty. In November 1978, large posters were hung on public walls in Beijing, calling for freedom and democracy. Wei Jingsheng, a leader of the so-called **Democracy Wall movement,** declared that the government's economic reform program, the Four Modernizations, would be meaningless without the addition of a Fifth Modernization, namely democracy.

The Democracy Wall movement persisted for a few months, but was crushed in April 1979, shortly after Wei Jingsheng criticized Deng Xiaoping by name. Wei was sentenced to 15 years in prison, the posters were removed

---

[26]This is the original form of the quotation, from a speech on July 7, 1962, as translated by Ross Terrill and recorded in *Bartlett's Familiar Quotations,* 16th edition (Boston: Little, Brown and Co., 1992), 712. When the quotation is repeated, the cats are usually said to be black or white. For additional background, see Steve Ball, "Deng's Will to Power," *South China Morning Post,* August 27, 1994, 8.

from the walls, and Deng issued a new ideological decree. According to the new formulation, truth should still be sought from facts, but only within the fence of **Four Cardinal Principles:** China would continue to follow the "socialist road," it would be governed by a "dictatorship of the proletariat," it would be led by the Communist Party, and it would be guided by Marxist-Leninist and Mao Zedong thought. The Four Cardinal Principles were enshrined in the 1982 constitution and invoked in the 1986 campaign against "bourgeois liberalization." In June 1989, the doctrine was used again to justify a bloody crackdown on the democracy movement in Tienanmen Square.

In 1983, Deng Xiaoping formulated a principle of pragmatic ideology that has continuing significance for China's domestic and foreign policies. In an extraordinary meeting with Professor Winston Yang of Seton Hall University, who was born in mainland China and raised in Taiwan, Deng declared that Taiwan would be able to maintain a high level of independence if it reunited with the Chinese mainland. During a 100-year period of transition, Deng said, "The mainland will continue its socialist system while Taiwan may continue its capitalism."[27] This policy of **one country, two systems** was quickly broadened to include Hong Kong, and it gained prominence in May 1984, when Premier Zhao Ziyang outlined China's policies toward Taiwan and Hong Kong in his speech to the National People's Congress.[28] Seven months later, Zhao and Margaret Thatcher signed the historic agreement that provided for Hong Kong's transfer from British to Chinese rule in 1997.

Also beginning in 1984, Professor Li Yining developed a Marxian rationale for a wide range of market reforms and ownership arrangements on the Chinese mainland. All these are acceptable, he reasoned, because China is still operating at the **primary stage of socialism.** China did not achieve a high level of capitalist development before its socialist revolution, so it must employ institutions usually associated with capitalism to prepare it for a higher stage of socialism. This is essentially the reasoning Lenin used in the early 1920s to justify his New Economic Policy in Russia. Nevertheless, when Li presented his primary stage thesis to the Chinese public, he caused a sensation; in mid-1987 his lectures were attended by thousands of students at Beijing University.[29]

In October 1987, Premier Zhao Ziyang made the primary stage thesis the centerpiece of his report to the Thirteenth Party Congress. Zhao predicted that China would continue to operate in the primary stage until at least the year 2050. Until that time, to develop **socialism with Chinese characteristics,** the government should encourage individuals to engage in market

---

[27]Michael Weisskopf, "New Proposals from Peking Being Offered to Taiwan," *Washington Post*, July 30, 1983, A20.

[28]The Chinese policies toward Taiwan and Hong Kong are different in several respects. Both can retain a capitalist system, but China has also pledged that Taiwan, unlike Hong Kong, can retain military independence if it does not threaten the mainland.

[29]"University Lectures on Primary Stage of Socialism," Xinhua General Overseas News Service, November 23, 1987. Also, see the comments of You Lin, "'Hong Qi' Forum on Theoretical Work and Spiritual Civilization," BBC Summary of World Broadcasts, FE/8336/BII/1, August 13, 1986.

exchange and pursue individual wealth, but it should carefully preserve the political monopoly of the Communist Party:

The basic line of the party in this stage is as follows: to . . . turn China into a prosperous, strong, democratic, culturally advanced and modern socialist country by making economic development the central task while adhering to the Four Cardinal Principles and persevering in reform and the open policy. . . . The purpose of reforming the political structure is to promote what is beneficial and eliminate what is harmful and to build a socialist democracy with Chinese characteristics.[30]

The primary stage thesis provided an ideological basis for economic liberalization, but, at the same time, the Communist Party leadership strengthened its opposition to democratic reform. Between 1986 and 1989, the Party initiated an "anti-bourgeois liberalization" campaign, dismissed General Secretaries Hu Yaobang and Zhao Ziyang for their permissive treatment of student protesters, used deadly force to end the democracy movement in Tienanmen Square, and placed new limits on freedoms of assembly, the press, and the academic community.

Between 1989 and 1991, when Communist regimes collapsed throughout the Soviet Union and Eastern Europe, Chinese leaders condemned Mikhail Gorbachev for his failure to maintain political stability in the region. In August 1991, when Soviet hard-liners attempted to overthrow Gorbachev, Chinese officials quickly affirmed the legality of the coup, and evidently were disappointed when it failed.[31] Fearing that the popular rebellion would spread eastward into China, Deng Xiaoping and his followers recommitted themselves to a stern political stance. When the Soviet Union disintegrated, they placed police and military units on a high state of alert and strengthened the "combative powers" of rural party cells.[32]

The Chinese leaders apparently were unified on the necessity for political stability, but deeply divided on economic issues. Economic conservatives, led by the octogenarian central planner, Chen Yun, and the propaganda chief, Deng Liqun, argued that the stability of Chinese communism was threatened by the growing concentration of wealth in the hands of private enterprise owners and by the troublesome influence of foreigners, permitted through the Open Door of foreign trade, travel, and investment.[33]

Economic pragmatists, led by Deng Xiaoping, argued that the failure of the Soviet economy demonstrated the inherent weakness of central planning. Early in 1992, Deng made a highly publicized tour of the Shenzhen and Zhuhai special economic zones in southern China, where economic reform

---

[30]"Zhao Ziyang Delivers Work Report at Party Congress," Xinhua General Overseas News Service, October 24, 1987.

[31]Yvonne Preston, "Coup Was Legal, Says China," *The Age* (Melbourne), August 21, 1991, 1; and John Kohut, "Beijing Dismayed at Coup Failure," *South China Morning Post*, August 23, 1991, 1.

[32]"Qiao Shi Urges Armed Police to Safeguard Social Stability," Xinhua General Overseas News Service, December 28, 1991; and Willy Wo-Lap Lam, "Party Orders Village Cells Strengthened," *South China Morning Post*, December 26, 1991, 1.

[33]Hsü, *The Rise of Modern China*, 944–945; and Chris Yeung, "Activist Tactics Still a Threat," *South China Morning Post*, December 20, 1991, 1.

and foreign participation were most extensive and economic growth was most rapid. He encouraged provincial officials to create Asia's fifth "little dragon," following the examples of Hong Kong, Singapore, Taiwan, and South Korea. Evidently, his public relations exercise was successful. In October 1992, at the Fourteenth Party Congress, Deng was able to force the retirement of old conservatives and the appointment of a new generation of pragmatic leaders. At the same time, he had the Party Congress declare its support for construction of a socialist market economy in China.

Also in 1993, the constitution was amended to acknowledge that China was operating in the "primary stage of socialism," that its immediate goal was to build a "socialist market economy," and that effective reform would require continued "opening to the outside world." When Deng Xiaoping died in 1997, at age 92, the Party rededicated itself to his ideology and strategy:

> The theory of building socialism with Chinese characteristics established by Comrade Deng Xiaoping and the Party's basic line formulated under the guidance of this theory are the guide for action which we must adhere to. In the new march into the next century, it represents the unswerving determination and faith of the leading collective of the Party Central Committee, as well as the common understanding and aspiration of the whole Party, the whole army and people of all nationalities of the whole country, to hold higher the great banner of Deng Xiaoping's theory of building socialism with Chinese characteristics and better carry out the Party's basic line.[34]

Despite these affirmations, Deng's successors continue to face opposition from the ideological left. President Jiang Zemin has been accused of reviving the "two whatevers"; that is, he has exalted the ideas and actions of Deng Xiaoping in the same uncritical way that previous generations worshipped the ideas and actions of Chairman Mao. Serving as the leader of the Left faction in the Communist Party and an "underground general secretary," Deng Liqun claims that the market-oriented policies of Deng and Jiang have caused a level of political corruption in China "at least several times worse than during the days of the Kuomintang," before the 1949 Revolution.[35]

CHINA AND CENTRAL EURASIA: INITIAL CONDITIONS

Unlike the "shock therapy" programs of price reform and industrial privatization in Russia and elsewhere in Central Eurasia, China's approach to market reform since 1979 has been characterized by gradualism and an initial emphasis on agriculture. When we speak of Chinese **gradualism,** we do not mean that its reforms have been undramatic, but, instead of a Big Bang, China has detonated "a series of small controlled explosions, which maintained the momentum of change while minimizing the risk of instability."[36]

---

[34]"Eternal Glory," 1.

[35]Willy Wo-Lap Lam, "Jiang's Claim to Power," *South China Morning Post,* May 21, 1997, 23; and "Sidelined Chinese Veteran Cadre Deng Liqun Reportedly Moving Against Jiang Zemin," BBC Summary of World Broadcasts, FE/D2904/G, April 28, 1997.

[36]Shahid Yusuf, "China's Macroeconomic Performance and Management During Transition," *Journal of Economic Perspectives* 8 (Spring 1994): 71.

Chinese leaders and some Western economists believe that the wisdom of the gradual strategy has been confirmed by its results; the Chinese economy has grown rapidly while most of the Central Eurasian economies have passed through deep downturns. Thus, some conclude that shock therapists have provided "the wrong type of policy advice in Eastern Europe."[37] Others believe that the differences between Chinese and Central Eurasian transition strategies have arisen primarily from dissimilar initial conditions:

- The economic reforms in Central Eurasia proceeded in an environment of political revolution, disintegration of political and economic institutions, disruption of existing production and supply relationships, and heavy international indebtedness. Drastic circumstances required drastic measures in Central Eurasia, but not in China.

- In 1980, when agriculture employed about 74 percent of the labor force in China, its share in Central Eurasia was about 18 percent, ranging from 13 percent in the Czech Republic to 16 percent in Russia and 57 percent in Albania.[38] Agricultural production was less mechanized in China than in Central Eurasia, so it was possible to yield large improvements in productivity with relatively simple reforms that divided farms into smaller units. These reforms immediately improved the living standards of the large rural population and provided resources for subsequent reforms in industry.

- Because of its enormous territory and population, its communal structure, and its limited capacity to gather, communicate, and manipulate large quantities of economic information, China's system of central planning and management never was fully developed at a national level.[39] Because the national economy was not fully integrated, it was possible to proceed with a gradual series of local and regional reforms (see "Chinese Statistics: Seeking Truth from Facts and Fantasy").

- Unlike the Czech Republic, Slovenia, and some of the other high-income countries in Central Eurasia, China had little experience with political democracy or capitalist institutions during the years before its socialist revolution. Unlike those countries, China could not attempt to quickly recapture its history.

- In comparison with the smaller countries in Central Eurasia, China had relatively little dependence on foreign trade. It was able to introduce an Open Door policy gradually, experimentally, and selectively, beginning with a small group of Special Economic Zones.

Of course, the conditions that preceded reform in China and Central Eurasia were also similar in many respects. The industrial sectors were owned by

---

[37] Pradumna B. Rana and J. Malcolm Dowling, Jr., "Big Bang's Bust," *International Economy* 7 (September–October, 1993): 40.

[38] World Bank, *World Development Report 1996* (Oxford: Oxford University Press, 1996), 194–195.

[39] Thus, in 1979, before industrial reforms began in China, 64 percent of cement, 41 percent of coal, and 23 percent of steel were already allocated outside the national planning system. See sources cited in Gary H. Jefferson and Thomas G. Rawski, "Enterprise Reform in Chinese Industry," *Journal of Economic Perspectives* 8 (Spring 1994): 49.

CHINESE STATISTICS: SEEKING TRUTH FROM FACT AND FANTASY

According to Deng Xiaoping's famous dictum, Chinese leaders should "seek truth from facts." Unfortunately, in the world's most populous country, the most basic facts about population, income, unemployment, and poverty are seldom known with certainty. Like its counterparts in other developing countries, the Chinese State Statistical Bureau is understaffed, underequipped, and underfunded. Statistical reporting from the provinces is encumbered by primitive postal and telecommunications systems and distorted by widespread suppression and falsification of data.

Deficiencies in the statistical system have figured prominently in China's postwar economic history. During the 1950s, when it became clear that a Soviet-style central planning system could not operate effectively without a more sophisticated system of centralized information, China shifted to a more decentralized system of administration, based on a Maoist philosophy of local self-reliance. Between 1959 and 1961, in connection with the so-called Great Leap Forward, a horrible famine was caused, in part, by the actions of local officials who claimed that their regions had successfully fulfilled enormous grain production targets. To cover their false reports, the officials had to sell large quantities of grain to the state, leaving insufficient local reserves.

In 1979, when major economic reforms were launched by Deng Xiaoping, the implementing agencies had to cope with a shortage of reliable population data. The most recent census had been taken in 1953, and its results had been questionable from the beginning. Until a new headcount was taken in 1982, each government agency formulated its own estimates; their calculations of the total Chinese population differed by more than 100 million people. As President Li Xiannian publicly lamented, "Unfortunately, there are no accurate statistics in this regard."

In 1984, a State Statistics Law was adopted to prevent false reporting, but it apparently had little effect; a 3-month investigation in 1994 uncovered more than 60,000 falsifications. According to an analysis of these findings in the *China Daily*, "Some officials are expert at misrepresenting information about local grain production and reserves, birth rates, commodity prices, and the improvement in farmers' living conditions."

The statistical picture is equally unclear in foreign research on the Chinese economy. During recent years, for example, several international organizations, governmental agencies, and individual economists have prepared U.S. dollar estimates of Chinese national income. With price and volume indexes, it is possible to move all these estimates to a common year and price level (1994 GDP in 1994 U.S. dollars).

Continued

CONTINUED

■ **TABLE 20.1**

NATIONAL INCOME IN CHINA AND SELECTED COUNTRIES, 1994

Country/Source	Per Capita GDP 1994 U.S.$	Aggregate GDP billion 1994 U.S.$
China:		
Kravis (1981)	8,942	10,649
Penn World Table 5.0 (1991)	4,893	5,763
U.N.D.P. (1996)	2,650	3,156
Rouen and Kai (1994)	2,593	3,088
World Bank, PPP method (1996)	2,510	2,989
Taylor (1991)	2,007	2,390
Penn World Table 5.6 (1996)	1,800	2,144
Wu (1993)	1,632	1,944
World Bank, Atlas method (1996)	530	631
United States	25,880	6,744
Japan	21,140	2,643
Germany	19,480	1,588
Czech Republic	8,900	92
Russia	4,610	684
Philippines	2,740	184
Pakistan	2,130	269
India	1,280	1,169

SOURCES: World Bank estimates for China and estimates for all other countries, valued at purchasing power parity, are from World Bank, *World Development Report 1996* (Oxford: Oxford University Press, 1996), 188–189. Other estimates for China are from Irving B. Kravis, "An Approximation of the Relative per Capita GDP of the People's Republic of China," *Journal of Comparative Economics* 5 (March 1981): 60–78; Robert Summers and Alan Heston, "The Penn World Table (Mark 5): An Expanded Set of International Comparisons, 1950–1988," *Quarterly Journal of Economics* (May 1991): 327–367; United Nations Development Program, *Human Development Report 1996* (Oxford: Oxford University Press, 1996), 136; Ren Rouen and Chen Kai, "An Expenditure-Based Bilateral Comparison of Gross Domestic Product Between China and the United States," *Review of Income and Wealth* 40 (December 1994): 377–393; Jeffrey R. Taylor, *Dollar Estimates for China,* Center for International Research Staff Paper No. 59, U.S. Bureau of the Census, March 1991; "How Poor Is China?" *The Economist,* October 12, 1996, 35; and Harry X. Wu, "The 'Real' Chinese Gross Domestic Product (GDP) for the Pre-Reform Period 1952–1977," *Review of Income and Wealth* 39 (March 1993): 63–86.

In the accompanying table, we find an enormous range of income estimates. As we would expect from our discussion of these issues in Chapter 2, the lowest measures of Chinese income (World Bank, Atlas

Continued

method [1996] and Wu [1993]) are derived from relatively simple market exchange rate conversions of Chinese GDP, measured in yuan. The seven higher estimates are based on purchasing-power-parity (PPP) valuation methods, which differ from one another according to base years, sampling methods, data sources, and other details of calculation.

In 1981, in an early attempt to construct a PPP estimate for China, Irving Kravis derived an income estimate that is now understood to be far too high. Adjusted forward in time, the Kravis estimate implies that China had a 1994 per capita income comparable to that of the Czech Republic or an aggregate income 58 percent larger than that of the United States.

In subsequent PPP studies, Chinese income was found to be substantially smaller. For example, the estimates included in the 1996 *World Development Report*, published by the World Bank, and the 1996 *Human Development Report*, published by the United Nations Development Program, apparently were based on a 1994 study by Rouen and Kai, which placed China on a per capita GDP level with the Philippines and ranked China's aggregate GDP behind the United States but ahead of Japan and Germany.

During 1996, the Penn World Table 5.6 estimate for Chinese income was released, reportedly based on the most recent and reliable information. Surprisingly, it provided an estimate of 1994 income about 28 percent lower than the previous estimates. Thus, on a per capita basis, it placed China on a level below Pakistan, but well ahead of India. On a total GDP basis, it indicated that China had the world's third largest economy in 1994, well ahead of Germany but marginally smaller than Japan.

The 1996 revaluation of Chinese national income also caused the World Bank to revise its estimate of the proportion of the Chinese population living in absolute poverty. Instead of a rate of about 7 percent, as previously reported, the correct figure was reckoned to be closer to 33 percent.

The recent downgrading of China's income status does not seem to diminish its economic performance during recent years. By most estimates, Chinese growth rates have been among the highest in the world. Still, these adjustments illustrate the puzzling state of Chinese economic statistics, and they underline the fact that Chinese economic development has only begun.

SOURCES: Colina MacDougall, "Alarm Bells Ring as China Sets Out on Its Big Count," *Financial Times*, April 13, 1982, 3; "China Statisticians Overwhelmed," Associated Press, September 11, 1994; and "China Mulls Criminal Charges for Falsifying Statistics," Agence France Presse, May 9, 1996.

the state, and were rigidly controlled, overstaffed, and dependent on large budget subsidies. Commodity prices, exchange rates, interest rates, and other payments were distorted from market-clearing levels. Military expenditures absorbed large fractions of national income. Commercial banking, insurance, and other financial services were nonexistent or poorly developed.

PLAN AND MARKET

When Deng Xiaoping consolidated power at the end of 1978, his first actions were taken in the context of a planned economy. To allow an improvement in living standards and to provide resources for his agricultural reform, Deng quickly replaced the Seven-Year Plan (1978–1985) that had been issued one year earlier by Hua Guofeng with a Sixth Five-Year Plan (1981–1985). Deng reduced the annual industrial growth target from 10 percent to 8 percent, hoping to relieve chronic raw materials shortages, reduce inflationary pressure, and boost living standards by reducing the bite of capital investment. During later years, industrial growth targets were further reduced to 7.5 percent in the Seventh Five-Year Plan (1986–1990) and to 7 percent in the Eighth Five-Year Plan (1991–1995). Based on the country's surging performance, the planned industrial growth rate was raised to 12 percent in the Ninth Five-Year Plan (1996–2000).[40]

In early 1982, the vice chairman of the Communist Party, Chen Yun, announced that China would develop an economic system that he called the **bird in a cage;** the market mechanism, like a bird, would be brought to life, and would be allowed to fly freely within the cage of central planning. Still, according to Chen, the plan would be "primary" and the market would be "secondary."[41] During 1982, 1983, and 1984, price adjustments were very small, yielding consumer price inflation rates of about 2 percent (see Figure 20.2).

In 1984, when the initial phase of agricultural reform was complete, Deng and his moderate colleagues wanted to broaden their program to include industry. They knew, however, that industrial reform would be much more complex, and would require a more effective market mechanism to coordinate the production and utilization of millions of final and intermediate products. To this end, a major decision of the Central Committee in October 1984 called for development of a **socialist commodity economy** with four major features:[42]

- ■ China would continue "on the whole" to have a planned economy, but planning would become indicative; macroeconomic guidance would replace mandatory targets.

- ■ Markets would establish a "rational price system," which would be "the key to reform of the entire economic structure"; nevertheless,

---

[40]Qian Ning, "Arduous Tasks Ahead for Ninth Five-Year Plan Period," *Beijing Review,* January 8, 1996, 18.

[41]Susumu Yabuki, *China's New Political Economy: The Giant Wakes* (Boulder, Colo.: Westview Press, 1995), 41–43.

[42]*China's Economic Structure Reform,* October 1984 Decision of the CPC Central Committee (Beijing: Foreign Languages Press, 1984).

■ FIGURE 20.2

CHINA: CONSUMER PRICE INFLATION, 1975–1996

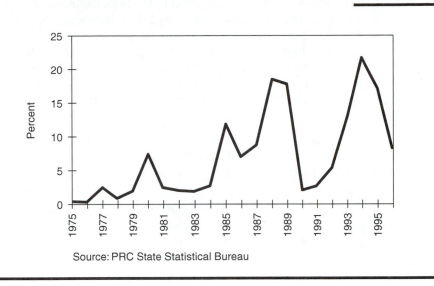

Source: PRC State Statistical Bureau

markets would not allocate or control the ownership of labor, land, mines, banks, railways, or state-owned enterprises.

■ The economic functions of the government would be defined more narrowly, and enterprises would be allowed to make more of their own decisions.

■ State enterprises would remain "the leading force" in the economy, but other forms of collective, individual, and foreign joint venture ownership would be encouraged.

After 1984, the scope of market activity grew very rapidly. During 1985, price controls were lifted from about 1,800 food items, food prices increased by about 14 percent, and the consumer price index increased by about 12 percent. By 1986, China had 66,000 free markets and bazaars. The proportion of retail sales conducted at state-controlled prices fell from 97 percent in 1978 to 35 percent in 1986. The number of industrial products controlled by the State Planning Commission's mandatory plan was cut from 120 in 1984 to 60 in 1986.[43]

An initial round of price increases was the natural result of price liberalization. Unfortunately, these increases were perpetuated by excessive monetary growth, driven by governmental budget deficits and central bank loans to unprofitable state enterprises. Between 1984 and 1988, the broadly defined money stock grew at an annual rate of about 28 percent while real GDP was

[43]James Sterba, "Peking's Streets Teem with Merchants Again as State Loosens Reins," *The Wall Street Journal,* June 16, 1986, 1; Gao Shangquan, "Progress in Economic Reform (1979–1986)," *Beijing Review,* July 6, 1987, 21; and Calla Wiemer and Mai Lu, "Prices: The Two-Tier Transition Process," in Walter Galenson, ed., *China's Economic Reform* (San Francisco: The 1990 Institute, 1993), 120.

growing at a rate of about 11 percent. Consequently, consumer price inflation continued, and escalated to a peak of 19 percent in 1988.[44]

The inflation of the late 1980s contributed to the political tensions that ultimately led to the Tienanmen Square tragedy of 1989. In reaction, the reform movement was placed on hold for a few years, and some price controls were reimposed. In 1992, however, Deng Xiaoping persuaded the Fourteenth Party Congress to establish the goal of creating a **socialist market economy** in China. According to a sweeping decision of the Central Committee, issued late in 1993, the socialist market economy would expand on the socialist commodity economy to include the following characteristics:

- The new system would include a wider array of modern institutions, including markets for credit and financial services, labor, real estate, technology, and information.

- Large and medium-sized state-owned enterprises would continue to be the "mainstay" of the economy, but these would be able to experiment with a corporate form of ownership with non-state participation, and smaller enterprises could be leased or sold to collectives or individuals.

- Property rights and responsibilities would be clarified for all enterprises, including the right to operate without day-to-day government interference and the responsibility to cover expenses or suffer bankruptcy.

- The scope of foreign trade and investment activities would continue to expand, governed by principles of comparative advantage in the marketplace, and generally would be regulated through exchange rates, taxes, loans, and other indirect economic levers.[45]

Approval of the new round of reforms was followed by another boom-bust cycle. Consumer price inflation climbed to a record-setting rate of 22 percent in 1994. Fearful that political instability would recur, Prime Minister Li Peng declared in September 1994 that control of inflation was the highest priority of the government. Inflation was fought primarily at the macroeconomic level, by regaining control of the money supply, but more direct measures also were taken:

During 1995, the government dispatched several price check groups to monitor market prices in major provinces and cities. Measures have been taken to combat illegal practices, such as wantonly raising prices, jacking up prices, reaping staggering profits, and monopolizing price rises.[46]

---

[44]Julia Leung, "Inflation in China Threatens to Worsen Unless Beijing Slows Its Money Presses," *The Wall Street Journal*, May 12, 1988, A12; and World Bank, *World Tables 1995* (Baltimore: Johns Hopkins University Press, 1995), 209.

[45]"Decision of the CPC Central Committee on Some Issues Concerning the Establishment of a Socialist Market Economy Structure," *Beijing Review*, November 22, 1993, 12–31.

[46]Qiu Xiohua, "Inflation Control: Review and Prospects," *Beijing Review*, December 25, 1995, 21.

Beginning in 1996, the task of price control was transferred to the provinces, with guidance from Beijing, under a "target responsibility system." For example, officials in Heilongjiang province were told to keep consumer price inflation below 8 percent in 1997. To do that, they established close supervision and control of prices for 30 categories of commodities and services, accounting for 80 percent of urban citizens' living expenses. According to the director of the Heilongjiang Provincial Bureau of Commodity Prices, "illicit price hikes" for grain, vegetables, pork, medicine, fuels, electricity, water, chemical fertilizer, and educational services "will be banned."[47]

AGRICULTURE

Traditional Chinese agriculture was based on small-scale subsistence farming. Even among the landlord class, who owned the largest properties, the average holding in 1949 was only 40 acres.[48] Between 1953 and 1957, the Communist government merged small peasant farms into Soviet-style collective farms with an average membership of 160 families. In 1958, the collective farms were merged into even larger people's communes, this time with a membership of 3,000 to 5,000 families. The communes and their constituent production brigades and production teams evidently were too large to operate efficiently, and their incentive system was notoriously deficient; the members metaphorically "ate from one big rice bowl."

Between 1961 and 1965, during the period of pragmatic recovery that followed the Great Leap Forward and preceded the Cultural Revolution, President Liu Shaoqi and General Secretary Deng Xiaoping adopted a policy of "Agriculture First." The average commune was reduced in size to about 1,700 households. Incomes were linked to the performance of the production team rather than the commune, and incomes were distributed to individuals within the team according to a work-point system. As they had been before 1958, families were allowed to operate small private plots on about 5 percent of the land area of each commune.

Between 1966 and 1978, progress toward significant agricultural reform was prevented by the Cultural Revolution and the post-Mao succession crisis. Furthermore, despite much that has been written to the contrary, the initial program of agricultural reform announced at the end of 1978, when Deng Xiaoping gained power, did not go far beyond the reforms of the early 1960s. Incentives would be strengthened, state procurement prices would be increased, and private plots would be protected, but the commune system would remain in place and the production team would serve as the basic accounting unit, and "this should remain unchanged."[49]

---

[47]"Heilongjiang Launches Price Control Program," Xinhua News Service, March 31, 1997.

[48]Hsü, *The Rise of Modern China*, 652.

[49]"Communique of the Third Plenary Session of the Eleventh Central Committee of the Communist Party of China," The Xinhua General Overseas News Service, December 24, 1978.

At the end of 1978, a small group of production teams in Anhui province secretly began to experiment with a system of contracting land and output quotas to individual households.[50] When the system produced large increases in agricultural yields, it gained the support of local officials; in 1979, national officials approved an expansion of the experiment to include poor agricultural regions in hilly and mountainous regions. In 1981, when Hu Yaobang replaced Hua Guofeng as Communist Party chairman, the leadership was united in support of agricultural reform. The **household responsibility system** was now actively promoted by the central government, and, within three years, it covered 98 percent of the rural population. Quickly reversing three decades of super-collectivism and returning the world's largest nation to a system of family farming, the responsibility system was "perhaps the most radical reform ever undertaken."[51]

Under the original form of the responsibility system, the huge communal fields were divided into small family plots, and each participating household contracted with the leaders of its production team to cultivate a tract of land for one year. In exchange for its allocation of land, the household was obligated to provide fixed quotas of certain agricultural products to the team at fixed prices. Any output in excess of the agreed quantity could be consumed by the household, sold on the free market, or sold to the state at negotiated prices. The land was still owned by the commune, but the household had an exclusive right to use it for the term of the agreement.

Several important modifications of the responsibility system were introduced in 1984. First, the communes were formally abolished; ownership of the land and the authority to negotiate contracts with households were transferred to the governments of local villages and townships. Second, to encourage long-term investments in irrigation and other land improvements and to encourage the planting of fruit trees and other slow-producing crops, the allowable terms of the contracts were extended to 15 years. In 1995, the term was again extended to 30 years. Third, with permission from the village government, a household could transfer its contracted land to another household. Thus, the door was open for creation of a rural market in real estate.

By most accounts, the household responsibility system was a big success. The annual growth rate of grain production rose from 2.1 percent during the period from 1957 to 1978 to 4.9 percent during the period from 1978 to 1984. According to econometric estimates, about three-fourths of agricultural productivity growth during 1978 to 1984 could be attributed to the responsibility system, and one-fourth was explained by a substantial boost in

---

[50]Much of the following discussion is drawn from Justin Yifu Lin, "The Household Responsibility System in China's Agricultural Reform: A Theoretical and Empirical Study," *Economic Development and Cultural Change* 36 (April 1988): S199–S244; Francis C. Tuan and Shwu-Eng H. Webb, "Agriculture: Past and Prospects," in Galenson, ed., *China's Economic Reform*, 81–117; and Hsü, *The Rise of Modern China*, 843–848.

[51]Jeffrey Sachs and Wing Woo, "Big Bang Smear Job," *International Economy* 7 (November–December 1993): 50.

agricultural procurement prices.[52] For the first time in 25 years, China became a net exporter of grain in 1985. Furthermore, the success in agriculture laid groundwork for subsequent accomplishments in industry.

How did the responsibility system generate such a large improvement in agricultural productivity? According to the usual analysis, the new system provided stronger incentives, so farmers were willing to work longer, harder, and with less need for supervision.[53] Robert Mead offers an alternative interpretation; instead of eliciting more work, the reform may have encouraged a more efficient allocation of work. Under the old commune system, farm workers spent inordinate amounts of time working on their private plots, and avoided work on the larger expanses of communal land. By removing the distinction between private and communal property, the responsibility system encouraged a more even distribution of labor effort over the land.[54]

Interestingly, during the early 1980s, the rewards for higher productivity were distributed rather evenly within each province. According to available evidence, the income distributions remained fairly stable during these years. After 1985, the benefits of the responsibility system had been reaped, and agriculture returned to a lower trend rate of growth. After that time, surging incomes in industry caused rising inequality within rural provinces, and contributed to an income gap between the cities and the countryside.[55] Thus, in 1995, average per capita incomes in the cities were nearly 150 percent larger than rural incomes. According to analysis by the World Bank, the gap between the city and the countryside is now the largest source of inequality in China.[56]

INDUSTRIAL REFORM

Under his policy of "agriculture first," Deng Xiaoping initially gave little priority to industrial development. His first enterprise reforms were designed to encourage the development of rural industries that supported farming. In 1978, 100 enterprises in Deng's native Sichuan province were allowed to experiment with profit retention schemes, and the early results were positive. Based on this experience, an **industrial responsibility system** was

---

[52]John McMillan, John Whalley, and Lijing Zhu, "The Impact of China's Economic Reforms on Agricultural Productivity Growth," *Journal of Political Economy* 97 (August 1989): 781–807.

[53]In simplified form, this is the reasoning presented, for example, in Lin, "The Household Responsibility System in China's Agricultural Reform," S219–S220; and McMillan, Whalley, and Zhu, "The Impact of China's Economic Reforms on Agricultural Productivity Growth," 782–783.

[54]Robert W. Mead, "An Examination of China's Agricultural Reforms: The Importance of Private Plots," Paper presented to the University of Pittsburgh Comparative and Development Workshop, October 1995.

[55]Scott Rozelle, "Rural Industrialization and Increasing Inequality: Emerging Patterns in China's Reforming Economy," *Journal of Comparative Economics* 19 (December 1994): 362–391.

[56]Ian Johnson, "Reform's Bloom Fades in Countryside as Chinese Peasants Train City Dwellers," *The Wall Street Journal*, February 21, 1997, A10.

formulated, whereby each state enterprise negotiated a "profit and loss contract" agreement with supervisory officials. The enterprise would remit an agreed quota of profit to the state, but would retain a portion of additional profits for payment of bonuses, employee benefits, and investments. By 1980, some 6,600 enterprises were operating under this system, and by the end of 1992 it covered all the state enterprises.[57]

In 1978 and 1982, when new drafts of the state constitution were adopted, they included language that affirmed the legality of small-scale private enterprise. The response was enthusiastic in both urban and rural areas. Between 1978 and 1983, the number of private businesses grew from about 100,000 to 5.8 million, and many of these were quite successful.[58] In 1984, when the Central Committee announced its plan to create a socialist commodity economy, it reaffirmed these enterprise freedoms, and also encouraged "diverse and flexible forms of cooperative management and economic association among the state, collective, and individual sectors of the economy."[59] For example, small state-owned enterprises could now be leased to collectives or individuals, or could be managed by individuals on a contract basis.

Also in 1984, when the rural communes were disbanded, ownership of their industrial holdings was transferred to the new units of local government. These became known as **township and village enterprises (TVEs)**, and they quickly became a major force in the industrial structure. Between 1980 and 1990, the share of TVEs in total industrial production jumped from 10 percent to 25 percent (Table 20.2). Between 1980 and 1995, they created 95 million new jobs in China, and their rates of productivity growth were twice as high as those in the state sector. According to analysis by the World Bank, several factors explain their rates of growth and efficiency:[60]

■ Strong kinship links among rural villagers create implicit property rights in a setting of collective ownership.

■ Chinese public finance has been decentralized since 1984, so financial benefits and burdens of the TVEs are felt locally.

■ Communities with TVEs engage in stiff competition with one another to attract local and foreign investment.

■ TVEs have acted flexibly to supply light industrial goods and services that were neglected by the state system.

---

[57]Barry Naughton, "Finance and Planning Reforms in Industry," in U.S. Congress, Joint Economic Committee, *China's Economy Looks Toward the Year 2000* (Washington, D.C.: USGPO, 1986), I, 608.

[58]Hsü, *The Rise of Modern China*, 852.

[59]*China's Economic Structure Reform*, 29.

[60]World Bank, *World Development Report 1996*, 51.

■ TABLE 20.2

CHINA: INDUSTRIAL PRODUCTION AND ENTERPRISE OWNERSHIP, 1980–1996 (PERCENTAGE SHARES OF CURRENT GROSS VALUE OF INDUSTRIAL OUTPUT)

	1980	1985	1990	1992	1996*
State	76	65	55	48	44
Collective:					
Urban	13	13	10	12	10
Township-Village	10	19	25	26	24
Other**	1	3	10	14	22
Total	100	100	100	100	100

*January–October
**Including private firms, joint ventures, foreign-owned firms, and others.
SOURCES: State Statistical Bureau, *Statistical Yearbook of China*, various years; and "Gross Value of Chinese Industrial Output in Ten Months," Xinhua News Agency, December 1, 1996.

■ Many of the TVEs have taken advantage of their freedom to form supply and technology alliances with state industries and foreign investors.

During the mid-1980s, when price controls were released to create a "socialist commodity economy," China was shaken economically and politically by recurring bursts of inflation. When the problem received careful analysis, Chinese economists quickly discovered that financial deterioration in the state-owned enterprise sector was a major source of inflationary pressure. Although many of the SOEs were able to contribute to the state budget, an increasing number of them required support. The proportion of SOEs that were unprofitable increased from about 10 percent in 1985 to 28 percent in 1990, and climbed to nearly 50 percent in 1995.[61] Money-losing enterprises became a serious problem because their losses were routinely financed with subsidies from the state budget and direct loans from the central bank. Extension of subsidies and loans usually involved emission of new money and acceleration of inflation.

In 1992, the State Council declared that *state-owned* enterprises no longer would be *state-run;* they would be free to make their own decisions in 14 areas of authority, including product mix, pricing, investment, personnel management, and foreign trade management.[62] In the Ninth Five-Year Plan (1996–2000), the state declared that it would continue to provide financial support to only

---

[61]Yabuki, *China's New Political Economy,* 51; and "Report of China's State-Owned Enterprises: A Progress Report of Oxford Analytica," *Transition* (World Bank), November–December 1995, 16.
[62]Wu Naitao, "State-Owned Enterprises No Longer State Run," *Beijing Review,* November 16, 1992, 17–21.

1,000 of the 13,000 large and medium-sized enterprises. The others would become candidates for merger, divestiture, management buyout, or bankruptcy. The SOEs would be encouraged to experiment with corporate systems of ownership and with other institutions of a "modern enterprise system." They would have new freedom to release redundant workers, create subsidiaries, and issue securities for listing on stock exchanges. A group of 100 enterprises were chosen for experimentation in November 1994; by the end of 1995, these had released 93,000 workers, and had increased their profits by nearly 13 percent.[63]

In September 1997, President Jiang Zemin reaffirmed his intention to maintain major shares of state ownership in the largest Chinese enterprises, but he also called for acceleration of the SOE reforms. The programs of enterprise independence, corporatization, merger and bankruptcy must move more rapidly, he said, to insure that most of the large and medium-sized SOEs will "markedly improve their operation" by the end of the century. Ziang acknowledged that enterprise reform would cause "temporary difficulties" for redundant workers who would lose their jobs, nevertheless, he argued, reform is "conducive to economic development, conforming to the long-term interests of the working class."[64]

FINANCIAL REFORM

Monetary and financial institutions have a long and troubled history in China. The Tang dynasty (618–907 A.D.) introduced the use of paper money in the world, and a ruinous inflation led to state bankruptcy in 845. Modern banking was introduced by British colonialists in 1845, when the Oriental Banking Corporation was established in Hong Kong, and, by the end of the nineteenth century, Shanghai and Hong Kong were teeming with European, Japanese, American, and Russian banks. To compete with foreign financiers, the Qing court in 1898 approved creation of the nation's first private bank; by 1914 there were 59 Chinese banks.[65]

After the 1949 revolution, the Communist leaders and their Soviet advisors installed a financial system—or the lack of one—that was characteristic of a centrally planned economy. The commercial banks on the mainland were merged into a monolithic **People's Bank of China (PBC),** which regulated and provided all the nation's banking services. Capital investment was regulated by the plan and was financed by budgetary appropriations and loans from the PBC. Interest rates and rates of return had little impact on investment decisions; bankers made few of their own lending decisions, and these did not hinge on the ability of the borrower to repay. Markets did not exist for stocks, bonds, or other securities.

In 1979, in connection with the broader program of economic reform, the PBC decentralized its activities by establishing a group of banks that handled

---

[63]Li Rongxia, "Progress in Reform of State-Owned Enterprises," *Beijing Review,* June 17, 1996, 15.

[64]"Text of Jiang Zemin's Report at Fifteenth Party Congress," Xinhua News Agency, September 21, 1997.

[65]Hsü, *The Rise of Modern China,* 432–433.

lending in agriculture, construction, communications, and other specialized areas.[66] In 1984, the government announced its intention to establish a two-level banking system: The PBC would restrict itself to central banking functions, including broad regulation of the specialized banks and oversight of monetary policy.

Beginning in 1992, the country was shaken by a series of well-publicized financial scandals, causing the dismissal and imprisonment of several government officials. In some of these cases, political influence was employed to obtain short-term loans from the state-owned banks, and the proceeds were used for speculation in financial, real estate, and commodity markets. In July 1993, the parliament dismissed Li Guixian, the governor of the PBC, and replaced him with Zhu Rongji, who concurrently served as the government's vice premier. Zhu initiated a financial rectification campaign that included, among other actions, the recall of illegal and unauthorized loans.

In November 1993, with the rectification campaign in progress, the Central Committee issued its blueprint for a socialist market economy. To reduce the likelihood of fraudulent lending, a clear line was drawn between **policy banks,** which would exclusively provide loans and services to support governmental development projects, and **commercial banks,** which ideally would provide business loans on an unsubsidized, independent, profit-and-loss basis. The plan called for establishment of three policy banks: a National Development Bank, an Agricultural Development Bank, and an Export–Import Bank.

The other specialized banks were converted into **state-owned commercial banks (SOCBs).** The Chinese banking market is dominated by the four largest SOCBs—the Agricultural Bank of China, the Bank of China, the China Construction Bank, and the Industrial and Commercial Bank of China. In 1994, these four had combined assets of more than $830 billion, controlled over 80 percent of the country's financial assets, operated 70 percent of its bank offices, and issued 60 percent of its loans. Unfortunately, despite their theoretical independence, the government has prevented the SOCBs from operating on a purely commercial basis; under duress, they have extended about two-thirds of their loans to state-owned enterprises, many of which are effectively insolvent. "The most serious threat to the safety of China's financial system," according to Raymond Blanchard, "is the possibility that a large number of state-owned enterprises would become unable to pay any interest on their bank debts, precipitating a grave liquidity crisis."[67]

The development of a Chinese **securities market** dates back to 1980, when a furniture store in northeastern Heilongjiang province and the nation's largest textile mill in Shanghai sold ownership shares to their workers. Initially, ownership of these shares was not transferable, but this limitation was lifted in 1986 when a secondary market was established in Shanghai. In 1986,

---

[66]This discussion of Chinese banking is drawn from Yabuki, *China's New Political Economy,* 133–136, 213–216, and 235–236; Jun Ma, *China's Economic Reform in the 1990s* <http://members.aol.com/junmanew/cover.htm>, Chapter 2; and Raymond J. Blanchard, Jr., "The Heart of Economic Reform," *China Business Review,* January–February 1997, 16–24.

[67]Blanchard, "The Heart of Economic Reform," 24.

China's first stock exchange opened on an unofficial basis in Shanghai, involving securities issued by 1,480 enterprises. Initially, though, the Shanghai market was described as a "fairly ramshackle affair, conducted across the counters of eight of the city's banks and on the pavement outside."[68]

In 1990, the Shanghai exchange officially opened its doors, with its trading dominated by shares of state-owned companies. During the following year, a market was established in Shenzhen, adjacent to Hong Kong, trading shares of joint venture companies with foreign participation. Both of these exchanges have developed rapidly; Shenzhen claims to have 1,800 computer terminals on a nationwide dealer network, with about 10 screens on each terminal.[69]

Late in 1996, in response to rising volatility in the markets, the Chinese Securities Regulation Commission (created in 1993) imposed a 10 percent limitation on the daily movement of each share price. Evidently, this action failed to dampen speculation in the booming Chinese market. During the first four months of 1997, stock prices surged more than 60 percent in Shanghai and Shenzhen. Again, the authorities took several steps to calm the markets, and finally interrupted the boom with a new financial rectification campaign. Stock prices fell 10 percent when it was announced that state-owned enterprises "should not be involved in stock speculation or provide funds for other institutions to speculate in stocks, nor should they use money loaned from state banks to purchase stocks."[70]

POPULATION GROWTH AND EMPLOYMENT

Chairman Mao and his leftist faction had little interest in controlling population growth. Mao once said, "It is a very good thing that China has a big population . . . as long as there are people, every kind of miracle can be performed."[71] Encouraged by this permissive policy, the Chinese population grew from about 542 million in 1949 to 937 million in 1976, the year of Mao's death—an annual growth rate of about 2 percent.

The post-Mao pragmatic leadership has regarded population growth a bane rather than a blessing. Surplus population exerts pressure on natural resources, slows the growth of living standards, and generates unemployment, crime, and other social problems. Rigorous birth control campaigns began in the cities in 1977 and in the villages in 1979. The authorities initially attempted to encourage two-child families—the guideline set by Liu Shaoqi before the Cultural Revolution. Since 1980 they have advocated one-child families.

---

[68]John Elliott, "Shanghai Stock Market Expected to Expand," *Financial Times*, November 9, 1988, 24.

[69]Marcus W. Brauchli, "China Is Imposing Stock-Trade Limits to Curb Volatility," *The Wall Street Journal*, December 16, 1996, A13.

[70]Francesco Lao Xi Sisci, "Beijing's Regulators Nip Speculation in the Bud," *Asia Times*, May 23, 1997, 12.

[71]Mao Zedong, "The Bankruptcy of the Idealist Conception of History," in Fan, ed., *Mao Tse-tung and Lin Piao: Post Revolutionary Writings*, 70–71.

To meet these goals, a broad range of actions have been taken. To provide positive incentives for compliance, bonuses are given to couples who pledge to have only one child, and they may also be publicly honored in their workplaces and neighborhoods. One-child families may have longer maternity allowances, larger pensions, and access to better housing, education, medical care, and low-interest loans. On the other hand, families with additional children may be subject to fines and taxes that are designed to compensate for the extra burden imposed on society. In Fujian, for example, the standard fine is twice a family's gross annual income. Failure to pay the fines may result in confiscation or destruction of personal property.[72]

On the medical front, family planning services, contraceptives, abortions, and tubal ligations are provided free of charge. During the period from 1989 to 1995, 83 percent of married couples of childbearing age in China were using contraceptives, compared with 43 percent in India, 18 percent in Haiti, and 6 percent in Nigeria.[73] According to official statements, participation in family planning programs is voluntary, but the programs are supported by strong material and moral incentives.

Particularly troubling is the evidence that population control programs in some localities have included performance of compulsory abortions and sterilizations.[74] In some rural areas, tight population controls and the traditional desire to have male children have combined to cause an epidemic of female infanticide. Alarmingly, every year the number of registered male births exceeds the number of registered female births by several thousand. These practices have been condemned officially and some of the perpetrators have been prosecuted as criminals, but the underlying causes persist.

In 1994, the government announced that it would take legal action to separate young people who live together before the allowable marriage ages of 22 for men and 20 for women. The Maternal and Child Care Law, which came into effect in June 1995, calls for premarital and prenatal examinations to determine whether couples have acute infectious diseases or certain mental illnesses, or are at risk for passing on debilitating genetic diseases. The Ministry of Public Health is responsible for implementing the law, which mandates abortion or sterilization in some cases. At least five provincial governments have implemented regulations seeking to prevent people with severe mental disabilities from having children.[75]

The population control measures have shown tangible results. The annual growth rate of the population slowed from 2 percent between 1949 and 1976 to about 1.5 percent between 1980 and 1990, and then to 1.2 percent between

---

[72]U.S. Department of State, "China: Country Report on Human Rights Practices for 1996," *Human Rights Country Reports, 1996* (February 1997).

[73]The World Bank, *World Development Report 1996* (New York: Oxford University Press, 1996), 198.

[74]For example, see Steven Mosher, *Broken Earth: The Rural Chinese* (New York: Free Press, 1983), 254f; and Nicholas D. Kristof and Sheryl Wudunn, *China Wakes: The Struggle for the Soul of a Rising Power* (New York: Times Books, 1994), Chapter 8.

[75]U.S. Department of State, "China: Country Report on Human Rights Practices for 1996."

1990 and 1994. The fertility rate has declined to a level comparable with that of the United States and France.[76]

The benefits that flow from a slower rate of population growth are clear enough, but China will also have to cope with some troublesome side effects. The one-child policy means that the working-age population will grow by only 41 percent between 1980 and 2000, while the elderly population will double. Thus, it will become increasingly difficult to provide for pensioners. Equally interesting, the Chinese are beginning to ponder the social and political consequences of raising a generation of only children. Will these stereotypically spoiled, self-centered, and demanding children be willing to submit to the authority structure and common will of the socialist state, or will they be more comfortable in a world of capitalist individualism?

Open Door Policy

After the isolationism of the Cultural Revolution, one of the most dramatic and significant shifts in policy during the post-Mao era has been the acceptance of foreign economic and cultural relations. The Open Door Policy has affected nearly every aspect of Chinese life. On a human level, the Chinese people have regained contact with the rest of the world. According to government reports, 51 million tourists visited China in 1996, making it the world's fifth destination in popularity, and adding $10 billion to the country's balance of payments.[77] At the same time, nearly 40,000 Chinese students were enrolled in American colleges and universities, and more than 9,000 Chinese scholars performed research or taught in American schools.[78] Foreign language instruction was restricted in China during the Cultural Revolution, but now, according to one rough estimate, about 200 million Chinese young people are studying the English language.

To pursue foreign business contacts, China opened its door to foreign investment, particularly in the five Special Economic Zones established after 1978, and extended trading rights to its enterprises that previously were monopolized by the Ministry of Foreign Trade and International Cooperation. It gained membership in the World Bank and the International Monetary Fund, and has opened sensitive negotiations to join the World Trade Organization. The results? The share of exports in Chinese national income increased from approximately 6 percent in 1980 to 24 percent in 1994. Direct foreign investment into China soared from an annual average of $2.3 billion between 1984 and 1989 to $37.5 billion in 1995; that makes China the largest recipient of foreign investment in Asia, and second largest in the world.[79]

---

[76]Joseph Kahn, "China Slices Its Population Growth Rate," *Dallas Morning News,* April 8, 1993, A1.

[77]"China Hits No. 10 Spot on Tourist Earnings," Agence France Presse, April 18, 1997.

[78]Institute of International Education data reported in *Chronicle of Higher Education,* December 6, 1996, A65 and A69.

[79]Nicholas Cashmore, "China's Great Leap Outward," *Asiamoney,* November 1996, 62–76.

HOW FAR CAN ONE LEG GO?

Since 1978, China has recorded an amazing record of economic growth and development with its policies of gradual market reform, agricultural priority, international openness, population control, and political conservatism. A few years ago, after the leadership announced its intention to build a social-ist market economy, *Business Week* declared that China was poised to be the "economic powerhouse of the twenty-first century."[80] Indeed, based on its prominent role in the history of human civilization, its surging performance, its untapped reserves, and its continuing record of economic reform, a very strong case can be made for a continuing Chinese miracle. According to a study prepared by China's Academy of Social Sciences, the country's "golden era of industrial revolution" should continue "well into the next century."[81]

A less glowing assessment of the gradual reform strategy is provided in a recent study by three prominent economists from Beijing University and the Chinese Academy of Social Sciences. They conclude that China's "boom and bust" cycle of rising and falling inflation, associated with cycles of liberaliza-tion and retrenchment, "is the result of institutional incompatibility arising from the piecemeal and partial approach to reform." To stay on a more stable path of growth and development, China must complete its transition from a planned economy to a market economy, and must "shift from a traditional anti-comparative-advantage, heavy-industry-oriented development strat-egy to a strategy that relies on the economy's comparative advantages."[82]

The preceding analysis raises another question: Will it be possible for China to abandon its heavy-industry orientation, supported by the leaders of state-owned industries and financial institutions, without rearranging the existing balance of political influence? In other words, as Li Honglin asks, how far can China go on the "one leg" of economic reform without accom-panying political reforms? Without a democratic government and a system of checks and balances, he argues, the country will never free itself from political corruption and errors of policy. If the country continues along its current path, he predicts, "the crisis will eventually culminate in a great upheaval."[83]

The Academy of Social Sciences "golden era" study concedes that China will face enormous challenges during the coming years. The most dangerous of these, it says, will be the huge displacement of surplus rural labor that will seek employment in the cities. According to Li Jingwen, the author of the report, China already has more than 100 million surplus farm workers, and

---

[80]"China: The Emerging Powerhouse of the Twenty-First Century," *Business Week*, May 17, 1993, 54.

[81]Tony Walker, "China's Golden Era to Last Well into Next Century," *Financial Times*, August 26, 1994, 4.

[82]Justin Yifu Lin, Fang Cai, and Zhou Li, "The Lessons of China's Transition to a Market Econ-omy," *Cato Journal* 16 (Fall 1996): 202.

[83]Li Honglin, "China's Economy: How Far Can One Leg Go?" *Freedom Review* 27 (1996): 57.

15 million are added every year. The solution to the problem, he suggests, is continued industrial growth.[84]

Some Western specialists are less confident that the Chinese leaders will be able to cope with emerging economic, demographic, and political crises. According to Richard Hornick, "As long as China's leaders insist on complete political control, they will always choose loyalty over competence," and, he continues, "as long as that is the case, it is difficult, given its present political structure, to argue that China will replicate the economic success of its neighbors."[85] Jack Gladstone, an American sociologist, paints a gloomier scenario:

> In sum, China shows every sign of a country approaching crisis: a burgeoning population and mass migration amid faltering agricultural production and worker and peasant discontent—and all this as the state rapidly loses its capacity to rule effectively. . . . China's best long-term hope for stability during the difficult transition ahead is to begin democratic reforms and implement them gradually in tandem with economic reforms.[86]

Will China surge into the twenty-first century as a powerhouse of economic growth and reform, ready to play its part in a cooperative community of nations, or will it pass through another deep cycle of economic and political instability? The answer to this question will have critical significance far beyond the Asian frontier.

SUMMARY

China, a large country with a shortage of arable land, is the only giant of the ancient world to survive into the twentieth century. Flood control required the early development of centralized institutions. Grounded in Confucian philosophy, the country developed an elite civil service during the third century, and it provided surprising advances in technology between the ninth and thirteenth centuries. Subsequent stagnation may have been caused by excessive population growth, by Mongol domination, or by failure to develop a systematic scientific method. Rapid population growth began in the 1600s, and the standard of living as assessed by Adam Smith became stationary. This fact, together with political corruption, opium addiction, and foreign imperialism, combined to cause the dynastic system to collapse. After 38 years of political instability, civil war, and two world wars, the Communists took control in 1949.

From 1949 to 1957, the Chinese Communists emulated the Soviet economic system and followed that development model. Chairman Mao eventually decided it was inappropriate for Chinese conditions and launched his Great Leap Forward (1958–1960). The GLF was intended to give greater pri-

---

[84]Walker, "China's Golden Era," 4.

[85]Richard Hornick, "Bursting China's Bubble," *Foreign Affairs* 73 (May–June 1994): 42.

[86]Jack A. Gladstone, "The Coming Chinese Collapse," *Foreign Policy* 99 (Summer 1995): 51–52.

ority to small-scale industry and included campaigns to strengthen moral incentives and establish communes. These policies were implemented poorly and the economic results were disastrous.

During a period of recovery from the GLF (1961–1965), the systems of planning and material incentives were strengthened, and the economic, educational, and population policies turned to the right. Mao then staged a political comeback and launched the Cultural Revolution (1966–1976). This was a period of international isolationism, political and ideological fervor, and inquisitional purges. Its economic consequences were less harmful than those of the GLF, but they continued over a longer period.

Mao died in 1976, and, two years later, Deng Xiaoping and his moderate faction won the power struggle and gradually introduced their program of reforms. These include a shift from revolutionary to pragmatic ideology; a more moderate rate of economic growth; autonomy and responsibility of farms and enterprises; a shift from detailed central planning to broad indicative planning and macroeconomic control; greater reliance on the market mechanism and material incentives; emphasis on control of population growth; and expansion of foreign trade and foreign educational, cultural, technological, and military cooperation. Progress toward reform was disrupted by fluctuations in the inflation rate, and by the efforts of Party leaders to maintain political stability and hegemony in the face of popular democratic movements. The record of economic growth has been very strong, but political clouds continue to hang over the economic future.

DISCUSSION AND REVIEW QUESTIONS

1. According to Adam Smith, China was transformed from "one of the richest" to one of the "most beggarly" countries in the world between the sixteenth and eighteenth centuries. What were some of the possible reasons?

2. What were the people's communes? When were they formed? How did they differ from Soviet collective farms? How did they change through time?

3. What is the household responsibility system? How much, and by what mechanism, did it affect Chinese agricultural performance?

4. How does the "socialist market economy" differ from the "socialist commodity economy"? How much progress has been made toward implementation of the latter model?

5. What are the township-village enterprises? Why have they grown so rapidly?

6. How have the opinions of the Chinese right and left differed on the subject of population control? What methods have been used by the government in recent years to deal with this problem?

7. What are the economic arguments for and against democratic political reform in China?

SUGGESTED READINGS

Eckstein, Alexander. *China's Economic Revolution*. Cambridge: Cambridge University Press, 1977. *Written just before Deng Xiaoping ascended to power, this scholarly work gives a full description of the Chinese development model under Mao's leadership.*

Galenson, Walter, ed. *China's Economic Reform*. San Francisco: The 1990 Institute, 1993. *Reports of seven working groups, each including Chinese and American specialists, on major issues in Chinese economic reform.*

Hsü, Immanuel C. Y. *The Rise of Modern China*, 5th ed. New York: Oxford University Press, 1995. *A monumental account of Chinese political, economic, and social history from the Qing dynasty to the current age.*

Ikels, Charlotte. *The Return of the God of Wealth*. Stanford, Calif.: Stanford University Press, 1996. *Based on research conducted in Guangzhou in 1980, 1987, and 1991, including panel interviews of 200 households, this study provides an enlightening account of contemporary Chinese culture and a rare description of individual adaptations arising from market reform.*

Kristof, Nicholas D., and Sheryl Wudunn. *China Wakes: The Struggle for the Soul of a Rising Power*. New York: Times Books, 1994. *Written with insight, wit, and style by a pair of journalists for the* New York Times, *this is a provocative and informative analysis of recent developments in China.*

Lichtenstein, Peter M. *China at the Brink*. New York: Praeger, 1991. *The author, who was an eyewitness to the 1989 crackdown in Tienanmen Square, was "shocked . . . into the realization that all of the knowledge that I had acquired after years of reading about and traveling in China [was] superficial and grossly inadequate." This book, based on additional study and travel, is an attempt to "peel off a few more layers of the onion."*

Mosher, Steven. *Broken Earth: The Rural Chinese*. New York: Free Press, 1983. *Written by an anthropologist, this is an unvarnished account of the extreme privation that persists in the Chinese countryside.*

U.S. Congress, Joint Economic Committee. *China's Economic Dilemmas in the 1990s*. Washington, D.C.: USGPO, 1991. *Like all the JEC collections, this one provides a wealth of information, statistics, and analysis.*

Wang, Hui. *The Gradual Revolution: China's Economic Reform Movement*. New Brunswick, N.J.: Transaction Books, 1994. *An expanded version of a Ph.D. dissertation written at the RAND graduate school, this review of Chinese economic reform devotes special attention to the contribution of the "human factor."*

Yabuki, Susumu. *China's New Political Economy: The Giant Awakes.* Boulder, Colo.: Westview Press, 1995. *An update and translation of a popular Japanese publication, this is an excellent review of the contemporary Chinese economic system.*

INTERNET RESOURCES

Beijing Review
http://www.china.or.cn/bjreview/

Beijing University
http://www.pku.edu.cn/

Center for Modern China
http://www.cmcic.org/

China Business Net
http://www.business-china.com/

China Business Research
http://www.crl.com./~covnerjm/research/asia/china/

China Daily
http://chinadaily.com.cn.net/cndy/cd_cate1.html

China Dimensions
http://plue.sedac.ciesin.org/china/

China Economic Policy Analysis
http://www.mkeever.com/china.html

China Economic Window
http://www.chinaeco.com/

China Education and Research Network (CERNET)
http://www.cernet.edu.cn/index.html

China Health and Nutrition Survey
http://www.cpc.unc.edu/projects/china/

China Internet Directory
http://www.internet-directory.com/china/

China Investment Guide
http://202.96.21.241/eindex.htm

China Law
http://www.qis.net/chinalaw/

China News Digest
http://www.cnd.org/

Chinapages
http://www.chinapages.com/

Chinascape
http://harmony.wit.com/chinascape/china/economy/index.html

China Science and Technology Network
http://www.cnc.ac.cn/

China Today
http://www.chinatoday.com/

China Virtual Library
http://www.univie.ac.at/Sinologie/cn-wwwvl.htm

China Window
http://china-window.com/window.html

Chinese Constitution
gopher://emailhost.ait.ac.th/00/AsiaInfo/CountryInfo/China%20%28P.R.C.%29/Constitution%20of%20PRC

Chinese Economic Area
http://www.stat-usa.gov/bems/bemschi/bemschi.html

Chinese Finance Association
http://www.aimhi.com/VC/tcfa/

Condensed China: History for Beginners
http://www.hk.super.net/~paulf/china.html

Contemporary China
http://www.chinalink.com/intro.htm

Fairbank Chinese History Library
http://www.cnd.org/fairbank/

Gate of Heavenly Peace
http://www.nmis.org/gate/

Guanzhong, Luo. Three Kingdoms.
http://cougarnet.byu.edu/~nguyenkk/threekingdoms/

History of China
http://www-chaos.umd.edu/history/welcome.html

InfoChina
http://www.info-china.com/

Inside China Today
http://www.insidechina.com/

Ma, Jun. "China's Economic Reform in the 1990s"
http://members.aol.com/junmanew/cover.htm

Marco Polo (Business in China)
http://www.new-century-co.com/

Modern Chinese History
http://orpheus.ucsd.edu/chinesehistory/

Tax Law of China
http://www.hk.super.net/~bizchina/

Africa

21

AFRICA: THE CHALLENGE OF DEVELOPMENT*

> The challenge that confronts Africa is not between either
> the world market or African collective self-reliance. It is
> rather a struggle to avoid being completely marginalized,
> if not totally forgotten, and to undertake the herculean task
> required to launch and sustain the process of
> transformation so that it can emerge eventually as a true
> and respected player in the international economy.
>
> —ADEBAYO ADEDEJI
> "THE CASE FOR REMAKING AFRICA," 1993

frica is the world's second largest continent, following Asia in population and land area. Unfortunately, Africa is second to none in its incidence of absolute poverty. Tortured by warfare, famine, and pestilence, about half the Sub-Saharan population struggles for bare subsistence. Less than half have access to safe drinking water; one-third of urban dwellers have no public sanitation services. Rates of HIV infection are epidemic in some countries. Africa was the cradle of human civilization, but its economic and social crises, if unanswered, may imperil our future.

ENVIRONMENT AND HISTORY

The Sahara divides Africa into two major regions. To the north, five countries share a relatively homogeneous culture based on Islam and the Arabic language. These countries aren't rich, but their average income is about triple the Sub-Saharan average (Table 21.1). The North African countries have valuable petroleum and phosphate resources, accounting for half their exports, and close access to Mediterranean ports and European markets.

The Sub-Saharan region is larger and more diverse. Its geography spans the spectrum from well-watered highland to arid desert, and from dry savanna to tropical rainforest. The people are divided by tribal, ethnic, and

*This chapter was coauthored by Mahamudu Bawumia.

■ TABLE 21.1

AFRICAN REGIONS: POPULATION AND INCOME, 1995

	Population (millions)	GDP per Capita (dollars at PPP)		Population (millions)	GDP per Capita (dollars at PPP)
Africa	**710.3**	**1,860**			
Northern Africa	**126.6**	**4,230**	*East Africa*	*186.6*	*900*
Algeria	28.0	5,300	Burundi	6.3	630
Egypt	57.8	3,820	Comoros	0.5	1,320
Libya	5.2	6,130	Djibouti	0.6	1,270
Morocco	26.6	3,340	Eritrea	3.6	960
Tunisia	9.0	5,000	Ethiopia	56.4	450
			Kenya	26.7	1,380
Sub-Saharan Africa	**583.7**	**1,350**	Mauritius	1.1	13,210
West Africa	*227.8*	*1,280*	Rwanda	6.4	540
Benin	5.5	1,760	Somalia	9.5	750
Burkina Faso	10.4	780	Sudan	26.7	890
Cameroon	13.3	2,110	Tanzania	29.6	640
Cape Verde Is.	0.4	1,870	Uganda	19.2	1,470
Chad	6.4	700			
Côte d'Ivoire	14.0	1,580	*Southern Africa*	*117.9*	*2,570*
Gambia, The	1.1	930	Angola	10.8	1,310
Ghana	17.1	1,990	Botswana	1.5	5,580
Guinea	6.6	910	Lesotho	2.0	1,780
Guinea-Bissau	1.1	790	Madagascar	13.7	640
Liberia	2.7	830	Malawi	9.8	750
Mali	9.8	550	Mozambique	16.2	810
Mauritania	2.3	1,540	Namibia	1.5	4,150
Niger	9.0	750	South Africa	41.5	5,030
Nigeria	111.3	1,220	Swaziland	0.9	2,880
Senegal	8.5	1,780	Zambia	9.0	930
Sierra Leone	4.2	580	Zimbabwe	11.0	2,030
Togo	4.1	1,130			
Central Africa	*51.4*	*530*			
Central African Rep.	3.3	1,070			
Congo	2.6	2,050			
Congo D.R. (Zaire)	43.9	430			
Equatorial Guinea	0.4	1,670			
Gabon	1.1	3,752			
Sao Tome	0.1	1,700			

Source: World Bank, *World Development Report 1997;* United Nations Development Programme, *Human Development Report 1997;* and author's estimates. Regional averages are weighted.

religious traditions, by national boundaries drawn arbitrarily by European colonists, and by more in than 1,000 distinct languages. Of 46 Sub-Saharan countries, the largest 6 account for more than half the regional population. Their governments range from working democracies to authoritarian regimes. Some economies are tightly controlled; others operate largely on market principles.

For analytical purposes, Sub-Saharan Africa frequently is divided into four subregions. West Africa is largest among these, consisting of populous Nigeria and 16 other countries. Central Africa, dominated by the Democratic Republic of Congo (former Zaire), has the lowest average level of income. Southern Africa, supported by the mineral wealth and unique polity of the Republic of South Africa, is richest. East Africa includes many of the continent's most troubled countries, but several of these are showing signs of stability and growth under new political leadership.

INDIGENOUS CULTURES

Our first human ancestors evidently lived in East Africa, and the first major civilizations assembled in the Nile valley of Northern Africa. The Egyptians of the Old Kingdom (2700 B.C.–2200 B.C.) devised a hieroglyphic system of writing, established programs of lower and higher education, developed systems of mathematical analysis, plotted the movement of stars and planets, prepared a 365-day calendar, and organized construction of the massive stone monuments that stand today.

Farther down the Nile, in the territory of modern Sudan, the Kingdom of Kush developed alongside ancient Egypt. The merchants of Kush generated enormous wealth by selling their ebony, ivory, perfume, and gold in Egypt, in the Mediterranean area, and across the Indian Ocean. During the eighth century B.C., the Kushites conquered Egypt and controlled all northeastern Africa for about 80 years; they retreated when the Assyrians, armed with iron weapons, invaded Egypt. To their credit, the Kushites quickly discovered how to make iron for themselves; they developed a major industry and disseminated the new technology to other regions of Africa. When Kush declined a few centuries later, its neighbor Axum, in the territory of modern Ethiopia, gained control of a large trade network.

The first major power of West Africa was the **Kingdom of Ghana,** which emerged in territories of modern Mauritania and Mali during the fifth century A.D. Most of the people of Ghana were farmers, but their wealth and power derived from gold mining and iron production. Gold was exported to North Africa in exchange for salt, which reportedly was worth its weight in gold. The king regulated mining and exportation of gold to maintain a high external price. Early iron production contributed to the kingdom's military power, enabling it to demand tribute from neighbors.

The Ghana empire declined during the eleventh century, weakened by Islamic holy warriors from the north. The **Mali Empire** took its place, gained control of the lucrative gold–salt trade, and rose to dominance during the thirteenth century. At its height, Mali led a confederation of 3 independent states and 12 provinces. Mali's reputation spread through the Islamic and European worlds in 1324 when King Mansu Musa led a caravan of hundreds of camels and servants, laden with gold, on a well-publicized pilgrimage to Mecca.

In the late 1300s, when civil war weakened Mali, the **Songhai Kingdom**, based in Gao on the Niger River, gained control of the gold–salt trade. By the end of the fifteenth century, the Songhai kings had conquered most of the Mali territories and built the largest empire ever known in West Africa. They established an efficient system of provincial government and enforced an official system of weights and measures. Timbuktu, the former Mali capital, became an international center of Islamic learning. African farmers developed agricultural methods that were adapted well to local conditions.[1]

We can conclude that the African people, like the Asians and South Americans, had experience with political organization, economic development, international trade, and extractive exploitation long before the arrival of European colonists. Unfortunately, Western colonialism displayed its greatest cruelty in Africa.

THE TRANS-ATLANTIC SLAVE TRADE

For many centuries, commodity trade between Africans and Europeans was handled on a normal, mutually advantageous basis. After the Americas were discovered in 1492, this relationship changed abruptly. Decimation of native populations in the Western Hemisphere and rapid development of plantation agriculture created chronic shortages of labor in the West Indies and the American South. With North Africa under Turkish control, the rest of Africa, and especially West Africa, became a source of cheap labor. Thus, in 1510, slaves were first exported from Africa to the West Indies. More cargoes followed, and this "trade" continued for more than three centuries.

The impact of the slave trade on African social, economic, and political development is incalculable. About 23 million able-bodied men and women were exported, including many skilled workers and craftsmen. A similar number died in transit or in the accompanying slave wars in Africa.[2] By 1800, about half the inhabitants of Brazil and Venezuela were Africans.[3]

As industrial development proceeded in Europe, the slave trade grew increasingly inefficient on economic grounds and distasteful on moral grounds. The trade was abolished in England, the United States, Holland, and France during the early 1800s, and, in 1842, Great Britain and the United States agreed to post squadrons on the African coast to enforce prohibition of the trade. Sierra Leone was founded in 1787 to accommodate slaves returning

---

[1]Bill Rau, *From Feast to Famine: Official Cures and Grass Roots Remedies to Africa's Food Crises* (London: Zed Books, 1991), 12.

[2]Bade Onimode, *A Political Economy of the African Crisis* (London: Zed Books, 1988), 12–13.

[3]Basil Davidson, *The Growth of African Civilization: West Africa 1000–1800* (London: Longmans, 1965), 270.

from England and America; Liberia followed in 1831, providing another set-tlement for returning American slaves.

THE COLONIAL PERIOD

Following abolition of the slave trade, a system of "legitimate" commerce re-sumed between Africa and Europe; Africans supplied primary products in ex-change for manufactured goods. Unfortunately, the relationship soured again after 1870 when European governments adopted a more aggressive stance in international markets to address their domestic economic problems.

Africa was thought to be an appropriate colonial target because its indige-nous institutions were considered archaic and barbaric.[4] During the last three decades of the nineteenth century, all the African territories except Ethiopia and Liberia were divided into 23 colonial possessions, held by French, British, Portuguese, German, Italian, Belgian, and Spanish authorities. Each of the new African countries adopted the language and legal system of its colonizer.

As usual, the main purpose of the colonial effort was low-cost extraction of raw materials and other primary products. Later stages of processing and manufacture were undertaken in Europe. In most cases, a colony was devel-oped to provide only two or three crops or minerals. Roads, railways, and ports were built for a single purpose—to move the products of mines and plantations to their external destinations. Most African countries came to de-pend on primary products for more than 75 percent of their export earnings. By 1914, a pattern of dualism developed in most colonies: At the center were the export enclaves—cocoa and groundnut farms in West Africa, mines in Southern Africa, and sisal plantations in East Africa; peripheral territories provided migrant labor to the export enclaves.

The colonial partition of Africa created political boundaries that divided existing ethnic groups. The Ewes were split between the Gold Coast and To-goland, the Ibos between Nigeria and the Cameroon, the Hutus and Tutsis between Rwanda and Burundi, and the Somalis between Ethiopia, Somalia, and Kenya. The new boundaries also created unstable states that were popu-lated by traditional rivals: the Asante and Fantis in the Gold Coast (Ghana), the Yoruba and Hausa in Nigeria, and the Ndebele and Shona in Northern Rhodesia.

The colonialists devoted little attention to education in Africa, and their ef-forts were usually designed to maintain the status quo. Some Africans were trained for menial and junior administrative tasks, but the general popula-tion remained illiterate. The main hospitals, post offices, and hotels were lo-cated in urban areas; rural areas, where most of the population lived, had little access to social and physical infrastructure. These patterns have contin-ued during the post-colonial period.

---

[4]Forbes J. Munro, *Africa and the International Economy: 1800–1960* (London: J. M. Dent and Sons, 1976), 67.

INDEPENDENCE, STATE OWNERSHIP, AND IMPORT SUBSTITUTION

After World War II, independence movements gained strength in many African colonies. In most cases, these were led by small, élite groups of teachers, lawyers, and businessmen who had been excluded from participation in government, and barred from profitable areas of production and trade.[5] Many Africans believed that their condition would improve when the "parasitic" colonialists were expelled. Despite these beliefs, the independence movements succeeded more slowly in Africa than in Asia; colonialism continued in many African countries until the 1960s, and the last cases of European control were settled in 1980.

Immediately after independence, the new governments pursued the Africanization of their civil services. Overnight, Africans were lifted from relatively junior posts to positions of high responsibility. Furthermore, to protect their political independence and to introduce local control, many governments nationalized foreign industrial holdings. Between 1960 and 1974, 340 companies were seized by the governments of Sub-Saharan Africa, accounting for more than one-third of the nationalizations undertaken throughout the world during those years.[6]

Most of the new African leaders were persuaded by the interventionist arguments of the United Nations Economic Commission for Latin America (ECLA).[7] Thus, many of their countries pursued the path of state-led import-substituting industrialization. They introduced programs of national economic planning, import restriction, foreign exchange controls, and public investment in import-substituting industries.

State-owned enterprises (SOEs) dominated the industrial sectors of many African countries. Between 1978 and 1985, SOEs accounted for one-quarter of the national incomes of Guinea, Mauritania, and Tunisia; for one-third of the GDP of Egypt; and one-half the income of Sudan; and for 70 percent of total production in oil-rich Algeria (Table 21.2). If manufacturing is considered alone, SOEs accounted for more than 90 percent of production in Ethiopia, 80 percent in Somalia, and 50 percent in Zambia.[8]

As we might expect from the experience of other countries, the financial performance of African SOEs was disappointing. In a 1986 study of 16 Kenyan agricultural SOEs, pre-tax losses totaled $183.4 million.[9] During the late 1970s, one-third of all SOEs ran persistent losses in Tanzania, and more than 60 percent were unprofitable in Benin.[10] At the same time, SOEs

---

[5]Adebayo Adedeji, *Indigenization of African Economies* (New York: Africana Publishing Co., 1981), 20.

[6]L. L. Rood, "Nationalization and Indigenization in Africa," *Journal of Modern African Studies* 14 (1976): 431.

[7]Recall our discussions of import substitution and the ECLA in Chapters 5, 6, and 8.

[8]John R. Nellis, "Public Enterprises in Sub-Saharan Africa," in *State-Owned Enterprises in Africa,* ed. Barbara Grosh and Rwekaza S. Mukandala (Boulder: Lynne Rienner Publishers, 1994), 6.

[9]Barbara Grosh, "Agricultural Parastarals Since Independence: How Have They Performed?" Working Paper No. 435, Institute for Development Studies, University of Nairobi, 1986, 18–19.

[10]Nellis, "Public Enterprises in Sub-Saharan Africa," 13.

■ TABLE 21.2

STATE-OWNED ENTERPRISE SHARES OF
GDP IN AFRICA, 1978–1991

(percent)

	1978–1985	1986–1991		1978–1985	1986–1991
Northern Africa			*Central Africa*		
Algeria	70	58	Central African Republic	4	4
Egypt	37	30	Congo	10	16
Morocco	19	17	Congo D.R. (Zaire)	23	n.a.
Tunisia	30	31			
			East Africa		
Sub-Saharan Africa			Burundi	5	7
West Africa			Comoros	6	12
Cameroon	18	18	Kenya	10	12
Côte d'Ivoire	11	n.a.	Mauritius	2	2
Gambia, The	4	4	Rwanda	n.a.	10
Ghana	6	8	Sudan	48	48
Guinea	25	9	Tanzania	11	14
Mali	14	n.a.			
Mauritania	25	n.a.	*Southern Africa*		
Niger	5	5	Botswana	6	6
Nigeria	14	15	Madagascar	2	n.a.
Senegal	9	6	Malawi	7	4
Sierra Leone	20	n.a.	South Africa	14	15
Togo	12	12	Zambia	32	30

SOURCE: Adapted from World Bank, *Bureaucrats in Business: The Economics and Politics of Government Ownership* (Oxford: Oxford University Press, 1995), Table A.1.

accounted for at least one-fourth of total external debt in Algeria, Cameroon, the Central African Republic, Côte d'Ivoire, Zaire, and Zambia.[11]

SOCIALISM, CAPITALISM, AND AUTHORITARIANISM

At the time of independence, some African leaders were impressed by the record of the Soviet Union, where a backward agrarian economy quickly became an industrial superpower. Thus, in some African countries, the role of the government extended far beyond import substitution and basic programs of state enterprise. In Ghana, for example, when Kwame Nkrumah and his Convention Peoples Party (CPP) led the country to independence in

---

[11]World Bank, *Bureaucrats in Business: The Economics and Politics of Government Ownership* (Oxford: Oxford University Press, 1995), 308–311.

1957, they called for establishment of "a socialist state in which all men and women shall have equal opportunity and where there shall be no capitalist exploitation." The CPP Manifesto promised free education up to the age of 16, a free national health service, mechanization of agriculture, and rapid industrialization. Government expenditures on education, health, and physical infrastructure increased dramatically from their colonial levels.[12]

Initially, the quality of life improved markedly in rural Ghana. National income increased at an annual rate of nearly 6 percent between 1955 and 1960. The economy took a turn for the worse, however, in the mid-1960s. Deterioration of the international balance of payments caused external reserves to decline dangerously.[13] Between 1964 and 1966, the country registered three years of negative income growth while inflation sped to an annual average of 17 percent. In 1966, as the economy continued to deteriorate, the CPP was overthrown by a military junta.

The Republic of Tanzania was formed in 1964 by merging the former German colony of Tanganyika and the British protectorate of Zanzibar. President Nyerere declared that the country was suffering from rising inequality; his solution was the 1967 Arusha Declaration, a blueprint for socialist economic development. Firms occupying the "commanding heights" of the economy, including the major commercial and financial institutions and some private agricultural estates, were quickly nationalized. To collectivize peasant farming, most of the rural population was resettled from family homesteads to *ujamaa vijijini,* or **village socialism** settlements. The *ujamaa* program gave exclusive marketing rights to traditional agricultural cooperatives.

Again, the strategy paid off in the short run; donor assistance to Tanzania increased rapidly; real GDP grew just under 5 percent annually between 1967 and 1973; and gross investment rose to more than 20 percent of GDP.[14] Behind these gains, however, the *ujamaa* experiment displayed signs of weakness. The villages were meant to be self-reliant, but they required continual state funding and support. Agricultural production declined rapidly, and, by 1974, the food crisis reached famine proportions.[15] The oil price shocks of the 1970s and a war with Uganda only served to worsen Tanzania's economic crisis. Still, unlike Nkrumah in Ghana, Nyerere maintained control over Tanzania until he retired from the presidency in 1985, and even then he remained chairman of the Revolutionary Party until 1990.

Kenya attained independence in 1963 under the leadership of Jomo Kenyatta, a revolutionary leader who studied in Western Europe and in Moscow

---

[12]J. H. Frimpong-Ansah, *The Vampire State in Africa: The Political Economy of Decline in Ghana* (London: James Currey, 1991), 52.

[13]Tony Killick, *Development Economics in Action* (London: Heineman, 1978), 72.

[14]Darius Mans, "Tanzania: Resolute Action," in *Adjustment in Africa: Lessons from Country Studies,* ed. Ishrat Hussein and R. Faruquee (Washington, D.C. : The World Bank, 1994), 352.

[15]Michael F. Lofchie, "Agrarian Crisis and Economic Liberalization in Tanzania," *Journal of Modern African Studies* 16 (1978): 486.

between 1931 and 1946. Kenyatta introduced a system known as **managed capitalism** in Kenya.[16] The government favored private ownership in both agriculture and industry, but worked toward a more equitable system of ownership. A land reform redistributed much of the better property from large farmers to peasants, and the latter were encouraged to cultivate tea, coffee, and hybrid maize. Between 1965 and 1979, the small-scale farm area under improved varieties of maize increased about forty-fold.[17]

Kenya followed an import-substitution strategy that was largely regarded a success. Income per capita increased at a moderate pace between 1964 and 1970, and indicators of public health, housing, nutrition, and education steadily improved.[18] Like most countries, Kenya took a turn for the worse during the 1970s. The economy endured a series of volatile price movements related to oil imports and coffee exports. These shocks were compounded by poor macroeconomic management. During the early 1980s, government expenditures increased rapidly, and inflation, which had averaged 3 percent during the first ten years of independence, accelerated to 22 percent.[19]

On the political front, post-independence African governments established patterns of authoritarianism and, in some cases, outright dictatorship. Strong leaders were needed, it seemed, to build new nations in the presence of deep internal divisions, and to pursue aggressive programs of economic modernization. African leaders, including Ghana's Kwame Nkrumah, Zambia's Kenneth Kaunda, Malawi's Hastings Banda, Zaire's Mobutu Sese Seko, and Guinea's Sekou Touré, argued for and exercised broad authority in one-party states.

AGRICULTURE

Agriculture dominates the economies of most African countries. It employs about two-thirds of Africa's total labor force, accounts for about one-third of GDP, and provides about one-half of exports (Table 21.3). Agriculture is the principal source of foreign exchange earnings for the vast majority of African countries.

Over the centuries, a mix of farming practices have evolved in Africa. Until recently, when land was relatively abundant, a seminomadic system of **shifting cultivation** was practiced over large areas on a subsistence basis. Under this system, farmers would allow an area of land to lie fallow for up to 25 years to regain fertility. As populations have increased, and as new

---

[16]Frances Stewart, "Kenya: Strategies for Development," in *Development Paths in Africa and China,* ed. U. G. Damachi, G. Routh, and A. A. Taha (Colorado: Westview Press, 1976), 86.

[17]Gurushri Swamy, "Kenya: Patchy, Intermittent Commitment," in *Adjustment in Africa: Lessons from Country Studies,* ed. Ishrat Hussein and R. Faruquee (Washington, D.C.: The World Bank, 1994), 197.

[18]Ibid., 14 and 15.

[19]Swamy, "Kenya: Patchy, Intermittent Commitment," 199.

■ TABLE 21.3

AGRICULTURE: SELECTED INDICATORS FOR
AFRICAN COUNTRIES, 1970–1992

Indicator	1970	1975	1980	1985	1990	1992
Share of Agriculture (%)						
GDP	35	31	30	33	32	33
Labor Force	78	75	73	70	67	66
Exports	63	—	57	52	49	48
Indices of Output (1979–1981 = 100)						
Agriculture	—	93.9	100.5	111.0	127.9	135.0
Food	—	93.1	100.4	111.1	129.0	136.7
Crop	—	97.9	100.6	111.4	129.4	137.2
Food per capita	—	108.0	100.4	96.1	96.2	93.4

SOURCES: World Bank, *World Development Report,* various issues; United Nations Development Program, *Human Development Report,* various issues; World Bank, *World Tables 1994;* Food and Agriculture Organization, *Production Yearbook,* various issues.

agricultural techniques have been adopted, farmers have adjusted from shifting to a settled system of agriculture.

European colonialism caused a drastic restructuring of agriculture from subsistence farming to cash-crop production, regulated by the demands of European markets. Production of cocoa and palm oil developed in West Africa; coffee in many countries, but particularly Uganda and the Ivory Coast; tea in Malawi, Kenya, and Uganda; bananas in Somalia and Cameroon; and rubber in Liberia.

Colonial cash-crop production usually created a dual agrarian economy. A plantation sector devoted to large-scale production of export crops existed side-by-side with a peasant sector for production of local food staples. The plantations were more likely to benefit from modern agricultural services, technologies, and systems of organization. The peasant sectors, in comparison, remained hopelessly backward. Facilities for transportation and storage of crops were limited; agro-scientific inputs were extremely rare; and credit facilities were practically nonexistent.

The plantations became economically indispensable. With advantages of modernity and control of the best land, plantation production soared in volume and monetary value. Export crops came to account for an overwhelming proportion of foreign exchange earnings and tax revenues.[20] The

---

[20]Robert H. Bates and Michael F. Lofchie, *Agricultural Development in Africa* (New York: Praeger, 1980), 4.

food-producing sectors, on the other hand, suffered from underdevelopment. Food production became more susceptible to breakdowns caused by climatic irregularities and other factors.

LAND TENURE AND LAND REFORM

In African societies, arrangements for ownership, inheritance, sale, and tenancy of land are derived from a blend of ancient, colonial, and modern institutions. Together, these have created a bewildering number of land tenure patterns that vary between countries and regions. The most common landholding pattern in Africa is known as the **customary, or communal, system.** In this case, land is held collectively in family kinship, clan, or tribal units and is allocated to households without the right of disposition.[21] According to the central principle of this system, a resident can lay claim to an area of land only if he or she will use it personally to support a household.

When Europeans entered Africa in the nineteenth century, they seized the land they needed for commercial agriculture and held it under a system of individual ownership. Africans were generally allowed to maintain their customary land system for production of subsistence crops. Thus, in many countries, the dual agricultural system was accompanied by a dual system of communal and private land tenure. Again, the dual system persisted in many countries after independence.

In a few countries, the post-independence governments extended the private and individual systems of land ownership. In Kenya, for example, two reforms were introduced: the first allowed Africans to consolidate and gain individual legal titles to their landholdings and to become cash-crop farmers; the second enabled them to buy land from Europeans, many of whom wanted to liquidate their holdings during the post-independence period.

In Ethiopia, Nigeria, and Tanzania, agricultural land was taken by the state from the communal holdings and from private landowners. In Tanzania, for example, in one of its first actions after independence, the government abolished freehold tenures that emerged during the colonial period, placed the land under state ownership, and converted private titles to 99-year leases.[22]

During recent years, much of Africa has been passing through a slow transition from communal to individual systems of land ownership.[23] Many farmers have permanent rights over land, but have no legal title. Their tenure is uncertain. Without clear title, they are reluctant to invest in irrigation systems and other land improvements, and they are unable to offer their holdings as collateral for loans.

---

[21]H. K. Podedworny, "The Customary Land Tenure: Selected Problems of Agrarian Reforms and Agricultural Development in Sub-Saharan Africa," *Africa Bulletin* 15 (1971): 95–122.

[22]Government of Tanganyika, *Proposals of the Tanganyika Government for Land Tenure Reform* (Dar es Salaam: Government Printer, 1962), 1–13.

[23]Paul Harrison, *The Greening of Africa* (London: Paladin, 1987), 59.

INDUSTRIAL ORGANIZATION

In most African countries, industrial production is divided between three broad sectors.[24] First, the modern sector is usually composed of a few large enterprises, either state-owned or foreign-owned, plus a few medium-sized enterprises with private African capital. Second, an intermediate sector of locally owned small and medium-sized enterprises usually supplies goods and services that require little capital. Some of these enterprises fall within the formal sector and others are in the informal economy. The third sector is composed essentially of household or one-person enterprises, operating with virtually no capital in the informal economy.

THE INFORMAL SECTOR

The African informal sector is populated by thousands of unregistered businesses engaged in a wide range of legal and illegal, but unrecorded, activities. These activities include everything from petty trading and craft manufacture to smuggling, equipment repair, and coordination of savings clubs. According to estimates of the International Labor Office, the informal sector provides employment for more than half the labor force in the capital cities of Senegal, Nigeria, Burkina Faso, and Ghana.[25] In Kenya, informal activities employed an estimated 43 percent of the national labor force in the mid-1980s.[26] According to some estimates, the measured national products of African countries would be as much as three times larger if it were possible to include a full accounting of informal production.[27]

Two major explanations have been suggested for the rapid growth of informality in Africa.[28] First, the urban informal sector has provided a critical source of income for migrants from rural areas. During the late 1970s and early 1980s, declining prices of cash crops caused an exodus of labor to move from rural areas into towns. In Sub-Saharan Africa, the urban share of the total population increased from about 15 percent in 1960 to 27 percent in 1990, and it continues to grow (Table 21.4). A large segment of the informal sector has been created by these new urban residents, desperately seeking sources of income.

Government intervention provides a second source of growth for the African informal sector. When governments attempt to control prices, import purchases, and foreign exchange transactions, they encourage a wide range of underground and black market activities. The informal sector, according to this interpretation, was created by rent-seeking individuals seeking relief from government controls and restrictions.

---

[24]Jacques Giri, "Formal and Informal Small Enterprises in the Long-Term Future of Sub-Saharan Africa," World Bank, LTPS Background Papers (1990), 111.

[25]Ibid., 113.

[26]Ian Livingstone, "A Reassessment of Kenya's Rural and Urban Informal Sector," mimeographed, University of East Anglia, 1990, 3–4.

[27]Janet MacGaffey, *The Real Economy of Zaire* (London: James Currey, 1991), 13.

[28]Michael Barratt Brown, *Africa's Choices After 30 Years with the World Bank* (London: Penguin, 1995), 224–227.

■ TABLE 21.4

URBANIZATION IN SELECTED AFRICAN COUNTRIES

(urban population as percentage of total)

	1960	1970	1980	1990	2000 est.
Northern Africa	**32**	**39**	**43**	**47**	**52**
Algeria	30	40	43	52	60
Egypt	38	42	44	44	46
Morocco	29	35	41	46	51
Sub-Saharan Africa	**15**	**20**	**23**	**27**	**34**
West Africa	*14*	*19*	*25*	*32*	*42*
Burkina Faso	5	6	9	18	37
Cameroon	14	20	31	40	49
Côte d'Ivoire	19	27	35	40	47
Ghana	23	29	31	34	39
Guinea	10	14	19	26	34
Nigeria	14	20	27	35	43
Central Africa	*22*	*30*	*29*	*28*	*31*
Congo P.R. (Zaire)	22	30	29	28	31
East Africa	*7*	*10*	*14*	*18*	*23*
Ethiopia	6	9	11	12	15
Kenya	7	10	16	24	32
Sudan	10	16	20	23	27
Tanzania	5	7	15	21	28
Uganda	5	8	9	11	14
Southern Africa	*17*	*20*	*24*	*31*	*39*
Angola	10	15	21	28	36
Madagascar	11	14	18	24	31
Mozambique	4	6	13	27	41
South Africa	47	48	48	49	53
Zimbabwe	13	17	22	29	36

SOURCE: World Bank, *World Tables*, various years; and United Nations Development Program, *Human Development Report, 1996*, 176–177. Regional averages are unweighted.

THE LABOR MARKET

Like the industrial structure, the African labor market can be divided into three broad sectors: a traditional rural sector, an informal urban sector, and a formal urban sector. The traditional rural sector is dominated by agriculture, and is characterized by relatively large numbers of low-productivity workers.

Spanning the traditional and informal sectors, a **migratory labor system** operates in many African countries. To supplement their incomes, farm workers temporarily migrate to provide part-time wage labor in other areas of the economy. The gold mines of South Africa, the coffee plantations of Uganda, the cocoa farms of Ghana and Côte d'Ivoire, and the peanut farms of Senegal are all dependent on the availability of migratory labor.

Even in the urban formal sector, few labor unions operated in Africa before World War II, and organized collective bargaining between workers and employers was rare. The few unions that existed were established by European and Asian workers. Colonial authorities and white settlers discouraged any African attempt to organize.[29]

After the outbreak of war in 1939, recurring labor shortages strengthened the bargaining power of African workers. Thousands of Africans joined the armies of their colonial masters, ostensibly to fight for the survival of democracy. War production programs created new employment opportunities. Large numbers of people entered the formal labor market, and were required to work long hours under difficult conditions. Inevitably, conflicts developed between workers and employers.

Organization of trade unions began in earnest when the colonial powers enacted laws to legalize and regulate them. At about the same time, African politicians were organizing independence movements, and the two projects became intertwined. The new political leaders supported the development of trade unions, and the trade unions joined the independence movements with propaganda activities and sympathy strikes. Thus, the Ghana Trades Union Congress and CPP under Kwame Nkrumah's leadership formed a common platform, and the Kenya Federation of Labor became that country's major voice of nationalism.

During the years after independence, authoritarian and socialist regimes have imposed new controls on collective bargaining practices. In Ethiopia and Tanzania, for instance, labor organizations have been required to support the development of socialism, embodied in the economic development programs of the government. The parameters of negotiation have been set in laws, regulations, and economic plans. In many countries, including Botswana, Gambia, Kenya, Nigeria, and Zambia, collective agreements are valid only after approval by an appropriate government agency.[30]

More generally, the trade union movement in independent Africa has had a turbulent existence. Autonomous and effective unions have ceased to exist in many countries, replaced by puppets of politicians and military rulers. Trade unionists have been arrested and jailed without trial, detained for months, and summarily executed.[31]

During the 1980s and 1990s, relations between governments and unions have been strained by the implementation of austerity programs sponsored by international agencies. Cuts in public sector employment have led to strikes in many countries, including Nigeria, Zambia, Kenya, and Ghana. However, a few countries have implemented important labor market

---

[29]Wogu Ananaba, *The Trade Union Movement in Africa* (London: C. Hurst and Co., 1979), 1–15.

[30]International Labor Organization, *Collective Bargaining and Security of Employment in Africa*, Labor Management Series No. 69 (Geneva, 1988), 27.

[31]Ibid., 6.

reforms. In the late 1980s and early 1990s, Senegal and Côte d'Ivoire abolished government employment agencies that held legal monopolies over placement and hiring. Mali adopted a new labor code in 1992, substantially liberalizing the labor market.

DEBT, POVERTY, AND STRUCTURAL ADJUSTMENT

After moderate growth during the 1950s and 1960s, African GDP per capita slowed to a crawl during the 1970s and declined during the 1980s (Table 21.5). The reasons were many: oil price shocks during the 1970s, public and private corruption, rising debt burdens, recessions in Western export markets, sustained deficit spending by governments, overvalued exchange rates, protectionist policies, and continued support for inefficient state industries.

Hoping to address their mounting economic problems, African leaders met in Lagos, Nigeria, in 1980, under the auspices of the Organization for African Unity, and formulated the **Lagos Plan of Action.** The leaders set four major objectives:

- achievement of food sufficiency through domestic food production;
- satisfaction of critical needs for food, safe drinking water, clothing, housing, health care, education, and transport;
- elimination or alleviation of poverty; and
- achievement of effective regional integration through national and collective self-reliance.[32]

■ **TABLE 21.5**

AFRICA: AVERAGE ANNUAL GROWTH RATES, 1951–1996

	(percent)					
	1951–1960	1961–1970	1971–1980	1981–1990	1991–1995	1996
GDP	3.6	5.0	3.6	2.1	2.0	5.0
Population	2.3	2.4	2.8	3.2	2.9	2.9
GDP per Capita	1.3	2.6	0.8	−1.1	−0.9	2.1
Agricultural Production	4.8	2.6	1.7	2.7	1.4	n.a.
Consumer Prices	3.0	4.7	13.8	17.7	31.4	24.8

SOURCES: International Monetary Fund, *International Financial Statistics;* World Bank, *World Tables;* Food and Agriculture Organization, *Production Yearbook,* various years; and International Monetary Fund, *World Economic Outlook,* May 1997.

---

[32]Organization for African Unity, *The Lagos Plan of Action for the Economic Development of Africa, 1980–2000* (Geneva: International Labor Organization, 1981), 128.

The Action Plan stated laudable objectives, but it provided few specifics for implementation, and it had the support of few resources. In the end, little was accomplished under the plan.

STRUCTURAL ADJUSTMENT PROGRAMS

Confronted with large balance of payments deficits, African countries have been forced to borrow heavily on international markets to maintain modest rates of economic growth. African debt grew from about $25 billion in 1975 to $84 billion in 1980, and then climbed to $287 billion in 1996.[33] Although Africa accounts for only 16 percent of the developing world's debt, its ability to service the debt is limited. In 1994, when the average ratio of external debt to GDP for developing countries was about 38 percent, the average for Sub-Saharan Africa was 79 percent. For several African countries, this ratio exceeded 100 percent (Table 21.6). On the International Monetary Fund list of 38 "heavily indebted poor countries," all but 6 are found in Sub-Saharan Africa.[34]

With few options available, more than 30 African countries have turned to the World Bank and International Monetary Fund (IMF) for financial assistance. In 1983, Jerry John Rawlings, who assumed power in Ghana on a platform of a socialist transformation, captured the mood of many African leaders who were looking for a way out of the debt crisis:

> We can no longer postpone the time for halting the populist nonsense. . . . Production and efficiency must be our watchwords. Populist nonsense must give way to popular or unpopular sense . . . to scientific sense, whether it is popular or not. Many of us have spent too much time worrying about who owns what. But there can be no ownership without production first. The only resources which do not have to be produced are those given to us by nature. . . . Everything else has to be produced, and until we all fully recognize and act upon this fact, we shall be deceiving ourselves with empty theories.[35]

In return for loans from the IMF and World Bank, African countries have been required to adopt stabilization policies and **structural adjustment programs (SAPs).** A typical stabilization package is designed to handle the short-term international payments problem by devaluing the domestic currency, reducing and restructuring government expenditures, and introducing other programs of fiscal and monetary restraint. The SAP is designed to restore long-run economic growth and competitiveness. It typically includes programs of exchange-rate liberalization, trade liberalization, financial liberalization, and privatization.

---

[33]World Bank,*World Debt Tables, 1989–1990,* 6; World Bank, *World Development Report 1996* (Oxford: Oxford University Press, 1996), 221; and International Monetary Fund, *World Economic Outlook,* May 1997, 190.

[34]International Monetary Fund, *World Economic Outlook,* May 1997, 127–128.

[35]*West Africa,* September 12, 1983, 1586.

■ TABLE 21.6

DEBT INDICATORS FOR
SELECTED AFRICAN COUNTRIES, 1980–1995

	External Debt as Percent of GNP		Debt Service as Percent of Exports	
	1980	**1995**	**1980**	**1995**
Sub-Saharan Africa	**30.6**	**81.3**	**9.8**	**14.5**
Benin	30.2	81.8	6.3	8.4
Burkina Faso	19.5	55.0	5.9	11.1
Burundi	18.2	110.1	—	27.7
Central African Rep.	24.4	—	4.9	6.8
Chad	39.5	81.4	8.4	5.9
Ethiopia	—	99.9	7.3	13.6
Ghana	31.6	95.1	13.1	23.1
Guinea	—	91.2	—	25.3
Kenya	48.1	97.7	21.0	25.7
Lesotho	11.4	44.6	1.5	6.0
Madagascar	31.1	141.7	20.3	9.2
Malawi	71.2	166.8	27.7	25.9
Mali	45.4	131.9	5.1	12.6
Mauritania	125.5	243.3	17.3	21.5
Mozambique	—	443.6	—	35.3
Niger	34.5	91.2	21.7	19.8
Rwanda	16.3	89.1	4.1	—
Senegal	50.5	82.3	28.7	18.7
Tanzania	—	207.4	21.1	17.4
Uganda	54.6	63.7	17.3	21.3
Zambia	90.7	191.3	25.3	174.4

SOURCE: World Bank, *World Development Report, 1997*, 246.

EXCHANGE-RATE LIBERALIZATION

Prior to recent economic reforms, unofficial parallel markets for foreign exchange operated in most African countries. Official exchange rates were overvalued by an average of 300 percent between 1981 and 1986.[36] The World Bank and the IMF considered these overvalued rates to be an important cause of payment imbalances and slow rates of economic growth.

Although their inflation rates accelerated during the 1980s and early 1990s, many African countries made significant progress toward devaluation of their

[36]Miguel, Kiguel, and Stephen A. O'Connell, "Parallel Exchange Rates in Developing Countries: Lessons from Eight Case Studies," World Bank, Policy Research Department, Transition and Macro-Adjustment Division, Washington, D.C., 1993, 14.

real exchange rates. Between 1985 and 1994, parallel exchange-rate premiums fell from nearly 4,000 percent to 14 percent in Mozambique, from 1,200 percent to 10 percent in Guinea, and from 149 percent to 32 percent in Uganda.[37] Until they accepted a 50 percent devaluation in 1994, the 13 members of the CFA franc zone maintained a fixed exchange rate that had been pegged to the French franc at 50:1 since 1948.[38] For these countries, the SAPs were implemented under a fixed exchange rate regime. Until their devaluation, these countries were in a poor competitive position because of the strength of the French franc against the U.S. dollar.[39]

TRADE LIBERALIZATION

Under their import-substitution programs, many African countries employed nontariff barriers to protect domestic producers from foreign competition. These barriers usually took the form of government licenses or approvals for imports. The SAPs have required African countries to reduce or eliminate these barriers.

Accordingly, many countries have adopted an **open general license (OGL)** scheme under which a limited number of goods are placed on a "positive list" to be automatically approved for import. The list is gradually expanded until the allowable items are so numerous that it becomes more efficient to have a smaller "negative list" of products that are not automatically approved. In 1989, when Zambia established an OGL scheme, only 10 percent of imports were on the positive list; by the end of 1992, 95 percent of imports were covered (excluding petroleum and fertilizer). Tanzania established an OGL scheme in 1987 and moved to a negative list by 1991.[40]

While they are reducing nontariff barriers, governments implementing SAPs also are expected to reduce the average level, number, and dispersion of tariff rates. Ghana, Mali, Senegal, and Togo have simplified their tariff systems to include only four or five rates.[41] However, in many adjusting countries, average tariff rates have not been reduced substantially. This has proved difficult because tariffs provide an important share of government revenue in many African countries. If South Africa and Nigeria are excluded, Sub-Saharan Africa's dependence on international trade taxes actually increased between the late 1980s and the early 1990s, from 24 percent of total revenue to 26 percent.[42]

---

[37]World Bank, *African Development Indicators 1996* (Washington, D.C., 1996), 51.

[38]These countries are Benin, Burkina Faso, Cameroon, Central African Republic, Chad, Congo, Côte d'Ivoire, Equatorial Guinea, Gabon, Mali, Niger, Senegal, and Togo.

[39]World Bank, *Adjustment in Africa: Reforms, Results and the Road Ahead* (New York: Oxford University Press, 1994), 57.

[40]Ibid., 72.

[41]Godfrey Martin, "Trade and Exchange Rate Policy: A Further Contribution to the Debate," in *Crisis and Recovery in Sub-Saharan Africa*, ed. Tore Rose (Paris: Development Center of the Organization of Economic Cooperation and Development, 1985), 8.

[42]World Bank, *Adjustment in Africa: Reforms, Results, and the Road Ahead*, 74; and World Bank, *African Development Indicators 1996*, 191.

FINANCIAL LIBERALIZATION

Before the African countries implemented SAPs, their financial systems were imbalanced and heavily regulated. Typically, inflation rates were high, putting upward pressure on nominal interest rates, but the latter were held below market-clearing levels with state-imposed interest rate ceilings. As a result, real deposit rates and real lending rates were low or even negative (Table 21.7).

According to the neoclassical view, supported by the IMF and the World Bank, excessively low interest rates can inhibit economic development in several ways. Low deposit rates provide little incentive for domestic saving, which is needed to finance productive investments without excessive reliance on foreign capital. Low lending rates provide little incentive for efficient allocation and employment of borrowed capital; if money can be borrowed at bargain rates, scarce capital may be wasted on low-return investments. Furthermore, if domestic interest rates are low in relation to international rates, the natural result is a weak domestic currency, susceptible to overvaluation. An overvalued currency, in turn, may render the country uncompetitive in international markets.

For these and other reasons, an important financial objective of the SAPs was to liberalize interest rates, allowing them to rise to market clearing levels. Interest rate ceilings were removed in Burundi, Gambia, Ghana, Kenya,

■ TABLE 21.7

SUMMARY OF FINANCIAL REFORM MEASURES FOR SELECTED AFRICAN COUNTRIES

	Inflation Rate (percent)		Real Deposit Rate (percent)		Real Lending Rate (percent)	
	Before Reform	1994–1995	Before Reform	1994–1995	Before Reform	1994–1995
Botswana	17.9	10.5	−1.35	−0.3	1.1	3.6
Burundi	9.1	17.1	−4.6	n.a.	2.9	−2.4
Egypt	17.3	8.3	−4.6	3.1	−7.9	8.2
Gambia	9.0	4.4	−2.62	8.2	5.6	20.6
Ghana	110.6	42.2	−56.4	−16.3	−103.8	n.a.
Kenya	9.3	14.9	1.1	−1.3	3.3	17.6
Malawi	25.9	27.2	−5.1	3.9	−9.2	12.0
Nigeria	−2.0	64.9	4.05	−51.6	9.6	−44.6
Zimbabwe	3.0	22.5	−8.7	3.8	1.6	12.3

NOTE: "Before Reform" refers to the average of two years prior to initiation of the program.
SOURCE: International Monetary Fund, *International Financial Statistics*, various issues.

Madagascar, Malawi, Mauritania, and Zambia.[43] Still, the financial markets have responded slowly because governments continue to intervene and competition is limited. Among the countries listed in Table 21.7, Egypt, Gambia, Malawi, and Zimbabwe have made successful transitions from negative to positive real deposit rates. Deposit rates in Botswana and Ghana have remained negative, and the rates in Burundi, Kenya, and Nigeria have actually moved from positive to negative.

PRIVATIZATION AND STATE ENTERPRISE REFORM

For reasons that we have considered extensively in earlier chapters, the IMF and the World Bank have encouraged African countries to make privatization of state enterprises an important component of their SAPs. Privatization, it is argued, would improve the efficiency of enterprise management, and, in many cases, would remove a tremendous drain from the state budget.

The privatization process, however, has been far from uniform across countries. Of the countries listed in Table 21.2, the share of state-owned enterprises (SOEs) in GDP dropped in seven countries after 1985, increased in nine countries, and was unchanged in seven. Clearly, some countries were more willing to trim their public sectors than others.

In Côte d'Ivoire, instead of following the usual practice of identifying companies it was willing to privatize, the government announced that it would accept proposals from the private sector to purchase almost any SOE. In this way, the government sold about 90 enterprises during the mid-1980s, mostly in industry. These included buy-outs by Ivoirian managers, privatizations through the stock exchange, and purchases of local companies by their foreign competitors. Despite these sales, the number of public enterprises in Côte d'Ivoire increased from 113 in 1977 to 140 in 1990.[44]

When African countries have been unable or unwilling to sell their SOEs, frequently they have taken other steps to reduce financial losses. In Zimbabwe, for example, the government set a timetable for gradual elimination of direct subsidies by 1995.[45] In Uganda, government loans to public enterprises were extended on commercial terms, and SOEs were freed from some administrative controls.[46] Following the French example, several Francophone countries prepared contract plans for their SOEs and public utilities, setting specific performance goals and planned levels of financial support.[47]

---

[43]World Bank, *Adjustment in Africa: Reforms, Results, and the Road Ahead*, 114; and Diery Seck and Yasim H. Nil, "Financial Liberalization in Africa," *World Development* 21 (1993): 1869.

[44]Ernest J. Wilson III, "Privatization in Africa: Domestic Origins, Current and Future Options," in *Privatization and Investment in Sub-Saharan Africa*, ed. Rexford A. Ahene and Bernard S. Katz (New York: Praeger, 1992), 73.

[45]International Monetary Fund, *Country Report: Zimbabwe* (Washington, D.C., 1994).

[46]International Monetary Fund, *Country Report: Uganda* (Washington, D.C., 1994), 4.

[47]Alfred Saulniers, "Public Enterprise Reforms in Francophone Africa," in *State-Owned Enterprises in Africa*, ed. Barbara Grosh and Rwekaza S. Mukandala (Boulder: Lynne Rienner Publishers, 1994), 30–31.

Côte d'Ivoire and Guinea have experimented with leasing arrangements, transferring the control, but not ownership, of state facilities to private contractors.

ECONOMIC AND SOCIAL PERFORMANCE

The African SAPs have been controversial since their introduction, and the controversy continues today. According to their supporters, the SAPs have provided a framework for African countries to cope with their debt crises and rebuild their distorted institutions to survive in an increasingly competitive world economy. Countries that have implemented SAPs fully and consistently, according to this point of view, have registered significant gains. Admittedly, the results initially were small because a new Africa could not be built in a day. From the early 1980s to the years between 1987 and 1991, six countries that implemented SAPs most aggressively were able to raise their annual growth rates of GDP per capita from negative levels to a modest average of 1.1 percent.[48] By 1996, though, per capita growth rates in these countries increased to a more respectable 2.0 percent. According to Lawrence Summers, deputy secretary of the U.S. Treasury, prospects for economic growth in Africa are now "the brightest they've been in a generation."[49]

According to their critics, the SAPs are, at best, misguided austerity and debt relief programs that fail to address the more basic obstacles to African economic development, or, at worst, neocolonial programs of extraction, designed to serve international banking and industrial interests at the expense of the African population. The SAPs have been variously blamed for destroying traditional patterns of African life, for encouraging deforestation and other environmental crises, for restricting needed expenditures on health and education, for enlarging gaps between rural and urban standards of living, for encouraging rapid and excessive urbanization, for forcing the development of cash-crop agriculture at the expense of staple food production, and even for creating conditions that caused the AIDS virus to spread in Africa.[50]

---

[48]The six countries in question were Burkina Faso, Gambia, Ghana, Nigeria, Tanzania, and Zimbabwe. See World Bank, *Adjustment in Africa: Reforms, Results and the Road Ahead*, 138–143. For a similar study by the IMF, see M. T. Hadjimichael et al., *Sub-Saharan Africa Growth, Savings, and Investment, 1986–1993*, IMF Occasional Paper No. 118 (Washington, D.C.: International Monetary Fund, 1995).

[49]Quoted in Leo Abruzzese, "Africa Suddenly Takes Center Stage," *Journal of Commerce*, June 23, 1997, 3A. For a similar assessment from the director of the Africa Department of the IMF, see Evangelos Calamitsis, "Building on Africa's Progress," *IMF Survey*, July 7, 1997, 201–204.

[50]On this last point, see Peter Lurie, Percy Hintzen, and Robert A. Lowe, "Socioeconomic Obstacles to HIV Prevention and Treatment in Developing Countries: The Roles of the International Monetary Fund and the World Bank," *AIDS* 9 (May 1995): 1–8; and the response from the IMF discussed in John S. James, "World Bank in AIDS Prevention Controversy," *AIDS Treatment News Archive*, June 16, 1995 <http://www.immunet.org/atn/ZQX22514.html>. For additional criticism from the left end of the political spectrum, see Martin Khor, "Colonialism Redux: Reconquering the World with Protocols Instead of Gunboats," *The Nation*, July 15, 1996, 18. For criticism from the right, see *Perpetuating Poverty: The World Bank, the IMF, and the Developing World*, ed. Doug Bandow and Ian Vasquez (Washington, D.C.: The Cato Institute), 1994; and a review of this book by Amy L. Sherman in *Reason*, October 1995, 56.

According to indicators of basic needs, Africa and all its subregions have recorded long-term improvements in life expectancy, infant mortality, and adult literacy (Table 21.8). With the exception of Central Africa, all the subregions posted increases in GDP per capita between 1960 and 1993. Still, the improvements in Sub-Saharan Africa lagged far behind those in Asia and Latin America.

Again, the SAP experiences were different in each country. In Ghana, the macroeconomic results show a marked contrast in the performance of the economy in the pre- and post-SAP periods. The economy has recorded strong and sustained growth since the institution of the SAP in 1983. Inflation fell from 122 percent in 1983 to 10 percent in 1992; the transition toward multiparty elections in 1992 precipitated a new populism, and inflation climbed again to a peak of 60 percent in 1995. Ghana's macroeconomic success has allowed it to obtain generous donor support.

Ghana's SAP was somewhat unorthodox because its fiscal policy was expansionary rather than contractionary. Expenditures increased during the SAP on services and infrastructure benefiting the poor. Real per capita education expenditures increased by a total of 80 percent between 1980 and 1993, and real per capita health expenditures increased by 76 percent.[51] Even so, because of rapid population growth in the cities, the proportion of the urban population with access to safe water declined from 93 percent in 1985 to 63 percent in 1990.[52]

Côte d'Ivoire, once a success story among African economies, was forced by its balance of payments difficulties to adopt an SAP in 1981. Unlike Ghana, the SAP in Côte d'Ivoire entailed a dramatic cutback in investment and current expenditures.[53] The government also followed a contractionary monetary policy to bring the growth of the money supply under control. A sharp decline in commodity prices in 1987 worsened an already precarious fiscal situation. Although expenditures had been trimmed to the bone earlier in the decade, the SAP required an even more austere stance.

Under pressure from workers, the government drew back from its commitment to adjustment, and essentially abandoned the program in 1987. In response, the World Bank interrupted its lending to Côte d'Ivoire until 1989, when the SAP was resumed. The growth record of Côte d'Ivoire in the 1980s was dismal. Between 1983 and 1991, real GDP fell by 0.4 percent annually. At the same time, population growth increased steadily from 3.4 percent in the early 1980s to 3.9 percent in 1991.[54] The net result of these trends was a decline in per capita income. For the population as a whole, it is estimated

---

[51]World Bank, *African Development Indicators 1996,* 204 and 206.

[52]African Development Bank, *African Development Report 1996,* A54.

[53]Sylvie Lambert, Hartmut Schneider, and Akiko Suwa, "Adjustment and Equity in Côte d'Ivoire: 1980–1986," *World Development* 19 (November 1991): 1563–1576.

[54]Lionel Demery, "Côte d'Ivoire: Fettered Adjustment," in *Adjustment in Africa: Lessons from Country Studies,* ed. Ishrat Hussein and Rashid Faruquee (Washington, D.C.: World Bank, 1994), 113.

■ TABLE 21.8

BASIC NEEDS INDICATORS FOR SELECTED
AFRICAN COUNTRIES, 1960–1993

	Life Expectancy (years)		Infant Mortality (per 1,000 live births)		Adult Literacy (percent)		Real GDP per capita ($PPP)	
	1960	1993	1960	1993	1970	1993	1960	1993
Northern Africa	**47**	**65**	**170**	**62**	**27**	**50**	**1,029**	**4,213**
Algeria	47	67	168	54	25	59	1,676	5,570
Egypt	46	64	179	66	35	50	557	3,800
Morocco	47	64	163	67	22	42	854	3,270
Sub-Saharan Africa	**40**	**51**	**167**	**97**	**27**	**55**	**990**	**1,379**
West Africa	*39*	*51*	*177*	*97*	*22*	*45*	*925*	*1,660*
Burkina Faso	36	48	205	129	8	18	290	780
Cameroon	39	56	163	62	33	61	736	2,220
Côte d'Ivoire	39	51	166	91	18	38	1,021	1,620
Ghana	45	56	132	80	31	62	1,049	2,000
Guinea	34	45	203	133	14	34	1,323	1,800
Nigeria	40	51	190	84	25	54	1,133	1,540
Central Africa	*41*	*52*	*158*	*92*	*42*	*75*	*379*	*300*
Congo P.R. (Zaire)	41	52	158	92	42	75	379	300
East Africa	*41*	*51*	*150*	*93*	*25*	*62*	*503*	*942*
Ethiopia	36	48	175	118	n.a.	n.a.	262	420
Kenya	45	56	124	69	32	76	635	1,400
Sudan	39	53	170	77	17	44	975	1,350
Tanzania	41	52	147	85	10	66	272	630
Uganda	43	45	133	115	41	60	371	910
Southern Africa	*43*	*55*	*152*	*89*	*45*	*68*	*1,575*	*1,642*
Madagascar	41	57	220	91	n.a.	n.a.	1,013	700
Mozambique	37	46	190	147	22	38	1,368	640
South Africa	49	63	89	52	57	81	2,984	3,124
Zimbabwe	45	53	110	67	55	84	937	2,100
South Asia	**44**	**60**	**164**	**84**	**31**	**48**	**698**	**1,576**
East Asia	**48**	**69**	**146**	**42**	**88**	**98**	**729**	**2,681**
Southeast Asia, Pacific	**45**	**64**	**127**	**53**	**65**	**86**	**732**	**3,680**
Latin America	**55**	**69**	**107**	**45**	**71**	**85**	**2,138**	**5,816**

SOURCE: United Nations Development Program, *Human Development Report, 1996.* Subregional averages are unweighted.

that the proportion in poverty increased from 30 percent in 1985 to 46 percent in 1990.[55]

Tanzania adopted an SAP in 1985, after the apparent failure of its experiment with socialism. Its economic performance has improved dramatically since that time. Real GDP growth increased from an annual average of 1.1 percent between 1981 and 1985 to 4.5 percent between 1991 and 1996. The inflation rate and the central government's fiscal deficit have both declined.[56] Again, urban access to safe water has declined, but rural access has improved.[57]

The stories of these three countries illustrate the fact that it is difficult to make broad statements about the SAPs that are true throughout Africa. Undoubtedly, though, the SAPs represent a sharp movement toward market-oriented economic development in Africa. Many countries, including Burundi, Gambia, Mali, Mauritania, Sierra Leone, Uganda, and Zambia, have removed price controls on all goods except refined petroleum.[58] Under the leadership of a new generation of politicians who have learned to balance the demands of their domestic populations and those of the international financial agencies, Africa has shown new signs of hope during the mid-1990s.[59] After centuries of torturous development, however, our hope remains fragile.

SUMMARY

The African continent can be broadly divided into a northern region, a lower-income Sub-Saharan region, and several subregions. The indigenous cultures, including the ancient empires of Egypt, Ghana, and Mali, developed social, economic, and political institutions long before the arrival of European colonialists.

The transatlantic slave trade, which began in response to a shortage of labor in the Americas, resulted in the decimation of African communities and the forcible export of skilled labor. By 1850, however, the slave trade had largely ceased. Between 1870 and 1900, the African continent was partitioned, with boundaries haphazardly cutting across existing ethnic groupings, by the European powers. The African colonies developed as suppliers of primary commodities. The infrastructure and educational systems introduced by the colonial powers were designed to reinforce the status quo.

After World War II, the post-independence African governments pursued policies of import-substituting industrialization. In many countries, govern-

---

[55]Lionel Demery and Christian Grootaert, "Correcting for Sampling Bias in the Measurement of Welfare and Poverty in the Côte d'Ivoire Living Standards Survey," *World Bank Economic Review* 7 (1993): 290.

[56]Darius Mans, "Tanzania, Resolute Action," in *Adjustment in Africa: Lessons from Country Studies,* 384; and International Monetary Fund, *World Economic Outlook,* May 1997, 138.

[57]African Development Bank, *African Development Report 1996,* A54.

[58]World Bank, *Adjustment in Africa: Reforms, Results, and the Road Ahead,* 90–91.

[59]See Judith Matloff, "New Rulers, U.S. Plan Give Africa a Future," *The Christian Science Monitor,* June 19, 1997, 10.

ments undertook public enterprise investments, and industries were nationalized on a massive scale. The performances of state-owned enterprises and import-substitution programs were generally disappointing.

Agriculture dominates production in many African countries. The colonial emphasis on cash-crop production led to the emergence of a dualistic agrarian economy of cash crop and local food staple production. The former benefited from modern agro-scientific inputs, while the latter was starved of modern inputs. Farming practices have evolved from shifting cultivation to a more settled system of agriculture in response to population growth.

The traditional landholding pattern in Africa is the customary or communal system of kinship, family, clan, or tribal ownership. The Europeans introduced individual ownership rights to agricultural land and a few governments have also implemented land reforms. Thus, a dual land system, where private ownership, rights exist side-by-side with communal ownership, has emerged.

The informal economy dominates the industrial organization of many African countries. This sector is small-scale and largely unorganized as compared to the urban formal sector, which is characterized by modern production methods and various degrees of collective bargaining.

During the early 1980s, faced with declining production and rising poverty and debt, many African countries adopted stabilization and structural adjustment programs in exchange for financial assistance from the World Bank and International Monetary Fund. These programs sought to reduce the level of government intervention in African economies and to allow for the operation of market forces. The policies implemented by many countries included trade liberalization, devaluation, reductions in government expenditure, privatization, and financial liberalization. The experiences of countries with SAPs are varied, and the results are a matter of controversy. Early gains were small, but Africa seems to be showing new signs of hope.

DISCUSSION AND REVIEW QUESTIONS

1. Are the African economies influenced today by the legacies of slave trade and colonialism?

2. What factors led to the economic decline of most African economies toward the end of the 1970s?

3. Are the stabilization and structural adjustment programs in Africa any different from the economic reforms currently underway in the former Communist economies of Central Eurasia?

4. How does the land tenure system in Africa differ from that of Latin America? What are their respective impacts on agricultural productivity?

5. What are the origins and characteristics of the informal sector in Africa?

6. Is there any conflict between the goals of poverty reduction and democratic reform in Africa? Should one carry a higher priority than the other?

SUGGESTED READINGS

Adjibolosoo, Senyo B-S. K., ed. *The Significance of the Human Factor in African Economic Development.* Westport, Conn.: Praeger, 1995. *Based on 16 papers presented at a conference in 1993, this book approaches the problem of African development from a broad economic and sociological perspective.*

Ezeala-Harrison, Fidelis, and Senyo B-S. K. Adjibolosoo, eds. *Perspectives on Economic Development in Africa.* Westport, Conn.: Praeger, 1994. *A collection of 13 studies on a range of topics related to African development, including the urban informal sector, the role of political corruption in economic underdevelopment, the African debt crisis, and the role of education in African economic growth.*

Hussein, Ishrat, and R. Faruquee, eds. *Adjustment in Africa: Lessons from Country Studies.* Washington, D.C.: The World Bank, 1994. *A companion volume for the World Bank study described below, this book provides an enormous amount of information on the variety of experience in Burundi, Côte d'Ivoire, Ghana, Kenya, Nigeria, Senegal, and Tanzania before and during their structural adjustment programs.*

Rimmer, Douglas, ed. *Action in Africa.* London: Royal African Aid Society, 1993. *Fifteen studies written by people actively involved in African business and government and in international aid agencies.*

World Bank, *Adjustment in Africa: Reforms, Results, and the Road Ahead.* Oxford: Oxford University Press, 1994. *Based on a major study of the performance of 29 Sub-Saharan countries, this is the definitive statement from the financial community on the performance of structural adjustment programs in Africa.*

INTERNET RESOURCES

The Addis Tribune (Ethiopia)
http://etonline.netnation.com/addis-tribune/

Africa Information Center
http://www.hmnet.com/africa/1africa.html

African National Congress Newswire
http://www.bibim.com/anc/

Africa News Service
http://www.africanews.com/

Africa Notes
http://www.einaudi.cornell.edu/africa/notes/

Africa Online
http://www.africaonline.com/

Africa Search
http://www.woyaa.com/

African Development Bank Group
http://www.dfait-maeci.gc.ca/ifinet/afdb-e.htm

Africa 2000
http://www.africa2000.com/

Afrika.com
http://www.afrika.com/

CNN Interactive: Africa
http://www.cnn.com/WORLD/africa/index.html

Demery, Lionel, and Lyn Squire. Abstract of "Macroeconomic Adjustment and Poverty in Africa: An Emerging Picture," World Bank Research Observer (February 1996)
http://www.worldbank.org/html/extpb/ObserverFeb96.html#Macroeconomic

The Drum
http://www.mindspring.com/~thedrum/

Economic and Development Bulletin
http://www4.nando.net/ans/pana/ECO/PANAECO.html

Economic Commission for Africa, 21st Conference of Ministers
http://www.sas.upenn.edu/African_Studies/ECA/menu_ECAminst.html

Ghana Government
http://www.ghana.gov.gh/

Ghana Online
http://www.ghanaonline.com/

Horn of Africa Bulletin
http://www.sas.upenn.edu/African_Studies/Newsletters/menu_HAF_Main.html
http://www.nordnet.se/lpi/hab/

Iafrica.com
http://iafrica.com/

Kenya Web
http://www.kenyaweb.com/

Mail and Guardian (South Africa)
http://www.mg.co.za/mg/

Main Street South Africa
http://mainstreet.t5.com/

Nigeria (World Bank Research)
http://www.worldbank.org/nigeria/

Panafrican News Agency
http://www.africanews.org/PANA/

Merchant Bank Economic Report
http://www.rmb.co.za/report.htmlRand

Regional Bureau for Africa
United Nations Development Program
http://www.undp.org/undp/rba/rba.htm

Report on the Economic and Social Situation in Africa, 1995
http://www.sas.upenn.edu/African_Studies/ECA/AfEcMenu.html

Rubani: African Web Directory
http://www.rubani.com/

Senegal Online
http://www.teranga.com/index.html

South Africa Guide
http://www.southafrica.net/

Southern Africa Database
http://www.sas.upenn.edu/African_Studies/Country_Specific/menu_ZAdbase.html

South African New Economics Network
http://196.30.17.130/sane/

South African Yearbook
http://www.wna.co.za/govt/yrbook95/yrbook95.html

United Nations Economic Commission for Africa
http://www.un.org/Depts/eca/

USAfrica Homepage
http://www.usafricaonline.com/

World Bank, Adjustment and Growth in Sub-Saharan Africa
http://www.worldbank.org/html/edi/briefing/adj-grow/adj-grow.html

Yaker, Layashi. "Report on African Economy"
http://www.sas.upenn.edu/African_Studies/Padis/padis_eca.html

Zimbabwe Independent
http://www.samara.co.zw/zimin/

CONCLUSIONS AND PROSPECTS

22

THE ECONOMIC FUTURE:
COOPERATION OR CONFRONTATION?

Our little systems have their day; They have their day and
cease to be; They are but broken lights of thee, And thou,
O Lord, art more than they . . .Behold, we know not
anything; I can but trust that good shall fall At last—far
off—at last to all, And every winter change to spring . . .

—ALFRED TENNYSON, "IN MEMORIAM," 1850

eldom in history have people been more convinced that a new day is dawning. The end of a
Cold War, the unification and expansion of Germany, China, Europe, and the North Atlantic
Treaty Organization (NATO), the assimilation of
new information technologies, the conclusion of
regional and global trade agreements, and the
dawn of a new millennium have convinced us all
that something big is happening.

But what exactly is it? Are we entering an era
of relative peace, prosperity, and stability, a new
Pax Americana, characterized by the spread of Western technologies, democratic traditions, and market institutions, facilitated by global communication
in the English language? Is this a realistic hope, or is it a fantasy promoted by
Western, and particularly American, triumphalism and neocolonialism? Is it
more likely that global cooperation will be undermined by demographic,
ecological, cultural, macroeconomic, and financial crises?

As human beings, we are naturally interested in these issues. As students
of economics, we are doubly interested, because we understand the power
and importance of expectations. Our beliefs, plans, hopes, and fears of tomorrow can have a major influence on our behavior today.

Our vision of the future is usually rooted in our understanding of the past
and our perception of the present. From the past, we may draw helpfully, but
always selectively, on the record of historical experience. We also rely on the
concepts, abstractions, and historical interpretations that we inherit from our
intellectual ancestors. John Maynard Keynes clearly understood the contemporary power of historical ideas: "Practical men, who believe themselves to

be quite exempt from any intellectual influences, are usually the slaves of some defunct economist."[1]

Our vision of the future also is grounded in our assessment of the present. Scholars who have a relatively positive view of present performance will usually, it seems, offer an optimistic assessment of the future. Scholars who are troubled by the current state of economic, social, political, and environmental relations will usually project their concern into the future.

Indeed, in their long-range speculations, scholars typically are led by the **tyranny of extrapolation**—the tendency to overestimate the powers of a perceived status quo, suggesting that the future will be much like the present. Not long ago, few believed that the Communist leaders of the Soviet bloc would surrender their privileges without a major fight. As recently as 1994, a prominent futurist argued that the European Union would not adopt a common currency—"not in this century and beyond—because our money . . . is one of the things that distinguishes us from others."[2] This, to paraphrase Oliver Wendell Holmes, seems to be certitude masquerading as certainty.

A BRIEF HISTORY OF THE ECONOMIC FUTURE

Before we survey the current state of global expectations, it will be instructive to reconsider the futurologies of the past. We direct special attention to expectations concerning the evolution of economic institutions and systems.

Adam Smith, the father of classical economics, was a product of the Newtonian Age. Just as Isaac Newton formulated natural laws of gravity and motion to explain the behavior of planets in the solar system, Smith employed the laws of supply and demand to explain the operation of the economic system. To Smith, the market economic system was a permanent part of the natural world. He spoke of a system of natural liberty that was governed by a system of natural prices. Mercantilist restrictions could interfere with the natural progress of opulence, but they could not fundamentally change or replace the underlying laws of the system.

The Smithian view of the world and its future was quickly challenged. Hegel, the German philosopher, and Darwin, the British naturalist, introduced the dialectical and evolutionary modes of thought that questioned all static conceptions of life and social organization. The French and American revolutions demonstrated the feasibility of revolutionary action and led to demands for political, economic, and social equality. By 1846, Marx and Engels believed that the conditions already existed for a Communist revolution that would quickly spread around the world and "abolish the present state of things."[3] Writing two years later, John Stuart Mill was more uncertain: "We

---

[1]John Maynard Keynes, *The General Theory of Employment, Interest, and Money* (New York: Harcourt, Brace and World, 1935), 383.

[2]John Naisbitt, *Global Paradox* (New York: Avon Books, 1994), 3.

[3]Karl Marx and Friedrich Engels, "The German Ideology," in *The Marx-Engels Reader* 2d ed., ed. Robert C. Tucker (New York: W. W. Norton, 1978), 162.

are too ignorant either of what individual agency in its best form, or Socialism in its best form, can accomplish, to be qualified to decide which of the two will be the ultimate form of human society."[4]

The possibility of a socialist revolution was finally demonstrated in 1917, when the Bolsheviks seized power in Russia. From the beginning, observers in the West found it difficult to believe that the system would last. When Lenin established his market-oriented New Economic Policy in the early 1920s, many believed that the socialist experiment was over. From that point forward, every Soviet program of reform was greeted by many Westerners as a return to capitalism.

PROPHETS OF CONVERGENCE

During the Great Depression, the old conceptions of capitalism and socialism seemed to lose their meaning. In the Soviet Union, Stalinist repression of the workers made a mockery of socialist ideals. In the United States, the New Deal policies seemed to modify the nature of the market system. A pathbreaking study by Berle and Means revealed that many capitalist firms were no longer controlled by capitalists.[5] An elite corps of professional managers had taken charge, they said, because ownership of the large corporations was divided among thousands of powerless stockholders.

In 1941, James Burnham detected a common thread in the evolutions of Russia, America, and Nazi Germany; he argued that all the industrial countries were shifting away from capitalism and socialism toward a middle ground that he called the **managerial society.** In this new society, he said, the means of production would be owned by the state, enabling the government to eliminate the mass unemployment of the capitalist system, but no progress would be made toward a socialist classless society. The managerial and technocratic elite would "gain preference in the distribution of products, not directly, through property rights vested in them as individuals, but indirectly, through their control of the state."[6] Russia had already "advanced furthest along the managerial road," but all the other industrial societies were on the way. Burnham's gloomy view of the future was shared by Friedrich Hayek in his 1944 book, *The Road to Serfdom.*[7]

In the year that Burnham's work appeared, a far more significant event captured the attention of the world and temporarily changed the Soviet image. The German invasion of Russia broke the bond of totalitarianism formed between Hitler and Stalin in 1939, and the Soviet Union joined in an alliance against Hitler with the Western democratic forces. In 1942, Wendell Willkie—the Republican candidate in the 1940 presidential race—spent ten days in the

---

[4]John Stuart Mill, *Principles of Political Economy,* Books 4 and 5 (1848; London: Penguin Books, 1970), 360.

[5]A. A. Berle and Gardner C. Means, *The Modern Corporation and Private Property* (New York: Commerce Clearing House, 1932).

[6]James Burnham, *The Managerial Revolution* (New York: John Day, 1941), 72.

[7]Friedrich A. Hayek, *The Road to Serfdom* (Chicago: University of Chicago Press, 1944).

Soviet Union during a round-the-world ambassadorial trip for President Roosevelt. Upon his return, Willkie published his best-selling book, *One World*, which contained a plea for postwar cooperation between nations:

> *No, we do not need to fear Russia. We need to learn to work with her against our common enemy, Hitler. We need to learn to work with her in the world after the war. For Russia is a dynamic country, a vital new society, a force that cannot be bypassed in any future world.*[8]

Captured by that same wartime spirit of cooperation, a Russian-born Harvard sociologist, Pitirim Sorokin, argued that Russia and the United States "exhibit an essential similarity . . . in a number of important psychological, cultural, and social values."[9] Both countries, he noted, are continental in scope, are cultural and racial melting pots, and have similar family structures.

Because of their environmental similarities, Sorokin predicted a "mutual convergence" of the economic and social structures of the two countries. As cultural interchange expanded between Russia and the United States, each country would be influenced by the strengths of the other system.

> *Without even diplomatic pressure the United States will strongly influence the Soviet regime in the direction of terminating its dictatorial violation of the elementary rights of Russian citizens. . . . On the other hand, Russia will continue to fructify the culture—particularly the fine arts—of the United States; and it may facilitate a decrease of the commercial hypocrisy, selfishness, and exploitation inherent, to a certain extent, in any private business on a large scale.*[10]

This convergence, Sorokin believed, could provide a basis for international cooperation. He called on the American and Soviet leaders to create a framework for lasting peace by establishing a "real, efficient, and powerful international authority empowered with the right of decision in all international conflicts between all states."[11] One year later, his hopes were partially fulfilled when the United States, the Soviet Union, and 49 other countries signed the United Nations charter.

CONVERGENCE AND DIVERGENCE AFTER WORLD WAR II

After the war, several circumstances seemed to support the contention that capitalist and socialist countries were converging toward a middle ground. England and several other capitalist countries initiated large-scale nationalizations of industry, and countries such as France and Japan established systems of indicative planning. In West Germany, the new system of codetermination placed labor representatives on corporate boards of directors. The Yugoslavs broke from the socialist mainstream in 1950 to establish their system of workers' self-management and gradually replaced central planning with market exchange.

In 1956, three years after Stalin's death, Nikita Khrushchev delivered two historic speeches to the Twentieth Party Congress. The first speech, delivered

---

[8]Wendell L. Willkie, *One World* (New York: Simon and Schuster, 1943), 87.

[9]Pitirim A. Sorokin, *Russia and the United States* (New York: E. P. Dutton, 1944) 26.

[10]Ibid., 210.

[11]Ibid., 239.

publicly, proclaimed that Lenin's doctrine of the inevitability of war between capitalist and socialist countries was rendered obsolete by the danger of nuclear extinction. He announced a policy of **peaceful coexistence**—a shift from military confrontation to economic and political competition. Furthermore, he attempted to draw Yugoslavia back into the fold by recognizing the legitimacy of different roads to socialism. In his second speech, delivered to a secret session of the Party Congress, Khrushchev denounced the crimes of Stalin.

The Party Congress sent shock waves through the Communist world. The de-Stalinization campaign cleared the way for release of political prisoners and improvement of relations with the West. In the late 1950s and early 1960s, economic and political reforms were launched in Poland, Hungary, and Czechoslovakia. In 1962, an article in *Pravda* by Professor Evsei Liberman initiated the discussion of economic reform in the Soviet Union.[12]

In the West, the Kennedy–Johnson administration opened the 1960s with an emphasis on governmental activism and civil rights. In Great Britain, the Conservative government established the National Economic Development Council in 1962, influenced by the French record of rapid economic growth under indicative planning. Even in West Germany, a bastion of anti-Keynesianism, a Council of Economic Experts was established in 1963 to strengthen the nation's fiscal planning.

As the Eastern nations dabbled with markets and democracy and the Western nations enlarged the roles of their governments, the convergence theory gained broad acceptance in academic circles. Jan Tinbergen, who would later share the first Nobel Prize in economics, published his "Theory of the Optimum Regime" in 1959, suggesting the existence of a superior system somewhere between the poles of atomistic capitalism and centrally planned socialism. According to the usual formulation, this system would allow the market to prevent imbalances in the short run, and it would employ economic planning to coordinate long-term decisions. In 1961, Tinbergen argued that systemic changes "are in fact bringing the communist and free economies closer together," although he was quite aware that "there are very large differences still."[13]

The convergence theory reached a popular audience in 1967, when John Kenneth Galbraith published his international best-seller, *The New Industrial State*. According to Galbraith, the international dissemination of mass-production technologies, employed with enormous investments of time and money, required all countries to engage in planning of production, distribution, and pricing. To perform these tasks, it was necessary for a Burnham-style technocracy of industrial managers to gain authority in all industrial countries. Thus, technology was driving a convergent pattern of planning and management throughout the world. True, the planners in

---

[12]See our discussion of the Liberman reforms in Chapter 16, and see his original article, "Plan, Profits, and Bonuses," *Pravda*, September 9, 1992, reprinted in *Current Digest of the Soviet Press*, October 3, 1962, 13–15.

[13]Jan Tinbergen, "The Theory of the Optimum Regime," in his *Selected Papers* (Amsterdam, 1959); and Jan Tinbergen, "Do Communist and Free Economies Show a Converging Pattern?" *Soviet Studies* 12 (April 1961): 333–341.

some countries were employed by private corporations, and in other countries they were employed by the state, "but these, obviously, are differences in method rather than purpose."[14]

The convergence theory also drew attention from the Soviet side in the 1960s, but primarily in the form of condemnation. According to the official Marxian position, the capitalist countries were destined to experience socialist revolutions, not gradual transitions to mixed economies. The convergence theory was designed to "trick the toiling people, to lead them astray with pseudo-socialist slogans."[15] As Khrushchev told a group of diplomats who visited the Kremlin in 1956, socialism would not converge with capitalism, but it would eventually witness the submergence of capitalism: "Whether or not you like it, history is on our side. We will bury you."

A few voices in the Soviet Union drew inspiration from the idea of convergence. Andrei Sakharov, the dissident physicist who later received the Nobel Peace Prize, proposed a plan in 1968 for economic and political convergence and disarmament.[16] Thirteen years later, living in internal exile, Sakharov summarized his position as follows:

> My ideal is an open, pluralistic society, with an unconditional observance of the fundamental civil and political rights of man, a society with a mixed economy which would make for scientifically regulated, comprehensive progress. I have voiced the assumption that such a society ought to come about as a result of a peaceful convergence of the socialist and capitalist systems. That is the main condition for saving the world from thermonuclear catastrophe.[17]

Between the late 1960s and the late 1970s, the international trend seemed to turn from convergence to divergence. In 1968, although the Hungarians were able to introduce their New Economic Mechanism, Soviet troops crushed a more significant revolution in Czechoslovakia. In the United States, 1968 was the year the Republicans regained the White House and liberalism lost two of its most important spokesmen—Martin Luther King Jr. and Robert Kennedy. In the Soviet Union, some of the 1965 economic reforms were rolled back in 1971. When international oil prices shot upward in 1973, even the Hungarians were forced to scale back their reforms.

A new era of revolutionary reform began in the East in the late 1970s, and persisted through the 1980s, overpowering the forces of ideology, bureaucracy, martial law in Poland, and an attempted *coup d'état* in the Soviet Union. The outlines of this revolution have been described in earlier chapters. China, led by Deng Xiaoping, adopted a firm commitment to pragmatism in 1978, two years after Mao's death, and Hungary turned its attention

---

[14]John Kenneth Galbraith, *The New Industrial State* (New York: Signet, 1967), 396–397.

[15]L. F. Il'ichev, Soviet Party Secretary, quoted in Leon Goure, et al., *Convergence of Communism and Capitalism: The Soviet View* (Miami, Fla.: Center for Advanced International Studies, University of Miami, 1973), 41.

[16]Andrei Sakharov, *Progress, Coexistence, and Intellectual Freedom* (New York: W. W. Norton, 1968).

[17]Sakharov's open letter to the president of the Soviet Academy of Sciences, published in *The Wall Street Journal*, February 5, 1981, 22.

back to the New Economic Mechanism in 1979. The independent Solidarity union was established in Poland in 1980 and won a number of concessions from the Communist government.

In the United States, any hint of middle-ground convergence was dispelled in 1980 by the inauguration of the Reagan administration, and, in England, Margaret Thatcher initiated a privatization campaign that would quickly spread around the Western world. The Socialist government of François Mitterrand entered office in France in 1981, but its leftist programs were short-lived.

The degenerative rule of Leonid Brezhnev finally ended with his death in 1982, and Mikhail Gorbachev gained power in the Soviet Union three years later. After progressively more radical political and economic reforms, Communist governments were overthrown throughout Central Eurasia between 1989 and 1991, and the Soviet Union was dismembered. In retrospect, Khrushchev was correct in his 1956 prediction that a major social system would be buried, but he identified the wrong victim.

AFTER THE COLD WAR: ALTERNATIVE FUTURES

As we noted in the opening paragraphs of this chapter, the end of the Cold War and the attendant revolutions of world trade and communications prompted a torrent of speculation about the institutional architecture of the new millennium. An opening salvo was fired in 1989 by Francis Fukuyama, who was, at the time, a policy planning official in the U.S. State Department under the Republican administration.[18] We seem to be witnessing, he said, "not just the passing of a particular period of postwar history, but the end point of mankind's ideological evolution and the universalization of Western liberal democracy as the final form of human government." Deliberately borrowing the vocabulary of Hegel and Marx, he claimed that we may have reached "the end of history."[19]

Shortly after Fukuyama proclaimed the victory of liberal democracy and the **End of History,** his position seemed to be contradicted by the continuing flood of world events: the Tienanmen Square massacre, the Gulf War, and ethnic cleansing in Bosnia and Croatia. In response to his critics, Fukuyama said he had not predicted an end to "the occurrence of events, even large and grave events, but History," which, according to his reading of Hegel, could be understood more narrowly as the "History of Ideology."[20]

---

[18]Since that time, Fukuyama has held teaching and research positions at Johns Hopkins School for Advanced International Studies, at the RAND Corporation, and presently, at the Institute of Public Policy of George Mason University. His educational background stretched from philosophy and classics at Cornell and comparative literature at Yale and in Paris to international relations at Harvard. On his interesting intellectual biography, see James Atlas, "What Is Fukuyama Saying?" *New York Times,* October 22, 1989, Section 6, 38.

[19]Francis Fukuyama, "The End of History," *The National Interest* 16 (Summer 1989): 4.

[20]Francis Fukuyama, *The End of History and the Last Man* (New York: The Free Press, 1992), xii; and Francis Fukuyama, "Beyond the End of History," *Washington Post,* December 10, 1989, C1.

When it crushed the democracy movement in Tienanmen Square, for example, the Chinese government was not able to build a credible ideological case for its moral authority or legitimacy; it could not offer the world a credible alternative for liberal democracy. Liberal democracy, attended by liberal rules of property ownership and market activity, has proved itself the victor in a centuries-old contest of institutional legitimacy.

WESTERN OPTIMISM AND TRIUMPHALISM

We will return later to Fukuyama's philosophical argument, but suffice it to say that his essay set the tone for a series of optimistic, or sometimes triumphal, Western assessments after the Cold War. Chief among the optimists have been mainstream professional economists, the progeny of Adam Smith and David Ricardo, who are broadly dedicated to the proposition that expansion of domestic and world trade is mutually beneficial.[21] The destruction of the Berlin Wall was a symbol of the wider removal of barriers between people and their products during the 1990s, made possible by new political freedoms, by dramatic advances in information technology, by regional and global trade agreements, by programs of trade liberalization in transitional and developing economies, and by the spread of English as a world language.

The multilateral financial agencies, which generally reflect the views of mainstream economists, are public in their optimism. According to the International Monetary Fund, individual countries still must address their particular problems, but "there is no doubt that globalization is contributing enormously to global prosperity."[22] Long-term forecasts by the World Bank suggest that every major region of the world, except one, will experience an acceleration of economic growth during the years between 1996 and 2005. The exception is East Asia, where the annual GDP growth rate is expected to decline from 10 percent to about 8 percent, but that will continue to be the highest regional rate of growth in the world.[23] Even in the troubled case of Sub-Saharan Africa, international officials are more hopeful than they have been in a generation.

Likewise, according to Henry Rowen, a Stanford University economist who served as chairman of the National Intelligence Council, long-term forecasts for lower population growth, higher investment in education, and broader diffusion of technology, as well as government policies permitting direct foreign investment, should lead to improved standards of living in the developing world. Taking the argument a step farther, Rowen suggests that prosperity has been correlated in the past with stronger democratic governments, and democracies have seldom waged war with one another. Thus,

---

[21]Richard M. Alston, J. R. Kearl, and Michael B. Vaughan, "Is There a Consensus Among Economists in the 1990s?" *American Economic Review* 82 (May 1992): 204.

[22]International Monetary Fund, *World Economic Outlook*, May 1997, 3.

[23]World Bank, *Global Economic Prospects and the Developing Countries 1996*, 10. Also, see Table 5.5 of this book.

Rowen places a high probability on democratic reform in China by 2015, and he holds hope for a more peaceful world.[24]

The tide of optimism rides particularly high in the United States. In recent years, the United States has maintained low rates of inflation and unemployment and moderate rates of economic growth. It leads the world in development and utilization of key computing and telecommunications technologies. As a major superpower, the United States plays a powerful role in NATO, in the International Monetary Fund, and in the World Bank. Its popular culture blankets the world with motion pictures, music, television programs, and CNN news reports.

During the electronic age, the United States and other English-speaking countries enjoy a special advantage. About 80 percent of global electronic communication is thought to take place in English. The official language of eight major countries, English has some form of administrative status in about 70 countries. It is the first language of about 400 million people, and has been studied as a second or foreign language by as many as 1 billion others.[25]

A particularly assertive statement of American and Western triumphalism is found in the writing of David Rothkopf, an international affairs specialist at Kissinger Associates and Columbia University who once served in the Commerce Department of the Clinton administration. Rising "in praise of cultural imperialism," Rothkopf argues that Americans should not be indifferent about their position in the emerging world culture:

> [It] is in the economic and political interests of the United States to ensure that if the world is moving toward a common language, it be English; that if the world is moving toward common telecommunications, safety, and quality standards, they be American; that if the world is becoming linked by television, radio, and music, the programming be American; and that if common values are being developed, they be values with which Americans are comfortable.[26]

Because American culture has evolved from a mixture of all the major world cultures, Rothkopf argues that it is adapted unusually well to the needs of the whole world. In light of recent efforts in some countries to create barriers of cultural protectionism, Rothkopf argues that Americans should be assertive:

> Americans should not shy away from doing that which is so clearly in their economic, political, and security interests and so clearly in the interests of the world at large. The United States should not hesitate to promote its values. In an effort to be polite or politic, Americans should not deny the fact that of all the nations in the history of the world, theirs is the most just, the most tolerant, the most willing to constantly reassess and improve itself, and the best model for the future.[27]

---

[24]"Economists See 'Mosaic' of Factors Contributing to Prosperity," Business Wire, January 8, 1996; and "Preparing for China's Future after Deng," Federal News Service, March 18, 1997.

[25]David Crystal, "The Language That Took Over the World," *The Guardian*, February 22, 1997, 21.

[26]David Rothkopf, "In Praise of Cultural Imperialism?" *Foreign Policy* 107 (Summer 1997): 45.

[27]Ibid, 48–49.

THE END OF HISTORY, OR A NEW BEGINNING?

According to critics, Fukuyama's End of History thesis stands on a weak philosophical foundation. Alex Callinicos says that Fukuyama cannot claim support from Hegel, who had "no interest in the idea of the End of History," and, in fact, no real interest in the history of the objective world, operating below the sphere of Absolute Spirit.[28]

Even if Fukuyama's position is supportable on Hegelian grounds, it is opposed by other philosophies of history that question the existence of any single ideal social system for all people and places. Thus, Fukuyama's End may be criticized on the same terms as Tinbergen's Optimal Regime or any other simple model of convergence.

As we observed in the first chapter of this book, an optimal economic and social system may exist only in the context of a specified set of social objectives and a specified environment of cultural traditions, natural resources, and human abilities. The ideal system may differ for each country, and its advantage may exist only in the moral context of a particular culture.

Thus, in reaction to the optimistic predictions of a homogenized global culture of market democracies, an enormous literature has appeared in recent years to reaffirm the importance and persistence of cultural and religious traditions. Most familiar in this line is Samuel Huntington's provocative 1993 essay in *Foreign Affairs* and his 1996 book, claiming that a growing "clash of civilizations" has replaced ideology as the greatest threat to world peace and prosperity.[29] Similarly, Benjamin Barber argues that world conflict increasingly will arise from local tribalisms, rooted in religion and culture, and from the forces of global consumerism.[30]

Many social scientists and philosophers also emphasize the Malthusian limits of modern economic growth. According to Paul Kennedy, a prominent Yale University historian, population pressure, resource scarcity, and large-scale migration will be major sources of instability in the coming century.[31] Richard Rorty, one of the leading philosophers of our time, doubts that the optimistic scenarios of the World Bank can be realized within the resource constraints of planet earth:

> [N]obody has written a scenario which shows how the people in the lucky industrialized democracies might redistribute their wealth in ways which create bright prospects for the children of the undeveloped countries without destroying the prospects of their own children and of their own societies.[32]

---

[28]Alex Callinicos, *Theories and Narratives: Reflections on the Philosophy of History* (Durham, N.C.: Duke University Press, 1995), 22–26.

[29]Samuel P. Huntington, *The Clash of Civilizations and the Remaking of World Order* (New York: Simon and Schuster, 1996).

[30]Benjamin Barber, *Jihad versus McWorld* (New York: Times Books, 1995). For an excellent survey of the culture and civilization literature, see Michael J. Mazarr, "Culture and International Relations: A Review Essay," *The Washington Quarterly* 19 (Spring 1996): 177–195.

[31]Paul Kennedy, *Preparing for the Twenty-First Century* (New York: Random House, 1993).

[32]Richard Rorty, "Moral Universalism and Economic Triage" <http://www.unesco.org/phiweb/uk/2rpu/rort/rort.html>.

Rorty agrees with Henry Rowen's view that stable democracy grows out of material prosperity, so he doubts the universal adoption of democratic institutions. The "moral universalism" expressed by Fukuyama, Rowen, and Rothkopf is, in Rorty's view, "an invention of the rich:"

> Only people who were already exceptionally rich, and therefore exceptionally secure, could have taken the idea of democracy, much less of global democracy, seriously. Moral idealism goes along with economic success.[33]

Is Rorty correct in his belief that the rich are more idealistic than the poor? Perhaps, but it seems equally plausible to argue that political scientists and philosophers including Rorty, have a more pessimistic view of modern globalization than professional economists. Once known as the "dismal scientists," economists now seem to be among the most cheerful people on earth. Based on the teachings of Adam Smith and David Ricardo, and on evidence drawn from decades of research, mainstream economists tend to emphasize the mutual benefits that arise from international trade and other forms of global interaction. Conversely, in their professional training and research, political scientists focus on the conflicting claims of political and social groups. Economists, it seems, are trained to search for positive-sum games, and political scientists are inclined to emphasize the zero-sum contests. Which will predominate in the near future? Conflict or mutual benefit? Well, this book was written by a hopeful economist.

SUMMARY

To Adam Smith, the capitalist economic system was a permanent part of the natural world. Dialectical and evolutionary theories, including those of Karl Marx, challenged the conception of an economic universe governed by immutable economic laws. The Russian Revolution finally proved that capitalism could be replaced for an extended period of time on a national scale.

The traditional views of capitalism and socialism were confounded in the 1930s by Stalinist repression in the Soviet Union and the separation of corporate ownership from control in the West. Hence, Burnham predicted that a managerial revolution would invade all the industrial countries. The convergence hypothesis gained adherents during World War II, when the Soviet Union joined forces with the Western alliance against Hitler.

After the war, nationalization programs in Great Britain, indicative planning in France and Japan, codetermination in West Germany, and workers' self-management in Yugoslavia provided further evidence of convergence. Then, in the 1960s, the popularity of the theory peaked with the introduction of reforms in the East and social welfare programs in the West. Convergence seemed to give way to divergence beginning in the late 1960s, as the Czech reforms were crushed, the Soviet reforms were rolled back, and conservatism made new gains in the West. The Eastern reforms gained new life in the late 1970s, and led to the fall of communism a decade later.

---

[33]Ibid.

Since the Cold War, one broad vision of the global future has been offered by those who believe that democracy and markets have won the historic contest of institutions, and that globalism will lead to greater peace and prosperity. Another broad view, with many variations, is held by those who emphasize the importance of cultural differences and environmental limits.

DISCUSSION AND REVIEW QUESTIONS

1. How did the events of the 1930s and 1940s give rise to the convergence hypothesis?

2. Do you believe that technology is a force that encourages countries to adopt a common set of institutions, or does technology help countries to maintain their differences?

3. What will be the state of the earth and its population in 2050? Will the average standard of living be higher than it is today?

SUGGESTED READINGS

Burnham, James. *The Managerial Revolution.* New York: John Day, 1941. *One of the earliest, and gloomiest, predictions of convergence.*

Drucker, Peter. *Post-Capitalist Society.* New York: HarperCollins, 1993. *Primarily known as an expert on international management, Drucker surveys the social challenges confronting capitalism, calling for new commitments to effective government, citizenship, and community.*

Frank, Robert H., and Philip J. Cook. *The Winner-Take-All Society.* New York: Penguin, 1995. *Argues that rising income inequality is caused, in part, by falling transport and communication costs, which allow the top performers in many sectors to corner their markets, capturing large shares of national or global sales and income.*

Fukuyama, Francis. *The End of History and the Last Man.* New York: The Free Press, 1992. *This book amplifies and greatly extends the line of analysis introduced in Fukuyama's 1989 essay in* The National Interest.

Galbraith, John Kenneth. *The New Industrial State.* New York: Signet, 1967. *This book probably played the most important role in carrying the convergence hypothesis, based on technological determinism, to a popular audience.*

Goure, Leon, Foy D. Kohler, Richard Soll, and Annette Stiefbold. *Convergence of Communism and Capitalism: The Soviet View.* Miami, Fla.: Center for Advanced International Studies, University of Miami, 1973. *A documentary record of Soviet reactions, most of them denials.*

Greider, William. *The Manic Logic of Global Capitalism.* New York: Simon and Schuster, 1996. *Argues that global competition between multinational corporations and national labor forces is moving the world toward "an economic or political cataclysm." Supports transaction taxes to slow down the "furious pace" of computer-driven stock markets and debt forgiveness for poor nations.*

Huntington, Samuel P. *The Clash of Civilizations and the Remaking of World Order.* New York: Simon and Schuster, 1996. *Written by a Harvard professor of strategic studies who was formerly a national security adviser in the Carter administration, this book argues that world divisions based on ideology have given way to more persistent divisions based on religion and culture.*

Kennedy, Paul. *Preparing for the Twenty-First Century.* New York: Random House, 1993. *Written by a distinguished, British-born-and-educated professor of history at Yale, this book emphasizes the demographic challenges that threaten world peace and stability in the coming years.*

Melzer, Arthur, James Weinberger, and M. Richard Zinman, eds. *History and the Idea of Progress.* Ithaca, N.Y.: Cornell University Press, 1995. *Here, in a single volume, we find essays on the past and future of history by a diverse collection of authors, including Fukuyama, Huntington, and Rorty.*

Naisbitt, John. *Global Paradox.* New York: Avon Books, 1994. *Written by a leading futurologist, this book explores the paradoxical joint development of individualism and globalism.*

Sorokin, Pitirim A. *Russia and the United States.* New York: E. P. Dutton, 1944. *This book, emphasizing sociological similarities between Russia and the United States, helped launch the postwar analysis of convergence.*

Toffler, Alvin and Heidi. *War and Anti-War.* New York: Warner Books, 1993. *By the authors of* Future Shock *and* The Third Wave, *this book explores the impact of the information revolution on issues of wealth creation, war, and peace.*

INTERNET RESOURCES

Barber, Benjamin. "Jihad vs. McWorld"
http://www.TheAtlantic.com/atlantic/election/connection/foreign/barjiha.htm

Carnegie Endowment for International Peace
http://www.ceip.org/

Earth Times Daily
http://www.earthtimes.org/

Global Economic Prospects and the Developing Countries
World Bank
http://www.worldbank.org/html/extpb/gep96eng/gep96en-home.html

International Institute for Sustainable Development
http://iisd1.iisd.ca/

Internationalist
http://www.theinternationalist.com/

Magna Carta for the Knowledge Age
http://www.townhall.com/pff/position.html

Millennium Institute
http://www.igc.apc.org/millennium/

One World
http://www.oneworld.org/

Progress and Freedom Foundation
http://www.pff.org/

Resources for the Future
http://www.rff.org/

Rorty, Richard. "Moral Universalism and Economic Triage"
http://www.unesco.org/phiweb/uk/2rpu/rort/rort.html

The Third Wave
http://lorca.compapp.dcu.ie/hsheehan/students/ts/downes.htm

U.S. Global Change Research Information Office
http://gcrio.gcrio.org/

Vision of the Future
Philips Corporation
http://www.philips.com/design/vof/toc1/home.htm

World Economic Forum
http://www.weforum.org/basic/home_nf.htm

World Future Society
http://www.wfs.org/wfs/index.htm